BAFFLE MARKS AND PONTIL SCARS:

A READER ON HISTORIC BOTTLE IDENTIFICATION

Peter D. Schulz, Rebecca Allen, Bill Lindsey, and Jeanette K. Schulz, Editors

The Society for Historical Archaeology

Special Publication Series No. 12

2016

SOCIETY *for*
HISTORICAL
ARCHAEOLOGY

Annalies Corbin, Co-Publications Editor

Library of Congress Control Number: 2015960388

Cover illustration by Chris McClellan

Copyediting by Marianne Brokaw
Design and Composition by Jaynie McCloskey

© 2016 by The Society for Historical Archaeology
13017 Wisteria Drive, #375
Germantown, MD 20874
www.sha.org

Published in the United States of America

For cripes sake, Pete!

–Jeanette

CONTENTS

Foreword
Annalies Corbin, Co-Publications Editor

Glass bottles are one of the most ubiquitous finds on historic archaeological sites, no matter the locale. Hundreds of thousands of glass bottles have been recovered, and hundreds of thousands more were manufactured.

Having found a bottle, it is the archaeologist's challenge to sort out when the bottle was made, what it may have contained, and how its presence can be used to interpret past behavior. Identification is a key step to interpretation. An archaeologist needs tools to correctly identify the what, where, when, and why a product (conveniently packaged in a glass bottle) was created. Archaeologists also need to understand bottle manufacturing in order to predict when the bottle was manufactured and how it may have gotten to the archaeological site. New and reprinted articles (many long out of print or from little-known industry-specific sources) collected in this reader are intended to do just that.

This volume begins with an overview of bottle identification and dating, and a review of hand-production technology. After 1880, the mechanization of glass bottle manufacture revolutionized the industry. New manufacturing techniques, including new finishes, closures, design, and labels, allowed producers to exponentially bring more variety and numbers of products (and thus more bottles) to the consumer. This in turn greatly impacted the historical archaeological record. For the archaeologist, the underlying theme of this volume is that more variety and number of consumer goods equals more potential for the understanding of everyday life.

Artifacts matter to the interpretation of the past. That is a central tenet of historical archaeology, and many of the publications sponsored by the Society for Historical Archaeology, including this one, reflect that core value. This volume collects many of the standard resources, introduces new ones, and points researchers in many directions to further inquiry as well as the recognition and interpretation of material things.

Old Wine in New Skins
Peter D. Schulz and Rebecca Allen

It is probably the fate of all metaphors to be misused. With apologies to Jesus (Mark 2:21–22), whose point was very different, the title "Old Wine in New Skins" alludes to the republishing of a series of reports on the identification of glass containers and the history of the glass container industry. These publications—several of them classics long out of print—provide a fundamental understanding of the technological evolution that allows accurate analysis of historic archaeological assemblages. Articles included come from trade publications, government reports, and newspaper accounts; topical studies by archaeologists; and some new articles intended to assist in laboratory analysis. The unifying thread in these selections is the attempt to give the reader a clearer picture of both the glass container industry and its processes that left physical traces through various ages on the surfaces of the bottles themselves.

In particular, it is worth emphasizing the many publications by Julian H. Toulouse, some reprinted here and others listed in an annotated bibliography on Toulouse works included in this volume. Several of these reports, written for a popular audience, originally appeared in magazines published for glass and antique collectors. The articles are so clearly written and reflect so thorough an understanding of glass technology and the history of the industry that they serve today, with barely a quibble or exception, as introductions from which any student can benefit.

We also direct the reader's attention to the *Society for Historical Archaeology's Historic Glass Bottle Identification & Information Website* < http://www.sha.org/bottle/index.htm>. Bill Lindsey originally created these pages for the Bureau of Land Management. Today, these pages are by far the most visited reference on the SHA's website (former website editor Kelly Dixon and webmaster Christopher Merritt helped to make the transition to SHA). Fortunately, Lindsey continues to maintain this site and frequently updates it with new information. The SHA is grateful to be a permanent steward of these invaluable pages.

1. BOTTLE BASICS

Section one introduces the glass bottle and its purpose, giving the reader sufficient background information to begin the process of bottle identification. The first article (Schulz and Allen) discusses the cultural context of glass bottles and why they are so significant as a packaging material. The next article (Schulz et al.) is reproduced from *The Bottles of Old Sacramento* and provides an overview of glass bottle manufacture in the United States. We also reprint Lindsey's short article from the SHA's *Technical Briefs in Historical Archaeology* series that explains the workings of the website he created, as noted above. An article entitled "Bottle Anatomy" (Lindsey and Schulz) gives basic nomenclature, intended to help standardize terms. The "Summary Guide to Dating and Identifying Glass Bottles" (Lindsey) is excerpted from the SHA historic bottle website. Edited to suit a printed volume, rather than a website format, this information is then reinterpreted to create laboratory worksheets (Lindsey and Allen) for dating glass bottles. The section ends with an essay (Allen and Felton) on building a bottle type collection and lists categories thought to be critical for cataloging glass bottles. For clarification of any terms, refer to the "Bottle Glossary" link in the SHA's historic bottle website.

2. HAND PRODUCTION TECHNOLOGY

Beginning with a short series of 19th- and 20th-century newspaper and trade journal articles, section two highlights the evolution of hand-production technology. Two articles by Olive Jones discuss the physical evidence of hand manufacture: push ups, pontil marks, and scars from early molds. Reprinted articles by Toulouse discuss the use of molds, pontil marks, seams, and other manufacturing techniques. These techniques have implications for the archaeologist, as the evidence from manufacture is often key to dating a bottle and, by extension, an archaeological assemblage. "Debunking the Myth of the Side Seam Thermometer" (Lockhart et al.) offers further clarification on seams and their usefulness for dating. An article by Edward Staski, reprinted from *Historical Archaeology*, reminds the reader of the importance of cultural context for archaeological deposits and discusses what the presence of bottles can reveal about past behavior in the 19th century.

3. THE IRON COMRADE: MACHINE AGE TECHNOLOGY

The increasingly mechanized bottle manufacture brought social change to labor markets as well as an increased presence and plethora of glass bottles to consumer markets. Section three deals with the evolution of machine technology, which leaves new physical traces for dating glass bottles. In their reprinted classic, George Miller and Catherine Sullivan set the stage for understanding the revolution of technology from 1880 to 1920 that resulted from the mechanization of glass-container manufacture. In a reprint from *Northeast Historical Archaeology*, Miller and Tony McNichol present evidence left by the Owens Machine. Reprints of three articles from 1920s trade journals suggest that the industry concerned itself with not only manufacturing capabilities and the ability to bring more products to the consumer but also with how this shift in manufacture would affect the glass industry labor force. Lockhart explains in a reprinted article how the introduction of manganese to produce colorless bottles and the subsequent purpling of that glass when exposed to sun is one of the common hallmarks of dating late-19th to early-20th-century deposits. Schulz offers a new essay on the historical reasons for the use of manganese.

4. FINISHES AND CLOSURES

The appearance of finishes and closure is critical to the identification of bottle function as well as important diagnostic features for dating a bottle. In section four, Lindsey offers a primer on understanding the manufacture, terminology, and appearance of finishes. This article is also available for download from the SHA bottle identification website and is best used in conjunction with other components of that site. Several useful reproductions from early-20th-century manufacturer catalogs are included to give the reader an overview of the most common kinds of finishes and closures. A reprint on closures from the *Parks Canada Glass Glossary* (Jones and Sullivan) illustrates the most common types. Several reprints from trade journals give an industry perspective on why the evolution of finishes and closures was so central to the availability of products found within glass containers. These articles speak to the fundamental purpose of the glass bottle, that is, to serve as a container.

5. GLASS CONTAINER DESIGN

Section five continues with the theme of bottle as container. Reprints from trade journals discuss the evolution and consideration of the bottle as a package for delivering consumer goods. These articles highlight styling, shapes, and design of containers as well as the strength of glass—an important quality that allows the safe delivery of products in an aesthetically pleasing way. All of these considerations affect what goods were available to consumers and what subsequently appears in the archaeological record. Three reprinted articles by Toulouse highlight the styling, standardization, and delivery of beer bottles.

6. LABELS AND MARKS

Labels and marks are two of the most useful items for identifying and dating glass bottles. A series of reprints in section six highlights the most common manufacturers and their marks. An essay by Lockhart and Russ Hoenig on the Owens-Illinois Glass Company logos and codes highlights the most commonly found manufacturing marks in the glass-bottle archaeological record.

7. REFERENCES

The volume ends with section seven—a bottle glossary and two bibliographies that present a short list of bottle manufacturing terms as well as references on bottle identification and dating for the continually intrigued. The glossary introduces the most commonly used terms in trade journals and archaeological literature; the reader is encouraged to use this information in conjunction with the glossary found at the SHA historic bottle website <www.sha.org/bottle/glossary.htm>. Topics in the bibliography include dating and contents, hand-production technology, machine technology, bottle form, labels and marks, finishes and closures as well as available reprinted glassworks catalogs. The bibliography also lists archaeological reports that make accurate use of glass bottle assemblages, providing further illumination about the usefulness of bottles in their archaeological context. For readers who wish to further their study of glass bottles, Schulz provides a partial bibliography on the works of Toulouse. The SHA historic bottle website is an additional source of references and information.

ACKNOWLEDGMENTS

The Bottle Research Group is always a guiding force in archaeologically based glass-bottle research <http://www.sha.org/bottle/about.htm#Bottle%20 Research%20Group>. Membership in this group varies but always benefits from the leadership of Lindsey and Lockhart, as this volume has benefitted from their insights and articles. We also especially thank Jeanette Schulz, Larry Felton, and Glenn Farris, who dedicated so much of their careers to the California Department of Parks and Recreation. They always seem to be ready to lend a helping hand. George Miller offered words of encouragement when most needed as well as insights and comments as only he could. We could not have accomplished this volume without the patience and professionalism of the SHA publication team: Annalies Corbin (co-publications editor), Marianne Brokaw (copy editor), and Jaynie McCloskey (design and composition). To the others offering information, assistance, and encouragement, we hope that you know who you are and that we promptly offered you our gratitude.

1
BOTTLE BASICS

Glass-Blowing. (Drawing from Clara L. Matéaux with additions by Joshua Rose [ca. 1884], *The Wonderland of Work,* new and revised edition, Cassell & Co., Ltd., New York, NY, p. 307.)

Articles

The Bottle as Package, the Bottle as Product
Peter D. Schulz and Rebecca Allen

The fundamental purpose of a glass bottle is to serve as a package. Its object is to protect the product from contamination or deterioration, to partition it into easily handled units, to guarantee a certain quantity of contents, and to impart information about the product and its origin (Walstra et al. 1999:373). This may strike the reader as obvious, but the study of historic bottles too often loses sight of an important point: artifacts have meaning within the cultural and technological contexts wherein they function (Figure 1). Glass as a packaging material has always been in competition with other materials. The advantages and disadvantages of glass have determined how it fared in these competitive encounters. Bottles as products emerge from the technologies of those who make them, only to function within the technologies of those who use them.

The origin of modern glass containers arose in England in the 17th century in an attempt to grab the market for wine containers, which was then controlled by stoneware jars from the continent. This change was made possible by a combination of factors. First, the conversion of glass furnaces from wood to coal fuel provided hotter and more easily worked metal that could be rapidly free-blown into heavier and larger ware than was previously practical. This change resulted in containers substantially cheaper than those produced by the continental potters:

> After the Restoration ... (1660), wine flourished and so did the glass wine-bottle, and within a few years it had almost completely ousted the stoneware bottle, even though this too was by now being made in England. The main reason for this success, apart from any considerations of quality, was the price: glass bottles sold for as little as 2*d*. each, rising to about 6*d*. each for bottles decorated with the owner's name and family crest. This compares with 8*d*. to 10*d*. each wholesale for Fulham stoneware bottles... (Moody 1960:61).

Figure 1. Some bottles have immediately identifiable shapes and contents, characteristics that are useful marketing ploys. Shapes such as this Berkshire Bitters bottle are also useful as dating tools. Research shows that Anthony and Edmund Amann started making these bottles in Cincinnati as early as 1869. (Photo from California Department of Parks and Recreation, Bottle Type Collection Photo Gallery <http:// www.parks.ca.gov/?page_id=22304>.)

The success of these developments was delayed by Puritan antipathy to the wine trade during the Cromwell years but soon flourished. Cork stoppers came into use about the same time as modern glass wine bottles. While glass quickly dominated the trade for wine and liquor, bottles seem to have only held their own in the packaging of foods, pharmaceuticals, and malt beverages.

For many products, glass containers are nearly ideal—offering unmatched transparency to enhance product appeal or reducing transparency where the exclusion of light is needed to protect product quality, as with beer and some pharmaceuticals. Glass is chemically inert and impervious to both water and gases. Other advantages of glass are high strength (higher than most other forms of packaging) and ready adaptability to sterilization of the container or its contents through in-bottle pasteurization. Glass containers are adaptable to a wide variety of products since they can be produced in a great variety of shapes with either wide- or narrow-mouth forms. Because of a glass container's weight and strength, it can be easily used as a multi-trip or refillable container—and for most of its history it was indeed so used and used again. Glass has historically been the most readily and completely recyclable of packaging materials.

Disadvantages of glass include weight, brittleness, surface scratching, and production line efficiency, although these factors have mostly proved to be irrelevant for the majority of packaging purposes (Theobald 2006:103). Cost, of course, has varied over time and may be an advantage or not, depending on the price of other packaging materials. The advent of production-line efficiency also directly affected bottle shapes and elements as well as their popularity as a package. As filling, capping, and labeling lines became ever faster, bottle shape became a crucial issue.

Throughout the changes in glass bottle technology over time, the manufacturers kept in mind the *function* of their container. In most cases glass containers can be easily (and demonstrably) cleaned—an advantage that was crucial in the competition with stoneware bottles and metal containers in the late-19th and early-20th centuries. Metal cans could also deteriorate or add off flavors to food, creating a set of problems for grocers and consumers:

> Manufacturers of fruit jars... anticipate a larger sale of fruit jars this year as a result of complaint made by wholesale and retail grocers, who for a year or more have been noticing the degeneration of the tin can in the packing of fruits and vegetables. It is claimed that the new pack of fruits and vegetables will be even worse packages than last

year. A few years ago much better tin was used in the packing of canned goods. The tin coating has been getting thinner and thinner, so that now apples and other acid fruits, also tomatoes eat off the tin and leave the surface of the iron exposed.

The latter metal imparts a disagreeable flavor to the product within the cans. Last year many of these imperfect cans swelled and occasioned a loss. California packers use better tin than is used in the East or in the middle West. In fact, they send much of their pack abroad, where the goods must pass inspection, they use Welsh tin instead of American tin. As a result of the complaint on tin cans not only by the housewife, but by the wholesale packer, there has been a heroic demand of fruit jars to replace the tins (*Commoner and Glassworker* 1901).

Over time, glass has long retained a marketing advantage in terms of "high-quality image," which has made glass largely immune from competition. It is easily manufactured, long lasting, and decorated at a relatively low cost. Glass remains one of the most common packaging materials and will continue to be an important element of archaeological sites of the future.

REFERENCES

Commoner and Glassworker

1901   Tin Can vs. Fruit Jar. *Commoner and Glassworker* 22(50):6.

Moody, B. E.

1960   The Origin of the "Reputed Quart" and Other Measures. *Glass Technology* 1(2):55–68.

Theobald, Nigel

2006   Closures for Glass Containers. In *Packaging Closures and Sealing Systems*, Nigel Theobald and Belinda Winder, editors, pp. 101–117. CRC Press, Boca Raton, FL.

Walstra, P., T. J. Geurts, A. Noomen, A. Jellema, M. A. J. S. van Boekel

1999   *Dairy Technology: Principles of Milk Properties and Processes.* Marcel Dekker, Inc., New York, NY.

The American Glass Bottle Industry—A Brief History

Peter D. Schulz

THE BOTTLES OF OLD SACRAMENTO:
A Study of Nineteenth-Century Glass and Ceramic Retail Containers
Part I

PETER D. SCHULZ
BETTY J. RIVERS
MARK M. HALES
CHARLES A. LITZINGER
and
ELIZABETH A. McKEE

CALIFORNIA ARCHEOLOGICAL REPORTS
No. 20

Resource Preservation and Interpretation Division

CULTURAL RESOURCE MANAGEMENT UNIT

May 1980

State of California — The Resources Agency
DEPARTMENT OF PARKS AND RECREATION
P.O. Box 2390
Sacramento, CA 95811

THE AMERICAN GLASS BOTTLE INDUSTRY -- A BRIEF HISTORY

Glassmaking in North America began in 1609 in a wooded area one mile from Jamestown. The production of glass in America was inspired by the abundance of fuel, the great cost of importing bottles, in addition to the breakage that occurred in transport, and the desirability of glass beads for the Indian trade. The first factory was apparently well planned, and was staffed by trained German and Polish glassmakers, but it was no more successful than the rest of the initial settlement, and it had ceased operation within a year. A second attempt, in 1621, this time using Italian workers, lasted for several years but was plagued by natural disasters, inferior raw materials, and labor-management difficulties. It was consequently short-lived. Some window and bottle glass was blown, but there is no evidence that bead manufacture, which was a primary incentive for both of these early factories, was ever initiated.[1]

After the Jamestown attempts, the next documented glass factory was established in 1639 at Salem, Massachusetts. This enterprise was brief and unsuccessful and was followed by similarly-fated ventures in New Amsterdam and Pennsylvania.[2] Although window glass and other articles may have been made in some of these seventeenth-century factories, the major item of production in all of them undoubtedly was glass bottles.

The history of glassmaking during the colonial period was one of continual failure, even though there was an abundance of raw materials. Skilled workers were in short supply; English craftsmen had little incentive to move to America because conditions at home at that time were to their advantage. There was also little or no financial assistance for the early American industry, and the few skilled immigrants who arrived often found more lucrative prospects in agriculture or commerce.

By the middle of the eighteenth century, the increasing population of the English colonies had created an improved market, and difficult economic conditions in Europe made skilled workers more interested in emigrating to the New World. Two of the best known glass manufacturers of this period were Caspar Wistar and Henry William Stiegel. In 1739 Wistar built the first glassworks in Salem County, New Jersey, where he began making window glass and bottles. Wistar's enterprise failed about 1774, but one of his workmen, Joseph Stanger, established a new factory in Glassboro, New Jersey. The plant later became the Whitney Glass Works and operated as such until 1918 when it was purchased by the Owens Bottle Company.[3]

Henry William Stiegel was a German immigrant to Lancaster County, Pennsylvania, in 1750. After successful efforts in real estate speculation and in the operation of an iron foundry, he returned to Europe to study glassmaking. He brought several German and Bohemian workers back to Pennsylvania, began making glass in 1763, and soon had retail shops in several colonies. Prerevolutionary economic disturbances, however, proved disastrous, and the business ended in bankruptcy in 1774.[4]

During and after the revolution there were glass factories in Philadelphia, New Hampshire, and Massachusetts, in addition to the Stanger plant at Glassboro. At the beginning of the nineteenth century there were probably less than a dozen such factories in North America.[5] The War of 1812 cut the supply of glass from England, and the American industry expanded as a result; however, the following peace brought another flood of English imports. Yet by 1820, the industry was once more expanding. The demand for bottles increased greatly in the nineteenth century, and with this demand came changes in glass bottle technology.

1

The techniques in use at the beginning of the century were basically those which had been employed since the inception of glassmaking on the continent, and, indeed, long before in Europe. Glass for bottles was made from silica (usually local river sand), soda, and lime, together with various minerals for coloring. This material was heated in large pots in a huge brick or stone furnace to form the molten glass or metal. The blowpipe, which was invented sometime during the three centuries immediately preceding the Christian era, was still the indispensable tool for all glass manufacturers, and remained so until nearly the end of the century. The flared end of this tool was inserted into the pot through a window in the furnace by a worker and withdrawn with an attached gob or gather of molten glass. The worker then rolled the glass into shape on a marver, and blew the first small pocket of air into it. The glass was then shifted to the very end of the pipe and transformed into a pear-shaped form, the parison, by alternately blowing, rotating, and swinging the pipe. Next, with the aid of a mold and hand tools, the body of the bottle was blown into its final shape. A rod -- either another blowpipe or a solid rod, called a punty or pontil -- with a small gob of glass on its end was then pressed into the center of the base to form a new bond. The worker snapped off the blowpipe, and, using the pontil to hold the bottle, reheated the neck and applied a final bit of glass at the mouth to form a usable finish. Finally, the complete vessel was taken to an annealing oven, or lehr, the pontil was snapped off, and the bottle was left to cool gradually.

During the nineteenth century several modifications of this process were introduced, all directed toward greater efficiency. The first general improvement consisted of the proliferation of varieties of molds. Single-piece or dip molds for glassware had been in use in western Europe at least since the sixteenth century.[6] They were little used on bottles, however, until late in the eighteenth century, because they were not needed for the efficient production of the squat, bulbous vessels then in vogue. As taller and narrower bottles became popular, however, mold blowing became universal. Single-piece molds soon coexisted with two-, three-, and even four-piece modifications, and portable molds opened and closed by an assistant were in use at the same time as stationary models operated by the blower himself using foot pressure.[7] The primary purposes of mold blowing were to increase the speed of bottle production and to standardize vessel size. Manufacturers quickly learned, however, that molds could be used to produce embossed labels, and by midcentury bottles were well on their way to being a major means of advertising.[8]

Another improvement, along with molds, consisted of the lipping tool, a hand implement with a central guidepost and two specially shaped arms. After the body of the bottle was completed and detached from the blowpipe, an additional band of new glass was laid on around the opening. The post of the tool was then inserted in the mouth and rotated, the arms thus forming the new glass into a symmetrical finish of predetermined shape and size. This device was reportedly introduced about 1850,[9] and this seems to be a good enough date for its initial use on most categories of bottles. If we may judge from the Old Sacramento collections, however (and they are both large and representative), the lipping tool must have been in general use on French champagne bottles by the beginning of the California gold rush, since all of the early champagne bottles from Sacramento have a tipping-tool finish.[10] Bottles for still wines from Bordeaux, on the other hand, continued to be made with crude laid-on-ring finishes not only through the 1850s, but almost until the end of the century and perhaps beyond it.

A further technological development was the introduction of the snap case. This device consisted of a rod, on the end of which were four curved, padded arms that could be clamped around the bottle. This tool gradually replaced the pontil for holding the bottle while the finish was applied. Use of the snap case did not result in the unsightly and

2

potentially dangerous scars of glass previously left on the bottom of the bottle when the pontil was broken away during manufacture. It also, incidentally, produced yet another smooth surface where glassworks could emboss their names or initials, or those of their clients. The real advantages of the snap case, however, were probably economic. First, it saved the time formerly required to carry the pontil to the pot and obtain the small gather of glass necessary to bond it to the bottle. Secondly, the snap case eliminated losses resulting from bottle breakage when the pontil bond proved insufficient, or when the bottom came out of the bottle along with the pontil. It also seems likely that the snap case could be used by workers with less training.

A date of about 1857 is often given for the advent of the snap case, although we have seen no evidence cited to support this date.[11] Similar devices such as the post or sabot, which like the snap case left no identifying marks on the bottles they held, were being employed decades earlier in Europe. Indeed, a tool clearly identical to the sabot is depicted in a seventeenth-century Dutch treatise on glassmaking.[12] That this tool was not in common use for making bottles until the early nineteenth century can only be ascribed to the fact that efficient use requires a very close fit between bottle and sabot -- something that was not possible until straight-sided vessels became common, and, indeed, until mold-blown bottles dominated the market place. Until then, the more versatile pontil was decidedly more efficient.

Both the snap case and the finishing tool illustrate a caveat often ignored by students of glass history: innovations were not introduced simultaneously in different countries, nor even in different regions. Along with local products, the American market received bottles made in factories all over western Europe. For most of the nineteenth century, for example, the great majority of wine bottles used here were made in France, while a large portion of the black glass liquor bottles in use were imported from England. Indeed, until the beginning of World War I, the United States imported far more glass than it exported (Fig. 1). Consequently, even when the introduction of new techniques by American glasshouses can be closely dated, the information will not necessarily provide an accurate date on bottles excavated here.

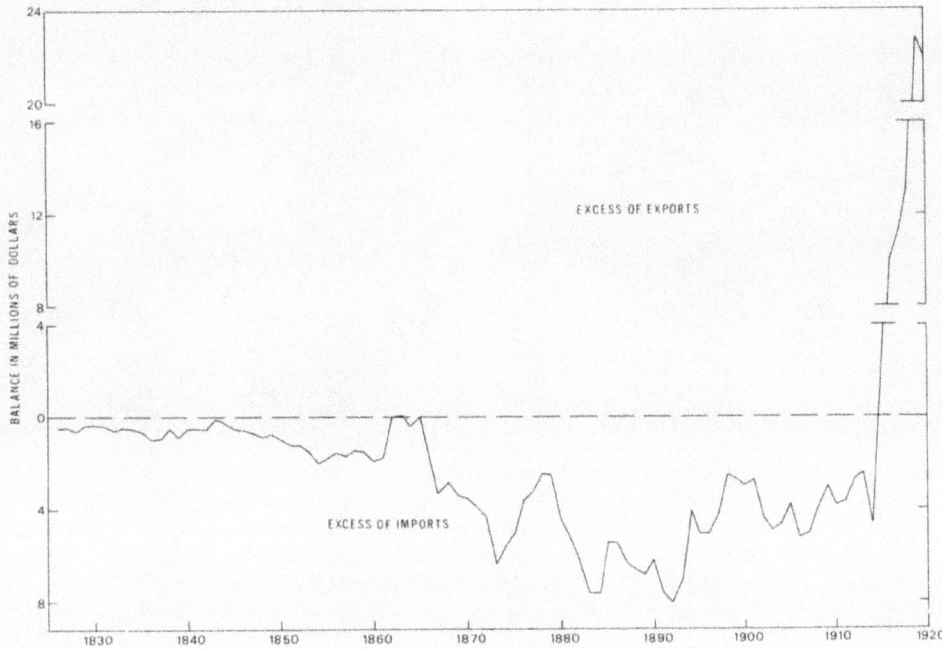

Figure 1. America's balance of trade in glass, 1826-1920 (after Scoville 1948). In 1873-1880 an average of 4,552,500 lbs of bottles filled with liquids and other products were imported annually, but these are not incorporated in the chart.

3

Other innovations involved the design of furnaces, replacement of pots with large tanks, and substitution of natural gas as a fuel source for the dirtier and more expensive coal.

One improvement involved not tools or equipment, but the organization of workers. This was the "shop system," a subdivision of labor supposedly introduced by the workers themselves after 1870.[13] Under this system each worker, instead of carrying out the whole process of bottle blowing, performed a specific task: the first (the gatherer) drew and marvered the gather; the second (the servitor) formed the parison; and the third (the gaffer) completed the blowing and formed the finish. In some factories even these last stages—mold-blowing and finishing—seem to have been handled by different workers. These men were all skilled glassblowers or apprentices. They were assisted by from three to five boys: a take-out, or molder, boy, who opened and closed the mold, applied the snap case and sheared or cracked the vessel away from the blowpipe; a cracker-off boy, who cleaned the residual glass from the pipes after each use; a snapper-up boy, who carried the incomplete vessel from the mold to the furnace to reheat the neck; and finally one or more carry-in boys, who took the reheated vessel from the furnace back to have the finish applied and then carried the finished bottle to the annealing oven. This team of adult and juvenile workers comprised a "shop" (Fig. 2); a factory had a shop for each pot in the furnace and for each ten-hour shift in operation.[14]

a

b

Figure 2. Glass shops at work: a) The worker partially obscured on the far right is gathering glass from the furnace; the apprentice standing in the center is rolling a gather on the marver, while blower on the left has just withdrawn a bottle from the mold. The can-shaped object projecting from the far left is a padded snap case. A molder-boy sits at the blower's feet, ready to shear the bottle off the blowpipe once it is placed in the snap case (from Stewart 1904). b) Carry-in boys placing finished bottles in the annealing oven (from Spargo 1909).

4

This system of organization was highly efficient: a single shop could be expected to produce 15 to 20 gross of pint bottles daily.[15] It was also highly rewarding for the glassblowers. The great stamina and high proficiency required for the job placed these skilled workers in a formidable position, and their average wages late in the last century were twelve times those of common laborers.[16] Glass blowers after the 1870s also had unusually strong unions.

Unfortunately, the position of the boys who worked in the factories was far less enviable. Their work was in some ways more demanding than that of the blowers:

> The earnings of the glass bottle blowers depends somewhat upon the speed of the boys who fetch and carry for them. These lads are, therefore, kept trotting at the highest speed that they can maintain for several hours. In inspecting the works, the writer found it impossible to get from a boy any consecutive statement as to his name, address, age, or parentage. A boy would say, "My name is Faber;" then run to the cooling oven with his load of bottles and returning say, "I live in a boat by the river;" then run to the moulder for another set of bottles and coming back say, "I'm going to be eight next summer," and so on. Among twenty-four lads questioned during one night-inspection, not one paused long enough to put together two of the foregoing statements.[17]

> Into the work of the snapping-up boy there enters the hardship of looking into the bright, glaring light of the glory hole... Not only is constant walking necessary, but also constant arm movement, some bending, and, in general, an incessant activity of the whole body... In a Pennsylvania establishment, where the temperature on the outside was 88 degrees, the temperature at the point where the snap-up [cracker-off?] rubs off the excess glass was 100 degrees; in front of the glory hole it was 140 degrees... The speed rate of the snapping-up boy is fixed by the output of the shop, and in case of such small ware as one ounce and under he must work with great rapidity.

> The carry-in boy, loaded and anxious, has perhaps the most mulish task of all. He must carry the red-hot bottles...on his asbestos shovel, with always an added danger of the slipping ware or the spattering glass; must hurry with his unstable, tormenting load on a slow run...

> In one factory...the distance from bench to oven was one hundred feet, and the carry-in boys made seventy-two trips an hour. In eight hours they thus ran twenty-two miles, half the time with a dangerous load, always in a Sahara of heat, always in a withering drift of glassy dust.[18]

Yet, since the labor performed required no special skills, wages of blowers' boys were as low as those of children in any other branch of American industry at the time. It is not surprising that the glass industry was for decades a major focus of the movement against child labor.

5

In spite of the innovations which had accompanied the expansion of the American glass industry during the nineteenth century, until 1915 more glass was still imported than was exported each year. Thereafter, however, this trend made a complete reversal and Europeans were striving to bring their factories up to the operating-efficiency level of those in the United States. From 1897 to 1905 the number of hand bottle blowers in the United States increased from six thousand to nine thousand men -- many of them highly specialized. In 1905-1906, skilled laborers blew most of the glass containers produced in the United States. Even at this late date semi-automatic machines, fed by hand, made only wide-mouthed jars, but the industry was on the verge of a technological revolution.[19]

The first patent for a bottle-making machine was issued in 1859, and several others were patented in the following two decades. None of these devices proved successful in practice. Philip Arbogast of Pittsburgh was the first to design a machine with the three essential steps for all successful bottle machines. Those steps are: formation of the top of the neck, formation of the parison, and blowing to the desired shape. In 1882, Argobast was granted a patent for his invention, but he was unable to develop a practical machine, and assigned his rights to the D. C. Ripley Company of Pittsburgh in 1885. The Ripley Company was taken over by the United States Glass Company, which then granted manufacturing licenses. By 1893, Vaseline jars were being made by the Enterprise Glass Company under license on Arbogast's press-and-blow machines.[20]

The plunger employed in the press-and-blow process, however, was too large to be used on narrow-mouthed containers. The first machine to make narrow-mouthed bottles was patented in 1886 by Josiah C. Arnall and Howard M. Ashley; this was the first blow-and-blow method. It incorporated three separate molds: one for the neck, a second for the initial form of the bottle, and a third for final shaping. Bottles were blown successfully, but the machine required a large number of workers to operate it. One skilled gatherer and six unskilled helpers could feed two of these machines and produce about one gross of soda water bottles per hour.

The Ashley blow-and-blow machine was one of the first of the "semi-automatics." This type of machine attracted considerable interest in France and Germany during the 1890s, but it was not commercially successful. In order for a machine to be fully automatic, a device had to be developed for both gathering and feeding.

There were two ways to solve this problem: suction feed, which vacuum-sucks just enough glass into a mold, and gravity feed, in which the glass flows out through a hole in the floor of a furnace extension and is sheared off when a sufficient amount to make a bottle, or the "gob," has flowed through. The latter method is that used by contemporary glass factories. Both techniques required large reservoirs of molten glass and could be developed successfully only after the regenerative tank furnace came into use. The semi-automatic machines at the end of the century were rather simplistic -- they made only one jar at a time, were frequently operated by hand, and required skilled gatherers. It was not until 1908 that the first satisfactory semi-automatic for making narrow-necked bottles was constructed. However, fully automatic machines were coming into use by this time, and the semi-automatic progressively declined in popularity, until in 1919 there were only ten such machines in use.[21]

The fully automatic bottle machine came about from work begun at the end of the nineteenth century by Michael J. Owens. In 1898 he began his experiments and within five years he had produced a commercially feasible machine. The Owens machine was a completely automatic unit -- it both gathered the glass by suction and finished the formation of the bottle mechanically. The original model was hand-held, resembling a

6

large bicycle pump or spray gun, but this was soon mounted on a column provided with wheels. Finally, a model was devised with six arms, each bearing a gathering and a finishing mold. Operation of this machine required less labor than a single hand-blowing shop: one man and five boys (none of them skilled craftsmen) spread over two labor shifts could adequately handle the machine. And they could produce in that time 70 gross of pint bottles.[22] The prospect of a 700% increase in productivity per (cheaper) man-hour was highly encouraging, and the Owens Bottle Company was incorporated in 1903 to produce the machines and license their use by other companies.

The Owens procedure for blowing bottles as practiced between 1903 and 1905 constituted by far the most important labor-saving technique introduced in the bottle industry. It was not at first, however, widely accepted; in fact, more than twenty years elapsed before its general acceptance in the glass container industry. The slowness of its adoption was due to several factors. First, though the Owens machine was of unparalleled efficiency in the manufacture of large quantities of containers of standardized size and shape, its economic advantage over hand and semi-automatic processes in small-lot production was not especially obvious. Product manufacturers were well aware of the marketing advantages of unique, eye-catching, or familiar bottles, and a redesigning campaign to conform bottles to a standard form made little headway. Therefore, large numbers of hand factories continued to exist for these increasingly specialized small orders of unusual-size or oddly shaped containers.

In addition, the Owens machines were very expensive, and in spite of their obvious merits, producers were hesitant to make the major capital investment necessary to install them. Not surprisingly, glass workers' unions, concerned about the replacement of workers by automation, resisted the use of the machine.[23] It has been estimated that in 1917 the Owens machine accounted for only 50% of all glass containers made in the United States and that skilled blowers and semi-automatics were responsible for almost all the rest.[24] Not until a declining market during Prohibition and the depression forced many small companies out of business was the change to automation by the commercial glass industry complete.

This mechanization revolutionized not only the glass industry itself, but also the ways in which the containers were used and their functional life expectancy. During the early and mid-nineteenth century, glass containers were such valuable commodities that they were used and reused continually. Generally bottles were not thrown away unless they were broken, and people frequently purchased their own bottles for home use. Small whiskey pocket flasks, for instance, were purchased for a good price for their convenience. Indeed, around 1870, an embossed pint bottle cost the liquor wholesaler twice as much as the whiskey it contained.[25]

Nineteenth-century druggists, in particular, faced a continuing problem with supplying vials, bottles, and tins for their products. These containers were a necessary but costly part of doing business, and once empty, they had to be stored and returned to their owners.[26] At times the problem of acquiring or disposing of containers was solved by trading them for other necessary items such as drugs, or other vials and tins. Similar problems were encountered by other merchants and manufacturers who dealt heavily in glass containers.

Until the arrival in the present century of automated mass production, bottles thus constituted a commodity of individually limited but real value. It is a fairly safe estimation, therefore, that most of them enjoyed years of usage before they finally ended up as components of a future archeological deposit.

7

A final note may be added on terminology. Technical terms used in this report for bottle parts or manufacturing techniques are generally those in common use in the glass industry or among glass collectors. Several of these terms are illustrated in Figure 3, while others are either defined in the text or will be readily apparent from the illustrations of individual bottles described. For those who wish a more detailed explanation of bottle characteristics and their chronology, several excellent papers by Toulouse review various aspects of nineteenth-century bottle production with clarity and authority, while many good books and articles are available for wider coverage.[27]

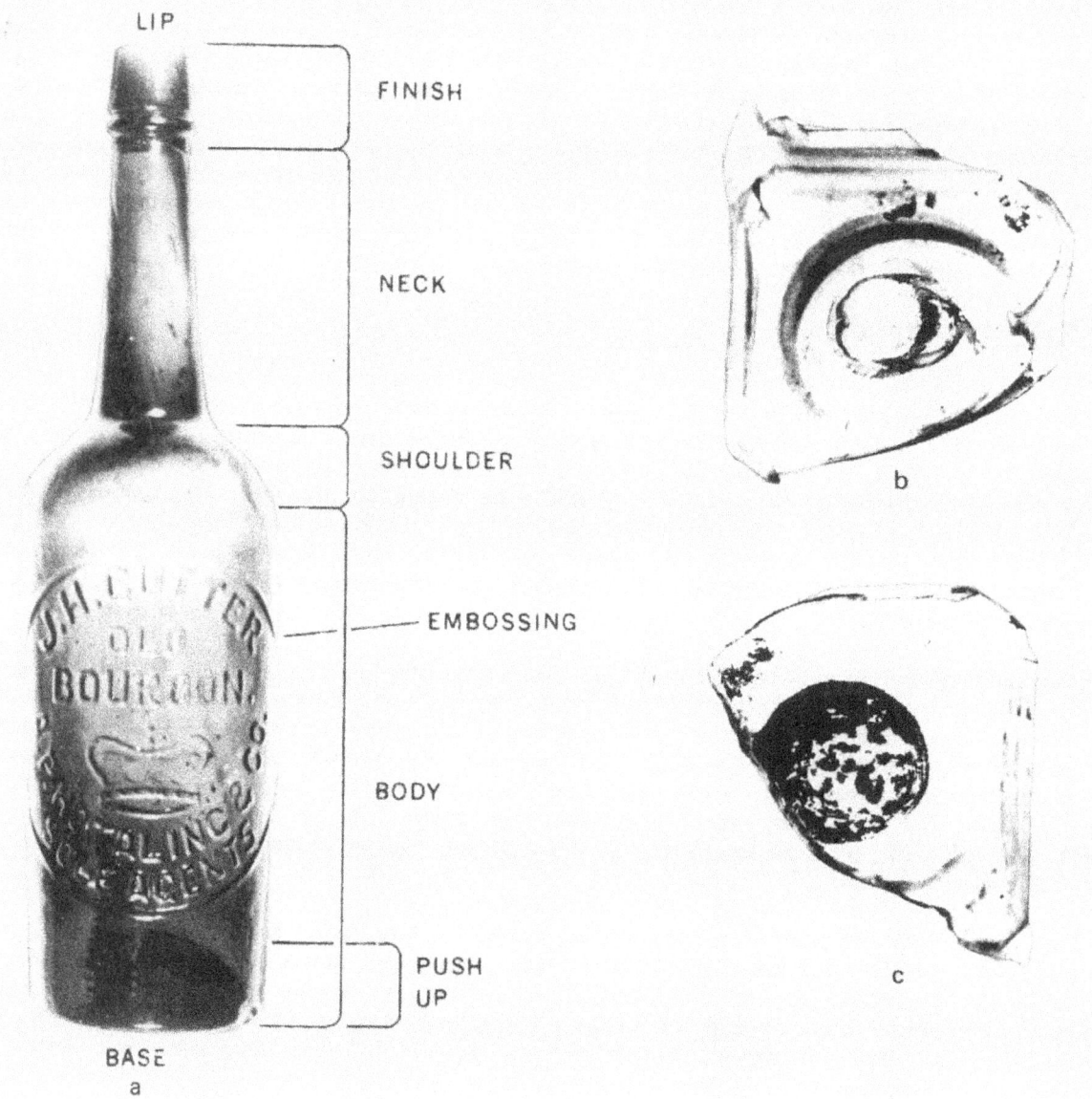

Figure 3. Bottle terminology: a) Parts of bottle; b) Bottle base showing pontil scar; c) Bottle base showing improved or bare-iron pontil scar.

8

Endnotes

1. Bishop 1864:232-233; Harrington 1952; Hudson 1964.

2. Bishop 1864:233; Glover and Cornell 1932:58.

3. Weeks 1883:316; Glover and Cornell 1932:580; Pepper 1971.

4. Heiges 1948.

5. Glover and Cornell 1932:580; Douglas and Frank 1972:36.

6. For a very clear description of hand blowing, see Kendrick (1968).

7. Cf. Douglas and Frank 1972:Fig. 28.

8. Readers desiring a fuller discussion of the use of molds, or wishing to use mold seams as dating tools, should see the excellent study of this topic by Toulouse (1967; 1969).

9. Lorrain 1968; Newman 1970.

10. It is noteworthy that a large collection of champagne bottles excavated from the hold of the storeship Niantic, which burned in the San Francisco fire of May, 1851, are also all made with lipping-tool finishes (Mary Hilderman-Smith, National Maritime Museum, San Francisco, personal communication).

11. Cf. Armstrong and Schulz 1980.

12. Cf. Douglas and Frank 1972:Fig. 1.

13. Keir 1928:536. Even if this date is correct for the introduction of a formally organized shop system in the United States, in principle it was hardly new. Some form of subdivision of labor appears to have been depicted by Diderot in 1772 (Diderot 1959:Plate 223) and the full shop system was in operation in England and Germany by the 1840s (Dodd 1845:92-93; Marx 1906:381).

14. Accounts of child labor in the glass industry often incidentally include descriptions of the division of labor involved (cf. Kelley 1903, 1905; Stewart 1904; Spargo 1909:154-205; Markham, Lindsey and Creel 1914:58-76). The working shift in American glass factories at the end of the century was ten hours long; this included, however, an hour off for lunch and two 15-minute rest periods (Barnett 1926:95).

15. Scoville 1948:159.

16. Keir 1928:535.

17. Kelley 1903:17.

18. Markham, Lindsey and Creel 1914:63-65.

19. Scoville 1948.

9

20. Douglas and Frank 1972:174.

21. Scoville 1948; Douglas and Frank 1972.

22. Scoville 1948:159.

23. Scoville 1948:105.

24. Lorrain 1968:43.

25. Wilson and Wilson 1968:21.

26. Porter and Livesay 1970:350.

27. Toulouse 1967, 1968, 1969, 1971; cf. Lief 1965; Ferraro and Ferraro 1966; Munsey 1970; Klamkin 1971; Stewart and Cosentino 1976.

Overview of BLM's Historic Glass Bottle Identification and Information Website

Bill Lindsey

Overview of BLM's Historic Glass Bottle Identification and Information Website

Bill Lindsey

ABSTRACT

The United States Bureau of Land Management (BLM) is creating a comprehensive internet website devoted to the dating and typing of glass bottles produced in the United States and to some degree Canada between 1800 and the 1950s. The BLM website provides information allowing users to determine a likely manufacturing date range and use for most U.S.-made bottles or substantial fragments. The website also provides in-depth information on an array of subjects related to the manufacturing of bottles. Currently, the BLM website is almost complete, with full completion expected in 2007, although most sections are fully useable now.

Introduction

The Unites States Bureau of Land Management (BLM) administers and manages the largest land base of any entity in the United States—261 million acres of public lands located almost exclusively in the American West and Alaska. Part of the mission of the BLM is the management and preservation of cultural and heritage resources found on public lands, both prehistoric and historic.

Discovering, studying, and understanding the evidence of past human influences on the land provides the BLM background information that is critically important in the process of determining appropriate land uses today and in the future. Many historic sites located on public lands contain information important to the understanding of a particularly vibrant era in American history—the trans-Mississippi migration and settlement of the American West. The recording, interpretation, and protection of historic sites are critical and mandated missions of the agency. The proper study and understanding of historic sites on public lands entails the use of analytical tools that assist in dating and interpreting occupation details and time period of a given site or landscape. Among the most common artifacts found on historic sites are discarded bottles and bottle fragments.

Currently, the information needed to have a reasonable chance at dating, typing or determining the likely use of historic bottles is scattered in hundreds of different, usually narrowly focused, professional and avocational publications, many of which are difficult to nearly impossible to obtain. A good example of a high quality but narrowly defined work is the classic *Bottle Makers and Their Marks* by the late Julian Toulouse (1971).

Few attempts have been made at consolidating these diverse works into a single user-friendly guide. Probably the most notable attempt was *The Parks Canada Glass Glossary* (Jones and Sullivan 1989). The *Intermountain Antiquities Computer System (IMACS) Guide*, to which BLM was a contributor, was another effort to create an interpretive aid for historic artifact identification through a section on bottles (University of Utah 1992). Both of these guides were attempts "... to provide archaeologists with a manual for a standard approach to arriving at historical artifact function and chronology" (University of Utah 2001). They are useful works but dated and constrained in scope. In addition, neither has been updated in recent years; Jones and Sullivan is out of print and largely unavailable.

BLM's Historic Glass Bottle Identification and Information Website

Simply stated, the BLM's Historic Bottle Website is an attempt to combine, consolidate, and interpret all pertinent and available historic bottle-related information into one source using the most modern and flexible of publishing forums, the internet <*http://www.blm.gov/historic_bottles/index.htm*>. This website is intended to provide a user-friendly information source that will allow both the cultural professional and general public a chance at greater understanding of the history and evolution of historic bottles in the United States and, to a lesser degree, Canada.

TECHNICAL BRIEFS IN HISTORICAL ARCHAEOLOGY, 2006, 1: 16–20

This history of American glass bottles touches on and connects with the transition from a craft-based to industrial based economy, 18th and 19th century technological change, the settlement of the United States, cultural patterns and changes, and more.

Nominally, the BLM has justified and facilitated the preparation of the Historic Bottle Website as an extension of agency responsibilities intended to assist internal and external cultural professionals, other employees, contractors, and volunteers in the pursuit of agency goals in the BLM's cultural resources management programs. The website does, however, have much broader external appeal and is already being accessed extensively by archaeologists, government and private institutions, and individuals throughout the world.

The information found on the BLM's Historic Bottle Website is presented via the Internet for several reasons. First, to answer or address questions related to the dating and typing of a bottle, an extensive amount of information must be presented in a way that is easily accessible to the user. A major benefit of using the Internet to accomplish this task is the ability to use hundreds or thousands of illustrative pictures—an attribute that would not be possible or affordable if in book form. The Internet also allows for ease of revising or adding new information as it becomes available. As soon as the information is incorporated into the webpage and reloaded on the BLM server, it is available to everyone immediately, another attribute not possible with a printed publication. Finally, the ability of the Internet to reach more potential users than any other communication medium makes it a most powerful tool for education and enlightenment today.

Goals of the Historic Bottle Website

The Historic Bottle Website is primarily designed for field archaeologists trying to identify and date bottles or bottle fragments that are found during cultural surveys and excavations in the United States and more generally for anyone trying to date a bottle, determine what it was used for, or begin a search for information on historic bottle types and technologies. Second, it is intended to provide a teaching resource for educators dealing with the subject of bottles in historic archaeology and material culture studies.

The overriding goal of the Historic Bottle Website is to enable a user to answer two primary questions about most utilitarian bottles and jars produced in the United States and Canada between the early 1800s and 1950s (see Figure 1 for a range of these types). These include:

1. What is the age of the bottle? (bottle dating)
2. What type of bottle is it? (bottle identification or typology)

The site also assists the user with three additional and related bottle questions:

3. What technology, techniques, or processes were used to manufacture the bottle?
4. Where did the bottle come from, where was it made and what is its distribution in the United States?
5. Where can more information on historic bottles and bottle manufacturing technologies be found?

How to Use the Historic Bottle Website

If a user is attempting to determine the approximate manufacturing date or age of a bottle or fragment with diagnostic features, the first page to visit is the Bottle Dating page and related subpages <*www.blm.gov/historic_bottles/dating. htm*>. This group of pages leads a user through a series of questions about the physical or morphological characteristics of historic bottles that helps to narrow down the age of an item. These pages are the major hub of the website and the best place to start a search. Also linked to the Bottle Dating page is a subpage called Examples of Dating Historic Bottles that tracks different bottles through a dating and general information quest to illustrate how the website works.

If a user is interested in identifying what a bottle was likely used for or what type of bottle it is, the Bottle Typing/Diagnostic Shapes page and related subpages should be visited < *www.blm.gov/historic_bottles/typing. htm*>. These include bottle type-specific subpages with extensive style and dating information. Beyond Bottle Dating and Bottle Typing, numerous other specialty pages cover various aspects of historic bottles in greater depth including Bottle Finishes and Closures, Bottle

Figure 1. Grouping of historic American-made bottles dating from the 1830s to 1930s. (Photo by author, 2003.)

Bases, Bottle Body Characteristics and Mold Seams, Bottle Glass Color and Glassmaking and Glassmakers. The site also provides an extensive Bottle Glossary and a comprehensive Reference Sources/Bibliography.

None of the Historic Bottle Website pages are fully inclusive since related information is typically spread over many pages. For example, there is information pertinent to dating bottles on virtually every page within the website, not just the Bottle Dating complex of pages. The title of any given page gives the predominant theme of that page and would be the first place to start when pursuing information on that particular subject. Because the processes of bottle dating and identification can be complex, there is a need for many web pages incorporating an abundance of descriptive information. Users need to spend some time viewing different pages.

Attributes and Limitations of the Historic Bottle Website

Since there were several hundred thousand different bottles produced in the United States between 1800 and the 1950s, it is beyond the capability of this or any website or book to provide more than a fraction of data and information related to historic bottles (Fike 1987). The BLM website primarily helps a user determine some key facts about a bottle—approximate age and function—based on observable physical characteristics.

Historic Bottle Website users will note that bottles produced in the United States are strongly emphasized. This geographical limitation is followed for the following reasons.

1. The art and science of bottle dating and typing is a very complex subject when focus is upon the history

of glassmaking for one specific country, in this case the United States. To cover all or most of the world would entail research that is well beyond the funding available for this project and knowledge base of the website's author. A broader geographical scope would entail the creation of a massive website with so many exceptions and regional variations as to significantly reduce the utility found in just focusing on American made bottles.

2. During the late-19th and early-20th centuries (1890 to 1920), American bottle manufacturing technology generally progressed faster than European and Asian glassmaking. This resulted in European and Asian bottles from the early-20th century showing some manufacturing-based traits that would date them as 20 or 30 years older if they had been produced in the US.

3. The Bureau of Land Management is an agency of government that manages lands exclusively in the United States - lands that are virtually all in the American West and Alaska. The bottles most likely to be found during cultural surveys on these lands are those produced in the United States. Although foreign produced bottles are found with regularity during surveys, they are typically a minority.

4. The United States government funds The Historic Bottle Website and it is appropriate that BLM place its emphasis on bottles with most interest to American citizens.

That said, the information on this website is generally applicable to many bottles produced in Canada since its glassmaking history closely parallels that of the United States. In fact, a significant amount of information used in the creation of this website was produced by Canadian historic archaeologists and collectors. It should be noted, however, that there are manufacturing and stylistic trends for Canadian bottles that parallel English bottle making and styles, particularly with many liquor, soda, and beer bottles (Watson and Skrill 1971; Watson et al. 1972; Urquhart 1976; Unitt 1980a, 1980b). What is generally true for Canada to the north is not necessarily true for Mexico to the south. Mexico was slower to implement new techniques and processes and in fact, continued to use mouth-blown processes

for many utilitarian bottles well into the mid-20th century.

Future of the Historic Bottle Website

Currently, the basic structure and content of the *Historic Bottle Website* is almost complete, with most portions fully functional to users pursuing historic bottle information relative to the noted goals. This website will also be, in a sense, always a work in progress as it is the intention of the website author to continually update, refine, and broaden the website's information base in the future with the ultimate goal of allowing all users an ever increasing opportunity to gain substantive information on the majority of bottles produced in the United States between 1800 and the 1950s. New or newly found information will always become available and will be incorporated into the site periodically and indefinitely. It is expected that the BLM will facilitate and sponsor this website on the internet indefinitely.

REFERENCES

Fike, Richard E.
1987   *The Bottle Book: A Comprehensive Guide to Historic Embossed Medicine Bottles.* Gibbs M. Smith, Inc., Peregrine Smith Press, Salt Lake City, UT.

Jones, Olive, and Catherine Sullivan
1989   *The Parks Canada Glass Glossary for the Description of Containers, Tableware, Flat Glass, and Closures.* National Historic Parks and Sites Branch, Parks Canada, Ottawa, Ontario, Canada.

Toulouse, Julian H.
1971   *Bottle Makers and Their Marks.* Thomas Nelson, Inc., New York, NY.

Unitt, Doris, and Peter Unitt
1980a   *Across Canada Bottle Price Guide*, revised edition. Clock House Publications, Peterborough, Ontario, Canada.

1980b   *Bottles in Canada.* Clock House Publications, Peterborough, Ontario, Canada.

University of Utah
1992   *Intermountain Antiquities Computer System User's Guide*, Bottle section, Part
472. University of Utah, Salt Lake City
<http://www.anthro.utah.edu/imacs.html>.

2001   Introduction. In *Intermountain Antiquities Computer System User's Guide*. University of Utah,
Bureau of Land Management, U.S. Forest Service
<http://www.anthro.utah.edu/imacs.html>.

Urquhart, Olive
1976   *Bottlers and Bottles, Canadian*. S. & O. Urquhart,
Toronto, Ontario, Canada.

Watson, George, and Robert Skrill
1971   *Western Canadian Bottle Collecting.* Hume Comp-
ton, Nanaimo, British Columbia, Canada.

Watson, George, Robert Skrill, and Jim Heidt
[1972–1973]   *Western Canadian Bottle Collecting, Book 2.*
Evergreen Press, British Columbia, Canada.

Bill Lindsey
Bureau of Land Management
Klamath Falls Resource Area
2795 Anderson Ave., Building 25
Klamath Falls, OR 97603
<William_Lindsey@or.blm.gov>

Bottle Anatomy
Bill Lindsey and Peter D. Schulz

The basic form of the bottle derives from a simple fact: all glass containers—whether called bottles, jars, flasks, vials, jugs, or any variety of other names—are hollow vessels. They are provided with a single opening capable of being sealed with some kind of closure. The basic terminology for the parts of such containers draws largely from the popular labels traditionally used by consumers. Terms like neck, shoulder, sides or body, heel, and base are readily comprehended by those with no prior knowledge of glass technology or the history of container forms (Figure 1).

Following the bottle from top to base, here is the most commonly used terminology for describing the basic physical parts common to most bottles.

BORE
The bore or orifice is simply the opening from which the bottle contents are accessed. Although a distinct bottle part, it could also be considered a part of the finish (described next).

FINISH
The finish comprises the uppermost part of a bottle from the lip to the upper part of the neck, including any modifications to strengthen the opening or adapting it to a particular closure. In hand manufacture, adding or tooling glass in this area to form a useable opening was the final modification before the bottle was completely formed (this volume, Bill Lindsey, "The Finishing Touch: A Primer on Mouth-Blown Bottle Finishing Methods with an Emphasis on 'Applied' vs. 'Tooled' Finish Manufacturing"), hence the name. In machine production the finish is the first part of the bottle to be formed, but the terminology continues regardless.

Although the term "finish" itself is standard throughout the industry and should be understood by archaeologists and collectors, its *components* have defied all attempts at standardized terminology. With regard to even the broadest concept of finish, the terms "lip" and "rim," "mouth" and "aperture," "bore" and "throat" and a variety of other synonyms have jockeyed for preference in the writings of different authors. If historical archaeologists consider the physical varieties of different *kinds* of finishes, the labels, in whole or in part, become legion.

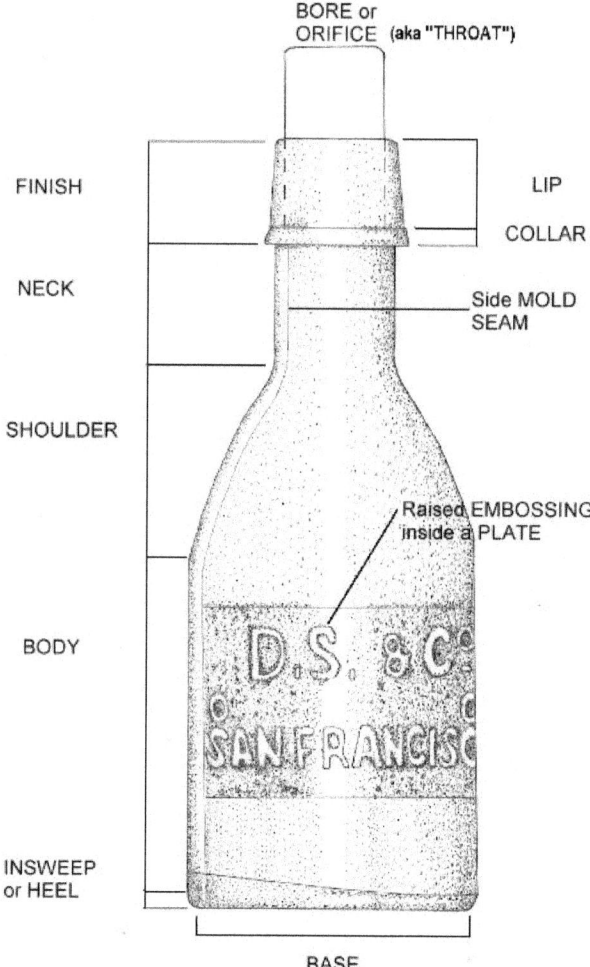

Figure 1. Commonly used bottle terms. (Drawing by P. Corson, 2003.)

One typically easy-to-see and describe differentiation among finish types, however, is that they can have distinctly one part, two parts (like in the illustration above), or three parts; rarely are there more parts (Jones and Sullivan 1989). A common differentiation between the parts of a two-part finish is to refer to the upper part as the lip and the *lower* part as the collar. As with most finish nomenclature, such labeling is not used universally because others refer to the *upper* part as the collar; however, if the finish is comprised of only one part, some refer to the entire finish as the collar. (For more information on this confusing subject, see the *SHA Historic Glass Bottle Identification & Information Website* <www.sha.org/bottle/glossary.htm>.)

RIM

The rim is the extreme upper surface of the finish where the bore begins. Simply put, it is the topmost portion of a bottle or jar. (Note: not illustrated in Figure 1.)

NECK

The neck is the (typically) constricted part of a bottle that lies above the shoulder and below the finish. There are exceptions in that many fruit or canning jars have no neck—like the ubiquitous 1858 Mason fruit jars. Instead, the jars transition from the base of the (external screw thread) finish to the very abbreviated shoulder without any distinguishable intervening neck.

SHOULDER

The shoulder is that portion of the bottle that lies between the point of change in vertical tangency of the body and the base of the neck. Similar to the heel of a bottle (covered below) the shoulder is a transition zone between two other major portions of a bottle.

BODY

The body is the main content-containing portion of the bottle that lies between the shoulder and heel.

HEEL

The heel (also called "insweep") is the lowest portion of the bottle where the body begins to curve into the base. The heel usually terminates at the resting point of the bottle, i.e., the extreme outer edge of the base. Put another way, the heel is the transition zone between the horizontal plane of the base and the vertical plane of the body.

BASE

The base is simply the bottom of the bottle—the surface upon which the bottle stands. The resting point of the bottle is usually the extreme outside edge of the base.

A base with a steep rise or pushed-up portion of the bottom is known as a "push-up" (Figure 2). This feature somewhat reduces the interior volume of the bottle, although it was created primarily for strength enhancing, stability, and possibly collecting content sedimentation (Jones 1971). The term "kick-up" is synonymous with push-up, and both terms may be used interchangeably. Some glassmakers also called this feature a "shove-up" (Illinois Glass Co. 1906).

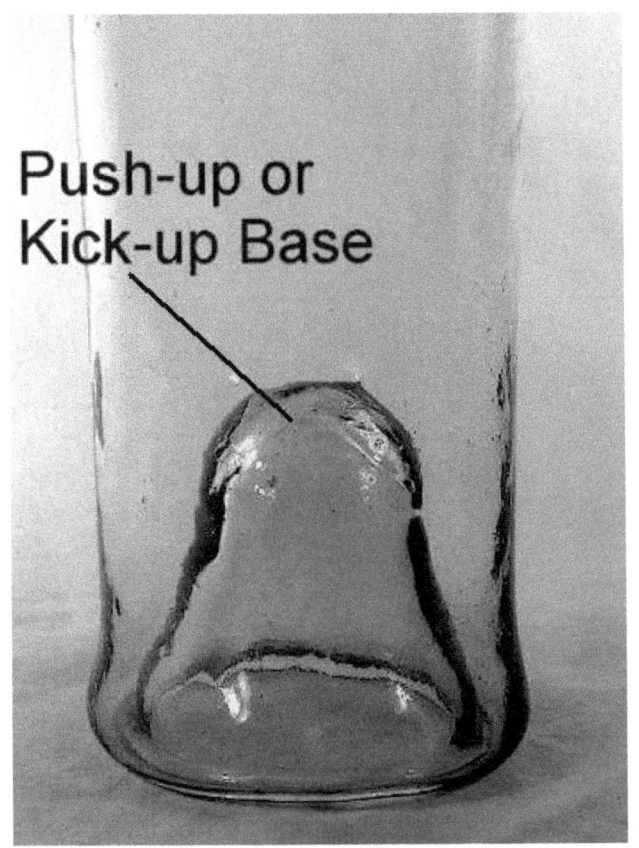

Figure 2. Common form of push-up base, pictured here on a mid-19th-century French wine (Muscat) bottle. (Photo by B. Lindsey, 2005.)

REFERENCES

Illinois Glass Company

1906   *Bottles of Every Description.* Catalog, Illinois Glass Company, St Louis, MO.

Jones, Olive

1971   Glass Bottle Push-Ups and Pontil Marks. *Historical Archaeology* 5:62–73.

Jones, Olive, and Catherine Sullivan

1989   *The Parks Canada Glass Glossary for the Description of Containers, Tableware, Flat Glass, and Closures,* revised ed. Studies in Archaeology, Architecture, and History. National Historic Parks and Sites, Parks Canada, Ottawa, ONT.

Summary Guide to Dating Bottles

Bill Lindsey

To misquote an old saying as rephrased by the Bureau of Land Management supervisor who facilitated the initiation of the *Society for Historical Archaeology's Historic Glass Bottle Identification & Information Website* project: "The universe (of bottles) isn't just more complicated than you think, it's more complicated than you CAN think." This is often true, although much information can be teased out of most bottles with a systematic approach to the matter. This concept is the crux of SHA's historic bottle website, and the reader should use that resource for a more detailed and interactive guide <http://www.sha.org/bottle/index.htm>. If the reader is uncertain of any terms, please see the bottle glossary (this volume) or the SHA historic bottle website for more information. The next article (Lindsey and Allen) is really a series of 3 worksheets and 18 questions designed to help those beginning the foray into bottle dating. Examples can also be found at <http://www.sha.org/bottle/examples.htm#Example%204>.

CAUTIONARY NOTES

- *Changes in technology are not immediate.*
  As the transition occurred from manual craft production to industrialization and automation, glass manufacturers did not always make an immediate leap to technological advances. There is often a technology lag, and acceptance of new technologies often occurred over a period of years, even decades in some cases. Some technological changes were expensive, thus not adopted by glassmakers until it became an "adapt or perish" issue. Many glass factories just perished. A classic example of technology lag is the shift to the fully automated bottle machine from mouth-blown and some semi-automatic methods in the early-20th century (Toulouse 1967, 1969a).

- *Consider the artisan effect.*
  All techniques of glass manufacture, once developed, have continued into the present. In short, there was (and is) nothing to stop a glassmaker

from using an obsolete method in the production of a bottle. Glassmaking and glassblowing induces uniqueness in the form of variations, errors, experimentations, and retrogressions.

• *Many bottles are recycled and reused.*
Glass bottles are an enduring form of storage. The same bottle could have been recycled and reused multiple times for many years before finally being discarded—entire or broken (Busch 1987). Reuse was almost universal with many beverage bottle types (e.g., soda, beer, milk) but was variably common with just about any type bottle, especially prior to 1920. When a likely or known "older" item is found in a known "newer" site, it is referred to as deposition lag.

• *Shapes can indicate manufacturing eras—or not.*
Some bottle shapes are indicative of a particular manufacturing era, such as late-17th to very early-18th-century English "onion" bottles; other bottle styles/shapes, such as square snuff bottles (early-19th century until the mid-20th), were used for so many years that the shape itself is not indicative of age. Other diagnostic tools must be used to date these items. Shape is more indicative of function, i.e., what the bottle was used for or contained, but even that has a myriad of exceptions.

A key concept in historic bottle dating is the high probability that the age range noted for a particular diagnostic characteristic is accurate for a given bottle with diagnostic features. This general probability is based on a merging of reliable references with empirical observations that are made by the author's affiliated consulting experts and by the author himself—all of whom have been students of historic bottle dating and identification for decades. What follows is a sort process using diagnostic characteristics of a bottle with diagnostic features.

The first step is to determine whether the bottle is mouth blown or machine made. Within each of those two categories there is a further sort process to narrow down the age range of the bottle.

INITIAL SORT—MOUTH BLOWN OR MACHINE MADE?

Question 1
Does the bottle have raised embossing on the body, shoulder, and/or neck OR a distinct vertical side mold seam (Figure 1) visible on the body, shoulder, and/or neck (or both features)?

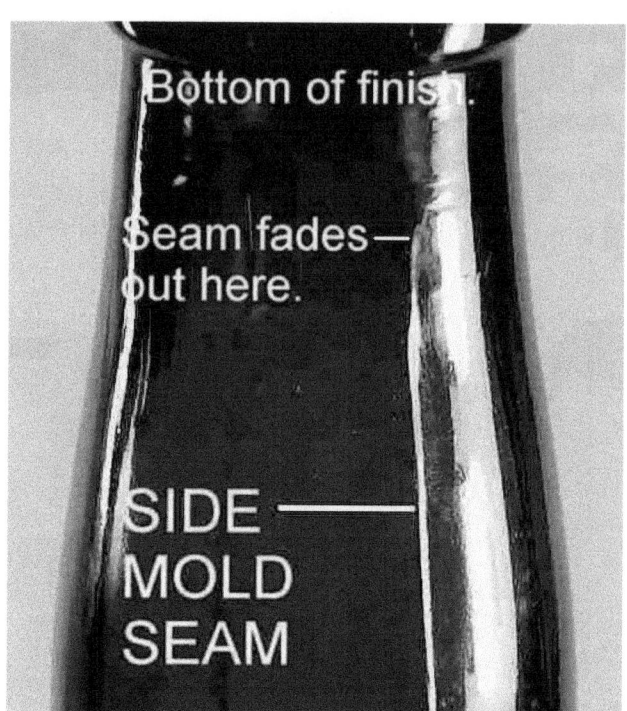

Figure 1. Vertical side mold seam on the neck of a beer bottle ending well below the tooled finish, indicating that it was at least partially handmade. This is a typical 11–12 oz. beer bottle, ca. 1905–1915. (Photo by Bill Lindsey, 2005.)

If YES: The bottle has embossing or visible, vertical side mold seams somewhere on the body between the heel and the base of the finish or lip. A bottle may have mold seams but no embossing, but *all* embossed bottles were molded and have mold seams, even if they are not readily apparent. The majority of the bottles made in the 19th and virtually all in the 20th century were made in molds so "YES" is the *most likely* answer to this question.

Move to Question 2.

If NO: The bottle has NO embossing and NO apparent vertical side mold seams on the body, shoulder, or neck. This bottle is either free-blown, "dip" molded, or was produced in a turn-mold (aka paste-mold) where the side mold seam is erased during manufacturing. A "NO" answer is *much less likely* than a "YES" for this question because a very large majority of bottles made during the 19th century and virtually all made during the first half of the 20th century were mold blown resulting in mold seams; see the note below.

Move to Question 3.

Question 2

Answer only if you said "YES" to Question 1. The bottle DOES have vertical side mold seams and/or raised embossing.

Do the vertical side mold seams go up to the highest vertical point of the finish (aka "lip") side and usually onto the finish rim itself AND the topmost surface of the finish (rim) is not visibly ground down, i.e., the bottle does not have a ground lip/rim?

If YES: The vertical side mold seam or seams go to the highest vertical point of the finish side and (usually) onto the top surface (rim) of the finish AND the top surface of the finish does not appear ground down.

This is a machine-made bottle or jar and will also usually have a highly diagnostic horizontal mold seam just below the finish that circles the neck. This is especially obvious with narrow-mouth or bore bottles but can also be found on wide-mouth/bore bottles, like canning jars.

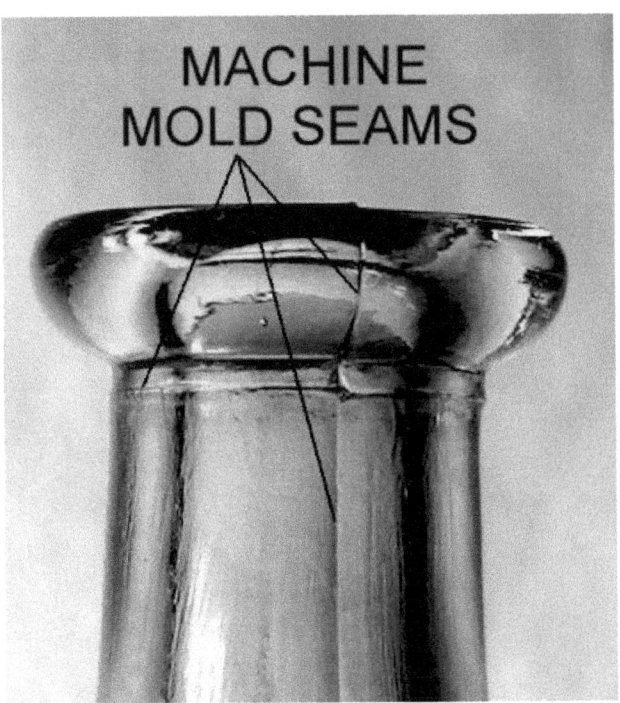

Figure 2. Close-up of the finish (lip) of an Illinois Glass Co. bottle manufactured on an Owens Bottle Machine (Toledo, Ohio), ca. 1915–1920. (Photo by Bill Lindsey, 2005.)

Figure 2 shows both of these mold seams. Bottles with these diagnostic mold seams in evidence were made by either semi-automatic or fully automatic bottle machines and virtually always date after 1900 (for wide-mouth bottles and jars) and after 1910 for narrow-bore bottles (Miller and McNichol 2002).

If NO: The top surface of the finish is either ground down (most commonly seen on canning/fruit jars but also on other types, including screw-thread-finish liquor flasks) or the side mold seam stops or fades out distinctly below the top of the finish and usually—but not always—below the lowest portion of the finish (i.e., collar) as shown in the Figure 1 above.

Bottles with this discontinuous or fading vertical side mold seams are referred to as mouth blown or handmade and typically date prior to 1915, although they could date back to at least 1800. The vast majority of U.S. manufactured, mouth-blown molded bottles were made between about 1820 and 1915. See Question 4 for more information on mouth-blown bottles portion of this key.

Exceptions to Question 2: One of the longest running myths in the world of bottle dating is that the side mold seam can be read like a thermometer to determine the age of a bottle. The concept is that the higher the side mold seam on the bottle, the later it was made or at least in the era from the early- to mid-19th century until the first few decades of the 20th century. For a broader discussion of this subject see "Debunking the Myth of the Side Seam Thermometer" (Lockhart et al., this volume).

The three most common exceptions to the side mold seam "rule" are a few types of machine-made bottles on which the vertical side mold seams do not quite reach the top edge of the finish, making them appear to be possibly mouth-blown.

- *Fire polishing*
  Occasionally encountered machine-made bottles may have fire-polished finish rims, a process that eradicated evidence of the neck-ring mold seam on the rim of the bottle. These bottles will not have the side mold seam proceeding from the upper finish side over and onto the rim itself.

- *Milk bottles*
  Many milk bottles made with press-and-blow machines from the very early 1900s into at least the 1940s resulted in vertical side mold seams that gradually fade out on the neck, distinctly below the base of the finish.

- *Ink/shoe polish bottles*
  Another common exception to this dating question deals with small inkbottles and similar small, moderately wide-mouth bottles (like shoe polish) made during the first half of the 20th century.

Question 3

Answer only if you said "NO" to Question 1. The bottle does NOT have vertical side mold seams.

Is the bottle cylindrical/round, exhibiting very symmetrical conformation and having faint concentric "rings" or striations on the glass surface going horizontally around the body and/or neck of the bottle as shown in the picture below (Figure 3)?

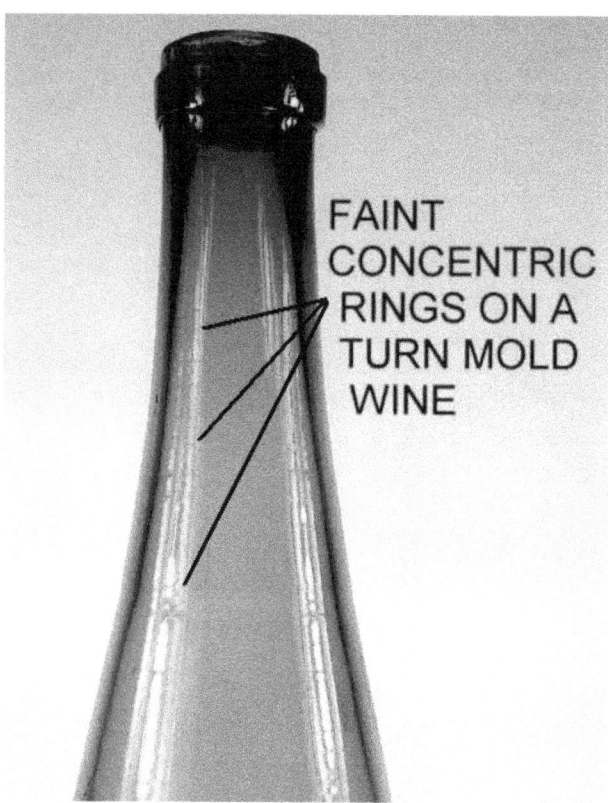

Figure 3. "Hock" wine bottle, ca. 1890–1915. The concentric rings are not always as obvious as the picture shows and sometimes not visible. Although if present this characteristic is a conclusive diagnostic feature. (Photo by Bill Lindsey, 2005.)

If YES: This bottle was produced in a turn-mold, which was also known in the glass industry as a paste-mold. The bottle literature variously refers to all turn/paste mold, free-blown, and dip-molded bottles as mouth-blown or handmade bottles. All turn-mold bottles are round in cross section and, unless stained (aka patinated), will usually have a polished-looking sheen to the glass surface. The large majority of turn-mold bottles date between 1880 and 1915, although they were produced as early as the mid-1850s and as late as the early 1920s (Switzer 1974; Deiss 1981; Jones and Sullivan 1989; Boow 1991; Gerth 2006; empirical observations).

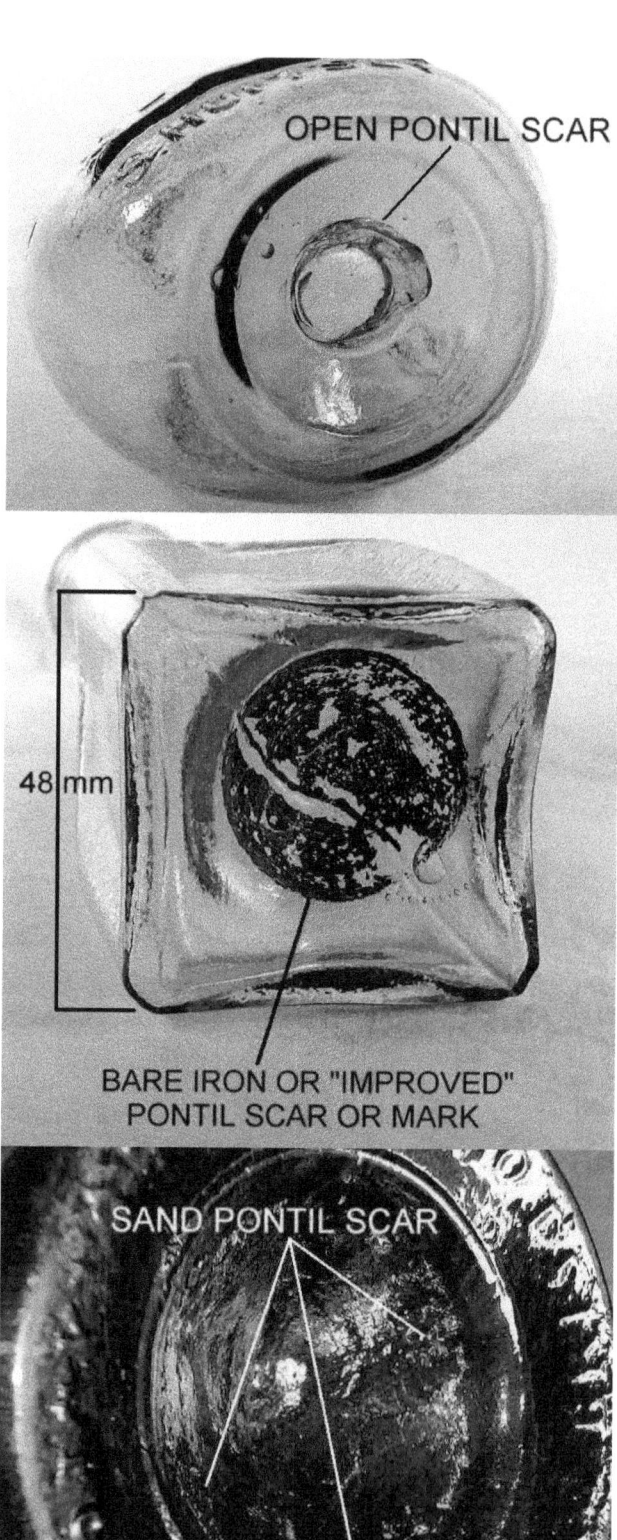

Figure 4. Examples of the three major pontil types: (a) glass-tipped or "open" pontil scar on a pictorial calabash flask from Isabella Glass Works, NJ, ca. 1850–1855; (b) iron or "improved" pontil scar; and (c) sand (disk) pontil scar on a "Rickett's Patent" liquor bottle, 1822 (this bottle has a dated blob seal). (Photo by Bill Lindsey, 2005.)

A "YES" answer to this question is more likely than a "NO." Go to Question 5 for a possible dating refinement based on the method of finish application, although turn-mold production process can mask some of the diagnostic features.

If NO: The bottle is either not round or, if round, is very crudely made and nonsymmetrical with no concentric body/neck rings. This bottle is probably free blown or dip molded. These two manufacturing types can be hard to differentiate from each other. Free-blown bottles are almost always round or oval in cross-section and have lines that are not sharp (i.e., a "flowing" look). Most free-blown bottles date prior to 1850 and can be much older. Dip-mold-produced bottles may be any shape in the body but have more distinct lines from the shoulder down since that portion was actually molded (Jones and Sullivan 1989). Dip-mold bottles usually date prior to 1865–1870 but can also be much older (back to early-18th century at least).

Note:
Questions 4–7 apply to diagnostic characteristics of mouth-blown bottles.

Questions 8–18 apply to diagnostic characters of machine-made bottles.

MOUTH-BLOWN BOTTLES

Question 4
Does the base of the bottle have some type of pontil scar or mark?

A pontil scar or mark is a very useful mid-19th-century diagnostic dating characteristic (Figure 4). Several different types of pontil marks exist, all of which are a mark or scar on the bottle base left by a type of pontil rod. A lot of variety is possible within each category of pontil marks. Between the mid-1840s and the mid-1860s, various snap-case tools that typically left no distinct markings on the bottle gradually replaced the pontil rod (Barber 1900; Jones and Sullivan 1989).

The SHA historic bottle website has much more information on pontil rods, pontil scars, and the empontilling process.

If YES: The base of the bottle does have a pontil mark. Utilitarian bottles with pontil marks usually date from or prior to the American Civil War era, i.e., ≤1860–1865, and almost always prior to the early-1870s, although bottles can date prior to 1800. Note that many specialty or artisan-made bottles can have pontil scars after this period.

If NO: The base of the bottle does not have any evidence of a pontil mark. The base may have a mold line(s) and/or embossing, or be totally smooth and unmarked. The vast majority (probably 95%+) of mouth-blown utilitarian bottles without pontil marks date after the Civil War, that is, they were made after 1865.

Question 5
Does the bottle finish ("lip") have an applied finish, tooled finish, or a finish that does not fit either of these categories or you do not know?

Unless familiar with these terms, a user must view the descriptions below for both applied and tooled finishes to properly differentiate those finishing methods from each other. The finish manufacturing technique can be difficult traits to differentiate from each other. The applied vs. tooled finish dating reliability is considered of moderate accuracy due to the wide time span that glassmakers adopted the new tooling methodology. A lot of finishing variability exists between types or classes of bottles, although within a given type of bottle, the finishing method can be a very helpful dating tool. For more information, see my reprinted article "Finishing Touch: A Primer on Mouth-blown Bottle Finishing Methods with an Emphasis on 'Applied' vs. 'Tooled' Finish Manufacturing" (this volume).

"True" applied finish—This finish is most accurately called an applied finish but is also referred to as an applied lip. Figure 5 shows a bottle with a distinct applied finish. This finish results from the separate application of hot glass to the unfinished bottle at the point where the bottle was removed from the blowpipe, i.e., the neck. After glass application, most applied finishes were also tooled to shape. Applied finish bottles typically date between 1820 and 1890, although there is much variety depending on type or class of bottles. In general, based on empirical evidence, the larger the bottle the later applied finishes were used.

Many collectors and archaeologists inaccurately use the term "applied lip" to refer to any finish on a mouth-blown (non-machine-made) bottle where the side mold seam does not terminate at the top of the finish. "Applied finish" should refer only to a separately applied finish, i.e., a "true" applied finish.

Diagnostic characteristics of an applied finish include several or all of the following:

• The mold seam ends abruptly at the lower edge of the finish (shown in Figure 5). Be aware that the mold seams in the upper neck portions of an applied finish bottle can be very hard to detect due to neck re-firing during the finish application process or just the emasculating effect of the hot glass to finer features like mold seams.

• There is usually a small quantity of excess glass slopping over onto the neck of the bottle just below the finish (Figure 5). Sometimes the excess slop-over is not evident or the finish glass was actually inadequate in quantity, resulting in a finish that is "missing" some portions, evidenced by unfilled spots on the top of the finish and/or ragged unevenness at the base of the finish.

Figure 5. "True" applied finish (lip) with the side mold seam stopping abruptly at the base of the finish. Bottle is a Lindsey's Blood Searcher (patent medicine from Hollidaysburg, PA), ca. 1855–1865. (Photo by Bill Lindsey, 2005.)

• The visual presence of a line or ridge inside the applied finish glass can often be confirmed and felt with the little finger inside the bore. (Note: this ridge is not visible in Figure 5 but can be distinctly felt on this bottle with ones finger.) This line/ridge is the "interface" between the blowpipe-severed neck and applied finish glass and can vary from distinct to virtually nonexistent.

• Concentric horizontal tooling marks from a finishing tool will be present on the finish itself but not on the upper neck just below the finish. Most applied finishes had to be hand tooled after the glass application in order to achieve the desired shape.

• On some applied finishes there will be a grouping of small, short fissures or cracks (crazing) in the area where the glass was applied to the sheared/cracked-off neck end. This feature is rarely seen on tooled finishes (next section) and typically quite indicative of an applied finish.

Tooled Finish—Figure 1 shows an early-20th-century beer bottle with a tooled finish. The sidemold seam fades out on the neck well below the finish. The tooled (aka "wiped" or "improved tooled") finish was usually a result of the glass for the finish being blown with the rest of the bottle in the mold, then the finish was hand tooled to a more precise shape once the still-hot (and pliable) bottle was removed from the mold, often after re-firing the bore at the blowpipe detachment point. In short, the finish glass was not applied to the severed neck of the bottle in a separate hand operation. The changeover from applied finishes to tooled finishes appears to have been in the 1880s, with a large majority of bottles produced after 1890 exhibiting this finishing method. Hand-tooled finishes largely disappeared between 1910 and the early 1920s with the ever-increasing dominance of fully automatic bottle-making machines.

Diagnostic characteristics of a tooled finish include several or all of the following:

• The side mold seam distinctly fades out on the neck of the bottle, typically within an inch of the bottom of the finish (Figure 1), although sometimes it will disappear within the finish itself but short of the rim. The terminal end of the seam will often bend slightly in the direction that the finishing (aka "lipping") tool was rotated.

• Concentric horizontal tooling marks are usually present on both the finish and the upper portion of the neck above the point where the side mold seam fades or disappears; these rings show faintly in the picture above. Sometimes the side mold seams can be observed faintly "underneath" or within the tooling marks or rings. The mold seam can occasionally proceed faintly almost all the way to the top of the finish. This residual seam evidence is likely a result of the glass beginning to cool and solidify while being hand tooled, allowing finish mold-seam traces to remain, and/or how tightly the finishing tool was pressed. Evidence of the mold seam within the confines of the finish positively identifies the finish glass as having been mold blown and not separately applied.

• The absence of a line or ridge inside the finish as would be found on a "true" applied finish since there was no separate application of finishing glass. The glass inside the neck at the finish/neck interface feels smooth to the touch with no ridge evident (not visible in Figure 1).

• There is often a visible change in the thickness of the glass on each side of the bottleneck inside the bore, beginning at the point where the seam disappears and the tooling marks begin. This is usually just a subtle "hump" on the inside surface of the glass where the tip of the finishing tool ended.

As usual with glass bottle manufacture, there was a lot of variation in the changeover from applied to tooled finishes, depending on the type or class of bottle. In general, based on empirical evidence, the smaller the bottle, the earlier that tooled finishes were generally adopted. For example, small proprietary drug store bottles appear to have almost totally made the changeover to tooled finishes by the late-1870s. Larger square "bitters" type bottles appear to have not completed this changeover to tooled finishes until the mid- to late-1880s, and beer bottles until the early- and possibly mid-1890s (Bill Lockhart 2006, pers. comm.).

Other Finishes or Do Not Know—The universe of mouth-blown historic bottles contains many finishes or finish processes that do not fit neatly into this key. An assortment of different finishes (e.g., sheared, laid-on rings) have features that defy specific categorization, although these bottles can be dating-diagnostic depending on the particular type or class of bottle on which the finish is found. If your bottle falls out here, the best course of action is to consult the "Bottle Finishes & Closures" link on the SHA historic bottle website.

Question 6
Does the bottle have some type of mold seam or seams within the extreme outside edges of the base?

Base mold seams can be indicators of age, although there are enough exceptions that the dependability of this diagnostic feature is only moderate. In addition, the mold seams on many bottles may be difficult or even impossible to discern for a variety of reasons. (Note: Base embossing is not pertinent to either a "YES" or "NO" answer here, as embossing can be present on bottles from any of the mold types.)

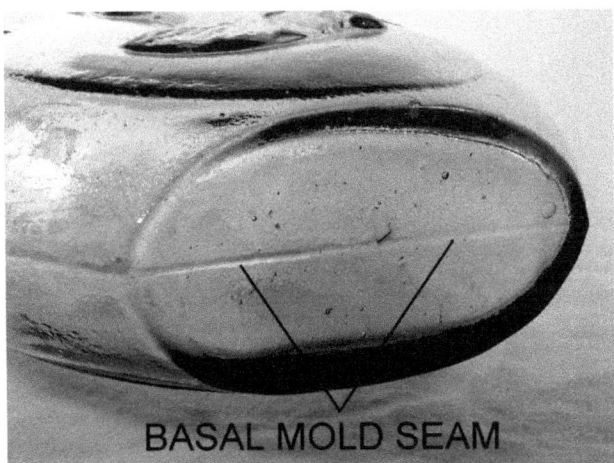

Figure 6a. Basal mold seam across the bottom of the bottle. Bottles produced in a simple two-piece mold with no separate base part have a mold seam that bisects the entire base. These are often referred to as hinge mold or snap-case bottles. This bottle is a Washington-Taylor figured flask (Philadelphia, PA), ca. 1860–1870. (Photo by Bill Lindsey, 2005.)

If YES: Within the confines of the bottle base, there is a mold seam or seams (Figures 6a and 6b). Base mold seams on mouth-blown bottles can be straight, round, oval, keyed, or notched. All versions include a continuation of the side (body) mold seams onto at least the outer edge of the base where the side seams merge with the base seams (post-bottom mold) or actually are the base seams (hinge mold). Bottles with these base types usually date no later than 1890–1895, although earlier cut-off dates are associated with certain mold types and within some bottle categories. On the SHA historic bottle website the links on "Bottle Bases" and "Bottle Typing & Diagnostic Shapes" cover exceptions to these rules.

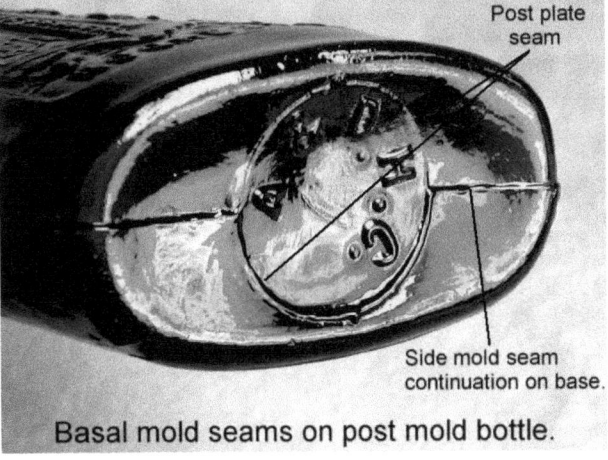

Figure 6b. Post-bottom mold produced bottle. The "post" seam is a result of a separate base mold section or plate. Bottle pictured is a Warner's Safe Tonic (Rochester, NY), ca. 1879–1883 (Seeliger 1974). (Photo by Bill Lindsey, 2005.)

Bottles with a centered round or oval mold seam within the base were produced in a post-bottom mold simply called a post mold (Figure 6b). With this mold type, a large section of the base is formed by a separate mold base plate or section. Post-bottom mold bottles (with no pontil scar) usually date between 1860 and 1890, although there are significant dating differences among different types of bottles.

Figure 6c. Cup-bottom mold-produced bottle with no mold seams within the base. Bottle pictured is a Cla-Wood Malt Tonic from Portland, OR (White 1974), ca. 1906–1916. (Photo by Bill Lindsey, 2005.)

If NO: If within the confines of the base there are no apparent mold seams, there will probably be a mold seam on the heel of the bottle at the lower edge of the body just above the base resting point (Figure 6c). This heel seam may be distinct but is often faint or invisible, as it is commonly hidden in the ridge or edge at the body/heel transition point or interface. Even if this base seam is not apparent, a cup-bottom mold is conclusively indicated by the side mold seams ending at the heel with no continuation around the heel edge and onto the base. Bottles with these diagnostic features were produced in a cup-bottom mold. These bottles can possibly date back to at least the 1870s (especially for druggist and smaller bottles), although the majority dates from the late-1880s to approximately 1915–1920, which is the effective end of the mouth-blown bottle era. Mouth-blown bottles from the early-20th century (1900–1920) were almost always produced in cup-bottom molds.

Cup-bottom molded bottles are produced in a mold where the base-forming portion of the mold "cups"

the hot glass for the base of the bottle to be (Figure 6d). This type mold was (and may still be) the dominant type used with automatic bottle machines (Toulouse 1969b), although the dates listed above are for mouth-blown bottles.

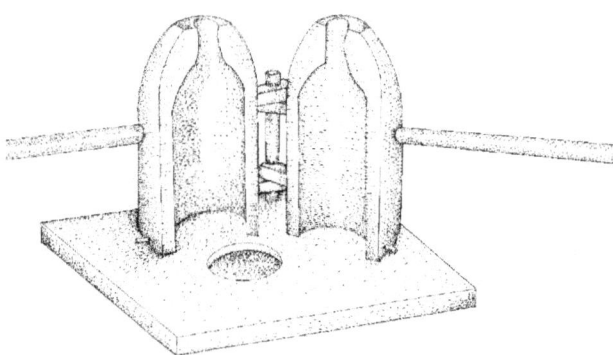

Figure 6d. Two-piece "cup-bottom" mold with separate base plate. (Drawing by P. Corson, 2003.)

Question 7
Are there mold-formed air venting marks on the shoulder, body, and/or base of the bottle?

Air venting marks are usually very small bumps that can be found just about anywhere on the surface of a bottle but are most common on the shoulders, corners, base, mold seams, (Figures 7a and 7b), and sometimes incorporated within the embossing pattern itself. Air venting marks can be found in several or even all of the locations illustrated in figures 7a and 7b and on the same bottle. Air vent bumps are typically smaller than a pinhead and appear like embossed "period" dots. These markings result from small holes drilled in the mold that allowed for the release of hot gases as the bottle was being blown and expanded. (Note: the information for question 7 was based largely on an amalgam of John Thomas (1974, 1977, 1998a, 1998b, 2002), Rex Elliott and Stephen Gould (1988), other references which provide company dating information, and empirical observations.)

If YES: There appears to be one or more air venting marks on the surface of the bottle. Mouth-blown bottles with air venting marks typically date from or after 1885–1890. Air venting began being used significantly in the early- to mid-1880s and appears to have been fairly quickly accepted, becoming an industry standard by about 1890. Few American-made mouth-blown bottles after 1890 are not air vented, although foreign-made items will often lack air venting into the early 1900s (empirical observations).

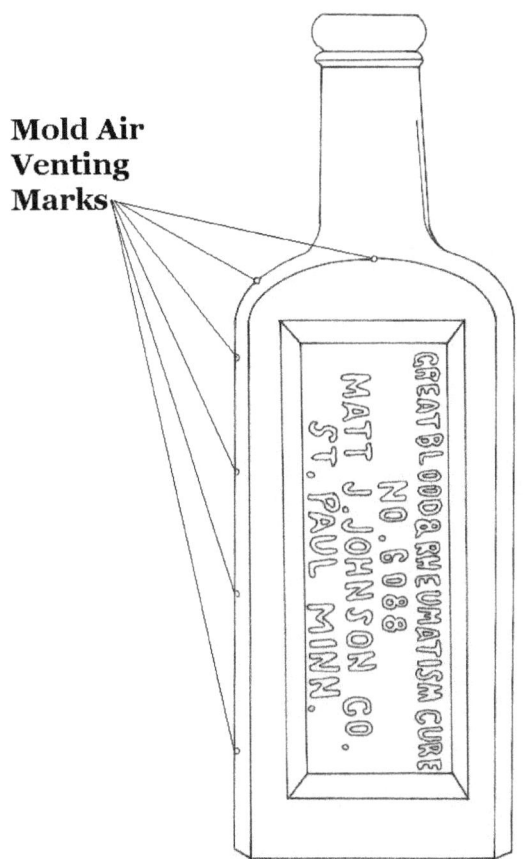

Mold Air Venting Marks

GREAT BLOOD & RHEUMATISM CURE
NO. 6088
MATT J. JOHNSON CO.
ST. PAUL MINN.

Figure 7a. This shows the most common places to look on a bottle, in order of likely probability of air venting marks being present: shoulders, on the body, vertical body edges (square or rectangular bottles). (Drawing by P. Corson, 2003.)

Depending on the location and type of mold air venting, additional dating refinement is possible. As a general rule, the more air venting marks present on the surface of a mouth-blown bottle, the later the bottle was likely produced. More specifically, just one air vent bump each on the front and back shoulder (cylindrical bottles) or the body shoulder corners opposite the vertical side mold seams (square or rectangular bottles) tend to be the earliest (mid- to late-1880s to mid-1890s). Those with multiple air-venting marks scattered around the bottle (including those integrated into the embossing pattern and/or on the base) tend to date to a later period (1905–1920).

Check the surface of the bottle carefully as air-venting marks can be very difficult to see and are sometimes easier to feel. One clue to consider in your search for vent marks is that bottles made in molds with air venting usually have sharper, more distinct

embossing than bottles without vent marks; although this characteristic can be difficult to discern except to the experienced eye.

Figure 7b. The base incorporates into the side mold seam (often hard to determine) or is integrated within the embossing pattern. (Photo by Bill Lindsey, 2005.)

The advent of air venting largely coincides chronologically with the adoption period for molded and tooled finishes, as described in question 5 above. Based on the author's observations, mold air venting appears to have been accepted by glassmakers for all types of bottles faster than tooled finishes replaced applied finishes. This makes the presence of air venting a somewhat more reliable diagnostic dating break for a wider array of bottle types than the finish method. (Of course, using both diagnostic features helps to better refine the dating.)

If NO: There appears to be no air venting marks on the body of the bottle. Mouth-blown American made bottles without air venting marks typically date from or prior to 1885–1890. Look closely at the entire surface of the bottle, as air-venting marks can be very difficult to discern and occasionally are not visible even though the mold may indeed have been vented. An additional diagnostic indication is that bottles produced in non-air-vented molds tend to have more rounded and flattened embossing; this characteristic can be difficult to discern even to the experienced eye.

Note: If your mouth-blown bottle has embossed (or labeled) volume capacity, consult question 16. If your bottle has any type of glass/bottle maker's marks embossed on the base or body, consult question 18 as well as the "Bottle & Glass Makers Markings" page on the SHA historic bottle website for dating refinements.

MACHINE-MADE BOTTLES

Question 8
What color is the bottle?

• *Aqua*
A machine-made bottle made of aqua glass (aquamarine of very pale green), which is NOT a soda bottle or canning jar, is most likely to date from or prior to the 1920s. Aqua pretty much disappears by the early 1930s as a bottle color with the notable exception of soda bottles (and many canning jars) that continued to be produced in various shades of aqua up until recent years.

• *Colorless*
Machine-made bottles with largely colorless (aka "clear") glass can date from any time after 1905, although there is a relatively reliable dating break possible, based on the type of colorless glass. In the production of colorless glass numerous methods—mechanical, physical, and/or chemical—were used to decolorize glass and could result in a slight color tint.

• *Lavender or Amethyst*
Manganese dioxide causes the glass to have a very slight lavender or amethyst tint which is amplified to varying degrees with exposure to sunlight (or artificial

radiation). Amethyst bottles generally date between 1905 and the early 1920s (Figure 8a), although some can date as late as the 1930s. Machine-made soda bottles were generally not decolorized with manganese after 1914 (Lockhart 2006a; 2006b).

Figure 8a. Small utility bottle made from manganese dioxide decolorized glass, exhibiting a slight lavender cast in the thick portions of the glass, ca. 1910–1920. (Photo by Bill Lindsey, 2005.)

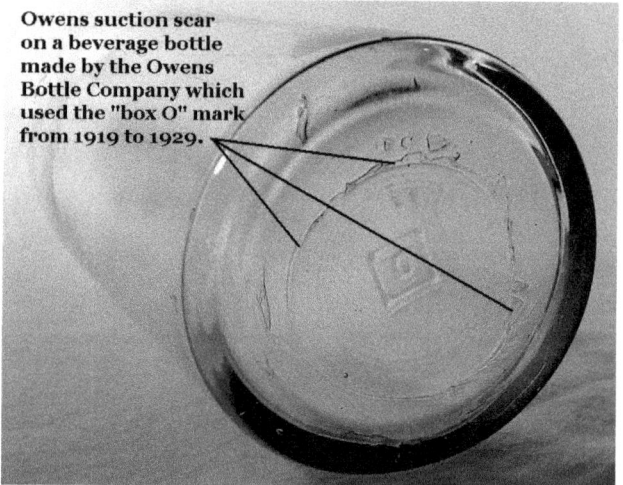

Owens suction scar on a beverage bottle made by the Owens Bottle Company which used the "box O" mark from 1919 to 1929.

Figure 8b. Beverage bottle made from arsenic and/or selenium decolorized glass, exhibiting a slight "straw" color in the thick portions of the glass, ca. 1920–1925. (Photo by Bill Lindsey, 2005.)

• *Straw*
When selenium or arsenic (or a combination of the two) is used to decolorize glass, it often leaves a very faint "straw" cast to the thick glass portions that is not affected or intensified by sunlight (Figure 8b). These bottles will date no earlier than 1912 (Lockhart 2006a and 2006b). One or both of these decolorizers are still in use today. Although after the 1960s other decolorizing agents and glass-producing processes were used, resulting in less abundant "straw" tinted bottles.

• *Other*

Bottle made of some other color of glass. In general, if the bottle has some other glass color, no useful general dating information is possible. See the SHA historic bottle website for more details on the exceptions, and move to questions below for more dating opportunities.

Note: As with all of the dating points on this page, color must be considered in conjunction with other diagnostic characteristics in arriving at a probable date or date range for any given bottle— the "preponderance of evidence" concept.

Question 9
Are there bubbles present in the glass? If so, how many and what size and shape?

Bubbles are air- or gas-filled cavities within the glass, caused by an assortment of irregularities in the production process, including a glass pot or tank that was too hot or not full enough, glass cut-off or shearing irregularities, and various gob feeder problems. Figure 9 is a close-up of a bottle with bubbles in atypically high quantity for illustrative purposes. In the glass-making industry, small bubbles were referred to as "seeds" and larger bubbles as "blisters" (Tooley 1953). Similar to the color question above, the presence of bubbles in the glass can help some in pinning down the date of a machine bottle, but this knowledge must be used in conjunction with other features to more confidently narrow down a date range because it is not conclusive by itself.

If YES: As a general rule of thumb, earlier machine-made bottles and jars (i.e., 1905–1910 [mid-1890s for wide-mouth ware] through the 1920s) will have more and larger bubbles than later machine-made bottles (early 1930s and later), when bubbles in the glass became a much rarer occurrence due to ever more-refined glassmaking technology. Larger bubbles (~1/8-inch and larger) and/or numerous bubbles of all sizes are more prevalent in bottles manufactured during the early machine period: 1890s (wide-mouth ware) to early 1920s.

If NO: The absence of bubbles or presence of only a very few small "seed" bubbles (less than a pin-head in size) or very narrow V-shaped bubbles, denotes a bottle that is more likely to date from or after the 1930s. Looking at glass bottles found in supermarkets today, one would be hard pressed to find even one bubble in all the observed bottles combined, as technology has all but eradicated this flaw in glassmaking.

Figure 9. Bubbles in the shoulder glass of a bottle. This is an extreme example of the number of bubbles to be found in a bottle. (Photo by Bill Lindsey, 2005.)

Figure 10. Bottle embossed with "FEDERAL LAW FORBIDS SALE OR REUSE OF THIS BOTTLE." (Photo by Bill Lindsey, 2005.)

Question 10
Does the bottle have the following statement embossed on its side or on the base? "FEDERAL LAW FORBIDS SALE OR REUSE OF THIS BOTTLE" (Figure 10).

In the U.S., National Prohibition was repealed in late 1933 and was subsequently followed by the passage of Federal laws prohibiting the reuse or sale of used liquor bottles. This requirement was intended to discourage the reuse of bottles by bootleggers and moonshiners, although the biggest discouragement to that illicit activity was that liquor was now legally available. On January 1st, 1935 all liquor sold in the U.S. was required to be in bottles that had the above statement embossed in the glass (Busch 1987). The statement was not required on wine or beer bottles, as the latter category was and to some degree still is bottled in reusable bottles.

If YES: If your bottle has this statement embossed in the glass, it is a machine-made liquor bottle that dates between 1935 and the mid-1960s. This inscription is found only on machine-made bottles, with the rare exception of some Mexican-made (for the U.S. market) bottle being mouth-blown during that era. In 1964, the law requiring this statement was repealed. Be aware, however, that for some years after 1964, liquor could still be found in bottles with this phrase, since not all liquor producers switched immediately to new bottles, either due to the expense of new molds or to deplete an existing supply of bottles (Ferraro and Ferraro 1966).

If NO: If your machine-made bottle does not have this phrase embossed in the glass, it is probably either not a spirits or liquor bottle, was made outside the era the statement was required, or was originally sold outside the U.S. If you know the bottle is a U.S. made/sold spirits bottle (i.e., distinctly a spirits bottle in shape or design or it has other conclusive features like brand embossing or labeling), it could date prior to 1935, although is more likely to be a post-1964 product. Visit the liquor bottle section of the "Bottle Typing/Diagnostic Shapes" link for more information on spirits bottles.

Question 11
Does the bottle base have similar markings to those shown in Figure 11?

The "Diamond O-I" maker's mark of the Owens-Illinois Glass Co. is shown in the picture within the white box. This mark is also known as the Saturn mark due to its stylized form. (Note: The "O" in the Diamond O-I marking is actually a vertically elongated oval, although referred to here as an "O" for simplicity.) This maker's mark is very common on bottles made during 1929–1930 to the mid-1950s.

Figure 11. Maker's mark showing manufacturer of bottle. Bottles with the mark in the image (see white inset box) date between 1930 and the mid-1950s, with some limited use of this mark until at least 1959. (Photo by Bill Lindsey, 2005.)

Figure 12. External (continuous) screw threads on a Heinz™ catsup bottle produced by the Illinois Pacific Glass Company (San Francisco, CA), ca. 1925–1930. (Photo by Bill Lindsey, 2005.)

Question 12
Does the bottle have a finish (lip) that was sealed with a cork, a threaded screw cap, or some other type of closure?

- *Cork*
  The bottle you have has a finish that accepted a cork as the closure and is not a soda, beer, wine/champagne, or liquor bottle. Cork closure, machine-made medicinal, food, inks, and some non-alcoholic beverage bottles usually date prior to the early-1930s, although there are numerous exceptions.

- *Screw cap*
  The bottle has external screw threads, which are usually either continuous (Figure 12) or non-continuous or variations on these themes. Most all types of machine-made bottles with external screw threads date from the late-1920s or after, although some types, like catsup bottles, were commonly screw-threaded from the beginning of machine manufacture in the early-1910s. Note that the Bakelite (plastic) cap for screw thread finishes made its debut in 1927.

- *Other closure*
  There are a lot of finish styles that accepted crown caps, lightening stoppers, or other types of closures that do not resemble either of the choices above. If your bottle does not fit cork or screw cap, consult the SHA historic bottle website.

Question 13
Does the bottle have what appear to be a painted or enameled label, lettering, and/or decoration?

Applied color labeling or lettering (also known as ACL or pyroglazing) was a common way of permanently labeling or owner marking a bottle without the use of fragile paper labels (Figure 13). It was most common by far on soda and milk bottles but can occasionally be found on other types of bottles. An ACL soda or milk bottle dates no earlier than 1934, when the ACL process was first adopted for commercial use in the U.S. (Giarde 1989) with almost complete acceptance by bottle makers (and users) by the early 1940s (Bill Lockhart 2003, pers. comm.). Many beverage and some other types of bottles are still produced today with ACL's (e.g., Corona™ Beer), so there is no termination date for this feature.

Question 14
Does the bottle have a shallowly incised circle on the base that is (usually) between 1/3-inch to 3/4-inch (10–18mm) in diameter?

A valve or ejection mark on the base of a bottle is a definitive indication of machine-made manufacture by a press-and-blow type machine (Miller and Morin 2004). This mark was formed by machines that used a push-rod valve to eject the partially expanded parison out of the one-piece blank mold (the "press" part of the process) to be grasped by transfer tongs when shifting the parison to the second blow mold (the "blow" part of the machine process) (Tooley 1953).

A valve mark is usually perfectly round and roughly 1/2-inch inch (12–14 mm) in diameter (Figure 14), although the marks can occasionally be a bit smaller (10–12 mm) or larger (up to at least 24 mm). The circle is incised or sharply indented into the surface of the glass and can be distinctly felt by running one's fingernail over the mark. On somewhat rare occasions (by a few different glass companies), the valve rod had a mold number incised in it that would emboss the base of the bottle with this number when ejecting the parison; these numbers will always be centered within the ejection mark (Bill Lockhart 2007, pers. comm.; empirical observations).

Figure 13. Applied Color Label (ACL) on a 10-oz. soda bottle from the Mission Bottling Co., Klamath Falls, OR. Bottle made by the Owens-Illinois Co. Oakland, CA, plant in 1946. (Photo by Bill Lindsey, 2005.)

Figure 14. Valve mark on the bottom of a Cloverdale Dairy bottle, ca. 1925–1930. (Photo by Bill Lindsey, 2005.)

Valve marks are almost exclusively found on wide-mouth machine-made hollowware: food bottles and jars, milk bottles, and canning/fruit jars. The mark is most commonly observed on wide-mouth milk bottles and food jars made between the early 1900s through the 1940s and occasionally after that. The mark is also common on canning jars, including many that were produced by semi-automatic press-and-blow machines, possibly as early as 1898 (Birmingham 1980; Leybourne 2001).

Valve marks are very unusual on narrow-necked/mouth (bore) bottle types, although there are some exceptions as valve marks are occasionally seen on early (1910s) machine-made beer and soda bottles. At least one manufacturer (Cumberland Glass Manufacturing Company, Bridgeton, NJ) invented and used a type of semi-automatic press-and-blow machine in 1910 that did produce narrow-neck bottles, most likely resulting in a valve mark on the base of the bottles produced in the early 1910s (Bill Lockhart 2006, pers. comm.; Roger Peters 2007, pers. comm.). Thus, the presence of a valve mark on a soda or beer bottle would indicate a narrow manufacture date in the early 1910s.

Question 15
Does the bottle have a narrow mouth (bore/finish) or does it have a wide mouth (bore/finish)?

- *Wide Mouth*
  During the mid-1890s, semi-automatic machines began to be used for the production of bottles and jars. The first known production bottles made on semi-automatic machines were wide-mouth Vaseline bottles made by the C. L. Flaccus Glass Co. in 1894 (Lockhart et al. 2007). For the first decade or so of use (i.e., up to about 1905), semi-automatic machines were useful almost exclusively for the production of wide-mouth bottles and jars (Figure 15a) due to the limitations of the press-and-blow machines in use at that time. Wide-mouth (bore) bottles and jars with machine-made characteristics can date from as early as the mid-1890s but primarily date after about 1900. These bottles/jars are usually food bottles and canning/fruit jars.

- *Narrow Mouth*
  Non-Owens machine-made bottles with narrow necks, like the medicinal bottles pictured below right (Figure 15b), will essentially always date after 1905 and virtually always after 1910. This also largely holds true for narrow-mouth bottles made by the

Owens machines, which began to dominate bottle production after about 1908–1910 (Toulouse 1967; Miller and Sullivan 1984; Jones and Sullivan 1989; Boow 1991; Miller and McNichol 2002; Bill Lockhart 2003, pers. comm.). Narrow-mouth machine-made bottles, regardless of the type machine they were produced on (e.g., blow-and-blow semi-automatic machines, Owens Automatic Bottle Machine), will essentially always date after 1905 with very few dating earlier than 1910.

Figure 15a. A wide-mouth machine-made canning jar. (Photo by Bill Lindsey, 2005.)

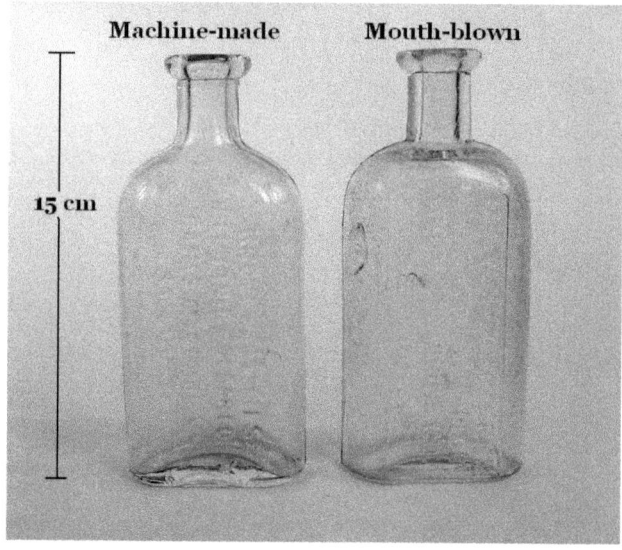

Figure 15b. (Left) narrow mouth machine-made bottle, produced by the Owens machine and likely dates between 1915 and the early-1920s; (right) mouth-blown bottle. (Photo by Bill Lindsey, 2005.)

Question 16
Does the bottle have embossed (or labeled) contents or volume-capacity information?

If YES: It was very uncommon until the early-20th century for the capacity or volume of the bottle contents to be noted in the embossing or on the label (or closure sometimes). Lockhart (2003) details the origin of volume designation: "On March 3, 1913,

Congress passed H.R. 22526, generally known as the Gould Amendment to the Pure Food and Drug Act of 1906. Although the Pure Food and Drug Act demanded a great deal of labeling information, it did not require the inclusion of volume specification. The Gould Amendment corrected that oversight..." (Figure 16a).

It appears that the majority of machine-made beverage, food, and medicinal bottles with embossed (or labeled) specific capacity or volume information likely date from 1913 or later. Note that the majority (*if not* all) of mouth-blown beverage, food, and medicinal bottles with embossed (or labeled) specific capacity or volume information also likely date from 1913 or 1914 or later. Since mouth-blown bottles largely disappeared by the mid-1920s, this gives a pretty tight timeframe for mouth-blown bottles with volume information.

There are several notable exceptions. Many later mouth-blown liquor or spirits bottles commonly had volume notations embossed in the glass (e.g., "FULL QUART," "ONE PINT") or on the label as early as at least 1900. Volume notation on liquor bottles was apparently a marketing issue and seems to be related to the rise of mail-order liquor. The other important exception is with mouth-blown druggist/prescription bottles, which had volume notations commonly embossed on them beginning very close to 1900 as well as gradation markings (Figure 16b).

Note: Keep in mind that bottles without volume embossing may have once had a paper label with volume information.

Question 17
Does all or a portion of the bottle base have a textured pattern, i.e., stippling or knurling?

The bases of mid- to late-20th-century, machine-made bottles commonly have a textured effect covering all or a portion of the base (Figure 17). There were several practical reasons for this feature: (a) reduced base surface contact, decreasing drag on the conveyor belts moving them within the factory and by purchasers/users; (b) hide product-related sediment; (c) hide the suction scar (primarily on Owens Automatic Bottle Machine products); and (d) for at least one specific machine operational reason (Phil Perry, engineer with the Owens-Illinois Glass Co., 2010, pers. comm.). The noted conveyor belt utility would only involve the stippling on the resting surface of the bottle base (like that on Figure 11) where the stippling pattern is just on the outside base edge where contact would

occur. Various stippling patterns were also added to bottle bases for largely aesthetic reasons (Figure 17).

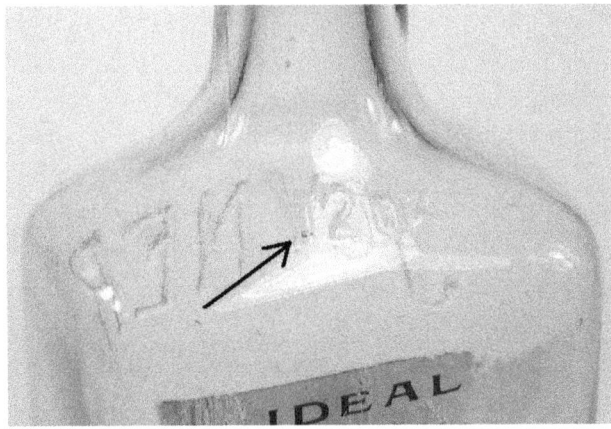

Figure 16a. This is a very late mouth-blown druggist bottle (1914 to early 1920s) from Spokane, WA, that has the volume capacity (12 oz.) embossed on the shoulder. (Photo by Bill Lindsey, 2005.)

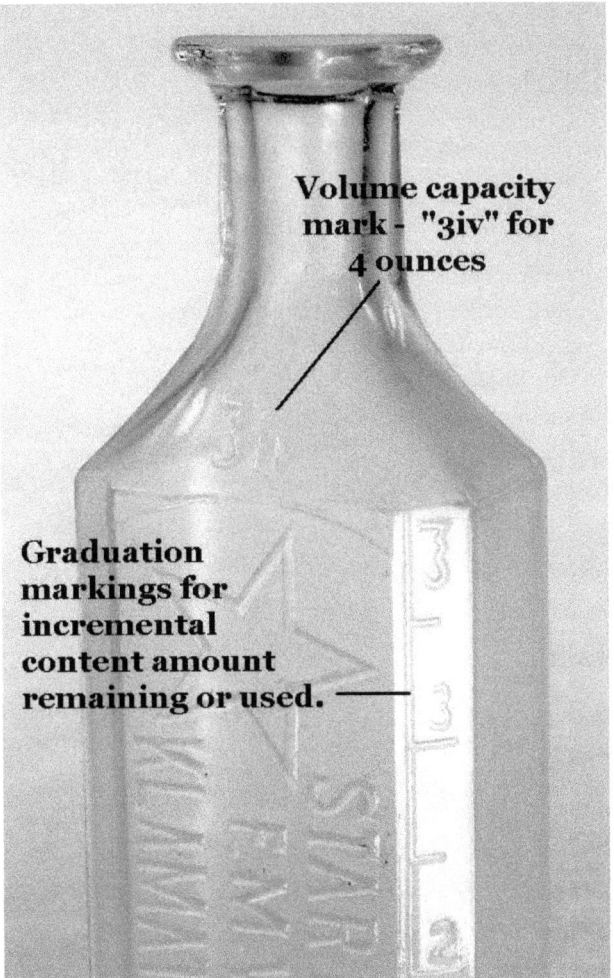

Figure 16b. Example of volume notation and gradation marking embossed on prescription/druggist bottle. (Photo by Bill Lindsey, 2005.)

Figure 17. Stippled base on the bottom of a 1959 soda bottle. (Photo by Bill Lindsey, 2005.)

Stippling was typically produced by hand punching the base plate of the bottle mold. Knurling was machine impressed on the base plate. Practically speaking, the difference between the two is unimportant, and the precise look of these base designs varies quite a bit over time, with different bottle types and among bottle makers. If one has a machine-made bottle with a stippled base, one can be quite certain that it dates from 1940 or later.

Question 18
Does the bottle have any type of glass/bottle maker's marks embossed on the base (typically) or body (occasionally)?

Machine-made (and often mouth-blown) bottles will frequently have embossing on the base (the most common location; see figure 11), base heel, and/or body that identifies the actual manufacturer of the bottle. Be aware that many times the embossing on a bottle base is not a manufacturer's or maker's mark but, instead, is either related to the product the bottle contained, the user of the bottle, or is for internal manufacturer-related tracking (e.g., mold or catalog designations). These latter markings are of little use in dating or typology.

When present, maker's marks (in hand with answers to the other questions) will often allow for a distinct narrowing of the date range in which a given bottle was likely produced. For example, the mark shown in *Figure 11* (C. C. G. C.) is on the base of a quart-sized mouth-blown export-style beer bottle manufactured by the Cream City Glass Company (Milwaukee, WI), which operated from 1888 to 1894 (Toulouse 1971; Bill

Lockhart 2007, pers. comm.). When present, maker's marks can be one of the best dating refinement tools of all. Incidentally, the no. 1 on this bottle base is of unknown meaning; it could be for the first mold made for this style or for the intra-factory bottle-blowing group (shop no. 1) that used the mold at the glass company ... or something else totally unrelated.

To assist with identifying marks and manufacturer-related dates, consult the "Bottle & Glass Makers Markings" link on the SHA historic bottle website, an interactive page that links to scores of articles <http://www.sha.org/bottle/makersmarks.htm#makersmarkinglogotable>. The articles were largely produced by members of the Bottle Research Group (BRG) and deal with specific maker's markings and the history of the companies behind those markings. The SHA site will be a work-in-progress over the coming years as scores more BRG articles (including revisions and updates of past articles) are planned to be e-published via this website on an array of other bottle makers.

If the marking is not clearly identifiable alphabetical letter or letters (like A. B. Co. for the American Bottle Company) but is, instead, a distinct logo or symbol, consult the "Manufacturer's Marks and Other Logos on Glass Containers" <http://www.sha.org/bottle pdffiles/SymbolsLogoTable.pdf>.

REFERENCES

Barber, Edwin A.
1900   *American Glassware Old and New.* David McKay & Co., Philadelphia, PA.

Birmingham, Frederick A.
1980   *Ball Corporation: The First Century.* The Curtis Publishing Co., Indianapolis, IN.

Boow, James
1991   *Early Australian Commercial Glass: Manufacturing Processes.* The Heritage Council of New South Wales, Australia.

Busch, Jane
1987   Second Time Around: A Look at Bottle Reuse. *Historical Archaeology*, 21(1):67–80.

Deiss, Ronald W.
1981   *The Development and Application of a Chronology for American Glass.* Master's thesis, Illinois State University, Normal, IL.

Elliott, Rex R., and Stephen C. Gould
1988   *Hawaiian Bottles of Long Ago*, revised edition. Hawaiian Service Inc., Honolulu, HI.

Ferraro, Pat, and Bob Ferraro

1966 *A Bottle Collector's Book*. Western Printing & Publishing, Lovelock, NV.

Gerth, Ellen C.

2006 *Bottles from the Deep—Patent Medicines, Bitters & Other Bottles from the Wreck of the Steamship Republic*. Shipwreck Heritage Press, Las Vegas, NV.

Giarde, Jeffery L.

1989 *Glass Milk Bottles: Their Makers and Marks*, 1st edition, 2nd printing. L. G. Enterprises, Redlands, CA.

Jones, Olive, and Catherine Sullivan

1989 *The Parks Canada Glass Glossary for the Description of Containers, Tableware, Flat Glass, and Closures*. Studies in Archaeology, Architecture, and History, National Historic Parks and Sites, Parks Canada, Ottawa, ONT.

Leybourne, Douglass M., Jr.

2001 *The Collector's Guide to Old Fruit Jars: Red Book 9*. D. Leybourne, Jr., USA.

Lockhart, Bill

2003 Exploring the Chronology of Soft Drink Bottles from El Paso, Texas, Part 2: Embossed, Machine-Made Bottles from El Paso's Three Largest Bottlers. *The Artifact* 41:21–45.

2006a A Tale of Two Machines and a Revolution in Soft Drink Bottling. *Bottles and Extras* 17(2):19–25.

2006b The Color Purple: Dating Solarized Amethyst Container Glass. *Historical Archaeology* 40(2):45–56.

Lockhart, Bill, Carol Serr, and Bill Lindsey

2007 The Dating Game: De Steiger Glass Co. *Bottles and Extras* 18(5):31–37.

Miller, George L., and Tony McNichol

2002 *Dates for Suction Scarred Bottoms: Chronological Changes in Owens Machine-Made Bottles*. Paper presented at the 2002 Society for Historical Archaeology meeting, Mobile, AL.

Miller, George L., and Ed Morin

2004 A Household Cleanup Assemblage from ca. 1938–1941, Raritan Landing, New Jersey, site 28Mil78: Feature 8, the well, 14 June. Authors' notes.

Miller, George L., and Catherine Sullivan

1984 Machine-Made Glass Containers and the End of Production for Mouth-Blown Bottles. *Historical Archaeology* 18(2):83–96.

Seeliger, Michael W.

1974 *H. H. Warner: His Company & His Bottles*. Michael W. Seeliger, Greenville, PA.

Switzer, Ronald R.

1974 *The Bertrand Bottles—A Study of Nineteenth-Century Glass and Ceramic Containers*. National Park Service, U.S. Department of the Interior, Washington, DC.

Thomas, John

1974 *Picnics, Coffins, Shoo-Flies*. Preuss Press, San Luis Obispo, CA.

1977 *Whiskey Bottles of the Old West*. Maverick Publications, Bend, OR.

1998a *Whiskey Bottles and Liquor Containers from the State of Oregon*. Privately printed, Scotts Valley, CA.

1998b *Whiskey Bottles and Liquor Containers from the State of Washington*. Ananta Printing & Publishing, Soquel, CA.

2002 *Whiskey Bottles of the Old West*, revised and updated edition. Boyertown Publishing Co., Boyertown, PA.

Tooley, Fay V. (editor)

1953 *Handbook of Glass Manufacture: A Book of Reference for the Factory Engineer, Chemist and Plant Executive*. Ogden Publishing Co., New York, NY.

Toulouse, Julian

1967 When Did Hand Bottle Blowing Stop? *The Western Collector* 5(8):41–45.

1969a *Fruit Jars*. Thomas Nelson & Sons, New York, NY.

1969b A Primer on Mold Seams, Part 1. *The Western Collector* 7(11):526–535; Part 2. *The Western Collector* 7(12):578–587.

1971 *Bottle Makers and Their Marks*. Thomas Nelson, Inc., New York, NY.

White, James Seeley

1974 *The Hedden's Story Handbook of Proprietary Medicines*. Durham & Downey, Portland, OR.

Bottle Dating Worksheets
Bill Lindsey and Rebecca Allen

WORKSHEET 1:
INITIAL SORT: MOUTH-BLOWN
OR MACHINE-MADE BOTTLE?

Circle Yes or No and note relevant dates.

Question 1:
Does the bottle have raised embossing on the body, shoulder, and/or neck OR a distinct vertical side mold seam visible on the body, shoulder, and/or neck (or both features)?

> *If YES: Continue to Question 2.*
> *If NO: Skip to Question 3.*

Question 2:
(Use when the bottle DOES have vertical side mold seams.) Do the vertical side mold seams go up side of the finish to the highest vertical point (rim or lip) and usually onto the finish (rim) itself AND the topmost surface of the finish (rim) is not visibly ground down, i.e., the bottle does not have a "ground rim"?

If YES: This is a *machine-made* bottle or jar. Bottles with these diagnostic mold seams in evidence were made by either semiautomatic or fully automatic bottle machines and virtually always date after 1900 (for wide-mouth bottles and jars) and after 1910 for narrow-bore bottles.

> *SKIP to Questions 8–18, completing Worksheet 3.*

If NO: Bottles with this discontinuous or fading vertical side mold seams are referred to as "mouth blown" or "handmade" and typically date prior to 1915, although they could date back to at least 1800. The vast majority of U.S. manufactured, mouth-blown molded bottles were made between about 1820 and 1915.

> *Continue to Question 3 AND Questions 4–7, completing Worksheet 2.*

Question 3:
(Use when the mouth-blown bottle DOES NOT have vertical side mold seams.) Is the bottle cylindrical/round, exhibiting very symmetrical conformation, and with the body and/or neck having faint concentric "rings" or striations on the glass surface going horizontally around the body of the bottle?

If YES: This bottle was produced in a turn mold. The majority of turn-mold bottles date between 1880 and 1915, although they were produced as early as the mid-1850s and as late as the early 1920s.

If NO: The bottle is either not round or if round is very crudely made and non-symmetrical with no concentric body/neck rings. This bottle is probably free-blown or dip molded. Most free-blown bottles date prior to 1850 and can be much older. Dip-mold bottles usually date prior to 1865–1870 but can also be much older (back to early–18th century at least).

Circle Yes or No and note relevant dates.

Question 4:
Does the base of the bottle have some type of pontil scar or mark?

If YES: Utilitarian bottles with pontil marks usually date from or prior to the American Civil War era, i.e., ≤1860–1865, and almost always prior to the early 1870s, although bottles can date prior to 1800. Note that many specialty or artisan-made bottles can have pontil scars after this period.

If NO: The vast majority (probably 95%+) of mouth-blown utilitarian bottles without pontil marks date after the Civil War, that is, they were made after 1865.

Question 5:
Is the bottle finish (a) applied, (b) tooled, or (c) unknown?

a.   Applied-finish bottles typically date between 1820 and 1890.

b.   The changeover from applied finishes to tooled finishes appears to have been in the 1880s, with a large majority of bottles produced after 1890 exhibiting this finishing method. Hand-tooled finishes largely disappeared between 1910 and the early-1920s with the ever-increasing dominance of fully automatic bottle-making machines.

c.   Does not fit A or B and is unknown to you. Continue with questions, and later consult the "Bottle Finishes & Closures" page on the SHA historic bottle website.

Question 6:
Does the bottle have some type of mold seam or seams within the extreme outside edges of the base?

If YES: Bottles with these base types usually date no later than 1890–1895, with some exceptions. Note that post-bottom mold bottles (with no pontil scar) usually date between 1860 and 1890.

If NO: If within the confines of the base there are no apparent mold seams, there will probably be a mold seam on the heel of the bottle at the lower edge of the body just above the base resting point (called a cup-bottom mold). These bottles can possibly date back to at least the 1870s (especially for druggist and smaller bottles), although the majority dates from the late 1880s to approximately 1915–1920, which is the effective end of the mouth-blown bottle era. Mouth-blown bottles from the early-20th century (1900–1920) were almost always produced in cup-bottom molds.

Question 7:
Are mold-formed air venting marks visible on the shoulder, body, and/or base of the bottle?

If YES: One or more air venting marks appear on the surface of the bottle. Mouth-blown bottles with air-venting marks typically date from or after 1885–1890. Air venting began being used significantly in the early- to mid-1880s and appears to have been fairly quickly accepted, becoming an industry standard by about 1890. Few American-made mouth-blown bottles *after* 1890 are not air vented, although foreign-made items will often lack air venting into the early 1900s.

More specifically, just one air vent bump each on the front and back shoulder (cylindrical bottles) or the body shoulder corners opposite the vertical side mold seams (square or rectangular bottles) tend to be the earliest (mid- to late 1880s to mid-1890s), while those with multiple air venting marks scattered around the bottle—including those integrated into the embossing pattern and/or on the base—tend to date to a later period (1905–1920).

If NO: No air venting marks appear on the body of the bottle. Mouth-blown American-made bottles without air venting marks typically date from or prior to 1885 to 1890.

SUMMARY OF FINDINGS
Start date (earliest date of manufacture possible):

End date (latest date of manufacture possible):

Note: If your mouth-blown bottle has embossed (or labeled) volume capacity, consult Question 16. If your bottle has any type of glass/bottle maker's marks embossed on the base or body, consult Question 18 as well as the "Bottle & Glass Makers Markings" page on the SHA historic bottle website for dating refinements.

WORKSHEET 3: MACHINE-MADE BOTTLES

Circle Yes or the appropriate letter and note relevant dates.

Question 8:
What color is the bottle?

Aqua—a machine-made bottle made of aqua glass—which is *not* a soda bottle or canning jar—is most likely to date from or prior to the 1920s. Aqua pretty much disappears by the early 1930s as a bottle color with the notable exception of soda bottles (and many canning jars).

a. Colorless, slight lavender, or "straw" cast—machine-made bottles with colorless glass can date from any time after 1905. Clear bottles with a slight lavender tint (amethyst) generally date between 1905 and the early 1920s, although some can date as late as the 1930s. Machine-made soda bottles were generally not decolorized with manganese after 1914. Clear bottles with "straw" cast will date no earlier than 1912, and that color was less common after the 1960s.

b. Some other color—in general, if the bottle has some other glass color no useful general dating information is possible. Move to questions below for more dating opportunities.

Question 9:
Are "bubbles" present in the glass? If so, how many and what size/shape?

If YES: Generally, more and larger bubbles (~1/8-inch and larger) and/or numerous bubbles of all sizes are more prevalent in bottles manufactured during the early machine period—1890s (wide-mouth ware) to early 1920s.

Question 10:
Does the bottle have the following statement embossed on its side or on the base? "FEDERAL LAW FORBIDS SALE OR REUSE OF THIS BOTTLE"

If YES: With rare exceptions (bottles made during late 1934 and after 1965), this is a machine-made liquor bottle that dates between 1935 and the mid-1960s.

Question 11:
Does the bottle base have a Diamond O-I maker's mark?

If YES: This Owens-Illinois Glass Co. maker's mark is very common from 1929–1930 to the mid-1950s.

Question 12:
Was the bottle sealed with (a) cork, (b) screw cap, or (c) other?

a. For machine-made medicinal, food, inks, and some non-alcoholic beverage bottles, these usually date prior to the early 1930s, although there are numerous exceptions. Does not apply to soda, beer, wine/champagne, or liquor bottles.

b. Most all types of machine-made bottles with external screw threads date from the late 1920s. Catsup bottles were commonly screw threaded from the beginning of machine manufacture in the early 1910s. Note that the Bakelite (plastic) cap for screw thread finishes made its debut in 1927.

c. Consult the SHA historic bottle website.

Question 13:
Does the bottle appear to have a painted or enameled label, lettering, and/or decoration, known as an applied color label (ACL)?

If YES: The ACL was most common by far on soda and milk bottles, but can occasionally be found on other types of bottles, and dates no earlier than 1934 with almost complete acceptance by bottle makers (and users) by the early 1940s. This process is still in use.

Question 14:
Does the bottle have a shallowly incised circle—a valve mark—on the base that is (usually) between 1/3- to 3/4-inch (10–18mm) in diameter?

If YES: Valve marks are most common on wide-mouth milk bottles and food jars made between the early 1900s through the 1940s and occasionally after that. A valve mark on a soda or beer bottle indicates a narrow manufacture date in the early 1910s.

Question 15: Does the bottle have a (a) wide-mouth or (b) narrow-mouth bore/finish?

a. Wide-mouth (bore) bottles and jars with machine-made characteristics can date from as early as the mid-1890s but primarily date after about 1900.

b. Narrow-mouth machine-made bottles will essentially always date after 1905.

Question 16: Does the bottle have embossed or labeled contents/volume capacity information?

If YES: The majority of machine-made beverage, food, and medicinal bottles with embossed or labeled specific capacity/volume information likely date from 1913 or later.

Question 17: Does all or a portion of the bottle base have a textured pattern, i.e., stippling or knurling?

If YES: The bottle dates to 1940 or later.

Question 18: Does the bottle have any type of glass-maker's or bottle maker's mark embossed on the base (typically) or body (occasionally)?

When present, maker's marks—in hand with answers to the other questions—will often allow for a distinct narrowing of the date range in which a given bottle was likely produced. Consult the "Bottle & Glass Makers Markings" page on the SHA historic bottle website.

SUMMARY OF FINDINGS

Start date (earliest date of manufacture possible):

End date (latest date of manufacture possible):

Bottle Identification and Cataloging Considerations
Rebecca Allen and David L. Felton

BUILDING A BOTTLE IDENTIFICATION COLLECTION

Collections of artifacts particularly selected as examples for identification can be one of the most useful tools in the archaeological laboratory. There are many ways and reasons to build an artifact identification collection—often called a "type" collection. Perhaps two of the most common needs for a glass bottle collection are to illustrate the different kinds found in archaeological collections and various the characteristics used for dating purposes.

All archaeologists are aware that while hands-on artifacts and visuals are key to learning, not every archaeologist may own or have access to artifact collections. In most cases, combinations of actual bottles and digital photographs (or online collections) may be used. Many agencies have existing type collections that are available for use, such as the State Archaeological Research and Collections Facility of California State Parks <http://www.parks.ca.gov/?page_id=22203>, a collection that can be visited online and in person. Because every region will have a different time period that is most common to its archaeological record, every collection will vary. For the most part, examples to include in an identification collection are the most common bottles and bottle parts (e.g., finishes, closures, manufacturing marks) as well the most unusual. A useful identification collection will be cataloged for easy searching and reporting.

Almost by definition, an identification collection assumes some underlying organizing structure, a "typology" by which the specimens included are grouped and classified to help the user identify, understand, and interpret them. Sorting, grouping, and classifying artifacts is second nature to most archaeologists, and the authors suspect more ink has been spilled in the archaeological literature debating approaches to classification than most other topics (cf. Read 2007). In spite of this attention, too often the underlying assumptions upon which classification systems are based are not explicitly documented.

While identifying a single, standardized classification system for a group of artifacts (e.g., glass bottles) might seem inherently desirable, it is an elusive goal. Different typologies are often developed to meet differing research goals, collections, or researchers' perspectives and biases. The focus here is to identify key dates in the development of bottle manufacturing, discuss several classification systems that have been developed for glass bottles, and suggest ways that one or more of these might be used in conjunction with a bottle identification collection, especially for searching, organizing, and reporting the associated catalog records.

TABLE 1. *Terminus Post Quem* Dates for 19th- and 20th-Century Glass Bottles.

TPQ YEAR	BOTTLE MANUFACTURING TECHNOLOGY
1821	Rickett's style three-piece mold used
ca. 1825	Lipping tool finish on bottles
ca. 1845	Iron pontils used on American bottles
ca. 1850	Snap-case-held bottles made
1858	Screw top jar, ground lip (Mason jar)
1864	Colorless soda-lime glass made
1873	Codd's patent ball stopper used on American bottles
1874	Charles Fox patents vented molds
1876	H.J. Heinz company begins to use traditional ketchup bottle
1879	Hutchins stopper "blob top"
ca. 1880	Manganese used to decolorize glass ("amethyst" after exposure to sun)
1882	Bail and yoke "lightening stopper"
1886	Introduction of the milk bottle
1889	Semiautomatic machine-made production of narrow-mouth bottles
1892	Introduction of crown bottle cap
1893	Semiautomatic machine-made production of wide-mouth bottles
1903	Owens bottle machine patented
1906	Lug finish on machine-made bottles
1935	Applied color labels appear on commercial glass containers
1933–1964	"Federal Law Forbids Sale or Reuse of the Bottle" embossed on liquor bottles; regulation ends in 1964.
1935	Lightweight nonreturnable beer bottle introduced
1938	Stippled bases appear on lightweight beer bottles
1948	Nonreturnable soft drink bottle

Primary sources: Jones and Sullivan (1989); Miller (1993); and Miller et al. (2000).

Table 1 illustrates common bottle manufacturing dates that are typical for 19th- and 20th-century bottles. These dates are *terminus post quem (TPQ)*, that is, dates after which a manufacturing method first appeared. Depending on cataloging needs, it may be useful to have examples of each manufacturing method or technology in the identification collection.

ORGANIZING PRINCIPLES

Figures 1 and 2 illustrate the drawer layout for the "Bottle Type Collection" at the State Archaeological Research and Collections Facility of the California State Parks <http://www.parks.ca.gov-/?page_id=22207>, compiled largely by Peter and Jeanette Schulz. An online presentation of a few of the specimens in this collection is found at the "Bottle Type Collection Photo Gallery" <http://www.parks.ca.gov/?page_id=22304>. This particular collection is physically organized by bottle function—the original contents that were distributed in bottles of specific, recognizable shapes. The primary purpose of this organization is to place like bottles together in storage, so the broad categories used reflect the makeup of the California collection, rather than a more comprehensive typological schema.

- ale/beer
- bitters
- food
- liquors
- patent medicine
- perfumes and cosmetics
- pharmacy medicine bottles
- soda water
- wine (and shoulder seals)

The California State Parks bottle type collection also includes examples of common manufacturer marks and date ranges for each.

The Society for Historical Archaeology's *SHA/BLM Historic Glass Bottle Identification and Information*

Figure 1. Bottle Type Collection at State Archaeological Research and Collections Facility of the California Department of Parks and Recreation. (Photo by R. Allen, 2015).

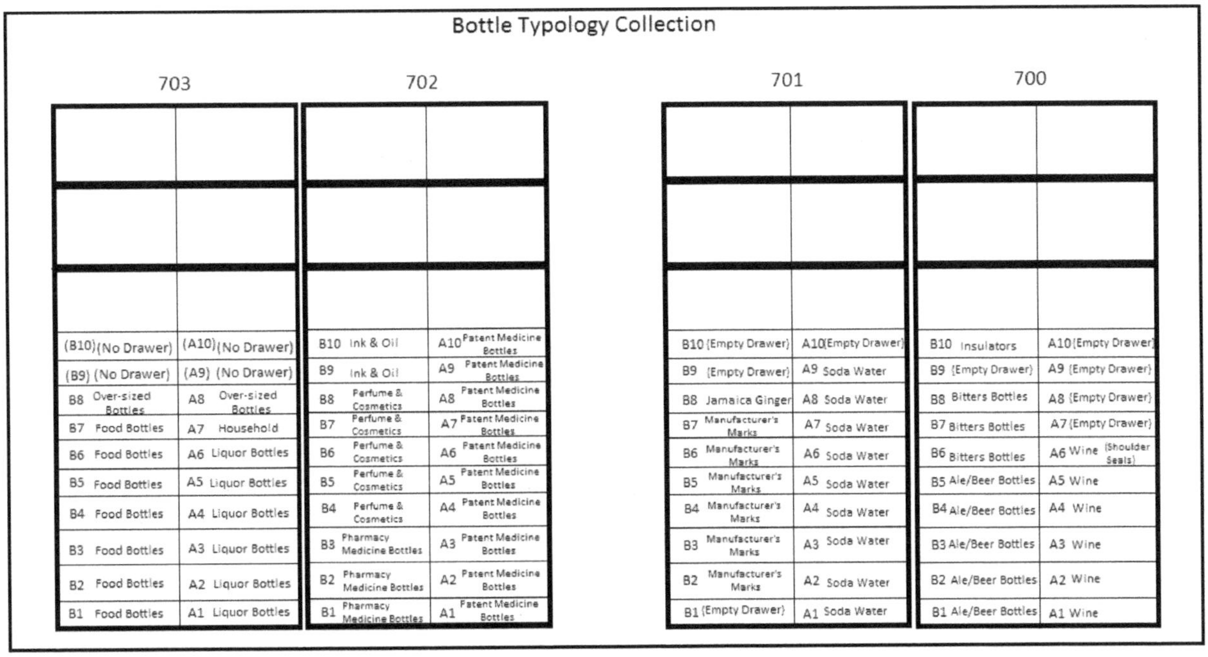

Bottle Typology Collection

703		702		701		700	
(B10) (No Drawer)	(A10) (No Drawer)	B10 Ink & Oil	A10 Patent Medicine Bottles	B10 (Empty Drawer)	A10 (Empty Drawer)	B10 Insulators	A10 (Empty Drawer)
(B9) (No Drawer)	(A9) (No Drawer)	B9 Ink & Oil	A9 Patent Medicine Bottles	B9 (Empty Drawer)	A9 Soda Water	B9 (Empty Drawer)	A9 (Empty Drawer)
B8 Over-sized Bottles	A8 Over-sized Bottles	B8 Perfume & Cosmetics	A8 Patent Medicine Bottles	B8 Jamaica Ginger	A8 Soda Water	B8 Bitters Bottles	A8 (Empty Drawer)
B7 Food Bottles	A7 Household	B7 Perfume & Cosmetics	A7 Patent Medicine Bottles	B7 Manufacturer's Marks	A7 Soda Water	B7 Bitters Bottles	A7 (Empty Drawer)
B6 Food Bottles	A6 Liquor Bottles	B6 Perfume & Cosmetics	A6 Patent Medicine Bottles	B6 Manufacturer's Marks	A6 Soda Water	B6 Bitters Bottles	A6 Wine (Shoulder Seals)
B5 Food Bottles	A5 Liquor Bottles	B5 Perfume & Cosmetics	A5 Patent Medicine Bottles	B5 Manufacturer's Marks	A5 Soda Water	B5 Ale/Beer Bottles	A5 Wine
B4 Food Bottles	A4 Liquor Bottles	B4 Perfume & Cosmetics	A4 Patent Medicine Bottles	B4 Manufacturer's Marks	A4 Soda Water	B4 Ale/Beer Bottles	A4 Wine
B3 Food Bottles	A3 Liquor Bottles	B3 Pharmacy Medicine Bottles	A3 Patent Medicine Bottles	B3 Manufacturer's Marks	A3 Soda Water	B3 Ale/Beer Bottles	A3 Wine
B2 Food Bottles	A2 Liquor Bottles	B2 Pharmacy Medicine Bottles	A2 Patent Medicine Bottles	B2 Manufacturer's Marks	A2 Soda Water	B2 Ale/Beer Bottles	A2 Wine
B1 Food Bottles	A1 Liquor Bottles	B1 Pharmacy Medicine Bottles	A1 Patent Medicine Bottles	B1 (Empty Drawer)	A1 Soda Water	B1 Ale/Beer Bottles	A1 Wine

Figure 2. Schematic of Organizing Principles, State Archaeological Research and Collections Facility of the California Department of Parks and Recreation. (Illustration by Abigail Schmenk, 2015).

Website has a page entitled "Bottle Typing (Typology) & Diagnostic Shapes" <http://www.sha.org/bottle/typing.htm> that offers a somewhat different and more comprehensive approach to organizing by bottle types, necessitated by the number of examples presented and its nationwide scope. Author Bill Lindsey makes the underlying assumptions about the classification system used explicit at the outset on a page entitled "Bottle Typing/Diagnostic Shapes" (bullets added here for clarity):

- The shape of an historic bottle is usually indicative of what the bottle was most likely used for, i.e., what it contained.

- What a bottle was used for is referred to on this website as a "bottle type" or "type of bottle", i.e., liquor, mineral water, druggist, food, etc.

- The process of ascertaining what a bottle was used for is termed typology or simply "typing" and is the subject of this webpage and the many connected sub-pages.

- Since it was the contents of a bottle that guided the consumer in making a selection, not the bottle itself, contents are the most important consideration in establishing categories for bottle classification (Herskovitz 1978)....

- The major bottle type categories used here are based on an amalgam of dozens of references ... but does not align precisely with any one of these references.

- Some users of this site will inevitably disagree with what bottle types were included—or not included—in the broad categories used.

- The point behind these typology pages is not to establish a hierarchal classification system for bottle types but, instead, to help users identify what the most likely function or use was made of the specific bottle shape or type they are interested in...

- This complex of "Bottle Typing/Diagnostic Shapes" pages will always be a "work-in-progress" for the author as the diversity of bottle types and shapes is almost endless. Thus, these pages will never be considered "complete" and are, in fact, designed to be added to continuously over time.

With those assumptions stated, the SHA website author organizes the bottle types represented predominately as a two- or three-level hierarchy:

- liquor/spirits bottles
- wine and champagne bottles
- beer and ale bottles
- soda and mineral water bottles
- medicinal/chemical/druggist bottles
- food bottles and canning jars
- household bottles (non-food related)
- miscellaneous and foreign bottles
- labeled bottles

Typically a second-level exists within each major group that identifies shape categories. For example, within liquor/spirits bottles, shape styles include the following: figured flasks, cylinder styles, square/rectangular styles, flask styles (not considered figured), and other miscellaneous shapes/styles. Finer breakdowns describing more specific shapes are often included as a third level of this hierarchy.

Both The California State Parks and the SHA type collections are organized primarily on the most common bottle uses/contents/functions, as inferred from the shape of the bottle. Keep in mind, however, when interpreting site activities using these classifications, that bottles are often reused and similar bottle shapes can be used for different kinds of products.

The classification approaches described above were developed specifically for glass bottles. Historical archaeologists often also work with more general "functional" artifact classification systems, designed to help researchers group wide arrays of historical artifacts used for similar purposes (functions), do intersite comparisons, and infer site activities represented by those artifacts. Stanley South (1977) developed such a classification system in his seminal volume *Method and Theory in Historical Archaeology*. This methodology has been redefined and refined for many Western U.S. historic sites (e.g., Praetzellis 2004:116–117; see also an example of an artifact catalog system known as SHARD, Sonoma Historic Artifact Research Database, available online at <http://sha.org/resources/artifact-cataloging-system/>). In this classification scheme, very broad artifact "groups" are subdivided into more specific "classes:"

- activities
- domestic
- indefinite use
- industrial
- personal
- structural
- undefined use

While many archaeologists will ultimately want to integrate their glass bottle data with those from other artifact categories, a system such as this is so general that it may prove of relatively little utility in the initial organization and analysis of bottle glass identification collections. We suggest that these classification approaches (particularistic bottle typologies and more general functional artifact groupings) serve

different purposes, but that both are worth recording as separate data elements in the catalog records for the bottle identification collection.

CATALOG DATA

Databases allow searching, sorting, categorizing, re-categorizing, and analyses of data. While many commonalities exist among databases, each project and institution has its own nuances and cataloging needs. Researchers will also find it expedient to have a database that allows for easy translation of data into tables, charts, or other ways of presentation.

For comparative purposes, it is useful to find database structures most commonly used in the surrounding state or region. Universities, state and federal agencies, and private consulting firms typically have their own cataloging systems. Researchers should determine what database and categories of information are critical for building their own sets of data but should avoid too many idiosyncrasies. The end goal is a dataset that other researchers can easily access and use for comparative purposes.

Ideally, catalog databases (and forms, if printed) are designed to gather groups of information in several categories:

- catalog number (unique identifier for keeping track of each artifact; typically includes accession, collection identification, as well as individual artifact number)
- archaeological provenience and data collection information (e.g., project name, unit, feature, level/context, depth, other provenience information, date recovered, recovery method, cataloger's name, date of entry)
- object identification and classification (artifact group, subgroup, object name)
- object information and description (marks, finish styles, origin, manufacturer, dimensions, etc.)
- quantification (percent complete, fragment description, count, etc.)
- dating and references (dating criteria, starting and ending dates, references)
- lab or repository staff information (a category often needed for supervisorial and quality review)
- comments

Much of the information on the catalog form and database can and should be standardized. Having catalogers select from controlled vocabulary (a set of standardized terms) whenever possible will decrease the number of errors and inadvertent variation in terms. Standardizing the logic of the data (e.g. classification schemes, vocabulary, etc.) is often more important than the specifics of the underlying database. Some fields, such as description and comments, do not lend themselves to standardization and need to be entered as free text narratives. Database creators should consider when standardized formats are appropriate and then use them.

Finally, the authors recognize that identification and classification systems are always in flux, "a work in progress" as Bill Lindsey attests. Builders and users of identification collections and catalog data should try to maintain the integrity and logic of whatever organizing principles are employed. Researchers should make additions or changes only after careful consideration and in consultation with others also using that system. To do otherwise will largely destroy the utility of a particular collection for comparison with others or for making more general inferences about the archaeological universe (be it large or small) for which it was devised.

NOTE ON CURATION:
DISCARDING GLASS BOTTLES AND FRAGMENTS

Archaeological investigations of 19th- and early-20th-century sites have the potential to recover large quantities of the same kinds of glass bottles, large numbers of unidentified glass sherds, and many other artifacts that have little information potential and occupy a lot of space or are otherwise difficult to curate. Government agencies and other researchers have recently recognized this dilemma and created guidelines for the collection, curation, and selective discard of materials from their archaeological collections. Such guidelines acknowledge the current problem of finding acceptable curation facilities and accept the premise that not all materials have equal curation value.

Researchers should use systematic guidelines when making decisions to not collect certain glass artifacts during fieldwork and should do the same when discarding glass artifacts after analysis is complete. Any resulting reports should explain the rationale, typically in terms of research potential, for both material retained and discarded. All uncollected or discarded objects should be documented in the catalog itself. By doing so, future researchers are made aware that the extant collection does not represent all of the materials originally excavated.

REFERENCES

Herskovitz, Robert M.

1978   *Fort Bowie Material Culture.* Anthropological Papers of the University of Arizona, No. 31, University of Arizona Press, Tucson, AZ.

Jones, Olive Jones, and Catherine Sullivan

1989   *The Parks Canada Glass Glossary for the Description of Containers, Tableware, Flat Glass, and Closures.* Studies in Archaeology, Architecture, and History. National Historic Parks and Site, Canadian Parks Service, Ottawa, ONT.

Miller, George L.

1993   TPQ List. "Glass Bottle Identification," Pete Schulz, editor. Manuscript handbook for Society for California Archaeology Training Class, 2005. California Department of Parks and Recreation, Sacramento.

Miller, George L., Patricia Samford, Ellen Shlasko, and Andrew Madsen

2000   Telling Time for Archaeologists. *Northeast Historical Archaeology* 29(1):1–22.

Praetzellis, Mary, editor

2004   SF-80 Bayshore Viaduct Seismic Retrofit Projects. Report on Construction Monitoring, Geoarchaeology, and Technical and Interpretive Studies for Historical Archaeology. 04-SF-80 PM 3.9/5.0, EA: 441011. Anthropological Studies Center, Sonoma State University, Rohnert Park, CA. Available online at <http://sonoma.edu/asc/publications/sf80bayshore/index.htm>.

Read, Dwight W.

2007   *Artifact Classification. A Conceptual and Methodological Approach.* Left Coast Press, Inc. Walnut Creek, CA.

South, Stanley

1977   *Method and Theory in Historical Archaeology.* Academic Press, New York, NY.

2
HAND PRODUCTION TECHNOLOGY

Glass Blower and Mold Boy. (Photo from Library of Congress, Prints and
Photographs Division, Washington, DC, 1908.)

Burst off: The blower gathered the melted glass, rolled it on a marver, blew into it slightly, then dropped it, in
a long, purse-shaped, glowing lump, into the open mould. This was immediately closed by the boy; then the
blower blew until a bubble, pushed up on the top of the mould, expanded to the size of a football, and to the
thinness of the thinnest transparent film, and finally burst with a loud pop, flying into shreds of tinsel, light as
feathers. The mould was then opened and a caster-vial with figured sides was exposed. This was taken up by a
second boy on a "snap-dragon,"—a rod something like a ponty, but with a socket at the end for holding articles
of glass,--and carried to a glory hole, where the round, open top was heated. It was then passed to a workman
seated in a chair, who shaped the top, and pressed into it a piece of iron called a "ip-maker." The top was then
a mouth, and the vial became a "vinegar," as the boys called it. Another man was blowing "mustards" in the
same way; and a third was blowing "inks."

Trowbridge, J. T. (1870:70) *Lawrence's Adventures among the Ice-Cutters, Glass-Makers, Coal-Miners, Iron-Men,
and Ship-Builders.* Henry T. Coates & Co., Philadelphia.

Articles

The Manufacture of Glass in San Francisco
[**Transcribed** from 1867, *Daily Alta California* 21 April, 19(6252):1.]
Daily Alta California

Glass-Making: III—The Evolution of a Glass Bottle
[**Reprint** from 1890, *Popular Science Monthly* 36(2):154–169.]
C. Hanford Henderson

Blowing Bottles by Hand
[**Reprint** from 1927, *Productivity of Labor in the Glass Industry*, Bureau of Labor Statistics, Bulletin, No. 441, U.S. Department of Labor, Washington, DC, pp. 28–31.] Available online <https://fraser.stlouisfed.org/title/?id=4043>.
Boris Stern

Glass Bottle Push-Ups and Pontil Marks
[**Reprint** from 1971, *Historical Archaeology*, 5:62–73.]
Olive Jones

The Contribution of the Ricketts' Mold to the Manufacture of the English "Wine" Bottle, 1820–1850
[**Reprint** from 1983, *Journal of Glass Studies* 25:167–175.]
Olive Jones

Debunking the Myth of the Side Seam Thermometer
[**Reprint** from 2005, *Bottles and Extras*, 16(4):14–15, 41.]
Bill Lockhart, Bill Lindsey, David Whitten, and Carol Serr

Whittled Molds
[**Reprint** from 1966, *Western Collector* 4(10):27–28.]
Julian Toulouse

When Did Hand Bottle Blowing Stop?
[**Reprint** from 1967, *Western Collector* 5(8):41–45.]
Julian H. Toulouse

Empontilling: A History
[**Reprint (two parts)** from 1968, *Glass Industry* 49(3):137–142; and 49(4):204–205.]
Julian H. Toulouse

A Primer on Mold Seams
[**Reprint (two parts)** from 1969, *Western Collector* 7(11):526–535; and 7(12):578–587.]
Julian Harrison Toulouse

The Pontil As a Tool for Holding Glassware during Finishing
[**Reprint** from 1973, *Federation of Historical Bottle Clubs Journal* 1(2):8–10.]
Julian Harrison Toulouse

Just What Can a 19th Century Bottle Tell Us?
[**Reprint** from 1984, *Historical Archaeology* 18(1):38–51.]
Edward Staski

The Manufacture of Glass in San Francisco
Transcribed from 21 April 1867, *Daily Alta California*

The two glass factories in the city are in a prosperous condition. They give employment to about one hundred men, and the quality of ware produced is considered fully equal, if not superior, to the manufacture of other countries. The Pacific Glass Works confine their operations to making liquor and spice bottles. The San Francisco Glass Works produce a greater variety; but, as yet, neither establishment has engaged in the manufacture of window glass, or of decanters, tumblers or dishes. It is expected, however, that the latter branch will be soon introduced, and be made successful. A visit to a glass factory will afford much valuable information, as many are not aware of the unimportant material that is used, and the process of converting it into multitudinous and wonderful forms. Visitors are always welcome at the works, and as the persons in charge are obliging and attentive, a spare hour could not be spent more pleasantly or usefully.

The invention of glass dates back from the earliest antiquity, and the honor of its discovery has been contested by many nations. As the oldest known specimens are Egyptians, the people of antiquity most renowned for glass were the Phoeniceans. Certain of their merchants, it is said, retuning in a ship laden with soda, and having been compelled by stormy weather to land on a sandy tract under Mount Carmel, placed their cooking pots on lumps of soda on the sand, which fused by the heat of the fire, and formed rude glass. The body of Alexander the Great was shown to Augustus in a glass coffin. As early as fifty-eight years before the Christian Era, the theatre of Scaurus, in Italy, had been decorated with mirrors, or glass plates disposed on the walls. Window glass does not appear before the third century, the houses at Herculaneum being glazed with talc, and some doubt remaining as to the use of glass for this purpose at Pompeii. The art of manufacturing glass progressed, and the article made in Venetia enjoyed for a long time the monopoly of commerce – their mirrors, goblets and cups being exported all over the world:

but it has been superseded by the manufactures of Germany and England. In 1771 the Company of British Plate Glass Manufacturers was established in Lancashire: and in 1728 plate glass was made at South Shields, and by the Thames Plate Glass Company in 1835. The first attempt to establish glass works in the United States was at Jamestown, Virginia, in 1746: and afterwards, in 1780, at Temple, N.H.: in 1789 at New Haven, and a year later at Boston. The first plate glass works were established at Berkshire, Mass., in 1853. The larges and most numerous factories in the United States, are at Pittsburg, Penn., and Cambridge, Mass.

No material invented by man is to be compared with glass in the service it has rendered. Chemistry and Astronomy are essentially indebted to its aid for their advancement. It has served alike to bring within the knowledge of man the solar system too remote for unassisted vision to detect, and to open new worlds of living creatures too minute for their forms to imprint a sensible image upon the delicate mechanism of the eye. In every direction we find it applied to add to the physical comforts of man. In his habitation it is used to admit the light of day, while it serves as a screen from the wind, rain, and cold. As a mirror it is made to throw back the rays that fall upon it, and perfectly reflect the images of objects, while through its transparent sheets every ray is transmitted. The manufacture of glass has always attracted attention. The production of each kind is a separate branch, involving numerous curious details and processes.

One of the first essentials to a successful manufacture of glass is the preparation of the melting pots. These pots are composed of clay, which is required to be as free as possible from lime and iron. The clay is carefully dried and sifted, after which it is mixed with hot water and worked into a past: it is then transferred into a kneading trough, and when sufficiently kneaded – which is done by men treading it with naked feet oo it is laid in masses in a room to ripen. When required for forming pots, a sufficient quantity is again taken and kneaded with one fourth of its quantity of the material of old pots, which are ground to fine powder and carefully sifted: the material gives firmness and consistency to the paste, and renders it less liable to be affected by heat. The pots are of two kinds – open and covered. The first is used for melting common glass, such as window and bottle ware: the other for flint glass. In each case the pots are made by hand and require great care. The bottom is first moulded on a board. When the bottom is finished, the workman begins to build up the side of the pot by first forming a ring of the same height all around, and so continues, leaving off occasionally to allow the clay to dry and the form to be kept. After the potter has finished his work, the pots are removed into the first drying floor, where they are protected from draughts so that the drying may be conducted with the greatest possible uniformity. When they have processed sufficiently, they are removed to the second drying floor, which is heated with a stove, and the drying is here completed. Both factories in San Francisco keep on hand a large supply of pots, as many as forty or fifty. Those in use are liable at any moment to crack. The open pots are used by the Pacific Glass Works: the covered pots by the San Francisco Glass Works. The clay is imported from Germany and after thorough scraping shines like marble. When pots are required for use they are placed four or five days in the annealing furnace, which is on the reverberatory principle, and there kept at a red heat. This furnace is so situated that when the pots are ready they can be quickly transferred to the main furnace. This operation is exceedingly difficult and requires skill and dexterity, as they have to be removed while red hot, and it must be done so quickly that no sudden cooling injure the pot. This operation will take place at five o'clock this evening at the San Francisco Glass Works.

THE PACIFIC GLASS WORKS

The Pacific Glass Works commenced operations in 1860. A factory was opened at North Beach, one of the objects being to determine by experiment the practicability of manufacturing glassware successfully and profitably. The results were satisfactory, and two years later Messrs. Robt. Turner, Caleb S. Hobbs, John Taylor, H.C. Hudson and Joseph S. Garwood formed a corporation, with a capital of $100,000 (since increased to $125,000) to manufacture all kinds of glass and glassware. A tract of land on the Potrero, containing ten acres, was purchased: a large factory with necessary outbuildings erected, and the machinery and appliances necessary for the business secured. The factory has been in operation since. Last year, however, the works were leased for a limited period to Messrs. Bennett & Co., who have long experience in the manufacture of glass.

The works are very eligibly situated, close to the Bay, and within a few minutes' walk of Long Bridge. The main building, where the huge furnace is located and where the blowing is performed, is 55 feet square and 45 feet high. It Is well ventilated – a provision that is necessary in consequence of the intense heat of the fires. The chimney stack in 14 feet square at the base, and stands on four iron columns, each 8 feet long and 8 inches in diameter. The furnace is 9 feet by 11 feet inside, and has seven pots, two having been added during the year. The latter stand on benches 8 feet long, 2 1/2 feet wide, and 26 inches high. There are eight outbuildings which are used for blacksmith's shop, mixing room, packing room, storehouse, and several are occupied for making pots. The land belonging to the corporation is occupied only to the extent of the ground covered by the works and the residences of a few of the employés, and it is understood that a portion of it will soon be placed in the market for sale.

The materials used, consisting of sand, soda-ash and lime, are to be found in the mixing-room, where the initatory steps are taken in the manufacture of glass. The sand is brought from Oakland, and a fine quality from Monterey: the lime is from Mount Diablo and the soda ash is imported from England. The lime, before mixing with the other two, is carefully sieved. A mixture is then made of the three materials in the proportion of 40 per cent sand, 40 soda, and 20 lime. This constitutes the ordinary batch for the pots, and as there are 7 in use and it requires 500 pounds for each, the amount prepared in 3,500 pounds daily. The color of the glass when cooled, after melting is green, and to alter this to blue, cobalt and zaben are use: to black, manganese and blacklead: to white, arsenic and saltpeter in small quantities. The operations at these works are confined to making wine bottles, pickle jars, carboys, soda water bottles, etc., and consequently the preparation of material is very little varied. Last year, over $100,000 worth of this class of ware was made and sold, and at present the factory works to its fullest extent to fill all the orders received. As mentioned below, the men leave off work at four in the afternoon, for the purpose of allowing the material to be melted for the next day's work. The Master Shearer, as he is called, at that hour with his assistants cleans the furnaces and fills in the batches of material for melting (sand, lime and soda), which remain five hours and until they have been brought to a liquid condition. The heat required is intense – more than tenfold that at which water boils. The pots are again supplied to their full capacity, and fires dept up, to the time the glass-blowers resume work at seven

o'clock next morning, when the pots are full of the molten metal. The furnace is taken down once a year, during the winter season, for the purpose of supplying defects and repairing damages. It is, besides, the dull season, and it is called "going out blast."

The scene presented on entering the main building where the glass-blowers are at work in highly interesting, and is apt to excite sentiments of wonder in a person who never witnessed such before. Thirty men and boys surround the circular furnace at the Pacific Glass Works, in which there are seven small apertures: the men stand upon a flat form about two feet above the floor, and hold in their hands hollow iron tubes six feet in length. The point of the latter having been first heated, which is done almost momentarily, is inserted in the pot containing the molted glass, and turned around by the workman until he gathers enough metal at the end as is sufficient to form a bottle of the size required. He then blows gently down the pipe and having distended the bulb of red-hot plastic glass, he places it upon a plate of polished iron. On this he turns it around, shaping the lump of glass into a conical shape, and then places it in a mould which imparts the form and size required. The neck in then rounded and finished, after which the bottles are removed on long sticks by boys to the annealing oven close at hand, where they remain several days subject to a moderate heat. The rapidity with which this work is performed is astonishing. Every minute the white metal, as soft and liquid as honey, is changed into bottles of various sizes. The small quantity that is removed each time from the pot in instantly spread out at the end of the tube by the action of breath into a fiery globe of large size: and as the boys are passing in a continual procession from one furnace to another with their light but warm burthens, a spectator will, notwithstanding interest in the proceedings, keep at respectful distance from the busy and skilful glass-blowers, and the boys who so industriously and unconcernedly perform their duties. A remarkable feature in the workshop is the cheerfulness that obtains among the men and boys. The employment is seemingly more an amusement than labor. Singing and lively conversation were general, and even occasionally a number joined in some popular ditty, a key note having been struck by one acquainted with the musical taste of the light hearted blowers. Work commences at seven in the morning and contunes until four in the afternoon – three quarters of an hour being allowed for dinner. The men generally work by the piece, or else perform an allotted amount of labor, that is, to blow a specified number of bottles. The average wages earned is about four dollars per day, though superior glass-blowers, when working on large ware can make eight dollars. The number of men and boys employed at the Pacific Glass Works is fifty, and in dismissing this part of the subject, it may be proper to add that the relations that evidently exist between the employés and Mr. Taylor, the President of the Company, and Mr. Bennett, one of the lessees of the factory, are most cordial and agreeable.

Messrs. John Taylor & Co., No. 514 Washington street, are the sole agents for the Pacific Glass Works. The ware is considered as clear and strong as is to be found in any market. It has stood the test of years, and is rapidly filling the place of foreign articles of like description. The manufacture of pickles, which is a large interest, requires a vast number of bottles, as well as the makers of soda water, mustard, etc. They are furnished in large quantities by this establishment. Parties requiring bottles with inscriptions, designs or trademarks are also furnished, and the moulds used are considered the private property of those ordering. The following shows the average daily manufacture of bottles at the Pacific Glass Works, with prices:

DOZENS.		PER GROSS.
Half gallon pickle jars	50	$18 00 to $00
Wine and brandy bottles	120	11 00 to 12
Mustard and spice bottles	250	5 00 to 6
Soda bottles (blue and green)	50	10 00 to 00
Jamaica ginger bottles	72	4 00 to 00
Panel (four ounce) bottles	60	4 50 to 00
Schnapps (one quart)	60	12 00 to 00
Holland gin	60	12 00 to 1¢

Gallon demijohns are sold at $7 50 to $9 per dozen. The willow work is put on the glass at the factory by men who are kept constantly engaged. This is an important branch, and is growing in importance every day.

SAN FRANCISCO GLASS WORKS

These works are on Townsend street, between Third and Fourth, and engage forty men and boys. The amount of ware manufactured is large and includes a great variety. Eight covered pots are used in the furnace, and the flint glass produced is not alone elegant in finish, but very durable. Messrs. Newman &

Brannan, the proprietors, are carrying on the business for two years, and from rather a small beginning have created an extensive factory. The main building is 110 feet in length and 50 feet wide, and there are store-houses, blacksmith-shop, pot-houses, etc. The smoke-stack is 70 feet high. Sand is obtained from Monterey. No trace of iron can be found in it, and by the addition of ten or fifteen per cent of nitre a flint glass is made of a superior description. All classes of druggists' and chemists' ware are produced at this factory, as well as lamp chimneys, funnels, carboys holding twenty-five gallons, ink bottles, soda water bottles and phials from half a drachm up to the largest description in endless lots. The work of the glass-blower here differs in some respects from the other factory. The tunnels [funnels], lamp chimneys, and other articles are made without the assistance of moulds: they are produced by the manipulation of the tube, to which the molten glass adheres, upon the smooth iron. A correct taste and a quick eye and hand are essential to do this work. The ginger and spice bottles are put in moulds, of course much smaller than those required for wine bottles, and here a boy is required to cut the glass close to the neck, while in the other case the man who blows does this work himself. On Monday last, the hands were engaged in making phials, funnels and tubing. On Saturday there were manufactured 200 dozen lamp chimneys, 120 dozen mustard bottles, and 170 dozen prescription phials, besides a large quantity of brandy and soda bottles.

The lamp chimneys made by Messrs. Newman & Brannan are of an excellent description. For the purpose of causing them to withstand great heat, [?]o percent. red lead is used in the batch. They are worthy the attention of consumers, and are sold at prices ranging from 60 cents per dozen, for the ordinary kind, up to $1 75 per dozen for the large mammoth. The San Francisco Factory excels especially in the capacity it possesses of furnishing all kinds of vessels required in chemical operations. The Golden City Works were provided with a complete set of retorts, tubes and glass vessels used in the manufacture of gases and acids, and hardly a day passes that orders are not received for some article of curious design. The San José Railroad Company is supplied by this establishment with cylinder chimneys for their cars, of a thick and heavy kind; the contract for furnishing glass to the light houses in this district has been awarded to Messrs. Newman & Brannan.

The arrangement of works for facility in producing ware is certainly very complete. The smoke in the furnace is consumed, and the residium of distilled coal oil used in the annealing furnace is in a tank under ground in the yard. It is pumped up from there to a second tank, and conveyed through a tube, 130 feet long, to the furnace. Old or broken glass is purchased and melted with the batch, as a certain portion of the article is found to improve the quality of the ware. The frosting, or light gassamer particles of glass, that accumulate about the work tables, are sold to scenic painters. Sydney coal is used in both factories.

Mr. Newman has had patented an improvement in the covered pot for making flint glass. It is the first introduced strange to state, in a hundred years, and is intended to save considerable time in melting the batch. The heat, in the old style of pots, penetrated the sides, and consumed thirty hours in bringing the metal to a condition for the blower. The new invention causes the flame to be directed into an aperture which is brought into contact with air passing through tubes on the top of the pot, which converts the unburnt particles of carbon into pure gas, which gas is carried up the stack by two flues that connect in front of the pot with large cone of furnace. This pot generates such great heat that it vaporizes the salt that usually accumulated upon the glass and carries it off. This is alone a great saving, besides the pot melts fifteen

hours sooner than the old covered style. It is especially intended to make common qualities of glass, such as black and green, in a flint glass furnace.

The principal wholesale druggists in San Francisco are supplied with glassware by Messrs. Newman & Brannan. The number of phials and bottles required is immense, and the orders received daily indicate the extent of this trade. Besides what have been mentioned large globes for street lamps; long, curved tubes; ornamental turrets provided with basins; one above the other, for fish; fancy vessels for fruit, and ornaments of every kind, large and small. The annealing oven in these works is fifty feet long, and is provided with an iron moveable bed, that forms an endless chain. Ware is placed in the oven as rapidly as it passes from the workmen's hands, and as the front is filled up, a windlass at the end is used to draw the bed forward. This is constructed of several pieces, held together by hinges. Space is thus made at the mouth of the oven and the piece removed is put in so as to receive fresh additions of ware. The manufacture of pressed ware, which includes drinking glasses and goblets, will be soon introduced at these works. It is stated that the quantity of chimney lamps required for this market is so great that the entire force of the factory, kept continually employed, would be necessary for the supply.

Glass-Making: III—
The Evolution of a Glass Bottle

C. Hanford Henderson

ESTABLISHED BY EDWARD L. YOUMANS.

THE

POPULAR SCIENCE

MONTHLY.

EDITED BY WILLIAM JAY YOUMANS.

VOL. XXXVI.

NOVEMBER, 1889, TO APRIL, 1890.

GLASS-MAKING.

By C. HANFORD HENDERSON,

PROFESSOR OF PHYSICS AND CHEMISTRY IN THE PHILADELPHIA MANUAL TRAINING SCHOOL.

III.—THE EVOLUTION OF A GLASS BOTTLE.

TO a little sand, a little alkali, and a little limestone, add considerable heat and a still greater amount of skill, might be taken as a brief recipe for the manufacture of a glass bottle.

But to know in just what proportions to mix these several ingredients, how to produce and manage the requisite heat, and particularly how to cultivate that most essential part of the whole process, the manual dexterity which gives value to these other factors, are matters less briefly disposed of. Their consideration has made the evolution of a glass bottle a history covering several thousand years. The importance of this modest process will appear, if one is not already persuaded of it, when one recalls for an instant the multitudinous uses to which bottles are now put. It is difficult to fancy the confusion which would result were so simple an article of commerce suddenly withdrawn from the world of fact, and society called upon to manage without its service. Great would be the consternation of a host of manufacturers, and loud the outcry of a larger host of consumers.

The earlier man, it is to be remembered, had his herds always with him, his spring of water near his tent-door. He knew no tonic save the air of the desert, and few other beverages than the wine which was stored in sacks of goat's skin. To him bottles and their contents were matters of little moment. It is true that, in the storage of the one liquid which he preserved in this way, he did have to be careful not to put new wine into old bottles, but the proverb was easily recalled, and its precaution not difficult to carry out. He contented himself with his sack of skin, and found, in the projection which had once been the leg or neck of the animal, a mouth to his bottle sufficiently convenient to serve his purpose.

It was from receptacles such as this that the tired heroes of the *Iliad* regaled themselves, and the aged Noah partook too generously.

Even now this primitive bottle is largely used for the transportation and storage of water by the people of western Asia, and the usage seems to possess enough inertia to carry it forward several centuries further. Invading Americans may find the bottle of skin still in vogue, when their restless westward-moving activity carries them across the Pacific.

The substitution of glass bottles was effected but slowly even among the more progressive of ancient peoples. In the use of glass, the idea of beauty and decoration long remained paramount to considerations of utility. It was an article of luxury rather than of necessity. Darwin observed with amazement that when the weather was warm and fair, the Fijians paraded their coats of furs and feathers with all the pomp and pride of the Parisian *beau-monde*, only to stand naked and shivering in times of storm. It seems to have been much the same thing among the ancients with respect to their glass bottles. It was ornament in place of use. They were quite willing to get along without them in the economy of every-day life, provided they could have a few rare vases and gold-mounted amphoræ in the early *salons* where Rameses gossiped about Egyptian politics, and Potiphar discoursed upon the mysteries of metempsychosis.

It must be confessed that, in the pursuit of this one idea, they were eminently successful. Their glass trinkets were beautiful, both in outline and in color, even if their bottles for real service were made of skin, and liable to rip and tear. The glass *bric-à-brac* of antiquity, its bottles and vases and jars, was not of large dimension, but it possessed a profusion of color which we have only of recent years been able to imitate.

With us moderns, however, life is much more complex, and the case is quite different. We are not insensible to ornamentation, but we are more keenly alive to comfort. In the absence of a king's taster, we are disposed to guard what we eat and drink. The majority agree with Charles Lamb, that poisoning is "a nasty death," and so we eschew the use of metals in contact with our foods, and much prefer glass. We want milk miles from where it is produced, and fruits and vegetables months after their harvest. We want medicines for health, balms for bruises, tonics for appetites, mineral waters for digestion, wines for strength, condensed products for our travel. We want to separate with acids and put together with glues. We want a host of other things which come in bottles. We even bottle our electricity—if so unscientific an expression may be applied to the storage-battery. There is, in fact, scarcely a single department of life, either social or industrial, where some product is not needed which must be kept or carried in some form of glass bottle or jar. The manufacture of so useful an article is thus brought into relation with all of our many-sided activity. It forms a distinct and very important branch of the glass industry.

In America, the process of bottle-making is nowhere carried on more extensively or more successfully than in the neighborhood of Philadelphia. Much of the sand of southern New Jersey is sufficiently pure to make an excellent bottle-glass. Its adaptability for this purpose seems to have been appreciated by the early colonists, for the oldest glass-works in this country are those established in 1775 at Glassboro. They are still in operation, and are at the present day the most extensive of American bottle-works, employing as they do some six hundred persons in the conduct of their operations. It is a significant fact, showing the force of modern progress, that after existing for more than a century, the capacity of the "plant" was increased over fifty per cent during a recent period of three years. It is one of several establishments which have grown up in that neighborhood, and which have been attracted by the same cause, the abundance of a fair quality of sand. There is, moreover, something highly gregarious about modern industries. It frequently happens that many other localities offer quite as favorable conditions as the one selected; but the simple presence of a successful industry seems to turn men's thoughts in that direction, and lead them to undertake similar enterprises rather than to attempt the dangerous experiment of importing a new manufacture. To this principle of gregariousness, as well as to the wide wastes of sand, must the community of glass-workers in southern New Jersey be attributed. Like apparently begets like.

FIG. 1.—A GLASS-BOTTLE FACTORY IN SOUTHERN NEW JERSEY.

There is little that is attractive about the exterior of such a bottle-factory. One finds it set down in the midst of a flat, monotonous country, and surrounded by indifferent wooden houses with bare, sandy door-yards which bespeak small appreciation of the element of beauty. That these houses are homes, and are for the most part owned by those who live in them, adds immensely to their interest, but it does not conceal the fact that life here is material and ugly. It is not a beautiful or an inspiring thing to blow bottles all day long, unless one does it remarkably well; but the industry remaining, the life in these towns might still be made much less bare than it is, could that gospel of happiness and culture which Mr. Walter Besant and others are preaching in the East End of London find here some good apostle who would make it the burden of a new evangel.

In the larger bottle-works there are generally several melting furnaces, but each is complete in itself, a unit from which a larger or smaller plant may be constructed, according to the requirements of the case. Each furnace is lodged in its own building. A certain symmetry is loaned to these low, rectangular wooden structures by the tall brick furnace-shaft which rises through the center of the roof, and by the numerous smaller chimneys scattered around the edge. The sides of the building are movable on pivots, and when open give the factory somewhat the appearance of the Japanese houses pictured by Mr. Morse.

Inside of the factory all is life and movement. But, amid the dirt and confusion which characterize such an interior, there are the order of active money-getting and the beauty of a long-practiced dexterity.

If one follow the crude materials from the time they enter the building until they finally emerge in the form of many-shaped bottles, he will begin his inspection at the mixing-room, where the questions of content and proportion are decided. Large wooden wheelbarrows come and go, stopping long enough only to have their weight taken, and to dump their thoroughly ground contents into one of the bins on the side of the room. Patient old men, with hoe and shovel, mechanically mix together the stuff for the "batch." This varies in its composition according to the sort of bottles that are to be made. Three grades of bottle glass are recognized. The ordinary green glass is obtained from a mixture of about thirty-eight parts of soda and twenty parts of marble-dust to every hundred parts of sand. The glass is essentially a lime-soda glass, not dissimilar to window glass in its composition. The sand used comes from the neighborhood, and contains a little iron. As no bleaching agents are employed, this gives the glass its characteristic light green color—the bottle-green of our colorists. The second grade, the amber glass, has about the same composition, only it is colored by the addition of a little ground coke, black-lead, or some other form of carbon, about eight ounces to every hundred pounds of sand. This makes a much less innocent-looking bottle than the sea-green tint of the first glass. The finest grade, the so-called flint glass, contains about the same ingredients as the ordinary bottle glass, but the materials used are purer, and some such bleaching agent as manganese dioxide, arsenious acid, or nitrate of soda is used to make the glass color-less. Blue bottles are occasionally wanted, and in that case a little peroxide of cobalt is added to the customary batch to give the required color.

To obtain the best results, it is essential that the grinding and mixing of the crude materials be carefully looked after. At Glass-boro the mixing as well as the grinding will soon be done by ma-chinery in one central mixing-room, and the batch conveyed to the different furnaces by means of endless belts. It is believed that this improvement will insure a better product as well as more economical working.

The batch having been prepared, the next step in the develop-ment of the bottle is to change this dull-white powder into clear, fluid glass. Such a metamorphosis is accomplished in the melt-ing furnace, which forms very naturally the central feature in a bottle-factory. The gratifying increase in the capacity of the Glassboro works is largely if not entirely due to the introduction of improved furnaces invented by the chemist of the works, Mr. Andrew Ferrari. They are continuous tank furnaces heated by gas—that is to say, the melting is carried out in large fire-clay tanks, and proceeds without interruption. There are other tank furnaces in use in America, but these are probably the only works where the melting is carried out continuously. Neither the em-ployment of a tank in place of separate crucibles, nor the substi-tution of a gaseous for a solid fuel, is in itself new; but the details of the Ferrari furnace are quite novel. In Europe, the regenera-tive system of Siemens has been employed with marked success in the manufacture of glass; but, unfortunately, the Siemens fur-naces are expensive in their construction and require some de-gree of skill to insure their best working. The Ferrari furnace, on the other hand, is an inexpensive affair and is easily worked. The gas generator is the usual inclined or " step " grate employed by Siemens, but it is placed directly alongside of the furnace, thus obviating the transportation of the gas, and the consequent neces-sity of reheating it before combustion.

At one end of the building one sees an elevated platform on which are stacked large blocks of bituminous coal. About six tons are daily required for each furnace. From this platform a line of low, irregular brick-work extends to the central stack. It contains the gas generators, three to each furnace, and beyond them the melting tank, which communicates on the other side with what is known as the working part of the furnace, lying directly under the central stack. The coal is fed directly into the generators from the platform, and on the inclined grate is com-pletely burned—that is to say, it unites with all the oxygen possi-ble, forming carbonic-acid gas. The supply of air may be regulated by dampers, so that the generator yields more or less gas according to the requirements of the furnace. But the carbonic-acid gas thus produced would be of no value as fuel, for it is totally incombustible. Rising, however, through the mass of incandescent fuel above it, the gas is speedily reduced to the condition of carbonic oxide, that combustible gas whose blue flame plays over

Fig. 2.—An Interior View, showing the Brick-work which contains the Gas Generators and Melting Tank.

the surface of an anthracite fire just after fresh fuel has been thrown on. This mixes with the volatile hydrocarbons—the coal-gas given off when fresh coal is introduced into the generator—and the mixture passes at once to the chamber above the melting tank. The air necessary for the burning of these generator gases is first heated by passing through a number of chambers in the lower part of the furnace. It is mixed with the gases to be burned just before they reach the fire-clay bridge separating the gas generator from the melting tank. The main combustion takes place right at this bridge, and produces an intense heat in the melting chamber, for both the gas to be burned and the air to burn it are highly heated before they are allowed to combine. The effect is the same as would be produced on a small scale if one fed his stove with the hot air from a register. This arrangement removes in a simple and inexpensive way one of the chief objections to the use of gas in glass-making. The fuel is so exceedingly convenient that its use in the industry was proposed, and indeed attempted, years ago, but a sufficiently intense heat could not be thus obtained.

The furnaces are in continuous operation for ten months in the year. Every three hours during the entire twenty-four a charge of a ton and a half of the batch is added to the melting tank. In an atmosphere so intensely heated as this, it does not take very long for the crude materials to fuse and form a glass quite as liquid as water.

Picture for a moment the white-hot caldron in which this transformation of the opaque into the transparent takes place. It is an oblong tank, some eight by ten feet, in which the glass in various stages of fusion stands to a depth of nearly three feet. Above this seething mass there is a low arch which deflects the long, curling flame as it comes over the bridge from the generators, until it bathes the entire contents of the tank in its Plutonic breath. As the materials of the batch unite and melt—alone, they would be for the most part entirely infusible—the liquid glass sinks to the bottom of the tank and flows through small openings into the gathering chamber beyond. The glass resulting from the union of sand and alkaline bases is heavier than the crude materials from which it is formed, and consequently seeks the lowest level. In this way the tank, although filled with material in all stages of transformation, has always at the bottom a bath of thoroughly fused glass. The communication between tank and gathering chamber is arranged at such a level that the fluid glass alone can pass from one to the other.

This central gathering chamber and the busy life surrounding it are the points of chief interest to the visitor who wishes to see the scenic part of bottle-blowing, and is willing to take the chemistry and some of the more occult parts of the process on faith. The chamber itself is circular, usually about sixteen feet in diameter, and contains a bath of molten glass nearly two feet deep. The temperature of this fiery lake is kept above the fusing-point by the hot gases which come from the melting tank and rise into the high shaft immediately over the gathering compartment. It takes only from two and a half to three hours for the crude materials of the batch to pass to the condition of perfectly fused glass. This is pretty quick glass-making.

A little sand, a little alkali, a little limestone, and considerable heat have so far been expended, and the result is fluid glass. It is that greater amount of skill which is now needed to transform the glass into a bottle.

There is a series of openings, some sixteen in number, around the sides of the gathering chamber and a little above the level of the molten glass. Through these the glass-blower draws his supply, but he does not dip his blowpipe directly into this glowing reservoir. Such an arrangement would cause too great a loss of heat, besides interrupting the furnace-draught, and would be a source of constant annoyance to the gatherer on account of the impurities which float as a scum on the surface of the bath. To avoid these evils, each gathering hole has its "boot," a rounded hood of fire-clay which surrounds the hole on the inside of the chamber, and extends downward to the bottom of the bath in the shape of an oval cylinder. An opening near the bottom of the cylinder admits the fluid glass into the interior of the boot, and

Fig. 3.—The Operation of "Marvering."

permits it to stand always at the same level there as in the gathering chamber outside. Thus the gatherer draws his burden from this little bucket-like reservoir, but, like the widow's cruse of oil, the supply never gives out.

Outside of the furnace the agencies of heat and chemism are replaced by that of human dexterity. The men work in companies, which are known in the glass-maker's parlance as "shops." And very busy companies they are. They resemble nothing so much as a swarm of bees, as they hurry to and fro about the gathering holes. The condition is one of almost nervous activity. The men toss their blowpipes hither and thither in the operation of forming the bottles, and boys dart in and out of the crowd carrying bottles in all stages of development. There is complete singleness of purpose. They are all intent on turning out the largest number of bottles possible—for the pay is largely by the piece. Where the bottles are very small, one man has been known to blow as many as two hundred dozen in a day, but this is exceptional activity.

There are, all told, seven persons in such a shop: three men, of whom two blow the bottles, while a third, the gaffer, forms the necks, and four boys who gather the molten glass, open the molds, and carry away the finished products. The gatherer is a somewhat older boy than the others, and stands in direct line of promotion; is, in fact, a blower or gaffer in embryo. He aspires—the others but distantly. One shop is attached to each boot; and occasionally, when work presses, there are two shops to a boot, but this is rather crowding things and is not favorable to the best working. The process begins with the gatherer. His blowpipe is a tube of wrought iron, five or six feet long, and of lighter weight than the pipe used in blowing window glass. He dips the end of his pipe into the molten contents of the boot, and brings out a mass of red-hot plastic glass. If the bottles to be blown are small, one gathering suffices, but, for larger wares, two or even three gatherings may be necessary to get the requisite supply of material on the end of the blowpipe. When the gathering is done properly, this lump of red-hot glass is a perfectly homogeneous mass. Its subsequent fortunes rest with the blower. He takes the blowpipe from the gatherer, and, resting the plastic glass against a marvering table of stone or cast iron, he gives the pipe a few adroit rotations, thus fashioning the glass into an even cylindrical shape. By further rolling it along the edge of the table he forms the smaller prolongation of glass which is afterward to become the neck of the bottle. Lifting the still red-hot glass from the table, he blows through the pipe, forming a small bubble of air in the interior of the mass of glass. This is afterward extended until it becomes the inwardness of the bottle.

The partly fashioned bit of glassware is now introduced into the mold which one of the "shop" boys has already opened to receive it. For convenience in working, the mold is placed on a somewhat lower level than that on which the blower stands. It is made of cast iron, and is commonly formed in two pieces. One of these is stationary, while the other opens outward, its motion being controlled by a foot-lever. When the blower places his incomplete bottle, still attached to the blowpipe, into the mold, he closes the mold with his foot, and blows through the pipe until the plastic glass is everywhere forced against the sides of the mold, and has impressed upon it the form of its prison. Then with a quick motion the blower detaches his blowpipe from the projecting neck of the bottle—the glass is still plastic—hands it over to the gatherer, and with a fresh blowpipe repeats his labor. Such constant blowing largely develops the muscles of the cheek, but the exercise is not unwholesome. It is impossible by methods like these to obtain bottles of uniform thickness, yet the variations are much less than one would suppose.

FIG. 4.—PUTTING THE BOTTLE IN THE MOLD PREPARATORY TO THE FINAL BLOWING.

In contact with the iron of the mold the bottle cools very rapidly. Almost as soon as the blower takes away his pipe, the mold may be opened and the bottle removed. The little fellow who does this is called a "snapper." He seizes the bottle with his iron forceps and transfers it from the mold to a pair of scales near by. A small square of asbestus cloth remains permanently on the scale-pan, as contact with the cold iron would be apt to crack the glass. All bottles, except the very small ones, are thus weighed, and any that show either a deficiency or an excess in weight are rejected. There will always be a slight variation, but it must be within narrow limits, not exceeding, for instance, an ounce in bottles intended to weigh seventeen ounces. Comparatively few bottles are rejected for this cause. The bottle of approved avoirdupois is placed in a closely fitting case of wrought iron mounted on a long handle. Only the neck of the bottle is allowed to project. Thus blanketed and mounted, the hot glass is easily handled.

It goes now to the gaffer, to have its neck properly shaped. He is found at no great distance, sitting before a little side furnace which affords three openings—" glory-holes "—large enough to admit the necks of the bottles, and a heated atmosphere of sufficient intensity to make the glass necks plastic and workable.

FIG. 5.—BLOWING A FLASK IN THE AIR.

Crude petroleum is the fuel used. It is stored in a tank to one side of the furnace, and trickles down, drop by drop, into a tube which brings a strong blast of air from a distant fan. In this way the oil is vaporized, and mixed with such proportions of air that the mixture is highly combustible, and in burning produces an intense heat. Three tongues of yellow flame thrust themselves out of the glory-holes and leap toward the gaffer sitting before them. In England this member of the shop is known as the chairman, a term which refers to his bodily rather than to his official position. He thrusts the necks of the incased bottles into the glory-holes, and then one by one withdraws them from their aureole and forms the necks. This he does by means of a convenient implement known under the generic name of tool. It consists of a central stopper, kept moist with oil, which is thrust into the mouth of the bottle, thus determining its gauge; and of two outside arms of iron, which, by the rotation of the case, the tool remaining stationary, form the smooth ring commonly adorning the necks of glass bottles. The gaffer, like the blower, is a quick workman, and does the finishing for both blowers belonging to his shop. He does not leave his chair, the glass being brought to him and carried away again by the little boys who have been noticed as darting about in such a lively fashion.

The bottle is now finished, so far as its form is concerned, but, like the window-pane under similar circumstances, it would have scant value if sent out into the world in its present condition. It would be too brittle, on account of its sudden cooling, and must therefore first be annealed. This operation is simply one of gradual cooling, and is carried out in ovens or in annealing leers.

FIG. 6.—A VIEW OF THE GAFFER AT WORK, SHOWING HIS TOOL AND MANNER OF HOLDING THE BOTTLE WHEN FORMING ITS NECK.

The oven is a roomy chamber of brick-work, in which a wood fire is permitted to burn for a couple of hours in the early part of the day. It is opened when the blowers begin work, and during the remainder of the day it is gradually filled with bottles as the different gaffers finish them. At night it is closed and permitted to remain so for three days. At the end of that time the oven has become quite cold, and the bottles are thoroughly annealed.

The leer is a later invention and carries out the same process, only it acts continuously and is in so far an advance. It also consists of a roomy chamber of brick-work, but the fire is permanent and is located at one side of the chamber. A long brick passage-way extends for eighty feet from the back of this receiving chamber. The bottles are not piled directly on the floor, but are placed in low sheet-iron cars which move on a track extending the length of the passage-way. As soon as a car is filled, it is moved along the passage-way in order to make room for an empty car in the receiving chamber. In this gradual way the loaded cars are moved along the passage farther and farther from the source of heat, and finally discharge their loads at the cold end of the leer. It takes from forty-eight to sixty hours to accomplish the journey, though this is simply a matter of convenience, as the annealing process itself would not require more than from nine to ten hours, if so long as that.

Ordinarily the bottles, just as they come from the ovens and leers, are ready to be packed and shipped to their purchasers. In case, however, a seal has been blown in the side of the bottle and its prospective contents are of an effervescent character, the strength of each bottle must be carefully tested, as the glass forming the seal is apt to blow out thinner than the rest, and thus be a source of weakness. The testing is carried out by filling the bottle with water and then subjecting it to the pressure of a column of water equal to eighty pounds to the square inch. Only a few of the bottles, however, break under this ordeal.

But in case the bottle has a screw top, as in fruit-jars and the like, or is to have simply a plain ground edge, as in electric-battery jars, it is manufactured with a slight excess of glass on the top. This is known as a "blow-over." In this event the bottle does not pass through the hands of the gaffer, but goes directly from the blower to the ovens or annealing leers. In the grinding department the blow-over is knocked off and the rough edges ground smooth in a rotary grinding machine. In this the bottles or jars are put in upside down, eleven at a time, and have their edges pressed against the face of a large horizontal iron wheel which is rotated by steam-power. The framework in which the jars are held also rotates, and, in addition, each individual jar turns on its own axis. The iron wheel is supplied with a constant stream of sand and water, and this, with the triple motion of the machine, does very effective work. As many as sixty dozen jars can thus be ground in an hour.

The products of such a bottle-factory are as varied as the processes by which they are fabricated. There are large bottles and small bottles, tall bottles and short bottles, thick bottles and thin bottles, ugly bottles and pretty bottles—in fine, all sorts of bottles, according to the taste and requirements of the purchaser. He may order anything, from the tiny vial of one-drachm capacity up to the ungainly carboy holding fourteen gallons. He may have any tints desired, from the colorless flint glass through all shades of green and brown and blue to the bottle of absolute blackness. Or

FIG. 7.—THE ANNEALING LEER, AS SEEN FROM THE FRONT.

he may have any shape or form he pleases. Few if any bottles are kept in stock or made until ordered. Nearly all of the work is the direct filling of orders.

It is only by comparison with the older order of things that one can appreciate the large improvements that have recently been introduced into the process of bottle-making. In the Glassboro works the Ferrari furnace has effected many changes and many economies. I am told, on very reliable authority, that not only is the quality of the glass much improved by the employment of these furnaces, but that in addition the experience of five years has shown their maintenance and operation to be notably less expensive than the old-style pot furnaces. In the matter of fuel the saving is said to have been more than fifty per cent. The repairs have also cost as much less in proportion. When the melting was done in pots, the cost of these alone made an appreciable item in the year's expenses. Each one cost about fifty dollars, and their average life was only two months. Occasionally one was known to last nine months, but for every such exception there were from two to three dozen which failed in less than a month. The four furnaces in operation would require in all about forty pots, and these renewed every two months would mean during the working year an expenditure for pots alone of ten thousand dollars. The present tank furnaces are out of blast during July and August, but the year's repairs are only a nominal expense. The hot season is chosen for renovation for very obvious reasons, though the heat alone is not sufficiently intense to make the cessation of work a necessity.

In thus following the evolutionary process by which a glass bottle is produced, one meets with many ingenious contrivances and many shrewd adaptations of means to ends, but he will scarcely meet with any problem of quite such deep interest as that presented by the people who carry out this process. Particularly is one struck with the large number of boys, scarcely more than children, who are employed in such a factory. About the furnace proper there are even more boys than men. The law does not permit the employment of children under twelve years of age, but exceptions are sometimes allowed by the labor inspector in case a boy has a widowed mother, or some other particular demand upon his early activity. New Jersey further attempts to protect her children by making an annual school attendance of five months compulsory for them. In the glass-blowing districts this requirement is met by the establishment of night schools supported by the State. The term lasts only for the allotted five months, the daily session being for two hours, from half-past six to half-past eight o'clock. My own limited observation of the working of night schools has led me to believe that they are but poor substitutes for work done earlier in the day when the boys are fresher and more buoyant; but the superintendent of a large factory, to whom I spoke on the subject, was of the opinion that these childish glass-workers are doing very satisfactory work in such schools. It is hard, nevertheless, that childhood should be made so short, and that the work-a-day life should begin so early for these little people. They seem, it is true, a very happy, merry set of youngsters, and, if one may judge from the tricks they are constantly playing on one another, they manage to get a fair share of boyish fun; but they can not fail to lose much in being so soon harnessed. As a class, these lads seemed to be finer looking and in many ways better conditioned than the older workers, so that one would naturally fancy that the hard work was leaving its landmarks. Men who have known them longer tell me, however, that it is a new generation, and one that has been reared under more favorable conditions of life.

They are comparatively well paid. The little boys make three dollars a week, and the larger ones six; modest sums admittedly; but large enough under the circumstances of country life to permit a little laying by. I felt curious to know what aspirations were most favored in such a community, and to what ideals the boys looked up. The story was soon told: to become glass-blowers, and to have plenty to eat—that was all; a life centered about bottles. Yet, among so many bright-faced lads, there are doubtless many of considerable promise, could their imaginations only be fired by some well-directed effort. Some one with a passion for culture and a big human heart could do great things, it seemed to me, with such quick, observant material.

With the older workers the dice have been cast, and life is well crystallized. It has left them divided into two classes: the green-glass blowers, who are chiefly Americans, and the flint-glass blowers, who are more largely Germans. Both bodies of men are closely organized, and as a result make excellent wages. The union to which they belong will not permit more than two apprentices a year to a single furnace. Such a regulation, with the annual increase of the industry and the inevitable deaths, practically excludes competition. The blowers make on an average five dollars a day. In rare cases as much as three hundred dollars a month has been paid to a single man. So large returns, however, are only possible for blowers and gaffers. The other members of the shop, as well as the numerous helpers employed in the conduct of such large enterprises, receive regular wages.

One other feature deserves mention. Throughout the entire works there is observable that marked tendency of modern industrial life to substitute continuous, automatic processes for those which are periodic and manual. The continuous annealing leer is taking the place of the oven; the steady flow of gaseous fuel is replacing the oft-repeated shovelful of coal; the continuous melting tank has been substituted for the discontinuous reservoir system represented by the crucible pots; the uninterrupted automatic charging of the furnace is about to do away with the manual feeding of the batch every three hours; and similarly, in all departments, the change is in progress. The operations of blowing have not yet been made automatic. Bottles but an inch long are still produced by the blower's breath, and little boys dispose of them one by one. But it is not improbable, in spite of the difficulties in the way, that a patent bottle-blowing machine will some day take the place of the army of workers who now swarm around the gathering chamber of a glass-furnace. Such a machine already exists in the brain of a man. When it is materialized into a working fact, the last step in perfecting the evolution of a glass bottle will have been taken, and any further development will be along lines already laid down.

11*

Blowing Bottles by Hand

Boris Stern

BLOWING BOTTLES BY HAND

Since time immemorial the operation of blowing bottles by hand has been performed by a group of workers, constituting a unit termed the "shop." The composition of a shop has varied from time to time, depending entirely upon the nature and the size of the bottles blown. For an average size bottle, ranging in contents from less than an ounce to a quart, a normal shop in this country has since 1870 consisted of three skilled workers and four helpers. Of the three skilled workers, two blowers usually gather the molten glass and blow the bottles independently of each other, while the third worker finishes the necks of the bottles made by the two blowers. In most cases the three workers are equally skilled in all three operations of gathering, blowing, and finishing, and when working in this order interchange occupations every 20 minutes.

The helpers to the blowers derive their names from the nature of their work, being termed mold boy, cleaning-off boy, snapping-up boy, and carry-in boy. The mold boy sits on a low stool at the foot of the blower's bench and opens and closes the molds as required by the two blowers. The cleaning-off or knocking-off boy stands near by and receives the pipe after it is disconnected from the bottle in the mold, and with a small iron tool resembling a file cleans the pipe of the bit of glass which solidifies around the blowing end. The snapping-up boy puts the bottle which has just been taken from the mold into "the snap" and places it into the "glory hole." [1] The carry-in boy carries the bottles from the finisher to the leer to be annealed.

The process of blowing bottles by hand may be briefly described as follows: Standing in front of the working hole of the furnace, the blower dips his pipe into the white mass of molten glass and by skillful movements of his hand gathers on the end of the pipe the exact quantity of glass necessary for the size of the bottle to be made. This he quickly removes from the furnace and rolls and smooths it on a flat piece of iron called the "marver." While thus marvering the glass the blower also gently blows into the free end of his pipe and by introducing a few puffs of air into the solid mass of glass forms the initial cavity in the prospective bottle. When the glass is marvered sufficiently the worker, while continuing to blow into the pipe, swings it forward and backward a few times. As a result of these operations the bit of glass suspended at the end of the pipe assumes a pear-shaped form, with a small central air cavity inside.

The mold boy now opens one of his two iron molds, the blower lowers the partially formed portion of glass into it, and the mold boy then closes the two halves of the mold. Continuing to blow into the pipe, the blower blows with sufficient force to distend the glass to the exact shape patterned in the mold, after which the pressure of the blowing on the small amount of glass remaining above the mold causes it to distend to a mere film, which breaks readily and

[1] For explanation of these terms see p. 31.

thus disconnects the pipe from the bottle in the mold. The film of glass above the mold, which is so thin and light that it actually floats in the air, is known as the "blow-over."

FIG. 1.—BLOWING BOTTLES BY HAND

While the bottle remains a short time in the mold until it solidifies sufficiently to be handled, the mold tender prepares the other mold for the second blower. Then he opens the first mold, takes out the

40780°—27——3

FIG. 2.—VIEW OF A HAND BOTTLE AND BLOWN-WARE PLANT

bottle with a pair of pincers, and places it on a stand at his side. Frequently he also weighs the bottle on a small scale standing near by.

At this stage of the process the bottle still needs to have its neck finished and the "lip" on the top formed. The snapping-up boy picks it up with a pair of pincers and puts it in a heavy can-like receptacle with a long handle, known as the "snap." He then places the snap with the bottle in the reheating furnace, termed the "glory hole," in order to reheat the neck of the bottle and thus make it ready for the finisher. The latter usually sits on a bench near the "glory hole," so that he may easily reach the snap and place it back in the fire when the bottle is finished. The work of the finisher consists of shaping the lip on the neck of the bottle, which he does very skillfully with a special wooden tool usually improvised by himself.

Next the snapping-up boy releases the finished bottle from the snap and places it on a stand for the carry-in boy, who picks up two or more bottles with a special iron fork and places them in the leer to be annealed.

While the normal shop is thus made up of seven workers, there are variations, in which the number of skilled workers as a rule remains the same while the number of helpers varies, depending upon the kind and size of bottles made. Quite often the cleaning-up boy is dispensed with. When an automatic mold is used which, operated by means of a treadle at the blower's foot, shuts and opens up by itself, the mold boy, too, is eliminated and the snapping-up boy adds to his duties the work of a take-out boy. Again, sometimes only one or two carry-in boys are used for as many as 10 shops or more. In such cases the snapping-up boys place the finished bottle in a large pan kept in a small iron oven termed the "peanut-roaster." The carry-in boy takes a full pan of bottles to the leer at one time and is thus enabled to serve all his shops in rotation.

The average daily productivity of the hand shop varies considerably with the size of the bottle, the condition of the glass, the skill of the workers, and the weather. In the case of small ware, ranging in contents up to 3 or 4 ounces, 30 to 35 gross constitutes a fair output for a shop of seven men during an eight-hour shift. As the weight of the bottle increases the output becomes smaller and smaller, so that in the case of quart jars 15 to 16 gross represents a very good output for an eight-hour day.

In the production of very large ware of a gallon and over, such as packer jugs, water bottles, carboys, etc., the total number of workers constituting a shop is considerably increased, although the number of skilled workers generally remains the same. Thus in the case of 5-gallon water bottles, which are still being made in large quantities by the hand process, a shop is made up of 13 workers, namely, 3 skilled blowers, 2 gatherers (who are as a rule apprentices to the blowers and are paid at a rate higher than the other helpers), 1 mold boy, 1 cleaning-off boy, 3 snapping-up boys, and 3 carry-in boys. The daily production of 5-gallon bottles by such a shop ranges from 250 to 350 bottles, depending on the skill of the blowers, the condition of the molten glass in the tank, and the weather.

Glass Bottle Push-Ups and Pontil Marks

Olive Jones

62

GLASS BOTTLE
PUSH-UPS
AND
PONTIL MARKS

OLIVE JONES

INTRODUCTION

Originally this study started as an attempt to explain the varied markings on bottle bases found in the National Historic Sites Service collection. These markings appeared to have been left on the glass by glassmakers during the formation of the base and while holding the bottle on the pontil. In the process of identifying the marks, some relationships between the marks and certain types of bottles and their country and date of manufacture became apparent.

Because most modern authors, with the exception of Dr. Julian Toulouse, have not discussed in detail the question of base formations and empontilling techniques, I have had to concentrate on bottles excavated by the Canadian National Historic Sites Service. I have also looked at some local private collections and the "wine" bottles in the Bristol City Museum and the Guildhall Museum in London. In general, these collections corroborated some of the conclusions in this paper.

The National Historic Sites Service collection has a built-in bias because very few of our excavated sites predate the 1720s and from that date to 1760, the predominant trading influence was French. After 1760, when New France passed into British control, the trading emphasis shifted to Great Britain. This means that there are few English bottles in the collection from before 1760, and after that date, very few French bottles. Because of this situation, the attempt to assign the different tools and techniques to specific countries and dates should be regarded by the reader as a question and a challenge, rather than as an immutable fact.

Although there are many variations in technique, a bottle is made in the following basic manner (Figure 1). A sufficient amount of glass is gathered on the end of a blowpipe. The glass is given a preliminary shape, called a parison, by marvering (turning) on a flat stone or metal slab and by preliminary insufflation. The parison is then usually inserted in a mould which may form only the body or almost the whole bottle. After the partially formed bottle is removed from the mould, if the base has not already been mould-formed, the base is pushed up. A tool, such as a pontil or a sabot, then holds the bottle at the base while the blowpipe is detached from the bottle. Extra glass is added at the mouth and then the glassmaker forms the finish (Figure 9). The completed bottle is carried to the annealing oven where it is slowly cooled to remove the stresses in the glass.

The two stages of the bottle-making process that are discussed in this paper are the formation of the base and the techniques used to hold the bottle while the finish is being made.

FIGURE 1. *Interior of a 19th century French bottle factory (Peligot 1877:299).*

PUSH-UPS

One of the familiar aspects of bottles is the base that has been pushed up into the body cavity. This formation is called a "push-up" (Toulouse: personal communication; Moody 1963:303) or "kick". Several explanations have been given for its presence:

1) Because glassmakers had difficulty making a bottle base flat enough for a bottle to stand upright without wobbling, they partially solved the problem by indenting the base.

2) A push-up helped to produce a stronger bottle. Part of the reason was that the glassmaker, while the bottle was being made, often rested the bottle on its base which allowed the glass to flow towards the basal area (Bontemps 1868:510). In pushing up the base, the glass was redistributed and thinned. If glass is too heavily concentrated in one place the annealing process is less effective and stresses are set up in the bottle which make it weaker. It is also possible that the push-up is structurally useful in helping the bottle withstand great internal pressure from contents such as sparkling wines.

3) Many authors suggest that push-ups were made deliberately deep, particularly in dark green glass bottles, so the bottles looked much larger than they actually were.

4) Many people also believe that the push-up assists in the sedimentation of wines (Mendelsohn 1965:51).

The practice of making a deep push-up probably continued long after its need was over because of conservatism on the part of the glassmakers and the consumers.

The push-up seems to have been formed by a variety of tools. In Diderot's *Encyclopédie* (1967:109), the base was formed by a mollette, *"morceau de fer plat, d'environ un pié de longueur"* (Figure 2). As forming the push-up could cause distortion in the body of the bottle, it was rolled again on the marver. Although there were no really distinguishing marks left by this process, bases which were formed in this way probably resemble those in Figure 3. This type of base is found on the familiar French "flower pot" wine bottles (Noël Hume 1970:71; Diderot 1772: Pl. V, VI) which have been excavated on many sites in Canada that were occupied by the French. The bases are normally very regular, with symmetrical, rounded conical profiles and a small pontil mark, usually between 25 mm. and 35 mm. in diameter, in the top of the push-up.

FIGURE 2. *The glassmaker forming the bottle base with the mollette and then remarvering the bottle to restore its symmetry (Diderot 1772: Pl. V).*

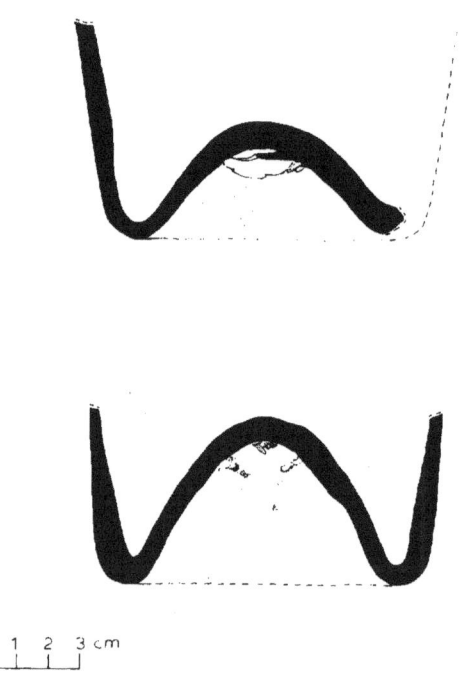

FIGURE 3. *Two bases, probably formed by a mollette, showing the regular, rounded conical profile and the*

FIGURE 4. *An 18th-century French "flower pot" wine bottle excavated from a site dating from 1732 to 1745.*

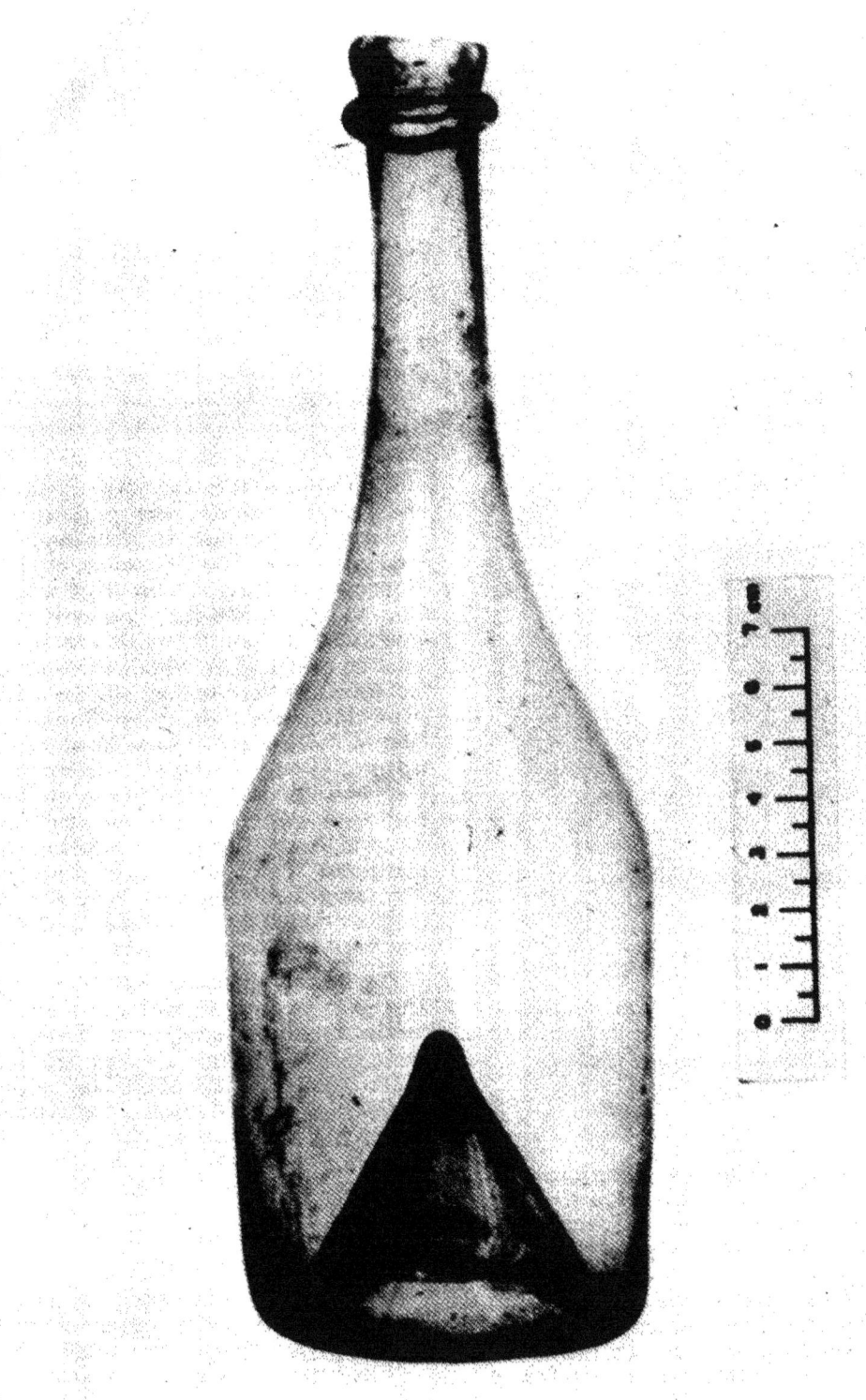

FIGURE 5. *A bottle showing how the base has been indented by a sharply pointed rod and the position of the pontil mark partway down the push-up.*

Another tool used to form the push-up appears to have been a thin, sharply pointed rod of wood or metal. As shown in Figure 5, the tip of the push-up often has a distinct, sharp point, visible on both the exterior and interior surfaces. The pontil mark is visible about two-thirds of the way down from the tip. On some small bottles, the push-up was so narrow that the pontil had to be applied on the resting surface. These sharply pointed push-ups appear primarily on medicine bottles and vials, occasionally on small rectangular bottles with chamfered corners and on olive oil bottles. Push-ups formed in this way are never found on the "wine" bottles. The use of this tool appears to have become less common during the 19th century as it was replaced by moulding techniques.

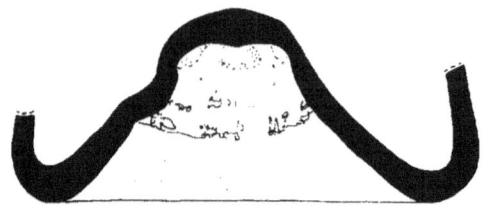

0 1 2 3 cm

FIGURE 7. *The same base as Figure 6 showing the relationship of the quatrefoil impression and the pontil mark. Note the distortion in the profile.*

sion (Toulouse 1968:140, 141). From above, on the interior surface, the push-up top often looks roughly square. In 75 examples from one Canadian site, the diameters of the impressions ranged from 16 mm. to 51 mm. In addition to the quatrefoil impressions, there is invariably a pontil mark consisting of an area of rough glass which encircles the push-up towards the resting surface. The pontil mark diameters range from 38 mm. to 64 mm. Figure 7 illustrates a base in which the push-up profile was distorted both by the forming tool and by the application of the pontil. Although split iron rods are still used today as pontil rods, the presence of both a distinct pontil mark and the quatrefoil impression on the same base suggests that the quatrefoil mark is logically explained if the split rod was used to indent the base.

The quatrefoil marks have been appearing almost exclusively in dark green glass "wine" bottles manufactured in the English shapes, such as Noël Hume's types 12, 15, 21, 22 (Noël Hume 1961:100-101). The earliest bases in the National Historic Sites Service collection with these marks date from the 1720s and they continue throughout the 18th and into the 19th century. Generally speaking, as the diameters of the bottles decreased towards the end of the 18th century, the quatrefoil marks also became smaller.

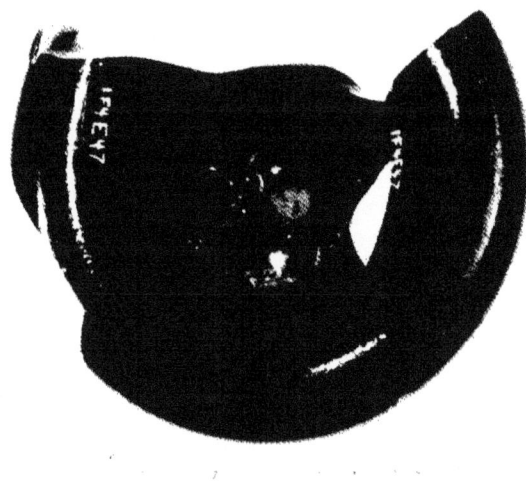

FIGURE 6. *The basal view of a bottle showing the quatrefoil impression in the tip of the push-up. The pontil mark can be seen as rough chips of glass.*

A third type of tool used to form push-ups appears to have been a circular iron rod, like a pontil, with the working end split into quadrants. The Canadiana Gallery of the Royal Ontario Museum, Toronto, has such a rod about 34 in. long with a working end about 7/8 in. in diameter. The separated quadrants left a quatrefoil impression in the top of the push-up. On some kicks the mark can barely be felt and on others, as in Figure 6, it is unmistakeable, even to the extent of distorting the profile. Occasionally iron oxide deposits from the iron tool are found in the impres-

A fourth way of forming the push-up was by using a specially designed mould part which fit into the bottle mould. An example of this method was developed by the H. Ricketts Company of Bristol in 1821. The patent included a lettered ring which could be placed close to the circumference of the base and "according to the thickness or

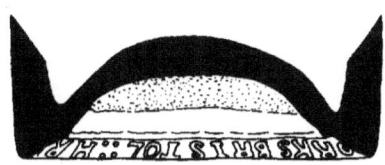

FIGURE 8. *The base of a bottle formed in the Ricketts mould showing the marks left by the device.*

thinness of the said ring is the body of the mould shortened or increased, and the various sizes of bottles produced'' (Ricketts 1821: 3). On the ring could be cut such information as the address of the manufacturer or the volume of the bottle.

As the Ricketts "three-piece" mould formed only the base, body and shoulder, the neck and finish were completed in a separate operation by hand. After a bottle was withdrawn from the mould, therefore, a pontil was attached to the base while the neck was finished. The base in Figure 8 illustrates the different markings left by the manufacturing process. The speckled area is the pontil mark and the raised ridge inside the lettering is the edge of the removable lettered plate. There is also a raised mould line on the resting surface which is not visible in the draw-

ing. Incidentally, these bottles negate a popularly held belief (Kendrick 1968:138) that basal lettering and pontil marks cannot be found on the same bottle.

Originally the Ricketts mould was "An Improvement in the Art or Method of Making or Manufacturing Glass Bottles, such as are used for Wine, Porter, Beer, or Cyder;'' (Ricketts 1821:1) in other words, it was used to make the dark green glass "wine" bottle. Later in the 19th century and even in the early 20th century, however, this mould type was used for bottles holding other products, including solids. The Ricketts mould was used very widely. The French writers De Fontonelle and Malepyre (1854:272) recommended the Ricketts mould because it made bottles of exact capacity and was easy to use, saving of both time and fuel. As well as in France, the Ricketts type of mould appears to have been used in the United States by several companies (McKearin 1970:106-7).

In Figure 12,*d* is another example of a base formed in what appears to be a special multipiece conical tool which may have been part of the mould or which may have been used separately. This type of base has distinctive characteristics. A distinct mould line is visible as a slight projection at the base of the body. A rounded ridge is visible on the push-up close to the resting surface. A small but distinct impression is located in the tip of the push-up. This mark is usually dome-shaped, as in Figure 12,*d*, but may be slightly square or pointed and will sometimes have an iron oxide deposit caused by being formed by a hot bare iron tool. All these marks have obviously been made deliberately but why this somewhat complicated arrangement was chosen is not known. In addition, the glass distribution is often very uneven and, if a pontil mark is present, it is usually large and consists of many sharp bits of embedded glass or sand. These bases, found mainly on dark green glass "wine" bottles, were probably manufactured during the second and third quarters of the 19th century. Their country of origin is not known.

Obviously the above discussion does not include all of the tools or moulds that have been used to form bases. For example, Bontemps (1868:509) mentions that the glassmakers used the handle of the battledore (see McKearin and McKearin: 1948, xv) or "*un crochet special*", and Peligot (1877:301) writes, "*il comprime le fond plat de la bouteille avec un crochet en fer.*" The bases made with these tools may or may not be

FIGURE 9. *The bottle is being held on the pontil while additional glass is added to the neck (Diderot 1772: Pl. VI).*

identifiable. Toulouse, in his article on mould seams, mentions other types of moulds used to form bases (Toulouse 1969:526-35, 578-87).

PONTIL MARKS

The pontil is a long iron rod used to hold a glass article during the finishing process after it is detached from the blowpipe (Mc-Kearin and McKearin 1948: xvi). In Figure 9, from the Diderot *Encyclopédie,* the bottle is empontilled while the bottlemaker adds additional glass to the neck to form the finish. When the pontil is detached from the bottle, usually by a sharp tap on the rod, there is a scar left in the base which is called a pontil mark. Figure 10 illustrates four empontilling techniques: (a) the plain glass-tipped pontil; (b) the sand glass-tipped pontil; (c) the blow-pipe as pontil, and (d) the bare iron pontil. Each of these processes leaves a characteristic pontil mark.

The plain glass-tipped pontil (Fig. 10,*a*), hereafter called a "glass-tipped" pontil, con-

sists of a solid iron bar with a slightly widened end which is dipped in molten glass. The glass on the pontil rod adheres to the glass of the base. The mark left by the glass-tipped pontil is comparatively small, usually no larger than 30 mm., although this will vary according to the size of the vessel being held. Usually there is evidence within the pontil mark that the whole area has been in contact with other glass, either because there is excess glass left when the pontil is detached (Figure 11) or because bits of glass are torn out of the base. This empontilling technique was commonly used on tableware, medicine and toiletry bottles, and on flasks. The small glass-tipped pontil mark in the centre of the push-up is not found after the 1720s on dark green glass "wine" bottles manufactured in the English tradition (see Noël Hume 1961:100-101, Types 12-16, 19-22). Some of the French "flower pot" wine bottles discussed in the push-up section do appear to have been empontilled in this way (Figure 3). The technique is still used for objects manufactured by hand.

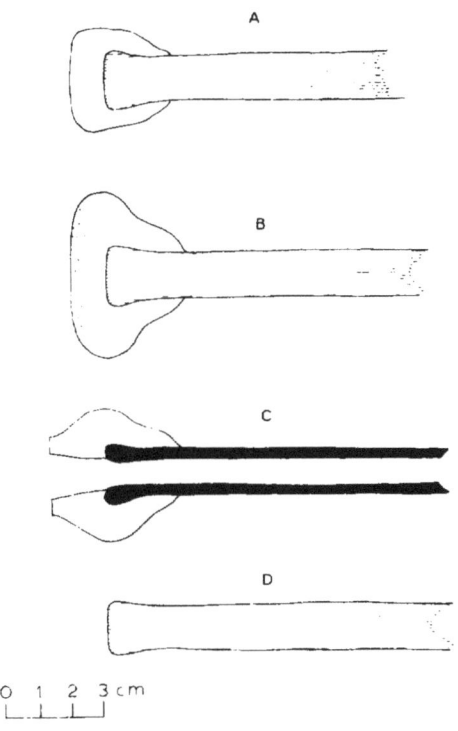

0 1 2 3 cm

FIGURE 10. *Four empontilling techniques: a) the glass-tipped pontil; b) the sand pontil; c) the blowpipe as pontil; d) the bare iron pontil.*

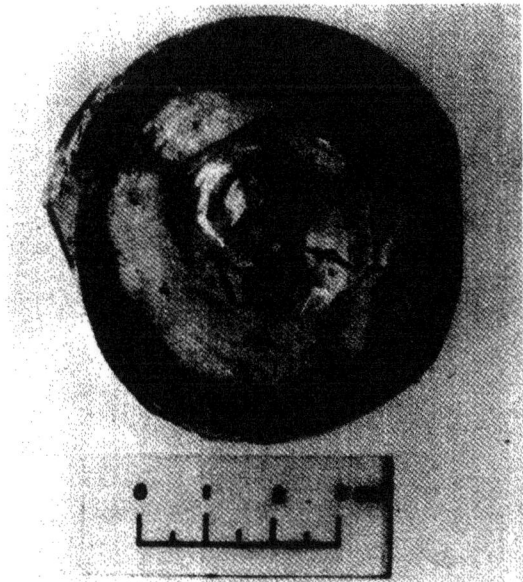

FIGURE 11. *Tumbler base showing excess glass left on the base after removal of the pontil.*

The sand glass-tipped pontil (Figure 10,*b*), hereafter called a "sand" pontil, consists of a gather of glass on the pontil which has been shaped to conform to the basal profile and then dipped in sand (Toulouse: personal communication; Larsen, Riismøller and Schlüter 1963:397). The sand prevents the glass on the pontil from adhering too closely to the bottle.

The sand pontil mark is larger than the glass-tipped one, although again the size varies according to the size of the bottle. It consists of a thin line of glass chips encircling the push-up and enclosing a pebbled surface caused by the grains of sand (Figure 12). Some of the sand may also be embedded in the base (Toulouse: personal communication). Toulouse also points out that this type of pontil will conform to the shape of the already formed base without distorting it.

Sand pontil marks are very common on English dark green glass "wine" bottles, octagonal bottles and occasionally case bottles. The four "wine" bottle bases in Figure 12 have sand pontil marks (Toulouse: personal communication). In the upper two, dating from the 18th century, the pontil has been applied closer to the top of the push-up, which is usually hemispherical or dome-shaped. In 128 examples from one Canadian site, the diameters of the sand pontil mark ranged from 40 mm. to 71 mm., but 86 per cent were between 50 mm. and 64 mm. Sometimes one can feel a quatrefoil mark in addition to the pontil mark, but more often there is a pinch mark or wrinkle in the centre of the push-up which may be indicative of the tool used to form the push-up. In the lower pair (Figure 12, *c,d*), dating from the late 18th and 19th centuries, the sand pontil mark is less distinctive. Almost the entire basal surface is disturbed and is frequently roughened by embedded grains of sand or glass chips. The pontil mark usually begins close to the resting surface. In 76 examples from the same site, the pontil mark diameter ranged from 46 mm. to 71 mm., but 80 per cent were between 50 mm. and 60 mm. Sand pontils are still used on glass manufactured by hand (Toulouse: personal communication).

The third type of empontilling technique (Figure 10,*c*), probably no longer in use, consisted of using the glass left on the blowpipe after the bottle had been snapped off. In other words, the blowpipe itself was used as a pontil. The bottle was laid on a V-shaped structure (Figure 13) while the glass-

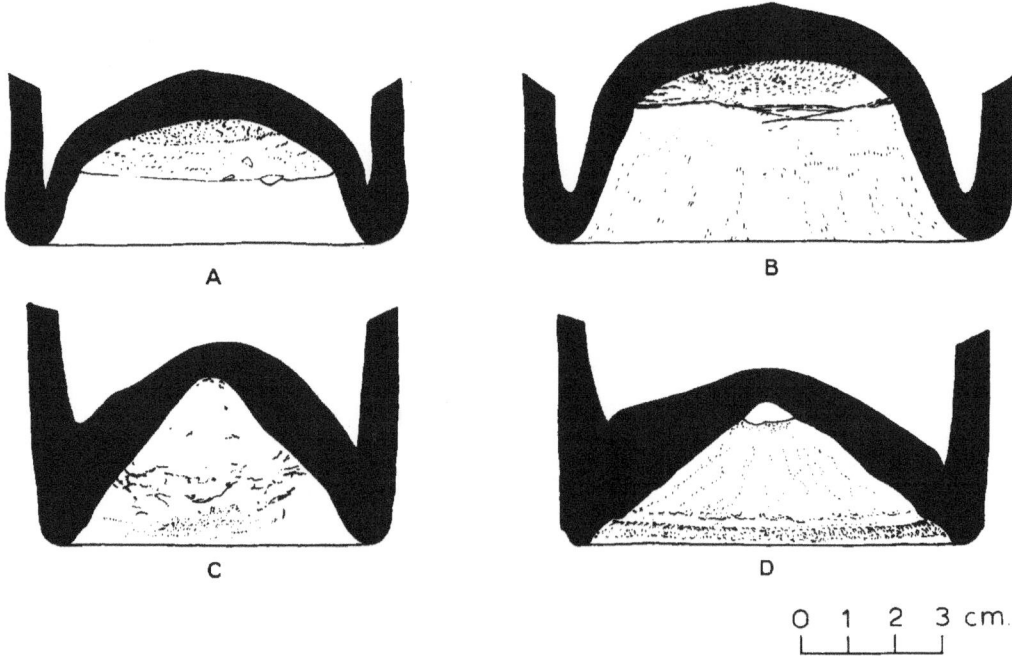

FIGURE 12. "Wine" bottle bases with sand pontil marks: a) and b) 18th century; c) late 18th, early 19th century; d) 19th century.

FIGURE 13. Bottle lying in a V-shaped structure while the blowpipe is attached to the base (Diderot 1772: Pl. V).

0 1 2 3 cm.

FIGURE 15. *"Wine" bottle base showing distortion which may have been caused by using a bare iron pontil.*

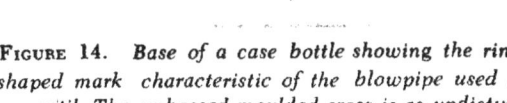

FIGURE 14. *Base of a case bottle showing the ring-shaped mark characteristic of the blowpipe used as a pontil. The embossed moulded cross is as undisturbed inside the ring as outside.*

maker applied the blowpipe with its excess glass to the base of the bottle. The pontil mark is a distinct ring-shaped mark about the same diameter as the neck (Toulouse 1968:139). When the blowpipe was removed from the base it either tore glass out with it or left extra glass behind. As the only area of contact is the ring of glass, any mould lines, embossed markings, and distinctive surface textures remain as undisturbed inside the ring as they do outside (Figure 14) (Toulouse 1968:139).

These ring-shaped marks are found on case bottles, champagne bottles, flasks, medicine bottles and other small vials, but they are not found after 1720 on the dark green glass "wine" bottles manufactured in the English tradition illustrated by Noël Hume (1961:100-101). This empontilling technique, described by Diderot (1772: Pl. V), was used for the French "flower pot" wine bottles, although the distinctive ring shape is not always obvious. Bottles of this type have appeared on a Canadian site occupied by the French be-

tween 1732 and 1745. The French writers Peligot (1877:300) and Bontemps (1868:509) described this technique, but whether this was straight copying from Diderot or whether the practise was still common has not been determined. Certainly it was still being used in the United States in the 19th century (Mc-Kearin 1970:89-91).

The fourth empontilling technique (Figure 10,*d*), probably discontinued, consisted of using a bare iron pontil with a suitably shaped end, usually a shallow arch, which was heated red hot and applied directly to the base of the bottle (Toulouse 1968:140). The pontil mark is a distinct circular mark covered with a reddish or black deposit which, when tested, indicated the presence of ferric oxide and occasionally ferrous exide (Toulouse 1968:141). Toulouse (personal communication) also suggests that the bare iron pontil tended to distort the push-up more than any of the glass-tipped pontils (Figure 15). Some of the marks that I have seen on bottles in local collections are unmistakeable, but others in the National Historic Sites Service collection have iron oxide deposits spread unevenly over the pontil mark area (Figure 15). The deposit could be explained in a number of ways. Possibly a bare iron pontil was used to hold the bottle; the push-up may have been formed by a bare iron tool, or the bottle may have been buried next to an iron object.

The distinct form has been found in American flasks, fruit jars and carbonated beverage bottles dating from about 1845 to 1870 (Tou-

0   1   2   3 cm.

FIGURE 16. *Moulded lettering in the centre of the base, a position formerly occupied by the pontil mark.*

louse 1968:141-2). The indistinct marks in the National Historic Sites Service collection occur in 18th- and early 19th-century dark green glass bottle bases. Obviously further investigations will have to be carried out on this technique.

The pontil was gradually replaced by other tools, such as the sabot (Figure 1) and the snap case (Kendrick 1968:128), which held the bottle around the body and did not leave disfiguring scars in the base. These tools were introduced sometime between the late 1840s and the 1850s (Bontemps 1868:511; Larsen, Riismøller, and Schülter 1963:389; McKearin 1970:107; Scoville 1948:17), and by the 1870's had superceded the pontil for holding bottles during the finishing process (Toulouse 1968: 204). With the disappearance of the pontil mark, the glassmakers began to use the centre of the base for moulded lettering and numbers (Figure 16).

CONCLUSIONS

Several relationships became obvious during the course of this study. Different empontilling techniques and methods of form-

ing push-ups were used for different types of bottles. Possibly these differences can be related to the size of the bottle.

A regular, rounded, cone-shaped push-up, probably made with a mollette, as described by Diderot, in combination with a small pontil mark, either from a glass-tipped pontil or from a blowpipe used as a pontil, occurs on 18th-century French wine bottles. I have seen the same combination on 18th-century European spa water bottles and suspect that the Belgian wine bottles illustrated in Chambon (1955: Pl. T, facing p. 113) were formed in a similar way. The combination, therefore, should probably be regarded as Continental rather than strictly French in origin.

The glass-tipped pontil or the blowpipe as a pontil appear to have been favoured by the French, and possibly the Continental glassmakers, for holding all bottles, even those of larger capacity (about 26 oz.). The English, however, favoured these two methods for their smaller bottles and used the larger sand pontil for bottles of larger capacity (about 26 oz.).

A separate mould part designed specifically to form the push-up appears to have been first introduced in England in the 1820s for the dark green glass "wine" bottles. Afterwards, however, this technique was used in many countries for most types of bottles.

The bare iron pontil appears to have been used in the 19th century. Iron oxide deposits on the bases of earlier bottles may be from the use of this type of pontil or from a tool used to form the push-up.

Obviously there are a great many questions left unanswered by the above study. The relationships between different bottle types, techniques, country and period of manufacture are very complex. Often the different types of marks are difficult or impossible to identify, and available literature on glass has, with few exceptions, not covered this aspect in detail.

In combination with other criteria such as body shape, size, and finish formation, the formation of the push-up and the empontilling techniques can be used as additional evidence in determining bottle types made during the 18th and 19th centuries.

ACKNOWLEDGEMENTS

My appreciation and thanks are extended to Dr. Julian Toulouse, retired glass Consulting Engineer, for his inestimable help and comments in the preparation of this article. I would also like to thank the National Historic Sites Service for permission to publish the information relating to the archaeological collections made by the Service. The photographs were done by Georges Lupien and the drawings by Mrs. Jane Moussette, both of the National Historic Sites Service.

REFERENCES

BONTEMPS, GEORGES
1868 *Guide du verrier, traité historique et practique de la fabrication des verres, cristaux, vitraux.* Librairie du dictionnaire des arts et manufactures, Paris.

DIDEROT AND D'ALEMBERT
1967 *Encyclopédie, ou dictionnaire raisonné des sciences, des arts, et des métiers.* Facsimile reprint of 1765 ed. of Vol. 17, text. Friedrich Fromann Verlag (Gunther Holzboog), Stuttgart.

1772 "Vetterie en bouteilles chauffée en charbon de terre." *Recueil de Planches sur les sciences, les arts libéraux et les arts méchaniques, avec leur explication.* Vol. 10. Briasson, Paris.

CHAMBON, RAYMOND
1955 *L'Histoire de la verrerie en Belgique du IIme siécle à nos jours.* Editions de la Librairie Encyclopédique, Bruxelles.

DE FONTONÈLLE, JULIA, AND F. MALEPEYRE
1854 *Nouveau manuel complet de verrier et du fabricant de glaces, cristaux, pierres précieuses factices, verres colorés, yeux artificiels, etc.* Vol. I. La librairie encyclopédique de Roret, Paris.

KENDRICK, GRACE
1968 *The Mouth-Blown Bottle.* Grace Kendrick, Fallon, Nevada.

LARSEN, ALFRED, P. RIISMØLLER, AND M. SCHLÜTER
1963 *Dansk Glas 1825-1925.* Nyt Nordisk Forlag Arnold Busck, Copenhagen.

McKEARIN, GEORGE, AND HELEN McKEARIN
1948 *American Glass.* Crown Publishers, New York.

McKEARIN, HELEN
1970 *Bottles, Flasks and Dr. Dyott.* Crown Publishers, New York.

MENDELSOHN, OSCAR A.
1965 *The Dictionary of Drink and Drinking.* Macmillan, Toronto.

MOODY, B. E.
1963 *Packaging in Glass.* Hutchinson and Co., London.

NOËL HUME, IVOR
1961 "The Glass Wine Bottle in Colonial Virginia." *Journal of Glass Studies,* Vol. 3, pp. 91-119. The Corning Museum of Glass, Corning, New York.

1970 *A Guide to Artifacts of Colonial America.* Alfred A. Knopf, New York.

PELIGOT, E.
1877 *Le verre: son histoire, sa fabrication.* G. Masson, Paris.

RICKETTS, H.
1821 *Ricketts' Specification: An Improvement in the Art or Method of Making or Manufacturing Glass Bottles, such as are Used for Wine, Porter, Beer, or Cyder.* British Patent, No. 4623.

SCOVILLE, WARREN C.
1948 *Revolution in Glassmaking: Entrepreneurship and Technological Change in the American Industry.* Harvard University Press, Cambridge, Mass.

TOULOUSE, JULIAN
1968 "Empontilling—A History." *The Glass Industry,* Pt. I (March), pp. 137-42; Pt. II (April), pp. 204-5. New York.

1969 "A Primer on Mold Seams." *The Western Collector,* Pt. 1, Vol. 7, No. 11, pp. 526-35; Pt. 2, Vol. 7, No. 12, pp. 578-87. San Francisco.

The Contribution of the Ricketts' Mold to the Manufacture of the English "Wine" Bottle, 1820–1850

Olive Jones

JOURNAL OF GLASS STUDIES

VOLUME 25 · 1983

THE CORNING MUSEUM OF GLASS

THE CONTRIBUTION OF THE RICKETTS' MOLD TO THE MANUFACTURE OF THE ENGLISH "WINE" BOTTLE, 1820–1850

OLIVE JONES

Parks, Canada, Ottawa, Ontario, Canada

IN December of 1821 Henry Ricketts of Henry Ricketts and Company, the Phoenix Glass Works, Bristol, England, patented a mold for "An Improvement in the Art or Method of Making or Manufacturing Glass Bottles, such as are used for Wine, Porter, Beer, or Cyder."[1] The mold consisted of a dip mold body, two hinged shoulder parts, and a movable base part which included a removable letter plate. The mold was placed in a specially designed frame, and the various parts of the mold could be moved by means of levers activated by the glassblower pressing caps or knobs set in the floor (Fig. 1). In the patent specifications Ricketts gave the following introduction:

> My Invention comprises an improvement upon the construction of all moulds heretofore used in the manufacture of bottles, whether of black or other description of glass or metal, of which bottles can be made by means of an entirely new method in the construction and operative movements and appendages of such moulds, particularly in reference to the casting or making of bottles, such as are used to contain wine, beer, porter, cyder, or other liquids. By this my sole Invention, the circumference and diameter of bottles are formed nearly cylindrical, and their height determined so as to contain given quantities or proportions of a wine or beer gallon measure, with a great degree of regularity or conformity to each other, and all the bottles so made by me after this method present a superior neatness of appearance and regularity of shape for convenient and safe stowage, which cannot by other means be so well attained.[2]

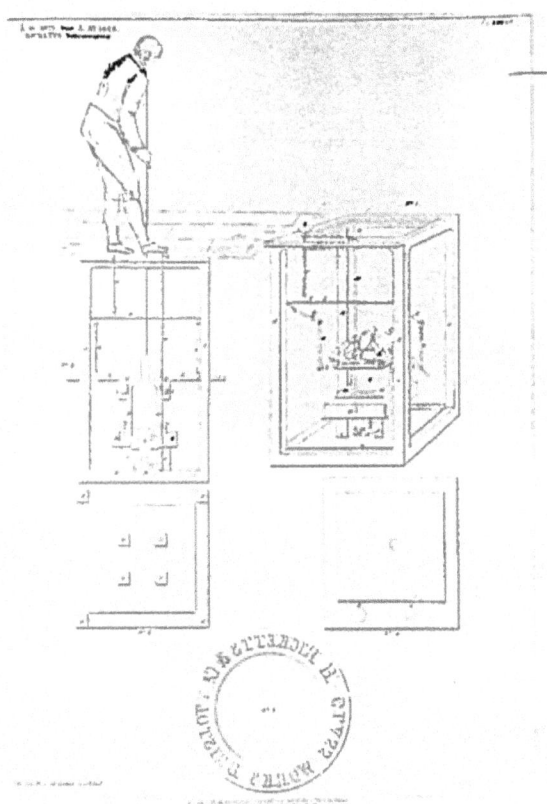

FIG. 1. *Drawings from the Ricketts' patent specification showing the construction and mechanical movements of the mold.*

1. Great Britain. Patent Office, A.D. 1821, No. 4623, *Glass Bottles, Ricketts' Specification*, London, 1857.

2. *Ibid.*

167

John Cave, one of the partners in the Phoenix Glass Works, wrote to Henry Ricketts on November 6, 1821, making the following comments concerning the patent:

Dear Ricketts

In reply to Henry Glascodines letter on the subject of the Patent for our Bottles, I can have no objection to the expenditure of £135– to take out the patent, provided the Sale could be increased to pay soon the expense of it, I should almost doubt the propriety of granting a Patent for so trifling an improvement, yet if it is our interest to obtain it You have certainly my consent, I am happy to find by his letter every thing is going on well at the Works, as to exports to the West Indies being small I am only surprised the Planters are able to pay for anything during the low price of Sugars....[3]

At the time Cave may have been right in regarding the improvements as "trifling"; however, in retrospect the mold can be seen to have had a profound effect on both the manufacture and appearance of the dark green glass English "wine" bottle. Ricketts appears to have introduced open-and-shut molds into the English bottle glass factories. He is certainly responsible for introducing the formation of the push-up inside the mold by means of the movable base part. The concept of the removable letter plate also seems to have been new. The operative movements of the mold streamlined the manufacturing process and were much admired in the technical literature. The mold regulated the appearance of the bottles, setting new standards which were soon followed by other glassmakers. It was also credited with producing bottles of standard capacity.

The Patent

During the 1829 investigation into the patenting process in Britain, witness after witness stressed that patents were for new inventions, not for the processes or techniques already known or in use.[4] Although as a general rule no official inquiry was made into the novelty of the invention, several practical considerations kept any but the most serious patentee from attempting to take out a patent. The cost and trouble involved were considerable. For example, Ricketts paid £135 for protection in England, Wales, and His Majesty's colonies and plantations abroad, but not Ireland or Scotland, at a time when the glassworks was in financial difficulties. Because he was located in Bristol, he would have had to employ an attorney or patent agent in London to shepherd the application through at least eight different government offices, a process frequently taking two months or more.[5] To offset this were the anticipated financial rewards to be gained from having fourteen years of exclusive rights to the patented process. These rights often had to be protected from infringers through negotiations or in the courts. Any hint of prior use, manufacture, or sale of the invention before it received official approval would be the basis of nullifying the patent at any time.[6] The suggestion by some authors[7] that Ricketts used his mold before receiving the patent cannot, therefore, be accepted. The patentee also had to be careful in his specifications not to lay claim to parts of his invention which were known before. The wording of the Ricketts' patent gives an indication as to what he thought he had invented.

Open-and-Shut Molds

From the 1730s onward British manufacturers made dark green glass bottles in a variety of forms —square case bottles, true and flat octagonals, cylindricals—by using the dip mold technique. In this technique the paraison is inserted through

3. Bristol City Archives Office, 12143(43)–23 Henry Ricketts & Company, Correspondence, etc.

4. Irish University Press Series of British Parliamentary Papers, *Inventions: General, Reports from Select Committees on the Law Relative to Patents for Inventions with Minutes of Evidence Appendices and Index*, vol. 1, Shannon, 1968.

5. *Ibid.*, pp. 16–26, 48–54, 66, 82, 126.

6. *Ibid.*, pp. 18, 80, 82, 114, 152.

7. Helen McKearin and Kenneth M. Wilson, *American Bottles & Flasks and Their Ancestry*, New York: Crown Publishers, 1978, pp. 216–218; Ivor Noël Hume, "The Glass Wine Bottle in Colonial Virginia," *Journal of Glass Studies* 3, 1961, p. 105.

168

the top of the mold, the bottle is blown and then withdrawn through the top of the mold. The mold may be in several parts but is not opened and shut during the blowing process. Dip molds form the body of the bottle and sometimes the base, but the shoulder, neck, and finish and often the base were formed outside the mold. The resulting bottles were irregular, and the acceptable range of variability both in shape and capacity seems to have been high.

In the tableware manufactories, however, full-size, open-and-shut molds had been utilized for centuries, not only in England but also in Europe. For example, molded lion-mask stems, dating from the mid-sixteenth to mid-seventeenth century,[8] were clearly made in this type of mold, as were the "Silesian" stems of the first half of the eighteenth century.[9] Completely molded objects such as small vials and tumblers were being made in full-size, two-piece bottom-hinged molds by 1750 and possibly earlier.[10] In Britain the use of this type of mold appears to have been confined to the flint and vial factories and to have been completely ignored by the dark green glass manufacturers. There are a number of possible reasons for this. The dip molds were probably cheaper to make and operate, they left no unsightly vertical mold lines on the body of the bottle, and they may have been more suited to the manufacture of larger bottles. In addition, the various parts of the English glass industry (crown, flint and vial, plate and bottle factories) were rigidly divided from each other by established working patterns and by the excise laws.[11] Transference of technology from one type of factory to another, and the concomitant change in working patterns, would have been difficult, time-consuming, and expensive, and not worth the effort without some strong economic incentive.

The first type of full-size open-and-shut mold to be used in the English bottle factories was the so-called three-piece mold, consisting of a dip mold body part and two open-and-shut shoulder parts (Figs. 1 and 3). These mold parts leave a horizontal mold line encircling the body-shoulder

FIG. 2. *A bottle blown in a Ricketts' mold showing the typical embossed marks and mold lines.* H. 270 mm. Parks Canada Archaeological Collections.

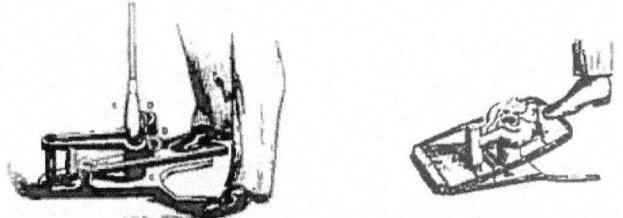

FIG. 3. *Two "three-piece" molds of differing construction and mechanical movements. a) Apsley Pellatt,* Curiosities of Glass Making, *London: David Bogue, 1849, p. 103. Original on file, The Corning Museum of Glass; b) Charles Tomlinson,* Cyclopaedia of Useful Arts, Mechanical and Chemical, Manufactures, Mining, and Engineering, *London: James S. Virtue, 1852–1854, vol. 1, p. 768.*

8 Noël Hume, "Some English Glass from Colonial Virginia," *Antiques* 74, no. 1, July 1963, pp. 68–71; Stephen Moorhouse, "Finds from Basing House, Hampshire (ca. 1540–1645): Part 2," *Post-Medieval Archaeology* 5, [1972] 1971, pp. 63, 65.

169

FIG. 4. *Bottle blown in a "three-piece" mold with a bulged heel and a finish formed by a finish-forming tool, a combination of features suggesting that the bottle was made during the 1820s. It represents an attempt to imitate the concept but not the technique of the Ricketts' mold while the patent was still in force. Although the shoulder has the typical "three-piece" mold lines, the push-up was obviously formed outside the mold. H. 245 mm. Parks Canada Archaeological Collections.*

FIG. 5. *An English "wine" bottle in a marked Ricketts' mold. H. 232 mm. Jones Collection.*

junction and two vertical mold lines going from this line over the shoulder to the neck (Figs. 2, 4, and 5). This particular mold construction is an integral feature of the Ricketts' mold (Fig. 1), although he does not lay specific claim to it, probably because the concept of the open-and-shut mold was already so well-known. By claiming as his "sole Invention," however, that his mold controlled capacity and height and that the bottles presented a "superior neatness of appearance and regularity of shape,"[12] Ricketts, by implication, did claim the hinged shoulder parts, as these were instrumental in achieving the stated results.

Weiss and Morgan[13] credit the discovery of the three-piece mold to a Charles Chubsee of Stourbridge in 1802. However, they illustrate a mold very similar in construction and operation to types which date to the mid-nineteenth century (Fig. 3). Other authors[14] have credited Charles Chubsee with introducing "open-and-shut" molds in

9. Paul McNally, "Table Glass from the Wreck of the *Machault*," *Occasional Papers in Archaeology and History* 16, 1977, pp. 38–39; E. M. Elville, *English Tableglass*, London: Country Life, 1951, pp. 48, 80–81.

10. E. Ann Smith, "Glassware from a Reputed 1745 Siege Debris Context at the Fortress of Louisbourg," *History and Archaeology* 55, 1981, p. 218; Noël Hume, "Glass in Colonial Williamsburg's Archaeological Collections," *Colonial Williamsburg Archaeological Series* 1, 1969, pp. 43–44.

11. Great Britain. Parliament. Laws and Statutes, 35 George 3, C.114, S.23; Great Britain. Commission of Enquiry into the Excise Establishment and into the Management and Collection of the Excise Revenue throughout the United Kingdom. Glass Branch. *Report Number 13*, London, 1835.

12. Great Britain. Patent Office, *op. cit.*, full text quoted above.

13. Gustav Weiss, *The Book of Glass*, New York: Praeger, 1971, p. 323; Roy Morgan, *Sealed Bottles: Their History and Evolution (1630–1930)*, Burton-on-Trent: Midlands Antique Bottle Publishing, 1976, pp. 20–21.

14. D. N. Sandilands, "The Last Fifty Years of the Excise Duty on Glass," *Journal of the Society of Glass Technology* 15, 1931, p. 238; Elville, *op. cit.*, p. 218, who refers to Charles Chasbie; G. Bernard Hughes, *English, Scottish and Irish Tableglass from the Sixteenth Century to 1820*, New York: Bramhall House, 1956, p. 299.

1802. Hughes suggests that they were of a two-piece type that "enabled the form of the vessel and elaborate, closely-spaced designs in relief to be applied to the outer surface of flint-glass tableware in a few simple hand operations."[15] This type of technology had, of course, been available and utilized in the glass industry long before 1802. The only nineteenth-century reference to Chubsee located to date is in some notes written in 1886 by Benjamin Richardson the First:

> In 1814 there was a flint Glass Works built at Wolverhampton and was carried on by Mr. Burkle, and Charles Chubsey was his Manager. Charles Chubsey was very hand in turning patterns . . . and also a good mould maker, principally for diamond mould. . . .[16]

It is likely, therefore, that the Chubsee mold was a full-size mold in two or more parts designed to impart complicated geometric motifs, modeled on contemporary cut motifs, onto the surface of a variety of tableware forms. This type of ware is familiar to collectors of American table glass as "blown three-mold"[17] but was also being made in the early years of the nineteenth century in Irish and English flint glass houses.[18] Chubsee can, therefore, be eliminated as the inventor of the "three-piece" bottle mold.

There is still some suggestion that the "three-piece" mold may have been in use before the Ricketts patent in 1821, either by Ricketts himself or by some other glassmaking firm. One occasionally sees undated bottles with the characteristic "three-piece" mold lines which could date earlier than 1821, but these usually have other odd features which make their date of manufacture uncertain. There is no doubt that other types of "three-piece" molds were in use during the 1820s (Fig. 4).[19] Because Ricketts did not lay specific claim to the "three-piece" mold, other glassmakers in England could have used the concept, but not the exact method, to make bottles. Glassmakers in Ireland and Scotland would have been able to imitate the Ricketts mold exactly, as he had no protection in either country.

Because of the lack of concrete evidence to the contrary, I think Ricketts can be credited not only with introducing the open-and-shut mold into the English bottle glass factories but also with introducing the "three-piece" mold.

The "three-piece" mold did not immediately replace the dip mold, which continued to be used for "wine" bottles even into the 1850s.[20] It did, however, become widely used in the industry and was particularly popular for the production of cylindrical pharmaceutical bottles because it left no disfiguring mold lines on the body of the bottle and produced bottles of uniform size.[21] Several different types were in use (Fig. 3), but as they all left the same type of mold marks in the shoulder area, one cannot discern which particular type was used to form a particular bottle.

Forming the Push-up in the Mold

> The act of treading upon the mushroom-shaped cap of M, marked O, so raises the knocker-up N against the punty S under the mould, as to produce the concavity usually formed at the bottom of the bottle, and which by this my Invention effectually secures a symmetry of shape.[22]

15. Hughes, *English Glass for the Collector, 1660–1860*, London: Lutterworth Press, 1958, p. 153.

16. I am deeply indebted to Mr. Herbert Woodward, Brierley Hill, West Midlands, England, for this reference.

17. George and Helen McKearin, *American Glass*, New York: Crown Publishers, 1948, pp. 240–331.

18. Phelps Warren, *Irish Glass: The Age of Exuberance*, London: Faber & Faber, 1970, p. 93, pl. 41D; McKearin and McKearin, *op. cit.*, pl. 124, nos. 1–4; W. A. Thorpe, *English Glass*, London: Adam & Charles Black, 1961, 3rd ed., p. 234.

19. See, for example, Olive R. Jones, "Catalogue of the Glass Bottles and Other Miscellaneous Glassware Excavated at Coteau-du-Lac, Quebec," ms. on file, Parks Canada, Ottawa, 1975.

20. Pierre Beaudet, "Bottle Glass from a Privy at Fort George Military Reserve, Ontario," *History and Archaeology* 45, 1981, pp. 116–117.

21. Georges Bontemps, *Guide du verrier: traité historique et pratique de la fabrication des verres, cristaux, vitraux*, Paris: Librairie du dictionnaire des Arts et manufactures, 1868, pp. 511–512; Apsley Pellatt, *Curiosities of Glass-Making . . .* , London: David Bogue, 1849, pp. 103–104; Edward Parrish, *An Introduction to Practical Pharmacy . . .* , Philadelphia: Blanchard & Lea, 1859, 2nd ed., p. 35; Beaudet, *op. cit.*, pp. 116–117.

171

The movable base part, used to form the push-up, was one of the innovative features of the Ricketts' mold. It also marked the first time that the push-up of the dark green glass English "wine" bottle was formed while the bottle was still in the mold.[23] Shallow push-ups could easily be formed inside the mold, but deeper push-ups, of the type found on "wine" bottles, had to be formed in a separate operation to avoid problems with uneven glass distribution. While the bottle was still in the blowpipe, a tool was used to indent the base and form the push-up.[24] This action frequently caused the lower edge of the body—the heel—to bulge outward.[25] French glassmakers remarvered their bottles to eliminate this bulge,[26] but the English had never bothered. As a result, the heel area on English "wine" bottles frequently bulged outward and frequently gave a very uneven resting surface (Fig. 4). By forming the push-up in the mold, Ricketts virtually eliminated these irregularities (Fig. 5).

The "superior neatness of appearance and regularity of shape"[27] of the Ricketts' bottles seem to have had a profound effect on the market. By the early 1830s the bulged heel had ceased to be a characteristic feature of the English "wine" bottle.[28] Even bottles blown in dip molds had abrupt heels and regular, well-defined resting points.[29]

How this was achieved is not clear, although it is clear that glassmakers had adopted other methods than those used by Ricketts. One description of the dip mold technique, given in 1842 by Barret and Clay, London wine merchants, states:

> . . . the *push*, as it is called, at the bottom of the bottle, may be pushed in too much or not enough; the bottom in the mould is of this shape [illustrates a rounded bottom], and it is pushed in afterwards by means of a conical mould. . . .[30]

A mold having a rounded rather than a flat or indented base should have given comparatively even glass distribution, and the push-up could have been made quite deep.

In the 1860s British glassmakers[31] mentioned that new techniques for forming the push-up had helped to cut the time and skill needed to do this task. The exact nature of these techniques is not clear, but some appear to have been done outside the mold in a way which controlled the lower body and eliminated the bulged heel. Others appear to have been blown with the push-up form already in place and stationary (Fig. 6e–i).[32]

Removable Letter Plate

The ability to emboss lettering onto the surface of the glass was available in the glass industry through the use of full-size contact molds. It was quite possible to emboss the base using dip molds, as the action of withdrawing the bottle from the mold did not affect the basal surface.[33] These

---

22. Great Britain. Patent Office, *op. cit.* A mold line, marking the junction of the base and body parts, encircles the resting point, and another mold line marks the junction of the stationary mold part and the movable base part (see Figs. 1 and 2).

23. Olive R. Jones, "The English Dark Green Glass 'Wine' Bottle, 1740–1850," ms. on file, Parks Canada, Ottawa, 1982.

24. Olive R. Jones, "Glass Bottle Push-ups and Pontil Marks," *Historical Archaeology* 5, 1971, pp. 62–73.

25. Personal communication, the late Julian H. Toulouse, August 31, 1972.

26. Denis Diderot, "Verrerie en bouteilles chauffée en charbon de terre," in *Recueil de planches, sur les sciences, les arts libèraux, et les arts mécaniques, avec leur explication*, vol. x, planche v, Paris: Briasson, 1772; Eug. Peligot, *Le Verre, son histoire, sa fabrication*, Paris: G. Masson, 1877, p. 301; Jeanne Alyluia, "Eighteenth-Century Container Glass from the Roma Site, Prince Edward Island," *History and Archaeology* 45, 1981, figs. 20–34, 39–43.

27. Great Britain. Patent Office, *op. cit.*, quoted above.

28. Jones, "The English Dark Green Glass 'Wine' Bottle." This conclusion is based on observations made on sealed and dated examples as well as on bottles from dated archeological contexts.

29. Beaudet, *op. cit.*, fig. 11.

30. Great Britain. Parliament. Sessional Papers, *Report of the Commissioners Appointed to Consider the Steps to be Taken for Restoration of the Standards of Weight & Measure*, London: HMSO, 1842, p. 353.

31. Great Britain. Parliament. Sessional Papers, *Children's Employment Commission, Fourth Report of the Commissioners*, London: HMSO, 1865, p. 407 (see below).

32. Jones, "The English Dark Green Glass 'Wine' Bottle."

33. Jane E. Harris, "Eighteenth-Century French Blue-Green Bottles from the Fortress of Louisbourg, Nova Scotia," *History and Archaeology* 29, 1979, figs. 5–7; Noël Hume, "The Glass Wine Bottle in Colonial Virginia," p. 106.

172

markings could be simple or elaborate. Decanters and other vessels made in the Irish glass factories from about 1790 onward often had the company name embossed on the base and vertical ribbing on the lower body.[34] In these examples only the lower portion of the vessel was formed and decorated in a shallow dip mold while the remainder was formed by hand.

The unique feature of the Ricketts' mold was that the letter plate could be removed or changed without affecting the rest of the mold:

> The Drawing or Plan No. 4 represents a ring or washer placed at pleasure within the bottom of the mould. . . . Upon the surface of this ring can be engraven the address of the manufacturer, together with figures or marks indicating the size of the bottle, and which exhibit the same by a projection of the characters in the glass.[35]

This feature of the Ricketts' mold is not one that seems to have received immediate attention in the glass industry, although removable letter plates which fitted into molds for stock bottle shapes became very popular in the last third of the nineteenth century for beer, soft drink, pharmaceutical, and toiletry bottles. Glass manufacturers offered them as inexpensive alternatives to having complete molds made.[36] Small local companies made use of this service until fully automatic machine production made small individual orders impractical.[37]

Operative Movements

It is very clear in the patent specification that Ricketts was patenting the frame for holding the mold and the mechanisms for moving the various mold parts. Although not mentioned in the patent, the successful use of his mold eliminated two steps in the process of making "wine" bottles that were necessary when the dip mold was used—forming the push-up and the shoulder.

Georges Bontemps mentioned that he saw "three-piece" molds being used in England in 1828 and that three workers could make 90–100 madeira bottles in an hour.[38] Knapp, writing in 1849, states:

Attempts have consequently been made by many inventors to furnish the bottle-maker with a mould of such construction as would enable him to secure the formation of a bottle, perfect both as regards form and capacity, at one single operation, without reliance upon his own correctness of sight. The use of moulds of this description, like that of Ricketts, which is easily managed, affords a great saving of time and renders the repeated heating of the bottles unnecessary.[39]

By 1865 open-and-shut molds (possibly also a type having two parts to form the body-shoulder and a third part to form the base of the bottle, this being the commonest mold type in use in Britain and North America during the last third of the nineteenth century) were recognized by British glassmakers as having made significant improvements in the time needed to manufacture bottles:

> The time has been gained in different ways. Less time is now taken in the preparation of the metal. The bottle-makers have better implements. . . . The open and shut moulds now in use enable them to make probably a dozen in an hour more than they could with the old open mould, with which the shoulder has to be formed by blowing. They can make now from nine to 10 dozen in an hour. Formerly they made only seven or eight dozen in the same time.[40]

> The amount of work turned out in a week has much increased from what it was formerly here [Glasgow], and is in parts of England. This is partly owing to mechanical causes, such as the open and

34. Warren, *op. cit.*, pp. 67–79.

35. Great Britain. Patent Office, *op. cit.*

36. See, for example, *Whitall, Tatum & Co. 1880—Flint Glassware, Blue Ware, Perfume and Cologne Bottles, Show Bottles and Globes, Green Glassware, Stoppers, Druggists' Sundries*, Princeton: Pyne Press, 1971. pp. 8–11.

37. George L. Miller and Antony Pacey, "Impact of Mechanization in the Glass Container Industry: The Dominion Glass Company of Canada, A Case Study," ms. on file, Parks Canada, Ottawa, 1982.

38. Bontemps, *op. cit.*, p. 512.

39. F. Knapp, *Chemical Technology; or, Chemistry, Applied to the Arts and to Manufactures*, trans. & ed. by Edmund Rolands and Thomas Richardson, Philadelphia: Lea & Blanchard, 1849, vol. II, p. 49.

40. Great Britain. Parliament. Sessional Papers, *Children's Employment Commission . . .*, p. 395.

173

shut, instead of the simple open, mould, and a mould in which the kick at the bottom is formed by the putter up, instead of by the finisher at the marver.[41]

Capacity

Ricketts claimed that the capacities of bottles blown in his mold could be made "with a great degree of regularity or conformity to each other."[42] While the exterior dimensions of the bottle were controlled by the confines of the mold, the interior was not. It was the opinion of Bontemps[43] and of Apsley Pellatt, both of them practicing glassmakers, that it was impossible to rigidly control the capacities of bottles.

> The cause of variation arises from the difficulty of gathering one uniform weight of metal; also with the greatest practice, from the thickness of metal being often greater in one part of the bottle than another (and although there could always be the same quantity of metal), a variation of contents would thus be caused; indeed the accuracy required for Excise inspection cannot be secured by any process of manufacture with which I am acquainted after an experience of above thirty years.[44]

In his book, however, Pellatt stated that the "three-piece" mold (Fig. 3a) "produces excellent apothecaries' phials of uniform size and capacity."[45] The London wine merchants Barret and Clay were of the opinion that the "patent" [Ricketts] bottle varied nearly as much in size as those blown in dip molds.[46]

Nevertheless, the Ricketts' mold acquired a reputation, whether deserved or not, for producing bottles of regulated capacity.

> Such a mould [Ricketts] ought to be prescribed by legislative enactment, with an excise stamp to define the capacity of every bottle, and thereby put an end to the interminable frauds committed in the measure of wine and all other liquors sold by the bottle.[47]

"superior neatness of appearance and regularity of shape"

Bottles blown in the Ricketts' mold set new standards for the acceptable appearance of the dark green glass English "wine" bottle. By forming the push-up in the mold, the bulge at the heel was virtually eliminated, and glassmakers who continued to use the dip mold were forced to follow the appearance if not the technology of the Ricketts' mold. From the evidence on sealed and dated bottles of the 1820s and 1830s, the bulged heel had virtually disappeared from the English "wine" bottle by the early 1830s.[48] Even the shoulders of bottles blown in dip molds were more regularly formed.

Another development in the 1820s helped to contribute to the regularity of the dark green glass English "wine" bottle. This was the finish-forming tool. Bontemps mentions having seen them in use in English and Scottish glass factories that he visited *"il y a quarante ans"* [i.e., 1828]. The type he illustrates consisted of a central mandrel which fitted into the bore and two arms which closed around the outer finish area.[49] Evidence for its use can also be observed on sealed and dated "wine" bottles from 1822 onward.[50] The finish-forming tool regulated the shape of the lip and string rim (Figs. 4 and 5), generally giving them a uniform appearance which they had not had prior to the 1820s.

In the 1820s, through the introduction of the

---

41. *Ibid.*, p. 406.

42. Great Britain. Patent Office, *op. cit.*

43. Bontemps, *op. cit.*, p. 498. Bontemps felt that it was more important to be sure of the quality of the product being purchased than its quantity.

44. Great Britain. Parliament. Sessional Papers, *Report . . . for the Restoration of the Standards of Weight & Measure*, pp. 362–363, evidence given by Pellatt to the Commissioners.

45. Pellatt, *op. cit.*, p. 104.

46. Great Britain. Parliament. Sessional Papers, *Report . . . for the Restoration of the Standards of Weight & Measure*, pp. 353.

47. Andrew Ure, *A Dictionary of Arts, Manufactures, and Mines: Containing a Clear Exposition of their Principles and Practice*, London: Longman, Orme, Brown, Green & Longmans, 1839, vol. 1, p. 161. This is the earliest reference to the Ricketts' mold that I have seen in the technical literature. Julia de Fontenelle and F. Malepeyre, *Nouveau manuel complet du verrier et du fabricant de glaces, cristaux, pierres précieuses factices, verres colorés, yeux artificiels, etc.*, Paris: Roret, 1854, vol. 1, pp. 272–273, also mention that the Ricketts' mold gave bottles of uniform capacity.

48. Jones, "The English Dark Green Glass 'Wine' Bottle."

49. Bontemps, *op. cit.*, pp. 512, 513.

50. Jones, "The English Dark Green Glass 'Wine' Bottle."

174

Ricketts' mold and the finish-forming tool, the English "wine" bottle lost its handmade look and assumed the regular, well-defined shape it was to continue to have into the twentieth century.

Conclusion

The success of the Ricketts' mold can be gauged by a number of factors. Embossed examples, although never in large numbers, have been found in Canada and the United States[51] and in South America. The change in appearance of the "wine" bottle after the introduction of the Ricketts' mold demonstrates that consumers in the liquor trades were eager to have bottles of regular shape. Another measure of success was the number of imitators. In addition to unmarked examples of "three-piece" molded bottles, at least nine United States firms marked their "wine" bottles in a similar style to the Ricketts' bottles, many of them embossing PATENT on the shoulder.[52] These factories generally dated after 1840. One English example, with PATENT on the shoulder, was embossed WEAR GLASS Bo. Co. DEPTFORD, a firm in Sunderland dating between 1814 and 1892.[53] "Three-piece" molds of a variety of types became widely used in the glass industry, as did mechanical methods of forming deep push-ups. Both of these improvements contributed significantly to increased productivity and gave the illusion, if not the fact, of reducing capacity variations.

The Ricketts' mold influenced the manufacturing techniques used by glass bottle manufacturers in Britain and changed the acceptable standards for the overall appearance of the English "wine" bottle—certainly no small contribution for "so trifling an improvement."

Appendix: Dating Ricketts' Bottles

Several authors have suggested that bottles embossed PATENT on the shoulder and H. RICKETTS & CO. GLASSWORKS BRISTOL on the base were being made prior to the patent date of 1821.[54] In order to apply for the patent in the first place and to maintain exclusive rights to the patent mold, however, Ricketts could not have made bottles in the mold prior to receiving the Great Seal in December 1821. All bottles embossed PATENT and H. RICKETTS & CO. GLASSWORKS BRISTOL must date after 1821.

Shoulder Markings

PATENT (Figs. 2 and 5): Began in 1821 and continued to be used after Ricketts' exclusive rights were finished in 1835. It was also used by American glass manufacturers and by at least one other British glass manufacturer.

IMPERIAL PATENT: Observed on two examples, both of which had an embossed crown in the center of the base (Fig. 6b). The imperial gallon was made into law in 1824 but came into effect May 1, 1825.[55]

Base Markings (Fig. 6)

No embossing: Examples embossed PATENT on the shoulder sometimes have no embossed marks on the base.[56] As the base ring was removable, no company can be assigned to these. They would date after 1821.

---

51. Beaudet, *op. cit.*, fig. 5; Jones, "Catalogue of the Glass Bottles . . . Excavated at Coteau-du-Lac, Quebec"; personal communication, Mary Hilderman Smith, December 10, 1979, concerning bottles from the *Niantic*, 1849–1851.

52. McKearin and Wilson, *op. cit.*, pp. 220–221.

53. Geoffrey Wills, *The Bottle-Collector's Guide*, London: John Bartholomew & Son, 1977, pp. 56–57.

54. McKearin and Wilson, *op. cit.*, pp. 216–218; Noël Hume, *op. cit.*, p. 105.

55. Great Britain. Parliament. Laws and Statutes, 5 George IV, C.74, S.6.

56. Beaudet, *op. cit.*, fig. 6.

Debunking the Myth of the Side Seam Thermometer

Bill Lockhart, Bill Lindsey, David Whitten, and Carol Serr

Debunking the Myth of the Side Seam Thermometer

by Bill Lockhart, Bill Lindsey. David Whitten and Carol Serr
© Bill Lockhart 2005

One of the longest running myths in the world of bottle dating is that the side mold seam can be read like a thermometer to determine the age of a bottle. The concept is that the higher the side mold seam on the bottle the later it was made – at least in the era from the mid-19th century until the first few decades of the 20th century. This dating tool was apparently devised by Grace Kendrick in her 1963 book *The Antique Bottle Collector*. This book was a pioneering effort and was reprinted many times into the 1970s. It is probably the most common and widely quoted bottle book ever written – by collectors and archaeologists alike. Kendrick's exploratory efforts were well done – for the time period. She was at the forefront of bottle researchers. However, we *have* learned a few things in the past 22 years.

The concept of the side-seam thermometer was articulated by Kendrick in her chapter entitled "The Applied Lip" that contains a chart, "Age Gauge: Mold Seams of Bottles" (Kendrick 1963:46). Kendrick explains in the text: "It is true that the mold seams can be used like a thermometer to determine the approximate age of a bottle. The closer to the top of the bottle the seams extend, the more recent was the production of the bottle" (1936:45-47).

The chart accompanying this statement notes that bottles made before 1860 have a side mold seam ending on the shoulder or low on the neck; between 1860 and 1880, the seam ends just below the finish; between 1880 and 1900, the seam ends within the finish just below the top lip surface; and those made after 1900 have mold seams ending right at the top surface of the finish, i.e., lip (Kendrick 1963).

Although there are examples of bottles having mold seams that fit these date ranges properly, the issue of dating bottles is vastly more complex than the simple reading of side mold seams. If it were that simple, much of the succeeding literature and research would have been unnecessary. For example, the process that produces a tooled

finish frequently erases any trace of the side mold seam an inch or more below the base of the finish; whereas, the typical applied finish has the seam ending higher – right at the base of the finish. Often the issue is the skill of the individual craftsman. A highly-skilled bottle maker obliterated less of the mold seam than one who was more sloppy in his work.

In addition, there are three other points pertinent to side seam height. First, on many 19th century bottles, the side seams are a different height on each side. According to the thermometer, the bottle halves would have been made during different years. Again, this is a result of the individual skill of the craftsman. Second, all glass techniques changed over a period of time. Not all mold makers produced molds with higher seams during the same period. Even if the chart were a good indicator, it would have to have a period of overlap for each line height during which the industry standards changed. Finally, most bottles made by hand throughout the mouth-blown bottle era (antiquity through the first quarter of the 20th century) received varying amounts of re-firing of the upper neck and/or finish. This reheating often erased traces of the side mold seams – further confounding the "thermometer" dating guide throughout the entire mouth-blown bottle era.

The final sequence in the chart, the side seam extending to the top of the finish after 1900 is extremely faulty. Many figured flasks (like scroll flasks) were simply cracked off from the blowpipe at the point where the top of the mold ended, with no re-firing of the lip. This leaves a relatively sharp, round lip surface to the bottle but also often results in a bottle where the side mold seams ends right at the top edge of the lip (but of course, does not go over the top of the finish like a machine-made bottle). Although these flasks date to the "before 1860" period, the "thermometer" would date them into the 20th century!

In 1881, Phillip Arbogast invented a semi-automatic bottle machine, a device

that reversed the process of bottle making by creating the "finish" first (Meigh 1960:3). Forming the finish first created side seams that extended to the top of the bottle. These early machines only worked on wide-mouth bottles and jars, but the technique was improved to make small-mouth bottles by late 1887 (Meigh 1972:28). Even when Michael J. Owens invented the Owens Automatic Bottle Machine in 1903, that did not mean that *all* or even most bottles began to have the seams extend to the top of the finish during that period. Many bottles continued to be mouth blown, meaning that the finish was created last, and side seams terminated *below* the finish, until the mid-1920s (see Miller & Sullivan for a good discussion about the transition period).

The seam that extends into the finish, a process Kendrick dated 1880-1900, is somewhat unusual and is found in relatively few bottles. Lindsey (2005) describes this as an "improved tooled" finish that is most commonly (but not exclusively) seen on bottles produced towards the end of the mouth-blown bottle era, i.e., 1890s to 1910s. While this can be dated reasonably well to that time period, it was clearly not a defining technique for that or any other period of time.

It is unfortunate that this fiction keeps popping up in the literature of bottle dating and identification ranging from Sellari's books (Sellari and Sellari 1970:5 and others) published shortly after Kendricks book to as recent as Fike (1998:4) and Heetderks (2002:15). It is also frequently noted by sellers on eBay® when describing their offerings. The most recent repetition (with the 1880-1890 form slightly altered from the original Kendrick chart) was published in the Summer 2005 issue of *Bottles and Extras* (Munsey 2005:31). The rest of Munsey's article, by the way, is excellent.

There is, of course, some truth in the thermometer concept. Over time, two improvements in bottle manufacture continued to advance. First, molds actually did improve, gradually creeping up the side seams ever higher. While this *idea*, the basis of the side-seam thermometer concept, is correct, it is not clearly articulated enough in the actual practice of 19th century bottle makers to be a usable, dating concept, especially not with clear-cut starting and stopping dates. Second, finishing techniques improved. As both tools and the techniques of the bottle makers became more refined, less of the bottle necks were affected by the finishing process. Once again, however, this was highly dependent on individual gaffers (glass blowers) and the tools provided by specific factories. It was not clear cut, and there are literally dozens of examples in the collection of only one member of this research group that refute the side-seam thermometer fiction. Between the four of us, we could probably provide literally hundreds of examples that are exceptions to the "thermometer" dating guide.

Examples of these are a bottle from M. H. Webb, Druggist, of El Paso, Texas. Webb was only at the address on the bottle (220 San Antonio St.) from 1900 to 1903. According to the thermometer, this bottle should have a side seam that extends to the top of the finish. In reality [**Figures 1 - 2**], the side seam terminates less than halfway up the neck. If the thermometer were to be believed, this bottle would date 1860-1880, at least 20 years too early.

A bottle from the Rio Grande Pharmacy [**Figures 3 - 4**], one of El Paso's oldest drug stores, is embossed with the signature of Stafford Campbell, Ph.G., Prop. Campbell was first listed as the proprietor in the El Paso city directories in 1896, and he took on a partner in 1901. Thus, the bottle was made during the 1896-1901 period and should have a side seam extending to the top of the finish (according to the thermometer). The actual side seam terminates slightly above the shoulder. According to the thermometer, that would date the bottle before 1860.

A third example comes from the Economical Drug Co., open in El Paso from 1915 to 1930 [**Figures 5 - 6**]. The style of this bottle, with graduations in ounces on the left and cubic centimeters on the right, was first offered in the 1902 Whitall Tatum catalog and was used until at least the 1930s. The seam on this bottle extends to the bottom of the finish on one side and less than halfway up on the other – clearly not to the top of the finish. These examples, alone, clearly refute the accuracy of the side-seam thermometer concept.

Two final examples are found on soft drink bottles from the Magnolia Coca-Cola Bottling Co., El Paso. The company was founded in late 1907 or early 1908 and obtained the Coca-Cola franchise in 1911 (Lockhart 2001:83-98). Magnolia's second bottle style [**Figures 7 - 8**] was used from about 1909 to 1911. On all examples of the bottle, the side seams extend more than

Figure 1: M. H. Webb Drug Store Bottle (1900-1903)

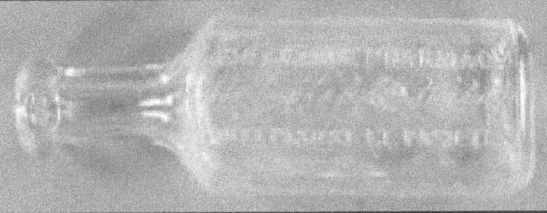

Figure 3: Rio Grande Pharmacy Bottle (1896-1901)

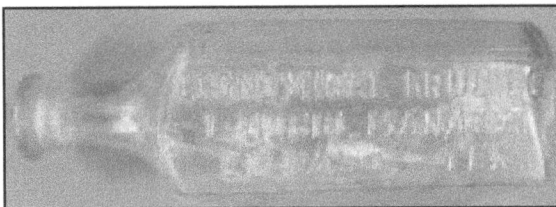

Figure 5: Economical Drug Co. Bottle (1915-1930)

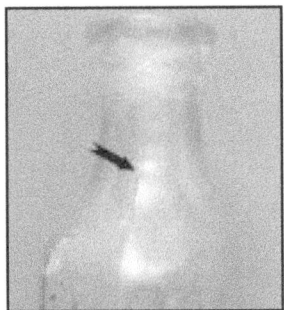

Figure 6: Side Seam – Economical Drug Co. Bottle

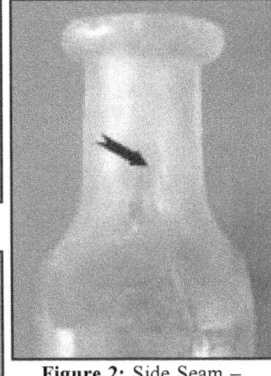

Figure 2: Side Seam – Webb Bottle

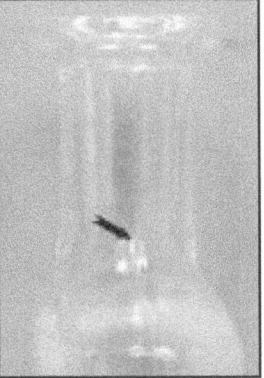

Figure 4: Side Seam – Rio Grande Pharmacy Bottle

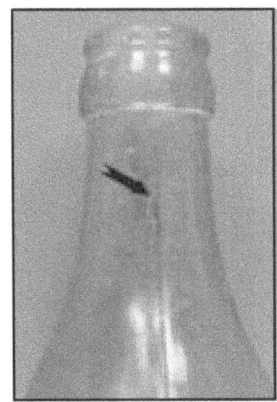

Figure 8: Side Seam Magnolia Bottling Co. Bottle

halfway up the neck but end well below the finish – a format that fits the 1860-1880 identification on the "thermometer" – at least 29 years off. A straight-sided Coke bottle [**Figures 9 - 10**] has a side seam that extends into the finish, an idea that on Kendrick's original thermometer would have dated the bottle between 1880 and 1890. Because Magnolia did not acquire the Coke franchise until 1911, this date range, too, is incorrect by at least 21 years. The evidence speaks for itself.

We hope this helps clarify bottle dating a bit and will help persuade more people to

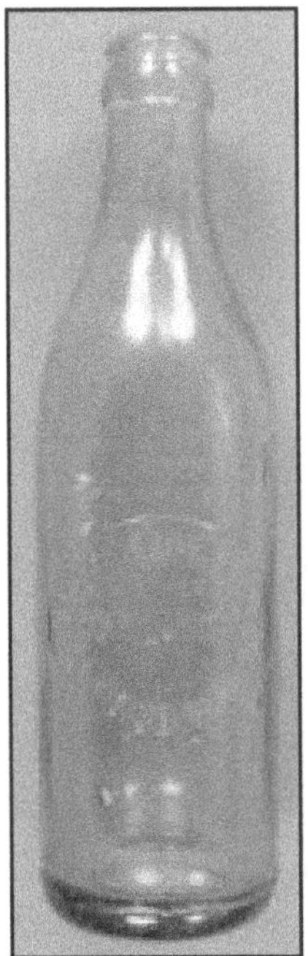

Figure 7: Magnolia Bottling Co. Bottle (1909-1911)

stop repeating this outdated dating technique. Kendrick's ideas were well thought out – for the 1960s. However, researchers of the 21st century need to update our body of dating tools to reflect more recent discoveries. For more discussion on this aspect of bottle dating and identification, see Bill Lindsey's "Bottle Body Characteristics & Mold Seams and Bottle Bases" webpages.

References:

Fike, Richard E.
  1998 "A Guide to Identification and Dating of Historic Glass Bottles."   Unpublished manuscript. Bureau of Land Management., Colorado. Used in the CDF Archaeological Training Program Reference Manual.

Kendrick, Grace
  1963 *The Antique Bottle Collector*. Old Time Bottle Publishing Co., Salem, Oregon.

Lindsey, Bill
  2005   "Bottle Body Characteristics & Mold Seams and Bottle Bases." http://www.blm.gov/historic_bottles/body.htm   and   http://www.blm.gov/historic_bottles/bases.htm

Lockhart, Bill
  2001 "Magnolia Coca-Cola Bottling Company." *Password* 46(2):83-98.

Meigh, Edward
  1960 *The Development of the Automatic Glass Bottle Machine*. Glass Manufacturers' Federation, London.

  1972 *The Story of the Glass Bottle*. C. E. Ramsden & Co., Stoke-on-Trent, England.

Miller, George L. and Catherine Sullivan
  1984 "Machine-made Glass Containers and the End of Production for Mouth-Blown Bottles."   *Historical Archaeology* 18(2):83-96.

Munsey, Cecil
  2005 "'The Smallest Bottle Ever Made on an Owens Automatic Glassblowing Machine.'" *Bottles and Extras* 16(3):28-31.

Sellari, Carlo and Dot Sellari
  1970 "Eastern Bottles Price Guide." Vol. 2. Area Printing Co., Dunedin, Florida. [The thermometer was repeated in Volumes 3 and 4, 1971 and 1972.]

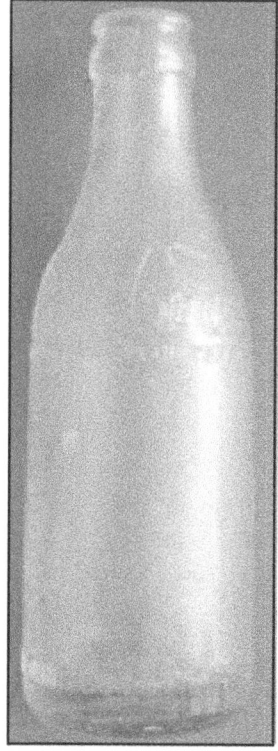

Figure 9: El Paso – Straight-Sided Coke Bottle (1911-1918)

Figure 10: Side Seam – Straight-Sided Coke Bottle

Whittled Molds

Julian Toulouse

BOTTLE WORLD

Whittled Molds

by Dr. Julian Toulouse

When we moved to California three years ago and attended our first Bottle Workshop, conducted by the Eastern California Museum under the direction of Mrs. Dorothy Cragen, at Bishop in March of 1964, I heard the term "whittled mold" for the first time. Since then I have read the term in some western books and letters, but nowhere else. Neither Mrs. Knittle or the McKearins mention whittle molds or their effects.

I did see what, during my thirty-seven years in the glass making and glass using industry, I had come to know as "cold" mold or "cold" glass effects—that is to say, glass whose surface was so cold when it was finally blown that it could not be blown up properly against the surface of the "finish" mold. Generally

in the hand blowing days it was caused by excessive "marvering," or the shaping of the gob on the blowpipe on a marble (marvre or marbre or other stone or metal surface, until the outer surface or "skin" had become so chilled that it would not be plastic enough to blow smooth in the final process. This could also be caused by excessive cooling of the finish mold by over-long dipping into water, which was done in order to cool the mold between blowings. Both were matters of skill, training, and judgment of the operator, the blower, or the mold boy.

In machine bottle blowing it occurs generally at the start-up of the machine after the molds, or part of the molds, have been changed. Not only are the new molds colder than the working tem-

perature, but those not changed at this time have had an opportunity to cool down while the machine is out of production. Particularly in the "blank" mold, which gives the preliminary shaping to the gob, or "parison," just as marvering did in the hand blowing days, the glass surface is chilled on contact and is, in the portion we call the "skin," below good operating temperature. In practice the machine is operated until the molds have taken up enough heat from the glass to operate properly.

After forming the shape and acquiring the "skin" in the blank mold, the parison or blank molded glass is transferred to the second mold of the series, the finishing mold, and inflated by air to the shape of that mold's interior, which is the final shape of the bottle. Because the glass surface temperature is quite variable in these cold glass conditions, and because the diameter of the blank is less than that of the finish mold, colder portions of

the skin never distend to the inner diameter of the finish mold. The result is a mottled, "hammered" or "whittled" appearance.

In June of 1965, returning from the Sacramento meeting of the Antique Bottle Collectors Association, I asked the manager of a glass bottle factory if he would send me some of the worst "cold mold" bottles that they might encounter during the next several months. Such occasions are few nowadays, since the conditions of their cause are well known, and both the mold change is fast, and the molds are well preheated before being placed on the machine. If a delay occurs in restarting there may be a few "cold mold" bottles made, but these are rejected as cullet either by the machine operator or the inspectors, and almost never get into the pack.

Several months later the plant encountered a condition that enabled them to send me a few cold mold bottles. I sent nearly two dozen to different bottle collectors for an opinion. The results were about fifty-fifty. Some agreed that these bottles looked like whittle mold bottles—others did not.

Then I found in my files of clippings and other information about glass and bottles this excerpt from the August, 1890, issue of the National Bottlers Gazette, the oldest journal of the carbonated beverage industry, and a journal which in the older days published many critical references to the materials and supplies that carbonated beverage bottlers might use. Remember also that this was a time of almost universal hand blowing of bottles, for only a beginning of semi-automatic machine bottle making was then being made:

"The hammered look that some bottles present is not a sign of weakness except so far as the appearance of the bottle is concerned. The cause of this 'Hammered' appearance is that the glass has been put into a mould which has not been sufficiently hot, and the steam from the surface has imprinted itself upon the bottle."

A "cold mold" bottle.

Therefore, it seems that the cause of this appearance was known to be a "cold mold" over seventy-five years ago. In those days the molds were momentarily dipped into water between blowings — they became much more heated by the blowing of the bottle than even now because the glass was in contact for a much greater, and more uncontrolled, length of time. But who could measure a moment? Who could tell, except by long experience, just how long to "marve" the gob, and how much of a "skin" to develop?

The quotation also speaks of the "steam from the surface" imprinting itself upon the bottle. Today, water is not used, and the molds are vented at many points by very small holes that allow the air entrapped between the expanding gob and the inside of the mold to escape. Otherwise the entrapped air would gather at the last part of the glass-mold interspace to be blown up, and prevent complete conformation with the mold. We know a great deal about all the technology of bottle making. I have no idea how and when venting was put into use, but "steam imprinting itself on the bottle" was probably a very real thing then.

The term 'whittled' assumes that molds were made of wood for many years. In the period just after 1800 and up to perhaps 1830, wood was quite commonly used for plain, unlettered bottles, especially round bottles, and those without sharp design features. Any lettered mold had a short life from charring of the wood, and in particular, letters were never sharp or very clear after a short time of use of the mold. Hard woods had to be used, with apple and beech wood the choices for most molds.

Brass, though expensive, had been introduced during the eighteenth century, and was necessary for any design where sharpness of detail was desired. It was being used for many of the historical flasks, along with some wood, in the 1820s. Joseph Magoun patented a method for making iron molds in 1847, and in 1866 Sweeney patented the chilled iron mold. Now, neither brass nor iron could be very well "whittled," so that bottles of any marked, and especially intricate, designs had to be of these metals, whether or not the bottles made in them might look whittled. They do scale, and the marks left on glass by scale on the molds is quite different than those shown to me as whittled. Inept removal of the scale might leave deep gouges, or indentation, but these would not be in the overall and random pattern of most "whittling."

Another proof that metals were used for glass making in the early 1800s is that pressed glass, with very intricate and lacy designs, was being made in the early years of the century. Bakewell of Pittsburgh patented a method of pressing glass in 1825. Henry Whitney of Glassboro, New Jersey, in 1826, Phineas Drummond of Jersey City in 1827, and Deming Jarves of Boston and Sandwich in 1828 brought it into perfection. Metal just had to be used.

It is hardly conceivable that the glass blower would get out his trusty pocket knife to make a minor correction in the mold, when his pay (and the pay of all the others in his "shop" or team working with him who would be standing idly by while he whittled) was based upon the number of bottles that he could produce; when he was content otherwise to make seedy bottles because he was in too much of a hurry to wait for the glass to "fine"; and when he was also content to make bottles that were out of capacity, and lopsided and otherwise imperfect, in order that he could make his quota. The idea that he would stop all this in order to improve the mold just has to be completely wrong. He couldn't care less! ∎

When Did Hand Bottle Blowing Stop?

Julian H. Toulouse

WHEN DID HAND BOTTLE BLOWING STOP?

by Dr. Julian H. Toulouse

There seems to be the feeling among some bottle collectors that the year 1904 was the final year for commercial hand bottle blowing in the United States and the beginning year for machine bottle making. This is far from true. It took fifty years to make the complete change.

It is impossible to look at the finish of a bottle, and from the disappearance of the side seam and the showing of rotation marks of the finishing tool, both at the neck to say, "this bottle was made before 1904" or, not finding these marks, to say, "this bottle was made after 1904." Jars with pressed finishes have their side seams intact to the point of pressing, ground lip jars to the point of grinding —and "turn mold" bottles have no side seam!

All bottles are made in a series of related steps. In hand blowing the steps are taken at different places around the "shop," or area occupied by a single team of workers. The blowpipes and pontils are carried from one place to an-

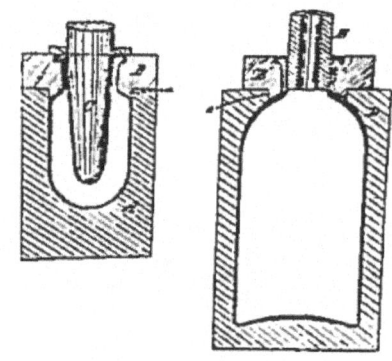

Arbogast patent drawing showing blank and plunger at left, finishing mold air-blown at right.

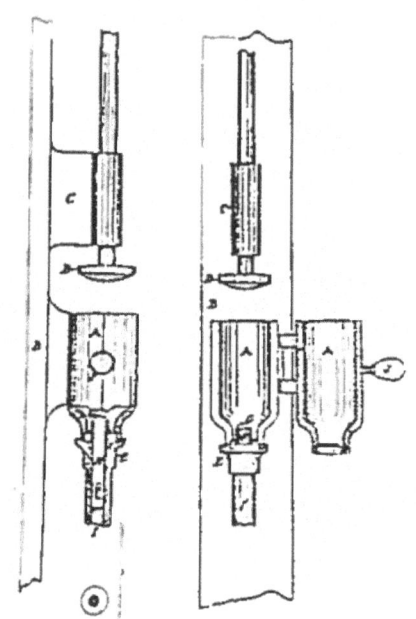

Ashley patent drawing.

Dr. Julian Toulouse is one of the outstanding authorities in the glass and bottle field. Prior to his retirement he was chief engineer of the Owens-Illinois Glass Company and has served as advisor to numerous governments including that of the United States.

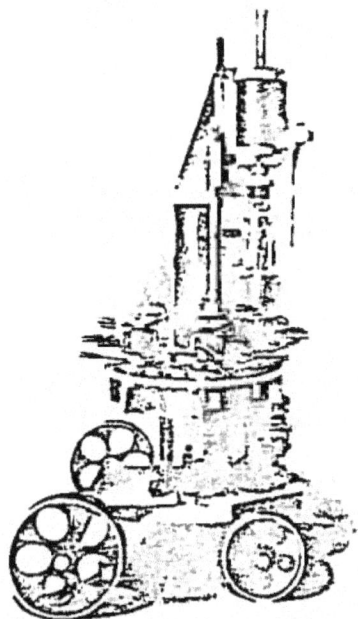

Blue.

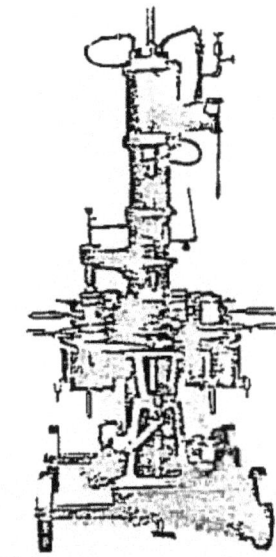

Cox-Winder.

other, and handed from one workman to another. Mechanization involves not only arranging the entire operation of forming the bottle in the same steps, although sometimes differently arranged in sequence, on one mechanical frame, but also the movement, or "transfer" of the bottle parts between stations on the machine. The several types of machines arise by their doing this by different means, or with different specialties for types of bottles.

First we must eliminate reference to "off hand" bottle blowing, or forming the bottle without the use of a mold. When the end use of a bottle was to be a container for a commercial product, at low cost, when there had to be a considerable degree of being alike, and when they had to be stoppered uniformly to preserve the contents, molds necessarily came into use.

So long as human lungs inflated the glass into the shape of the inner cavity of the mold, and human hands manipulated the shaping tools, the process has been called "hand-blown" in the glass industry, or in the collector's terminology, "blown - molded," which excludes "off hand" blowing. But "blown-molded" does not distinguish between machine and hand blowing in molds, and "hand-blown" does not distinguish between mold and off-hand blowing, unless qualified. It is in the sense of hand blowing into molds versus machine blowing into molds with which we are concerned.

Hand blowing starts at the pot with a gathering of glass on a blowpipe by a junior workman, who carries the gather to the marvering table where he rolls the gather into a desired shape and makes a few "puffs" into the mouthpiece in order to start the "bubble." Then he hands the blowpipe to the blower, who inflates the "parison" to the inner shape of the mold, where it chills and "sets." The partially completed bottle is then handed to the finisher or "gaffer" at the chair.

First he attaches a pontil at the bottom and snaps off the blowpipe. Then he must reheat the neck at the furnace. If a laid-on-ring is to be applied, he does this when he returns to his chair. After this the neck is shaped by hand tools, the bottle detached, and carried to the lehr.

Machine operation merged these steps into a sequence in a single mechanical frame. Glass was gathered at the pot as usual, brought to the machine, and a portion was severed by a pair of shears, held in such a position that a "gob" fell into a newly added "blank" mold. So long as glass had to be brought to the machine in this fashion, the machine was called "semi-automatic." The 1904 patent of the Owens machine was the transfer of glass to the machine mechanically, leading to the first "automatic" machine. But semi-automatics had long been in use by that time.

The first operation was the use of a plunger which was forced down into the mold to press the gob into the shape of the blank mold. It also forced glass into the inner contour of the "neck ring" which was placed above the blank mold and in close contact with it. This not

42

only performed the shaping formerly done at the marvering table, but also the entire operation of the finisher, even the thickening made by the laid-on-ring. The plunger was first operated by a hand press, then by an air, steam or mechanically driven cylinder.

The parison was then hand-transferred to the finishing mold, a blowing "head" applied at the top, and air introduced by a hand-operated valve. When finished, the mold was opened by hand and the bottle taken to the lehr. The entire "machine" was but little more than a grouping of hand operated tools and molds. It was now possible to make glass faster, and by the employment of only a man and a boy. Bottles so made had no turn marks, or loss of side seam; the seam

chine. But they were still semi-automatic in this function.

The object of this inquiry is: when did even semi-automatic bottle blowing start, and as a corollary, what led up to it?

Obviously the term "machine" cannot be applied to the hand-held tool used for finishing, even though composed of springs and linkages. Such a tool dated from the 1830s in England and from the 1850s in the United States. Nor can it be applied to the "sabot" of Bontemps (1860s) used to grip the bottom instead of using a glass-tipped pontil, nor to the later ones with springs and cups. But the several presses beginning in the 1820s to imitate cut glassware by a single pressing operation, hand levered,

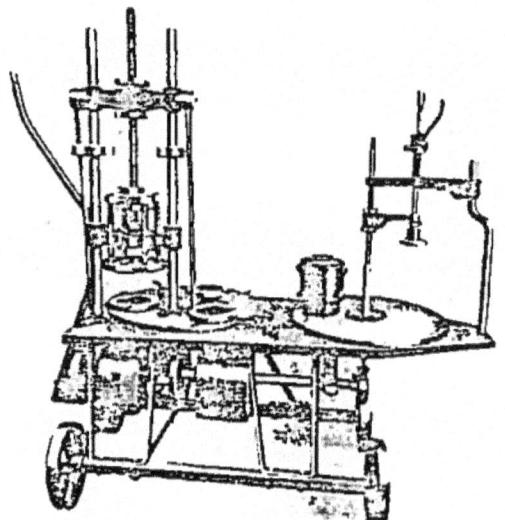

Teeple-Johnson, large ware.

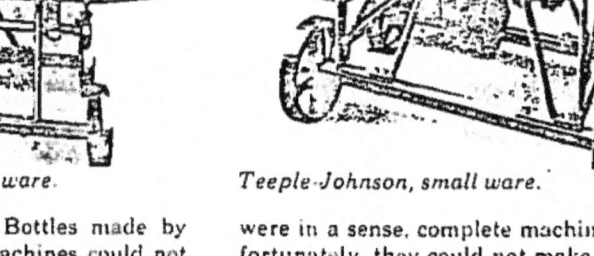

Teeple-Johnson, small ware.

went over the finish. Bottles made by the earliest of these machines could not be distinguished *by the finish* from today's machine-made bottles—they looked like, and were, machine made.

When it was realized that one bottle could be in the finishing mold while another was starting in the blank mold, production almost doubled. When it was realized that the blank mold operations could be subdivided into a series, and finishing mold operations as well, from three to five separate blank molds were arranged to form a ring on a rotating table, together with as many finishing molds, and production took another increase. Finally, power driven machines eliminated all the human operations except that of feeding glass to the ma-

were in a sense, complete machines. Unfortunately, they could not make bottles. The virtue of mentioning them here is that they were steps in the beginnings of shaping glass by mechanical contrivances.

The beginnings of the machine might also be set with Alexander Mein's British Patent No. 680 of 1859 for a so-called machine, or to Kilners' of Yorkshire, in 1860, or to Bowner's British patent of 1861, or to Gillender's U. S. patent for forming a finish in 1865. These were all machine elements, rather than machines in completeness.

The date might well be 1866 when Portmaster Josiah Arnall, of Ferrybridge, Yorkshire, imparted an idea to bottlemaker Edgar Breffit, but Breffit

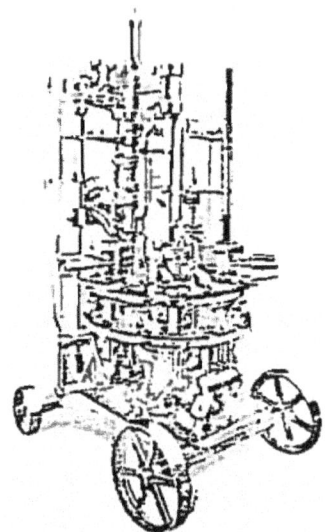

Miller.

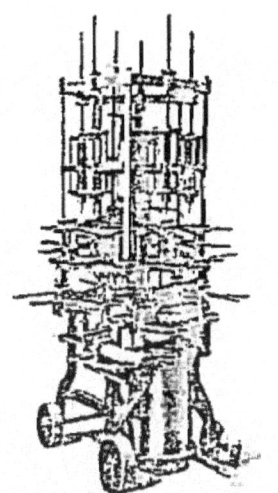

Johnson-Fry.

man's rates demanded by the unions made the machine unprofitable. In 1891 Ripley was absorbed into the United States Glass Company's combination of companies, and this non-union group was able to use the machine at a profit over hand making, even with single molds then used. In 1893, the Enterprise Glass Company, owned by the C. L. Flaccus Glass Company, made the first commercial ware—a vaseline jar.

In England, Postmaster Arnall had not been quiet. About the time that Arbogast was giving up his efforts, Arnall was "bending the ear" of his boarder, H. M. Ashley, manager of a Ferrybridge foundry. Together they took out B. P. No. 8677 on July 2nd, 1886. The idea was not quite successful, but the effort brought about new ideas and

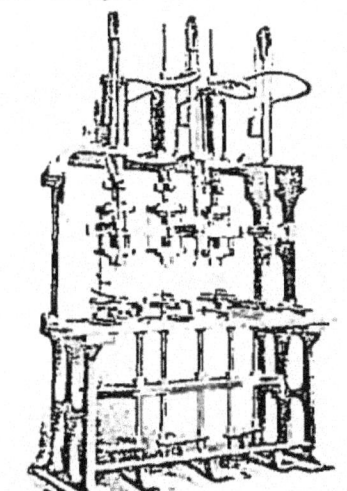

Pancoast.

did not buy it and the idea lay dormant for twenty years. Then, Atterbury obtained a U. S. patent in 1873. Bottlemakers began to think machines.

The real start appears to have been in two places independently. First of record came U. S. Patent No. 360,819, by Phillip Arbogast, of Pittsburgh, Pa., on July 11, 1882. It has already been described: a hand gather, a gob placed into a blank mold, pressed into shape and into finish rings simultaneously by a plunger-press, transferred to a finishing mold and blown.

Arbogast was not able to make bottles, although time proved that he was on the correct track. After three years he sold the patent to the Ripley Glass Company of Pittsburgh. In time they were able to make bottles, but the work-

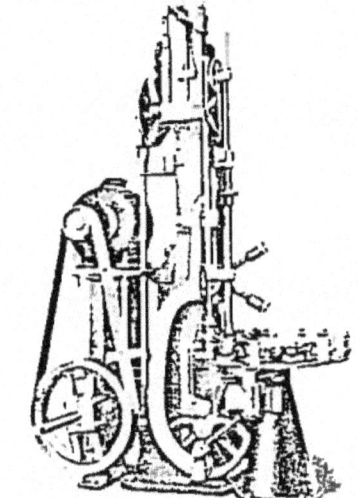

O'Neil-Gordon.

Ashley made improvements that resulted in his receiving B. P. No. 3434 on
March 7th, 1887. Based on it he made
bottles after a fashion.

Changes and additions now came fast.
The C. L. Flaccus Company had used a
machine for small ware in which the
blank mold was directly under the plunger in a fixed position, and the finishing
mold merely placed beside it as a convenience. Ashley's had first placed the
two molds one above the other. Charles
E. Blue, of the Wheeling (West Virginia) Mould and Foundry Company is
credited by Edward Meigh with the development of the Blue rotating table,
five position machine in 1896; but John
Algeo, former sales manager of Hazel
Atlas, gave me the date of 1894 and
stated that President C. N. Brady of
Hazel Atlas had subsidized Blue's work.
The earlier date may be logical because
Brady founded the Atlas Glass Company in 1896 in order to use the machine, and some lead-time would have
been necessary. At any rate, Atlas was
the first glass company to have been
formed for the exclusive use of machines.

It was reported that Ball Brothers
bought or leased Blue machines. However, Ball Brothers soon brought out
their own machines: first the F. C. Ball
hand indexed machine in 1898, and then
the Ball Bingham, Patent No. 610,515, in
1900, as the first power-driven machine.

Power perfected the semi-automatic
machine. When the operator brought
the gather of glass to the machine and
placed the pontil in a certain position,
he tripped a lever that started the machine into operation. It sheared the gob
free, dropping it into the blank, pressed
it, transferred it to the finishing mold,
applied the air pressure, blew the bottle, and opened the finishing mold so
that the "taker in" could remove the
bottle to the lehr. It indexed the machine into each new position as it rotated the table that held the molds. It
was making several bottles, in different
stages of bottle blowing, at the same
time.

In rapid succession other machines were
developed. In America there were the
"Cox," the "Winder" and then the "Cox-
Winder," followed by the "Teeple-
Johnson" or Johnny Bull (an American
version of the Ashley), the "Miller," the
"Johnson-Fry," the "Pancoast,", the

"O'Neill," the "Jersey Devil," the "Morrison," the "Butler" and later the
"Lynch," the "Brockway," and several
others. Several other machines were developed in England, Germany and
France. Thus there was no lack of
machines making bottles before the
Owens machine of 1904. The bottles
were in every sense machine made in
appearance and fact, and the first of
them goes back to about 1886 or 1887.
This gives us our first date.

Hand bottle blowing did not end with
the first usages of the machine. Machines were expensive by the money
standards of that day. Companies would
buy one machine and then struggle to
learn how to use it. When they mastered
the first machine, and if business justified it, or they could afford it, or if the
unions accepted it, they could buy another. They did not at once drop hand
operation—at first they needed it to
fulfill their production requirements.
The Glass Factory Directory, an annual
listing of all glass plants since 1924, has
many references to pot furnaces, even
to the late 1930s. Generally the use of
machines accelerated the changeover to
day or continuous tanks.

One present-day important company,
by private communication, has stated
that they used hand bottle blowing for
making some of their short run and specialty items until 1938. Thus we have a
usable second date in the transition.

Many companies never installed machines. They kept on making bottles by
hand until the lower priced machine
made bottles made hand blowing unprofitable and forced them into bankruptcy. One by one they dropped away.
During prohibition, when a considerable portion of the market vanished,
some fifty or more glass companies, both
hand and machine operating, closed.

It is thus apparent that machine operation started about 1886 in a semi-
automatic way, and hand bottle blowing practically ceased about 1938, a
span of fifty-two years. Therefore, it is
difficult to say that hand operation ceased
and machine operations started when
Michael Owens received Patent No.
774,690 on November 8th, 1904, important though that patent was as one
basis for the first completely automatic
bottle-blowing machine.

The semi-automatics had their day,
too.   □

Empontilling: A History

Julian H. Toulouse

EMPONTILLING: a history Part one

by Dr. Julian H. Toulouse

The research for this article on empontilling techniques was started as a result of the term, "Graphite Pontil," a completely incorrect name that has arisen among lay collectors for the red-to-black iron oxide deposit which is found on the bottoms of some Western ghost-town bottles. Helen McKearin suggested to the author that he attempt to emphasize the incorrectness of this term by explaining the empontilling method and the deposit of the oxides. This, in turn, led him to a chain of investigations and literature search which has now increased the known methods of empontilling bottles to at least six. It is the purpose here to outline these methods as a contribution to glass-making history.

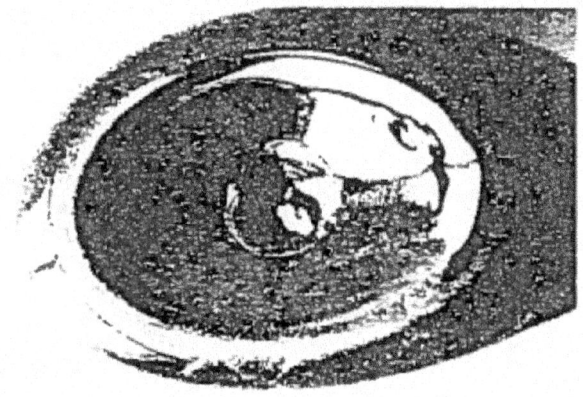

Fig. 1. Glass-tipped solid iron bar pontil. Entire area of scar has evidence of broken glass.

In hand glass blowing—both off-hand, and mouth-blown in molds—it is necessary to transfer the article being blown from the blowpipe to some sort of holding device. In this way, the workman can perform those operations needed at that part of the glass which was first attached to the blowpipe. Since it was the earliest method, and so often described, most people assume that the only way this was done was by sticking the bottom of the piece to a pontil, or solid iron bar, on whose working end a small bit of glass had been gathered. When the tooling or pressing operation had been finished, this temporary adhesion at the bottom was broken free. It is also generally understood that, beginning in the mid 1850's, in the United States, some sort of grasping tool replaced the glass-tipped pontil in the making of cheaper ware, such as bottles—although the "snap tool" was not necessarily confined to making low-cost ware.

On pieces of very fine glassware the roughened area left by breaking off the glass-tipped pontil was sometimes ground away and polished smooth. For most glassware, and especially on low cost bottles and flasks, the pontil mark was left untouched, unless it was too jagged or protruded so far beyond the bottom that the piece was "rocker bottomed." Strangely enough, after the snap tool replaced the pontil, many bottles—even the cheaper ware —were made with the contour of the bottom resembling the ground pontil mark, by means of a small round "push-up" in the bottom plate of the mold.

Western mining towns grew up, and were abandoned, during a time of rapid change in the glass-making industry. Their household trash disposal places became depositories of bottles that have remained undisturbed until the present time. These bottles which are now being found by collectors in these western ghost towns, illustrate some of the changes in glass-blowing techniques. Some bottles have red, reddish black, black, and even white areas covering a part of the bottoms. Collectors began calling the red-to-black discolorations "graphite pontil" marks, and the name has persisted even though the deposit is not graphite.

This led to a chain of investigations and literature search which has now increased the known methods of empontilling bottles to at least six. It is the purpose of this article to outline these methods as a contribution to glass making history.

Much of this information presented in this article is not truly new, for it comes from a study of old writing on practical glass making. Some of it is new only in the sense that century-old bottles have just come to light and, since they have just recently been studied, the six methods of manufacture can now be partially explained:

1. Glass tipped solid iron bar pontil.
2. Blowpipe as a pontil.
3. Bare iron pontil and the red-black bottom deposits.
4. Bare iron pontil and the white coated bottom.
5. "Post" of Pellatt and the "sabot" of Bontemps.
6. Snap tool or snap case.

1. Glass tipped solid iron bar pontil.

For centuries the classical method of empontilling, and so often the only one described, was done with a solid iron bar, slightly enlarged at one end and about the length (4-6 ft) of its companion blowpipe. It had to be long enough so that heat transfer from the hot end would not make it uncomfortable to hold—and even then it was often cooled, as was the blowpipe, by a specially shaped water container that cascaded water along its length in the form of a thin broad stream. The enlarged end was first dipped into the pot in order to gather a small quantity of glass on its tip. This glass-tipped end was then applied to the bottom of

Photographs by the author, from his private collection of bottles and glass-making tools.

EMPONTILLING
CONTINUED

the glass piece still on the blowpipe. The latter may have been completely blown in a mold, except for the "finishing," or bringing into conformation that part still attached to the blowpipe. Or it may simply have been an enlarged bubble awaiting further manipulation or shaping off-hand after cracking off, or severing of the piece from the blowpipe. In any event, the purpose of empontilling was to transfer the piece to a temporary holding device for further manipulation.

The operation was performed at the chair, a seat equipped with broad, level arms across which the pontils and blowpipes could be placed so that they could be rolled. By thus rotating the glass piece, the glass man could counteract the tendency of the hot glass piece to sag, and he could carry out the necessary manipulations in order to form the glass properly.

The master workman seated himself at the chair and placed the blowpipe across the arms with the piece extending (usually, if right-handed) to his right. His 'servitor' approached that side with his hot-glass-tipped pontil and placed the hot tip against the bottom of the piece on the blowpipe. With a few rolls of the blowpipe back and forth along the arms of the chair, the centering was adjusted so that the pontil was approximately matched with the axis of the piece, and the piece firmly adhered to the pontil. When this had been accomplished the piece was cracked off, or severed from the blowpipe by touching it at the proper place with a wetted tool, leaving a small portion called the moile on the blowpipe.

The important considerations in this operation were (1) that the centering be well done so that the piece would be rotated on a true axis with the pontil in order that the

Fig. 2. Glass-tipped pontil. Note iron that migrated into glass from unclean glass tip.

finishing operations be more easily and more precisely done; and (2) that the pontil be adhered well enough to hold the piece through the finishing operations, but not so firmly as to prevent snapping the piece free later, since normally wetting off cannot be done. Generally this latter operation was also performed at the chair, and the piece was carried to the lehr, but Bontemps' *Guide du Verrier* (Paris, 1868) indicates that the French practice was to carry the piece to the lehr while still on the pontil, and have the lehr attendant snap it free.

The detachment of the piece from the pontil often left a scar of broken glass (Fig. 1, 2), either from the glass tip on the pontil, or from the bottom of the piece itself, or both. Many pieces are found on which the scar manifests itself

merely as a matte surface in the plane of the bottom of the piece—perhaps an indication that the piece and the hot glass tip of the pontil were widely different in temperature, and thus had different rates of expansion and contraction. For some very fine glassware this scar was ground until it was completely obliterated. On most ware the scar was left untouched unless it was too jagged, or

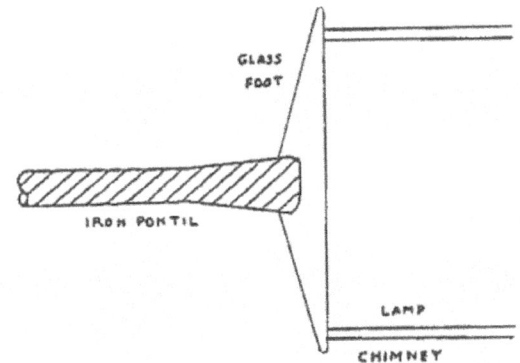

Fig. 3. Glass-tipped solid iron bar pontil (after Pellatt).

protruded below the plane of the bearing surface of the piece, so as to make it rock.

There is a tendency among western collectors, without regard for long-established names, to refer to this as an "open pontil." What is "open" about it and, pray tell, what would be called a "closed pontil"? Of course it is not a pontil that one sees, but a mark left by a pontil. The term, pontil mark, is long established and generally accepted. The McKearins, in their *American Glass* (Crown Publishers, 1941), Rhea Mansfield Knittle, in *Early American Glass* (The Century Co., 1927), and N. Hudson Moore, in *Old Glass* (Tudor Publishing Co., 1935) all use the term, pontil mark, and Stephen Van Rensselaer refers to it as a "scarred base." Perhaps for closer definition of the marks left by other types of pontils, we should use the terms "glass tipped pontil mark," "bare iron pontil" and "white coated pontil mark," when more complete distinction is necessary.

The glass tip was not merely a blob (another western term that I detest), but it could be shaped for special applications. Pellatt, in his *Curiosities in Glassmaking* (London, 1849), briefly mentions that the glass on the end of the pontil might be formed into disk shape to hold the open end of a partially formed cylindrical lamp chimney (Fig. 3). The method is more completely described in *The Commoner and Glassmaker* (Pittsburgh, Pa.,) in the Oct. 21, 1903, issue:

" . . . the foot-maker takes an iron rod, about the length of a blowing iron, on the end of which he gathers a small mass of metal, which he squeezes between a pair of wooden foot-boards while revolving the glass . . . made sufficiently wide to cover the edges of the fitting of the shade to which it has to be attached. The post is first heated to a red heat and then pressed gently against the edges of the fitting, which also has to be at the same heat, until the two are united."

(Then follows details of the wetting off and the formation of the crimping.)

"The article is then lifted off the crimper and detached

from the post by gently tapping the point of a knife blade between the edge of the fitting and the post, and giving the iron rod a sharp tap, which causes the shade to become detached."

This method must have been old when Pellatt gave his lectures in 1845, from which the 1849 book stems, since he also illustrates a pontil whose working end was an iron disc (which may or may not have been used bare), and also a "spring cradle," both of which will be discussed later in their proper places. His objections to the glass disc method were that it often broke into the body of the chimney and destroyed it, or "is very liable to cut or scratch the hand in cleaning."

Under various names, the pontil, puntellium, punte, pontie and punty (also 'broche' for spit or spindle) has been mentioned in the literature since the early sixteenth century. Perhaps the Anglicized versions, ponte, punty, and puntie, of the French pontil are the roots of the English use of the word "punt" for the bottom of a bottle.

2. Blowpipe As A Pontil.

The following is my translation of a portion of the chapter in the book on glassblowing by the French glassmaker, Bontemps, (*Guide du Verrier*):

"Then, cracking off the neck by contact with a wet iron, he detaches the bottle into a depression in the ground, formed with two inclined continuing surfaces. Next, turning the bottle end for end, he empontils it with that part of the neck that stayed on the blowpipe, placed at the bottom part."

Kenneth M. Wilson, Curator of The Corning Museum of Glass (he had photostated the original French for me), he quickly associated this use of the blowpipe with circular

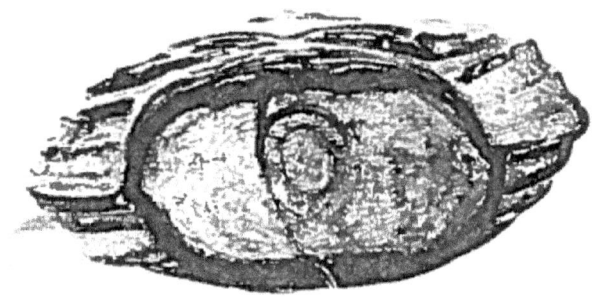

Fig. 4. Blowpipe as a pontil (scroll flask). Distinct ring is inside and out.

marks that appeared on the bottoms of some bottles in the Museum's collection. Subsequently, I found this circular mark on a number of my own bottles—a ring enclosing an area that showed no contact with the glass of the pontil.

In the past I had considered this central area as a place where the glass had broken off more deeply. Closer inspection now shows evidence of a ring contact only. The following could be considered criteria in estimating the use of the blowpipe as a pontil:

That the scar itself be ring shaped, or approximately so (Fig. 4).

That the continuing surface within the ring be the same as the bottom of the bottle.

That the enclosed surface exhibit the same surface characteristics as the surface outside the ring of the pontil scar (Fig. 5, 6).

That a cross-bottom mold parting line, if present, continue inside of the ring as without it (Fig. 7).

That the diameter of the scar be approximately the same as that of the neck.

That when the scar is a ring of glass adhered to the bottom, the contact point be as 'square' on the inside junction as on the outside junction.

Fig. 5. Blowpipe as pontil. "Success to the Railroad," horse-drawn.

One or more of these criteria are met by several of my bottles. In one, a pebbly surface as a continuance of the bottom, and of the same character, is evidence that the middle part within the circle of the contact area was not touched by glass. Several, including an "A. A. Cooley, Hartford" amber, sheared-lip snuff bottle (circa 1840), in particular show the mold seam passing through the ring unchanged. By contrast, a Fahnstock & Albree half pint "Union" flask shows by its matte surface within the ring a full area glass contact (another Fahnstock & Albree pint Union has a false ground pontil mark, as illustrated.) Both F. A. & Co. flasks had to be made during the two-year existence of this firm (1860-1862). A "Success to the Railroad" flask (horse drawn) also shows the cross-bottom mold seam intact within the ring of the scar. Can it be that the use of the blowpipe as a pontil in the making of ordinary bottles has been more extensive here than we thought?

There seems to have been but one fault—the method frequently left considerable amounts of jagged glass on the bottom of the bottle, particularly on light ware. The glass has a tendency to break just before the point of contact, leaving a portion of the moile on the bottom of the bottle. This may be a function of the coldness of the moile at the time it was pressed against the bottom of the bottle. Bottles which I believe to have been made by using a hot-glass-tipped pontil, and particularly in light-weight bottles, seem to break at the plane of the bottom, with re-entrance into the bottle glass in the center. Hot-glass-tipped pontils also seem to break away with less breakage of a jagged nature.

The use of the blowpipe as a pontil would have certain appeal costwise. It would be a one-man operation, considering that the master glassblower could make the transfer unaided. He would simply crack off the blowpipe at the

EMPONTILLING
CONTINUED

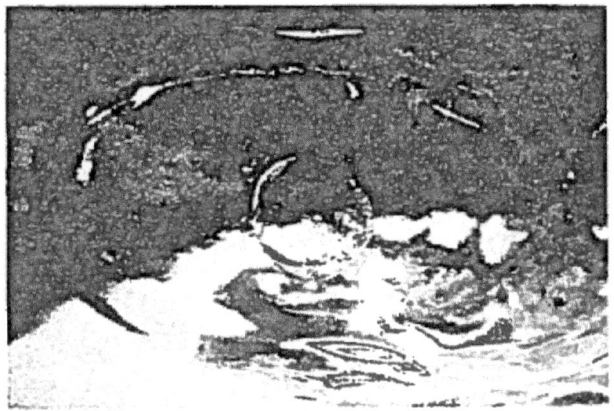

Fig. 6. "Checkered diamond" flask of uncertain age (1830-60?) with sheared lip.

moile, quickly turn the bottle, and then press the still hot moile against the bottom of the piece resting in the angled depression in the floor. He would have to do this very rapidly since the moile, already cooled by heat transfer up the iron pontil, would be further cooled by the wetting off. Since the workman not used would have been a servitor, whose pay would be next in rank to that of the master workman, the labor part of the manufacturing cost would be greatly reduced. This would make the use of the blow-pipe as a pontil very desirable.

3. Bare Iron Pontil and Red-black Markings

The next advance made in empontilling low-cost bottles was in the use of the solid iron pontil without bothering to tip its working end with glass. Pellatt may have been referring to this use in his drawing of a post-type pontil (Fig. 8) for holding cylindrical lamp shades, in which both the rod and the flared fitting at its end were of iron. This would have been the next step after the use of the flared glass foot on the end of the usual pontil, and before the spring cradle. Bontemps may have been referring to this use in his book:

"But one has abandoned this crude method of empon-

Fig. 7. Note ring shape of glass contact. Open center did not obliterate cross-bottom mold seam.

tilling the bottle with the neck end still fastened to the blowpipe. There always remains a bit of broken glass on the bottom of the bottle. In certain factories one empontils the bottle with an iron pontil, curved or flat in a manner to cover the circumference of the bottom of the bottle, which only adheres long enough to form the neck and detaches without leaving traces when one carries the bottle to the annealing oven."

The pontil was heated red hot and applied directly to the bottom of the bottle. In heating, the iron oxidized, and a scale of iron oxides was adhered to the glass, and almost fused to it.

The characteristic sign, or mark, of the use of the bare iron pontil is a red, reddish black, or black deposit (Fig. 9) usually circular, on the bottom of the bottle. There is indication, as will be shown under Method 4, that the original deposit is ferroso-ferric-oxide, or magnetite, which is black. In the bottles made under Method 3, in which the oxides are left exposed to the atmosphere, the oxygen of the air slowly reacts with the ferrous oxide to form ferric oxide, a red material. Thus, as time passes, all

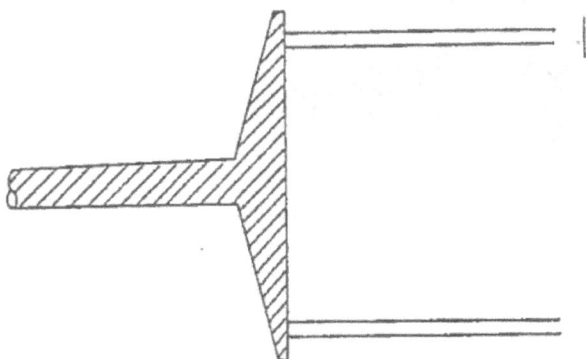

Fig. 8. Bare iron pontil (after Pallett). Probably used without glass tip.

gradations from black to red may be found.

Some individual, without benefit of either knowledge of the chemistry involved or regard for accuracy, gave this deposit the name 'graphite pontil' and the name has persisted. Pontils could never have been made of graphite as it is carbon, and such a pontil would burn in the heat of the furnace, as the glass is gathered. If the mark had actually been graphite, it would have burned at the temperature of the annealing oven. It was careless thinking to have used the technical word, graphite, just because the deposit was black in color, without having made a chemical test, particularly since the nature of the deposit has already been described in books and in articles about glass.

The McKearins, in *American Glass* (Crown Publishers, 1911), in reference to certain Jenny Lind bottles state:

"On the base of the Ravenna bottles, black or reddish coloration is usually present due to the method of heating punty rods and using them without dipping the ends of the punty into glass. The cause of the black color was due to the oxide from the punty rod being in a low state of oxidation or what is called the ferrous state. When the red coloration is present then the black oxide has turned through oxidation into the ferric, or red, oxide."

Miss Helen McKearin, in private communication, has

stated that Mr. Frederick Carder, of Steuben explained the cause of the deposits. Dr. Robert H. Brill, of The Corning Museum of Glass, made a number of chemical analyses. In twenty three specimens on which I, myself, made qualitative tests, only five showed any traces of ferrous oxide,

Fig. 9. Bare iron pontil and red-black bottom deposit. Note evenness of deposit.

and only one gave more than a faint trace. All twenty three gave strong tests for ferric oxide.

The fact that in my tests the discoloration was dissolved merely by adding a small quantity of hydrochloric acid into the cup-shaped bottoms of the inverted bottles proves that the oxides were not fused into, and glazed over, by glass, but merely adhered to its surface. The fact that the oxides reacted with the oxygen of the air also indicates that the oxides were not originally fused into the bottom. The solution of the oxides made in preparation for my tests was always yellow—a partial indication of ferric iron. There was never an undissolved portion, or free-floating black specks that *might* have been carbon.

The McKearins also list discolored pontil marks on their GIX-34, an Eagle flask made by the Louisville Glass Works, their GX-8, a small scroll flask by the same maker, and on GIX-29, a large scroll flask. I have verified the presence of ferric oxide in the discoloration on the bottom of a GIX-29 large scroll flask owned by Marje and Jack Slattery, and on a GVI-42, Union and Clasped Hands, reverse Eagle, that they also own.

The reddish-black deposit appears on one of my cork-stoppered fruit jars, perhaps made before the Robert Arthur patent No. 12,153 of Jan. 2, 1855, which converted the cork stoppered fruit jar into the groove ring wax sealer that practically all Pittsburgh, and many other glassmakers were producing by the mid 1860's. Mr. Alex Kerr has two very similar fruit jars with the bare pontil mark, and a groove ring wax sealer lettered for RAVENNA OHIO. Note, above, that the McKearins' Ravenna Jenny Lind also had discolored bottoms due to iron oxide.

This gives us a fairly good approximation of the period during which this technique was used. The Jenny Lind's would have been made during, or just after her 1850-51

*Page 533

visit to the United States. The 'Union' motif would date from the early 1860's. I feel that the practice was used from about 1845 to about 1870, or perhaps twenty five years. It was followed by the brief period of coating the bare pontil mark with a white paint, as is discussed in method 4.

All of the bottles involved had bottom constructions in the form of a shallow arch—almost saucer shaped. The contact area of the pontil was very broad. This may have been for the reason that the hot, bare iron did not adhere to the bottom glass as well as the hot, glass-tipped pontil. Bontemps stated that the pontil ends used for this process were flat or curved to "cover the surface of the bottom of the bottle." The arch of the end of the pontil and that of the mold bottom plate were probably closely matched.

There were, other shapes used for the bare pontil. An early patent is reported in which the pontil, very broad at the working end, had been divided into four quadrants, which were spread apart and held in that position by a piece of ceramics, or a marble, forced down the center line. Bottles have been described which had oxide deposits on the bottom in the form of similar four quadrants. No doubt this pontil made for easier and quicker heating of the thinner cross-sections, and may have facilitated separation from the bottom of the bottle. It may have aided attachment to the exact center by providing a target. It is not as easy to adjust the bare iron pontil for good centering, as with the glass-tipped pontil, in which the plastic nature of the glass tip allows some side movement before it 'sets.'

Under the direction of Paul Close, Chief of the Inorganic Analytical Laboratory, Owens Illinois Technical Center, Ron Hall made emission spectrographic analyses of the white substance from five bottles with the white-coated bottoms. In four of them, the white substance contained lead and barium oxides in large amounts; calcium, silicon, iron, magnesium, aluminum, and phosphate in lesser amounts; and traces of tin, titanium and zinc. The other coating, which may have been selectively leached during its 80 or more years in the ghost town dump, was composed chiefly of aluminum, calcium and titanium, with smaller amounts of other chemicals. The first four coatings could have originally been lead-barium-titanium paints, and the fifth possibly the residue of a titanium-clay paint. The material, as found, was not glazed and was probably not ceramic in character, nor had it been through the annealing lehr.

Beneath the white coating was a black metallic coating which adhered tightly to the glass bottom. The position of the metallic coating between the white coating and the glass disproves one theory—that the white coating was an application to the pontil before it was heated and fastened to the glass bottom. The metallic coating, tested spectrophotographically, was apparently 100 per cent Fe in mineral content, indicating a very low alloy steel. The coating was magnetic, and therefore a great part magnetite, or Fe_3O_4.

Evidently a very hot, bare pontil was used to hold the bottle during the finishing operation, and the white coating applied afterward. Just why and when we can only guess, since I have found no literature references. The coatings are uniform and thin, not spilled over any other

EMPONTILLING
CONTINUED

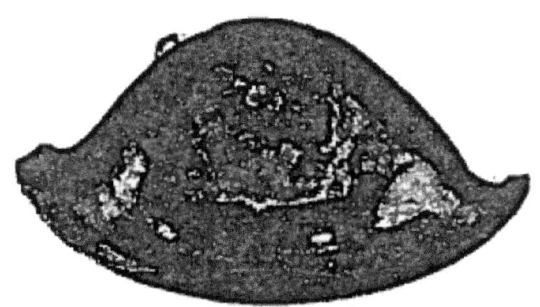

Fig. 10. Bare iron pontil and white-coated bottom.

part of the bottle, yet completely covering the metallic undercoating. It is unlikely that the coating could have been applied to the hot bottle before annealing, not only because the attendant breakage from heat shock would be almost certain, but also because any vehicle for the paint, either as a water slurry or in oils, would have steamed off immediately, or would have caught fire. Therefore, it seems most likely that the coating was brush-applied, as a paint, after annealing.

Only dark green bottles have been found with the white coating. Since the bottles were for carbonated beverages and mineral waters, they would not be critical in appearance, so that the substituting of a white inside-pushup for a black one would not have been considered important. But the type of bottle on which the white coating is found is used over and over, after washing in a hot alkali solution. While today, solutions of caustic soda are used in the machine washers, in the day of this bottle little more than a hot solution of sodium carbonate was used. The edge of the metallic coating would be under stress because of the difference in the rates of expansion between glass and the metallic layer. This could cause breakage during washing. Even a thin layer over the metallic layer could retard the shock of the heat change, both going into the hot solution, and being rinsed later by a cold solution. I remember performing just such a test of a similar nature with beneficial effects by a coating.

A coating of oxides would resist solution in mild alkalies, just as it would more readily dissolve in mild acids.

Fig. 11. Bare iron pontil and white-coated bottom. Note ridge of glass forced out at arrow.

4. Bare Iron Pontil and White-coated Bottom.

In a number of soda and mineral water bottles found in western ghost towns, the oxide deposit was found covered by a soft, white material, which adhered very closely but which, in the condition found, could be easily scraped off. It was easily soluble in hydrochloric acid with the evolution of gas, indicating the presence of carbonates. Since the white substance was soluble in hydrochloric acid, it merely indicates that its chlorides were soluble, as most chlorides are.

All of the bottles seen have been sodas and minerals of about 12-oz capacity, and heavy, for the purpose of holding the pressure due to carbonation. They were variously lettered for different companies, or plain. All were finished for cork stoppers. All have the deep push-ups illustrated. There is evidence in the form of slight ridges of glass at the edge of the deep push-ups, as illustrated in

Fig. 12. Cross section showing area of white coating.

Fig. 10, 11, and 12, that while the shape of the push-up in the mold bottom plate must have matched the round, 1-in.-diameter of the hemispherical end of the pontil, the latter must have been very hot and must have been pushed firmly into the bottom cavity of the bottle. The narrow diameter of the bottle would have precluded the broad coverage of the bare pontil mentioned under Method 3. It is therefore felt that the deep push-up was necessary to hold the heavy bottle on the pontil during the finishing operation.

Because the laid-on-rings that all of these bottles had were better finished than in the case of the bottles described under Method 3, they are considered to be of a later period. They are so smoothly tooled, almost without traces of the underlying glass, that they must have been made with much hotter glass, probably after the advent of the coal- or gas-fired glory hole. None of the patented closures that took over so quickly after their inventions in the mid- and late-1870's were found. Therefore I place this technique in the 1870-80 period. ■■■■■

(To be concluded next month)

EMPONTILLING: a history
conclusion

by Dr. Julian H. Toulouse

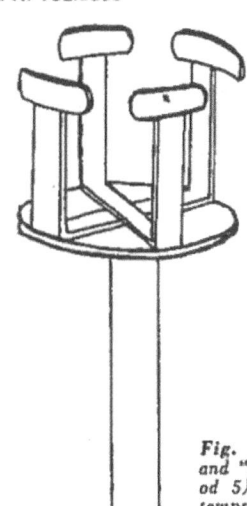

Fig. 13. The "post" of Pellatt and "sabot" of Bontemps (Method 5). After drawings by Bontemps, as used for bottles, 1868.

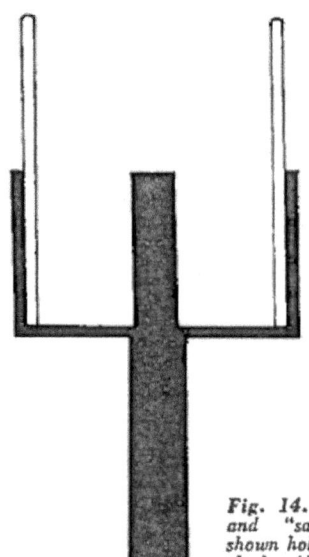

Fig. 14. The "post" of Pellatt and "sabot" of Bontemps— shown holding a cylindrical lamp shade. After drawings by Pellatt, 1849 (Method 5).

5. "Sabot" of Bontemps, and the "Post" of Pellatt

It was a long chain that led to the literature reference to *un pontil appele sabot*. In seeking information about the bare pontil and any literature about it, I inquired of Norman Densem, Managing Director of the Scottish Division of United Glass Limited, Great Britain, with whom I have been a consultant in Engineering for several years. Professor Douglas, of Sheffield University, gave him the Bontemps reference to the sabot, which he forwarded to me. Kenneth M. Wilson supplied me with photostats of the chapter of George Bontemps' *Guide du Verrier* (Paris, 1868), *Travail du sufflage*, or *The Work of Blowing Glass*, and the rest was translation. The Pellatt reference was to his *Curiosities of Glassmaking*, (London, 1849) or almost 20 years earlier—actually 23 years earlier, since the Pallatt book was a compilation of lectures given in 1845.

Both Pellatt and Bontemps picture the instrument as a simple cage made from two pieces of spring strap iron, crossing each other at right angles (Fig. 13, 14), with the four ends at a distance from their common center of half a bottle diameter, turned upward at right angles for about 3 in. Since Pellatt refers to it as a spring cradle, the four side-tines must have been movable enough to place some restraint on the sides of the lamp chimney or bottle that it held. This cage was fastened onto the end of an iron rod.

Bontemps ascribes the tool to France in the 1860's, but he states that it had been in use in England for over 30 years, which would place it in the 1830's. Mrs. Rhea Mansfield Knittle, in her *Early American Glass* (The

Century Co., 1927), places the tool in the United States about the mid-1850's, and that may well have been through the migration of glass workers from English and Scottish factories. If through migration, or through the visits of American glass house managers, the knowledge of it would have slowly disseminated from one factory to another, so that the exact American dates are unlikely.

Pellatt traces the development: through 1. The use of a foot prepared from a glass gather on a pontil in ring form for temporary attachment to the lamp chimney, which left an undesirable roughness; and 2. A pontil made with a permanent end-disk of iron which he pictures but does not describe as being used either with a gather of glass or bare; to 3. The more mechanical cradle. Bontemps describes it only as a device to hold the bottom of the partially finished bottle while it is being "finished," and that it does away with any kind of scar on the bottle.

In use, the bottle was first blown in a mold using the blowpipe, and Bontemps emphasizes that the mold is essential in order to keep the bottle diameter within the limits of the device. The blowpipe is then carried to the chair as usual, and placed across its arms. The servitor, perhaps first warming the sabot so it would not crack the glass, would thrust it over the bottom of the bottle. The piece would be cracked off the blowpipe in the usual manner, and the neck and rim of the finish tooled in the normal manner. The same would be true in the finishing of a free-blown, cylindrical lamp chimney.

By the mid-1860's almost all bottles were being made with the use of this, or the snap case that succeeded it. By the mid-1870's the changeover was virtually complete. I

204

Fig. 15. "Snap case" closed (Method 6). Note end of sleeve at arrow, and position of bottle in case.

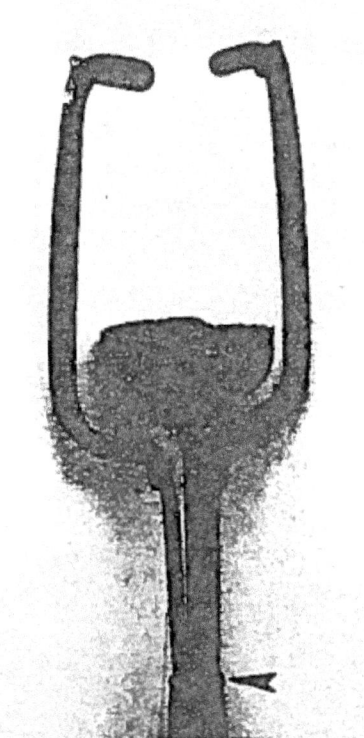

Fig. 16. "Snap case" open. Note end of sliding sleeve at arrow, and division into three arms, of which central arm is cupped (Method 6).

cannot recall ever seeing a bottle with the smooth-finished laid-on-ring, made possible by the coal-fired glory hole, that showed evidence of being held for finishing, by any other method.

6. Snap Tool or Snap Case.

Just when Bontemps' sabot was changed from a spring cradle to a tool employing a sliding sleeve that would be 'snapped' into place has not yet been established. In my own collection of glassmaking tools there is a snap case known to have been used in the late-1890's. It is of a design suitable for handling a small range of diameters about the size of beer and soda bottles, but it is undoubtedly late in the series.

Esentially, the snap case or tool (Fig. 15, 16) is a pontil which has been split lengthwise at the working end for about 12 in., and into three elements—a central post and two parallel matching side bars. The central post ends in a heavy cup which encircles the bottom of the bottle. The side bars extend beyond the cup for several inches, and end in two right-angled wings, slightly curved to follow the contour of the bottle. The side bars spring outwards, and are compressed together by a sliding sleeve which is pushed along the bar toward the cup, so as to squeeze the side bars together and toward the central post. This grips the bottle just below the shoulder. Since the sleeve "snaps" into place, this is probably the origin of the name of the tool.

Many variations of this tool exist, and have existed over the years. Some of the more modern have elaborate linkage systems for holding fine glassware, and often are only the gripping part of a rotational device such as a lathe.

Many of those in use now are lined with asbestos, but the early ones were not insulated. Variations are being used in such exacting operations as those required in the joining of parts for television picture tubes, and in the holding of tumblers for flame cut-offs of the rim, but for the common bottle, the snap tool 'went out' with the advent of machine blowing.

7. Summary

The holding of a partially finished glass piece, especially in order that the 'finishing' operation could be made of the part originally on the end of the blowpipe, has gone through several changes. The first method involved a separate tool, in the form of an iron rod, or pontil, to whose working end a small bit of hot glass had been gathered. During the early and mid part of the nineteenth century, the blowpipe from which the piece had just been cracked off, was used immediately to attach to the bottom of the bottle, and its use may have been greater than ordinarily thought. At mid-century the pontil, shaped to the bottom of the bottle and somewhat large in diameter to increase holding power, was employed, followed by using the same technique, but with deeply indented push-ups, and covered with a white paint, in the 1870's. Even earlier, a metal spring cradle was used, followed by a mechanically operated gripping device, for a total of at least six methods of empontilling during the same century.

Acknowledgment
The author wishes to thank Helen McKearin, Kenneth M. Wilson, and A. Christian Revi, both for suggestions during the research and during the preparation of the first draft of this manuscript.

A Primer on Mold Seams
Julian Harrison Toulouse

A PRIMER ON MOLD SEAMS

by Dr. Julian Harrison. Toulouse

PART 1

AUTHOR'S NOTE: This discussion is primarily concerned with glass in the form of a container. The object is to enable the bottle collector to ascertain the general mold type used to make his bottle, and form it to supplement other knowledge by reasonable guesses as to the period of time within which his bottle might have been made.

The several mold replicas pictured are based on publications by certain nineteenth century writers, modified by the author so that they would all produce the same bottle shape for direct comparison.

Mr. Alex Kerr arranged to have the wood turning done at the Santa Ana plant of the Kerr Glass Company. The author shaped and fitted the hinges, pins, dowels, stops and carvings; made the final assembly; and painted the molds. Black was used on the sides which went together to form seams; silver was used for the highly polished glass contacting surfaces; and gray was

BOTTLE WORLD Edited by Cecil Munsey, *Associate Editor*

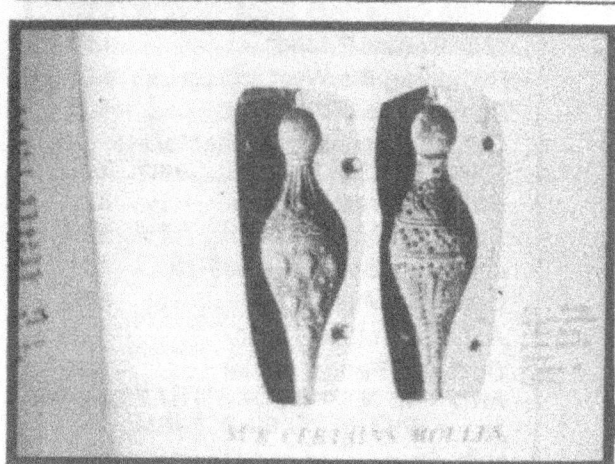

Figure 2. Four part molds of stone, from early Islamic period. Use for glass open to proof. From: Journal of Glass Studies, The Corning Museum of Glass. P. 55, Vol. I, 1959. Sur Certains Moules, Trouves A Milet by Henri Seyrig

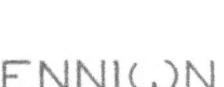

ENNIⲰN EⲠOIEI

Figure 1. Mold seams in first century A.D. Sidonian Glass. Three-part mold. Note heavy seam in neck, traceable vertically. Signed: ENNIⲰN EⲦⲦOIEI (Ennion made it). Photo courtesy of The Corning Museum of Glass. One of three known bottles from this mold.

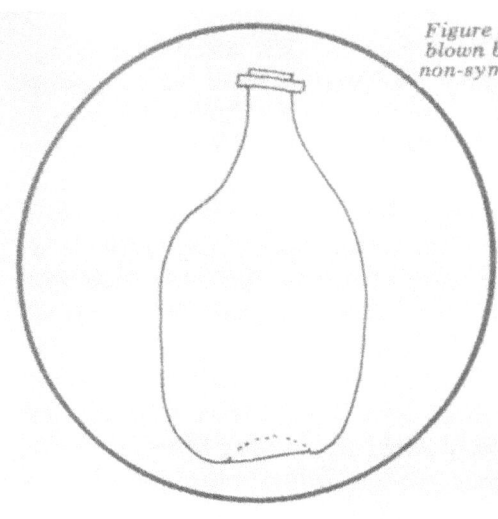

Figure 3. The completely free-blown bottle will have areas of non-symmetry, and no mold seams.

Figure 4. Replica of tapered dip mold from the author's set.

used on the rest to represent normal cast iron. Black was also used on supporting members not normally part of a mold.

While in general they are both seams, the glass making fraternity usually refers to the vertical junctures between matching mold halves, as seams, but horizontal junctures, as between non-matching mold elements, as parting lines. Thus "neck ring seams" would refer only to the vertical seams at the neck ring area, while "neck ring parting lines" would refer to the juncture between the neck ring and the body mold, or the neck ring and the collar above it.

❖❖❖❖❖❖❖❖❖

No matter how carefully molds are made, the junction of two separate pieces (often called 'parts') of the composite mold leaves a mark on the surface of the glass piece that is blown within it. The marks of repairs, such as the peening of a mis-cut or unwanted letter or element of decoration, are examples of the faithfulness with which hot glass will mirror the surface condition of the metal. Even a deep scratch in the mold may show on the surface of the glass, and metal scale, or oxides of iron formed in use from the repeated heatings and coolings, and only a few thousandths of an inch thick, can leave visible marks. The double seam, when machine made bottles may have been made using both a seamed blank mold, and a seamed finishing mold, is another example of the impression of a discontinuity on the glass piece. In hand blowing, the momentary touching of the parison to the lettered bottom, then

lifting it for better adjustment, leaves an impression as a ghostly set of letters beside the wanted ones.

The cyclic heating of the mold, followed by cooling each time a bottle is blown, and the unavoidable unevenness in temperature at the edges of the mold (seams) warps the mold ever so little but enough to disturb alignment and alter the gap between mold parts. This repeats every time a bottle is blown, and much of this alteration takes place while the hot bottle is within the mold and is being expanded into final shape. Finally, the glass maker depends in part, and with other 'vents', upon the small distance between iron faces as an air exit. If the air within the mold cannot escape ahead of the 'balloon' of glass advancing toward it a pressure will build up and prevent the glass from reaching the mold wall in some area. This causes a condition called 'not blown up", and the bottle shape departs from that wanted.

Thus, what the glass maker calls seams or parting lines on the mold, and seams on the glass, is an inevitable result of the necessary use of separate mold parts.

By discovering the position and the extent of mold seams as marked on the glass surface (and there also called 'seams') one may surmise much about the molds used to make a particular piece of glassware, no matter how old. In this study we are concerned chiefly with hand blowing of bottles, more especially in the nineteenth century. The reasoning will apply equally well to other years, and to art and table glassware as well.

147

Molds are Centuries Old

When the blowpipe came into use some twenty centuries ago, man was already familiar with the use of molds. In the sense that it was a fixed form or shape, the sand core about which the ancients wound threads of glass as early as forty centuries ago, then followed by fusing the threads together by heat, and finally digging out the sand core, was a mold of an internal sort. It had no seams. The shallow bowls that they formed by placing bits of broken glass and powdered glass on the surface of an open, bowl-shaped, and necessarily shallow mold, usually cut and carved with a design on that surface, then heating the glass to fusion, was another use of a mold that left no seam.

It can be argued that their use predisposed man to the use of molds for shaping glass, so that the introduction of the blowpipe (said to be about the middle of the first century B.C.) could have been first for the blowing of glass into shapes determined by molds, rather than for free-hand blowing which would have taken time to determine as a technique, both as to the manipulation and as to the auxiliary tools.

Be it as it may, the use of the external mold introduced a new problem, with a difficulty all its own—how to get the piece out of the mold. The mold had to be with separating, and matching, parts. Man soon solved this problem to some extent by making the mold in parts keyed together with dowels. By the end of the first century A.D. he was using two, three, four and even six part molds — having so many separating leaves whose composite made the completed shape of the glass piece.

Figue 1, by courtesy of The Corning Museum of Glass, is of a piece signed by the Sidonian, ENNION, known to have made glass in the first century, A.D., and is one of at least three pieces from the same mold. Note the seam in the neck, traceable down the side. It was blown in a three part mold.

How do we know it was a three part mold, and how do we know others to have been blown in two part, four part, and six part molds? Because we are able to find that number of mold seams on the glass surface.

The object of this discussion is to identify the type of mold by the mold seams on the piece. The mold seams will tell us that much—but little else— not the mold material or the exact method of the mold's use and construction. The mold seams may give us a generality about the date—at least the *earliest* date we can apply to the piece, but with no certainty as to how late after the known beginning of the use of the mold type. Methods may be used in hand blowing shops long after the techniques are considered obsolete.

Figure 5. Bottles from a tapered dip mold will have no seams unless caused by a slight 'blow-over' at the base of the shoulder, or widest point. This is shown by the dotted lines.

We cannot tell if the molds were hinged, or of what material they were made, so far as the seams of the bottles are considered. Wooden molds intended to define the final shape would have quickly burned away, or became so charred in use that any designs would have become progressively dimmer. Successive pieces would have become larger in dimensions. (The possibility that pieces were annealed in the mold would have ruled out wood.) If the glass vessel were heavy walled, holding a considerable amount of heat, the wood would have charred most rapidly, and fewer pieces would have been possible than with thin walled pieces. This does not preclude the use of wood for 'turn-mold' bottles, where no lettering is involved, nor as preliminary shaping tools prior to further blowing free-form. It does mean that sharp lettering and design, and the use of wood molds, are not compatable.

Ceramic and clay molds have been used for centuries, and are still being used. M. A. Bezborodov and A. A. Abdurazakov, writing in the *Journal of Glass Studies*, p. 64, Vol. VI, 1964 (The Corning Museum Of Glass) report finding three scorched clay molds, made with relief patterns, found with other glass making artifacts in a third century, A.D. glass plant in Russia. The ease with which bronze could have been remelted, to make other molds or other things as a salvage of its value, would account for failure to find such molds today.

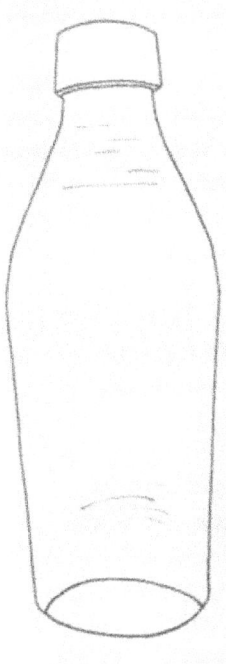

Figure 6. The turn-mold bottle will have no mold seams, but may have horizontal score-marks from an uneven mold surface.

Stone may have been used. One small group of stone molds, which may or may not have been used for glass blowing, is known. They are shown in *Figure 2*, taken from Vol. I, p. 55, 1959, of the *Journal of Glass Studies* "Sur Certaines Moules Trouves A Milet" by Henri Seyrig. Each mold appeared to have been made with four leaves, or separating parts, keyed for register by lead dowels or plugs. There is no indication of any hinging or other method of holding the parts in either an open or a closed position. Although use for glass blowing or casting is but one guess, the stone was a type that would resist the action of moderate heat.

It is not known whether these ancient glass blowers arranged to "quick-open" the mold in order to transfer the piece alone to the lehr, or whether they annealed the piece while still in the mold.

During the growth of technology during the past two or three hundred years, and the more recent acceleration, many types of molds have been developed. One product of change was the way in which the molds opened—especially in respect to the place of hinging. Each type left a characteristic, though different, seam pattern on the resulting glass. Usually the presence of a seam in a specific area of the bottle, regardless of the more common seams in other areas, is an indication of the kind of mold-part separation.

In this discussion, therefore, we will dwell upon the seam positions that are different for each type of mold design, together with a suitable name for the mold. The illustrations will be, in part, by photographs of the author's replicas of nineteenth century mold designs. Bottle outlines, with exaggerated mold seams will illustrate the positions of the characteristic seams.

1. Bottles Without Mold Seams

a. Free Blown Without Molds.

Off-hand, or free-blown, bottles are initially blown as the "natural" almost globular shape that glass assumes because of surface tension when the gather is inflated free from any restraint save the necessary attachment to the blowpipe. Modification of this shape may come through tooling and the manipulation of the blowpipe during the blowing process, and by the forming of the 'push-up' or 'kick-up' to provide it with a plane bearing surface on which to stand. The height may be made tall by swinging the blowpipe to allow centrifugal force to stretch out the gather, or made short by holding the blowpipe in a vertical position with the gather at the top so that gravity can compress the pattern. Additional effects are obtained by rolling in the glassmaker's 'block' or by marvering or rolling on the stone or metal flat surface known as the 'marvre'. The many tools that the glassmaker has developed over the years all could be brought to make further modifications.

Squeezing the bottle between two paddles, or by resting opposite sides briefly on the marvre produce the 'chestnut' shape—left alone or with a long neck, it would be called a 'calabash'. The gather could be pressed into a dip mold having an incised design, before blowing or at a stage of partial blowing, in order to impart a pattern to the surface of the gather before the final blowing without the benefit of restraint of a mold.

Free blown bottles differ to some degree from each other even when made by the same workman. Their common similarity, to this discussion's interest, is that they have no seams. *Figure 3* illustrates with a little exaggeration the lack of symmetry that is one indication of a free blown bottle.

There is nothing about the fact that there are no seams that will give us a useful date. (Other conditions and logic may do this.) Free blown bottles were being made almost a score of centuries ago—they are being made today.

b. Dip Mold Body—Free Blown Shoulder.

Bottles otherwise free blown may have been modified by one restraint— the use of a 'solid' or one-piece *dip mold*, tapered with the small diameter near the bottom of the bottle, and with a straight taper to the widest point at the open top of the mold, at the base of what will be the curve into the shoulder. When the bottle being blown nearly fills the dip mold, the blowing pressure is reduced as the blowpipe is carefully lifted in order to draw up the shoulder. When this is shaped to the satisfaction of the blower he stops blowing and carefully lifts the bottle out of the tapered mold. He transfers the bottle to a pontil or snap and completes the shaping of the finish at that part which had hitherto been attached to the blowpipe.

Thus the bottle body will be closely constant in dimension while the shoulder slope and the height will vary. The action of pressing the hot-glass tipped pontil against the bottom both to adhere it and to form the push-up, as well as setting the hot bottle upright, both contribute o a common bell-bottom appearance. *Figure 4* illustrates the dip mold in my set, and *figure 5* is drawn to show only the possibility of a mark around the middle, as defined by the top of the dip mold, when the glass might be blown with a slight 'blowover'.

The fact that the tapered mold-blown bottles, hitherto regarded as free blown, were actually blown in a dip mold has also been recently advanced by James F. Shaffer, II, writing under the title: "Free Blown Bottles" in the June, 1969, *Western Collector*. Shaffer's argument agrees with those I have often expressed—that the smooth tapers and wrinkle-free surfaces of such bottles could not have been produced on the marvering table. It is quite a different thing to roll a relatively cool bottle on the table than the relatively hot gather. It is quite different as to the rest of the shape than rolling a blown cylinder on the half cylinder block. From other considerations it would appear that the mold used for many 18th century wine bottles was a dip mold.

Shaffer adds a missing proof, in that he has found such bottles with a line similar to a mold seam line around the point of widest diameter. Such a line could be produced by a slight 'blowover' during the blowing operations if the glass blower had continued the glass blowing over-long. It would have bulged the glass over the top edge of the mold—a tight belt around the waist would be a good comparison. Even if the glass were then drawn up in shaping the crease would persist.

The employment of the dip mold was greatly aided by a phenomenon that aids the blowing of many types of glassware—the fact that a piece will blow 'from the bottom upward'. What is meant is that since the glass is hottest on the blowpipe away from the cooling effect of contact with the blowpipe, the end of the parison away from the blowpipe begins to swell first when blowing starts, and a ball will form at the *end* of the parison. This is at the bottom when the blowpipe is held vertically over, and into, the mold. The ball swells outwardly until it meets the restraint of the mold wall and becomes fixed in shape at the point of contact. The bubble then enlarges progressively higher in the mold as a sort of rolling motion. The glass blower can watch the progress of expansion as he blows the piece in the open top mold, and diminish his effort as the bubble approaches the top of the mold.

Open top molds (either dip molds or shoulder height hinged or keyed molds when the ware was lettered or highly decorated) were among the earliest of molds. Molds of this description were used in the first century, A.D., at Sidon.

The art seems to have been forgotten for many years. Of particular importance to the bottle collector, the use of the tapered dip mold seems to have been a transition between the bulb and onion shaped bottles of the 16th and 17th centuries, to the tall shapes with dip mold bodies and sectional mold shoulders of the late 19th century. Traditionally the wine bottle is not lettered —pragmatically the wine bottle could not be lettered so long as it was blown in the 'solid' tapered dip mold.

Turn mold bottles were blown in molds which had a special surface treatment for those surfaces contacting glass. This surface was generally wetted between each blowing. The water flashed into steam as the hot glass contacted it, so that the bottle 'rode' on a cushion of steam. This facilitated the rotation and it gave the bottle a high polish.

The surface was covered with a 'paste' of an organic fiber, even sawdust, in a binder that was evaporated

Figure 7. Replica of hinged shoulder height mold: Note lettering which makes a tapered dip mold impossible to use, even for a tapered bottle.

c. **Turn-Mold Bottle.**

First to correct any false impression by this traditional name—the bottle is normally rotated within the mold and the mold does not rotate. One or two patents called for rotating molds, but there is no evidence that the practice was successful.

While the molds in which turn-mold bottles were blown had to be in separable parts in order to define the body and shoulder contours, and while ordinarily these parts would leave impressions of their junctions as seams on the bottles, the rotation of the bottle during the blowing operation eliminated all seams. The rotation against the sides of the mold simply rubbed them out while the glass was still plastic.

No lettering or decorative design could be used. The bottle had to be circular in cross section at all horizontal levels. It could have any vertical contour.

by the heat of the baking process that was part of the preparation of the mold. This left the surface coated with a soft, water absorbent, layer. There was almost no wear on the iron that backed the 'paste', so that molds had long lives. The 'paste' did wear rapidly (a day in modern machine tumbler making) but upon wear, the remaining paste was removed and a new facing prepared.

It was also possible to make molds of hard wood for turn-molding of bottles. Generally these are not treated with the 'paste' since the natural charring supplies the effect gained by paste on iron. Wood molds were often boiled in chemical solutions as a preparation. The paste coated iron mold was probably an outgrowth of the wooden mold used for the same purpose. As noted, the iron mold could be re-coated almost indefinitely—the wood mold might be burned out after making six to eight dozen *heavy* bottles. The wood mold could make several times that many thin walled bottles or "shell" tumblers. *Note that this use of wood is solely to make bottles which have no lettering or design, and which are rotated during the blowing process.*

The turn mold bottle acquired a high polish during the turn-blowing operation, but it also acquired horizontal grooves or scratches, sometimes best visible by reflected light. Thus the turn mold bottle, while having no seams, carries its own positive identification as such. *Figure 6* attempts to show these turning lines. Irregularities in the surface burned away as the mold was used, and because of this action the so-called "Whittled Mold Bottles" could never have been made in a wooden mold.

Turn mold bottles became popular in the United States beginning in the 1870s and were produced possibly as late as the 1910-20s, going out with the last of the hand blowing shops. Several United States patents were granted in the 1870s and 1880s for 'seamless bottles' with and without turn molding. The period was probably earlier in Germany, whence came many of our turn mold (or twister) blowers. A section of Streator, Illinois, where a number of German 'twister blowers' settled in the 1880s became known as "Twister Hill".

The popularity, and possibly the novelty, of turn mold bottles is attested by the fact that many glass companies used the term 'seamless' as a part of their corporate name. Perhaps, also, their salesmen were not above pointing out that the bottles would not split because they were not stuck together at the seams!

2. Hinged Shoulder Height Mold
Identifying Seam Characteristic:
Seam on Side Disappears at or Just Above the Widest Diameter

Bottles have been made in this fashion for nineteen centuries (ENNION and JASON, first century A.D.) although their mold parts must have been keyed or dovetailed or dowelled to register together rather than hinged. This style has the same general operating functions already described for the dip mold, except that the shoulder height hinged mold is opened on its hinged support today in order to remove the bottle. The operator may watch the progress of the blowing as with the dip

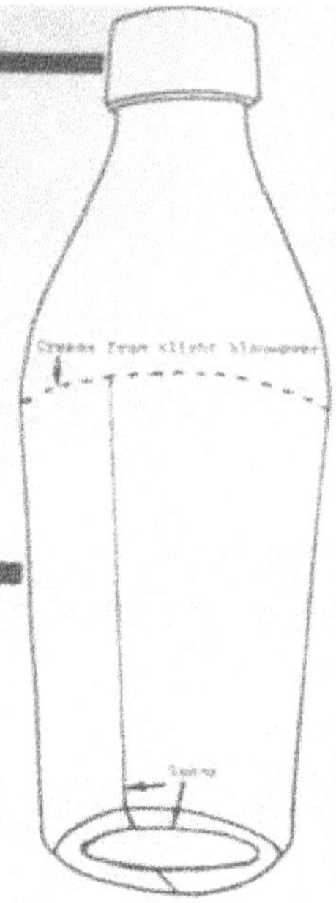

Figure 8. Shoulder height hinged mold. Not necessarily tapered, the hinged shoulder height mold could be opened to free bottle with letterings, or shape not adaptable to a tapered dip mold. Dotted line shows possible 'blow-over' mark.

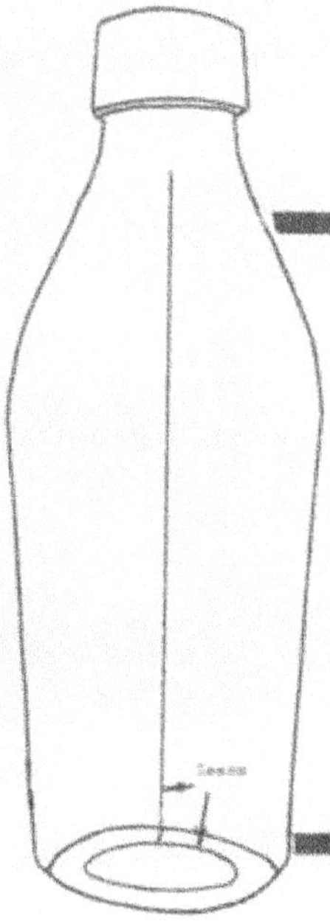

Figure 9. Mold seam is rubbed out just below the finish by the jaws of the finishing tool. Exact level at which the seam disappears is immaterial in this hand operation.

mold, and he must likewise shape the shoulder by his own skill.

The mold differs from the shoulder height dip mold in that it may be lettered and decorated. It need not be tapered. Its side wall need not be a straight line, and the design need not be symmetrical or 'regular' in any way. *Figure 7* shows a replica of such a mold, open to show a monogram and tapered only because all the mold replicas are made relative to the same bottle design. *Figure 8* illustrates the seams on a bottle from such a mold. Only the disappearance at the shoulder is important —the design of the rest is not.

The object of this mold design was to avoid the limitations just mentioned for the dip mold. While decorations could be made, as they were made in the 1st century, A.D., with clay and stone molds, production was limited both in speed and number produced. The advent of the brass mold, perhaps in the 17th or 18th centuries, followed by the iron mold possibly in the 18th century, and definitely by the 19th, made a new kind of mass production of decorated and lettered bottles possible. Much occurred in the newly opening age of the commercial demand for a container, and glass was already used as a container. The evolution of the wine bottle was followed by the development of other shapes for other products.

(Skeptics who believe that all merchandising is modern should read page 457 of McKearins' *American Glass*, Crown Publishers, New York, for the advertisement of Thomas W. Dyott, of Philadelphia, 1825. It starts with offering 20,000 gross of apothecaries vials and 15,000 gross of patent medicine bottles. It includes at least ten other classifications of bottles *now named for the product they were identified with*. So quickly did glass bottles become traditionally named, as part of their commercial use. To become identified, the shape had to be reproducable.)

Such molds were not limited to a separation into two halves. Even in ENNION's time three to six parts were used. The choice of the mold structure was a function of the severity of the lettering, area coverage by the decoration, closeness to seams for decorating elements, and the like, which will be shown under "6. three part molds" later. A shoulder height mold was not limited as to the number of leaves making up its girth.

3. Mold Type Not Material
Identifying Characteristic:
Seam Disappears in the Neck.
a. Action of the Finishing Tool.

This seam condition, and the two others that follow under group 3, does not come from the mold design but from treatment of the bottle after it has been removed from the mold. So far as the mold is concerned, it may be two-part or any number of parts, and with a 'cup' bottom, a 'post' bottom, or any construction whatever, just so the bottle has side seams that go all the way to the finish as the bottle comes out of the mold and is prepared for the hand finishing operation.

The seam structure is shown in *figure 9*. The important thing is the disappearence of the seam in the neck. It is

there rubbed out by the finishing tool, a hand held clamp whose jaws, closing about the finish area and which have the contour desired in the finish, also contact the neck area. It is rotated, or the bottle is rotated during this operation so that turn lines *in the neck only* (as contrasted with turn mold bottles) are produced. This is the last operation generally performed in hand bottle making, after which the bottle is 'finished', with that word then becoming generic for the result the tool produced.

While the glass worker could use his pucella or other hand tools for this contouring operation, and did so before the tool was developed in England in the 1830s (circa 1850-55 here), the tool most likely to rub out the seams was the jawed 'finishing tool' — a sort of pliers-shaped clamp having a central mandrell to enter the bottle mouth and prevent it from collapsing under the pressure from the jaws, and two opposing jaws that were cut with the desired finish contour on their inner surfaces. The jaws were squeezed together while the bottle (or the tool) was being rotated between them, so that the contour was impressed as a complete circle about the neck of the bottle. It is apparent from the author's collection of about a hundred such patents that the tools became increasingly complicated as time passed — finishing tools were still being patented even sixty years after Amasa Stone received his patent (the first in the U.S.) for such a tool in 1856. Probably tools were in use even before Stone's patent as they could have been imported, or copied, from England.

Generally, but not always, a quantity of glass was added to the bottle lip before applying the tool. This is often evident by the folds of glass where the neck meets the added glass and where the tool rubs the glass of both. There are often signs of two surfaces of glass within the mass at the bulb of the finish. The proper name of this condition is 'laid-on-ring' — 'applied lip' tells us nothing of the method, while 'laid-on-ring' tells us it is ring-shaped and 'laid' as the glassworker calls this method of adding glass. This name also does not imply that all such additions are at the lip of the bottle. The first such additions of glass were slightly below the lip

(McKearins' *American Glass*, p. 424, Plate 221 and 222). Laid-on-rings are also used for decorative purposes, with several often being spaced at various levels on the neck of a bottle, or a vase.

As noted, the tool was first used in England — Bontemps, writing in 1869 said that the tool had been used in England for over 30 years. Amasa Stone's 1856 patent may or may not have been the first to be used here as the tool could have been imported from England, or copied from English sources without patenting here. Until the 1870s the application was apt to be crude and rough under commercial bottle making demands because the use of the furnace opening as a gloryhole was insufficient as a heating device unless the bottle was held in the heat so long that the bottle shape softened. Since corks were the chief closures, the neatness of the finish was of less concern.

Demand creates ingenuity, and by the 1870s there began a thirty year rush of new closure invention. With it came a great elaboration of the finishing tool. With that came the development of the separate coal and gas fired glory hole (often 'sweetened' by the addition of pine knots and resin) with which to give intense localized heat to the finish while keeping the rest of the bottle to its wanted shape. We can use this as a rough date. From the 1830s to late 1870s the result of the use of the finishing tool was often rough, confined largely to cork finishes, apt to show laps in the neck attachment of the laid-on-ring—any of these might date the bottle as pre-1870. After the late 1870s the greater heat made for finishes so smooth that the laid-on-ring was virtually undetectable—the two glasses appear as one. Finish designs became more complicated.

b. Action of a Pressing Tool.

Instead of the rotating, hand-held tool, a press could be used for much the same purpose. Many were patented in the 1880s and later. Almost all were bench mounted because of their weight or to free one of the glass workers hands in order that he could operate the lever. Both presses and bench-operated rotating finishing tools grew up together, with some presses either rotating in the press-jaws, or having the bottle rotate with them.

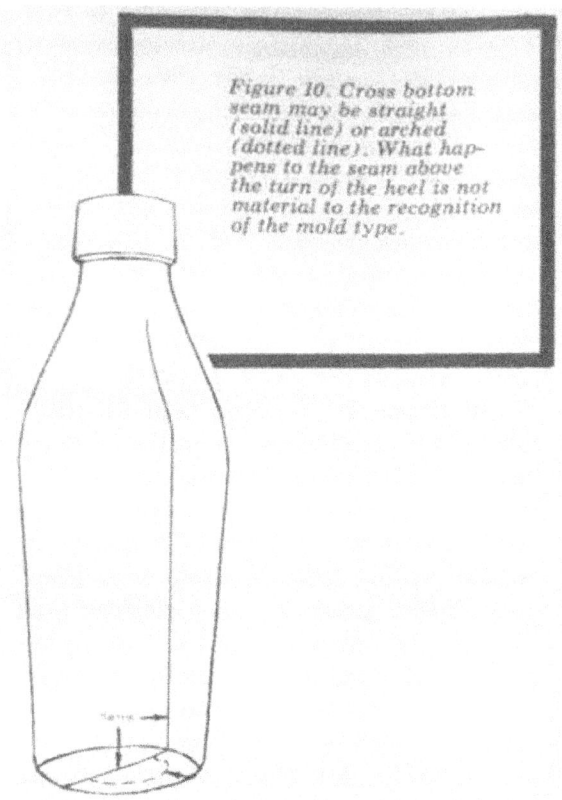

Figure 10. Cross bottom seam may be straight (solid line) or arched (dotted line). What happens to the seam above the turn of the heel is not material to the recognition of the mold type.

Most press jaws had seamless tops, being in one piece, but necessarily had to have seamed halves for that part of the bottle contact that was made below the bulge of the finish. This meant that there was a horizontal seam around the widest part. Even when the press jaws, or the bottle, did not rotate, the clamping of the press-jaws against the neck eliminated the seam at that point.

One design making the groove ring wax sealed fruit jar clamped the finish below, and scribed the groove by a rotating piece above, thus making a seamless finish top.

c. Flared or Fired Lip.

Especially when a cork was to be the closure, a bottle could be finished either as a straight neck (often termed sheared even when not obviously trimmed with the use of a pair of shears), or flared and fire-polished. In either case the finish portion of the bottle was first heated at the glory hole. For a straight neck only enough heating was applied to round off the edges where the bottle cracked off the blow pipe. For the flared neck the heating was prolonged until the neck was made plastic enough so that the application of a tool, even a wooden stick, would make the

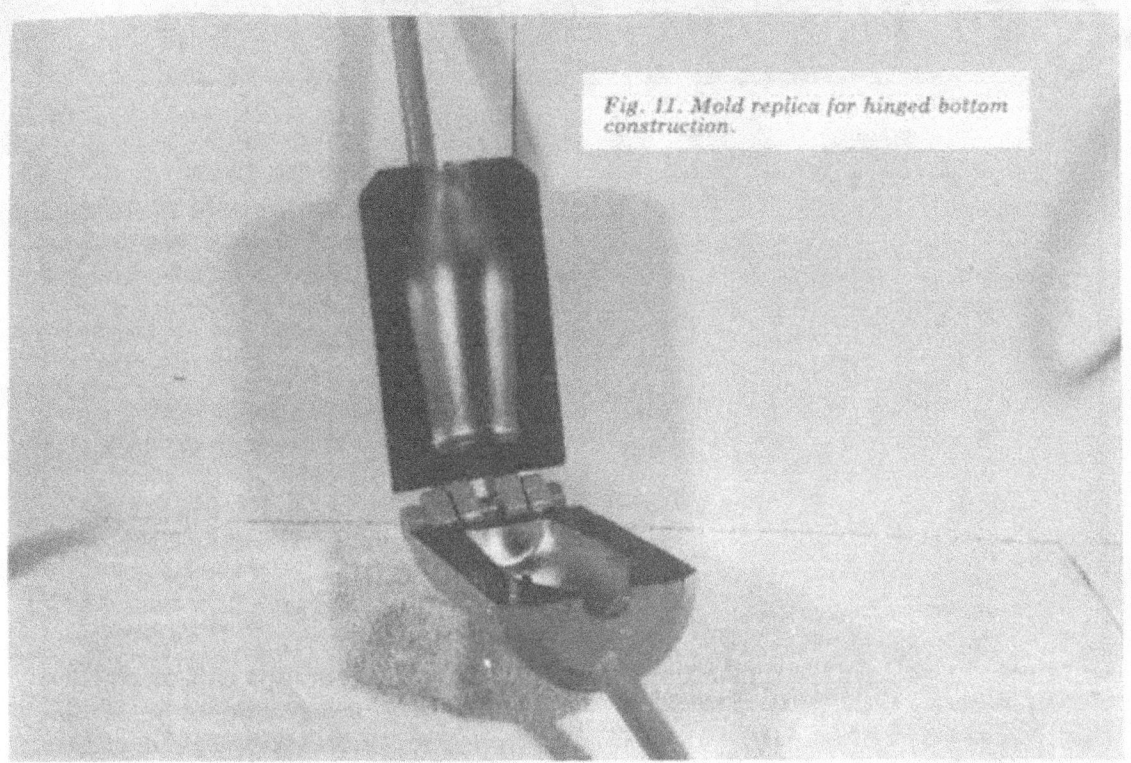

Fig. 11. Mold replica for hinged bottom construction.

flair while the bottle was being rotated in a snap at the chair. A certain amount of the seam would disappear due to the fusion of the glass.

There is no 'date' for this technique. It was already old in the first century, A.D.—it is still being used today. Make no estimates of antiquity solely on the presence of a flared or fired neck.

4. Hinged Bottom Mold
Identifying Seam Characteristic:
Seam Crosses the Bottom of the Bottle

The cross bottom seam may be straight or it may take a half-circle about the central push-up. In either case, the ends turn the heel and proceed upward toward the finish where they may be modified by other conditions. The thing that counts is that only in the hinged bottom mold does the seam cross the bottom. *Figure 10* illustrates the bottle and *figure 11* the mold. The half circle sometimes found is shown as a dotted line. This mold form was in use by 1810 since bottles known to have been made about this date are seen with cross-bottom seams. In some bottles of this period the seam is partly obliterated by a pontil scar. In other bottles,

as in some rairoad flasks, the cross-bottom seam intersects a ring shaped pontil from the use of the blowpipe as a pontil — see: "Empontilling," by Julian Harrison Toulouse; *The Glass Industry*, March and April, 1968, page 137. This would represent dating about 1830.

The seam position is also seen on bottles that must have been made subsequent to 1850-55 since there are no pontil scars—hence probably held in a snap case for finishing. Even later, as in the 1870s-80s, the bottom hinge construction was shown in patents for foot-operated mold opening and closing. Hence the cross bottom mold seam could be considered common from 1810 to 1880.

(Treat terminal dates with care. We can always have some indication of a starting date for a technique if we can find who first put the idea into practice. But any technique, once developed, can be used right up to the present — as many collectors know who have been so unfortunate as to rely too heavily on a popular termination date as sure evidence of true antiquity — and thus acquired 'quick-aged' antiques. □

(To be continued next month)

A PRIMER ON MOLD SEAMS

by Dr. Julian Harrison Toulouse
(Continued from last month)

5. Three Part Mold, With Dip Mold Body
Identifying Seam Characteristic:
Lowest Seam Circles Body at Widest Point—Two Seams from This Seam Upward.

This is the 'three-part mold' best known to the collector of utility bottles, such as the wine bottle already mentioned in connection with dip molds. It was most popular, subject to the limitations just mentioned, about 1870 to 1910. The body of the bottle was tapered and without lettering or decoration. It would be possible to letter the shoulder but this was seldom done. One patent lettered the top area of the body by means of a hinged plate that swung out after the bottle was blown.

The mold represents an important step from the simple dip mold, with its more satisfactory control of the shoulder contour and bottle height in a growing trend of mechanized bottle filling. *Figure 12* shows the position of the seams, considering hand held finishing tools rubbing out part of the upper neck seam.

There are at least two designs for molds that will impart mold seams to the bottle in the manner shown by *figure 12*. The bottle cannot tell us which one might have been used to make it. In one type the two mold halves that shape the shoulder are hinged by a vertical pin at the back of the body (dip) mold. The two halves open and close by a horizontal movement as shown in *Figure 13*.

In the other two part mold giving the same seam arrangement on the bottle, each shoulder half-mold is separately hinged by a horizontal hinge on either side of the top of the dip mold section. Each half moves in a vertical plane in order to open or close. *Figure 14* illustrates this design.

6. Three Part Mold With Three Body-Mold Leaves.
Identifying Seam Characteristic:
Three or More Vertical Seams from Near Base to Near Finish Depending on Other Factors.

This is the three-part mold more commonly known to the collector of art glass, but it is occasionally found used with highly decorated bottles. Each part is a complete segment (or leaf) of the body mold from base to neck. The bottom may be either 'post' or 'cup' design. Generally the post design was favored for hand operated, three part molds.

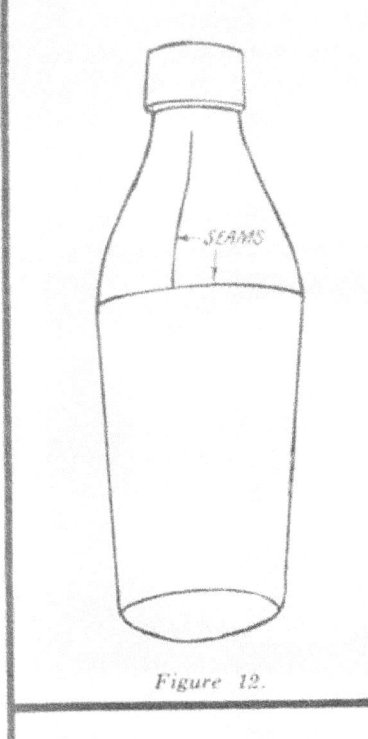

Figure 12.

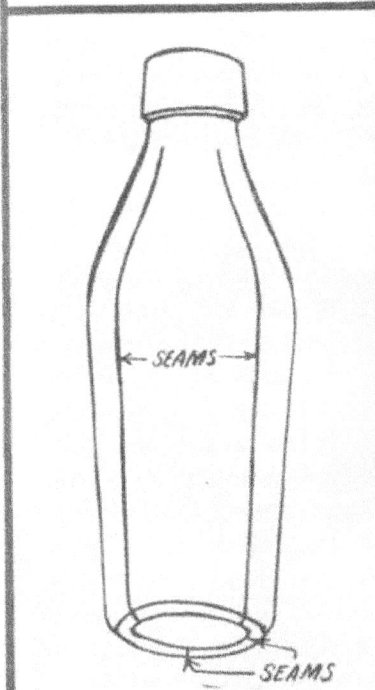

Figure 13.

Figure 12. Wine bottle type of three part mold. Seam around shoulder and seams from shoulder to neck, on opposite side—disappearing at the neck if finished with a hand tool.

Figure 13. Alternate mold design for wine-type bottle making in three-part mold. Hinge is vertical.

Figure 14.

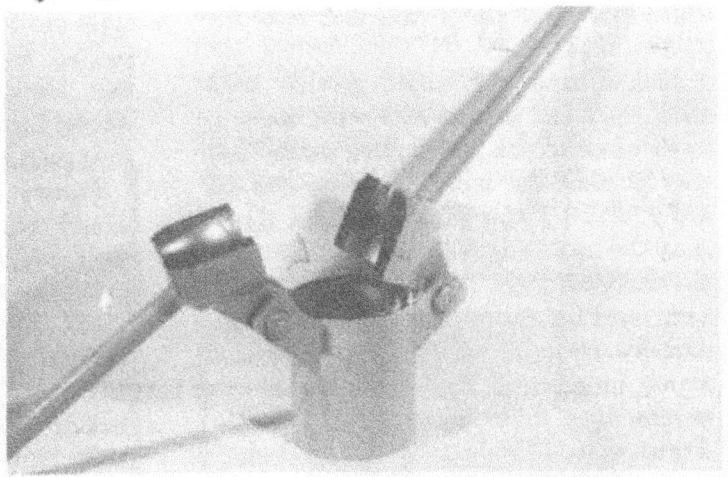

Figure 15.

Figure 14. Alternate mold design for wine-type bottle making in three part mold. Hinges are horizontal.

Figure 15. Seam position in highly decorated types of glass ware, shown as in three part mold. Third vertical seam is behind the bottle because they are generally, but not absolutely required to be, 120 degrees apart.

Figure 16. Radii of gyration and theoretical depth of letters, two-part mold.

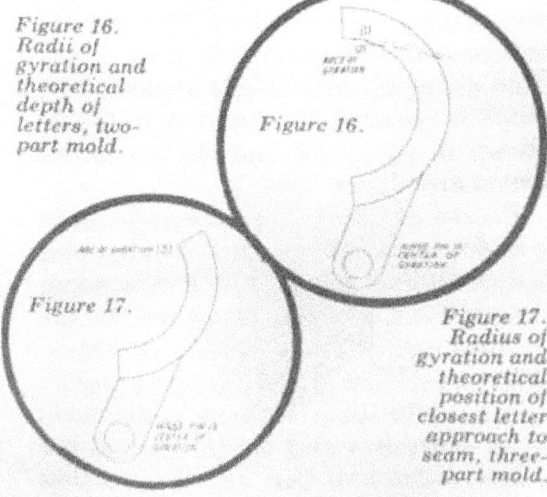

Figure 16.

Figure 17.

Figure 17. Radius of gyration and theoretical position of closest letter approach to seam, three-part mold.

There are two alternate objectives in deciding to use three, or more, parts in the designing of the mold. First is that a poly-part mold enables deeper cut letters and decorations, and a closer approach to the seams. A three part mold almost meets these objectives, and a four part mold should satisfy them completely. The second objective is that three sided, or four, or five, or six, or seven or eight-sided pieces may have to have an equal number of parts in the mold because of the angles involved. A greater number of sides than eight would easily be handled as a paneled piece with two sides to a mold leaf.

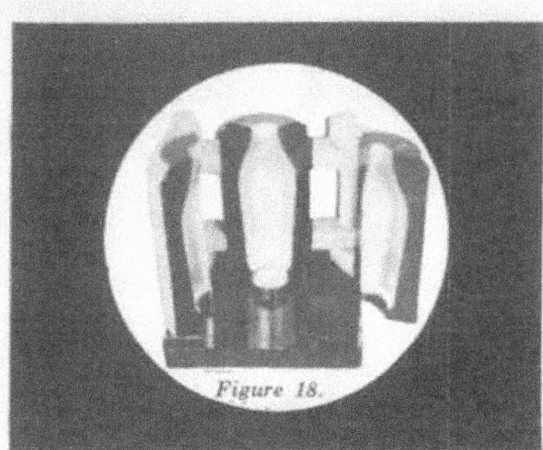

Figure 18. Three part mold type for decoration close to seams.

Figure 19. Radius of gyration and theoretical position of closest letter approach to seam, four-part mold.

Practically speaking the same is true even of an eight sided bottle.

Three part molds are not uncommon, four part molds are infrequent, and more than four parts rare and only for special reasons.

Round and poly-sided pieces, both with deep cut letters and with decorations close to the seams, are made that way so that the molds may be opened after blowing the piece, without dragging the mold edges through letters and decorations. Poly-part molds are therefore used for esthetic reasons of design and decoration, except for the polysided group mentioned. *Figure 15* shows two seams of a three part molded bottle. *Figures 16, 17 and 18* show the conditions that obtain at the critical edge areas with two part, three part and four part molds, respectively.

Figure 16 shows the radii of gyration about the hinge pin of the mold for the areas near the edge of the mold, for a two-part mold. The radius describing arc (1) crosses the face of the mold at so shallow an angle that it indicates that almost no shallowness of cut of a letter would prevent the metal edge at the edge of a letter near the mold edge from dragging across that letter and smearing it as the mold was opened. By going to arc (2) some depth of cut would be possible, but a wide area between that arc and the edge of the mold could not be utilized. The width of the 'no-mans-land' varies with the bottle diameter and the distance from the hinge pin center to the cavity center, and could range from a half-inch to well over an inch.

Not only is there an area of the mold face that cannot be lettered but the letters and decorations must be noticeably more shallow for an additional distance. This dictation of design by the limitation of the two part mold would be very undesirable in many instances. It would seldom be of moment in the making of commercial containers —

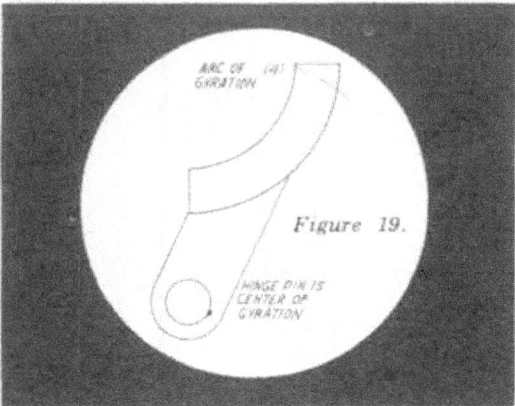

Figure 19.

hence three and four part molds of this type are rarely met with in commercial bottles. Such a curb on the designer by the mechanics of this mold design would be met by the use of a three or four part mold.

Figure 17 shows the conditions that would obtain if the circumference of the mold were to be divided into three sections, usually, but not essentially, equal. The art glass collector calls this a three-part mold, and we will follow this convention although it ignores the fact of a bottom plate as another mold part. Now the radius of gyration may be drawn almost to the edge of the mold face to indicate the extreme letter position. The cutting angle may be moderately steep right up to this point, given sharp letters and design. Position (3) shows the probable limiting radius of gyration. A three part mold of this type would satisfy almost any demand for decorations approaching the seams, and would allow good detailing.

In general, one leaf of the three part mold is secured to the bottom plate, shown in *figure 18*, and the two other leaves are hinged to it.

Figure 19 shows the comparisons in a mold composed of four leaves making the complete circle. Using the same descriptions, position (4) shows the arc of gyration which would allow letters and decorations to approach practically to the mold seam without restrictions as to sharpness and depth—except for a new restriction that any thin section of metal, as when a deep-cut letter is set too close to the edge of the mold must be kept within limits or a section of the metal will 'burn', or oxidize, rapidly.

Bottles were made from molds having three and more parts at least by the first century, A.D. Ironically we would have trouble today approaching the side seams so closely with machine bottle making; first because mass production machines are generally limited to two-part molds; and second because the hotter glass temperatures (and different composition) used for machine made glass would burn out the small wall between letters and mold edge much faster than in hand blowing.

Indirectly this indicates that the early highly decorated molds could not have been made of wood since thin wood partitions left by any close approach to the seam would have burned away almost at first use.

The use of the terms: 'two-part', 'three-part', 'four-part' and the like may not be completely definitive of the way the mold is constructed. They are descriptive terms that depend upon an understanding of just what parts of the mold are being counted. The wine bottle mold previously described as a three-part mold (circular seam at widest diameter) was truly made in three parts. The art glass designation of three part mold ignores the fact of a bottom plate as a fourth part. This without moment so long as we know just what we mean. Calling such a mold a four-part mold now, after so long in designation as a three-part mold, would be even more confusing. It is probably best to continue the present semantically incorrect nomenclature.

A modern mold for the manufacture of bottles, under a correct counting of all the parts in contact with glass at the final blowing stage (i.e., not including the three or more parts in the parison forming stage) might have to be called a *nine part* mold: the bottom plate, two side plates inserted in the two body mold halves, two neck ring halves, a collar, and a plunger tip. It would very likely be called a two part mold since the body was formed from two matching halves, and therefore presented two side seams.

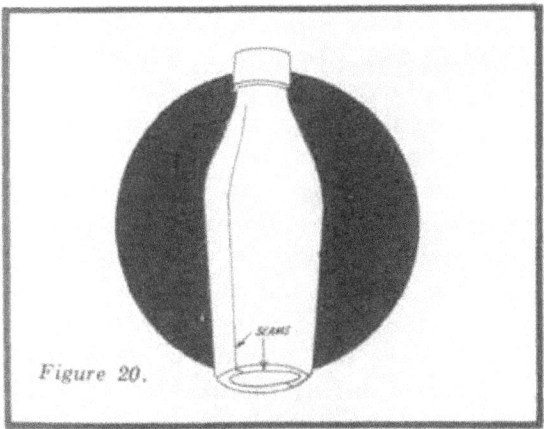

Figure 20.

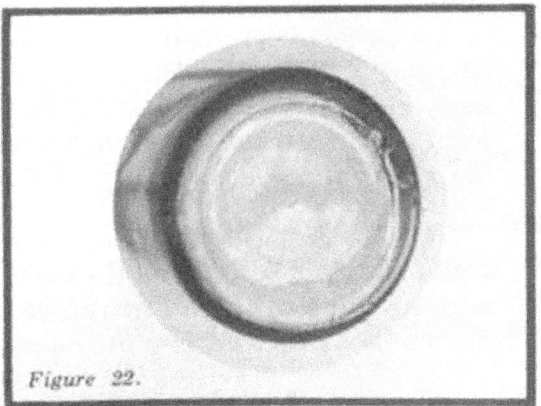

Figure 22.

Figure 20. The seam characteristic from a post bottom mold is a circle symmetrically placed on the bottom, no matter what other seams show.

Figure 21. A post bottom mold. Note the central pillar on the bottom plate, about which the side mold halves close.

Figure 22. Feathery form of suction machine 'cut-off' scar. Since it is formed as part of the 'blank' mold operation it is stretched by the blowing after it is formed, and it is generally not centered.

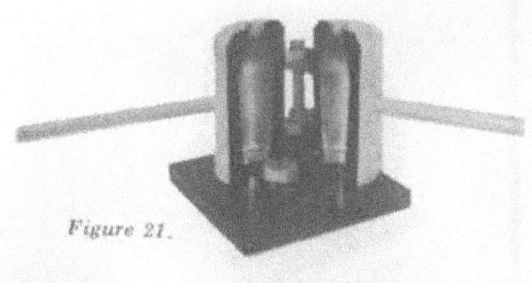

Figure 21.

7. Post Bottom Mold
Identifying Seam Characteristic:—
A Circular Seam Symmetrically Placed on the Bottom of the Bottle, Either Coincident With the Bearing Surface (or Bottom Contact Area on Which the Bottom Stands) or With a Slightly Larger (Never Smaller) Diameter. Side Seams Join the Bottom Circle.

The circle formed by the seam on the bottom will always be centered. This will distinguish it from other bottom seams or pseudo-seams. From this bottom seam the two or more side seams branch off, turn the heel, and rise to the top of the bottle. Post bottom molds may be used with any of the poly-part molds.

The name 'post bottom mold' comes from the design of the bottom plate. It has a raised platform in the center of the bottom-forming area, and this is called the post. Its top surface is shaped to the desired contour of the bottom of the bottle within the ring seam formed by the post.

The two, or more, parts of the side mold close about the post, and include all of the radius of the heel of the bottle, or nearly all since the post *may* be slightly larger than the contact circle. This takes the seam slightly away from the bottom contact circle and renders the bottle more stable, and less likely to rock should a worn mold make a projection in the seam. *Figure 20* shows the seam pattern; *figure 21* the mold.

This construction was much favored during the hand blowing days, and was already old when Mason showed it in the fruit jar mold he patented on November 23, 1858, one week before his famous jar. The virtue of the construction was that it allowed automatic alignment of mold parts when the 'boy' closed the mold. The bottle would then be blown without 'off-sets' which is the name given to a part of a bottle where mold parts were out of alignment and the glass formed a stepped bridge at some seam.

While the modern machine can make a post bottomed bottle (and the author once participated in an experiment to see whether either method produced a stronger bottle—negative) the cup bottom described later has been preferred. Machines may be adjusted to prevent off-sets, and the incised form of the cup

bottom is easier to use and handle.

There are at least two 'pseudo-seams' to consider in connection with the post bottom mold seam. Note in *figure 20* that the bottom circle is *symmetrically placed and branched into the side seams.* The pseudo-seams are neither.

8. Suction Machine 'Cut-Off' Scar Identifying Seam Characteristic: Irregular, Often Feathered, Bottom Circle, Varying From Faint and Wide Spread to Strong and Small (Inch) Diameter.

This mark may be considered to be a 'blank' seam showing through, and intersecting, the finishing mold seams. It is made as the junction between the knife that severs the glass from the pot, and the side of the bottom opening of the blank mold. The junction is actually a shearing action. The featheryness comes from the sliding action of the knife and the rolling of slivers of glass in the narrow clearance between knife and mold. The formation dates from the 1904 development of the first suction machine and continues to the present time since the machine type is still in use. The cut-off scar is definite proof of machine manufacture.

Several conditions may vary the size and character of the mark. With heavy weight ware the parison is not much stretched in the blowing operation, so the cut-off circle is more apt to be nearly round, and the seam is more pronounced and rather 'hard'. On very light ware the parison is much more stretched during the blowing. The diameter of the mark becomes quite large, the circle may become distorted, and the whole appearance is lighter. The mark may even extend around the curve of the heel to the lower sidewall. *Figure 22A* shows a 'hard' scar and

Figure 23A. A 'hard' suction cut-off scar, sometimes mis-called a 'pontil' scar. Note feathers.

Figure 23B. A 'spread' suction cut-off scar. Note 'feathers.'

Figure 24. A common valve mark, as found on a milk bottle.

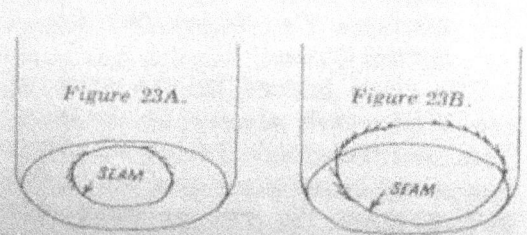

Figure 23A. Figure 23B.

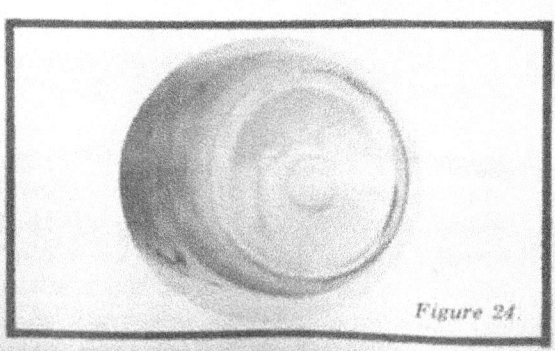

Figure 24.

Figure 22B a 'spread' scar. *Figure 23* is a photograph of a suction machine 'feather'.

9. Machine Made 'Valve' Mark
Identifying Seam Characteristic:
> A Circular Bottom Mark, Seldom Centered, and Formed as an Indentation Into the Glass Surface.

Generally the diameter is from ½ to ⅞ths of an inch. It is most often found on wide mouth foods of the 1930s and 1940s and even later, and on many milk containers. The aspect is *hard*, i.e., strongly marked, often indented deeply enough that a fingernail may follow it as an indented groove. A typical valve mark is shown as *figure 24*, taken from a milk bottle.

The name is a reference to a device used on those machines that used a solid, or dip, mold in which to form the blank or parison, and then pushed the blank up in the mold by a push-up plunger, or 'valve' in the bottom so it could be grasped by tongs for transfer to the finishing mold.

Amateur collectors sometimes refer to this as a *pontil* mark.

10. Cup Bottom Mold
Identifying Seam Characteristic:
> Lowest Bottle Seam Is a Circle Around the Heel at, or Just Below, the Tangent of the Heel Radius and the Side-Wall.

In contrast with the post bottom mold, the part that shapes the bottom of the bottle is cut into the bottom plate as a small depression or cup. The construction requires some sort of limiting stops in order to center the body mold halves over the cup without off-set.

The cup bottom is the more common machine mold type. *Figure 25* shows a cup bottom mold and *figure 26* the seam structure of such a bottle.

Figure 25. Cup bottom mold. Note the depression that shapes the bottom of the bottle.

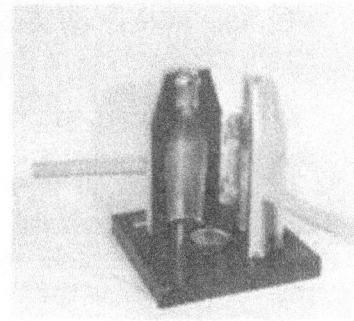

Figure 26. Seam structure on a bottle made in a cup bottom mold. The lower seam circles the bottle in the heel-side tangent area. From it the side seams rise.

Figure 27. Blow-back mold. The blow-back is the small, bulb-shaped, part almost at the top of the mold.

Figure 28. Seam structure goes to the top of the finish in bottles from a blow-back mold.

Figure 29. One form of plated mold. The replaceable 'plate' is the round part in the center, but the plate may have other shapes.

Figure 30. Plated mold, showing one plate in place and other alternate plates. Shown as with post bottom mold.

11. Blow-Back, and Blow-Over Molds
Identifying Seam Characteristic:
> Seam Goes All the Way to the Top of the Bottle, Which Is Usually Ground or Fired.

Mason secured a patent claiming the blow-back feature in his fruit jar mold patent of November 23rd, 1858, and Homer Brooke later claimed that it was well known in the industry and that the technique had been imparted to Mason by his father and himself. It was used so long as hand made finishes were blown in the mold in order to standardize their forms. This included screw threads and other complex forms such as external lugs, ramps or spirals, or sharp cornered ledges for wire and other clips.

The purpose of the blowback was to provide a place where the glass would blow thinner, and be easily cracked off without making cracks that might extend into the wanted part of the bottle.

The blow-back itself was a circular, bulb-like formation above the finish, as *figure 27;* seams as in *figure 28.*

The "blow-over" was another means of accomplishing the same thing and the bottle cannot tell us which method was used to make it. A small fraction of an inch of straight metal was designed into the mold above the top of the finish. When the bottle was blown to the extent that the mold was filled, and by keeping on blowing, helped somewhat by a wiping action of the blowpipe across the face of the top opening of the mold, the glass blower would balloon the glass above the mold and 'pop' it free. The method was simple and easy to do—also it was dangerous to safety of the blower, and frequently distorted the glass inside the mold.

Collectors often state that the difference between hand blown and machine blown bottles is that the seams on a machine made bottle go all the way to the top of the bottle. This all-important exception negates that premise. Many finish contours other than this were also made by hand tooled methods with the seam going to the top of the finish.

12. Plated Mold

Identifying Seam Characteristic:
A Circular or Oblong Seam on Either or Both Side Walls, Not Touching any Other Seam, and Appearing in Round, Oblong and Panelled Bottles.

This seam is caused by the junction of the body-mold part and a removable insert, called a plate, placed in a hole in the body mold part. It enabled the glassmaker to blow personalized bottles for a buyer whose needs were too small to justify the expense of a complete mold. This same body mold could then serve many customers who would agree to the same arrangement. In addition to the personalized part on the plate, the mold might also carry standardized information common to all users, such as capacity, weight and product (if a product-associated design).

The Foster Sealfast fruit jar used many interchangeable plates in order to personalize fruit jars for many grocers and wholesalers. Dairy bottles are often made with such plates in order to satisfy the needs of the small dairy. The many patents concerned with the difficulties of fitting oblong plates to panelled bottles for medicinals and prescriptions indicate that these were 'small lot' items. In the panelled bottle an object was to hide the seam in a corner of the panel.

Unfortunately a very common decoration not at all connected with the use of plated molds is the line of a circle or an oblong or the like, incised into the mold, surrounding the letters. There seems to be no sure way in which to tell these decorative lines from plate seams. Only if the seams are ragged, have evidence of fins or broken tops as when the hot glass penetrated deeply into a seam, or otherwise grossly made (and this would be a rarity) can we even suspect, let alone prove, the use of a plated mold. *Figure 29* shows the seam position; *figure 30* shows the mold and parts.

Some people refer to this as the use of a 'slug plate'. Since the two words mean essentially the same thing, the phrase is redundant. In addition the phrase seems not to have been used in the glass making industry but only by collectors, where I first heard it after thirty years in the glass industry. I made a survey of all the patents I have been able to find on plated mold use in the United States and *did not* discover the word 'slug' in a single patent by the men who used the plates.

The first patent involving a plated mold appeared in 1867, but it was for details of holding the oblong plate in place. Evidently the idea of plates was old by that time, and I would estimate that plates were in use before 1860. They are still being used today.

13. Separate Neck Rings

Identifying Seam Characteristic:
A Parting Line (Seam) Between Finish and Body Mold.

This horizontal seam is in itself not a proof of machine made bottles. It only indicates that the neck rings (finish rings) were separate parts from the body mold—but it does not indicate that these neck ring halves opened separately from the body mold halves.

The first such patent was by Robert Hemingray on Sept. 18, 1860. Pat. No. 30,063, and it was for a mold with a separate neck ring which opened by lifting, to make the groove for the fruit jar often identified as "Patent Sept. 18, 1860" and as often made with mis-

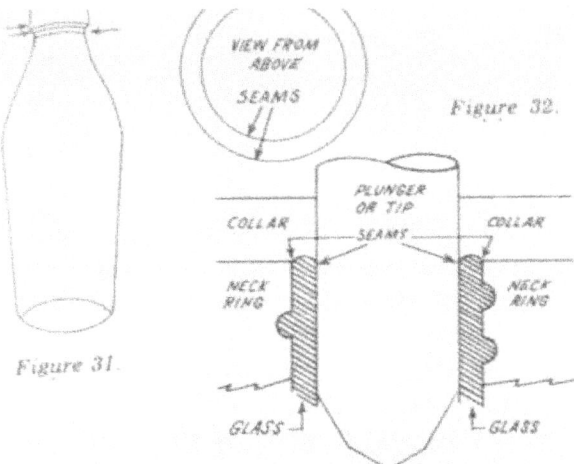

Figure 31.

Figure 32.

Figure 31. Parting line (or seam) between finish and body mold is no an exclusive indication of machine made bottle.

Figure 32. The seams on the top of the finish, and how they are formed in a composite machine bottle design.

Figure 33.

Figure 34.

Figure 33. Relation of plunger tip, collar, pressed parison in half a neck ring, and the blank mold in the press operation of press-and-blow machines. The push-up bar in the center-bottom would make a valve mark if the blank mold had been one-piece. Press-and-blow operation is generally used for wide mouth ware.

Figure 34. Relaion of neck ring (half ring is shown), blown bottle in the ring, and the body molds in the blow operation of press-and-blow machine operation.

Figure 35.

Figure 36.

Figure 35. Relation of plunger tip, collar, neck ring (showing parison in half ring) and blank mold in the first blow operation of blow-and-blow machine operation as used for narrow mouth ware.

Figure 36. Relation of neck ring, blolwn bottle (in a half ring) and finishing mold in the second blow operaion of blow-and-blow machine operation.

dated lettering. Most of the patents that followed called for neckrings that were separable, but bolted to the body mold so that the two operated as one unit.

Hence, the finding of a parting line between finish and body mold parts must have other confirmation before deciding whether the bottle is hand or machine made.

Figure 31, right hand arrow and line, shows one position of such seams, slightly below the angle that starts the bulge of the finish. The seams can be at the angle just mentioned, or it can be on the lower part of the bulge itself, as shown by the two other arrows.

14. Machine Made Bottle
Identifying Seam Characteristic:
One or More Seams Circle Top of Finish.

Warning: there is an important exception—beverage and beer bottles are often 'firepolished' to smooth the top of the finish.

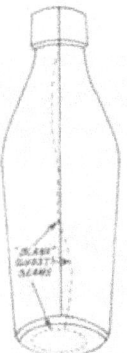

Figure 37. Ghost seams from the machine made blank or parison, near their counterparts from the finishing mold. Note that they join in the vicinity of the finish, which is formed as part of the blank, and has no finishing mold counterpart. Ghost seam is shown by dotted lines.

One thing almost all machines have in common is a 'tip' or 'plunger' which merely defines the inner throat diameter of the finish in the case of narrow mouth 'blow-and-blow' bottles, or also presses the parison into shape in the wide mouth 'press-and-blow' jars. In either case the tip necessarily contacts glass. Since to guide the tip a collar also descends into contact with the glass —therefor the junction between tip and collar leaves a seam, and this seam is circular in form.

Since the collar also contacts the neck rings, their junction also produces a seam that is circular, concentric with, but larger and outside of, the tip-collar seam. These two seams can be a mark of a machine made glass piece (container) with certainty. If they are smoothed over by firepolishing, other signs must be relied upon to indicate machine making for the bottle.

If the seams on the side of the finish disappear into a smooth and highly polished, shining area on the top of the finish, firepolishing can be verified. Hand blown bottles were firepolished also, but they would lack the seams on the side of the finish. Since the crown beverage finish came into important use only some years after it was patented, and since hand held, rotating, finishing tools were used for the crown finish until the machine production started, a firepolished crown finish is almost certain to be machine made.

Figures 32-36 show a plan view and an elevation of a magnified arrangement of tip, collar and neck rings and the various relationships of the tips, collars, neck rings and molds for press-and-blow and for blow-and-blow machine operation. In the plan view the two circles are the two seams, although some designs may depart from this exact relation. In the elevation, the junction of the tip and collar is shown as the locus of one of these seams; the collar-neck ring junction is the other.

There are details that form a third seam in the concentric series, but that is only an addition that does nothing to add to any proof of machine operation.

Press-and-blow operation is that generally used in the making of wide mouth ware, in which the plunger can be large enough to enter deeply into the mold and actually shape the parison in the first stage of the machine opeartion. It is a pressing operation, but in the second stage the bottle is *blown* into shape by air pressure. Thus it is associated with wide mouth jars.

Blow-and-blow operation is that generally used in the making of narrow mouth ware, or bottles. The plunger cannot be large, so air pressure is used to blow the glass into the shape of the finish. It is followed by a blowing operation in the finishing mold just as in Press-and-blow.

15. Machine Made Bottle
Identifying Seam Characteristic:
Irregular 'Ghost Seams' Beside the Normal Seams.

Not until after the advent of the Arbogast principle of a separate 'blank' mold to shape the finish and to do the work that the marvering table does in hand blowing of bottles, was the first semi-automatic bottle blowing machine possible. In most, but not all, of the machine designs that followed, the 'blank' mold was made in two hinged halves—the exceptions were largely those already mentioned under 'valve marks'. These halves resulted in

blanks, or parisons, having seams. When the blank was transferred to the finishing, or blow, mold slight movements of the blank in transfer, centrifugal action in rotary machines, irregularity in heat balance and resulting irregularity in blowing, and the fact of stretching the 'skin' of the glass itself, all generally cause the blank mold seams to fail to register in position with those of the finish mold. The blank seam usually is still seen as a faint, irregular imagery of the lines of the finishing mold, as in *figure 37*. The blank and finishing mold seams appear to cross one another; the latter is superimposed on the blank seam. The irregular 'ghost' seam appears both alongside the side seam in the body area, but also appears on the bottom, where the seam appears very like the post bottom seam except that it is quite faint, and not centered, or symmetrical. The blank seam is at the bottom of the blown bottle because the blank is very much smaller in diameter than the finishing mold, and does not stretch large enough to disappear up the side wall. The blank is smaller because it need only be large enough to contain the glass volume needed for the bottle, which also must be large enough to hold the bottle's intended capacity. *Figure 33* shows some ghost seams.

SUMMARY.

The seams on a bottle tell us much, and have been discussed as follows:

1. When there are no seams whatever:
   a. the piece may be free blown without molds, or
   b. it may have been blown in a shoulder height dip mold with hand shaped shoulder, or
2. A seam disappearing at the shoulder means a bottle blown in a shoulder height hinged mold.
3. Seams disappearing in the neck area may be blown in any mold, but the seam rubbed out with a hand held finishing tool.
4. If a seam crosses the bottom the mold was a two piece, hinged bottom type.
5. A horizontal seam around the widest point, with two side seams going upward means a three part mold based on a dip mold bottom.
6. Three or more side seams from heel to finish means a three part (or more) mold for decorative designs.

7. Circular seam symmetrical with bottom, joining two or more side seams means a post bottom mold.

8. Irregular, feathery, non-symmetrical bottom seams usually mean a machine made bottle from suction machine equipment.

9. Small diameter, *indented* into surface rather than extending, non-symmetrical, on the bottom, usually is the valve mark of a press-and-blow machine.

10. Circular seam in heel-side wall tangent area means a cup bottom mold.

11. Seams to top of finish, which is then ground to level, usually indicate hand blown in blow-back mold, or snapped off by blow-over method.

12. Circular or oblong seams in side wall, not connected with other seams are made by plated molds.

13. Horizontal seams below finish area mean separate neck rings but do not prove manchine manufacture.

14. One or more seams circling top of finish show machine manufacture.

15. 'Ghost seams' seams come from the use of a separate blank mold—hence indicate machine manufacture □

The Pontil As a Tool for Holding Glassware during Finishing

Julian Harrison Toulouse

Federation of Historical Bottle Clubs Journal 1(2):8-10   November, 1973

THE PONTIL AS A TOOL FOR HOLDING GLASSWARE DURING FINISHING

By Julian Harrison Toulouse

[Julian Harrison Toulouse is one of the nation's leading glass experts. Dr. Toulouse was Chief Engineer and Manager of Quality Control and Operations Research for the Owens-Illinois Glass Company where he worked for over 30 years as a glass engineer. Since his retirement he has spent his time researching and writing about glass containers. Bottle collectors are familiar with his numerous writings which have appeared in such leading magazines as *Western Collector* and *Spinning Wheel*. In addition to nearly 300 technical and historical papers for glass industry periodicals and three technical books, Dr. Toulouse has written two books for bottle collectors: (1) *Fruit Jars* – Thomas Nelson, Inc., 1969; and (2) *Bottle Makers and Their Marks* – Thomas Nelson, Inc., 1971.]

It has always fascinated me to watch a glass- blower attach the piece on which he is work-ing to a bit of hot glass on the end of an iron rod and then sever the piece from the blow-pipe for further shaping and tooling. The operation is often called "sticking" in the glass house, and the solid iron rod a pontil. For eighteen centuries only one method seems to have been used, but in the past two centuries several modifications came into being. The method was only partially super-ceeded by the "snap," earlier called the "snap-dragon" but never the "snap-case" by glass men.

We believe that the blowpipe came into use during the first century before Christ. By the middle of the first century after Christ, ENNION, JASON, and ARISTEAS, to name three who signed their ware, were producing incredibly fine ware blown in molds. It is not apparent that they used pontils, but from a cemetery in Samothrace of about the same time, bottles with pontil scars were found. Thus the pontil must date about the same time as the discovery of the blowpipe, and possibly even before it.

Pontil tipped with hot glass.

For eighteen centuries the practice was to touch the end of the pontil to the top of the molten glass and rotate it to gather a small amount of glass on the very end - the pontil was not "dipped" into the glass. This hot tip was then pressed against the bottom of the piece on the blowpipe, trued to its axis and allowed to set, after which the piece was severed from the blowpipe. There must have been other methods since glassware is known without pontil marks, and even with decora-tions over the entire bottom, from even before these early times.

Glassmakers tried to find a better way because there was always some loss of ware held by the hot tipped pontil. It could come free by tearing a large piece of glass form the piece being worked, or the break-off might leave a sharp, jagged glass from that on the pontil. In either case the rough scar was not desired.

Sand coated, hot tip.

Some say that early in the 1700s glassblowers began to dip the hot tipped pontil in sand before "sticking." I believe it was more like the extreme end of the 1700s and more than likely in the early 1800s. The reason is that the dip mold method of shaping bottles came in about the middle of the first half of the eighteenth century and prevailed until the beginning of the nineteenth century. Bottles made in the dip mold were almost always placed on the push-up spindles after blowing and this left a characteristic bulge at the heel. I have seen only two or three sand-pontil bottles with evidence of this procedure. Dozens had the shallower push-ups (a glass man never says **kick**) that come from mold operations such as Henry Rickett's 1821 full-mold patent, in which the push-up was in the mold.

The sand tipped pontil always left the center of the attachment area quite pebbled in appearance, with sometimes a small ring of adhered glass around it. Grains of sand often imbed in the glassware.

Blowpipe as a pontil

In the first half of the nineteenth century there began a practice of severing the piece from the blowpipe, into a trough in the earthen floor of the glasshouse, reversing it, and then sticking it quickly with the glass still on the end of the blowpipe. It left a circular scar, whose center was the same surface as that part of the bottom of the piece outside of the circle. Bontemps described it in his 1869 *Guide du Verrier* as a "former method." Many of our historic flasks show this kind of a scar. Unfortunately someone called it an open pontil mark. There is an open pontil but it did not leave this kind of a mark.

The sand tipped pontil, and the blowpipe as a pontil began a trend toward spreading the contract area which gave greater support to the piece while making for less sold adherence. The outer edge of the contact area is where the support lies – the center gives little support to the piece. Most subsequent methods followed this lead.

Bare iron pontil.

About 1845 in this country, but earlier in France according to Bontemps, glassmakers began pressing a red-hot pontil against the bottom of the glassware being made, without first tipping the pontil with glass. For cheaper ware this made little difference, even though the bottom of the piedce was left with an adherent layer of iron scale. Generally speaking it was used on heavy mineral water bottles, but it was also used on ware such as the Jenny Lind bottles made about the time she visited this country, in 1850 and 1851. The original iron layer was the magnetic ferri-ferroso-oxide but exposure during many years resulted in further oxidation to simple ferric oxide, a red material.

Bare iron pontil, coated.

Later, about 1870, heavy mineral water bottles were first made by using the bare iron pontil, then coating the annealed bottles with a lead oxide, or similar, paint. Many of these still exist. Under the paint has been found unchanged magnetic iron oxide as first deposited by the hot pontil.

There seems to be only one good reason for coating the iron deposit left by the use of the bare iron pontil. The edges of such discontinuous surfaces can develop tension as with the heat shock due to washing these return- able bottles. In work by my laboratory in earlier years it was found that even a thin layer across a known area subject to heat shock would provide enough insulation to allow the evening of temperature to become beneficial.

Open pontil.

There is a tool called the "open pontil." It was a tool for special purposes, usually made in the factory blacksmith shop, hence had no required dimensions. One that I have seen was a flat annulus, or ring, about five inches in diameter and with the ring about three-quarters of an inch wide. This left a circular hole about three and one-half inches across. This is what made it **open**. What is so often called "open pontil" by collectors is, as already stated, the result of using the blow-pipe as a pontil. A pontil made as a miniature of the true open-pontil, to fit the size of the rings left by using the blowpipe, would fill completely with glass on gathering and leave no such ring.

The open pontil was used to "stick" heavy objects, such as very large bowls, platters, and the like. The ring was gathered with glass.

Clay head (or ball) pontil.

Spurred by photos of an odd looking pontil, having a crossbar at the end, I have been lately searching for its use, and particularly its origin. The crossbar, of "X" shape or as more elaborate whorls outlining a sphere, were covered with clay, baked more or less in the heat of the furnace, and used as gathering irons for transferring glass in quantity. The earliest use I have found was about 1912 when it was used to feed semi-automatic or hand powered bottle making machines. Several references to this use in the United States and Great Britain have been found, but no patents have been discovered. With the development of automatic feeding, this use of the clay head pontil phased out.

At the same time another use became vastly more important. In the pressing of fine crystal glass automatic machines are less used, and glass must be transferred from pot or tank furnace in quantities. The clay head became most valuable for this and is used today. The glass is hotter, has less tendency to show wave marks, and, above all, is not apt to be contaminated with streaks of iron that came from the use of an iron ball or normal pontil. In addition, any burning off of the parts to fall into the pot, which would be disastrous if of iron, would give only minor trouble with the clay head, which would float until fished out.

Modern "shaped" pontil tips.

If the use of the glass tipped pontil ever waned, it has gone through a great revival today. Not only are there a number of commercial shops producing fine art ware, but scores of one-man and two-man shops make ware that commands high respect as completely hand made ware. Most of them use the glass tipped pontil, but a method of shaping has added greatly to its efficiency.

Earlier I spoke of spreading the contact area and reducing the adherence of glass-to-glass as a means of holding ware on the glass tipped pontil. Knowingly or not, the methods most favored do just that.

The earliest and simplest was to press the hot tip against a small iron bar to divide the face of the tip into two hemispheres before attach-ing it to the piece. Alternately the tip was pressed once, then rotated ninety degrees and pressed again, leaving quadrants instead of hemispheres. That balanced the attachment and left the useless center without contact.

Next came several versions of a checkerboard design, leaving the contacts either as squares, or as the bars between squares when the glass tip was pressed against a form before attaching to the glassware being shaped. A diamond grid is very popular, leaving in one case, only diamond points as contacts, or the reverse, fine lines left with sunken diamonds – the die for this is easier to machine. An imitation of the blowpipe as a pontil is made by pressing the hot tip against the proper form. There is really no limit to the possible shapes for the hot tip, pressed against a die before "sticking."

Abridged from book in progress: *Backgrounds for Glass Collectors*.

Just What Can a 19th Century Bottle Tell Us?

Edward Staski

EDWARD STASKI

Just What Can A 19th Century Bottle Tell Us?

ABSTRACT

Like all artifacts, 19th century bottles reveal different kinds of information. Formal characteristics, contextual patterns, and behavioral correlates to patterns of material culture, are all familiar avenues of inquiry in archaeology. An ongoing project at the University of Arizona depends on the analysis of bottles in large measure, in order to study patterns of alcohol consumption among selected ethnic and economic groups. The actual amount of alcohol consumed appears to be an individual decision. The results support treatment programs for alcohol abuse that focus on the individual and not the group.

The title of this article is not a trivial question. Much current research in historical archaeology depends on the interpretation of bottles. Research designs are becoming quite sophisticated. The question—what can a 19th century bottle tell us— is of necessary interest and relevance to many archaeologists. Rephrasing the question in general terms underscores its importance. What is the informational value of our artifacts? This article begins with a brief exploration of the kinds of information bottles supply. It goes on to discuss how this information can play a part in the study of complex human behaviors. An ongoing study of the role of alcoholic beverages among selected urban ethnic and economic groups is discussed in some detail. Contributions to modern society that archaeologists can make with the results of this and similar studies are considered.

Bottles have formal characteristics noted by every archaeologist, including size, shape, volume, color, weight, and historical information. All measurements of form help classifying artifacts, recognizing bottle types, dating periods of manufacture, understanding technological change and documenting industrial development. Even the physical properties of fluids can be ascertained by an examination of form (Jones 1971; Lorrain 1968;

Miller and Sullivan 1981; Newman 1970; Switzer 1974; White 1978; Wilson 1961). Much of the needed information is found in studies dedicated specifically to the collector of glass antiques (Cohen 1975; Colcleaser 1965, 1966; Davis and Davis 1967; Ferrars and Ferrars 1966; Freeman 1964; Kendrick 1963; Lyons and Lyons 1967; Munsey 1970; Toulouse 1969a, 1969b, 1971; Yount 1967). Additional information is presented in histories of glass manufacturing (Angus–Butterworth 1948; Meigh 1972; Scoville 1948).

Study of the provenience of bottles, their condition, and the association of these bottles with other recognizable artifacts, suggests patterns of use and preservation. Once manufactured, bottles are not necessarily emptied immediately. When emptied of original contents, bottles are often recycled and reused. Those which finally enter archeological context are often smashed, and the remaining pieces may be moved about extensively. Investigating the paths of bottles from initial systemic context to final location in the ground allows an understanding of site formation and past behavior (Hill 1982a, 1982b). In methodological terms, the information gained from observing formal characteristics is compared to what is learned from analyzing context and association to arrive at statements concerning complex behavioral and formation processes (Fontana 1968; Staski and Wilk 1981).

A third category of information revealed by bottles is that which can be used to make significant contributions to modern society. Historical archaeologists and other scholars who depend to a large degree on information from bottles are asking some very interesting questions about trade and economics, political organization, social stratification, household variability, ethnicity, and conditions of life on the frontier (Fontana 1968; Schuyler 1972; Staski and Wilk 1981; Switzer 1974; Toulouse 1970; Wilson 1981). A thorough review of these and other studies is beyond the scope of this article. It is clear, nevertheless, that a general pattern of research is developing. The significance of understanding human behavior, revealed to archaeologists by the formal characteristics and contexts of bottles, is becoming the focus of many studies.

This third kind of information has significance in that it has the potential of contributing to the improvement of the current human condition. One of the paramount values of archaeology (as with any science) lies in its potential ability to help improve aspects of our own lives (King 1981; Staski 1983a). In accordance with this philosophy, one project at the University of Arizona deals explicitly with this potential contribution. The topical focus of this research involves the delineation of how patterns of alcoholic beverage consumption and drinking pathologies correlate with patterns of ethnic affiliation, socioeconomic status, and family structure. Initial investigations have concentrated on the refuse of living residents of Tucson, Arizona. Continuing research (described below) in part focuses on urban populations from the late 19th century. The goals of this study include accurate descriptions and useful explanations of drinking behavior, along with evaluations of various solutions to present–day problems of alcohol abuse.

This study of alcohol consumption emerged from a larger modern material culture research program. "Le Projet du Garbage" has been conducting urban archaeology of living groups for over 10 years. The "Projet" has emphasized, theoretically and methodologically, the use and comparison of diverse measures: attitudes, observed behavior, and material culture (Rathje 1974, 1978, 1979; Rathje and Hughes 1975; Rathje and McCarthy 1977). Although there are complexities in the data analysis, several interesting patterns regarding drinking behavior have emerged.

Early analysis was limited to a consideration of beer consumption. Residents of a sample of households (N = 73) were questioned about a number of consumption habits. Refuse from these same households was collected over a five week period. Comparisons of interview and refuse data revealed certain discrepancies. It was initially believed that accuracy in reporting rates and quantities of consumption to interviewers varied most along ethnic lines (Le Projet du Garbage 1978:50–65). Analyses of responses and trash from three census tracts in Tucson that differ in ethnic and economic composition show this clearly. In middle-income Anglo Tract 40.05, only two families out of 10

reporting no beer purchased had beer containers in their trash. In Tract 38, a low–income Mexican-American and Anglo neighborhood, 10 of the 12 households that claimed not to buy beer threw out beer containers. The low–income Mexican-American community of Tract 11 contained nine "never purchase" families out of 11 sampled that discarded beer containers. That ethnicity is the crucial independent variable, and not income, was apparently confirmed by individual household analysis. In fact, 18 of the 19 "non-reporting" households that consumed beer are Mexican-American (Le Projet du Garbage 1978:61, 64).

Why Mexican–Americans should under-report beer consumption significantly more often than Anglos was not entirely clear. Regrettably, the literature concerning Mexican–American mental health issues in general, and Mexican–American attitudes toward alcohol use and abuse in particular, is scant indeed (Boulete 1976; Vega 1980:3–5). It is possible, however, to suggest tentatively a number of attitudinal factors that may influence responses. The relatively low utilization of mental health facilities by Mexican–Americans (Vega 1980:10) reflects the perceived capacity of the family and community either to prevent mental problems or to absorb such problems should they occur (Jaco 1959, 1960; Madsen 1964; Miranda 1980:27–29; Valle and Vega 1980). It has also been suggested that mental illness, including drinking pathologies, is a highly stigmatized condition within the Mexican–American community (Vega 1980:6). The combination of these two related attitudes might explain why Mexican-Americans give inaccurate descriptions of their drinking behavior. A similar situation is found among Jewish–Americans, who are considered in more detail below.

The role of ethnicity in reporting accuracy has recently been questioned (Staski 1983b). When all alcohol types are considered (beer, wine, and hard liquor—see below) degree of reporting accuracy does not appear to follow ethnic lines. What is more, a certain number of household residents appear to *over-report* the amount of alcohol consumed as determined from refuse. Over-reporting, and the unclear realtionship between reporting accuracy and ethnicity, appear to be results of recycling behavior which cannot be measured systematically. Nevertheless, it still appears that general attitudes about alcohol use are ethnic phenomena (MacAndrew and Edgerton 1969; Staski 1983b).

Initially, actual drinking consumption rates and quantities were thought to vary most directly with income and wealth. Average consumption of beer per household for the entire sample is 21.0, 93.56, and 93.19 ounces per week for Tracts 40.05, 38, and 11, respectively. It is notable that there is little difference between Tracts 11 and 38. Both are low–income (median annual income, approximately $4,500, 1970 census) though 38 is mixed Anglo and Mexican–American. Tract 11 is exclusively Mexican–American. Tract 40.05 stands out because it is middle–income (median annual income approximately $10,709, 1970 census). Income appears to be the crucial independent variable here. Poorer people seemingly drink more, at least in so far as beer is concerned.

However, further analysis of total alcohol consumption as suggested by household refuse once again does not support earlier findings. A goal of this research is to estimate from refuse data the incidence of drinking pathologies among groups, and determine how incidence relates to various social variables such as ethnicity and economic status. Medical literature strongly suggests that, within populations, the average per capita intake of the drug ethyl alcohol is highly correlated with the incidence of pathologies (Clark and Kricka 1980; World Health Organization 1980:19–21). Therefore, material evidence for the three types of alcoholic beverages—beer, wine, and hard liquor—should be combined for this analysis. Suggested rates of intake are converted to amounts of ethyl alcohol. Beer is most often 4.5% ethyl alcohol, while wine averages 12%. Hard liquors range from 35 to nearly 80%, although most have an average of about 40 to 45% (Stables 1979:5). Fortified wines, such as sherry (20% ethyl alcohol) are included in the hard liquor category. However, they make up less than 5% of the hard liquor sample. An estimated average is that ethyl alcohol composes 40% of hard liquor. By simply multiplying the quantities for beer, wine, and hard liquor

intake by 0.045, 0.12, and 0.4, respectively, and combining these amounts for each household, an estimate is derived for the average total of ethyl alcohol consumed per household per week (Figures 1–3).

At first glance, it appears that the middle-income residents of Tract 40.05 consume more alcohol than the lower–income residents of the other tracts. However, the Mann Whitney U Test (for distributions that are not normal) shows the differences between tracts to be insignificant. These results can be explained in two ways. First, variation of income within tracts may be so great as to mask a correlation of income and quantity of alcohol consumed. Second, income and quantity of consumption of the drug might not be significantly correlated when total alcohol intake is considered. Comparisons of alcohol intake and income at the level of the individual household support the second of these explanations. At this stage of analysis, absolutely no correlation between income and amount of drinking whatsoever has been found.

Analysis of individual households now indicates that no available social measure correlates signifi-

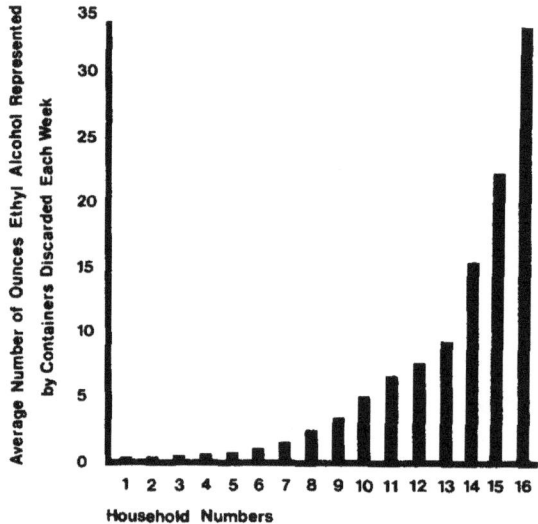

FIGURE 1. Average weekly rate of household ethyl alcohol consumption as indicated by refuse, for a sample of households from Tract 11, Tucson, Arizona.

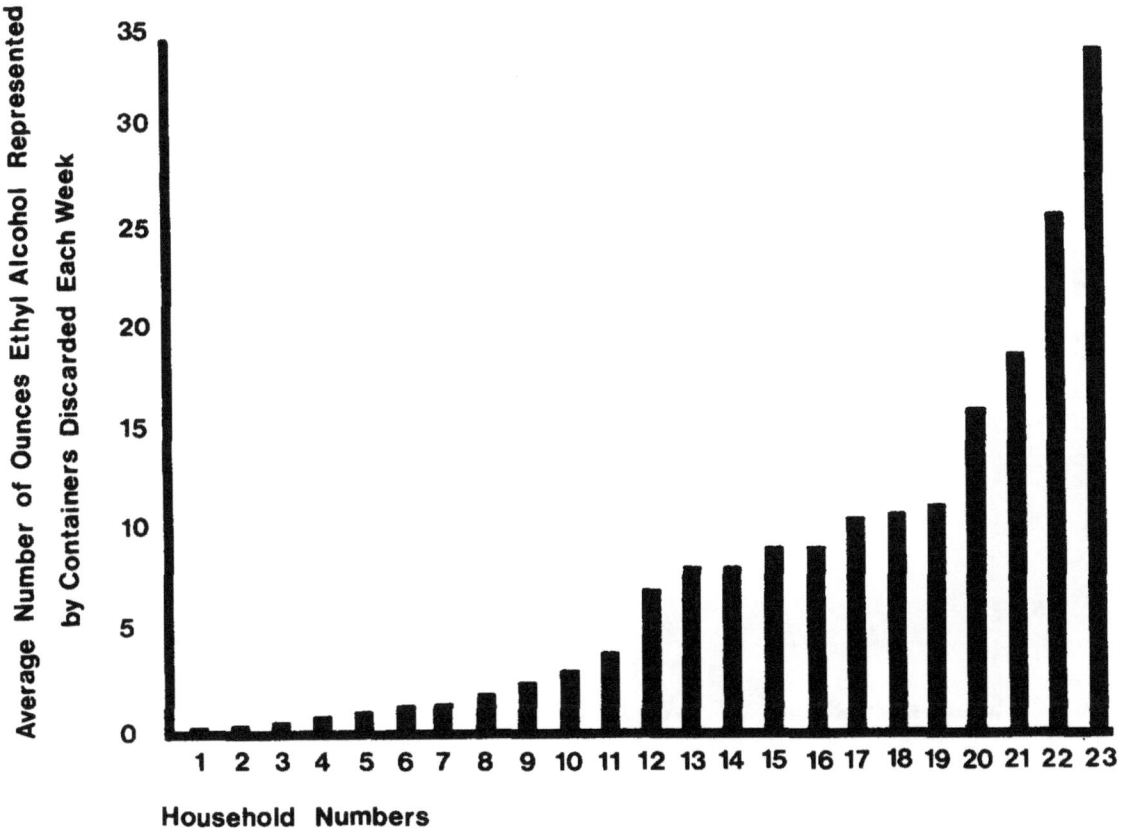

FIGURE 2. Average weekly rate of household ethyl alcohol consumption as indicated by refuse, for a sample of households from Tract 38, Tucson, Arizona.

cantly with the actual amount of ethyl alcohol consumed. Variables studied so far include income, wealth, education level, ethnic affiliation, size of family, and number of adults in household. Analysis is continuing, and the possibility of sample error has not been ruled out. However, this startling result, should it be confirmed, is not very disquieting if a number of facts are considered. The data suggest that quantities of alcohol consumed, and thus the incidence of pathological drinking (Clark and Kricka 1980; World Health Organization 1980), is determined for the most part by individual and not social characteristics. This conclusion is supported by the majority of practitioners in the field who are treating problem drinking on a daily basis. Those who treat alcohol

problems recognize that they occur in all kinds of people. The most efficacious treatment consists of small group and "one–on–one" counseling programs. Educating the individual patient about the harm of excessive drinking, not changing his or her social roles, is most effective (Davies 1980). On the other hand, social responses to alcohol consumption, such as Prohibition and the various attempts to raise the price of alcohol to levels that would discourage use (The Royal College of Psychiatrists 1979:96–97) have met with failure.

Thus, the results of the project at this time support the clinical literature and contradict the majority of the sociological literature (see below). This phase of the alcohol study suggests that treatment programs that focus on the individual are more

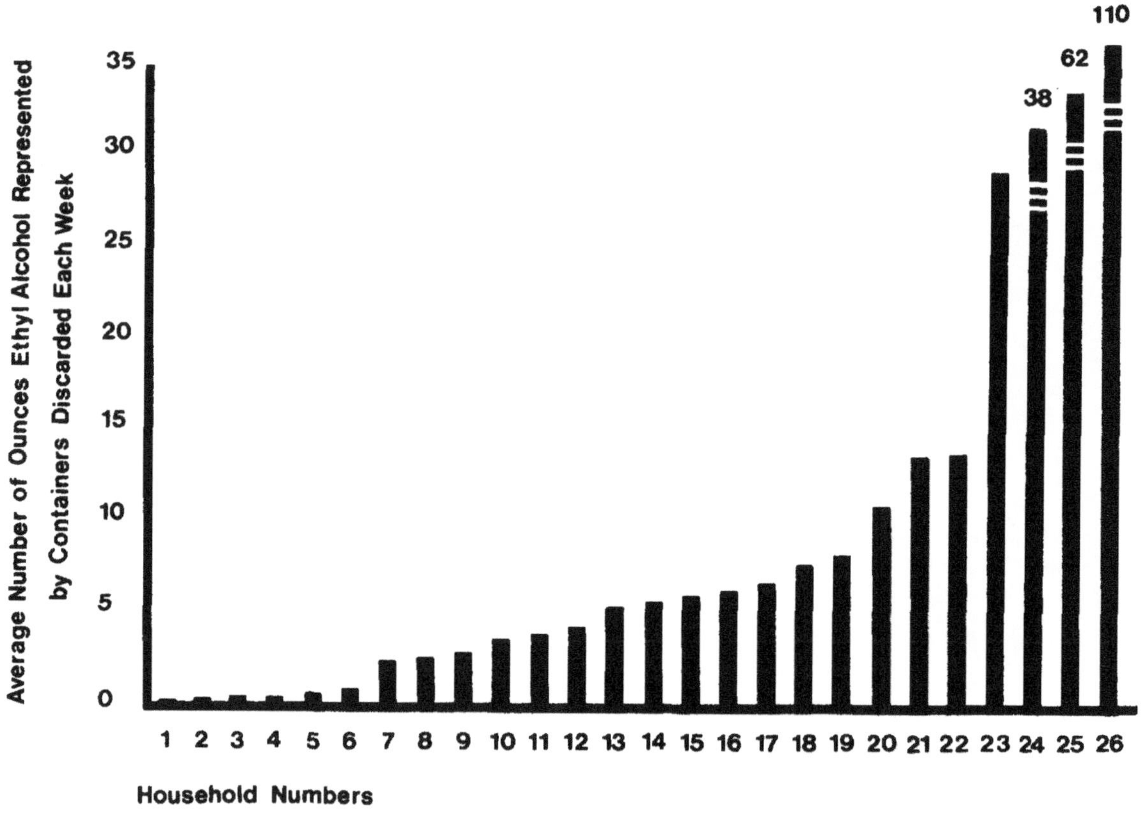

FIGURE 3. Average weekly rate of household ethyl alcohol consumption as indicated by refuse, for a sample of households from Tract 40.05, Tucson, Arizona.

useful than social reform movements when it comes to treating alcohol–related problems. It also shows that groups of people—ethnic, economic, or otherwise—are not made up of certain kinds of drinkers. The origin of drinking patterns and problems is neither found in the nature of ethnic groups nor, apparently, in economic conditions. Of course, the social nature of alcohol consumption cannot be denied, as many patterns of drinking and responses to the effects of drinking are social in nature (MacAndrew and Edgerton 1969; see below). All that is suggested is that the extent of ethyl alcohol consumption, and thus the incidence of pathological drinking, might be determined by characteristics of individuals.

Recent analysis suggests that household structure and composition may play important roles in determining an individual's use of alcohol. It appears that the degree of "internal social heterogeneity" within a household—the difference in social positions of related household heads—strongly correlates with both the choice to use alcohol and the amount of alcohol consumed (Staski 1983b). Social position is measured by consideration of occupation type, age, and years of education. Households in which husband and wife hold similar social positions are scenes of very little or no drinking. Households in which the social positions of spouses are quite different all exhibit heavy drinking behavior relative to the balance of the sample. Although this analysis is preliminary, it can be interpreted in a way consistent with previous findings. Individuals in households with great internal social heterogeneity might experience high degrees of stress, since different social positions lead to different expectations and thus to conflicting views and opinions. Heads of households with similar social positions apparently are under less stress and demonstrate greater stability throughout their lives. Elevated alcohol consumption may be a response to stress by some household heads with different social positions.

This study of alcohol consumption is now moving into a second phase, which involves the archaeological analysis of household trash from late 19th century urban sites. The goal is to ascertain the amount of ethyl alcohol consumed among certain immigrant groups from that time. The research design is in the final stages of development. Emphasis is given to patterns of alcoholic beverage consumption among Jewish–Americans and Irish–Americans.

Social historians and sociologists have consistently accepted as fact that these two ethnic groups represent the extremes in terms of amount of alcohol consumed and incidence of drinking pathologies (Bales 1944, 1946; Glad 1947; Skolnick 1957). Jewish–Americans are described as rarely suffering the effects of problem or heavy drinking, despite regular consumption of alcoholic beverages (Cheinisse 1908; Glatt 1970; Landman 1952; Snyder 1954, 1958). Irish–Americans are depicted as always having experienced an incidence of drinking pathologies far above that of other groups (Bales 1962; Stivers 1976). The reason for the purported difference is said to be located in the nature of the ethnic groups.

Obviously, the results of research with refuse from Tucson, Arizona, show that these descriptions should not be accepted uncritically. What historians and sociologists have done, it appears, is to accept popular stereotypes of ethnic drinking patterns, originally formed in Europe (Jellinek 1941; Stivers 1976) and reinforced after immigration to the United States (Bernheimer 1905; Fishberg 1911; Riis 1890; MaGuire 1868).

By doing so, the stereotypes have been given legitimacy and have been perpetuated to the present.

Investigations have traditionally focused on expressed attitudes, not behavior. Using the traditional survey methods of interview and questionnaire, scholars have tended to simplify the role of attitudes to the point that patterns of cognition are assumed to be directly translatable into patterns of action. Degrees of cooperation, bias, and recall—all factors that influence the accuracy of information given by respondents—are not taken into account (Sinaiko and Broedling 1975). Actual behavior is seldom observed. Material culture is never studied. Interviews seemingly reveal that American Jews drink regularly, but rarely overindulge. However, they also show that Jews abhor drunkenness, especially among themselves. The Irish, on the other hand, have never held such a strong sentiment. Undoubtedly, attitudes about drinking and drunkenness affect what people say about their drinking habits. Many scholars fail to acknowledge that all attitudes held by a group work as a system and influence what people remember to tell, and choose to tell, the interviewer.

Other sources of data, such as hospital admission records for alcohol–induced diseases and arrest records for drinking–related crimes, are also inadequate. In these cases, scholars have tended to ignore the role of attitudes in shaping behavior. To the Irish, drinking has for several hundred years been considered a social, public activity. In Ireland during the 18th and early 19th centuries, the consumption of alcohol was an integral part of a number of social events, including marriages, births, funerals, and significant economic transactions. Drinking was also institutionally associated with many occupations, serving the function of linking new workers with the corporate work group (Stivers 1976:15–22). The pub served a crucial sociopolitical role by integrating the community, allowing communication and the exchange of ideas among many individuals. Later in the 19th century, this role was transferred to America. Public drinking met an important social need of the Irish–American immigrant. These drinking patterns did not necessarily involve heavy drinking or develop into pathologies. Yet, the behavior was considered repugnant by the Anglo–Protestant majority (Fallows 1979:36, 50–51) and the stereotype of the ''drunk Irishman'' spread.

Jews, on the other hand, have tended to confine drinking to the privacy of the home, among family members. Religious doctrine, combined with the realization that the dominant society must not be given perceived license to persecute them, have led the Jews to conceal any and all unacceptable behavior (Patai 1977:433–447). Public admission of drinking heavily or having a drinking problem—allowing oneself to be arrested for drunken behavior or seeking out medical help— has been and continues to be more difficult for Jewish–Americans than for Irish–Americans. The Irish appear to have a greater incidence of drinking problems because culturally it is not as difficult to let the presence of the pathology be known.

A study conducted several years ago shows that similarly distinguishable behavior patterns among the Navajo and Hopi lead to similarly differing stereotypes. The publically drinking Navajo are popularly believed to have a much greater problem with alcohol than the privately drinking Hopi. Interestingly, records of deaths due to cirrhosis of the liver do not indicate that the former have a greater incidence of drinking pathologies than the latter. In fact, the Navajo are slightly below the national average, while the Hopi exhibit nearly the highest rate for the disease (Kunitz et al. 1968; Kuntiz et al. 1971; Levy and Kunitz 1971, 1974). Incidence of cirrhosis is the only behavioral measure that does not *intrinsically* suffer from bias or cultural loading. Among scholars in the health fields the most widely used method of estimating the prevalence of alcoholic pathologies has been the ''Jellinek Estimation Formula,'' which is based on cirrhosis mortality data (Jellinek 1947; Jolliffe and Jellinek 1941; Keller 1962; Pearl et al. 1962). With some minor revisions, mortality rates from cirrhosis continue to be the best measure of the rate of alcohol abuse (Brenner 1975; Terris 1967). The distinction between pure physiological effect, which is reflected in cirrhosis rates, and culturally determined patterns of drunken comportment,

which is reflected in rates of public drunkenness, attitudes towards drinking, hospital admission and crime rates, must be kept in mind (MacAndrew and Edgerton 1969).

Using rates of death by cirrhosis can, nevertheless, be problematic. Complexities arise when the accuracy and precision of older records are considered. Room (1968) uses rates of death due to alcohol and liver diseases to show that at the turn of the century Irish–Americans died from cirrhosis at a disproportionally high rate, while the Jewish–American rate was exceptionally low. His data came from the 11th United States Census of 1890, the first to include detailed information on ethnic groups (United States Government 1892:xix), chiefly because of the invention of electrical card sorters which could handle great amounts of data rapidly (United States Government 1892:xvii; Wright 1900:74). The mortality data indeed reflect the traditional view of Irish–American and Jewish–American drinking habits (United States Government 1895:40–43, for example). Yet, even census officials at the time recognized certain shortcomings of these records (United States Government 1892:xxi). Approximately two–thirds of the mortality data were recognized at the time of their collection to be unreliable. Rates of mortality differed so drastically in similar areas of the country that the only explanation possible was recording error (United States Government 1896:264; Wright 1900:71).

What is more, the lack of medical sophistication in 1890 led to what are now recognized as arbitrary and inaccurate determinations of cause of death. Doctors and hospital staff were subject to their own cultural biases and stereotypes, and these affected their judgments (Chase 1980:220). Among the poor, many deaths remained hidden, never to be recorded. In general, the accuracy of death records from the late 19th century is in doubt.

Essentially, then, the ways that 19th century Irish–Americans and Jewish–Americans really ''handled'' alcohol remain unclear. These ways may have been far different than traditional descriptions. There is an obvious need for an archaeological study of these drinking patterns.

Material culture from 19th century urban contexts can be approached in the same way Le Projet du Garbage studies the trash of today. Modern refuse is equivalent to 19th century refuse recovered from urban backyards, privies, and wells in socially and behaviorally meaningful ways. Both assemblages consist of domestic trash. The roles of formation processes (such as scavenging) and socio–technological changes (such as the introduction and development of municipal sanitation services) can be controlled. Many urban backyards are well-protected sites (Staski 1982). Sanitation services had little impact on 19th century urban slums (Melosi 1981).

The excellent dating capabilities of historical archaeology, due mostly to the presence of documentation and historic information on material culture, also allow temporal correspondences of modern and 19th century deposits to be made. Dates and durations of dumping can be measured with assurance. Furthermore, the presence of documentation allows the control of certain 19th century demographic variables. For example, the approximate number of people involved in forming any particular backyard trash deposit can be known. Ethnicity, wealth, income and occupation of occupants are also available from historic records. Population correspondence between modern and 19th century trash is achievable.

A number of potential distortions in the archaeological record must be mentioned. Seasonal variations in consumption rates, and holiday drinking, might both be controlled by careful analysis of the patterns of material culture. These distortions have been accounted for in modern material culture and are found to be insignificant in their effects (Staski 1983b). A more powerful distortion, the role of public drinking, creates a more problematic issue. As discussed above, public drinking appears to be an attitudinal factor that correlates with ethnicity. At this time, no systematic archaeological method to control for the role of public drinking is available. Many 19th century bars can be linked historically to specific ethnic groups. Refuse from such bars can be located and used to measure neighborhood consumption rates more accurately. Still, the amount of drinking done in back alleys, front stoops, and on the street, and the number of bottles discarded away from household domestic refuse, remains unknown.

A possible solution to this problem is found in the fact that certain behaviors vary according to the quantity of alcohol consumed. A recognizable pattern of behaviors is associated with an increasing rate of alcohol consumption, and these behaviors can be seen in patterns of material culture. The number of bottles that originally held alcohol is thus only part of an archaeological measure of the quantity of alcohol consumed. Other items of material culture—categories of objects that reflect other, though related, behaviors—apparently have patterns in the archaeological record that reflect the amount of drinking that took place.

Preliminary study of modern material culture from Tucson, Arizona, and a review of the medical literature, suggest that decreasing intake of protein, increasing intake of sugar and medical products, and increasing waste of edible food all relate directly to the amount of alcohol consumed. These trends occur at the level of the household, not the individual drinker (Thomson et al. 1980; Wallgren and Barry 1970; Westcenter of Tucson n.d.). Analysis of household ethyl alcohol and medical product consumption rates, for instance (from the same sample of households discussed above) clearly shows a positive correlation. From the total sample of 73 households, there are 32 for which reliable measures of total ounces and number of items of medical goods are available. Over 90% of these medical products are high turnover, over–the–counter items. When weekly average intake of medical products is plotted against weekly average ethyl alcohol consumption, a highly dispersed but positive trend is apparent (Figure 4). High dispersion is to be expected, since there are a number of reasons besides the consumption of alcohol that lead people to use medical products.

In order to determine whether the differences in medical product use are significant for groups of drinkers, it is necessary to compare the rates of use for such groups. The sample of 32 households is divided at the median into "light drinking" and "heavy drinking" populations. The comparison of amounts of medical products consumed shows an

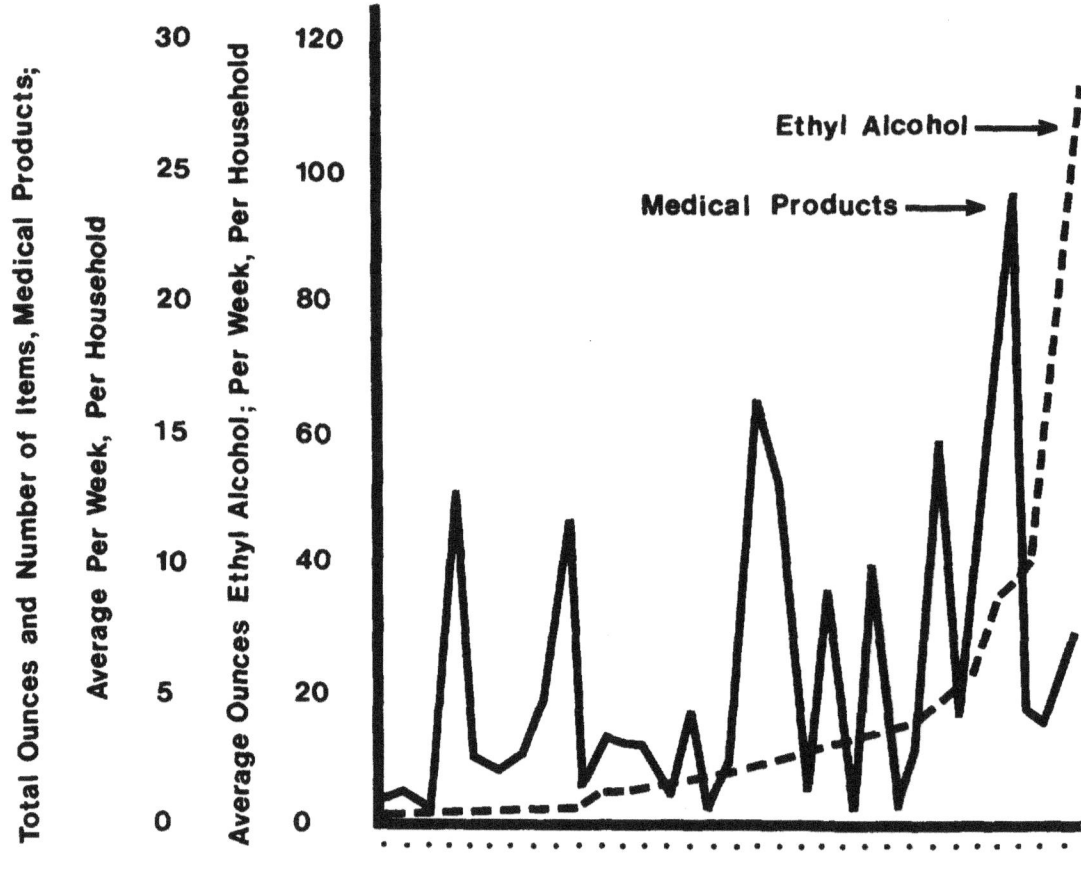

FIGURE 4. Number and total ounces of medical products found in household refuse, for a sample of households from Tracts 11, 38, and 40.05, Tucson, Arizona.

obvious difference now (Figure 5) which is, moreover, statistically significant (Mann Whitney U Test, significance at the .05 level). Considering again the fact that people change their rate of consumption of medical products for a number of reasons highlights the powerful nature of this correlation. Recognizing this and other behavioral trends archaeologically is difficult; nevertheless, progress is being made. The relationships between ethyl alcohol consumption on the one hand, and sugar and protein ingestion on the other, remain unconfirmed at this time. Analysis of domestic faunal remains, once further systematized, will be the major approach to measuring protein consumption. Patterns of Patent and Proprietary medicine use as revealed in the archaeological record will aid in measuring the consumption of medicines. Other behavioral correspondences are presently being developed.

The archaeological study of 19th century Irish–

American and Jewish–American patterns of drinking is designed to accomplish a number of objectives. A more accurate description of how these immigrants used alcohol will arise. The patterns suggested by the first phase of this project (i.e., the modern material culture study) will either be strengthened or weakened. If strengthened, suggestions made earlier in this article regarding patterns of alcohol consumption will be fortified.

A methodological goal of this project is a better understanding of the degree of heterogeneity exhibited by household material culture and how this compares to the patterns and range of behaviors among residents. Measuring and accounting for variability in household material culture are fundamental objectives of much archaeological research. Only a small number of the kinds of material items and behaviors that pertain to households are considered by this project. A more complete understanding of how people live and lived will require many more.

Bottles, as well as all other items of material culture, have the potential for saying a significant amount about human behavior if the right questions are asked and addressed properly. Historical archaeologists can study material culture, documents, behavior, attitudes—the entire range of human endeavors—and arrive at intriguing and meaningful statements about many human issues. Such statements lead the way to social solutions, and the solving of social and individual problems is what archaeologists more often should be attempting to achieve.

ACKNOWLEDGEMENTS

The theme and ideas of this article were generated after conversations with a number of people. Deserving special mention are P. Darcy, A. Greeley, W. L. Rathje, M. B. Schiffer and G. D. Stone. A shorter version of this paper was presented at the symposium "Urban Archaeology in the United States," held at the 47th annual meeting of the Society for American Archaeology. All participants are to be thanked for their contributions.

REFERENCES

ANGUS-BUTTERWORTH, L. M.
    1948   *The Manufacture of Glass*. Pitman Publishing Corporation, New York.

BALES, ROBERT FREED
    1944   *The "Fixation Factor" in Alcohol Addiction: an Hypothesis Derived from A Comparitive Study of Irish and Jewish Social Norms*. Unpublished Ph.D. dissertation, Department of Sociology, Harvard University.
    1946   Cultural Differences in Rates of Alcoholism. *Quarterly Journal of Studies on Alcohol* 6:480–499.
    1962   Attitudes Toward Drinking in the Irish Culture. In *Society Culture and Drinking Patterns*, edited by D. J. Pittman and C. R. Snyder, pp. 157–187. Southern Illinois University Press, Carbondale and Edwardsville.

BERNHEIMER, CHARLES S. (EDITOR)
    1905   *The Russian Jew in the United States: Studies of Social Conditions in New York, Philadelphia, and Chicago, with a Description of Rural Settlements*. Winston Press, Philadelphia.

BOULETTE, TERESA RAMEREZ
    1976   *Comprehensive Interventions in Behalf of the Spanish-Speaking Surnamed*. Report Commissioned by The Children's Bureau, September, Washington, D.C.

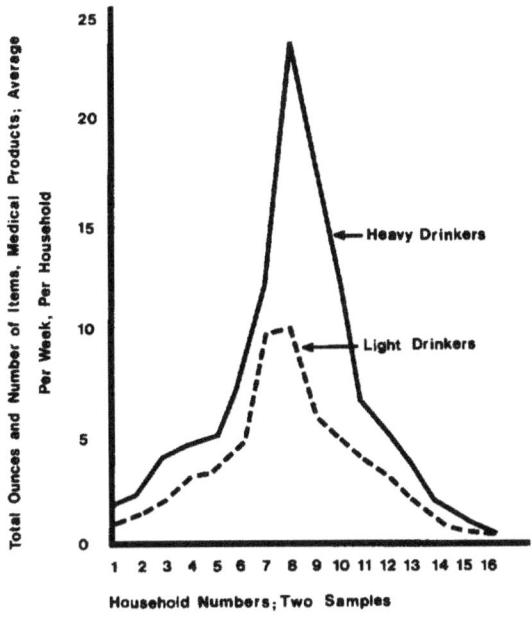

FIGURE 5. "Light Drinkers" vs. "Heavy Drinkers" compared in relation to the number of medical products and total ounces of medical products found in household refuse.

BRENNER, M. HARVEY
   1975   Trends in Alcohol Consumption and Associated
          Illnesses. *American Journal of Public Health*
          65:1279-1292.

CHASE, ALLEN
   1980   *The Legacy of Malthus: the Social Costs of the New
          Scientific Racism*. University of Illinois Press,
          Urbana.

CHEINISSE, L.
   1908   La Race Juive, Jouit-elle d'une Immunité à l'Égard
          de l'Alcoolisme? *Seminaire de Medical* 28:613-615.

CLARK, P. M. S. AND L. J. KRICKA
   1980   Introduction. In *Medical Consequences of Alcohol
          Abuse*, edited by P. M. S. Clark and L. J. Kricka, pp.
          17-22. John Wiley and Sons, New York.

COHEN, HAL L.
   1975   *Official Guide to Bottles Old and New*. House of
          Collectibles, Florence, Alabama.

COLCLEASER, DONALD E.
   1965   *Bottles of Bygone Days, Part 1*. Betty's Letter Shop,
          Vallejo, California.
   1966   *Bottles of Bygone Days, Part 2*. Betty's Letter Shop,
          Vallejo, California.

DAVIES, D. L.
   1980   The Treatment of Alcohol Dependence. In *Medical
          Consequences of Alcohol Abuse*, edited by P. M. S.
          Clark and L. J. Kricka, pp. 261-276. John Wiley and
          Sons, New York.

DAVIS, MARTIN AND HELEN DAVIS
   1967   *Antique Bottles*. Gandee Printing Center, Medford,
          Oregon.

FALLOWS, M. R.
   1979   *Irish Americans: Identity and Assimilation*. Prentice-
          Hall, Englewood Cliffs, New Jersey.

FERRARS, PAT AND BOB FERRARS
   1966   *A Bottle Collector's Book*. Western Printing and
          Publishing Company, Sparks, Nevada.

FISHBERG, MAURICE
   1911   (reprinted 1975) *The Jews: a Study of Race and En-
          vironment*. Arno Press, New York.

FONTANA, BERNARD L.
   1968   Bottles and History: the Case of Magdalena de Kino,
          Sonora. *Historical Archaeology* 2:45-55.

FREEMAN, LARRY
   1964   *Grand Old American Bottles*. Century House, Wat-
          kins Glen.

GLAD, D. D.
   1947   Attitudes and Experiences of American-Jewish and
          American-Irish Male Youth as Related to Differences
          in Adult Rates of Inebriety. *Quarterly Journal of
          Studies on Alcohol* 8:406-472.

GLATT, MAX M.
   1970   Alcoholism and Drug Addiction Amongst Jews. *Brit-
          ish Journal of Addiction* 64:297-304.

HILL, SARAH H.
   1982a *A Consideration of Manufacture Deposition Lag in
          Urban Site Formation*. Paper Presented at the 47th
          Annual Meeting of the Society for American
          Archaeology, Minneapolis.
   1982b An Examination of Manufacture-Deposition Lag for
          Glass Bottles from Late Historic Sites. In *Archaeolo-
          gy of Urban America, the Search for Pattern and
          Process*, edited by Roy S. Dickens, Jr., pp. 291-328.
          Academic Press, New York.

JACO, E. GARTLY
   1959   Mental Health of the Spanish-American in Texas. In
          Culture and Mental Health, Cross-Cultural Studies,
          edited by M. Opler, pp. 467-485. Macmillan, New
          York.
   1960   *The Social Epidemiology of Mental Disorders: a Psy-
          chiatric Survey of Texas*. Russell Sage Foundation,
          New York.

JELLINEK, E. M.
   1941   Immanuel Kant on Drinking. *Quarterly Journal of
          Studies on Alcohol* 1:777-778.
   1947   Recent Trends in Alcoholism and in Alcohol Con-
          sumption. *Quarterly Journal of Studies on Alcohol*
          8:1-42.

JOLLIFFE, NORMAN AND E. M. JELLINEK
   1941   Vitamin Deficiencies and Liver Cirrhosis in Alcoho-
          lics, Part VII, Cirrhosis of the Liver. *Quarterly Jour-
          nal of Studies on Alcohol* 2:544-583.

JONES, OLIVE
   1971   Glass Bottle Push-Ups and Pontil Marks. *Historical
          Archaeology* 5:62-73.

KELLER, MARK
   1962   The Definition of Alcoholism and the Estimation of
          its Prevalence. In *Society Culture and Drinking Pat-
          terns*, edited by D. J. Pittman and C. R. Snyder, pp.
          310-329. Southern Illinois University Press, Carbon-
          dale and Edwardsville.

KENDRICK, GRACE
   1963   *The Antique Bottle Collector*. Western Printing and
          Publishing Company, Sparks, Nevada.

KING, THOMAS F.
   1981   The NART: a Plan to Direct Archaeology Toward
          More Relevant Goals in Modern Life. *Early Man*
          3(4):35-37.

KUNITZ, STEPHEN J., JERROLD E. LEVY AND
M. EVERETT
   1968   Alcoholic Cirrhosis Among the Navajo. *Quarterly
          Journal of Studies on Alcohol* 30:672-685.

KUNITZ, STEPHEN J., JERROLD E. LEVY, C. L. ODOROFF
AND J. BOLLINGER
1971   The Epidemiology of Alcoholic Cirrhosis in Two
       Southwestern Indian Tribes. *Quarterly Journal of
       Studies on Alcohol* 32:706–720.

LANDMAN, R. H.
1952   Studies of Drinking in Jewish Culture 3. Drinking
       Patterns of Children and Adolescents Attending
       Religious Schools. *Quarterly Journal of Studies on
       Alcohol* 13:87–94.

LE PROJET DU GARBAGE
1978   *The Socioeconomic Correlates of Household Re-
       siduals, Phase 2.* Report to the National Science
       Foundation, Directorate of Applied Science and Re-
       search Applications, Washington, D.C.

LEVY, JERROLD E. AND STEPHEN J. KUNITZ
1971   *Indian Drinking: Problems of Data Collection and
       Interpretations.* Paper Presented at the First Annual
       Conference of the National Institute of Alcohol
       Abuse and Alcoholism, Washington, D.C.
1974   *Indian Drinking: Navajo Practices and Anglo–
       American Theories.* John Wiley and Sons, New
       York.

LORRAIN, DESSAMAE
1968   An Archaeologist's Guide to Nineteenth Century
       American Glass. *Historical Archaeology* 2:35–44.

LYONS, BILL AND JEAN LYONS
1967   *Bottles From Bygone Days.* Beeyay Publishers,
       South Vienna, Ohio.

MACANDREW, CRAIG AND ROBERT B. EDGERTON
1969   *Drunken Comportment: a Social Explanation.*
       Aldine, Chicago.

MADSEN, W.
1964   Value Conflicts and Folk Psychiatry in South Texas.
       In *Magic, Faith, and Healing*, edited by A. Kier, pp.
       470–488. The Free Press, New York.

MAGUIRE, JOHN FRANCIS
1868   (reprinted 1969) *The Irish in America.* Arno Press,
       New York.

MEIGH, EDWARD
1972   *The Story of the Glass Bottle.* C. E. Ramsden and
       Company, Ltd., Stoke-on-Trent, England.

MELOSI, MARTIN V.
1981   *Garbage in the Cities: Reform and the Environment;
       1880–1980.* Texas A & M University Press, College
       Station.

MILLER, GEORGE L. AND CATHARINE SULLIVAN
1981   Machine-Made Glass Containers and the End of Pro-
       duction for Mouth-Blown Bottles. *Research Bulletin*
       171. Parks Canada.

MIRANDA, MANUAL
1980   The Family Natural Support System in Hispanic
       Communities. In *Hispanic Natural Support Systems*,
       edited by R. Valle and W. Vega, pp. 25–32. Depart-
       ment of Mental Health, California.

MUNSEY, CECIL
1970   *The Illustrated Guide to Collecting Bottles.* Haw-
       thorne Books, Inc., New York.

NEWMAN, T. STELL
1970   A Dating Key for Post–Eighteenth Century Bottles.
       Historical Archaeology 4:70–75.

PATAI, RAPHAEL
1977   *The Jewish Mind.* Scribner's, New York.

PEARL, ARTHUR, ROBERT BUECHLEY AND
WENDELL R. LIPSCOMB
1962   Cirrhosis Mortality in Three Large Cities: Im-
       plications for Alcoholism and Intercity Comparisons.
       In *Society Culture and Drinking Patterns*, edited by
       D. J. Pittman and C. R. Snyder, pp. 345–352. South-
       ern Illinois University Press, Carbondale and
       Edwardsville.

RATHJE, WILLIAM L.
1974   The Garbage Project: a New Way to Look at the
       Problems of Archaeology. *Archaeology* 27(4):236–
       241.
1978   Archaeological Ethnography . . . Because Some-
       times it is Better to Give than to Receive. In *Explora-
       tions in Ethnoarchaeology*, edited by R. A. Gould,
       pp. 49–76. University of New Mexico Press, Albu-
       querque.
1979   Trace Measures. In *Unobtrusive Measures Today,
       New Directions for Methodology of Behavioral Sci-
       ence*, edited by L. Sechrest, pp. 75–91. Jossey-Bass,
       San Francisco.

RATHJE, WILLIAM L. AND WILSON W. HUGHES
1975   The Garbage Project as a Nonreactive Approach. In
       Perspectives on Attitude Assessment: Surveys and
       Their Alternatives, edited by H. W. Sinaiko and
       L. A. Broedling, pp. 151–167. *Manpower Research
       and Advisory Services Technical Report* 2. Smithso-
       nian Institution and the Navy Manpower R and D
       Program, Washington, D.C.

RATHJE, WILLIAM L. AND M. MCCARTHY
1977   Regularity and Variability in Contemporary Garbage.
       In *Research Strategies in Historical Archaeology*,
       edited by S. South, pp. 261–286. Academic Press,
       New York.

RIIS, JACOB
1890   *How the Other Half Lives.* Scribner's, New York.

ROOM, ROBIN
1968   Cultural Contigencies of Alcoholism: Variations Be-
       tween and Within Nineteenth Century Urban Ethnic

Groups in Alcohol–Related Death Rates. *Journal of Health and Social Behavior* 9:99–113.

SCHUYLER, ROBERT L.
1972 Sandy Ground: Archaeological Sampling in a Black Community in Metropolitan New York. In *The Conference on Historic Site Archaeology Papers Volume 7*, edited by S. South, pp. 13–51. University of South Carolina, Columbia.

SCOVILLE, WARREN C.
1948 *Revolution in Glassmaking: Entrepreneurship and Technological Change in the American Industry 1880–1920*. Harvard University Press, Cambridge.

SINAIKO, W. H. AND L. A. BROEDLING (EDITORS)
1975 Perspectives on Attitude Assessment: Surveys and Their Alternatives. *Manpower Research and Advisory Services Technical Report* 2. Smithsonian Institution and the Navy Manpower R and D Program, Washington, D.C.

SKOLNICK, JEROME H.
1957 *The Stumbling Block: a Sociological Study of the Relationship Between Selected Religious Norms and Drinking Behavior*. Unpublished Ph.D. dissertation, Department of Sociology, Yale University.

SNYDER, CHARLES R.
1954 *Culture and Sobriety: a Study of Drinking Patterns and Sociocultural Factors Related to Sobriety Among Jews*. Unpublished Ph.D. dissertation, Department of Sociology, Yale University.
1958 *Alcohol and the Jews: a Cultural Study of Drinking and Sobriety*. The Free Press, Glencoe, Illinois.

STABLES, RUTH L.
1979 *Alcoholism*. Blue Cross and Blue Shield Association, Chicago.

STASKI, EDWARD
1982 Advances in Urban Archaeology. In *Advances in Archaeological Method and Theory*, edited by M. B. Schiffer, pp. 94–149. Academic Press, New York.
1983a *What Can We Give the Tourist Besides a Tour?* Paper Presented at the 48th Annual Meeting of the Society for American Archaeology, Pittsburgh.
1983b *Patterns of Alcohol Consumption Among 19th Century Irish– and Jewish–Americans: Contributions from Archaeology*. Unpublished Ph.D. dissertation, Department of Anthropology, University of Arizona.

STASKI, EDWARD AND RICHARD WILK
1981 *The Material Culture of Poor People and Marginal Areas: a Case from Toledo District, Belize*. Paper Presented at the symposium "La Arqueologia Historica en el Area Maya," 17th Meeting of the Mexican Society of Anthropology, Chiapas, Mexico.

STIVERS, RICHARD
1976 *A Hair of the Dog: Irish Drinking and American*

Stereotypes. The Pennsylvania State University Press, University Park.

SWITZER, RONALD R.
1974 *The Bertrand Bottles: a Study of 19th Century Glass and Ceramic Containers*. National Park Service, United States Department of the Interior, Washington, D.C.

TERRIS, MILTON
1967 Epidemiology of Cirrhosis of the Liver: National Mortality Data. *American Journal of Public Health and the Nation's Health* 57:2076–2088.

THE ROYAL COLLEGE OF PSYCHIATRISTS
1979 *Alcohol and Alcoholism*. The Free Press, New York.

THOMSON, A. D., S. A. RAE AND S. K. MAJUMDAR
1980 Malnutrition in the Alcoholic. In *Medical Consequences of Alcohol Abuse*, edited by P. M. S. Clark and L. J. Kricka, pp. 103–156. John Wiley and Sons, New York.

TOULOUSE, JULIAN H.
1969a A Primer on Mold Seams. *The Western Collector* 7 (11, Pt. 1):526–535.
1969b A Primer on Mold Seams. *The Western Collector* 7 (12, Pt. 2):578–587.
1970 High on the Hawg: or How the Western Miner Lived, as Told by Bottles He Left Behind. *Historical Archaeology* 4:59–69.
1971 *Bottlemakers and Their Marks*. Thomas Nelson, Inc., New York.

UNITED STATES GOVERNMENT, DEPARTMENT OF THE INTERIOR, CENSUS OFFICE
1892 *Compendium of the Eleventh Census: 1890, Part 1: Population*. Government Printing Office, Washington D.C.
1895 *Report on Vital and Social Statistics in the United States at the Eleventh Census: 1890 Part 4—Statistics of Death*. Government Printing Office, Washington, D.C.
1896 *Abstract of the Eleventh Census: 1890* (2nd edition). Government Printing Office, Washington, D.C.

VEGA, WILLIAM
1980 Mental Health Research and North American Hispanic Populations. In *Hispanic Natural Support Systems*, edited by R. Valle and W. Vega, pp. 3–14. Department of Mental Health, California.

VALLE, RAMON AND WILLIAM VEGA (EDITORS)
1980 *Hispanic Natural Support Systems*. Deparment of Mental Health, California.

WALLGREN, HENRIK AND HERBERT BARRY III
1970 *Actions of Alcohol* (two volumes). Elsevier Publishing Co., Amsterdam.

WESTCENTER OF TUCSON
n.d. *Understanding Ourselves and Alcoholism*. Westcenter of Tucson, Tucson.

WHITE, JOHN R.
1978   Bottle Nomenclature: a Glossary of Landmark Ter-
        minology for the Archaeologist. *Historical Archaeol-
        ogy* 12:58–67.

WILSON, REX L.
1961   A Classification System for 19th Century Bottles.
        Arozoniana 11(4):2–6.
1981   *Bottles on the Western Frontier*, edited by Edward
        Staski. University of Arizona Press, Tucson.

WORLD HEALTH ORGANIZATION
1980   Problems Related to Alcohol Consumption. Report of
        a WHO Expert Committee. *World Health Organiza-
        tion Technical Report Series* 650, Geneva.

WRIGHT, CARROLL D.
1900   *The History and Growth of the United States Census.*
        Government Printing Office, Washington, D.C.

YOUNT JOHN T.
1967   *Bottle Collector's Handbook and Pricing Guide.* Ac-
        tion Printery, San Angelo, Texas.

EDWARD STASKI
DEPARTMENT OF SOCIOLOGY AND ANTHROPOLOGY
    CULTURAL RESOURCES MANAGEMENT DIVISION
NEW MEXICO STATE UNIVERSITY
LAS CRUCES, NEW MEXICO 88003

3
THE IRON COMRADE: MACHINE AGE TECHNOLOGY

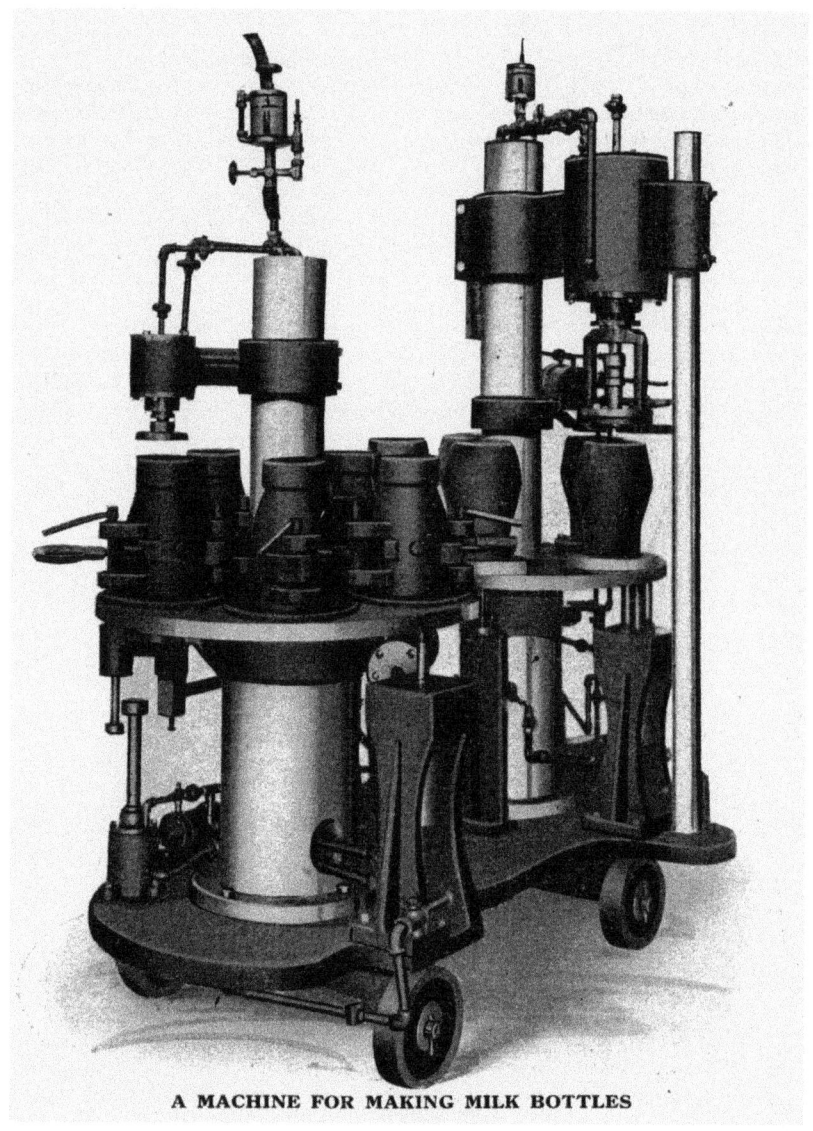

A MACHINE FOR MAKING MILK BOTTLES

When it is remembered that there are now nearly two hundred machines in successful operation in the United States, all of them making jars or wide and medium mouthed ware formerly blown exclusively by hand, the extent of the machine invasion of the bottle making craft will readily be understood by all fair minded observers. (1902, [untitled editorial note] *National Glass Budget* 18[14]:6.)

The Shirley-Johnson machines which were installed at the Heinz bottle works... are turning out excellent ware and the management of the factory is well pleased with their operation. The flint and green unions had a tilt over which would furnish men to operate the "iron comrades," the greens coming out second best. (1903, [untitled note on machines at Sharpsburg] *National Glass Budget* 18[37]:10.)

Articles

Machine-Made Glass Containers and the End of Production for Mouth-Blown Bottles
[**Reprint** from 1984, *Historical Archaeology* 18(2):83–96.]
George L. Miller and Catherine Sullivan

Dates for Suction Scarred Bottoms: Chronological Changes in Owens Machine-Made Bottles
[**Reprint** from 2012, *Northeast Historical Archaeology* 41:18–38.]
George L. Miller and Tony McNichol

Aspects of Bottle Machine Operations
[**Reprint** from 1928, *Glass Industry* 9(7):143–148.]
B. M. Pearson

Volume Variation of Bottled Foods
[**Reprint** from 1921, *Bulletin* 1009:1–20, U.S. Dept. of Agriculture, Washington, DC.]
H. Runkel and J. C. Munch

Displacement of Labor by Machinery in the Glass Industry
[**Reprint (two parts)** from 1927, *Glass Industry* 8(5):110–115; and 8(7):161–164. Originally published as 1927, *Monthly Labor Review* 24 (4): 1–13.]
U.S. Bureau of Labor Statistics

The Color Purple: Dating Solarized Amethyst Container Glass
[**Reprint** from 2006, *Historical Archaeology* 40(2):45–56.]
Bill Lockhart

Manganese, Glass Technology, and the Giant Hand, 1914–1918
Peter D. Schulz

Machine-Made Glass Containers and the End of Production for Mouth-Blown Bottles

George L. Miller and Catherine Sullivan

GEORGE L. MILLER
CATHERINE SULLIVAN

Machine-Made Glass Containers and the End of Production for Mouth-Blown Bottles.[1]

ABSTRACT

Between 1880 and 1920 a major revolution in the production of glass containers transformed the glass industry and launched an ancient craft into a modern "mechanized engineering activity" (Meigh 1960:25). The number of patents for and improvements of semi-automatic and automatic bottle blowing machines in this period is very confusing. This discussion is an attempt to outline these developments with an emphasis on their chronology and impact on bottle and jar production. Although this discussion is limited to containers, it should be borne in mind that similar mechanization was occurring in other branches of the glass industry.

Introduction

During the late 19th century, improvements in the finish portion of glass containers in combination with the development of convenient, reliable closures, helped increase the demand for glass commercial containers. Two very important closures were the crown top for bottles and the Phoenix cap for jars, both patented in 1892 (Lief 1965:17–20). During this same period, automatic canning and bottling machinery was being developed, along with better knowledge of sterilization and a wider availability of refrigeration (Hampe & Wittenberg 1964:115–21). All of these developments were part of a broad change in food consumption patterns and emerging brand-name products.

Statistics illustrating the impact of these developments on glass container demand and production for Canada and England are very limited; however, in the United States, container production increased 50 per cent between 1899 and 1904, that is, before the development of the fully automatic machine (Barnett 1926:70). From 1897 to 1905 the number of hand bottle-blowers in the United States increased from 6000 to 9000, which matches the 50 per cent increase in glass container production (Barnett 1926:71). By 1919 the amount of glass containers produced was 180 per cent higher than the number produced in 1904 (Barnett 1926:70, 89). The increasing market for glass containers helped provide the capital necessary for mechanization and the drive for its success.

All glass-blowing machines (semi-automatic and automatic) that have been successfully taken into production, have involved three separate molding steps. These involve a ring mold which shapes the finish, a parison or part-size mold to give initial shape to the hot glass, and a blow or full-size mold to form the container's final shape, size and any embossed letters or designs it might have. Machine production follows these steps:

1. A gob of molten glass enters the ring and parison mold and is forced by air pressure, suction, or a plunger to take the shape of the full-sized finish mold and that of the part-sized parison mold. The role of the parison mold is to distribute the glass into the shape needed for blowing the full-sized container.
2. With the finish ring mold still attached, the parison mold is removed. In some cases, the body of the parison is allowed to elongate.
3. The full-sized or blow mold is joined to the ring mold around the parison and the bottle is blown to full size by air pressure.

While both semi-automatic and automatic machines went through the above steps, there was a fundamental difference recognized by the glass industry. Semi-automatic machines were supplied with gobs of molten glass and operated by semi-skilled laborers. Fully automatic machines, on the other hand, gathered glass directly from the furnace and all processes in molding and blowing were independent of human labor. Semi-automatics were limited in their production capacity by the speed with which the worker could feed glass to the machine and run the machine through the molding sequence. Limited production capacity and the cost of labor led to the elimination of

[1]This article is reprinted by permission of Park Canada, Ottawa, Ontario k1A1G2, from *Research Bulletin* Number 171.

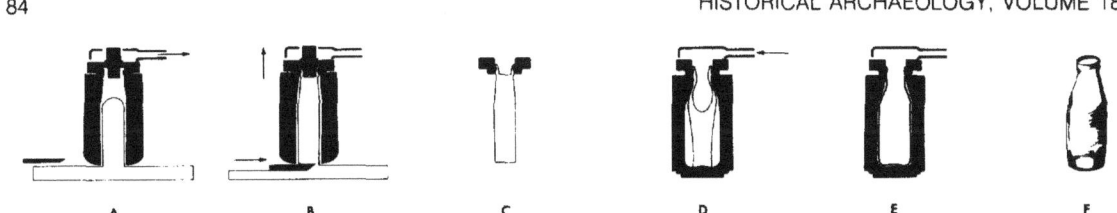

FIGURE 1. The Owens suction-and-blow process (*Drawing by S. Epps*). A. Gob sucked up into blank mold; B. Neck formed and gob sheared off at base; C. Blank (parison) shape with ring mold still attached; D. Blank shape transferred to full size mold; E. Final shape blown; F. Finished bottle

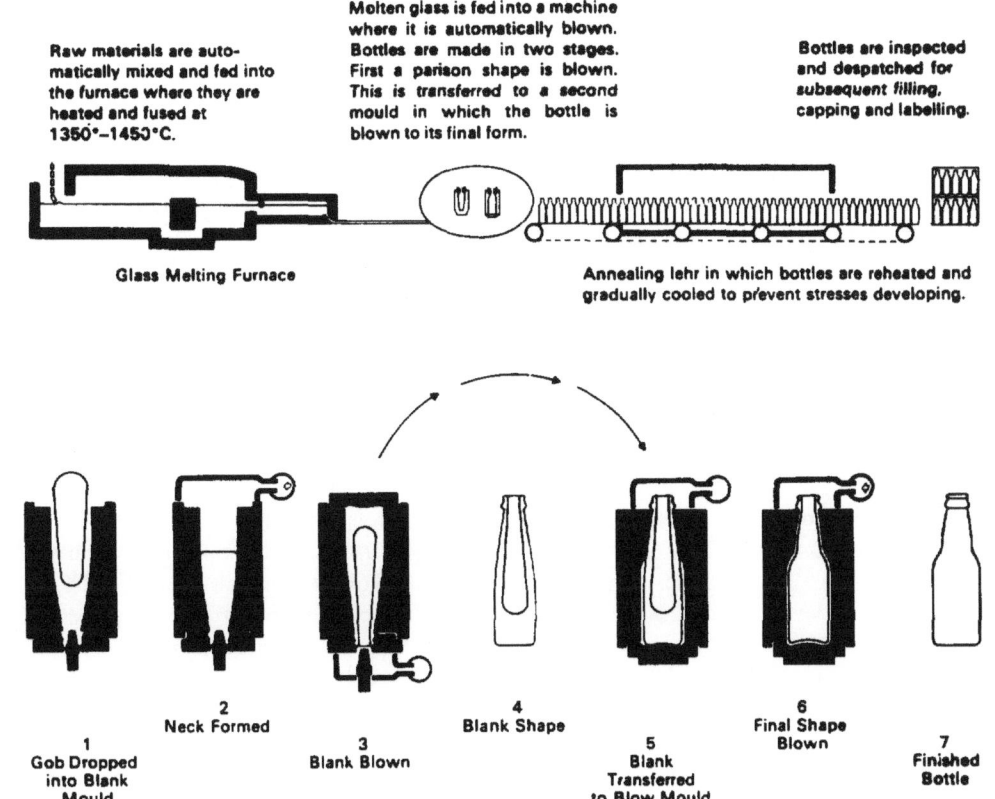

FIGURE 2. Blow-and-blow process (Published with permission of *Glass Manufacturers Federation 1973:25*).

semi-automatic machines in favor of the more productive automatic bottle-blowing machines.

In the hand-blowing process, the glass blower gathered a gob of molten glass on the blow pipe, shaped it and then blew it into shape with or without molds. After the vessel was fully blown, the bottle was disconnected from the blowpipe and then the neck was shaped. Because the mouth of the container was the last part completed, it became known as the finish. A major development

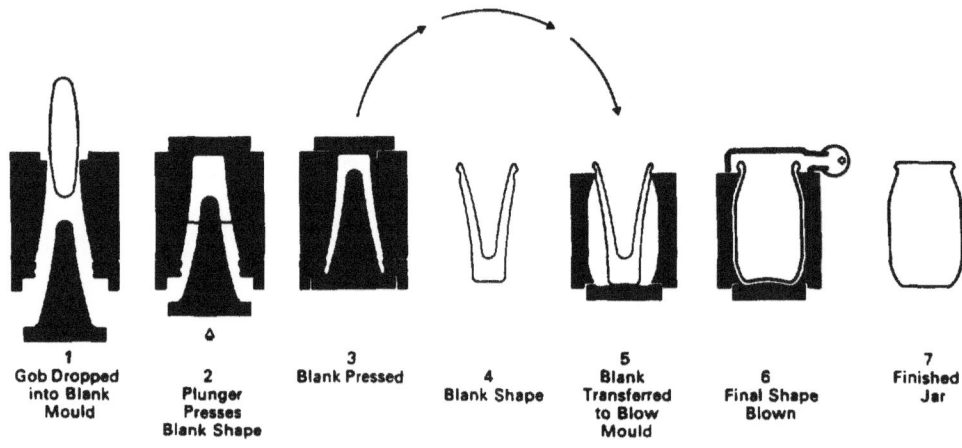

FIGURE 3. Press-and-blow process (*Glass Manufacturers Federation* 1973:25).

towards machine-made glass bottles was the recognition that the finish had to be the first part formed rather than the last. It is the finish that provides the momentary connection of the glass to the machine for blowing of the container. Two American patents, Gillender's in 1865 and Atterbury's in 1873, both described molding processes where the finish was formed as the first part of machine blowing; however, neither of these patents seems to have come into production (Barnett 1926:67).

Two semi-automatic blowing machines were developed in the 1880s—one, by Philip Arbogast, patented in 1881 in the United States, and the other, by Howard Ashley, patented in 1886 in England (Meigh 1960:26–27). Use of machines was limited by strong glass blowers' unions in their respective countries. Arbogast's machine established the principle of using a parison and a blow mold in a press-and-blow method which formed wide-mouthed containers. Use of his machine did not enter large scale production until 1893 when it was used in a non-union shop to make vaseline jars, and, later, fruit and other jars as well (Meigh 1960:27). The Ashley machine used a blow-and-blow process with a parison and full-sized mold to produce small-mouthed containers (Meigh 1960:28). Its successful application to mass production of containers did not take place until 1899 (Meigh 1960:27).

After the development of these prototypes, several other machines were developed in quick succession. These have been well described by Edward Meigh (1960) in "The development of the automatic glass bottle machine: a story of some pioneers." The 1890s was a period of revolution in glass technology; however, the new technology did not begin to cut down on the number of hand glass blowers until after 1905, because expanding demands for glass containers accommodated both the new technology and the old (Barnett 1926:71). This situation could not last forever.

In 1903 Michael Owens of the Libbey Glass Works in Toledo, Ohio, patented his fully automatic glass-blowing machine. He had been making a series of improvements towards machine-blown bottles since 1898 (Meigh 1960:29–31). The machine Owens developed was a major advance over the semi-automatic machines, and in 1903 The Owens Bottle Machine Company was organized with a capital of $3,000,000 to license rights to the machine to various glass companies for production of specific types of bottles (Walbridge 1920:67–68). By 1909 three other companies had taken up licences to use the machine and had put 46 machines into production (Scoville 1948:105, 115). Their success with the machine and further improvements by Owens increased the number of glass companies taking out licences. In the two years from September 1909 to September 1911, the number of Owens machines in production doubled from 51 to 103.

Between 1903 and 1923, Owens designed a series of 12 automatic bottle-blowing machines which increased productivity and expanded the types of containers that could be produced from three-ounce bottles to carboys (Meigh 1960:33). By 1917 half of the production of glass containers in the United States was done on Owens machines (Barnett 1926:88).

The spread of the Owens Bottle Machine to other countries was fairly rapid. In 1906 a licence from the Owens Company was issued to the Canadian Glass Manufacturing Company for a glass works in Hamilton, Ontario (King 1965:90). By 1914 there were 60 Owens machines in Europe (Barker 1968:317).

During the period when the Owens machine was being developed, semi-automatic machines were being improved and automatic feeding devices were being invented. These devices, such as the Brooke's continuous stream-feeding device and the Peiler Paddle Gob Feeder, transformed semi-automatics into automatic glass bottle-blowing machines (Meigh 1960:35–40). They were much simpler than Owens machines and much less costly to build and operate. The feeding devices took a small amount of glass to the machines, whereas the Owens device took the whole machine to the glass. Owens machines could weigh up to 120 tons and were raised and lowered by counterweights to suck up the molten glass (Walbridge 1920:93). Each arm of the Owens machine was dipped into a revolving circular tank furnace to suck glass up into the mold. Each mold-filling required the whole machine to move up and down (Figure 1). Some Owens machines had up to 15 arms and could produce 350 gross pint bottles in 24 hours, production equal to the output of 50 glass workers (Meigh 1960:33).

While the Owens machine was highly successful in large production runs, it was of limited use for short runs due to the necessity of shutting down the whole machine to change a mold on any one arm. As well, the larger the Owens machine, that is the greater the number of arms, the larger the revolving tank needed, which meant that fuel costs were higher for the more complex machines (Meigh 1960:34).

Rapid adoption of machines for manufacturing glass containers was a matter of economics. Semi-automatic and automatic glass bottle-blowing machines worked in two ways to lower the cost of glass container production. First, mechanization greatly increased the productivity of the workers making glass containers, and second, it eliminated the need for highly-skilled craftsmen. Prior to the development of bottle-blowing machines, glass blowers were very well paid, for their skills were essential to produce bottles and jars. Minimal skill was needed to operate semi-automatic machines, and the fully automatic machines almost completely replaced laborers.

In terms of productivity, the machines greatly increased output of containers per man-hour. Boris Stern's 1927 study of *Productivity of Labor in the Glass Industry* established that semi-automatic machines were between 42 and 171 per cent more productive per man-hour than hand production methods and that fully automatic machines were between 642 and 3806 per cent more productive than hand manufacture (1927:8). These ranges relate to the size of containers being produced and differences in the capacity of the various types of bottle-blowing machines.

The same study indicates that the labor cost per gross of bottles produced on the semi-automatics were from 23 to 52 per cent cheaper than hand-blown bottles. Labor costs per gross of bottles produced on fully automatic machines were between 90 and 97 per cent lower than hand-blown bottles (Stern 1927:8). Lower labor costs were of course offset by the capitalization necessary to acquire the machines.

Development of the Semi-Automatics into Automatic Bottle-Blowing Machines

Semi-automatic bottle-blowing machines which began development before the Owens machine had their significance eclipsed by the speed and efficiency of the Owens machine. The step needed to make the semi-automatic fully automatic was the development of automatic feeding devices. One of the earliest such devices to be successfully developed was the Brooke's stream feeder, patented in 1903 (Scoville 1948:182–83). Between 1911 and 1915 the Graham Glass Company adapted the stream feeder to their semi-automatic machine. When it became apparent that the Graham Glass Company had developed a workable automatic glass-blowing machine, the Owens company bought them out. However, attempts to further the production of this machine met with limited success (Scoville 1948:182–83). Brooke's feeder used a gravity flow of glass in a stream from the glass furnace. The flow was husbanded in a cup until the desired quantity was collected and it was then dumped into the mold. Cooling of the glass in the cup caused it to be stringy and often entrapped air blisters. These defects did not stop Hazel-Atlas from using a stream feeder to produce pressed jar lids (Meigh 1960:36).

The Hartford-Fairmont Feeding Devices

An engineering firm in Hartford, Connecticut, and a glass company in Fairmont, West Virginia, were incorporated in 1914 to develop an automatic feeding device to be used with semi-automatic bottle-blowing machines (Meigh 1960:36–37). The engineer who developed the feeding device was Karl E. Peiler, with an engineering background from the Massachusetts Institute of Technology rather than from the glass industry. The first successful feeder he developed used a fire clay paddle to push a gob of molten glass from the furnace onto a metal chute kept moist to create a cushion of stream for the gob to ride on into the mold (Meigh 1960:37–38). In 1915 this device was put into use for the production of milk bottles and Hartford-Fairmont began marketing it to other glass manufacturers.

The gob feeder was limited to the production of wide-mouth glass containers. To overcome this limitation, Peiler created an improved gob feeder, a Paddle-needle Feeder that came into production in 1918 (Meigh 1960:38). It had a lip on the tank furnace with a hole at its base, through which a plunger needle fed the glass. Success of Peiler's feeding devices led to their wide usage. In fact, the Owens Company entered into an agreement with Hartford-Fairmont and became a major lessee of gob feeders in 1924 (Meigh 1960:39). By 1925, in the United States, the gob feeders working with various glass bottle- and jar-blowing machines were producing approximately 8,500,000 gross of glass containers as compared to roughly 12,500,000 gross by the Owens machine (Scoville 1948:185).

Use of the gob feeders with bottle-blowing machines involved mechanical alignment of parison and blow molds, usually by means of one or two rotating tables. This complexity was simplified by the I.S. or Individual Section Machine developed by Henry Ingle of the Hartford Empire Company in 1925 (Meigh 1972:62). Instead of moving molds to the feeding device, the I.S. feeder had a bank of parison and blow molds in a straight line on a fixed-bed plate. Gobs of hot glass were delivered to each mold in sequence and any one section of the machine could be shut down to change the molds without stopping production in the other sections (Meigh 1972:62–64). This was a great advantage over other automatic machines and by 1960 there were 1250 I.S. machines in production (Meigh 1960:47).

Because the various machines with gob feeders were less expensive than the Owens machine and more versatile for small orders, they began to supersede the Owens machine during the 1920s. Sometime between 1927 and 1930, the number of glass containers produced on gob feeder machines surpassed the amount produced on the Owens machines (Meigh 1972:57). By 1947, in the United States, it is estimated that only 30 per cent of production was on the Owens machine while the gob feeders produced 67 per cent of the glass containers (Phillips 1947:188–89). Meigh estimates that over 90 per cent of world production of glass containers by the early 1970s was produced on gob feeder machinery (Meigh 1972:58). Whether any Owens machines are still in production today is not clear from the literature. In Canada the Owens machine stopped being used at Dominion Glass Company in about 1945.

Impact of the Machine-made Glass Container

The impact of automatic machine production of glass containers was extensive and rapid. Hand production of bottles and jars declined rapidly from the second decade of the 20th century. For archaeologists, two immediate questions come to mind: when did hand production stop, and what characteristics might be used to identify bottles from the various machines that came into production? Much broader than these questions is the impact of cheap glass containers on society.

The period of overlap for hand and machine production is fairly long. Types of bottles being blown by hand were continually being reduced as semi-automatic, automatic, and feeding device machines were developed. Barnett's *Chapters on Machinery and Labor* (1926) estimates the number of hand glass bottle-blowers working in the United States during the period when bottle-blowing machinery was being developed:

Year	No. of Blowers	Page Ref.
1896	6229	83
1897	6000	70
1905	9000	71
1917	2000	90
1924	1000	86

Declines in the number of bottle blowers were occurring at a time when glass container production was rapidly increasing. Once again, Barnett provides the statistics on container production used below:

Year	No. of Gross Produced	Page Ref.
1899	7,777,000	70
1904	11,942,000	89
1909	12,313,000	89
1914	19,288,000	89
1917	24,000,000 est.	89
1919	22,289,000	89
1924	18,000,000 est.	85

The drop in production reflected in the figures for 1919 and 1924 was caused by prohibition which began in 1919 in the United States. Rising glass container production from the beginning of the 20th century was of course related to increased use of semi-automatic and later fully automatic bottle-blowing machines: in 1900 there were 80 semi-automatic machines producing wide-mouthed glass containers; by 1904 when Owens machines came into production there were 200 semi-automatics in production and the number increased to a high of 459 in 1916 (Barnett 1926:69, 92). After that, the Owens machine and gob feeding devices adapted to existing machines cut into bottle production by semi-automatics. By 1924 there were only 72 semi-automatics in production (Barnett 1926:111). Impact of the automatics is reflected in a 1927 government study by Boris Stern, *Productivity of Labor in the Glass Industry*, which states that:

In 1926, out of 25 bottle plants inspected only one plant was found using the semi-automatic to a large extent. In another plant the semi-automatic was found standing by the furnace but dismantled and ready to be displaced by an automatic. In still another plant a semi-automatic machine had recently been consigned to the scrap heap (Stern 1927:35).

Adoption of Owens machines was retarded by the leasing system used by the Owens Company. In the 1905–06 period there were only eight Owens machines in production. By 1916–17 there were 200 in production (Barnett 1926:88). It was shortly after this period that the gob-feeding devices and the Individual Section Machine began making inroads on the market serviced by Owens machines. As mentioned earlier, by 1917 the Owens machine was producing half of the glass containers made in the United States. The other half was produced by 2000 hand blowers and 2000 operators of semi-automatic machines. According to Barnett, the 12,000,000 bottles produced by glass blowers and semi-automatic machine operators in 1917 was equal to the 12,000,000 bottles produced by 9000 glass blowers and 1000 semi-automatic machine operators in 1905 (Barnett 1926:88–89). Stated as mathematical equations, these figures come out as follows:

1905

9000 blowers' production + 1000 machine workers' production = 12,000,000 gross

1917
2000 blowers' production + 2000 machine workers' production = 12,000,000 gross

Assuming that productivity for blowers remained the same and solving the above equations gives the following results:

Hand-blown   Semi-automatic
1905 7,714,000 gross + 3,286,000 gross = 12,000,000 gross
1917 1,500,000 gross + 10,500,000 gross = 12,000,000 gross

Total 1917 production
1,500,000 gross by hand blown methods
10,500,000 gross by semi-automatics
12,000,000 gross by Owens machines

These figures are rather rough, but they suggest that hand-blown containers made up between 5 and 10 per cent of all the bottles and jars produced in the United States in 1917.

One of the myths about the Owens bottle-blowing machine is that it greatly lowered the cost of glass containers and thus expanded the demand for them. In reality, the price of bottles made on Owens machines fell only about 15 per cent from 1905 to 1914 (Barnett 1926:130). Thus, the cost of production was a marginal consideration in expanding the use of glass containers. More important was that machines could produce highly standardized, reliable finishes and sizes that could be used on the automatic machines that filled the containers. These developments combined to meet and change consumer demands for products put up in glass containers.

The types of bottles produced on the Owens machine were limited to those for which there was a fairly large demand. Stern's 1927 report sums up the machine-made bottle market as follows:

The principle advantage of the machine lies in mass production. The high cost of making the necessary number of molds and the time required in adjusting the machine and changing molds make it uneconomical for large machines to work on orders less than 1,000 gross of bottles. Even for the smaller six-arm machines the order has to be at least 250 gross to make production economical. Hence the smaller orders, especially those below 100 gross, necessarily go to the hand plants. Among bottles of this kind the principle place is occupied by perfumery and toilet ware, individually shaped bottles being used as a means of identifying and advertising their contents.

As a competitive factor in the bottle branch of the glass industry hand production is absolutely non existent. At best it fills the gaps left by the machine and must therefore be considered as supplementary to the machine rather than competitive (1927:55).

Some idea of just how costly the molds for the Owens machine were is given in B. E. Moody's *Packaging in Glass:*

A 'single' mould, i.e., the equipment required for one head on a machine, consists of at least nine separate parts, . . . and a complete set for a six-head machine could cost well over £1000. It is clearly vital that the bottle maker should be able to obtain a long working life from the moulds; a single mould may be capable of producing something like a million bottles before it has to be scrapped (1963:21).

The minimum number for an economical run of glass containers appears to have increased between 1927 and 1963 when Moody wrote his book. He states that:

We have seen above that it is not an economic proposition to run a bottle machine for short periods, and generally a run of about three days would be regarded as an absolute minimum. The output from a modern bottle machine might be in the region of 100 to 1200 gross per day, depending on the size of the bottle and size of machine, so the minimum number of bottles which can be made economically in a run is of the order of 1,000 gross (1963:20).

The economics of machine production changed the characteristics of bottles. Prior to machine domination of glass container production, the industry produced a wide variety of bottles and jars for small companies such as local breweries and soft drink bottlers. Through the use of plate molds, glass manufacturers made distinctive bottles for small pharmacies and medicine companies. These small-run orders were not compatible with machine production. Barnett summarizes the situation in 1926.

Many articles put up in glass containers have a small market and the orders of the makers of these articles are for only a small number of bottles. The Owens machine is an instrument of large scale production, and the manufacturers who were using the older methods of manufacture—hand and semi-automatic—were able, therefore, to hold the orders for small lots of special bottles. This advantage has been less important in recent years, as the small user of glass containers, in order to secure cheaper bottles, has become willing to use standard sizes and to rely on the label for his distinctive mark (1926:91).

Hand-blown tradition for commercial containers was still going on in 1934 for "small orders and oddly-shaped bottles" (Jerome 1934:106).

World War II further consolidated the standardization of glass containers when the American federal government, with the glass manufacturers, reduced the number of types and varieties of bottles to maximize production.

> Prior to the war, there were many odd shapes and sizes of bottles. War standardization, and elimination of small sizes, provided an increased output with the same production machinery. Janssen stated in 1946 that a return to the prewar pattern would cut output by 20% in grossage, or 40% in gallonage (Holscher 1953:375).

Hand-blowing of commercial containers in the United States probably was close to non-existent by World War II, and in the period between the World Wars it was limited to odd shaped containers, perfumery, toiletware and carboys.

Machine-made Glass Containers in England

Information for countries other than the United States is not as easy to locate. In England, according to Angus-Butterworth, mechanization of the glass industry was fairly complete by 1924 (Angus-Butterworth 1948:177–78). Mechanical production of glass containers in England began with the use of the Ashley semi-automatic machine in Castleford in 1887. Further modifications produced several models, one of which, the Plank machine, had 20 units in commercial operation by 1889. A semi-automatic jar machine was in production in the early 1890s, and before the end of the 19th century, three factories had put bottle machines into operation and a further three or four had used jar machines (Turner 1938:251–52).

Shortly after the Owens automatic bottle-blowing machine was developed in the United States, the Owens Company attempted to lease rights to it in Europe. Not finding a buyer, they formed the Owens European Bottle Machine Company and built a factory at Manchester, England, which was in production by 1907 (Meigh 1960:34). Successful demonstration of the machine's capabilities in the mass production of cheap glass containers convinced the European manufacturers to speedily form a cartel, the *Europaischer Verband der Flaschen-fabriken Gesellschaft* (E.V.), to purchase the European rights to the Owens machine for 12 million gold marks (Meigh 1960:34). The English part of the cartel was the British Association of Glass Bottle Manufacturers Ltd.

The E.V. cartel was interested in minimizing the impact of the Owens machine on glass production and union resistance to it. Therefore, they set goals of 10 per cent of glass container production for the first year with an increase of 5 per cent for the following two years of each country's production (Barker 1968:317). If they had continued to increase at the rate of 5 per cent a year, then 100 per cent automation would have occurred around 1925. Angus-Butterworth suggests that by 1924 the English glass container industry was under "fairly complete mechanization" (1948:177–78). Supporting this is Meigh's statement that the English glass container industry was fully automated by the early 1920s (1960:34). However, Meigh, writing in 1934, indicates that a small number of hand-blown bottles was being produced in England for "special bottles and those used in small quantities" (1934:123–24).

One of the English companies that continued hand production on a large scale was Beatson, Clark & Company Ltd., a large manufacturer of druggists' ware. Their production in 1929 was 98 per cent mouth-blown and 2 per cent semi-automatic, with an output of 1100 gross per week (Beatson, Clark & Co. Ltd. 1952:40). While this seems like a large production, it would be less than one per cent of the British glass container production which was over eight million gross in 1928 (Meigh 1960:43). In 1929 Beatson, Clark and Co. began building a glass works capable of fully automatic production and by 1949, 80 per cent of their production was fully automatic, 19 per cent semi-automatic and less than 1 per cent mouth-blown

(Beatson, Clark & Co. Ltd. 1952:30–40). As in the United States, it was the pharmaceutical and cosmetic bottles that were the last types to be mouth-blown.

Machine-made Glass Containers in Germany

For the rest of Europe, the history of the transition to machine-made glass is much more sketchy. Germany had the largest glass container production in Europe prior to the introduction of the Owens machine and was the major shareholder in the E.V. cartel formed in 1907 to purchase European rights to the Owens machine (Barker 1968:317). Before the Owens machine came on the scene, a very successful device known as the Schiller Semi-Automatic, a press-and-blow machine, was in 1906 put into commercial use in Germany. Between 1906 and 1932, it is claimed, 1150 Schiller Semi-Automatic bottle-making machines were installed throughout Europe, 223 of them in Germany itself (Turner 1938:257).

The first Owens fully-automatic bottle-blowing machine was installed in Germany in 1907, the year the E.V. cartel was formed (Turner 1938:58). As mentioned earlier, the E.V. cartel attempted to minimize the impact of the Owens machine by limiting its production to 10 per cent of the glass containers for the year of introduction with 5 per cent increases for the following two years. If this schedule were followed by Germany, then roughly 40 per cent of German bottle production by 1914 would have been made on fully-automatic machines. In 1914, half of the 60 Owens machines authorized by the E.V. cartel were in Germany (Barker 1968:317), a higher proportion than the original agreed-upon distribution of machines based on pre-machine production for each country in the cartel. This suggests that Germany may have been ahead of England in the proportion of Owens machine-made bottles being produced. What happened to the German glass industry during World War I is not clear, and it is difficult to say when mouth-blown bottle production ended in Germany.

Machine-made Glass Containers in France

Prior to the introduction of Owens machines into Europe, the French production of glass containers almost equalled English production, making France the third largest European producer of such wares (Barker 1968:317). Like manufacturers in the United States, England, and Germany, the French had developed a successful semi-automatic bottle machine. Claude Boucher began developing his machine in 1894 and was successful by 1897 (Turner 1938:253). According to Henrivaux, the Boucher bottle machine was used in countries other than France, and he estimates world-wide production by this machine to have been in excess of 200,000 bottles in 1909 (Henrivaux 1909:395). Unfortunately, figures are not given for French production of machine-made vs. hand-made glass containers.

French glass manufacturers joined the E.V. cartel in 1907 and then withdrew from the agreement (Barker 1968:317). How long they remained outside the cartel is not clear; however, the first Owens machine was installed in France in 1910, following installations in England, Germany, Holland, Austria, and Sweden (Turner 1938:258). How fast the French industry converted to mechanized bottle production is not clear from the literature consulted.

Machine-made Glass Containers in Canada

Information on the transition of the Canadian glass industry from a craft to an automated industrial activity is very limited. For example, the available literature provides little information on the introduction of semi-automatic bottle machines into the Canadian market and no quantitative information on their output. The dramatic technological developments in the United States probably entered Canada much faster than England, due to physical proximity, the constant flow of information carried by glass workers moving between Canada and the U.S., and contact between the unions involved in setting wages in both countries.

For example, one of the early manufacturers of semi-automatic machines was Frank O'Neill (of Toledo, Ohio) who had one of his jar-lid power presses operating in Ontario by around 1901 (Scoville 1948:333 n42). Newspapers from Wallaceburg, Ontario, for 24 September, 1903, report fruit jar-making machines at the Sydenham Glass Works but unfortunately do not mention the type of machine being used (Stevens 1967:29). Among the types of semi-automatic machines documented in use in Canada are the O'Neill, Teeple-Johnson, Olean, and Lynch machines (Stevens 1967:20, 21, 54, 55, 88, 90, 91; King 1965:89; Meigh 1960:40). The relationship of Frank O'Neill with the Canadian glass manufacturers appears to have been fairly significant. After selling his United States interests in the O'Neill Machine Company in Toledo in 1912, he set up the O'Neill European Machine Company factory in Montreal (Meigh 1960:40). How much impact the semi-automatic machines had on hand-blown production of glass containers and how rapidly they spread in Canada is not documented in the literature.

Information on the introduction of the Owens machine to Canada is better documented, due to the leasing structure set up by the Owens Company, and, no doubt, also because of the great costs involved. Rights to the Owens automatic machine for Canada were secured before the European rights were leased. In 1906, for $104,900, the Canadian Glass Manufacturing Company purchased exclusive Canadian container rights on the Owens bottle machine (Scoville 1948:141, Table 14). This company was established specifically to lease Owens machines to operating glass plants in Canada. One of the prime movers in the company was George A. Grier who had acquired control of the Diamond Glass Company and changed its name to Diamond Flint Glass Company (King 1965:90). The first Owens machines in Canada were set up in the Hamilton Glass Works in 1906 (Stevens 1967:9–10).

Control of container rights for the Owens machines was instrumental in the amalgamation of Diamond Flint Glass, Sydenham Glass Company, and the Canadian Glass Company into the Dominion Glass Company in 1913 (King 1965:90). This was the dominant Canadian glass company until the founding of Consumers Glass Company in 1917 (Stevens 1967:54–55). By that time the feed-and-flow devices discussed earlier were being adapted to semi-automatics, such as the O'Neill, Hartford, and Lynch machines, which made them competitive with the Owens machine, and they were a great deal cheaper (Meigh 1960:39).

How long it took bottle-blowing machines to replace bottle blowers in Canada is not well documented. Because the Dominion Glass Company had a practical monopoly on glass production in Canada, it was not a case of hand factories competing against mechanized factories. When Dominion Glass built its new glassworks in Redcliff, Alberta, in 1913, the company combined production on the Owens machine with hand-blown shops. In 1915 the Redcliff operation had an Owens ten-arm machine, a lamp chimney machine, and three bottle shops in operation (Stevens 1967:69). The bottle shops would have produced orders that were too small for production on the Owens machine. Most likely these included such types as pharmaceutical bottles, cosmetic wares and probably demijohns. By the mid-1920s the amount of glassware being hand-blown in Canada was very small, as was the case in the United States and England. Gerald Stevens describes the declining role of glass blowers at the Redcliff plant in the 1930s:

Mechanization was to take its toll. A jurisdictional issue arose in 1937 and the last of the glass blowers declared a lengthy strike. Eventually, they returned to work, "but things were never the same. Their time had run out and they and their skills and songs are gone." (Stevens 1967:69–70).

According to E. G. Davis, manager of the Dominion Glass Works plant at Wallaceburg, Ontario, there were no glass blowers employed in Canadian glass factories in 1959 and the last hand-blowing operation at the Wallaceburg works was in about 1942 (Stevens 1967:91).

The Owens machine in Canada began being replaced by the Individual Section Machine in the 1940s (King 1965:91).

Discussion and Chronological Summary

For the purposes of archaeology, the machine-made bottle provides an excellent, readily-identifiable time marker. Because all semi-automatic and automatic bottle-blowing machines work on the principle of forming the finish first as an attachment to the blowing machine, and the use of a parison mold followed by a full-size mold, identification of the differences between bottles made on the various machines is limited. The major exception to this is the Owens scar.

Characteristics of Machine-made Bottle Manufacture

1. A large number of mold seams, particularly related to the finish.
2. Finish seams:—horizontal mold seam encircling the neck-finish junction. This seam must appear with other machine-made characteristics; an 1860 patent for hand-blown bottles features this seam (Toulouse 1969:584).—1 or 2 horizontal mold seams around the top of the finish or lip caused by a neck-shaping plug and a collar to guide it. On beer and beverage bottles these seams have sometimes been fire-polished off, so other evidence must be sought.—continuous vertical mold seams up the side of the body and over the finish (Figures 4 and 6).
3. Body seams:—wandering vertical "ghost" mold seams on the body of the container, left by the parison mold halves, which join the full-sized mold seams at the finish. A "ghost" seam is certain proof of machine manufacture (Toulouse 1969:585) (Figure 5).
4. Base:—either cup or post bottom mold seams can appear on machine-made bottles and should not be confused with the mouth-blown versions.
    —Owens scar, a distinctive, circular mark with "feathery" edges, caused by the shears that cut off the gob of glass in the suction

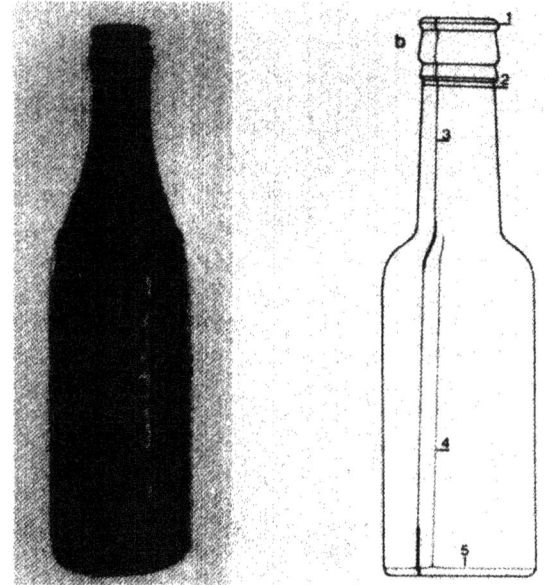

FIGURE 4. *a & b.* Two bottles showing typical machine-produced mold seams, including on *b* a "ghost" seam from the parison mold on the body (*Photo by R. Chan; Drawing by D. Kappler*).

machines. An Owens scar is usually off-center and may sometimes even extend onto the heel. It dates from 1904 until at least 1969 (Toulouse 1969:582) (Figure 8).
    —valve mark. A non-symmetrical indented groove on the base, found on wide-mouthed containers and milk bottles. 1930s into 1950s (Toulouse 1969:583) (Figure 7).
    —"ghost" seam from the base part of the parison mold.

The main difference between semi-automatic and automatic machines was the degree of mechanization and thus the rate of production, not the appearance of the container. Bottles produced by either method should look the same and have similar "typical" seams and evidence of manufacture.

Roughly speaking, the chronology of mechanization for production of glass containers is as follows:

FIGURE 5. Close-up view of a wandering "ghost" mold seam on the body of a container (*Photo by R. Chan*).

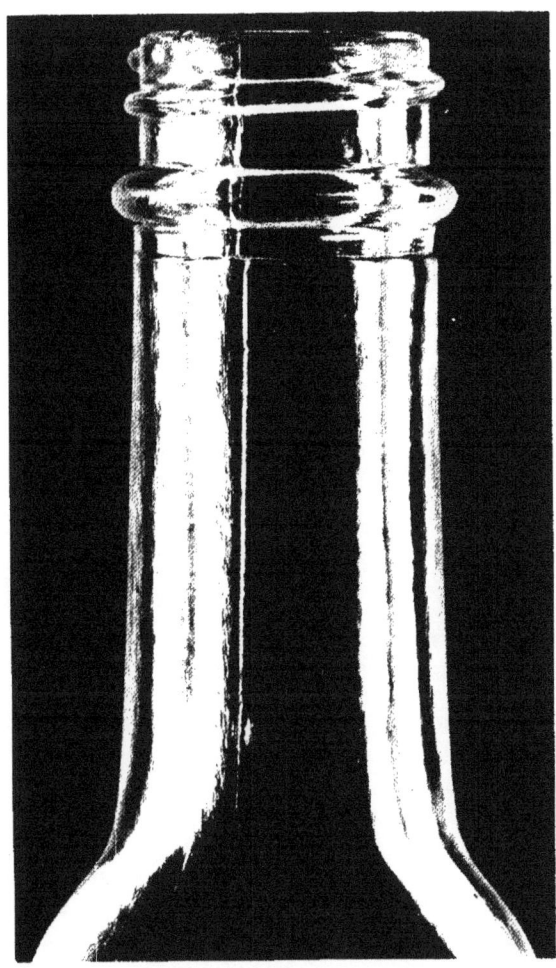

FIGURE 6. Close-up view of a container finish, showing the large number of seams left by the mold parts (*Photo by R. Chan*).

A. Semi-automatic machines for wide-mouthed containers: commercial production begins 1893, peak ca. 1917, end ca. 1926.

B. Semi-automatic machines for production of narrow-mouthed containers: commercial production begins 1889, peak ca. 1917, end ca. 1926.

C. Fully-automatic production on the Owens machine for narrow- and wide-mouth containers: commercial production begins 1904; by 1917 they were producing half of the bottles in the United States; began being replaced by feeders in the 1920s; end of production around the late 1940s or early 1950s.

D. Semi-automatic made automatic by flow-and-feed devices: introduced in 1917, continued to grow in importance and offered an inexpensive alternative to the Owens machine.

E. The Individual Section Machine: developed in 1925; by the 1940s this had become the machine most commonly used in producing bottles.

Hand-blown bottles, as discussed earlier, lasted into the 1930s but only for small run types such as pharmaceutical bottles, cosmetic wares and demijohns. Their quantities would be very small in any post-1920 archaeological assemblage.

REFERENCES

ARGUS-BUTTERWORTH, L. M.
  1948 *The Manufacture of Glass.* Pitman Publishing Corporation, New York.

BARKER, T. C.
  1968 The Glass Industry. In *The Development of British Industry and Foreign Competition: 1874–1914, Studies in Industrial Enterprise,* edited by Derek H. Aldocroft, pp. 307–25. University of Toronto Press, Toronto.

BARNETT, GEORGE E.
  1926 *Chapters on Machinery and Labor.* Harvard University Press, Cambridge.

BEATSON, CLARK & CO. LTD.
  1952 *The Glass Works Rotherham: 1751–1951.* Beatson, Clark & Co. Ltd., Rotherham, England.

THE GLASS MANUFACTURERS FEDERATION
  1973 *Making Glass.* Glass Manufacturers Federation, London.

FIGURE 7. Owens suction scar caused by shearing the glass when the mold is full. The shears leave a cooled glass surface, creating a scar from the cutting action; *a* also shows the base and heel mold seams from the parison mold (*Drawing by D. Kappler; Photo by R. Chan*).

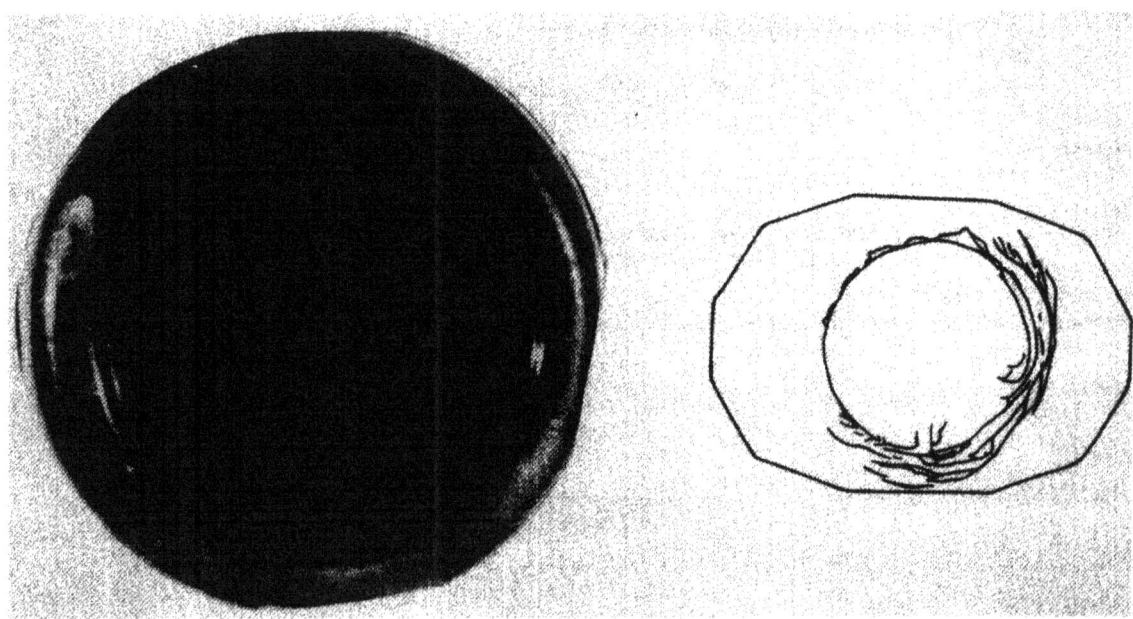

FIGURE 8. Valve mark on a bottle base. Toulouse (1969:583) says that this mark is caused by a valve that ejects the parison out of the mold so that it can be transferred to the blow mold for completion (*Photo by R. Chan*).

HAMPE, EDWARD C., JR., AND MERLE WITTENBERG
1964 *The Lifeline of America: Development of the Food Industry.* McGraw-Hill Book Company, New York.

HENRIVAUX, JULES
1909 Fabrication mecanique des bouteilles. *La Nature* 37:392–95.

HOLSCHER, H. H.
1953 Feeding and Forming. In *Handbook of Glass Manufacture: A Book of Reference for the Plant Executive, Technologist and Engineer,* compiled and edited by Fay V. Tooley, pp. 299–388. Ogden Publishing Co., New York.

JEROME, HARRY
1934 *Mechanization in Industry.* National Bureau of Economic Research, New York.

KING, THOMAS B.
1965 History of the Canadian Glass Industry. *Journal of the Canadian Ceramic Society* 34:86–91.
1977 19th century Bottle Moulds. *Glasfax 10th Anniversary Seminar, June 11, 1977,* pp. 53–59. Montreal.

LIEF, ALFRED
1965 *A Close-up of Closures: History and Progress.* Glass Containers Manufacturers Institute, New York.

MEIGH, EDWARD
1934 Notes on the Design of Glass Bottles. *Journal of the Society of Glass Technology* 18:122–127.
1960 The Development of the Automatic Glass Bottle Machine: A Story of Some Pioneers. *Glass Technology* 1:25–50.
1972 *The Story of the Glass Bottle.* C. E. Ramsden & Co. Ltd., Stoke-on-Trent, England.

MOODY, E. B.
1963 *Packaging in Glass.* Hutchinson, London.

PHILLIPS, C. J.
1947 *Glass the Miracle Maker: Its History, Technology and Applications.* Pitman Publishing, New York.

SCOVILLE, WARREN C.
1948 *Revolution in Glassmaking: Enterpreneurship and Technological Change in the American Industry 1880–1920.* Harvard University Press, Cambridge.

STERN, BORIS
1927 *Productivity of Labor in the Glass Industry.* Bulletin of the United States Bureau of Labor Statistics No. 441. Government Printing Office, Washington, D.C.

STEVENS, GERALD
1961 *Early Canadian Glass.* McGraw-Hill, Ryerson, Toronto.
1967 *Canadian Glass: c. 1825–1925.* Ryerson Press, Toronto.

TOOLEY, FAY V. (COMPILER AND EDITOR)
1953 *Handbook of Glass Manufacture: A Book of References for the Plant Executive, Technologist and Engineer.* Ogden Publishing Co., New York.

TOULOUSE, JULIAN HARRISON
1967 When did hand bottle blowing stop? *The Western Collector* 5 (8):41–45.
1969 A Primer on Mold Seams. *The Western Collector* 7 (12):578–587.

TURNER, W. E. S.
1938 The early Development of Bottle Making Machines in Europe. *Journal of the Society of Glass Technology.* 22:250–58.

WALBRIDGE, WILLIAM S.
1920 *American Bottles Old & New: A Story of the Industry in the United States.* The Owens Bottle Company, Toledo.

GEORGE L. MILLER
SENIOR LABORATORY ANALYST
OFFICE OF EXCAVATION AND CONSERVATION
COLONIAL WILLIAMSBURG FOUNDATION
WILLIAMSBURG, VIRGINIA 23185

CATHERINE SULLIVAN
1600 LIVERPOOL COURT
PARKS CANADA
OTTAWA, ONTARIO K1A 1G2

Dates for Suction Scarred Bottoms: Chronological Changes in Owens Machine-Made Bottles

George L. Miller and Tony McNichol

Dates for Suction Scarred Bottoms: A Chronology for Early Owens Machine-Made Bottles

George L. Miller and Tony McNichol

For much of the 20th century the Owens automatic bottle-blowing machines were used to produce glass containers around the world. This machine and others revolutionized glass production and led to the end of hand production of commercial glass containers. Bottles produced on the Owens machines have distinct suction scars on their bases that make them easy to identify. Because of the way the rights to the Owens machines were licensed, these licenses have a great potential to establish the dates when the production of major categories of glass containers on the Owens bottle-blowing machine began. The first lease for the use of the Owens machine was issued in 1904, followed by a number of leases issued in 1905 and a few subsequent years. Thus 1905 is a good terminus post quem for suction-scarred glass containers. The last Owens bottle-blowing machine went out of production in 1982.

Les machines automatiques de type Owens pour la production mécanique de verre soufflé ont été utilisées pour la production de contenants de verre partout au monde. Ces machines, de même que d'autres modèles, ont révolutionné la production de verre et ont mené à la fin de la production manuelle de contenants commerciaux en verre. Les bouteilles produites par la machine de type Owens sont facilement identifiables grâce à leur marque de succion distincte sous la base. Les modalités de la licence pour l'utilisation de la machine Owens offrent un excellent potentiel pour mieux comprendre la date de production des catégories principales de contenants de verre produits par cette machine. Le premier bail pour l'usage de la machine Owens a été octroyé en 1904 suivi de plusieurs autres pendant quelques années dès1905. On peut donc considérer l'année 1905 comme le début de la production de contenants de verre portant une marque de succion. La dernière machine Owens a cessé sa production en 1982.

Introduction

The Owens bottle-blowing machine was one of a series of inventions by Michael Owens that included semiautomatic machines for blowing light bulbs, patented in 1894 (Scoville 1948: 152). This machine was modified so that it could also blow tumblers and lamp chimneys. Experimentation toward these developments had two key elements. One was the fertile mind of Michael Owens, a practical glass man who began as a boy laborer in the glass industry in West Virginia, advanced to being a glassblower, and became the manager of the Libbey Glass Company of Toledo, Ohio. The other factor was the patronage and backing of Edward Drummond Libbey, who was the owner and main stockholder of the Libbey Glass Company (Scoville 1948: 95–97). Mr. Libbey had inherited the New England Glass Works from his father and in 1888 had shut it down and moved his company to Toledo to take advantage of newly discovered natural gas wells that cut the fuel costs for the production of glass (Paquette 1994: 15).

The Libbey Glass Company and its predecessor, the New England Glass Company, had a long history as manufacturers of table glass, but they did not have experience in the production of container glass. After the Libbey Glass Company was established in Toledo, Ohio, it was approached by the Corning Glass Works in Corning, New York, to fulfill a contract for light bulbs for the Edison General Electric Company. The production of light bulbs at Corning had been interrupted by a labor strike in 1890 (Paquette 1994: 24). To undertake this contract, Libbey Glass Company leased a closed glass factory and put Michael Owens in charge of producing the light bulbs.

While overseeing the light bulb production Owens invented and patented a machine for the blowing of light bulbs. That machine was later modified to blow tumblers and lamp chimneys (Scoville 1948: 152). This invention and the potential for further developments caused Edward D. Libbey to express an interest in expanding into the area of glassblowing machines. However, some of the other investors and members of Libbey Glass Company were leery of expanding into that area. Part of the problem was that Michael

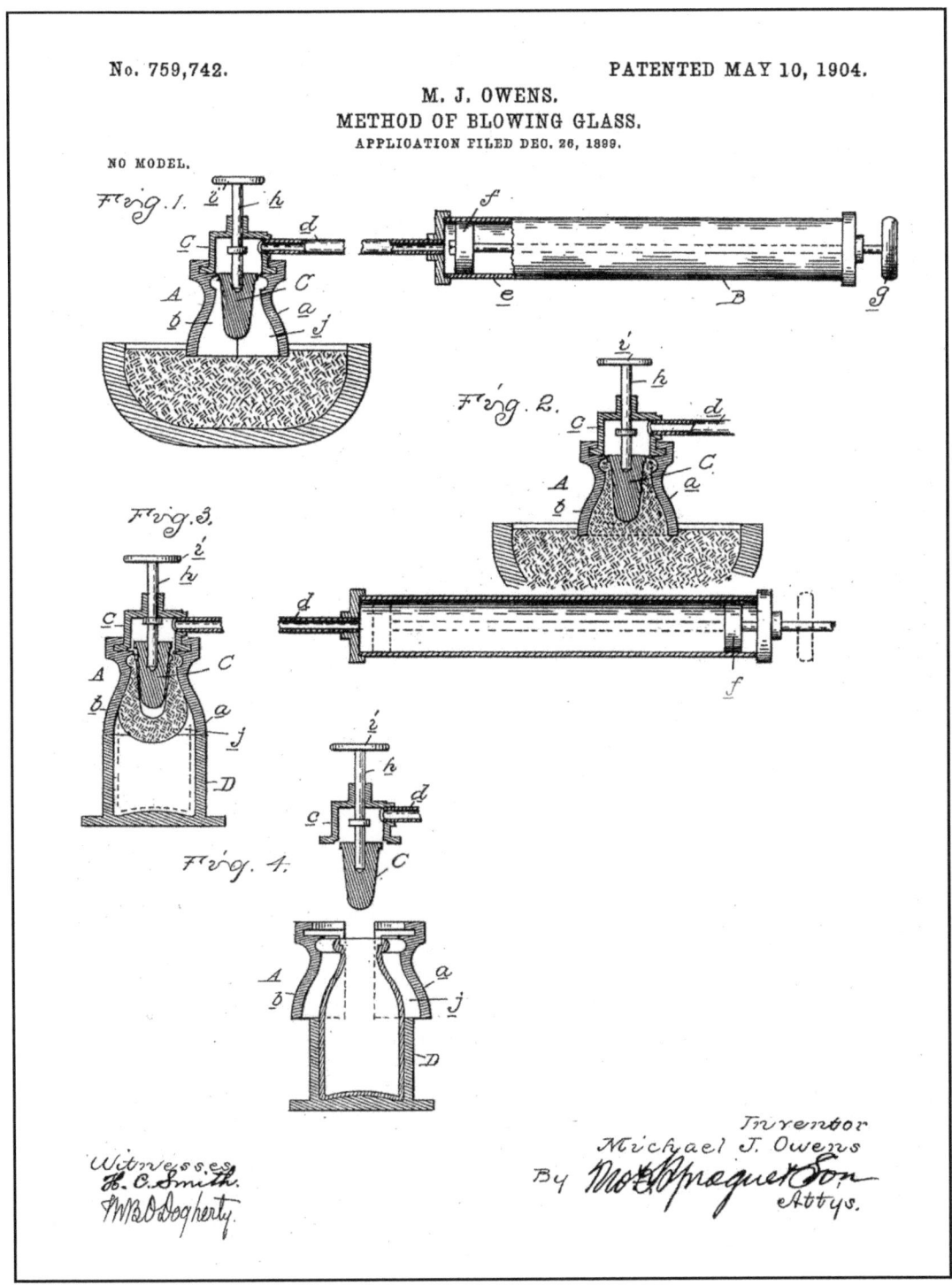

No. 759,742.

PATENTED MAY 10, 1904.

M. J. OWENS.
METHOD OF BLOWING GLASS.
APPLICATION FILED DEC. 26, 1899.

NO MODEL.

Figure 1. Handheld vacuum-pump machine, patent No. 759,742. The pump sucked up the molten glass into the upper half of the mold when the pump handle was pulled. When the upper half of the mold was full, it was carried to the bottom half of the mold and the handle was pushed in to blow the bottle. (Owens 1899)

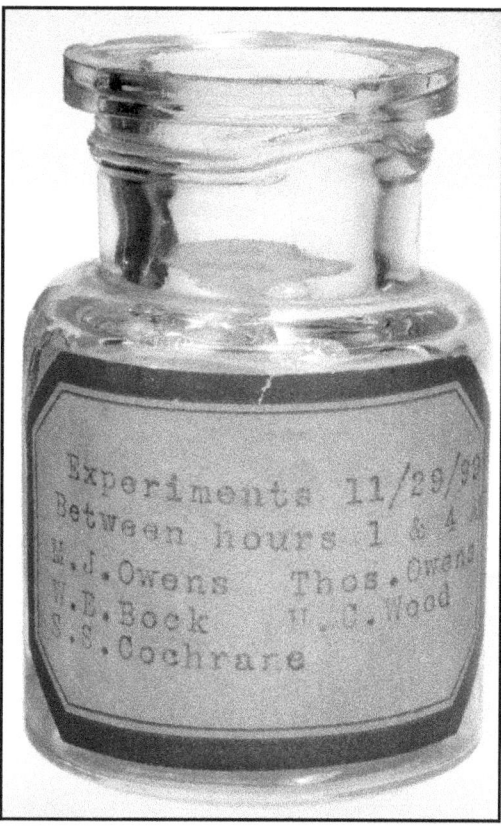

Figure 2. Photo of a bottle blown on the handheld pump machine. The paper label is dated "11/29/1899" (Floyd, Bowers, and Brownlee 2006). (Photo courtesy of the Owens-Illinois, Inc. Archives, MSS-200, Ward M. Canaday Center for Special Collections, University of Toledo.)

Owens was not an easy man to get along with and was rather gruff in dealing with those around him. While Michael Owens had a great understanding of working with glass and was visionary in terms of the mechanics of production, he was dependent on engineers and draftsmen to execute his ideas and on financial backing from Libbey to fund his experimentation and the development of the bottle-blowing machine (Paquette 1994: 21–26). Several of the more conservative partners in the Libbey Glass Company did not want to be involved with Michael Owens, nor did they want to take the risk of developing machines to produce glass containers (Scoville 1948: 279–281). Part of this reluctance may have been because, by this time, a number of semiautomatic machines had been developed and were already producing glass containers.

This led Edward D. Libbey, Michael Owens, and three other investors to establish the Toledo Glass Company in 1895 to follow up on the inventions of Michael Owens (Scoville 1948: 282–283; Paquette 1994: 31). The Toledo Glass Company built a factory with a 14-pot furnace and several machines for making tumblers. In 1897 the exclusive use of the tumbler machines in America was licensed to the Rochester Tumbler Company (Scoville 1948: 97–98). Later the Macbeth-Evans Glass Company purchased the rights to make lamp chimneys on the Owens machine (Paquette 1994: 31). Capital gained from the licensing of the production rights to tumblers and lamp chimneys, plus the investments made by Libbey and the other partners, enabled Michael Owens, the draftsmen, and an engineer the time needed to proceed with the development of bottle-blowing machines.

The first bottle-blowing machine Owens produced was submitted to the U.S. Patent Office in December of 1899, but the patent was not granted until May of 1904 (United States Patent Office 1904). This device was a handheld machine that used a long cylindrical pump to suck molten glass into the upper half of a bottle mold. When the half mold was filled with the hot glass it was hand carried to the bottom half of the mold. Once the two parts were connected the hand pump was reversed to blow the bottle (FIG. 1).

William Walbridge's book on American bottles illustrates a couple of small widemouthed jars blown on this handheld suction machine (Walbridge 1920: 61). One of the completed jars blown on this hand-pump machine is now in the Ward M. Canaday Center for Special Collections at the University of Toledo. A paper label on the jar reads: "Experiments 11/29/99 Between hours 1 & 4." The label goes on to list M. J. Owens, Thomas Owens, W. E. Bock, H.C. Wood, and S. S. Cochrane as witnesses to the production of the jars (FIG. 2). This handheld semiautomatic machine illustrated the principles and encouraged the further research that led to the fully automatic Owens bottle-blowing machines.

After establishing that a bottle could be made with the handheld suction device, the devise was mounted on a column on a three-wheeled cart that could be moved into the glass furnace to make the gather and then pulled back for completion of the bottle. This second machine is also illustrated in Walbridge (1920: 60) (FIG. 3). While it was still semiautomatic, the principle had been established for production of bottles by the suction process. An English patent for the second machine was applied for in 1902 and granted 18 December 1903 (Toledo Glass Company of Ohio 1903). The amended patent has a header that reads: "Reprinted as amended in accordance with the decisions of the Comptroller General dated the 10th day August 1903, and the Law Office dated 18th day of November 1903." One of the added sections of this amended patent reads:

> I am aware that the use of suction to pick up measured quantities of molten glass from a pool into a ladle or tool is not new, and that the use of suction for the purpose of removing air from the ends or portions of moulds so as to enable glass which has been poured into the moulds to penetrate into small parts or extremities is also old, and I make no claim to any such use of the process of suction. (Toledo Glass Company of Ohio 1903:7)

A device called a "tallyho" or "sucker-upper" was used in the Libbey Glass Company to consistently gather a given quantity of glass for tableware production (Scoville 1948: 327). Given that Michael Owens was a manager of this plant, he would have been familiar with this device and that may have been where he picked up the idea of gathering glass by suction to make bottles. The American patent on this machine was filed on 13 April 1903; Michael Owens filed a patent application for the first fully automatic bottle-blowing machine. It does not have the disclaimer on the previous use of suction devices to gather glass. That patent (No. 766,768) was granted on 2 August 1904 (Owens 1903) (FIG. 4). In September of 1903, Libbey, Owens, and others incorporated the Owens Bottle Machine Company to manufacture and license the newly developed automatic bottle-blowing machine (Scoville 1948: 101). It was the first and only automatic bottle-blowing machine at the time (Turner 1938: 257–258). The semiautomatic bottle-blowing machines then in use were limited to producing widemouthed jars, mostly fruit canning jars and packers' ware. The early semiautomatic machines used the press-and-blow process that did not work well with narrow-neck bottles (Miller and Sullivan 1991: 101).

Figure 3. The second Owens bottle-blowing machine, which is the vacuum pump mounted on a three-wheel carriage—still a semiautomatic machine (Floyd, Bowers, and Brownlee 2006). (Photo courtesy of the Owens-Illinois, Inc. Archives, MSS-200 in the Ward M. Canaday Center for Special Collections, University of Toledo.)

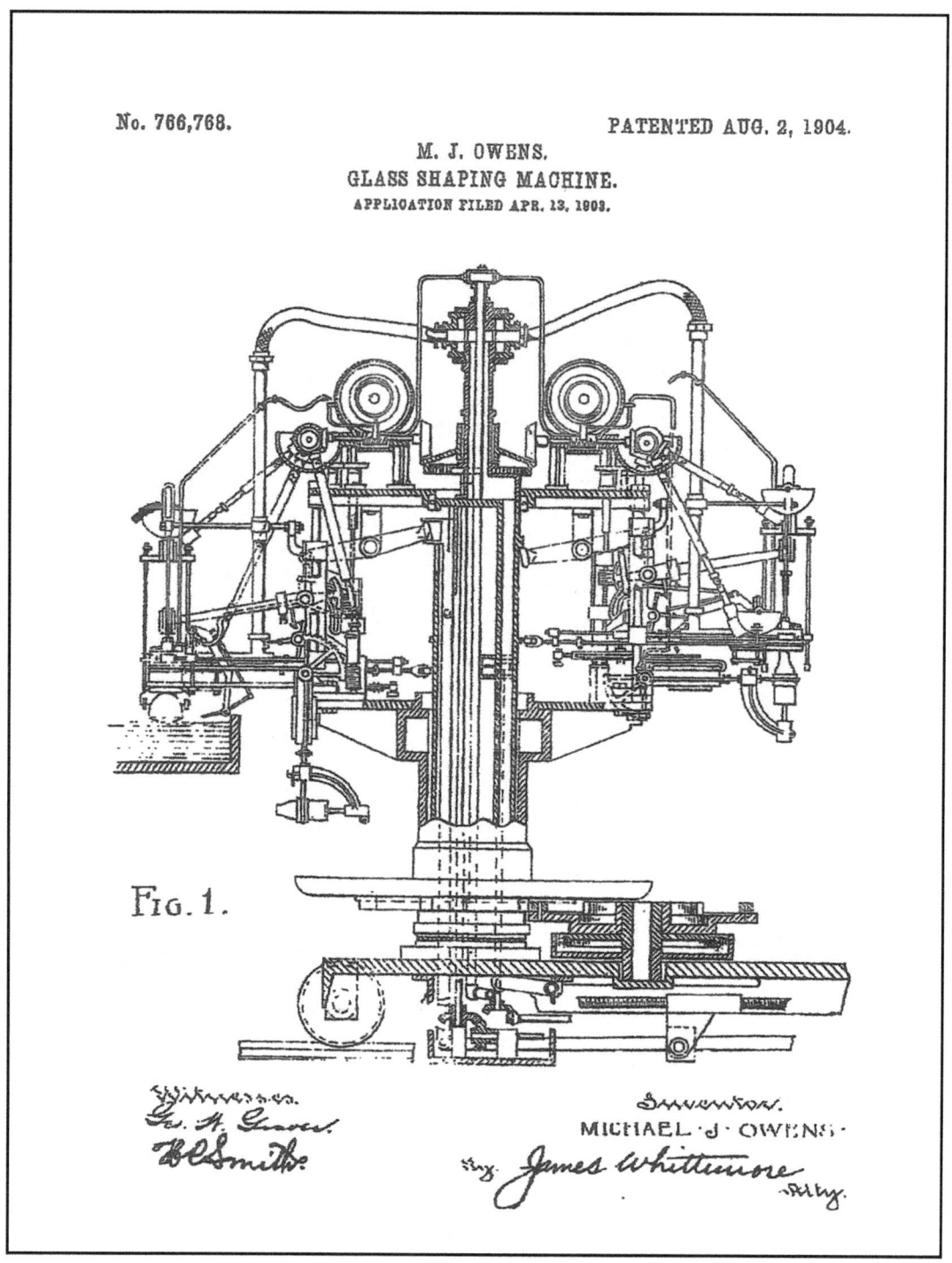

No. 766,768.   PATENTED AUG. 2, 1904.

M. J. OWENS,

GLASS SHAPING MACHINE.

APPLICATION FILED APR. 13, 1903.

Fig. 1.

Witnesses.   *Inventor.*

MICHAEL·J·OWENS·

James Whittemore

Figure 4. The first fully automatic Owens bottle-blowing machine, patent No. 766,768 granted 2 August 1904. Notice the blank mold on the left side of the machine resting on the surface of the molten glass in position to fill the mold and the blow mold below it. On the right side of the machine, the blow mold has been drawn up to replace the blank mold after the machine has rotated. (Owens 1903).

Northeast Historical Archaeology/Vol. 41, 2012 23

Figure 5. Photograph of Michael Owens holding a bottle taken hot off an Owens bottle-blowing machine (Floyd, Bowers, and Brownlee 2006). (Photo courtesy of the Owens-Illinois, Inc. Archives, MSS-200 in the Ward M. Canaday Center for Special Collections, University of Toledo.)

The Owens machine could produce narrow- and widemouthed bottles and jars, and because it was not dependent on skilled glassworkers to fill its molds, it had a much higher rate of production than was possible on the handfed semiautomatic machines (FIG. 5). When the Owens Bottle Machine Company was organized in 1903, the owners had limited capital and planned to maintain a demonstration plant in Toledo and to issue exclusive licenses to different glass manufacturers to produce limited ranges of bottle types on the Owens machine. Manufacturers that leased an Owens bottle machine would be given the exclusive license to produce a given type of bottle on that machine. In addition to the licensing fee, the companies receiving the lease would pay royalties equal to half the amount saved over the cost of hand production of the bottles they produced (Scoville 1948: 107). In August of 1903, Frank M. Gessner from the *National Glass Budget* visited the Toledo Glass Company plant as part of a demonstration of the Owens automatic bottle-blowing machine. His description of the machine, its advantages and potential, is quite informative:

> [The Owens machine] gathers its glass, forms its blank, transfers the blank from the gathering to the blow mold with a finished lip and ring, blows the bottle, and delivers the bottle automatically, without the touch of a human hand. ... Not only that, but it puts the same amount of glass into every bottle of the same exact length, finish, weight, shape and capacity. It wastes no glass, uses no pipes, snaps, finishing tools, glory-holes, oil, rosin, charcoal, and requires neither gatherer, blower, mold boy, snap boy, or finisher, and still makes better bottles, more of them, at a lower cost, than is possible by any other known process. (Gessner 1903a: 1)

He goes on to say that

> [w]arm weather does not reduce the factory output. The scarcity of blower or boys no longer results in spare pots and places. There is no wasted glass on the pipe-head, or the blow-over. There is no idle period between turns, and every hour of the 24 is continuously utilized, since the machine never gets hot enough to "horse," does not stop for lunch nor rest during dinner hour, registers no grievances, requires neither holiday nor summer stop, needs not glory-hole, and resorts to no strike for increased wages or less work. (Gessner 1903a: 4)

The average labor cost of the 7,877,308 gross of bottles made in the United States in 1902 was $1.53 per gross, and Gessner quotes the Owens company as saying that they could reduce the labor cost to produce bottles down to $0.06 per gross (Gessner 1903a: 1).

In 1903 and later, a number of bottle manufacturers were invited to attend demonstrations of the Owens machine producing bottles. Although impressed with the machine's capability and potential, manufacturers were slow to take up licenses. The only Owens machine in operation from 1903 through 1904 was the one at the Owens Bottle Machine Company demonstration factory in Toledo (Walbridge 1920: 99). While bottle manufacturers could clearly see the potential of the machine, it appears that none wanted to be the first company to take the plunge. Significant production of bottles on the Owens machine did not begin until 1905.

The Owens Bottle Machine Company would only license the use of its machines. Licenses came with an exclusive right to produce designated types of bottles. Some companies took out options on licenses but let them expire. For example, options on licenses to produce fruit jars were taken out in 1907 by James A. Chambers and later by the Ball Brothers Glass Manufacturing Company. Both of these companies let their options expire. Ball Brothers later purchased the Greenfield Fruit Jar Company for four times the cost of the original option to secure the rights to use the Owens machine for the production of their canning jars (Scoville 1948: 105).

Setting up to produce bottles on the Owens machine was an expensive and complicated process. Special tank furnaces had to be built that had a revolving runoff area from which the machines sucked up the glass, and lehrs, or temperature-controlled kilns for annealing the glass, had to be built to accommodate the machine. The first three manufacturers to be licensed for the Owens machine built new plants designed around the Owens machine (Scoville 1948: 103). In 1938, the Congressional Committee on the Investigations of Concentration of Economic Power called William Levis, the head of Owens-Illinois Glass Company, as a witness. In response to a question from H. B. Cox, special assistant to the attorney general, about the cost of setting up production with an Owens machine, Levis gave the following statement:

> Very briefly, sir—we have always analyzed it—it costs about $500,000 per furnace to go into the glass-container business; that is, the furnace that melts the glass, the forming device to make the ware, and the annealing ovens, with their buildings, and packing-house facilities. Another $100,000 should be added to cover compressors and office facilities and machine shop, and about half a million dollars working capital, or $400,000 to make a round number, requiring about a million dollars invested capital, which you turn once in the production of the furnace, about a million dollars in sales. That wouldn't make any difference, sir, whether you had our suction machine, on it, or say, we put two suction machines to draw 100 tons, or whether we put six of seven Hartford machines on it to draw the same tonnage. (United States Congress 1939:474-488)

No doubt the cost was much lower in 1905, but licensing an Owens machine still would have been a major investment. The expenses associated with the machines made the cost of the new technology seem prohibitive. In addition to these problems, there was resistance from the glassblowers' unions. Because the Owens bottle-blowing machine did not require any skilled glassworkers, the machine was a great threat to the economic position of glassblowers, who were among the highest-paid skilled workers in the country. The Owens bottle-blowing machine would be the death knell for their trade (Scoville 1948: 205–206). Thus, the high cost of setting up the furnace and Owens machines, along with labor resistance, made it difficult to place the machines in existing factories.

It appears that the glassworkers' unions recognized that it was going to be useless to fight the bottle-blowing machines. Rather than fight the introduction of the semiautomatic bottle-blowing machines, the Glass Bottle Association began bargaining with glass manufacturers in the 1890s. Bargaining with the Atlas Glass Works and the Ball Brothers Glass Works led to agreements that the union members would become the machine operators (Minton 1961: 21–22). By 1924–1925 the Glass Bottle Association reached agreements that extended its jurisdiction to 42 glass factories, however, there were 25 plants with automatic machines outside their jurisdiction (Minton 1961: 84–85).

William Walbridge, an early partner of the Owens Bottle Machine Company, wrote a company history in 1920 that illustrated one of the first bottles blown on the Owens automatic bottle-blowing machine. It was a beer bottle with a cork finish (Walbridge 1920: 65). This type of bottle was being produced in the demonstrations described in the *National Glass Budget* in 1903 and for the manufacturers who came to Toledo to see the new wonder machine. Unfortunately for the company, no one purchased a license until 1905, when three companies took out licenses and the number of Owens machines in production jumped from one to six (Scoville 1948: 115). For practical purposes, 1905 is probably a good *terminus post quem* (*TPQ*) date for the bottles blown on the Owens machine.

The Owens machine was an instrument of mass production best suited to making large quantities of standard bottles. The early machines had 6 arms with later machines having 10 and 12 arms. Each arm had a set of ring (the mold that created the finish), blank,

and blow molds; changing molds on any one of these arms required shutting down the entire machine. This lack of versatility meant that the Owens machines were not well suited for short runs of specialty bottles for small merchants, such as bottles embossed with the names of small-town druggists. Thus the first products produced on the Owens machine were common types such as bottles for beer, ale, wine, liquor, ketchup, and milk. Because semiautomatic machines were producing widemouthed jars at the time the Owens machine was introduced, it appears that the Owens Machine Bottle Company and those licensed to use the machine concentrated on narrow-mouthed bottles, rather than widemouthed jars. The first license for jar production was issued in 1910 to the Greenfield Fruit Jar and Bottle Company (Scoville 1948: 105).

The first Owens machines could make bottles that ranged from 4 to 40 oz. in size (Meigh 1960: 33). Early licenses (APPENDIX 1: TAB. 1) do not list anyone having the rights for small bottles such as pharmacy wares. Because small bottles have thinner walls, they had to be made with glass at a higher temperature due to the glass setting up much faster through the loss of heat to the molds. The early six-arm Owens machines could not be run fast enough to produce bottles less than 4 oz. in size. The development of ten-arm machines and the adoption of dipping head molds in 1911 speeded up production and enabled the Owens machines to produce bottles under 4 oz. in size. This change gives archaeologists a *TPQ* of 1911 for Owens-made

Table 2. Start dates for production of Owens machine-made bottles

Year	Bottle type
1905	Beer, porter, ale, soda water, wine, brandy, milk, patent medicines
1906	Ketchup
1908	Vinegar, grape juice, narrow-mouthed food bottles, European bottles
1910	Fruit jars, packers' ware, prescription ware, ammonia bottles
1910	Heinz bottles
1911	Whiskey, gallon packers
1911	Small bottles from 1/2 oz. to 6 oz. capacity
1912	Carboys

bottles smaller than 4 oz. in size. The 1916 report to the stockholders of the Owens Bottle Company states that the Owens machine could produce bottles ranging from 1/10 oz. to 13 gal. in size (Owens Bottle Machine Co. 1916: 1). Because of the exclusive licensing system used for marketing the Owens machine, it is possible to assign other *TPQ* dates based on the type of bottle produced on Owens machines (TAB. 2); see Table 1 for citations.

The share of the glass-container market produced on the Owens machine expanded rapidly from 1905 into the 1920s. By 1917, half the bottles produced in the United States were produced on the Owens machine, and hand production has been estimated to have been reduced to less than 10% of the bottles being produced (Miller and Sullivan 1991: 105). Leases to the American Bottle Company, Ball Brothers, Thatcher Manufacturing Company, Hazel-Atlas Glass Company, Illinois Glass Company, and others had begun to change the nature of the American glass industry. Those glass manufacturers left outside the chosen circle having access to the Owens bottle-blowing machine were in a tough spot. This situation brought about experimentation by other glass manufacturers and engineers to develop a range of different automatic glass bottle-blowing machines and feeders that could convert semiautomatic machines to being fully automatic.

Semiautomatic bottle-blowing machines worked well, but their production speed was limited by how fast skilled glassworkers could hand feed gobs of the right size and temperature into the machines. An article by Gessner in 1903 states that "[a]bout ten gatherings per minute on articles weighing up to 8 oz. is all that can be maintained regularly by competent workmen under good factory conditions" (Gessner 1903b: 6). The solution was to build feeding devices that could take the place of the skilled glassworkers and convert the semiautomatics into fully automatic bottle-blowing machines. Development of feeding devices by Hartford-Fairmount (later to become Hartford-Empire) and others after 1915 provided the first stiff competition to the Owens machine (Scoville 1948: 185–186). Hartford-Fairmount began leasing its gob-fed automatic bottle-blowing machines in 1915. That machine was less

expensive to operate than the Owens machines, and the company charged a lower initial licensing fee, along with a lower royalty fee on the number of bottles produced than that charged by the Owens Bottle Company (U.S. vs. Hartford-Empire Company 1939: 24). Hartford-Fairmount and its successor Hartford-Empire were in the business of developing and manufacturing bottle-blowing machines and feeders to bottle machines, and they did not go into the manufacturing of glass containers. Like the Owens Bottle Company, their leases were for specific types of bottles and sometimes included limits on the quantities that could be produced.

The Owens Bottle Company was also developing glass-feeding devices, and by the early 1920s it was involved in patent-infringement litigation with Hartford-Empire over the claims covered by the feeder patents. To resolve this problem the two companies formed a patent pool in April of 1924 entitled "General License Agreement" by which they cross-licensed each other's patents. The Owens patents for suction machines, however, remained limited to the Owens Bottle Company (U.S. vs. Hartford-Empire Company 1939: 26–27). Under this agreement, the two companies agreed to share the cost of purchasing patents from other companies and the cost of litigating patent infringement cases against other companies. The strength of this patent pool convinced most of the major glass-container producers to take out leases from Hartford-Empire. Part of the fees from these leases and royalties collected by Hartford-Empire were paid to the Owens Bottle Company. This revenue sharing led to the Hartford-Empire and Owens-Illinois companies, along with other companies, to be called before the Committee on the Concentration of Economic Power related to their abuse of patents to control the glass industry. These activities led to a U.S. Supreme Court case that forced the breakup of the patent pool and opened the use of the patents to anyone for a reasonable license fee (Hartford-Empire Co. et al. v. United States 1945).

After the Owens bottle-machine patents began to expire in the 1920s, anyone could build and use an Owens bottle-blowing machine, although the cost and learning curve would have been an impediment. By that time the Owens bottle-blowing machine was being supplanted by Hartford Empire's individual section machine (the I. S. machine), which went on to become the dominant machine for the production of glass containers, as it still is today. The Owens Bottle Company began leasing Hartford Empire's I. S. machine.

The existing Owens bottle machines continued in use because they were excellent for the production of long runs of bottles, and those companies using the machines continued to benefit from their large initial investment in this technology. The last two Owens machines went out of production in December of 1982 at the Owens-Illinois Company factory in Gas City, Indiana (American Society of Mechanical Engineers 1983: 6). These machines ceased production as part of the permanent closure of 42 domestic and foreign plants by Owens-Illinois during an economic downturn (Paquette 1994: 276).

The Owens Bottle Machine Company began to transition into the manufacture of bottles shortly after it began licensing the use of the Owens automatic bottle-blowing machines to others. In November of 1904 Libbey and some of the other investors in the Owens Bottle Machine Company began the Northwestern Ohio Bottle Company in Newark, Ohio, licensed by their Owens Bottle Machine Company to produce wine, brandy, and a few special "branded" bottles (Scoville 1948: 104). The Owens Bottle Machine Company purchased all the stock in this company in 1908 (Toulouse 1971: 329). In 1909 the Owens Bottle Machine Company built a

plant in Fairmount, West Virginia, that went into production in 1910 (Toulouse 1971: 394). Thus, by then it was well on the way to becoming a major glass-container manufacturer. The leases that had been issued to other companies for exclusive rights to produce certain types of bottles presented some limitations that were overcome by purchasing some of those companies (TAB. 3).

In 1919, the Owens Bottle Machine Company became the Owens Bottle Company (Lockhart et al. 2010: 51). The last lease granted by the Owens Company for use of an Owens automatic bottle-blowing machine was in 1918 (Levis 1938: 497). In 1929 the Owens Bottle Company merged with the Illinois Glass Company to form the Owens-Illinois Glass Company, which made it the largest glass-container manufacturer in the United States. In response to a letter written in 1935 asking about leasing an Owens machine, the assistant secretary to Owens-Illinois Glass Company responded as follows:

> Referring to your communication of June 8, this company is engaged in manufacturing and sale of glass containers, but we are not licensors of glass making machinery. We do construct certain glass-forming mechanisms, but such equipment is for use in our own factories exclusively. We are unable therefore, to render the service which you require. (Levis 1938: 517–518)

By the time the above letter was written, all the major patents on the Owens automatic bottle machine had expired. William Levis, in response to a question by counsel H. B. Cox about who controls the patents on the suction

Table 3. Companies having Owens Bottle machine leases later purchased by the Owens Bottle Company

Company	Lease to produce	Date purchased by Owens Co.	Source
Northwestern Ohio Bottle Co.	Wines, brandy, and special branded bottles	1908	Toulouse 1971: 329
Whitney Glass Works, continued under the Whitney name until 1918	Prescription ware and ammonia bottles	1915	Toulouse 1971: 524
American Bottle Co.	Beers, porter, ale, and soda bottles	1916	Toulouse 1971: 30–31
Charles Boldt Glass Co.	Whiskies	1919	Toulouse 1971: 91

machines for producing bottles, answered that "we" (Owens-Illinois Glass Company) did, but "I don't think there is much left of them," and went on to state: "I would say we had no very important patents after 1929" (Levis 1938: 467). After the patents had expired, anyone could have built an Owens-style suction machine if desirous of expending the funds to do the engineering to accomplish this task. However, by that time the Hartford-Empire Company's I. S. machine was beginning to replace the Owens machines. The last Owens suction machines were built in 1941 for the company's use (American Society of Mechanical Engineers 1983: 6).

Owens Bottle-Blowing Machines and the Suction Scar

Bottles made on the Owens machine are easy to identify because of their distinct suction-scarred bottom. With the Owens machine, the blank (or parison) mold is dipped into a revolving tank of molten glass from which it sucks up the glass to fill the mold. When the blank mold is full, it is lifted off the molten glass and a knife comes across the base of the mold to sever the glass in the mold from that in the tank. That cutting action drags glass across to one side of the base of the mold and creates what is called an Owens or suction scar. Suction scars are rarely centered on the base of the bottle. This is because the rotation of the machine causes the semi-liquid parison to move about and be off center when it is enclosed by the blow mold. Another factor is that the parison molds are round in cross section, and when the parison is blown into an oval or square bottle the suction scar commonly comes up on the side of the bottle. The visibility of the suction scars can range from being very obvious to being difficult to see. They are often more obvious on larger and earlier bottles. Some of the factors involved are described in the following quote:

> The cut-off will give trouble. The principal trouble is a dirty cut-off, resulting from bad condition of the blank noses, and a defective knife. The glass is not cut-off cleanly, and the flaky pieces remain on the bottom of the parison molds, and on the knife, and are incorporated in the next cut-off, fusing in on the bottom. The knife may be blunt, may be of the wrong angle, may be loose, and may not be cutting closely to the blank bottom. (*Glass Industry* 1928: 147)

The blank mold that creates the parison and the blow mold both join to the ring mold that forms the finish of the bottle. Where the blank and blow mold join the ring mold, the mold lines are in alignment, i.e., the lines from both molds will be on top of each other where they join the ring mold that creates the finish. However, because the parison is rarely centered when the blow mold closes around it, the mold lines from the blank mold will be out of alignment with those of the blow mold near the base of the bottle. This results in faint mold lines that are partly compressed by the surface of the blow mold. These parison mold lines are often referred to by bottle collectors as "ghost" mold lines. Parison mold lines are present on almost all machine-made bottles, so they cannot be used to identify an Owens suction machine-made bottle. To separate an Owens bottle from other machine-made bottles, one has to have the base of the bottle. Figure 6 shows the mold-filling sequence for an Owens machine (FIG. 6).

It is worthwhile to get to know what a suction scar looks like because it, in combination with the known information on licensing, can be used to provide some fairly tight *TPQ* dates for early Owens machine-made bottles. Figures 7 and 8 show very clear examples of Owens suction scars on bottles, but not all scars are this obvious (FIGS. 7 & 8). For more examples of Owens scars see Lockhart et al. (2010: 56–59) and Miller and Sullivan (1991: 111).

The Owens machine remained an important producer of bottles into the 1950s and later. Beyond the dates of licensing for production and changes in the Owens machine, there are other factors that can help date all machine-made bottles. The first bottles to be produced by machine production were the most common types for which there would be long runs. It made little sense to produce the complex set of molds for a bottle type that would have a short run. For the Owens machine the early focus was on beer, wine, brandy, soda-water, liquor, and food bottles. Companies using the Owens machine first produced small-mouthed bottles because the semiautomatic machines could not produce such bottles. However, by 1910, the Owens machine was producing canning jars, food-packing jars, and common pharmaceutical

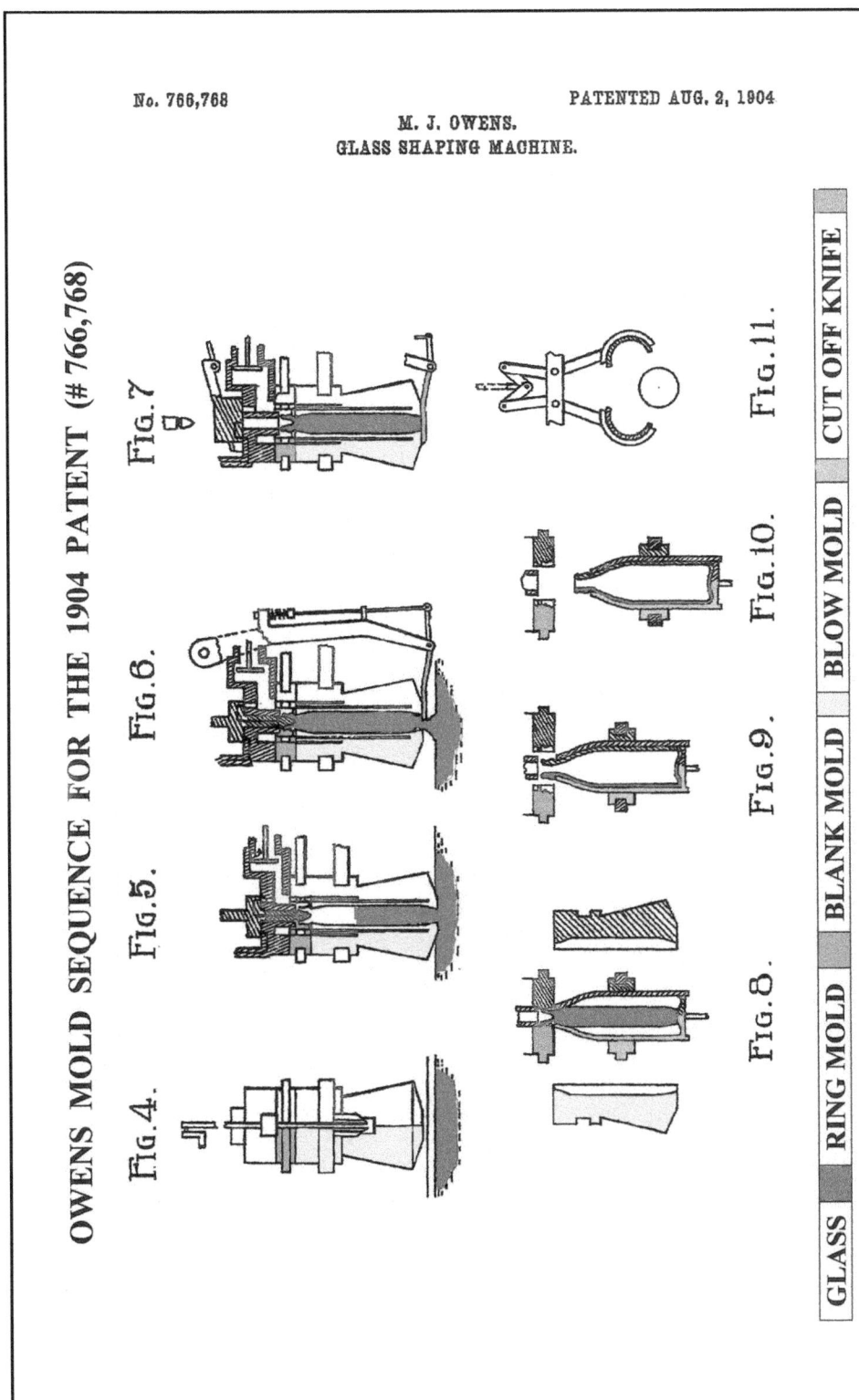

Figure 6. The Owens machine mold sequence: Fig. 4 shows the blank mold resting on the molten glass; in Fig. 5 the glass is being sucked into the blank mold. Fig. 6 shows the knife severing the glass from the furnace and the blank mold, which is then lifted in Fig. 7. Above Fig. 7 is a plug that creates the cavity in the neck for the blowing of the bottle. Fig. 8 shows the blank mold opening and the glass parison being held by the ring mold. Fig. 9 illustrates the bottle being blown in the blow mold. Fig. 10 shows the ring mold opening, and Fig. 11 depicts the blow mold opening to release the bottle. (Owens 1903).

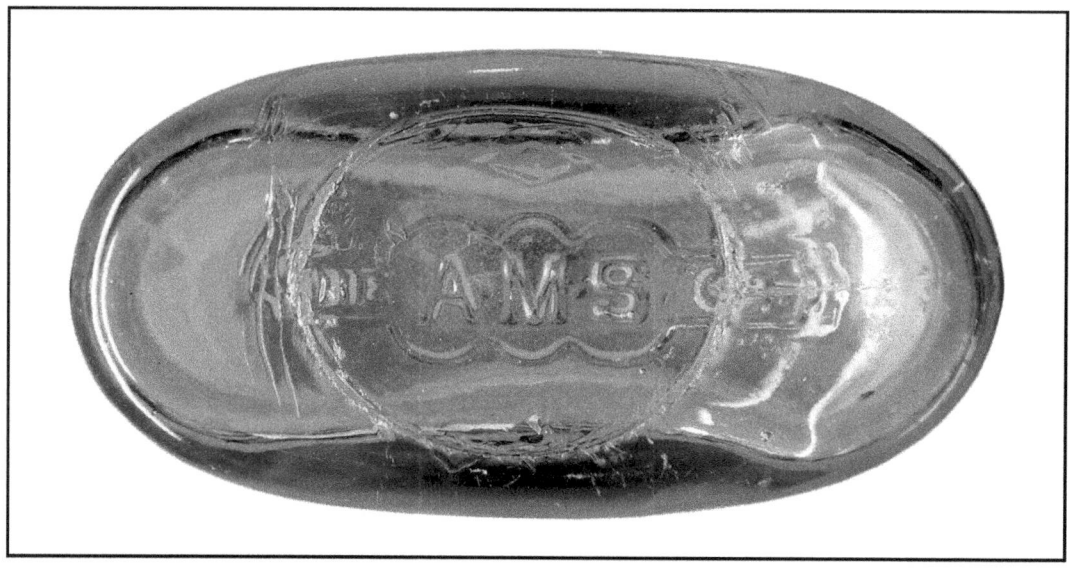

Figure 7. Owens suction scar on a "FULL PINT," cork-stopped, colorless glass liquor flask. There is a faint Illinois Glass Co. I-Diamond trademark above the bottler's mark: THE A.M.S. CO. (the American Medical Spirits Co.) which made medicinal whiskey during Prohibition. This information, plus the I-Diamond mark, dates the bottle to between 1919 and 1929. Notice the slightly oval mark, which is from the blank mold. The knife cutting off the glass created the Owens scar, dragging some of it off to the left side of the oval blank mold mark.(Photo by George L. Miller).

bottles. Most of the early bottles are what were called stock types. That is, they were not being made for a particular proprietary brand. Bottles for proprietary products are known as private molds, and they were not far behind in production. An early example would be those bottles produced by the H. L. Heinz Company for its own products. Major companies such as Chesebrough Vaseline, Lydia Pinkham's medicines, and Sloan's Liniment were not far behind. The Owens machine was one of mass production, and to shut the machine down to change molds was limited as much as possible.

Because the Owens bottle-blowing machine was best at long production runs of bottles, it eliminated many older types of bottles that were blown with letter-plate molds for pharmacies, breweries, and other small enterprises. These smaller companies were not able to absorb the minimum order size for special bottles made on the Owens machines. Shutting down an Owens machine to change molds was not practical for short runs. Thus ended a colorful period of bottle production that began in 1867 when James Christie of Baltimore, Maryland, took out a patent for plate molds for bottles (Christie 1867). He

referred to the plate as "a movable panel or slide." This is referred to as a "lettered plates" in the 1880 Whitall, Tatum & Company catalog (Whitall, Tatum & Co. 1971: 8–9). The plate mold led to many small pharmacies, breweries, and other companies ordering bottles with their names blown in the glass. These could be accommodated during the period of the mouth-blown bottles, however, the Owens and other automatic machines could not readily accommodate small orders because the changing of a mold would mean shutting down the machine. Minimum orders for machine-made bottles limited production to those companies that used large numbers of bottles. For a discussion of these changes see Miller and Pacey (1985: 41–44). Thus the period prior to the takeover of the Owens and the I. S. machines had many more varieties of bottles from smaller firms.

The second change that took place was in the color of the glass. When the Owens bottle-blowing machine began production the most common colors were a light green/aqua and amber brown. These colors came from iron that was commonly found in the sand that is used to make glass. The more iron in the sand, the darker the color. Colorless glass became common slightly later. Sand with low iron content could be used to produce colorless glass by the addition of manganese dioxide to the batch. Bill Lockhart has written a history of the use of manganese dioxide to produce colorless glass (Lockhart 2006). His research has shown that commercial containers in colorless glass created with manganese dioxide were being produced by the mid-1870s, which is well before the introduction of machine-made bottles (Lockhart 2006: 54). Glass made colorless with manganese dioxide will turn a light purple when exposed to sunlight.

For manganese dioxide to work as a decolorizer of glass, the glass batch has to be in reduction rather than oxidation. If the glass batch is in oxidation the glass will have an amethyst to purple color (Scholes 1941: 13). If the glass in a crucible is in oxidation, this can be remedied by the introduction of organic material into the batch. Rosenhain states: "Thus, a glass having a slight tinge of pink or purple derived from manganese can be rendered entirely colourless by the action of reducing gases or by introducing into the glass a reducing substance, such as a piece of wood" (Rosenhain 1908: 192–193). He also states that the introduction of organic materials can be used to get rid of bubbles in the glass:

> The most usual method is to place a potato in the crook of a forked iron rod and then dip the rod with the attached potato into the molten glass; the heat at once begins to drive off the moisture and to decompose the potato, so that there is a violent ebullition of the whole mass. ... It is, of course, further obvious that this process can only be usefully applied to glass melted in pots

[crucibles], since the bulk of molten glass in a tank furnace could not be reached at all in this manner. (Rosenhain 1908: 81)

The Owens machines pulled its gathers of glass from large tank furnaces. Controlling the reduction or oxidation of the batch in a tank furnace, as Rosenhain states, was not possible, as it was done in crucibles full of molten glass. Some early Owens-made bottles, such as milk bottles and pharmacy ware, were produced in glass that was made colorless by the use of manganese. These probably date before 1920. Another problem with manganese dioxide is that when it is exposed to high temperatures for prolonged periods, such as is common in a tank furnace, it tends to burn out in its ability to produce colorless glass (Angus-Butterworth 1948: 67).

The glass industry began switching to selenium as a decolorizer, which is much more

Figure 8. Owens suction scar on a dark-amber tapered gin bottle (Dutch gin bottle). No makers' or other marks. Probably made by the Illinois Glass Co. between 1910 and 1919. The slightly off-center round mark is from the blank mold. Again, one can see the glass dragged by the knife that cut the glass off when the blank mold was full. Not all Owens suction scars are this obvious; they are generally easier to see on larger bottles and those that are not round in cross section. (Photo by George L. Miller).

stable under the conditions in tank furnaces full of molten glass. Information on selenium as a decolorizer was being published as early as 1911 (Angus-Butterworth 1948: 68–69). Selenium was more expensive that manganese dioxide, although not as much was needed to create colorless glass. Less than an ounce of selenium per ton of sand in the glass batch was needed, whereas it took 15 lb. of manganese per ton of sand, in addition to large amounts of nitrate that had to be added, to create the reduction for the manganese to produce colorless glass (McSwiney 1925: 54). In tank furnaces the quality of colorless glass obtained from manganese was inferior to that obtained by using selenium (McSwiney 1925: 53–25). Selenium, on the other hand, works well in a slightly reducing atmosphere that is common in tank furnaces (McSwiney 1925: 56). Probably by 1920 selenium had replaced manganese as a decolorizer in tank furnaces used to feed the Owens bottle-blowing machines. Although light-green, aqua, and amber bottles continued to be produced, colorless glass became the dominant type. A 1933 inventory of the Hamilton plant of the Dominion Glass Company lists thousands of bottles, and the dominant color is listed as "flint," which would be colorless non-lead glass (Miller and Pacey1985: 45).

The next big change in machine-made bottles related to closures. Most of the illustrations of early machine-made bottle catalogs show cork or crown closures on the products (Illinois Glass Company [1915]; Owens Bottle Company [1925]). In 1906 the lug-top finish was introduced as a common bottle and jar closure (Leif 1965: 22). The great majority of bottles produced on the Owens bottle-blowing machines would have cork or crown closures. Initially the bottle companies did not produce their own metal caps, and they would have been ordered from companies that produced metal products. The end of the cork closure appears to have been brought about by the shortage of supplies of cork during World War II (Riley 1946: 209). Today, corks are rarely used for bottles, other than for wine and some fancy gourmet foods.

The last major change that is fairly easy to spot is the development of the lightweight bottle. It is our experience that the early bottles produced on the Owens machines appear to be rather heavy. By 1911 the company had developed an Owens machine that could produce bottles under 6 oz. in size (Walbridge 1920: 89). These bottles had thinner walls, and this may mark the beginning attempts to produce lighter-weight bottles. Beginning in the 1920s, the Bureau of Standards of the Department of Commerce began working with bottle manufacturers, bottlers, and other groups to establish recognized standard bottle sizes and shapes. This was meant to cut down on the number of types being produced in a move toward efficiency and economy. For example, the Bureau of Standards met with the American Bottlers of Carbonated Beverages at their 1929 annual meeting and attempted to set up standards for the industry. The recommendation was to cut the 15 available capacities of bottles down to 3, and to cut the 78 heights of the bottles being used down to 6. The government published the standards for soda-water bottles and other types of containers in the 1930s. Because these standards were not enforced by law, most of them did not come into effect until required by the government during World War II as part of the rationing of resources and energy (Riley 1946: 140). During the war, the number of bottle sizes, weights, and types of closures was reduced to cut down on the use of fuel, glass, shipping weight, and needs for warehousing. Lightweighting of bottles began around 1935 when the beer can came into production and began cutting into the bottle market share. The glass industry responded by making a lightweight single-trip bottle or a throwaway. Glass engineers began doing studies as to the best weight and shape for bottles without compromising strength. These standards became established during World War II. Lightweight bottles will have a fairly even distribution of glass on the sides and bottom of the bottle. A machine-made bottle with an irregular distribution of glass in the base most likely dates from before World War II. The war was a major turning point in bottle production, as was summed up by Holscher, who stated:

> Prior to the war, there were many odd shapes and sizes of bottles. War standardization, and elimination of small sizes, provided an increased output with the same production machinery. Janssen stated in 1946 that a return to the pre-war pattern would cut output by 20% in grossage, or 40% in gallonage. (Holscher 1953: 375)

The wide range of sizes is well illustrated by the ca. 1925 Owens Bottle Company catalog. It lists 29 sizes of "Standard Tablet Blakes Wide Mouth" ranging from 1/6 to 28 oz. in size. Seven of these available sizes were less than 1 oz. in capacity (Owens Bottle Company [1925]: 37). The range of small bottles being made after World War II was greatly reduced, and today plastic bottles have taken their place.

Acknowledgments

The senior author owes an intellectual debt to his glass mentor Olive Jones. My research on machine-made bottles began at Parks Canada in the early 1980s under her direction. Many others have contributed to this research, including Jack Paquette, whose book, The Glassmakers: *A History of Owens-Illinois Incorporated*, was of great help, along with other information that he sent to me. Peter Schulz provided copious photocopies from trade journals on the development of the glass industry. Gail P. Bardhan of the Corning Museum of Glass Library was very helpful in providing copies of Owens Glass Bottle Company documents and suggesting references. Kimberly Hieronimus Brownlee of the Ward M. Canady Center for Special Collections of the University of Toledo, Ohio, was most helpful in getting permission to use images from the Owens-Illinois, Inc. archives. I would also like to thank Stephanie Johnston from corporate communications of Owens-Illinois, Inc. for granting permission to use photographs from their archives. Dick H. Cole of the Minnetrista Museum in Muncie, Indiana, provided information on the use of the Owens machine in the Ball Brothers works. James C. Coleman, who worked in the general research department of Owens-Illinois, shared a biography he produced on the life and work of Michael Owens with me and provided some helpful comments on an earlier draft of this paper. Charles Depew, who worked his way up into management for Owens-Illinois and had worked with Owens and other types of bottle-blowing machines, provided helpful comments on a much earlier draft of this paper. J. William Barrett II told me about working with the I. S. bottle-blowing machines and about what it was like to work in a glass factory. Glenn Vogel was able to supply me with some glass factory ephemera that was greatly appreciated. Christopher Hogue, who

is using the process of production by the Owens machine to simplify the description of the molecule ATP phase in photosynthesis, provided some very thought-provoking discussions on the development of the Owens machine. I would like to apologize to those whom I have forgotten to mention for their thoughts and contributions to the development of this paper. The authors would also like to thank Bill Lockhart and two other reviewers for their comments on our study.

References

American Society of Mechanical Engineers
1983   *American Society of Mechanical Engineers Designates the Owens "AR" Bottle Blowing Machine as an International Historic Engineering Landmark.* American Society for Mechanical Engineers, New York.

Angus-Butterworth, Lionel M.
1948   *The Manufacture of Glass.* Pitman Publishing Corp., New York.

Birmingham, Frederick A
1980   *Ball Corporation:* The First Century. Curtis Publishing Co., Indianapolis, IN.

Christie, James J.
1867   Improved Glass-Bottle Mold. United States Patent 72,368, filed 10 October 1867, and issued 17 December 1867.

Coles, Jessie V.
1949   *Standards and Labels for Consumers' Goods.* Ronald Press Co., New York.

Floyd, Barbara, Ann Bowers, and Kimberly Brownlee
2006   Time in a Bottle: A History of Owens-Illinois, Inc. Ward M. Canaday Center for Special Collections, University of Toledo <http://utoledo.edu/library/canaday/exhibits/oi/OIExhibit/MainPage.htm>. Accessed 27 August 2013.

Franken, Richard B., and Carroll B. Larrabee
1928   *Packages that Sell.* Harper & Brothers, New York.

Gessner, Frank M.
1903a   The Owens Bottle Machine. Its Demonstrated Economy and Efficiency. *National Glass Budget: Weekly Review of the American Glass Industry* 19(15): 1, 4.
1903b   Weekly Review of the American Glass Industry. *National Glass Budget: Weekly Review of the American Glass Industry* 19(1): 6.

Glass Industry
1928   Aspects of Bottle Machine Operation. Glass Industry 9(7): 1,947.

Gooding, E. J., and Edward Meigh (eds.)
1951   *Glass and W. E. S. Turner* [1915–1951]. Society of Glass Technology, Sheffield, UK.

Holscher, Harry H.
1953   Feeding and Forming. In The Handbook of Glass Manufacture: *A Book of Reference for the Plant Executive, Technologists and Engineer.* Comp. and ed. by Fay V. Tooley, 229–388. Ogden Publishing Co., New York.

Illinois Glass Company
[1915]   *Illinois Glass Co. Bottles, "Diamond I"* Products, General Catalog "A." Illinois Glass Company, Alton.

Leif, Alfred
1965   *Closeup on a Closure.* Glass Container Manufacturers Institute, New York.

Lockhart, Bill
2006   The Color Purple: Dating Solarized Amethyst Container Glass. *Historical Archaeology* 40(2): 45–56.

Lockhart, Bill, Pete Schultz, Carol Serr, and Bill Lindsey
2010   The Dating Game—the Owens Bottle Co. *Bottles and Extras* 21(1): 50–62.

McSwiney, D. J.
1925   The Decolorization of Glass. *Glass Industry* 6(3): 53–57.

Meigh, Edward
1960   The Development of the Automatic Glass Bottle Machine: A Story of Some Pioneers. *Glass Technology* 1(1): 25–50.

Miller, George L., and Antony Pacey
1985   Impact of Mechanization in the Glass Container Industry: The Dominion Glass Company of Montreal, a Case Study. *Historical Archaeology* 19(1): 38–50.

Miller George L., and Catherine Sullivan
1991   Machine-Made Glass Containers and the End of Production for Mouth-Blown Bottles. *In Approaches to Material Culture Research for Historical Archaeologists.* Comp. by George L. Miller, Olive R. Jones, Lester A. Ross, and Teresita Majewski, 99–126. Society for Historical Archaeology, California, PA.

Minton, Lee W.
1961   *Flame and Hearth: A History of the Glass Bottle Blowers Association of the United States and Canada.* Merkle Press, Washington, DC.

Moody, B. E.
1963   *Packaging in Glass.* Hutchinson and Co., London.

Owens Bottle Company
[1925]   *Proprietary Owens Bottles: Owens Machine Made by Owens, Stock Catalog No. 2.* Owens Bottle Company, Toledo, OH. No. 30550, Corning Glass Museum Library, Corning, NY

Owens Bottle Machine Company
1916   Owens Capital Now $50,000,000. *National Glass Budget: Weekly Review of the American Glass Industry* 31(47): 1–3.

Owens, Michael J.
1899   Method of Blowing Glass. U.S. Patent 759,742, filed 26 December 1899, and issued 10 May 1904.

Owens, Michael J.
1903   Glass-Shaping Machine. U.S. Patent 766,768, filed 13 April 1903, and issued 2 August 1904.

Paquette, Jack K.
1994   *The Glass Makers: A History of Owens-Illinois Incorporated.* Trumpeting Angel Press, Toledo, OH.

Paul, John R., and Paul W. Parmalee
1973   *Soft Drink Bottling: A History with Special Reference to Illinois.* Illinois State Museum Society, Springfield.

Riley, John J.
1946   *Organization in the Soft Drink Industry: A History of the American Bottlers of Carbonated Beverages.* American Bottlers of Carbonated Beverages, Washington, DC.

Rosenhain, Walter
1908   *Glass Manufacture.* D. Van Nostrand, New York.

Scholes, Samuel R.
1941   *Handbook of the Glass Industry: A Book of Reference for the Factory Engineer, Chemist and Plant Executive.* Ogden-Watney, New York.

Scoville, Warren C.
1948   *Revolution in Glassmaking: Entrepreneurship and Technological Changes in the American Industry, 1880–1920.* Harvard University Press, Cambridge, MA.

Toledo Glass Company of Ohio
1903   Improvements Relating to the Production of Articles of Glass and Apparatus Therefore. British Patent 20,148, issued 1902, and amended specifications 18 November 1903. British Patent Office, London. Collection of George Miller, Newark, DE.

Tooley, Fay V.
1953   *Handbook of Glass Manufacture: A Book of Reference for the Plant Executive, Technologist and Engineer.* Ogden Publishing Co., New York.

Toulouse, Julian Harrison
1971   *Bottle Makers and Their Marks.* Thomas Nelson, New York.

Turner, William E. S.
1938   The Early Development of Bottle Making Machines in Europe. *Journal of the Society of Glass Technology* 22(52): 250–258.

Tutton, John
1994   *Udderly Delighful:* A Guide to Collecting Milk Bottles and Related Items. 3rd ed. John Tutton, Front Royal, VA.

United States Congress
1939   *Investigations of Concentration of Economic Power: Hearings before the Temporary National Economic Committee, Congress of the United States, Seventy-Fifth Congress, Part 2, Patents: Automobile Industry, Glass Container Industry.* United States Congress, Washington, D.C.

District Court of the United States
1939   *United States of America v. Hartford Empire Company et al., Complaint.* Civil Action No. 4426, District Court of the United States for the Northern District of Ohio, Western Division. Filed 11 December.

United States Supreme Court
1945   Hartford-Empire Co. et al. v. United States, 323 U.S. 386. Reargued and submitted 9 & 10 October 1944, decided 8 January 1945. Findlaw for Legal Professionals http://caselaw.1p.findlaw.com/scripts/getcase.pl?=us&vol=323&invol=368. Accessed 24 May 2005.

Walbridge, William S.
1920   *American Bottles Old and New: A Story of the Industry in the United States.* Owens Bottle Company, Toledo, OH.

Whitall, Tatum & Co.
1971   *Whitall,* Tatum & Co. 1880. Pyne Press, Princeton, NJ.

Author Information

George L. Miller
Retired
Newark, Deleware
miller.ccindex@gmail.com

Anthony J. McNichol
Principle Investigator
Chrysalis Archaeological Consultants
Brooklyn, NY
amcnichol@chrysalisarchaeology.com

Appendix 1: Table 1: Dates for Owens Machine-Made Bottles

Year	Company	Products	Source
1903	Owens Bottle Machine Co.	Organized with a capital of $3,000,000, took over the Toledo Glass Co. factory to set up a demonstration facility.	Walbridge 1920: 67
1903	Owens Bottle Machine Co.	Pint and quart **beer bottles**, demonstration of the machine described in National Glass Budget in August of 1903.	Walbridge 1920: 67
1904	Owens Bottle Machine Co.	Only one Owens machine in operation.	Walbridge 1920: 99
1904 16 Sept	Baldwin-Travis	License for **milk bottles** to Baldwin-Travis. It merged with Thatcher Manufacturing Co. less than a year later.	Scoville 1948: 104
1905	Thatcher Manufacturing Co.	Thatcher Manufacturing Co. was a distributor of milk bottles from different manufacturers to dairies. They merged with Baldwin-Travis to acquire the rights to produce **milk bottles** on the Owens machine. They installed a No. 6 machine in a factory in Kane, PA.	Walbridge 1920: 72 Toulouse 1971: 497
1904 1 Nov.	Ohio Bottle Co.	For exclusive rights to produce **Beer, porter, ale, and soda-water bottles** on the Owens machine. They used their license to bargain for a merger with Streator Bottle & Glass Co. and Adolphus Busch Glass Manufacturing Co. This license was consigned to this consortium called the American Bottle Company 7 Sept. 1905.	Walbridge 1920: 72 Scoville 1948: 104 Toulouse 1971: 399–400
1905 7 Sept.	American Bottle Co.	Product of a merger to have access to the license for the production of beers, **porter, ale, and soda bottles** on the Owens machine. Combination of the Ohio Bottle Co. with the Streator Bottle and Glass Co. and Adolphus Busch Glass Manufacturing Co. Owens Bottle Co. purchased American Bottle Co. in 1916. It continued to use the American Bottle Co. name until 1929 when Owens merged with Illinois Glass Co. Prohibition killed the demand for beer bottles.	Walbridge 1920: 72 Toulouse 1971: 30–31, 373
1904 1 Nov.	Northwestern Ohio Bottle Co.	"On Nov. 1, 1904 Libbey entered the bottle-making business as the Northwestern Ohio Bottle Co. of Toledo. The company had an exclusive license to make **wines** and **brandies** and a few "branded" (or "**proprietary**" medicine) bottles." Owens Bottle Machine Co. bought all of their stock in 1908. They added another furnace, two more Owens AD machines, and began making **vinegar, grape-juice, ketchup**, and other **narrow-neck food bottles**.	Walbridge 1920: 72 Scoville 1948: 104 Toulouse 1971: 329
1904–1912	Owens Bottle Machine Co.	Made **beer and sodas** for its licensee American Bottle Co. in 1905 and 1906 and then turned to **ketchups** until 1912, when it added **pharmaceutical and proprietary medicine**.	Toulouse 1971: 393
1905 19 Oct.	Owens European Bottle Machine Co.	The Owens European Bottle Machine Co. was formed to sell the machine to European manufacturers.	Walbridge 1920: 73 Scoville 1948: 118–119
1906	James A. Chambers	Took an option on a license for making **fruit jars**, but let the option expire.	Scoville 1948: 105
1906	Greenfield Fruit Jar Co.	"The former Greenfield Fruit Jar & Bottle Co. . . . installed Owens machines about 1906, had been acquired by Ball Bros. in 1912 and resold to Owens Bottle Co. In 1917." **Fruit Jars**.	Toulouse 1971: 396
1907 1 Feb.	Rhein-Ahr Glasfabrik	Rhein-Ahr Glasfabrik Gesellschaft mit beschränkter Haftung, license for making **Apollinaris** and other **mineral water bottles** only to make bottles for their own bottled mineral waters.	Walbridge 1920: 74 Scoville 1948: 122

Year	Company	Products	Source
1907 1 Oct.	Owens European Bottle Machine Co.	Plant at Trafford Park, Manchester, England, opened to demonstrate to European manufacturers. Turns $58,000 profit over operating expenses in 11 months.	Walbridge 1920: 73 Scoville 1948: 121
1907z	Ball Brothers	Took an option on a license for making **fruit jars**, but let it expire. They later purchased the right as an assignee from Greenfield Fruit Jar Co. in 1909, and it cost them more than four times the original license cost.	Scoville 1984: 105
1909 2 Jan.	Greenfield Fruit Jar Co.	Louis Hollweg took out a license for fruit jars and assigned the rights to Greenfield Fruit Jar & Bottle Co. in November. They sold the rights to Ball Brothers a week or so later.	Scoville 1948: 105
1909 Nov.	Ball Brothers	Purchased the license rights to the Owens machine for making fruit jars from Greenfield Fruit Jar and Bottle Co. in November.	Scoville 1948: 105
1909 20 May	Hazel-Atlas Glass Co.	For most kinds of **packers' ware**	Walbridge 1920: 79 Scoville 1948: 105
1909 19 July	H. J. Heinz Co.	For bottles to pack their own merchandize. **Heinz bottles.**	Walbridge 1920: 79 Scoville 1948: 105
1909	Owens-West Virginia Bottle Co.	Northwestern Glass and Owens-West Virginia consolidated with Owens Bottle Machine Co. A large factory was set up to make **prescription ware** in Clarksburg WV.	Scoville 1948: 110
1909 27 Dec.	Owens-West Virginia Bottle Co.	License for certain kinds of **beverage bottles.**	Scoville 1948: 105
1909 Dec.	Dec. Whitney Glass Works	For druggists' ware, had exclusive rights to **oval ammonia bottles**, but not exclusive rights to **"prescription ware."**	Walbridge 1920: 79 Scoville 1948: 106–107
1910	Whitney Glass Works	First to produce varied sizes on one six-arm machine: five **squares,** and one **oval** of three weights, three heights, and three capacities.	Walbridge 1920: 82
1910 11 June	Illinois Glass Co.	Licenses were issued to Illinois glass on 11 June 1910, 18 Jan. 1911, and 22 May 1914. **Whiskies.**	Scoville 1948: 106
1910 11 June	Charles Boldt	**Whiskies.**	Walbridge 1920: 79 Scoville 1948: 106
1911	Name changed to Owens Bottle Co.	United Owens-West Virginia and Northwestern Ohio Bottle Co. under the name Owens Bottle Co.	Toulouse 1971: 394
1911	Owens Annual Report	New machine to make **siphon bottles.**	Walbridge 1920: 89
1911	Owens Annual Report	New machine to make **gallon packers.**	Walbridge 1920: 89
1911	Owens annual report	Machine to make bottles ranging in size from **1/2 to 6 oz**	Walbridge 1920: 89
1911	Owens annual report	Machine to make **bottles** up to 8 in. in diameter and 17 in. height, larger than heretofore made.	Walbridge 1920: 89

Year	Company	Products	Source
1912	Owens annual report	Licensed to manufacture **prescription and proprietary ware**, to the Owens Eastern Bottle Co.; the plant was later acquired by Owens Bottle Co.	Walbridge 1920: 91
1912	Owens annual report	Projected development of a machine to make 5 to 13 gal. **carboys.** When developed, the lease went to Illinois Glass Co.	Walbridge 1920: 93
1912	Owens annual report	133 machines in production with a capacity of 7,000,000 bottles.	Walbridge 1920: 95
1913 Dec.	Maryland Glass	**Blue glassware**, particularly **Bromo-Seltzer bottles** license to Maryland Glass Corp. Illinois Glass Company contested the right of Maryland Glass to make Bromo-Seltzer bottles.	Walbridge 1920: 95–96 Scoville 1948: 106
1914	Owens Bottle Co.	Owens Bottle Co. purchased Owens Eastern Bottle Co. They had a non-exclusive license to make prescription and **proprietary** bottles.	Walbridge 1920: 101
1916	Owens Bottle Co.	Owens Bottle Co. purchased American Bottle Co., the largest manufacturers of **beer, carbonated-beverages, soda**, and **water bottles**. Their annual capacity was 2,000,000 gross.	Walbridge 1920: 104
1916	Owens annual report	Owens Bottle Co. sales of 613,959,696 bottles, a 66% increase over 1915. Became the foremost bottle producer in the country.	Walbridge 1920: 105
1917	Owens annual report	Total production on Owens machines by the company and licensees was 1,588,996,416 bottles.	Walbridge 1920: 108
1918	Owens Bottle Co.	Opened its Charleston, West Virginia, plant producing **prescription, proprietary, pharmaceuticals, household and chemical, toilet, and cosmetic bottles, and foods.**	Toulouse 1971: 397
1919	Box 0 trademark	The Box 0 trademark was registered on 16 March 1919.	Lockhart et al. 2010: 57
1919	Charles Boldt Glass Co.	Acquired by Owens Bottle Co.	Toulouse 1971: 397
1925	Thatcher Manufacturing Co.	They built a third furnace for their Elmira, NY, plant to install a **Hartford Empire Machine**. Thatcher Manufacturing Co. purchased other **milk-bottle** producers to secure the rights to use the Hartford milk-bottle machine and the Hartford feeder.	Toulouse 1971: 498
1941	Last Owens machine built	The last Owens suction machine built for the company's use was in 1941.	American Society of Mechanical Engineers 1983: 6
1982	Last two Owens machines	"The last two Owens machines in production, 15-arm 'AQ' models, were operated at Gas City, Indiana, until December 17, 1982." Gas City was an Owens-Illinois plant that probably was one of the 42 plants that Owens-Illinois permanently closed in 1982 during an economic downturn.	American Society of Mechanical Engineers 1983: 6 Paquette 1994: 276

Aspects of Bottle Machine Operations

B. M. Pearson

The Glass Industry

REG. U. S. PAT. OFF.

Vol. 9   JULY, 1928   No. 7

Aspects of Bottle Machine Operations

By B. M. Pearson

SINCE bottle making machinery has now come into universal use, a study of the operating conditions, with a view to the securing of the best working results should, of course, be a feature in any plant of size.

Machines can be semi-automatic or semi-automatic operated in a fully automatic manner by the incorporation of a feeding device and a blank transfer mechanism. Finally we have the fully automatic machine, as exemplified by the suction machine, in which class, the Owens machine, for years, held the field alone, but has now rivals in the similarly constructed English Redfern machine, and the smaller Continental and English 1, 2, 3 or 4 mold suction machines, such as the Wilzin, the Severin, the McNish, etc.

Semi-automatic narrow neck machines are being fast replaced by the fully automatic machines, principally of the flow type. These machines closely follow the fully automatic flow machine in principle. They are of the turnover, parison type. The glass is gathered on the end of a punty, and dropped into the upturned parison mold. The parison is then blown up, and the blank mold is opened and the blank is swung over by its ring mold, into the open blow mold, which is then closed on the parison, and the bottle is blown up. Being conducted with the aid of a fair concentration of labor, comparable to a hand bottle making unit, the results obtained are dependent, to some extent, upon the personal element. Thus, the degree of puff admitted to blow up the parison, the way in which the air is admitted, the length of time in which the blow is held, are all operations controlled entirely by the operator, usually a youth, and are operations upon which the quality of the finished bottle is dependent. There is an interesting psychological study involved, and the problem is not a little perplexing. Thus if the workers are paid on a time basis they will slack, invariably as much as possible, and the production will accordingly fall off. If they are paid on a production basis, they will tend to slack off, as far as quality is concerned, and to produce the greatest number of bottles. The only really satisfactory way is to pay the operators on production, and pay on results. Thus the bottles will be sorted into firsts and seconds, the top price being paid for the first quality, and a lower price for the second quality. The crew on the machine must be trained to work well together, as otherwise production will fall off seriously. One of the chief troubles in operating semi-automatic machines is to secure a good distribution. This arises from several causes. One is the personal element, as mentioned above, in the matter of introducing the blow air and securing the satisfactory blowing up of the bottle. It will be found that semi-automatic operatives are very versatile in this respect. They manipulate the compressed air valves with great cunning, and an extraordinary complexity of turning on and off. This is stated to imitate the hand blowing process as much as possible. The average hand-blown bottle is noted for its excellence of distribution. Another trouble is that owing to the slow speed, it is difficult to keep the molds satisfactorily warm, and bad distribution may accordingly arise from this case. The drawback of semi-automatic machines is the large amount of labor required to operate the machine, and the slow speed of working. For this reason they are mainly relegated to working on small orders, and specials, which are not of a sufficient size to warrant them being run on a large automatic machine, and which would otherwise have to be made by hand.

Flow Machines

The second class of machine to consider, or, as it is called, the feeder-fed or flow machine is very similar to the semi-automatic. The flow machine is simply a semi-automatic machine, with the glass fed by a feeder instead of a gatherer, and with the various forcing operations linked up, and performed mechanically. The construction of the machine is correspondingly strengthened, so as to enable the units to withstand the mechanical stresses imposed. The necessity for this strengthening of the constructional details was not sufficiently realized in the early days of flow machine design, and the machines were made very little stronger than the semi-automatic machines from which they were evolved. Consequently the wear and tear was very rapid, and the machines migrated with more or less celerity to the scrap heap. This has been remedied, and the march of progress has eliminated the "tinny" flow machine, and replaced it by a much more substantial mechanism altogether.

Flow machines must, of course, be considered from three distinct aspects—the press machine, the press and blow machine, and the narrow-neck bottle machine.

Press and Blow Machines

The press and the press and blow machines represented the earliest evolution of the flow machine, and they were turning out wide-mouth ware at a time when narrow-neck

O'NEILL STANDARD NO. 28, AND O'NEILL FEEDER
Installed in England

bottles were still being made by hand. The press and blow machine is simply a development of the press machine. The press machine is capable of making all ware with a smooth regularly shaped interior, and tapering somewhat toward the bottom, and without a finish. Examples of such ware are tumblers, fruit dishes, containers for preserves, etc. A water-cooled plunger is pressed down on to the glass, and forces it to take the shape of the mold. The plunger is preferably actuated by a toggle mechanism, and its motion so controlled by a suitable arrangement of powerful springs that it pauses, at the point of maximum pressure, in the mold. This pause may last for a few seconds, and serves to allow the glass time to accommodate itself to the mold. This pause is very necessary in the case of the pressing of ware with a more or less complicated exterior, such as the imitation cut glass, and also, in the case of ware with a plain exterior, such as tumblers, etc., serves to assist in giving a good distribution. The shape of the plunger in the case of a simple press machine must be regulated by the inside shape desired for the ware being produced. The pressure of the plunger is very important. Too low a pressure will give a badly shaped article, while too high a pressure will give trouble such as surface defects, crizzles. The correct plunger pressure to employ will vary with the shape of the article, and the weight, also the nature of the glass and with other similar considerations. It was stated above that a water-cooled plunger is employed; this is necessary to prevent the plunger becoming too hot, and letting the glass stick to it. Care is necessary, with the water used for this purpose. It must be as "soft" as possible, i.e., contain very little dissolved impurities, and be quite free from impurities

in suspension. If a hard water is employed, or one containing material in suspension, a heat insulating lining will be deposited on the inside of the plunger, and cooling will be impossible, with resulting trouble. The cooling of the plunger is more important still in the case of press and blow machines, which generally work at a higher speed than simple press machines. It is necessary to employ springs on the plunger head, so as to obviate "over-pressing." The charge of glass is not entirely uniform, so that unless definite means are adopted to afford a pressure relief, when, for instance, more glass than usual is in the mold, it is very probable that something will be broken. The incorporation of strong springs on the plunger head provides this mechanical safety valve, also allow for the plunger being gently brought to rest when it has reached its lowest point of travel, instead of stopping with a jar, and in addition, affords a ready means of providing for a pause in the plunger travel, at the position of maximum pressure.

As has been stated above, the press and blow machine is a development of the press machine. In the press and blow machine two mold tables are provided. On the first table are mounted the press molds, and on the second table the blow molds. The press molds are operated with a

WM. J. MILLER MODEL AGA
Motor Driven, High Power Toggle Press

plunger in the usual way. No special shape is, however, given to the blank pressed, that is the shape of this blank has little or no reference to the shape of the finished article. This is possible because the required shape can be imparted in the subsequent blowing operation. The pressing serves to form the finish. In general the parison is given a conical shape. As there is a considerable latitude as regards the shape which can be imparted to the parison, it is possible to vary the shape of the plunger on a press and blow machine. The variation will be found to be of great benefit, as when the correct shape is found, the machine speed possible will be found to be influenced very profoundly, as also will the quality of the ware. The speed of operation will be decided within limits by the shape of the plunger, as stated above, and also by the temperature of the glass among other things. Too high a temperature will enable the glass to flow very rapidly and conform to the shape of the parison molds very easily, but will slow up the machine,

feeble air pressure, giving defects such as not blown up, thin bottoms, uneven bottoms, bad distribution, thick shoulders, etc. If the glass is being delivered to the machine too hot, and the parison is being handled too quickly, it will most likely sag in the press-mold. When transferred, the finish will probably lie unevenly in the blow mold, and if the blowhead cannot from this cause, rest evenly on the

MODEL B-1. MILLER MACHINE AND MOLD WORKS

OWENS AUTOMATIC BOTTLE MACHINE
Plural 10-Arm, Latest Type

owing to the appreciably greater time required before the plunger can be withdrawn, without risk of the collapse of the parison in the blank mold, and before the parison has set rigid enough to be handled and transferred to the blow mold. Too high a temperature will tend to give blisters in the ware, a rough surface, and perhaps crizzles. Too low a temperature of the glass will give a very bad distribution, owing to the sluggish flow of the glass, and will form crizzles. Owing to the too high viscosity of the glass, the plunger must also rest in the mold for a lengthy period, to ensure really satisfactory ware. Defects in such ware, for example, as jam jars or fruit jars, i.e., ware which has a finish, will be not filled up in ring; split-rings. Regarding split-rings, also, unsuitable design or unsuitable operation of the plunger will be a prolific cause of split-rings. The remarks appertaining to the pressing of the parison can also be applied to press machines. After the parison has been pressed, it is transferred to the blow table. It is deposited in the appropriate blow mold, and a blow head is then placed on top of the finish, and the parison is blown up to conform to the finishing mold. Defects occurring during this procedure may chiefly arise from the chilling of the surface of the parison, which takes place during the transfer, and from the unsuitable application of the compressed air. If the surface of the parison is chilled during the transfer, the surface will be badly torn during the blowing up. Also the bottle will not take the shape of the mold very well and the distribution is certain to be bad. If the compressed air is not applied in a suitable manner, defects in the body of the bottle, below the mold parting line will be caused. Water in the air line will result in uneven or

parison, leakage of pressure will result, giving the defects referred to immediately above. If the parison is transferred, while too hot, thin shoulders and thick bottoms will

OWENS FLOW DEVICE—AY MACHINE—10 ARM

result in the finished bottle. The chilling of the parison, referred to above, occurs during the transfer from the press table to the blow table. Modern examples of press and blow machines cut down this chilling effect as much as possible, by placing the molds as close together on one table as possible. This is effected by alternating the two sets of molds. Examples of such machines are the W. J. Miller, P. C. E., P. C. D., and similar types. More attention could be paid to the cooling of the blank or press molds, on the press and blow machine. Thus, on the Daubenspeck ma-

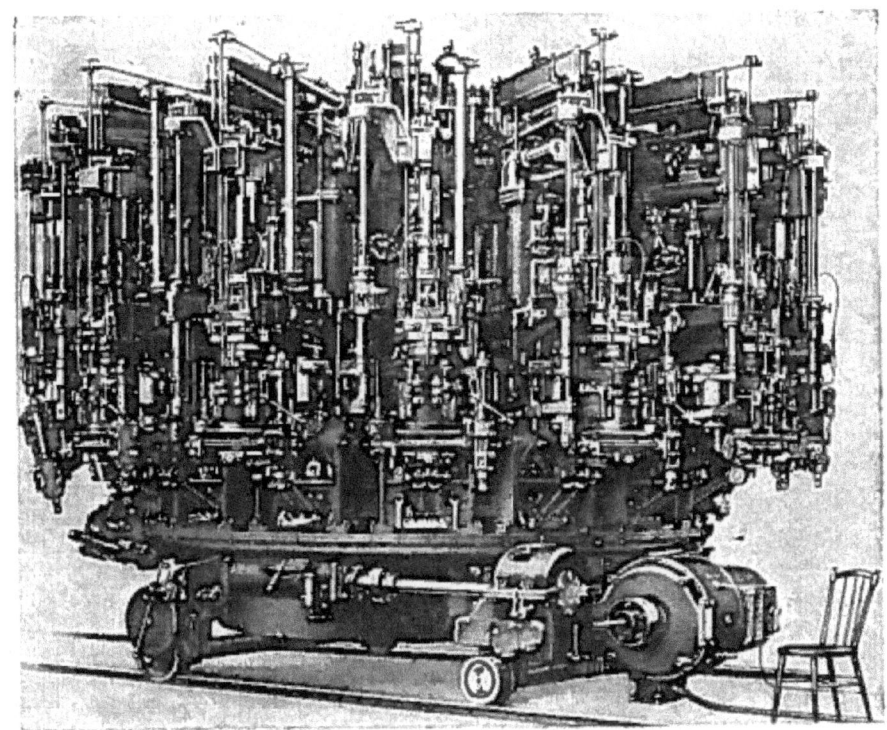

THE NEW REDFERN 15-ARM SUCTION BOTTLE-MAKING MACHINE

The sizes recommended are 6, 10, 12, or 15 units. Each of these sizes can be converted into any other of these recommended sizes in 2 days. A 15 unit machine can be erected in 2 days and completely dismantled in 8 hours. The units are interchangeable. A single unit can be replaced ready for work in 25 minutes.

Ten different bottles varying in size, shape weight and capacity can be made at the same time on the 10, 12 and 15 unit machines and six different bottles on the 6 unit machine

Operating speed 1½ to 6 revolutions, per minute.

closes on the parison, and the bottle is subsequently blown up by one or more blow-heads. The chief troubles arising with this class of machine are bad packing round the tip, giving thick and uneven necks, and choked and narrow bores, bad distribution, split rings, crizzles due to chilling during the transfer, uneven bottoms, not blown up, ring not filled up, thin seams, and blistered rings. This type of

chine, operating in England, there are 16 blank molds, with corresponding benefit to the operation. The writer has had considerable experience of press and blow bottle machines, including Daubenspeck, early Miller machines and the latest type of machine as exemplified by the Miller P. C. D. machine, and has yet to find a machine which will give a better quality line of wide mouth ware than this class will produce. The quality can be maintained at a higher pitch than on the Owens machine, even, with suitable operation, of course.

There is a limit to the amount of lime which can be used in press and in press and blow machines. Too high a lime content will result in a great amount of crizzles, and a large number of split rings. The best working figure will generally be round about 7.5 to 8 per cent of lime in the glass.

It will no doubt have been obvious that the press and blow machine is not capable of making a narrow necked bottle. These are now, by the flow process, invariably made on the turnover parison type of machine, either single table or double table. The gob or gather is dropped into the upturned parison mold, which is closed at the bottom by the tip or plunger. The glass is packed round the tip, and is then blown up by the puff. The parison mold is then turned over so that it is right way up, and opened. The parison is then taken by its ring mold over to the second table, into an open, waiting finishing mold, which then

machine has been successfully adapted for producing internal screws for beer bottles, etc., by imparting a rotatory movement to the tip, and in this case, the troubles with the rings, mentioned above, are accelerated. Chilling of the transfer is obviated by mounting all the molds on one table.

It will be obvious that to effect the various operations on these flow machines such as receiving the gob or gather, pressing, transferring from one table to another, etc., a pause must be made in the revolution, while the operation is proceeding. The machines are now made strong enough to withstand the mechanical strains imposed by this constant stopping and starting. Consequently, designers have turned their attention to obviating the necessity for such continual arresting of motion, and by mounting all the molds on one table, one set above the other set as in Owens practice, arrange for the machine to receive its gob and to make the transfer on the move, and so are able to arrange for the continuous rotation of the machine. In the case of the press and press and blow machine, the motion must be arrested during the pressing operation. For such machines, therefore, designers have evolved very ingenious systems, designed to ameliorate to a very considerable extent, the shocks arising from the stopping and starting. An example is the Geneva movement incorporated in a line of modern press and press and blow machines. By means of a continually rotating spider, driven by an electric motor, the machine is gently brought to rest, and gradually started up again.

Other designs of intermittent flow machines use a compressed air cylinder and a rack and pinion or a similar device, to move the machine a station.

Suction Machines

The suction type of machine, in the case of the fully automatic Owens and Redfern type is arranged for continuous

ONE OF THE REDFERN UNITS—DIPPING POSITION

rotation. The principle is well known. The glass is contained in a revolving basin, held at a suitable temperature, and the parison molds in turn, are pressed down on to the surface of this glass. A vacuum is applied to the blank mold then, and it fills itself with glass. The blank is formed, and subsequently transferred to the finishing mold. There are defects which are peculiar to the process and to the machine, and also a number which are common to other machines. The use of the vacuum will at times cause difficulties. Leaky blanks, for instance, will permit the vacuum to escape, and will result in insufficient glass being sucked into the parison mold, giving rise to thin bottoms and walls and over-capacity bottles. For the best results, the vacuum should be as high as possible, so as to get the glass into the mold as quickly as possible. The vacuum is stated by some authorities to be a prolific cause of blistered rings. Practically all the air is drawn out of the blank mold, and when the glass is drawn up it will make very close contact with the side of the mold. On cooling, the glass in the ring mold will contract and draw away from the side, leaving a space which will contain a vacuum, and will allow the dissolved gases in the glass to come out of solution, and to form bubbles or blisters in the ring. Blisters generally are rather

an obscure phenomenon, and it appears probable that there are several separate contributory causes. Carbon in the glass in the pot from oil off the machine, or from the gas or oil is known to cause blisters. If a low vacuum is used, resulting in a relatively slow filling of the parison mold, and the consequent long continued exposure of the glass to the vacuum, blisters will conceivably be formed. Blisters may

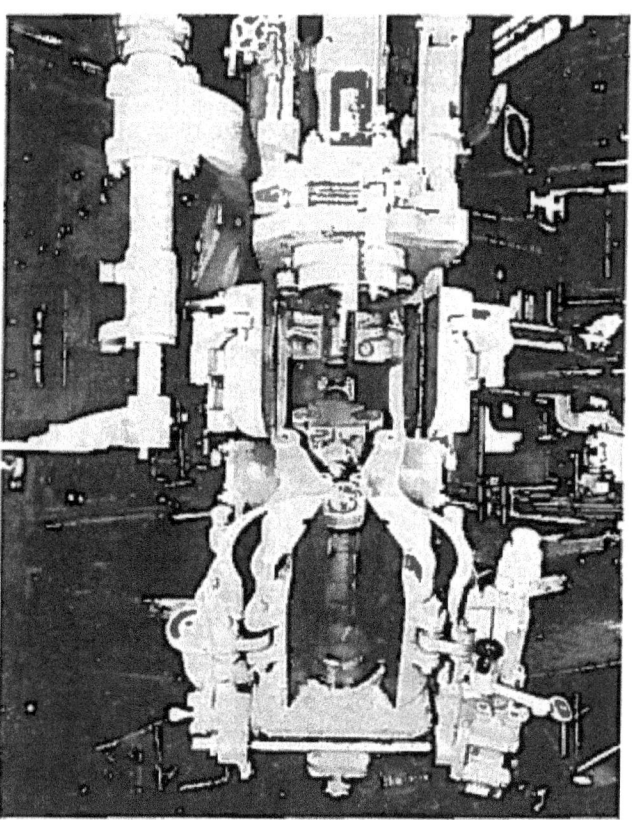

MOLD SYSTEM AND KNIFE—REDFERN MACHINE

also be formed in the pot by gas coming out of solution from the glass, by the agitation of the parison mold; by the lapping over of the cut-off, enclosing air-bubbles. Remedies for blisters are to work the revolving pot at a higher temperature, with the inevitable slowing down of the machine speed, and to alter the pot speed relative to the speed of the machine, giving time for any lapped cut-offs to be melted in before being again worked.

Common Defects

The cut-off will give trouble. The principle trouble is a dirty cut-off, resulting from bad condition of the blank noses, and a defective knife. The glass is not cut-off cleanly, and then flaky pieces remain on the bottom of the parison molds, and on the knife, and are incorporated in the next cut-off, fusing in on the bottom. The knife may be blunt, may be of the wrong angle, may be loose, and may not be cutting closely to the blank bottom. Air blisters occur with a lightly dipping parison mold, and are large air bubbles or inclusions, drawn up with the rest of the glass. An eccentric pot in the horizontal plane may also give this trouble. Blank seams are where the blank has too big a clearance. The remedy is to make an adjustment,

Typical Working Compositions Used on Various Types of Bottle Making Machines

	(1) O. M.	(2) O. M.	(3) O. M.	(4) O. M.	(5) Flow	(6) Flow	(7) Flow	(8) Flow	(9) Flow	(10) Flow
SiO_2	75.00	74.54	73.32	67.65	73.34	73.09	74.13	73.88	74.01	72.0
Al_2O_3	0.53	0.35	0.56	2.92	0.70	1.23	0.37	0.62	1.08	2.1
Fe_2O_3	0.048	0.06	0.25	2.30	0.054	0.36	0.06	0.06	0.17	0.15
CaO	5.10	10.70	7.80	11.32	8.49	8.61	7.90	7.65	7.21	8.5
MgO	3.32	0.05	0.77	0.12	0.13	0 06	0.11	0.16	0.06	0.2
Na_2O	16.00	14.30	16.75	13.55	17.29	16.34	17.43	17.63	17.47	17.0
MnO	....	....	0.55	2.14	....	0 31	....	....	....	....

(1) Owens Flint. (2) Owens Flint. (3) Owens Amber. (4) Owens Green. (5) O'Neill Flint. (6) O'Neill Amber. (7) Daubenspeck Pr. and Blow Flint. (8) Miller Press Flint. (9) Miller Pr. and Blow Pale Green. (10) Graham Flow. Pale Green.

or to change the blank. Hot blanks will give sticking, and thin shoulders and thick bottoms. Thin shoulders will occur both with cold glass and with hot glass. With cold glass, the metal will chill, and will not rise up the mold readily. With hot glass, in applying the puff, the glass may all be blown away from the shoulder. Thin seams are caused by hot glass. Cold glass will give very uneven distribution, and will cause the metal to blow up in lumps, and generally gives rise to thin bottoms. Tear under ring occurs with ware having an external screw on the finish, and may be remedied by adjusting and easing the mold, or by replacing the ring mold. Crooked necks are occasioned by bad registering of the finishing mold, with the ring mold. Mold marks show the marks of the mold tool on the bottle, and are disfiguring. In bad cases, the mold must be re-turned. Split rings are due to a cold tip, or a tip of too straight or too curved an outline, also to cold ring molds, and vibration of the mold carrier. Dannied or shouldered ware is generally ascribable to too sharp a curve on the shoulder of the mold. Tight bores are due to cold tips, to cold glass, to worn tips, and to inaccurate machin-

ing. High and thick seams are due to bad mold machining, and to bad registration on the machine, and will naturally invariably occur if the molds are neglected and are not kept in good condition.

It is amazing what a personality a glass bottle machine possesses, and while these notes will indicate the chief faults, and their eradication, and will serve as an outline for the manner in which glass bottle machines should be conducted, a considerable amount of detail of the actual manipulation of the glass to the machine and the operation of the machine can only come from experience of the local conditions.

With all bottle machines, the glass composition must be kept as constant as possible. The Owens machine may work with a wide range of compositions. In the following table is given the typical working compositions used on the various types of machines. It will be apparent that a fairly considerable diversity occurs in the composition used on any particular machine. However, within limits this is not so important as keeping the working composition, once it has been standardized, as constant as possible.

Volume Variation of Bottled Foods

H. Runkel and J. C. Munch

UNITED STATES DEPARTMENT OF AGRICULTURE
BULLETIN No. 1009

Contribution from the Bureau of Chemistry
W. G. CAMPBELL, Acting Chief

Washington, D. C.   **PROFESSIONAL PAPER**   December 16, 1921

VOLUME VARIATION OF BOTTLED FOODS.

By H. RUNKEL, *Assistant Chemist*, and J. C. MUNCH, *Junior Chemist*.

CONTENTS.

PURPOSE OF INVESTIGATION.

The amount of variation which occurs in the volume of bottled foods packed under conditions of "good commercial practice" is often the subject of controversy among the bottler, the food official, and the bottle manufacturer. The Bureau of Chemistry has made a number of investigations on this subject. Some of these investigations have been somewhat disconnected, but the gaps existing in the information thus obtained have been filled in, so far as possible, by supplementary investigations. The prevalence of various methods of packing bottled foods, prevalence of the various types of bottles used for foods, prevalence of the different types of bottles manufactured, types of filling machines, methods of manufacture, commercial methods of purchasing and testing bottles, variations in capacity of bottles, variations in volume of contents of bottles of food, and allied subjects have been studied to determine the difficulties involved in packing bottled foods with a uniform quantity of contents. Precaution has been taken to observe the obligations of the bottler, the bottle manufacturer, and the food official to the consumer.

68708°—21——1

Because the Net Weight Amendment to the Federal Food and Drugs Act and many State laws require that food in package form bear a statement of the quantity of contents, the obligation of the food official to the consumer includes the promotion of the delivery of bottles of food which vary as little as possible from the stated quantity of contents when the possibilities of good commercial practice are taken into consideration. The obligation of the bottler to the consumer calls for an effort to deliver bottled food products, such as flavoring extracts, mineral waters, carbonated and uncarbonated beverages, molasses, honey, maple sirup, vinegar, olive oil, essential oils, table oils, catsup, and salad dressing, which are as uniform in quantity of contents as is commercially practicable. The bottle manufacturer, therefore, is under direct obligation to the bottler and indirect obligation to the consumer to furnish bottles which are as uniform in capacity as it is commercially possible to make them.

It is the purpose of this bulletin to describe a commercial method of bottling which may be considered "good," to calculate maximum variations in the volume of bottled liquids used as foods when packed in accordance with specified good commercial practice, and to present data showing that the calculated maximum variations of the good commercial practice outlined can be met by the bottler.

The results of the investigation here reported are intended to be applicable to liquid foods only.

SOME CAUSES OF VARIATION IN VOLUME OF FOOD IN BOTTLES.

The variation of the quantity of food in the bottle depends on many factors, since various types of bottles are manufactured by various methods and filled by various methods. The causes of the variations are cumulative, extending far back into the history of the bottle. In order to direct attention to the relative weight of some of the causes, certain pertinent factors in bottle manufacturing, methods of bottling, and types of bottles used as food containers are mentioned

BOTTLE MANUFACTURE.

Bottles are manufactured by three processes: Hand, semiautomatic machine, and automatic machine. The processes vary in two particulars—first, the method of gathering the proper amount of glass to be blown into a bottle, and, second, the method of blowing the bottle.

Hand blowing is the oldest and simplest method of manufacture. In this process one end of the punty, a hollow tube about 6 feet long, is inserted in the molten glass and rotated until the amount of glass necessary to produce a bottle of the desired weight has been collected. The lump of glass attached to the punty is rolled into a pear-shaped lump on an iron plate, placed in a mould, and the glass expanded to the limiting mould walls by blowing through the punty. As soon as the mass has been expanded to the limits of the mould, the punty is detached, the mould opened, and the bottle removed. The neck is then reheated and finished and the bottle placed in a cooling chamber, where the temperature is gradually reduced.

The semiautomatic machine process embodies the first attempts to apply machinery to the blowing of bottles. A stream of glass falling into the mould is cut off by scissors operated by a foot treadle. Since practically all of the glass which falls into the mould is contained in the finished bottle, its weight depends upon the judgment of the operator of the foot treadle. The molten glass is formed roughly in a blank mould by a plunger, and it is then transferred by hand to the blow mould, where it is blown by compressed air to the limits of the walls of the mould.

The automatic machine process accomplishes all steps of bottle manufacture by machinery. The amount of glass is gauged by filling a hollow mould by suction and striking off the excess glass with a knife. The weight of the glass in the bottle is that measured into the mould. After forming the neck of the bottle in this mould the blow mould is brought into position around the pencil of glass, which is expanded to the mould limits by compressed air.

In both hand and semiautomatic machine processes the weights of the bottles are controlled by the accuracies of human judgment, in the first case in properly estimating the weight of molten glass on the punty, and in the second case in properly estimating the amount of glass which drops into the mould. In the automatic machine process the weight of the bottle depends upon the amount of glass measured into the mould by machinery and does not depend upon the accuracy of human judgment. So far as the manufacturing affects the weight of the bottles there are only two processes, hand and machine, the semiautomatic machine process falling into the first class.

In all processes the mould is manufactured according to strict specifications and tests. Its cavity, which controls the exterior dimensions of the bottle, is accurately machined to previously determined dimensions, and sample bottles are blown for weight and capacity tests before it is installed. With continual use a scum accumulates in the mould, slightly diminishing its interior dimensions. After this scum has been removed a sufficient number of times, the mould's dimensions become appreciably larger, so that a new mould must be substituted for it. Much attention is given to the cleaning of the mould and to the possibility of its replacement by the bottle manufacturer. One of the criteria for changing it is the increased weight of the bottle when bottles of a definite capacity are being blown.

To assist him in keeping the weight of the bottles as accurate as possible, the hand blower familiarizes himself with the weights of the bottles as he blows them and can at once adjust any tendencies toward overweight or underweight. In the Wage Scale and Working Rules of the Glass Bottle Blowers' Association the blower is continually cautioned to "work as close to weight given as possible." Similar precautions are taken in blowing bottles by the machine process. For the past 30 years at least (1) (6),[1] the National Glass Bottle and Vial Manufacturers' Association, composed of manufacturers, and the Glass Bottle Blowers' Association, composed of blowers, have held annual conventions, where questions pertaining to their several interests are discussed and agreements made by which each party should be governed. The limit of variation in weights which would be permitted during the ensuing year has been one of the questions decided at these meetings. This point became of special importance after the passage of the Net Weight Amendment to the Federal Food and Drugs Act, March 3, 1913, when the food officials were also consulted. The variations agreed upon and adopted in 1914 have been readopted annually without change. The manufacturer has the privilege of rejecting bottles whose weights fall outside these allowable variations. They are used in this bulletin in calculating the maximum variation in the volume of bottled foods.

To show the extent to which any allowable variation will be applicable to all bottles, it is necessary to note that the variation in the weight of hand-blown bottles is greater than that of machine-blown bottles. While this is generally an accepted fact (7), it has been further verified by 27 sets of data collected in the course of these investigations, each containing measurements on 25 to 50 bottles of 4, 8, and 12 ounce weights. It was found that the respective average deviations were 0.12, 0.24, and 0.37 ounce in hand-blown ware, and 0.03, 0.06, and 0.18 ounce in machine-blown ware. It is pertinent also to note that machine manufacture has had a steady growth. In 1912 (2) 33 factories in the United States were equipped with bottle-blowing machines. In 1913 (2) 37 factories and in 1914 (5) 54 factories, or 37 per cent of those in the United States, were so equipped. It has been estimated that 45 per cent of the bottles blown in 1917 (7, p. 129) and 60 per cent of those blown in 1918 [2] were made by automatic machines. This steady growth, together with the fact

---

[1] Figures in parentheses throughout this bulletin refer to the bibliography on page 20.
[2] Bureau of Chemistry surveys, unpublished.

that machine patents are now expiring, emphasizes the necessity for giving consideration to the smaller variations which may occur in machine-blown bottles.

BOTTLE FILLING.

The accuracy in bottle filling is affected by every operation of the bottler from the time he places his order for bottles until they are sealed and labeled. In placing the order the bottler has in mind, and sometimes states in his contract, the capacity which he desires. Upon receipt of the bottles the correctness of their capacity is ascertained by actual measurement, or else it is assumed that the manufacturer has delivered bottles having the capacity designated in the contract. According to the tests made the bottles are rejected or suitable arrangements are made for their use with respect to a proper declaration of quantity of contents. In a survey it was found that 10 of 16 bottling factories made tests on every lot of bottles received from the factories, and also that 10 of these bottlers did not specify in their contracts with the glass factories the capacities which they desired for their bottles. The transparent nature of the bottle compels the bottler to cater to a popular demand that the packages be reasonably full, which requires filling to a somewhat uniform height, leaving sufficient head space.

The liquid food is filled into the bottle by machines of various degrees of complexity. A general study of the catalogues of bottle-filler manufacturers has shown these fillers to fall into three general types. The first is practically a hand filler. It is equipped with a filling nozzle and a lever cut-off operated by hand. When bottles are filled to the desired filling point, as estimated by the eye or by comparison with a properly filled sample, the flow is cut off and the bottle corked. This type represents the simplest method of filling. The second type of filler works upon the siphon principle. The bottle is filled from a siphon tube connected with a constant level tank. As soon as the liquid in the bottle has reached the level of the liquid in the tank the flow ceases. The height of fill is adjusted by raising or lowering either the bottle or the delivery tube. The third type is a development of the second type in which the liquid runs into a measuring chamber of adjustable dimensions before delivery to the bottle. A uniform volume is thereby delivered into each bottle.

Of these types of fillers the second is most common. The third is used more generally for filling cans which are not transparent. Regardless of the type of machine used, the bottler is impelled to fill his bottles to a definite height in order that they may make a satisfactory appearance as a commercial article. It was found during the inspection of a number of factories that even where machines which measured the quantity to be delivered were used, continual attention was given to the height of fill of the bottle. The short-capacity bottles, which were always too full and filled high in the neck, were partially emptied into the over-capacity bottles, which were not full enough, in order to obtain a more uniform quantity of contents.

FIG. 1.—Long-necked bottles.

It is the custom of bottlers to label their products with the quantity of contents either by a paper label or by having the statement blown into the bottle. In each case the bottler must depend upon the uniformity of the bottle to secure accurate statements of the quantity of contents. This fact is considered in this bulletin in calculating the variation in volume of bottled foods.

FIG. 2.—Short-necked bottles.

TYPES OF BOTTLES.

Although foods are put up in a large variety of bottles, three surveys of the industry indicate that certain types are very prevalent. In view of the mooted questions concerning the panel bottle it has not been included in this study. Figures 1 and 2 illustrate the types which have been studied. The cross section of the bottle may be round, square, or oval, and the necks long and conical or cylindrical, or short and cylindrical. The type of shoulder shown in these figures, while of minor significance in some cases, is important in others and illustrates the type to which the data reported in this bulletin apply. It is intended that the results be applicable to the simplest and most prevalent types of bottles used for food purposes.

"GOOD COMMERCIAL PRACTICE" IN BOTTLING.

In considering the specifications which should be met by a commercial practice considered to be "good," the demands of the consumer and the law, as well as the ability of the bottler to meet the requirements, have been taken into account. Because of the transparency of the bottle, the bottler attempts to cater to the demands of the consumer that the bottle be as full as practicable, considering the necessary head space. When the bottler receives a shipment of bottles which are over capacity, he hesitates to fill the bottles with a larger quantity without changing the quantity of contents declaration on the label. On the other hand, when bottles which are under capacity are received the law demands that the contents declaration be changed to make the statement correct. If the true capacity of the bottle to the usual filling point differs only slightly from that desired, there is a possibility of making a slight increase or decrease in the height of fill. This change in the height of fill necessitates instructing a number of employees who have been trained to fill to a certain height. It also requires a change in the setting of filling machines if such are used. A further inconvenience is suffered by the necessity for the determination of the proper height of fill. A material change in height of fill, therefore, can be regarded only as a temporary expedient. It will be suffered by the manufacturer only long enough to permit him to give proper instructions to the bottle manufacturer from whom he makes his purchases. While readjustments are taking place, it is not considered that the bottler has yet attained conditions of good commercial practice.

It is evident that the first step of the bottler in eliminating his difficulties with respect to the variation in capacity of the bottles he receives is to make definite specifications in his orders. The law requires that the quantity of liquids shall be declared by volume. The height to which the bottler fills his bottles can be varied slightly, but to meet the demands of the law and the public he is required to demand of the bottle manufacturer a bottle with a definite capacity at a height of fill which will satisfy the public. This condition can be attained by inserting in the specifications in his orders the requirement that the bottle have a specified capacity at a definite height of fill. This is considered the first condition of good commercial practice.

When any lot of bottles is received, the best practice demands that they be tested. The test to be applied is whether they meet the specification as to capacity at the height of fill specified in the contract. If the bottles do not test correctly, two alternatives are possible. The bottles may be rejected or temporary expedients, such as changing the contents declaration on the labels, may be employed to use up the particular lot. Rejection of bottles involves the inconvenience of temporary loss of packages and friction with the manufacturer. It is for the bottler to decide which method will be employed. If the variation is excessive, good commercial practice would demand that they be rejected. Testing the capacity of a representative sample of each lot of bottles received and rejecting those lots with excessive variations from the contract specifications is the second step in the attainment of good commercial practice.

The testing of the bottles gives the bottler information as to his correct filling point. Whether or not the tests show a variation from his usual filling point wide enough to justify him in instructing his employees as to proper changes is a question for him to decide. The best practice would demand that the question of change of height of fill be given due consideration. The adoption of the process of making slight changes in the height of fill as indicated by the tests made on the various lots of bottles as received is the third step in the attainment of good commercial practice.

Printing labels with the quantity of contents before they are attached to the bottles is decidedly convenient. By making this statement beforehand the bottler determines the quantity of contents which he expects to fill into his bottles. The statement of quantity of contents is necessarily the same as that specified in his contract with the bottle manufacturer. The expediting of his business demands that labels be ordered before the bottles are received. There is always a possibility of altering the statement of quantity of contents by rubber stamp or by reprinting, but this is an inconvenience which will be suffered by the bottler only long enough to permit him to give proper instructions to his manufacturer to correct the capacity in the subsequent shipments. The application of labels bearing a definite, correct statement of the quantity of contents is regarded as the fourth step in the attainment of good commercial practice.

The development of good commercial practice is a growth and requires a sufficient amount of time for adjustment to proper conditions by the bottler. It involves the ordering of labels previous to the time bottles are ordered, and a requirement on the part of the bottler that his bottles be delivered to him as specified. Though this is an ideal condition and it is not conceivable that it could be continued without an occasional interruption, many factories are using this practice closely. For the purpose of this bulletin, therefore, good commercial practice in bottling foods is the attainment of conditions in the bottler's state of business in which he (*a*) includes in his orders for bottles the specifications as to capacity when filled to a specified height, (*b*) tests a representative sample of every lot of bottles received, and rejects those lots appreciably under capacity, (*c*) fills his bottles to a height determined from the results of his tests, and (*d*) has his labels printed with a definite, correct statement as to the quantity of contents and applies them unaltered to the bottles he fills, such statement to be correct within his required variations.

The calculated maximum variations computed in this bulletin are based on the assumption that this specified good commercial practice in bottling has been attained.

CALCULATED MAXIMUM VARIATION IN THE VOLUME OF BOTTLED FOODS.

The first and most important requisite in the carrying out of the good commercial practice plan in bottling is that the variation in the bottles shall be as small as commercially practicable. With the use of accurate bottles the bottler is able to adjust his filling process to any extent he desires and to produce bottles of food which, in quantity of contents, vary within limits as narrow as he may wish to have them.

The calculated maximum variation in the volume of bottled foods is computed in this bulletin on the basis of the usual variations in the bottles. It is defined as the volume which is equivalent to the allowed weight variation of the bottle as manufactured.

Variations in the weight of bottles which the manufacturer shall allow to the blower, as published in the Wage Scale and Working Rules of the Glass Bottle Blowers' Association, are given in Table 1.

TABLE 1.—*Variations in weight of bottles allowed by manufacturers.*

Weight of bottles.	Under.	Over.
Ounces.	*Ounces.*	*Ounces.*
½ and under		
[1] 1 to 1		
1 to 2		
2 to 4		
4 to 6		
6 to 8		
8 to 10		
10 to 12		
12 to 14	1	1
14 to 17	1	1
17 to 20	1	1½
20 to 25	1¼	1½
25 to 28	1½	1½
28 to 32	1½	2
32 to 40	2	3
40 to 50	3	4
50 to 60	4	5

[1] Inclusive. The following figures are not inclusive.

68708°—21——2

The variations as given in Table 1 are applicable to bottles of particular weights. While bottles of any capacity may be blown at any specified weight, if so ordered, the general practice is to follow the weights and capacities stated in the Wage Scale and Working Rules of the Glass Bottle Blowers' Association. Weights of bottles of various capacities as stated in the Wage Scale and Working Rules have been compiled in Table 2.

TABLE 2.—*Weights of bottles of various capacities.*[1]

Types of bottles.	Capacity (fluid ounces)—										
	½	1	2	4	6	8	12	16	24	32	64
	$Oz.$[2]	$Oz.$[2]	$Oz.$[2]	$Oz.$[2]	$Oz.$[2]	$Oz.$[2]	$Oz.$[2]	$Oz.$[2]	$Oz.$[2]	$Oz.$[2]	$Oz.$[2]
Round and fluted prescriptions...	1.25	1.50	2.0	3.5	5.0	6.5	9.0	11.0	15	18	......
Round castor oils, lemon sirups, olive oils, etc..................	1.00	1.50	2.25 2.5	4.0	5.0	6.5	9.5	11.0	16	20	......
Ovals, French squares, tall blakes, and oblongs..................	.75	1.25	2.0	4.0	5.5	7.0	10.0	12.0	18	20	......
Flats, short blakes, and oblongs...	1.00	1.50	2.5	4.5	6.0	8.0	11.0	14.0	18	22	......
Grape juices and catsups, champagnes, octagons, r o u n d s, squares..................	......	1.50	2.25	4.0	5.5	6.5	10.0	13.0	19	22	34
Tinctures, round and square......	.75	1.25	2.0	4.0	5.0	6.5	9.0	11.5	15	18	32
Range in weight.................	.75– 1.25	1.25– 1.50	2.0– 2.5	3.5– 4.5	5.0– 6.0	6.5– 8.0	9.0– 11.0	11.0– 14.0	15– 19	18– 22	32– 34
Corresponding range in Table 1...	½–2	1–2	2–4	4–6	4–6	6–8	8–12	12–14	14–17	17–25	32–40

[1] Compiled from text of Wage Scale and Working Rules of the Glass Bottle Blowers' Association, 1918–19.
[2] Avoirdupois.

The simple types of bottles listed in Table 2 are very common food containers. They are the types to which the results found in this bulletin are applicable. The weights of bottles of any given capacity are so uniform that they fall within one of the definite ranges in weight mentioned in Table 1. Each range in weight corresponds to a capacity. For example, a corresponding range in Table 1 of 1 to 2 ounces, avoirdupois, corresponds to a capacity in fluid ounces of 1. Therefore, there is an allowed variation in weight which corresponds to each capacity, that is, the first column of Table 1 has been converted from terms of weight to terms of capacity.

An increase in the weight of the bottle is caused by the use of more glass, which thickens the walls and decreases the capacity. Since the bottler is penalized for short capacity, the overweight limits as given in Table 1 were selected as the basis of computing the maximum variations in capacity. The overweight limits have been computed to volume equivalents by use of the factor, 1 ounce of glass is equivalent to 3.1 drams in volume, the usual factor used by glass blowers and manufacturers.[3] This factor has been further verified by measurements and computations based on the specific gravity of

[3] Bureau of Chemistry Hearing of Glass Bottle Blowers' Association, May, 1913.

glass given in literature, and is found to be sufficiently accurate for use in this bulletin. The volumes equivalent to the variations in overweight as given in Table 1 are computed by this factor and tabulated in Table 9 (page 20) under the heading " Individual bottles," opposite the various capacities given in Table 2. These are calculated maximum variations computed in this bulletin, on which further computations are based in Tables 4 and 6.

The blower is continually cautioned to " work as close to the weight specified as possible." Since those bottles which are outside the permitted variations in weight may be rejected, the blower will attempt to have them occur as seldom as possible. As a result of following this caution and attempting to keep within the limit, the weights of the bottles will be distributed in accordance with the normal law of errors. For example, if the blower intends to deliver a bottle weighing 8 ounces, most of his bottles will weigh close to 8 ounces and only a few will be over or under by large amounts. Their average weight will approximate 8 ounces and there will be about as many over as under weight. The allowable variations stated in Table 1 would probably occur very few times in the course of a day's work. These are the primary conditions for distribution according to the normal law of errors. In accordance with the principles of the law of errors, the variation of the average of the representative sample, which has the same chance of occurrence as the variation of an individual bottle, is equivalent to the individual variation divided by the square root of the number of bottles in the sample (3). In making observations of this type, it has been found that at least 50 bottles should be measured in order that the results may be accurately representative. The calculated maximum variation in the volume of a representative sample has been computed according to this rule and included in Table 9 under the column "Average of representative sample."

Data to show the possibilities of meeting these variations of the average volume are not presented in this bulletin. Studies of a similar nature (4) on other products have shown that variations computed by this method are within the range of commercial possibilities.

In the calculations of the maximum variations in Table 9 the assumption has been made that the bottler is able to limit his variations in filling to any desired degree. The figures chosen for the calculations are the weight variations allowed to hand blowers. Machine-blown bottles are more uniform in weight and also in capacity. Since the majority of the bottles are blown by machine, this calculated maximum variation is representative of the variations in the volume of bottle foods when they are packed under the specific good commercial practice conditions outlined, which require that the bottler give special attention to his methods of filling. Data are presented to show the possibilities of meeting the calculated maximum variations,

EXPERIMENTAL RESULTS.

The data which have been collected were taken for the purpose of showing the chance of occurrence of the calculated maximum variations in the capacity of the bottle and in the quantity of food therein. Other data were also collected to show the possibilities of meeting the calculated maximum variations by such temporary expedients as changing the height of fill or the declaration on the label.

VARIATION IN CAPACITY OF BOTTLES.

In order to determine the variations due exclusively to difference in the capacity of bottles, 22 representative glass factories located in Virginia, Maryland, Pennsylvania, New Jersey, West Virginia, and Ohio were visited, and 28 sets of measurements, including 1,090 bottles blown by hand and by machine processes, were taken. Certain conditions of blowing were prescribed before a set of bottles was selected for measurement. The moulds were noted to be in good repair and to have been in use at least one hour before the bottles selected for measurement were blown. It was stated that the glass was in good workable condition. All machines were operating under favorable circumstances and all blowers and gatherers were journeymen workmen. In the case of hand-blown bottles, measurements were made on a set which had been blown in a single mould. In the case of machine-blown bottles, a run of machine ware was measured. All measurements were made by pouring water from a standardized graduate into the bottles. A recapitulation of the results obtained is given in Table 3.

TABLE 3.—*Variations in capacity of bottles.*

[Data based on measurements in glass factories.]

Reference No.	Size of bottle.	Type.	Number measured.	Capacity at top.			Average deviation.	Average of average deviations of the size.
				Maximum.	Minimum.	Average.		
	Fl. oz.	HAND BLOWN.		*Fl. oz.*	*Fl. oz.*	*Fl. oz.*	*Fl. oz.*	*Fl. oz.*
1006–0	1	Shoo-fly flask.........	25	1.08	0.93	1.03	0.035	....
1006–1	1	.....do............	25	1.03	.90	.96	.032	0.033
1002–B	3	Oval prescription.....	25	3.55	3.31	3.47	.042	....
1002–S	3	.....do............	25	3.31	3.11	3.21	.039	....
1010–1	3	.....do............	25	3.21	2.99	3.11	.066	....
1010–2	3	.....do............	25	3.18	2.91	3.00	.055	....
1001	4	Round square.........	50	4.77	4.33	4.52	.099	....
1006–1	4	Shoo-fly flask.........	25	4.22	3.92	4.07	.074	....
1006–2	4	.....do............	25	4.29	3.89	4.12	.080	....
1008	4	Oval prescription.....	50	4.66	4.19	4.48	.071	.068
1001	8	.....do............	50	9.06	8.08	8.69	.15	....
1002	8	Tall blake...........	50	9.19	8.25	8.62	.13	....
1005	8	Soda water...........	50	8.92	7.67	8.32	.21	.16
1005	12	Beer................	50	13.58	12.71	13.18	.15	.15
1000–K	24	Brandy...............	25	24.84	23.49	24.24	.30	....
1000–P	24	.....do............	25	25.69	24.17	24.71	.36	.33
1005	64	Round packer.........	15	68.48	66.46	67.30	.41	.41

TABLE 3.—*Variations in capacity of bottles*—Continued.

Refer-ence No.	Size of bottle.	Type.	Number meas-ured.	Capacity at top.			Average devia-tion.	Average of average devia-tions of the size.
				Maxi-mum.	Mini-mum.	Average.		
	Fl. oz.	MACHINE BLOWN.		*Fl. oz.*	*Fl. oz.*	*Fl. oz.*	*Fl. oz.*	*Fl. oz.*
1004–M	2	Round packer.........	50	2.44	2.37	2.40	0.013	....
1004–1	2	.....do.......	50	2.44	2.37	2.40	.012	
1004–2	2	.....do........	50	2.42	2.37	2.40	.011	0.012
1004	4	Prescription...........	50	5.75	5.44	5.57	.068	.068
1015–A	8	Catsup...............	50	8.15	7.81	8.05	.06	....
1015–B	8	Grape juice...........	50	8.69	8.48	8.57	.04	
1004	8	Oval prescription.....	50	9.02	8.72	8.86	.07	
1014	8	.....do........	50	8.82	8.52	8.72	.04	.05
1004	12	.....do........	50	10.75	10.48	10.65	.05	.05
1004–U	16	.....do........	50	17.17	16.70	16.97	.09	....
1004–W	16	.....do........	25	17.58	17.31	17.47	.05	.07

Measurements were taken on a variety of types of bottles, the num-ber measured in every set was usually 25 or 50, and several sets of data were usually collected on one size of bottles. The maximum, minimum, and average capacities to the tops of the bottles show the usual range of capacities. The average deviation is the average of all the variations from the average capacity of the set as measured. The average of the average deviation of the various sizes, as shown in the last column, is an index of the variation of the bottles of the size mentioned. The figures in this column are used to compute the chance of occurrence of the calculated maximum variation in the capacity of bottled foods.

The chances of occurrence of variations in a normal frequency dis-tribution are calculated in accordance with the laws of probability as found in standard textbooks (3). The probability of occurrence of a given variation is found by the formula $f = \dfrac{x}{r}$, where f is a factor whose probability value is read from a table of probability integrals, x is the limiting variation whose probability of occurrence is de-sired, and r is the probable error of a single observation of the dis-tribution. The complement of the equivalent of f gives the prob-ability that variations greater than x will occur, and the resulting fraction, reduced until its numerator is one, gives the chances of their occurrence.

The variation for which it is desired to determine the chance of occurrence is the calculated maximum variation given in Table 9. This figure is given in Table 4 in the column headed "x." The prob-able error as found experimentally is computed from the last column of Table 3. For practical purposes, the probable error is equivalent to 0.8453 times the average deviation. It is so computed and in-cluded in Table 4, under the column headed "r." The remaining computations in Table 4 have been made according to the method outlined in the preceding paragraph.

TABLE 4.—*Chances of occurrence of variations in the capacity of bottles larger than the calculated maximum variations.*

HAND-BLOWN.

Capacity.	Calculated maximum variation, individual bottles.	Average deviation $\times$ 0.8453.	$\frac{x}{r}$	Probability.	Chance of occurrence based on observed data.
	(x)	(r)	(f)		
Fluid oz.	*Fluid oz.*				1 in:
1	0.10	0.028	3.58	0.9842	63
4	.24	.057	4.21	.9955	222
8	.29	.135	2.15	.8530	7
12	.29	.127	2.28	.8759	8
24	.39	.279	1.40	.6550	3
64	1.16	.346	3.36	.9766	43

MACHINE-BLOWN.

2	0.19	0.010	19.00	.9999+	over 10,000
4	.24	.057	4.21	.9955	222
8	.29	.042	6.90	.9999+	over 10,000
12	.29	.042	6.90	.9999+	over 10,000
16	.39	.059	6.62	.9999+	over 10,000

While the chances of occurrence of the calculated maximum variation, 1 in 7, 1 in 8, and 1 in 3, as shown for the hand-blown 8, 12, and 24 ounce sizes, respectively, are not very large, at least the table shows that they are far from even, and indicates that there is not an unreasonable possibility that hand blowers may meet the required calculated maximum variations, in a large percentage of cases. It is also possible that further data on other types of 8 and 12 ounce hand-blown bottles might reduce the chance of occurrence of the calculated maximum variation, since these sizes include soda water and beer bottles, in which exceptional care as to exact weight is not exercised in blowing. The 24 ounce size is not exceptionally common, and a majority of the other two sizes are blown by machine.

The averages of the figures in the last column of Table 4 are 1 in 58 for hand-blown bottles and 1 in more than 10,000 for machine-blown bottles. These figures show the reliability of the calculated maximum variations when used as limits of variation in the capacity of bottles. In view of the relative prevalence of machine-blown bottles and the possibilities of exceptional care in blowing hand-blown bottles, the data indicate that only a small percentage of the bottles as they occur on the market should vary in capacity by more than the calculated maximum variations.

VARIATION IN VOLUME OF BOTTLED FOODS.

In order to determine the variation in volume of the food filled into the bottle, 27 bottling establishments located at various points in Virginia, West Virginia, and Maryland were visited, and 20 sets of measurements, including 524 bottles, were taken. Rough measurements were first made on the bottles being used, from the result of which the bottler was given an aim in ounces by which to fill 50 bottles for measurement. The aim given was as consistent as possible with his declaration of the quantity of contents, but slight changes were often made, even though he were approximately following the good commercial practice outlined in this bulletin. The bottler was then requested to fill a number of his bottles with the specified number of ounces given to him as an aim, take the average of the distance from the top, and adjust his filling machine or filling system to fill to this average height. In cases where allowance for contraction due to change in temperature was necessary, he was instructed to deliver bottles which would be filled to this aim when cool. In cases where the bottles could not be opened, such as soda water, 50 empty bottles were selected at random, paired with full bottles, and filled to the same height by pouring water from a standardized graduate. The results so obtained were assumed to be equivalent to the volumes of food contained in the original bottles.

The results obtained are recapitulated in Table 5.

TABLE 5.—*Variation in volume of foods packed in bottles.*

Reference No.	Product.	Type of bottle. Manufactured.	Base.	Neck.	Number measured.	Aim.	Volume found. Maximum.	Minimum.	Average.	Average deviation.	Average of average deviations.	Average minus aim.	Average of average minus aim.
						Fl. oz.	Fl. oz.	Fl. oz.	Fl. oz.	Fl. oz.	Fl. oz.	Fl. oz.	Fl. oz.
1120	Flavoring extract.	H	Sq.	Con.....	25	0.75	0.88	0.66	0.76	0.034	0.034	0.01	0.01
1100	Soda water..	H	Rd..	Con.....	50	6.0	7.84	5.44	6.38	.29	.....	.39	.....
1110	Coca cola....	M	Sq.	Con.....	25	6.0	6.42	4.97	5.87	.27	.....	-.12	.....
1111	.....do.......	M	Sq.	Con.....	25	6.0	6.25	4.66	5.66	.25	.27	-.34	-.02
1105	.....do.......	H	Rd.	Con.....	50	7.0	7.54	6.42	7.07	.22	.....	.07	.....
1108	Soda water..	.....	Rd.	Cyl.	50	7.0	8.18	6.12	7.34	.37	.....	.34	.....
1109	.....do.......	H	Rd.	Con.....	50	7.0	7.77	6.56	7.01	.24	.....	-.02	.....
1113	.....do.......	.....	Rd.	Con.....	25	7.5	8.69	6.15	7.28	.63	.....	-.22	.....
1101	.....do.......	H	Rd.	Con.....	50	8.0	8.38	7.54	7.97	.15	.32	-.03	.04
1114	Vinegar......	H	Sq.	Con.....	10	15.0	15.68	14.94	15.51	.15	.15	.51	.51
1115	.....do.......	H	Rd.	Cyl. jar..	10	20.0	20.45	18.93	19.77	.34	.....	-.22	.....
1116	.....do.......	H	Rd.	Cyl. jar..	10	25.0	26.20	25.01	25.62	.27	.....	.63	.....
1124	.....do.......	H	Rd.	Cyl. jar..	20	25.5	26.70	25.52	26.30	.19	.....	.82	.....
1104	.....do.......	M	Rd.	Cyl. jar..	20	26.0	26.87	25.69	26.29	.31	.28	.30	.38
1103	.....do.......	M	Rd.	Cyl.	25	63.0	63.75	62.91	63.25	.19	.....	.25	.....
1117	.....do.......	H	Rd.	Cyl. jug.	10	63.0	65.61	63.75	64.25	.37	.....	1.25	.....
1123	.....do.......	H	Rd.	Cyl. jug.	19	63.0	63.24	61.22	62.22	.39	.32	-.78	.24
1102	.....do.......	M	Rd.	Cyl. jug.	20	128.0	130.70	126.82	128.02	.93	.....	.01	.....
1118	.....do.......	H	Rd.	Cyl. jug.	10	128.0	128.51	125.46	127.27	1.03	.....	.74	.....
1122	.....do.......	H	Rd.	Cyl. jug.	20	129.0	129.69	123.31	127.34	.47	.81	-1.67	-.80

With the exception of one set of data, measurements were taken on bottles of soda water and vinegar, and data were taken on hand-blown and machine-blown bottles, round and square bottles, bottles with conical and cylindrical necks, jars, and jugs. Some of these sets were filled by hand and some by machine. The maximum, minimum, and average volumes show the range of volume. As in Table 3, the average of the average deviations of various sizes is an index of the variation in volume of food in the bottles of the size mentioned, and the figures in this column are used to compute the chance of occurrence of the calculated maximum variations in the volume of bottled foods. By computations similar to those used in Table 4, the chance of occurrence of variations in the volume of food in the bottle larger than the calculated maximum variations has been computed and compiled in Table 6.

TABLE 6.—*Chances of occurrence of variations in the volume of food in the bottles larger than the calculated maximum variations.*

Capacity.	Calculated maximum variation, individual bottles. (x)	Average deviation ×0.8453. (r)	$\frac{x}{r}$ (f)	Probability.	Chance of occurrence based on observed data.
Fl. oz.	*Fl. oz.*	*Fl. oz.*			1 in—
0.75	0.10	0.029	3.45	0.9800	50
6	.24	.227	1.06	.5254	2
8	.29	.272	1.07	.5295	2
15	.39	.131	2.98	.9556	23
20–26	.39	.236	1.65	.7342	4
63	1.16	.269	4.31	.9964	278
128	1.94	.686	2.83	.9437	18

The results of the calculations in Table 6 are given in the last column. The average of the last column is 54, showing that, as a rule, one bottle in 54 will fall without the calculated maximum variation. With the exception of the 63-ounce size, where the chance of occurrence of the calculated maximum is 1 in 278, the results indicate that there might be a frequent occurrence of variations larger than the calculated maximum variation. It should be noted, however, that soda water is perhaps the most difficult food to bottle accurately, since it is carbonated. The vinegar bottled in the establishments in which these data were collected was bottled hot, thereby giving chances for additional variation due to cooling. When it is considered that the aim of the bottler was changed in some cases from his normal height of fill, it is evident that a number of factors have been introduced to cause variation which would not be met in bottling uncarbonated liquids under conditions which have been customary for some time, as would be the case if the bottler were following the good commercial practice outlined in this bulletin. These data represent variations which would be met under very extreme and difficult conditions. Under more favorable circumstances the chances of occurrence as calculated in Table 6 would be reduced.

The average deviations given in Tables 4 and 6 afford a comparison of variations in the capacities of the bottles and variations in volume of food after filling. The deviations are compiled in Table 7 for comparison.

TABLE 7.—*Comparison of the variation in capacities of bottles with the variation in volume of the bottled food.*

Capacity of bottles.	Average of average deviations in the capacity of hand-blown bottles.	Average of average deviations of the volume of food in the bottle.
Fluid oz.	*Fluid oz.*	*Fluid oz.*
0.75	....	0.034
1	0.033	....
4	.068	....
6	....	.269
8	.16	.322
12	.15	....
16	....	.155
24	.33	.279
64	.41	.318
128	....	.811

The average deviation in the capacities of the bottles of a given size is approximately equal to the average deviation of the volume of food contained in the bottles of that size. The fact that these two deviations are practically equivalent, supports the belief that the volume variation of bottled foods is approximately equivalent to the capacity variation of the bottles themselves when blown by hand. The calculated maximum variation apparently has about the same relation to the capacity of the bottle as to the volume of food in the bottle after it is filled.

In view of the unfavorable circumstances under which the data on the volume of bottled foods have been taken and the approximate agreement with the data on the variation in the capacity of bottles, the data indicate that only a small percentage of the bottled foods on the market should vary in quantity of contents more widely than the calculated maximum variations.

RELATION BETWEEN CALCULATED MAXIMUM VARIATION AND TEMPORARY METHODS OF MEETING DECLARED VOLUME.

The calculated maximum variation is not large enough to prevent the bottler from meeting it by the two temporary methods ordinarily used, namely, changing the height of fill or changing the declaration of the quantity of contents on the label.

In the course of the investigations, capacity measurements were made on bottles from the base of the shoulder to the usual aim in filling and to the top of the bottle. It is recognized that the base of the shoulder is not a definite filling point and that measurements will vary widely. However, the best estimate possible was made to determine this point, after which the measurements on 50 bottles were averaged. The aim, determined by the manufacturer of the bottles, was the height to which he usually fills to make his tests as to capacity. A recapitulation of the data, showing the average capacity of the bottles measured and the capacity from the base of the shoulder to the top and from the aim to the top, with their relations to the calculated maximum variations, is given in Table 8.

TABLE 8.—*Average shoulder to top capacity and head space (bottles with cylindrical necks and conical necks).*

Size.	Reference No.	Type.	Number measured.	Calculated maximum deviation.	Volume (shoulder to top).	Calculated maximum (shoulder to top).	Volume (aim to top).	Calculated maximum (aim to top).
Fl. oz.		CYLINDRICAL NECKS.		Fl. oz.	Fl. oz.	Ratio.	Fl. oz.	Ratio.
1	1006–0	Shoo-fly flask	25	....	0.39	0.3	0.09	1.1
	1006–1	.....do	25	0.10	.35	.3	.08	1.2
		Average	....	....	....	.3	....	1.2
2	1004–M	Round packer	50	....	.47	.4	.17	1.1
	1004–1	.....do	50	....	.47	.4	.22	1.6
	1004–2	.....do	50	.19	.44	.4	.11	1.7
		Average	....	....	....	.4	....	1.5
3	1002–B	Oval prescription	25	....	.45	.5	.33	.7
	1002–S	.....do	25	....	.37	.6	.30	.8
	1010–1	.....do	25	....	.61	.4	.21	1.1
	1010–2	.....do	25	....	.60	.4	.38	1.3
4	1001	Round square	50	....	.71	.3	.38	.6
	1008	Oval prescription	50	....	.55	.4	.16	1.5
	1004	.....do	50	.24	1.42	.2	.63	.4
		Average	....	....	....	.4	....	.9
8	1001	Oval prescription	50	....	1.19	.2	.71	.4
	1002	Blake	50	....	1.05	.3	.44	.7
	1004	Oval prescription	50	....	1.38	.2	.36	.8
	1014	.....do	50	.29	1.52	.2	.65	.4
		Average	....	....	....	.2	....	.6
10–12	1004	Oval prescription	50	.29	1.57	.2	.24	1.2
		Average	....	....	....	.2	....	1.2
16	1004	Oval prescription	50	....	2.86	.1	.36	1.1
	1004	.....do	25	.39	2.51	.2	.27	1.4
		Average	....	....	....	.2	....	1.3
64	1005	Round packer	15	1.61	10.65	.1	4.39	.3
		Average	....	....	....	.1	....	.3
		Grand average of individual observations.	....	....	....	.30	....	.97
		CONICAL NECK.						
4	1006–1	Shoo-fly flask	25	....	1.30	.2	.20	1.2
	1006–2	.....do	25	.24	1.35	.2	.23	1.0
		Average	....	....	....	.2	....	1.1
8	1005	Soda	50	....	1.87	.2	.66	.4
	1015–A	Catsup	50	....	2.68	.1	.19	1.5
	1015–B	Grape juice	50	.29	3.03	.1	.55	.5
		Average	....	....	....	.1	....	.8
12	1005	Beer	50	.29	3.15	.1	.78	.4
24	1000–K	Brandy	25	....	6.68	.6	.72	.5
	1000–P	.....do	25	.39	6.86	.6	.66	.6
		Average	....	....	....	.6	....	.6
		Grand average of individual observations.	....	....	....	.23	....	.76

The calculated maximum variations average nearly 0.3 of the available space from the base of the shoulder to the top in cylindrical-neck bottles and nearly 0.3 in conical-neck bottles; that is, the bottler has about three times enough room in his filling range to adjust his height of fill to meet the variations equivalent to the calculated maximum variations. The calculated maximum variations average about the same as the space in the bottle from the aim to the top, in the case of cylindrical-neck bottles and 0.8 in the conical-neck bottles (Table 8). Accordingly there is sufficient room in the bottles to permit changes from the usual height of fill to the limits of the calculated maximum variations.

The unit of change in declaration is of concern to the bottler when he receives bottles short of the capacity which he expects. It is the custom to declare the quantity of contents on bottled foods in whole units. In a survey of the bottling of flavoring extracts and similar products it was found that the prevalent sizes of bottles were 1, 2, 4, 8, and 12 ounces, 1 pint, 1 quart, $\frac{1}{2}$ gallon, and 1 gallon. In bottles containing less than 2 ounces some of the declarations varied by $\frac{1}{8}$-ounce units; in sizes from 2 to 8 ounces, some of the declarations varied by $\frac{1}{4}$-ounce units; and in sizes above 8 ounces, some varied by $\frac{1}{2}$-ounce units. The calculated maximum variations for 2 ounce, 8 ounce, and 1 pint capacities are 0.19, 0.29, and 0.39 ounce, respectively, which are approximately equivalent to the usual units of declaration for these sizes of bottles. The bottler would therefore meet the variations equivalent to the calculated maximum variations if he made the usual changes in his units of declaration. It follows that the bottler's usual temporary methods of meeting the proper declared volume can be governed by the calculated maximum variations as found in this bulletin.

PRACTICAL APPLICATION OF RESULTS.

The bottler will be able to apply the results of this investigation as outlined in Table 9 to guide him in making tests on bottles received. If the capacities of the bottles at his usual filling point vary from the capacity ordered by amounts greater than the results given in Table 9, he will necessarily feel that some further steps should be taken to meet properly the requirements of the law that the volume of food declared on the labels be correct. The bottle manufacturer will be able to use the results in Table 9 to guide him in determining whether or not any shortage found in the volume of bottled food may be due to unavoidable difficulties in the manufacturing or filling of the bottles.

SUMMARY.

Good commercial practice in bottling foods has been considered in this bulletin to be the attainment of conditions in the bottler's state of business in which he (a) includes in his orders for bottles the specifications as to capacity when filled to a specified height, (*b*) tests representative samples of every lot of bottles received, rejecting those appreciably under capacity, (*c*) fills his bottles to a height determined from the results of his tests, and (*d*) has his labels printed with a definite, correct statement of the quantity of contents and applies them unaltered.

The calculated maximum variations in the volume of bottled foods, as given in Table 9, have been computed from the weight variation allowed the blowers by the manufacturers, and by the use of the relation between the weight and volume of bottle glass.

TABLE 9.—*Calculated maximum variation in volume of bottled foods.*

Capacity of bottles.	Calculated maximum variation in volume.	
	Individual bottles.	Average of representative samples.
Fl. oz.	*Fl. oz.*	*Fl. oz.*
½	0.10	0.014
1	.10	.014
2	.19	.027
4	.24	.034
6	.24	.034
8	.29	.041
12	.29	.041
16	.39	.056
24	.39	.056
32	.58	.083
64	1.16	.17
128	1.94	.28

Data on the capacity of bottles and volume of food in bottles indicate that only a small percentage of the bottles of food filled in accordance with good commercial practice, as outlined in this bulletin, should vary in quantity of contents by more than the calculated maximum variations.

LITERATURE CITED.

(1) GLASS BOTTLE BLOWERS' ASSOCIATION OF THE UNITED STATES AND CANADA. Wage scale and working rules, 1914–15.

(2) HAMOR, W. A. The present status of the glass bottle and hollow ware industries in the United States. *In* J. Ind. Eng. Chem., 5 (1913): 951–954.

(3) MERRIMAN, MANSFIELD. A textbook on the method of least squares, 8th ed. New York, 1913.

(4) RUNKEL, H. Weight variation of package foods. U. S. Dept. Agr. Bull. 897 (1920), 20 pp.

(5) U. S. DEPARTMENT OF COMMERCE, BUREAU OF THE CENSUS. Abstract of the census of manufactures, 1914, pp. 209–210.

(6) U. S. DEPARTMENT OF COMMERCE, BUREAU OF FOREIGN AND DOMESTIC COMMERCE. The glass industry—Report on the cost of production of glass in the United States. *In* Misc. Series 60 (1917), pp. 303–306.

(7) U. S. TARIFF COMMISSION. The glass industry as affected by the war. Tariff Information Series 5 (1918), p. 147.

Displacement of Labor by Machinery in the Glass Industry

U.S. Bureau of Labor Statistics

Displacement of Labor by Machinery in the Glass Industry

From the Monthly Labor Review of the U. S. Bureau of Labor Statistics, Summarizing the Results of a Recent Investigation into Actual Conditions

In no other industry has the introduction of machinery had a more dramatic effect upon labor productivity than in the glass industry. Thus, to take an extreme example, in the blowing of 4-ounce prescription bottles, the average output per man is more than forty-one times as great with the automatic machine as with the hand processes which were in general use up to less than 20 years ago. This means a great reduction in the number of workers necessary to turn out a given quantity of product. It also means a great change in the character of the labor force. Instead of a group of very highly skilled glass blowers, assisted by a group of unskilled "boys," the automatic machine employs mechanics and machine operators, with little or no demand for child labor.

These revolutionary changes in the glass industry have taken place within a period of 25 years. The advent of the twentieth century found the glass industry in the United States still in the stage of hand production. With the exception of a few experimental semi-automatic machines used for the making of vaseline jars, the process of blowing bottles and other glassware was essentially the same as that used in Egypt some 3,500 years ago. In 1925, hand production had all but disappeared from the field. Its place was taken first by the semi-automatic and more recently by the automatic machines. The history of this change, and its effects on labor productivity and labor cost in the glass industry, are set forth in a bulletin soon to be published by the United States Bureau of Labor Statistics entitled, "Labor Productivity in the Glass Industry." The present article is a summary of that work.

Comparisons of Labor Output and Cost in Hand and Machine Production

How far-reaching these results have been will become self-evident from the following highly illuminating examples:

BOTTLES.—A hand "shop," consisting of 3 skilled workers (a gatherer, a blower, and a finisher) and 4 helpers, can produce on the average 3.75 gross of 4-ounce prescription ovals per hour. The 1925 average output of the most up-to-date Owens automatic machine was 69,754 gross of 4-ounce prescription ovals per hour. The average output of the hand shop is 0.536 gross per man per hour, while with the automatic machine the average is 22.028 gross per man per hour, or more than forty-one times as much as in the hand process.

Based on the 1925 wage rates, the direct blowing labor cost of a 4-ounce prescription oval made by hand would be $1.177 per gross. With the Owens automatic machine, the 1925 direct blowing labor cost of the same kind of bottle was 3.15 cents per gross. For every dollar spent on blowing a 4-ounce prescription oval by hand, the labor cost on the Owens automatic machine was but 2.70 cents.

PRESSED WARE.—In making 8-9 ounce common table tumblers on the side-lever press, a hand shop, consisting of 3 skilled workers (a gatherer, a presser, and a finisher) and 6 helpers, produced in 1925 an average of 278.96 pieces per hour, or 31 pieces per man per hour. The Hartford Empire twin press, operated with an automatic conveyor, produced in 1925 an average of 1,903.54 pieces per hour, or 380.71

pieces per man per hour, more than twelve times as much as could be produced with the hand press. The direct labor cost of pressing 100 of these tumblers was with the hand press, $1.95 and with the automatic press, 13 cents. Thus, for every dollar spent on the direct labor of pressing common table tumblers by hand it cost but 6.7 cents to press them on the automatic machine.

ELECTRIC-LIGHT BULBS.—A hand shop, consisting of a gatherer and a blower, assisted by a section boy and a cutting-off boy, can produce on the average 121.98 40-watt electric-light bulbs per hour, or 54.21 pieces per man per hour. The 1925 average output of the new type Westlake automatic machine was 2,342.44 bulbs per hour, or 1,703.59

window glass, per hour, or 0.709 box per man per hour. On the Fourcault automatic machine, the average 1925 output was 7.68 boxes per hour, or 1.85 boxes per man per hour, more than two and a half times as much as by the hand process. The average direct blowing labor cost by the hand process was 95.5 cents per box, as compared with the average cost of 29.9 cents per box made on the Fourcault automatic machine, the use of the machine meaning in this case a saving of nearly 70 cents on every dollar spent for blowing by the hand process.

PLATE GLASS.—The output of casting rough plate glass by the discontinuous process, which is still prevalent in the industry, is 43.89 square feet per man per hour; by the

ROLLING PLATE GLASS ON THE CASTING TABLE
Reprinted from a previous issue.

pieces per man per hour, more than thirty-one times as much as by the hand process. The average blowing labor cost by the hand process was $13.88 per 1,000 pieces, as compared with $0.470 by the machine process. The saving in labor cost effected by automatic machine was 96.61 cents on every dollar required for the hand process.

GLASS TUBING.—A hand shop, consisting of 4 skilled workers (a gatherer, a ball maker, a marverer, and a gaffer) and 4 unskilled helpers, can produce on the average 80.54 pounds of glass tubing, sizes 32 to 34, inclusive, or an average of 10.07 pounds per man per hour. In 1925, the Danner tube-drawing machine, working on the same sizes of tubing, produced on the average 300.70 pounds per hour or 75.17 pounds per man per hour, which is seven and one-half times as much as by the hand method. The blowing labor cost by the hand process averages $6.83 per 100 pounds, while with the Danner machine the cost is only $1 per 100 pounds. Thus, for every dollar spent for labor on blowing glass tubing by hand it costs but 14.7 cents to blow it by the Danner machine.

WINDOW GLASS.—A hand shop, consisting of one gatherer, one blower, and one snapper, can produce on the average 2.72 boxes, each containing 50 square feet of single-strength

continuous automatic process, recently introduced, the average is 63.63 square feet per man per hour, or 45 per cent more than by the old process. In the case of polished plate glass, the man-hour output by the discontinuous process averages 7.66 square feet, while that by the continuous process is 12.30 square feet, or 60.5 per cent higher. The total labor cost of casting rough plate glass by the continuous process is 25.1 per cent less than by the discontinuous process, and the total labor cost of making polished plate glass is on the average 43.3 per cent less than by the discontinuous process.

Development of Machinery in the Industry

The glass industry is composed of a number of branches whose only common characteristic is the molten glass from which the respective commodities are made. The nature of the ware made and the methods of production, whether by hand or by machine, are entirely different in the separate branches. The development of machinery also has not been uniform and simultaneous in all the branches. To all intents and purposes, therefore, the five separate branches may be considered as independent industries manufacturing, respectively: Bottles and jars, pressed ware, blown ware, window glass, and plate glass.

MANUFACTURE OF BOTTLES AND JARS

In his book, Machinery and Labor, Prof. G. E. Barnett, of Johns Hopkins University, distinguishes three periods in the development of machinery for the purpose of making bottles and jars: (1) 1898-1905, during which was developed semi-automatic machinery for the making of wide-mouth ware exclusively; (2) 1905-1917, characterized by the introduction of the Owens automatic machine for the making of all kinds of bottles, both wide and narrow mouth, and of semi-automatic machinery for the manufacture of narrow-mouth ware; (3) 1917 to date, during which time semi-automatic machinery has been made automatic by "feed and flow devices."

The first more or less successful semi-automatic machine was invented in 1882 by Philip Arbogast, of Pittsburgh, Pa.,

ROLLING PLATE GLASS BY THE FORD PROCESS
Reprinted from a previous issue.

and 11 years later this machine was successfully applied for the purpose of making vaseline jars. In 1896, a similar machine was invented for the purpose of making Mason jars. The growth of the semi-automatic machine from 1897 to 1905, as shown by the number of machines in use in each of those years, is given by Professor Barnett as follows: 1897, 20 machines; 1898, 50 machines; 1899, 60 machines; 1900, 80 machines; 1901, 90 machines; 1902, 100 machines; 1903, 150 machines; 1904, 200 machines; 1905, 250 machines.

But the first really revolutionary change took place in 1904, with the successful introduction of the automatic machine, invented by M. J. Owens. This machine, where used, at once displaces all the skilled blowers and most of their helpers in the shops. The output of the new machine was so much greater and the cost of production so much less than by the hand and the semi-automatic processes, that had it not been for the restrictive policies of the owners of the Owens machine, these less economical processes would at once have been displaced by the automatic machine.

As it happened, however, the period of the Owens automatic machine was also the period of the development of semi-automatic machinery. In 1917, there were 200 Owens machines in operation in this country, but there were also in use 428 wide and narrow mouth semi-automatic machines. At about this time, also, the "gob" feeder, which had been

experimented with for some time, became a commercial success. This appeared to have certain advantages over both the Owens automatic and the semi-automatic machines. In the course of the next eight years the majority of the semi-automatic machines were reconstructed and equipped with automatic feeders so as to become completely automatic. The Owens machine has also undergone a series of important changes, especially as to the number of arms and the number of molds on each arm. The most modern type of Owens machine has 15 arms, each equipped with two molds, and each mold containing cavities for two or three bottles, depending on the size of the bottle. At present, these automatic processes completely dominate the bottle-making industry. The semi-automatic process has disappeared entirely, but a

FORD CONTINUOUS GLASS GRINDING MACHINES
Reprinted from a previous issue.

small number of plants are still using the hand process for bottles which cannot be made more economically on the machine.

MANUFACTURE OF PRESSED WARE

Although the introduction of the side-lever press dates back to 1827, the general introduction of machinery in this branch of the industry took place much later and is less significant than that in the bottle industry. The side-lever press is still used in a large number of plants. During the first part of this century the semi-automatic rotary press was introduced, but the greatest change came with the introduction of feeding devices. Modern machines equipped with these devices are made after the pattern of the bottle-blowing machines, but are less complicated. They are used primarily for making pressed tumblers of all sizes, nappies and sherbets. The largest proportion of pressed ware, especially the so-called "novelties," is still, however, made either on the old-fashioned side-lever press or on the rotary press.

MANUFACTURE OF BLOWN WARE

In the field of blown ware, the development of machinery has been much more pronounced than in the case of pressed ware. The machines used are also more complicated and specialize in the production of some particular article, such as lamp chimneys, electric-lamp bulbs, punch tumblers, and tubes.

The lamp-chimney semi-automatic machine dates back to 1894. Since then it has undergone a number of changes, but on the whole very little progress has been made in this branch of the glass industry. Hand production, especially the off-hand method, is still an important factor, but the industry as a whole is diminishing in importance, as electricity is rapidly displacing the use of oil-burning lamps even in the most outlying and inaccessible districts.

On the other hand, the most amazing progress has been recorded in the making of electric-lamp bulbs. Since 1917, hand production has been almost entirely displaced, first by the semi-automatic Empire E machine, and more recently by the completely automatic Westlake machine and the Empire F machine operated with an automatic feeder. At present, more than 95 per cent of all the electric bulbs are made by the two automatic processes. The semi-automatic machine has been almost completely abandoned, while a few hand shops have been retained for experimental purposes, or for the purpose of making oddly shaped and colored electric bulbs.

THE WESTLAKE MACHINE

The Westlake machine, which revolutionized the bulb-making industry, has also recently invaded the field of punch tumblers. These are now made either on the Westlake machine or as a byproduct on the lamp-chimney semi-automatic machine. Only the most expensive tumblers, those decorated with special designs, are still made by the hand shops.

The year 1917, which brought with it so many revolutionary innovations in the bottle and pressed and blown ware branches of the industry, witnessed also the introduction of the Danner machine for the making of glass tubing. The new method was so superior to the old hand process that, in the comparatively short period of less than eight years, it so thoroughly displaced the old process that not a single shop can now be found making glass tubing by hand.

MANUFACTURE OF WINDOW GLASS

The introduction of the Lubber cylinder machine in 1905 was the first successful attempt to replace by machine the hand process of making window glass. The cylinder process may be called semi-automatic, as considerable handling of the glass is required in the various stages of its journey from the tank to the cutter's table. In 1917, the Colburn process of automatically drawing a continuous sheet of glass from the tank became a commercial success, while in 1921

the Fourcault automatic process, invented in Belgium, was successfully introduced into this country. As a result very little window glass is at present made in this country by the hand process. The cylinder machine is still the dominating factor in the industry, but the improved Colburn process and more recently the Fourcault machine have been rapidly gaining on the cylinder process and are becoming very important.

MANUFACTURE OF PLATE GLASS

The story of plate glass is essentially different from that of any other branch of the glass industry. It has been from the very beginning a nonskilled industry, and the many simple operations involved in the process of handling the large and heavy plates soon suggested the use of labor-saving devices. When the industrial revolution finally

DRAWING WINDOW GLASS CYLINDERS
Reprinted from a previous issue.

reached the other branches of the glass industry, plate glass had already become a progressive, well-integrated industry. Recently, however, the introduction of the continuous tank and the automatic process of casting rough plate, and the conveyor method of grinding and polishing the plates, have tended to bring about changes in the plate glass branch almost as revolutionary as those in the other branches of the industry. The continuous process has not yet reached the stage of unquestioned superiority over the older so-called discontinuous process, and some time will probably elapse before the industry universally adopts the new process.

The Monthly Labor Review from which this article is reprinted is published twelve times a year by the Bureau of Labor Statistics, United States Department of Labor, James J. Davis, Secretary. Copies may be obtained from the Superintendent of Documents, Washington, D. C., at 15 cents each.

Effects of Automatic Machinery on the Industry

In view of the tremendous changes in man-hour output and labor cost due to automatic machinery, it may be worth while to examine more or less in detail the effects of the introduction of machinery on the industry as a whole. Table 1, compiled from census reports, shows the growth of the industry from 1899 to 1925 (the period during which the change from hand production to semi-automatic and automatic machinery

this branch has an increased number of plants and wage earners, as well as an increase in the average number of workers per establishment. In the window-glass branch, the predominance of the cylinder-machine process has cut the number of establishments over half, somewhat diminished the total number of wage earners, and increased the average number of wage earners per plant nearly one and one-third times. In the plate glass industry, which until very recently wit-

TABLE 1—DEVELOPMENT OF THE GLASS INDUSTRY, IN SPECIFIED YEARS, 1899 TO 1925								
Item	1899	1904	1909	1914	1919	1921	1923	1925
Total number of establishments	355	399	363	348	371	329	333	310
Bottles and jars	147	158	166	150	145	(*)	117	120
Pressed and blown ware	84	103	114	107	130	(*)	127	123
Window glass	100	103	(*)	64	79	(*)	65	42
Plate glass	16	17	(*)	19	17	17	17	19
Total number of wage earners	52,818	63,969	68,911	74,502	77,520	54,748	73,335	69,371
Bottles and jars	28,370	(*)	(*)	(*)	(*)	(*)	24,010	21,704
Pressed and blown ware	12,546	(*)	(*)	(*)	(*)	(*)	27,196	21,507
Window glass	8,682	(*)	(*)	(*)	(*)	(*)	8,826	8,346
Plate glass	3,220	(*)	(*)	(*)	(*)	(*)	9,961	11,124
Output:								
Bottles and jars—thousand gross	7,780	12,005	12,316	19,290	22,295	(*)	28,393	26,044
Pressed and blown ware—million pieces	360	428	532	701	1,080	(*)	(*)	1,963
Window glass—thousand boxes	4,341	4,852	6,922	8,020	7,380	5,201	10,204	11,343
Plate glass—thousand square feet	16,884	27,293	47,370	60,384	56,823	56,239	94,470	17,369
Value of output (000 omitted)	$56,540	$79,608	$92,095	$123,085	$261,884	$213,471	$309,353	$295,959
Bottles and jars	21,677	33,631	36,018	51,959	94,670	(*)	107,231	100,301
Pressed and blown ware	17,076	21,956	27,398	30,279	70,749	(*)	77,279	72,085
Window glass	10,879	11,611	11,743	17,495	41,101	24,026	42,623	37,525
Plate glass	5,159	7,978	12,205	14,774	33,348	37,261	66,103	57,207
Wages (000 omitted)	27,084	37,288	39,300	48,656	87,527	68,224	89,898	86,736

(*) Not reported.

took place) for the industry as a whole, and also, where available, for the four principal branches whose combined output constitutes more than 90 per cent of that of the industry.

ESTABLISHMENTS AND WAGE EARNERS

As shown in the table, the glass industry in 1899 comprised 355 establishments, employing 52,818 wage earners, an average of 149 wage earners per establishment; in 1925 there were only 310 establishments, but these employed 69,371 wage earners, an average of 24 wage earners per establishment. In the course of the 25 years, the number of establishments decreased 12.7 per cent, while the number of wage earners increased 31.3 per cent, and the average number of wage earners per establishment increased 50.3%.

The figures for the industry as a whole, however, do not tell the story of what happened in the separate branches. In the bottle and jar branch, the general adoption of the automatic machines resulted not only in a diminution of the number of plants and wage earners in the industry, but also in a decrease of the average number of wage earners per establishment. Fewer workers are seen in a large up-to-date machine bottle plant than in a small hand plant. In the pressed and blown ware branch the automatic machines have so far invaded only a small part of the industry, and

nessed no revolutionary changes, the growth of industry more than tripled the number of wage earners and nearly tripled the average number of workers per establishment.

SIZE OF ESTABLISHMENTS

The number of workers employed and the average number per establishment cannot, however, be used as an indication of the change in the size of the establishment, for the reason that the primary object of the introduction of machinery has been to decrease the number of wage earners employed. This is especially true of the bottle and jar branch of the industry.

THE LIBBEY-OWENS SHEET GLASS DRAWING MACHINE
Reprinted from a previous issue.

A better means of measuring the size of an establishment may be found either in the quantity or the value of output. For a period of years the quantity of output is more effective, as it remains more or less untouched by changes in prices, which exert a disturbing influence on the value of the output.

In 1899, the average output per establishment in the four branches was: Bottles and jars, 52,925 gross; pressed and blown ware, about 4,286,000 pieces; window glass, 43,410 boxes; and plate glass, 1,055,200 square feet. In 1925 it was: Bottles and jars, about 217,000 gross; pressed and blown ware, 15,959,000 pieces; window glass, 270,100 boxes, and plate glass, 6,177,000 square feet. Thus, in 1925, the average output per establishment was 4.1 times as much as in 1899, in the case of bottles and jars; 3.7 times as much in the case of pressed and blown ware; 6.2 times as much in the case of window glass, and 5.9 times as much in the case of plate glass.

The distribution of total number of establishments and the value of their output on the basis of the value of output in each establishment is even more significant of the changes in the size of establishments than the actual output per establishment. Table 2 shows the total number of establishments in 1904* and 1925 divided according to the value of the yearly output.

As shown in the table, the tendency has been for the manufacturing units to become steadily larger. Thus in 1904 only 11.3 per cent of the total value of all glass products was produced in plants with annual products valued at $1,000,000 or over. In 1925 this percentage had grown to no less than 72.5.

Prior to the introduction of machinery, the glass industry was predominately a small-unit industry. The amount of capital needed for a plant was small, and the principal item of expenditure, outside of labor, was fuel. A cheaper rate on coal or natural gas was enough of an inducement for the removal of a glass plant from one locality to another and from State to State. The history of the discoveries of natural

TABLE 2.—NUMBER OF ESTABLISHMENTS IN THE GLASS INDUSTRY AND VALUE OF THEIR PRODUCT, 1904 AND 1925, BY CLASSIFIED VALUE OF PRODUCTS.

Establishments with yearly value of product of—	Number of establishments		Total value of product	
	1904	1925	1904	1925
Under $100,000	164	49	$8,341,000	$2,652,000
$100,000 and under $1,000,000	230	178	62,274,000	78,754,000
$1,000,000 and over	5	83	8,993,000	214,553,000
Total	399	310	79,608,000	295,959,000
			Per cent—	
Under $100,000	41.1	15.8	10.5	0.9
$100,000 and under $1,000,000	57.6	57.4	78.2	26.6
$1,000,000 and over	1.3	26.8	11.3	72.5
Total	100.0	100.0	100.0	100.0

gas in Pennsylvania, Indiana, West Virginia and Oklahoma also tells the story of the migrations of the glass industry to and from these States.

But with the advent of machinery, the situation changed

FOURCAULT SHEET GLASS DRAWING MACHINES AND TANKS
Reprinted from a previous issue.

completely. Fuel is still a very big item in the cost of production of glass, and is still considered as the factor determining the site of a new glass establishment. But once the plant is built, the capital outlay on the building, the furnaces, and the machines, and other items prevent the moving of the establishment irrespective of the cost of fuel. Thus, as migration was eliminated, the advantages of large-scale production were at once brought into play, with the result that in the short span of 25 years, the glass industry has been converted from a small and loosely connected industry into a large and well-integrated one.

[The concluding portion of this article will be given in an early issue: It treats of Output and Productivity; Value of Output; Wage Workers' Earnings; Child Labor in Industry.—Ed.]

*Data are not available for 1899.

Displacement of Labor by Machinery in the Glass Industry

From the Monthly Labor Review of the U. S. Bureau of Labor Statistics

(Concluded from the May issue)

Bulletin 441, "Productivity of Labor in the Glass Industry," mentioned on page 110 of the May issue, will contain more than 200 pages, crammed full of description, data and discussion of the glass industry, principally manufacturing operations, with particular reference to the cost and productivity of labor in this industry as affected by the introduction of machinery.

The investigation upon which this report is based was authorized by the United States Department of Labor, James J. Davis, secretary, and was conducted by the Bureau of Labor Statistics, Ethelbert Stewart, Commissioner. The bulletin was prepared by Boris Stern of the latter bureau, who evidently spent a great deal of time and an enormous amount of energy in the collection of information and preparation of this voluminous report of facts and statistics pertaining to the subject of the investigation.

Mr. Stern visited scores of glass factories and has thoroughly familiarized himself with all of the principal glass making operations as carried on today. He has compared them with former methods and treats of the effects of the introduction of machinery into glass-making processes from the time when mechanical inventions were first applied to the production of glass down to the present.

The exact date on which the bulletin will be issued by the Bureau of Labor Statistics has not been learned, but it is understood that copies will be available very soon. They will be obtainable through the United States Government Printing Office, Washington, D. C.

A large part of the material contained in the accompanying article was taken from matter prepared for Bulletin 441, which in reality is a more extensive treatment of the same subjects.

Output and Productivity

From the labor standpoint, the most important change directly connected with the introduction of machinery in the glass industry has been the increase in output per wage earner employed. Table 3 shows a comparison of output per man in the four principal branches of the glass industry in 1899 and 1925. As there shown, the increase in 1925 over 1899 was greatest in the case of bottles and jars, 338 per cent; and lowest in the case of plate glass, 101.3 per cent.

TABLE 3.—YEARLY OUTPUT PER MAN IN SPECIFIED BRANCHES OF THE GLASS INDUSTRY, 1899 AND 1925.

Branch of industry	Unit	1899	1925 Quantity	Per cent of increase over 1899
Bottles and jars	Gross	274	1,200	338.0
Pressed and blown ware	Pieces ...	28,694	91,272	218.1
Window glass	Boxes	500	1,359	171.8
Plate glass	Square feet	5,240	10,551	101.3

In the figures for the separate branches of the industry there exists a slight error, due to the fact that the hours worked per day in 1899 and 1925 are not strictly comparable. For instance, in the bottle industry the regular hours of work were eight and one-half in 1899 and only eight in 1925. On the other hand, in 1899 nearly all the plants, following a long-established custom, suspended production for a period of two months, while in 1925 only a few plants stopped producing for a month or more, because of repairs or the usual reconstruction of tanks, which must be done every 12 to 18 months. Similar or somewhat different discrepancies in the hours worked also exist in the other branches of the industry, but their general effect on the output was so slight as to exert very little, if any, influence on the validity of the figures of productivity given.

Value of Output

In 1899, the 7,780,000 gross of bottles and jars produced were valued at $21,677,000, an average of $2.79 per gross; in 1925, the value of the 26,044,000 gross produced was $100,301,000, an average of $3.86 per gross, and an increase of 38.4 per cent over the average value of 1899. In the pressed and blown ware branch of the industry, the 360,000,000 pieces produced in 1899 were valued at $17,076,000, an average of $4.74 per hundred pieces. In 1925, the 1,963,000,000 pieces produced were worth $72,085,000, making the average $3.67 per hundred pieces, or 22.6 per cent lower than in 1899. In the window-glass branch, the 4,341,000 boxes produced in 1899 were valued at $10,879,000, an average of $2.50 per box. In 1925, the 11,343,000 boxes were worth $37,525,000, an average of $3.31 per box, or 32.4 per cent higher than in 1899. In the plate-glass branch, the 16,884,000 square feet of polished glass produced in 1899 were worth $5,159,000, making the average $30.56 per hundred square feet. In 1925, the 117,369,000 square feet produced were worth $57,207,000, an average of $48.74 per hundred square feet, which is 59.5 per cent higher than the average of 1899.

Table 4 compares the trend of these average values in the four branches of the industries, and of wholesale prices of manufactured commodities, from 1899 to 1925.

In average unit values each branch of the industry seems to have a trend entirely different from any other branch, due to conditions inherent in that branch. For instance, window glass and plate glass as building materials are largely affected by the general conditions in the building industry. This accounts for the drop in their values in 1909 and the steep rise in 1919, as compared with the value of bottles and jars or of pressed and blown ware. Again, for a number of years plate glass has been in great demand for the automobile industry, and in 1921, in spite of the depression in the other branches of the glass industry and in the wholesale price index of manufactured commodities, the value of plate glass continued to rise through 1923, when the introduction of the continuous process began to exert its influence and values began to drop.

On the whole, however, the general trend of the four branches of the industry is unmistakably downward, and, with the exception of plate glass, none of the average unit value indexes rose during the period above the wholesale price index of manufactured commodities.

TABLE 4.—AVERAGE UNIT VALUES OF PRODUCT AND INDEX NUMBERS THEREOF AND OF WHOLESALE PRICES OF MANUFACTURED COMMODITIES IN SPECIFIED YEARS, 1899 TO 1925

| Year | Average value of product | | | | Index numbers of— | | | | Wholesale prices of manufactured Commodities[1] |
	Bottles and jars (per gross)	Pressed and blown ware (per 100 pieces)	Window glass (per box)	Plate glass (per 100 square feet)	Bottles and jars	Pressed and blown ware	Window glass	Plate glass	
1899	$2.79	$4.74	$2.50	$30.56	100.0	100.0	100.0	100.0	100.0
1904	2.80	5.13	2.40	29.23	100.0	108.2	96.0	95.6	109.8
1909	2.93	5.15	1.70	25.78	105.0	108.6	68.0	84.4	124.6
1914	2.70	4.33	2.18	24.47	96.8	91.4	87.2	80.1	128.7
1919	4.25	6.54	5.57	58.68	152.3	138.0	222.8	192.0	273.4
1921	([2])	([2])	4.61	66.25	....	....	184.4	216.8	188.2
1923	3.78	([2])	4.18	69.96	135.5	....	167.2	228.9	188.7
1925	3.86	3.67	3.31	48.74	138.4	77.4	132.4	159.5	203.3

[1] Recomputed from indexes given in U. S. Bureau of Labor Statistics Bul. No. 415, p. 31.
[2] Not reported.

Wage Workers' Earnings

A comparison of rates of wages in the glass industry in 1899 and 1925 is of no significance, for the reason that the nature of the work done and the kind of labor used in 1925 were entirely different from the work done and the labor used in 1899. Twenty-five years ago the majority of workers employed in the industry consisted of highly-skilled blowers, pressers, finishers, gatherers, flatteners, and cutters, and unskilled mold boys, snapping-up boys, warming-in boys, carry-in boys, carry-over boys, and the like. In 1925, only a small percentage of such labor had been retained even in the hand plants. The new class of glass workers is made up of tank men, machinists, machine foremen, machine operators, and helpers, with little if any preliminary training in handling machines. Again, in 1899 all skilled workers were paid on a piecework basis, while in 1925 the overwhelming majority of workers were paid on a time basis—by the hour, by the week, or by the month.

It is possible to compare the yearly earnings of the wage earners in 1899 and in 1925. In 1899 the 52,818 wage earners in the industry received a total wage of $27,084,000, an average of $512.78 per wage earner per year. In 1925 the 69,371 wage earners received a total wage of $86,736,000, an average of $1,250.32 per wage earner per year, or nearly 2½ times as much as in 1899. But in making these comparisons it must be remembered that the group of wage

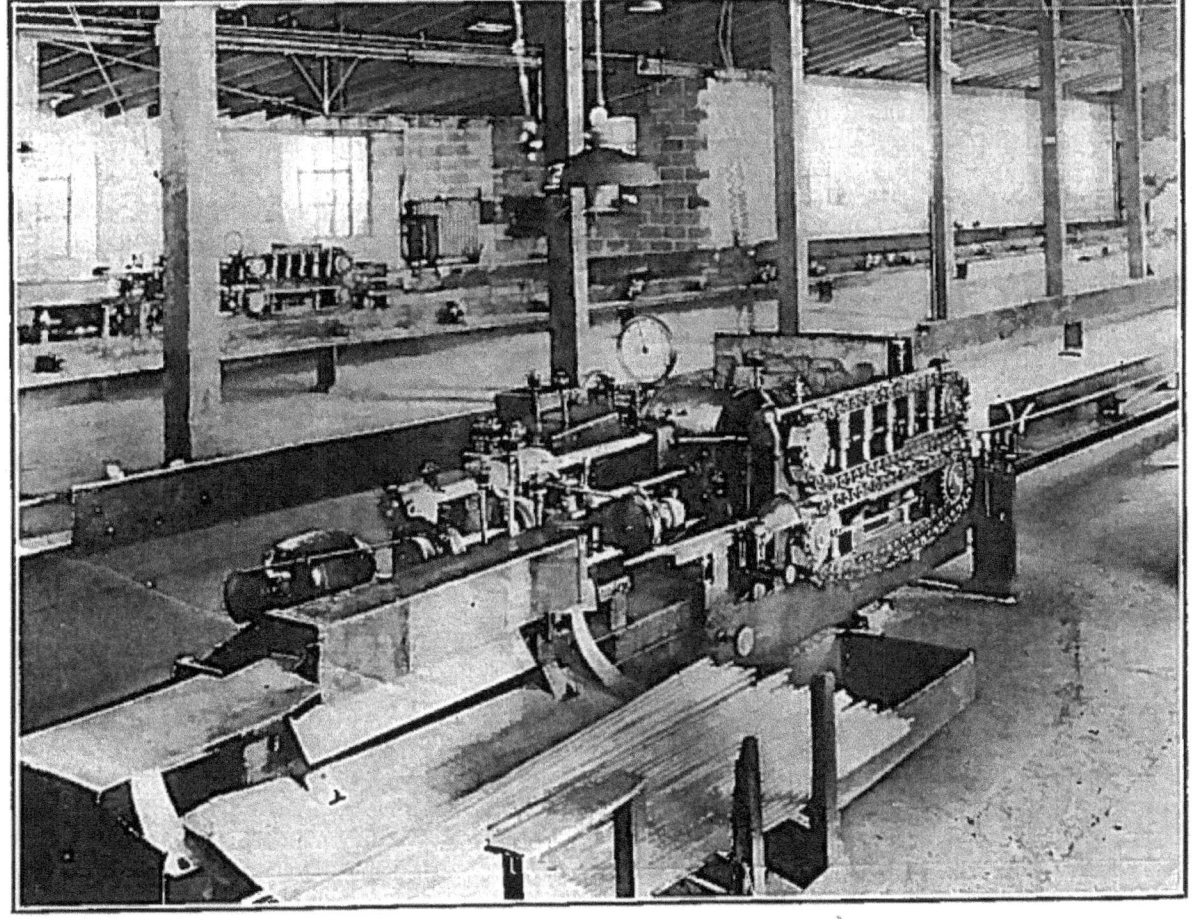

THE DANNER AUTOMATIC TUBE DRAWING MACHINE, WHICH IN A FEW YEARS DISPLACED PRACTICALLY ALL "HAND BLOWERS" IN THE TUBING FIELD. *Reprinted from a previous issue.*

earners in 1899 contained a large percentage of workers under 16 years of age, with extremely low wages; whereas in 1925 the number of minors under 16 years was practically nil. This difference would tend considerably to depress the average earnings per man in 1899 as compared with 1925. On the other hand, many of the skilled workers in 1899, working on a piece-rate basis, were earning exceptionally high wages. Fifty to seventy-five dollars a week was not an exceptionally high wage for a skilled bottle or window-glass blower in those days. In 1925 this extreme had also been eliminated.

Child Labor in the Industry

Prior to the introduction of machinery, the glass industry was one of the greatest exploiters of child labor. This was particularly true of the bottle and pressed and blown ware branches, for very few children had ever been employed in the making of window glass and none in plate glass. In 1899, of the total of 40,916 wage earners employed in making bottles and pressed and blown ware, 7,035, or 17.2 per cent, were children under the age of 16 years. These were employed chiefly as mold boys, cleaning-off boys, and snapping-up boys in the furnace room, and partly as burning-off girls, glazing girls, and selectors in the finishing department.

The conditions under which the children were employed are fully discussed in the Commissioner of Labor's Report on Condition of Woman and Child Wage Earners in the Glass Industry in the United States made at the request of the United States Senate and published in 1910. The following quotations are from this report. Referring to the work of the mold boy it says:

The mold rests upon or very close to the floor. As a result the mold boy must either squat upon the ground in an awkward, cramped position * * * or, standing, must stoop constantly to his work. When the mold boy must thus sit with his legs doubled under him, or sitting on a crude chair or box, stoop over almost to the floor to operate the molds, the occupation becomes one which, continued for any great length of time, undoubtedly tends to dwarf and deform the child.

He must necessarily be close to the mold, and for speed of working the mold is placed near the furnace, directly in front of the working hole and some 3 feet below the level of the hole. As the mold tender works he faces the furnace, and his face and shoulders at least are in direct line with the radiated heat from the working hole. In addition to the furnace, there are other sources of heat adding to the boy's discomfort: The blower in lowering the hot lump of glass into the mold necessarily swings it close to the boy's face; the mold itself, after a short using, becomes very hot and gives off considerable heat; in some factories the "glory holes," at which the finishing work is done, are crowded close to the furnace, and little space left between them and the mold boys (p. 48).

The heat conditions in the furnace room are thus described:

The generally accepted figures of the heat within a furnace during the "fusing" is 2,507° F. between the pots and 2,390° F. in the metal itself. These temperatures are reduced when the holes are opened for working to a standard of

1,913° F., although glass is commonly worked at a temperature of a hundred degrees less than these figures.

Factory No. 2 was examined June 18, at 12.25 p.m. with the outside temperature at 90°. The temperature taken at a point two feet from but directly in front of a working hole showed 142°, two others taken the same distance from but slightly to the side of the holes showed 135° and 137°. Temperature near cleaning-off boy, 105°; near the mold boy 113°; in front of the "glory hole," 116°; at finisher's bench, 104°; where snap-up boy stands to rub excess glass off neck of bottle, 103°; where carry-in boy picks up ware, 98°; in

MELTING AND DRAWING TANK, DANNER PROCESS.

front of lehr, where carry-in boy stands to deposit ware, 125°.

In warmer weather the ill effects of the heat show themselves directly in the form of prostration or affections directly due to the high temperature. In the winter the immediate danger to health arises from sudden changes in temperature. The boys, as a rule, have little or no extra clothing to protect them from the outside weather and rarely take the trouble to wait in the factory until their bodies are sufficiently cooled to bear the change. The danger is particularly acute when night work is being done.

With the introduction of machinery in the industry the child-labor situation changed. The mold boys, the cleaning-off boys, and the snapping-up boys were at once dispensed with, even in the case of the cruder and semi-automatic machines. The job of the carry-in boys was retained for some time, but the introduction of the Owens automatic machine, with its automatic conveyor, eliminated all the work formerly done by child labor. Even where no conveyors have been installed and the job of the carry-in boys has been retained, the output of the machines has proved to be too large to be handled by minors, and the job, though retaining the name of "carry-in boys," is actually performed by an adult unskilled man or woman.

Table 5 gives the total number of wage earners and of children under 16 years employed in the industry from 1880 to 1919, the last year for which figures are available from the census reports:

TABLE 5.—NUMBER OF WAGE EARNERS AND OF MINORS UNDER 16 YEARS EMPLOYED IN THE GLASS INDUSTRY. BY SPECIFIED YEARS, 1880 TO 1919.

Year	Number of wage earners	Minors under 16 years	
		Number	Per cent of total wage earners
1880	24,177	¹ 5,658	23.4
1890	44,892	¹ 6,943	15.5
1899	52,818	7,116	13.5
1904	63,969	6,435	10.1
1909	68,911	3,561	5.2
1914	74,502	1,992	2.7
1919	77,520	1,413	1.8

¹ Males under 16 years and females under 15 years.

From 1880 to 1899 the number of minors under 16 years increased from 5,658 to 7,116, but this increase was not so fast as that of the total number of wage earners in the industry. The percentage that minors formed of the total number of wage earners decreased therefore from 23.4 to 13.5, though the actual number increased 25.7 per cent.

Beginning with 1904, both the actual number and the percentage minors formed of the total decreased, while the total number of wage earners continued to rise rapidly. In 1919, the last year for which official figures are available, there were 1,413 minors, only 1.8 per cent of the 77,520 wage earners in the industry. Child labor in the glass industry has now become almost a matter of the past, and credit for this is due in no small measure to Michael J. Owens, the inventor of the Owens machine. As a boy of ten, in 1869, he joined the ranks of the thousands of children employed in the glass factories. He died in 1923, the genius of the glass industry, whose inventions contributed more than all other factors combined to the complete elimination of child labor from the industry.

The Color Purple:
Dating Solarized Amethyst Container Glass

Bill Lockhart

REPRINT—THE COLOR PURPLE: DATING SOLARIZED AMETHYST CONTAINER GLASS

Bill Lockhart

The Color Purple: Dating Solarized Amethyst Container Glass

ABSTRACT

From the late-19th century on, there was an increased production of colorless bottles for a wide variety of products. Producing colorless glass is not difficult if pure sand with a very low iron content is available. Iron in sand gives the glass a range of colors from light green to dark amber, depending on the amount of iron in the sand. To overcome this problem, some factories that used iron-bearing sands added manganese to their batch as a decolorizer. While this produces colorless glass, that glass will turn a light purple or amethyst color when it is exposed to sunlight. Dating of solarized glass by archaeologists has relied on information from a variety of sources, including books produced by bottle collectors. Some of this information is good and some of it, erroneous. The objective here is to provide a useful chronology of the development and use of manganese as a decolorizer and to dispel some of the myths that have crept into the literature.

Introduction

Historically, both container glass and window glass have generally been colored varying shades of green and aquamarine. This color was produced by the natural inclusion of iron impurities in the sand used to produce the glass (see detailed information below). Gradually, lead glass came to be used for fine tableware, but the process was too expensive for the general line of containers. Throughout the 19th century, a gradual trend occurred in the glass industry toward light shades of aqua and colorless glass. Relatively inexpensive means were sought to produce colorless bottles. One of the cheapest methods was to add manganese to the glass mixture to create a colorless environment. This additive generated an interesting side effect—the glass became purple with prolonged exposure to the sun.

The color purple (or amethyst), when created by the inclusion of manganese in the formula of container glass, has long been a source of fascination for the archaeologist and the bottle collector. Although scientists and collectors are often at odds over issues of curation, access, ownership, and techniques in dealing with historical bottles, both have contributed to the literature used by archaeologists in dating and researching glass containers. Often, collectors have been on the cutting edge of descriptive and historical research on the glass industry, local users and bottlers, and local/national containers (McKearin and McKearin 1941; Munsey 1970, 1972; Zumwalt 1980; Fowler 1986) and are frequently cited by archaeologists. In researching solarized amethyst glass, archaeologists and collectors alike have made contributions. Archaeological and collector literature as well as contributions by chemists, physicists, and the glass industry is examined to study the dating and use of manganese dioxide as a decolorizer for impure container glass.

Background

Chemical and Physical Properties of Manganese Decolored Glass

Sand is one of the basic ingredients in the manufacture of glass, and most sand contains iron impurities in varying types and quantities. These impurities impart a green, blue-green, blue, or yellow tint to the glass, depending on the percentage of iron in the glass mixture and whether the iron is ferrous (blue-green), ferric (yellow), or a combination of the two. Because container glass was generally made as cheaply as possible (especially prior to the 20th century), most bottles displayed the blue-green or greenish tints often referred to by archaeologists and collectors as aqua but known in earlier times as "common green" (Harrington 1952: 28). The use of the term was so prevalent that one of the unions was called The Green Glass Bottle Blowers' Association of the United States and Canada (Scoville 1948:201). In most cases, "the *colour* of the glass [was] nearly, or quite, immaterial so that the introduction of relatively

Historical Archaeology, 2006, 40(2):45–56.
Permission to reprint required.
Accepted for publication 16 November 2004.

large proportions of iron oxide [was] permissible [emphasis in original]" (Rosenhain 1908:96).

Colorless glass became important for use in windows and tableware before it was widely introduced to containers, requiring a method of eliminating the tint caused by the iron impurities. L. M. Angus-Butterworth (1948:64) suggested that there were three ways to overcome the problem of unwanted color: (1) use a pure grade of sand with as low a percentage of iron impurities as possible (the best solution, but frequently impractical); (2) use oxidation to reduce undesirable color; or (3) add complementary colors (usually purple or pink) to offset the green tint caused by iron. George Miller and Antony Pacey (1985:44) add that the color may be masked by adding "other metallic oxides, such as cobalt" to change the color, or the color could be accepted as is. Pure sand produces a glass without color, and some locations are noted for sands lacking in impurities. Glasshouses, located in such areas, generate colorless glass without the use of complementary colors or oxidizers. Benjamin Biser ([1899]: 28) noted, "American sands, especially, show supremacy over all others, many of them being free from excessive organic matter and in almost absolute state of purity, and the supply nearly always inexhaustible." He also notes that Minnesota, Missouri, Illinois, Pennsylvania, Maryland, New Jersey, and the New England states are especially good places to find pure sand.

Although the distinction is of little practical use to historical archaeologists (at least using currently practiced methods), chemically, glass is formulated in four basic ways: soda-lime glass, potash-lime glass, potash-lead glass, and lime glass. Each of these glass types can be produced in colorless form without the addition of decolorizers. Glassmakers of Venice discovered a method to create colorless soda-lime glass by the 13th century, and colorless potash-lime glass was produced by the 17th century (for a more detailed discussion, see Jones and Sullivan 1989:10–12). It is clear that colorless glass for containers (as well as other uses) has been available for some time.

Historically, the most common method used to produce colorless glass was to add complementary colors, often using the purple hue created by manganese dioxide (MnO^2). At the close of the 19th century, Biser ([1899]:

43) explained the decolorization process: "Manganese imparts to glass a pink or red tint, which being complementary to green, neutralizes the color and permits the glass to transmit white light." The required quantity of manganese varied with the amount of iron in the mixture along with the nature of other chemicals present. D. J. McSwiney (1925a:23) noted, "the desired results are actually achieved by adding more color to the glass instead of taking it away." F. W. Hodkin and A. Cousen (1925:133) noted, "manganese is a more successful decolouriser in potash glass than in soda glass," although that distinction is of little practical use to archaeologists. There is no doubt that manganese was the most successful decolorant used in the latter part of the 19th century and the early part of the 20th century (Rosenhain 1908:192–193; Scholes 1935:207). Manganese-decolored glass that has undergone a color change due to exposure to the ultraviolet rays of the sun is variously known as sun-colored amethyst (SCA), solarized amethyst, solarized purple, or irradiated glass.

Through the years, chemists have argued *why* mixing complementary colors green and purple result in (to the eye, at least) a colorless glass (Fettke 1918:83; Weyl 1959:500–507; Paul 1982: 260). For the archaeologist it is sufficient to note *that* the phenomenon takes place. For a more technical explanation of how manganese dioxide functions as a decolorant, see A. Paul (1982:260) and Woldemar Weyl (1959: 500–507).

J. F. White and W. B. Silverman (1950: 255,257) sliced thin layers of glass to reveal that the solarization of manganese-bearing glass extends through the entire body of the piece rather than just appearing on the surface. Although the color extends all the way through, C. R. Bamford (1977:51) records, "ultra-violet irradiation gives a purple colouration extending with decreasing intensity into the body of the glass from the glass surface." It is clear that direct sunlight (or artificial irradiation) is required to create the color change. In 1905, S. Avery (1905:910) noted that a partially-buried bottle "showed the greatest change of color where most exposed to the sun's rays." Charles Hunt (1959:10) also illustrated the phenomenon in a way that suggested solarization would not occur through soil packed into a bottle or fragment. Further confirmation was offered by Mary Zimmerman (1964:31) that "partially colored bottles, those that are half-purple-and-half-clear, are commonly found by bottle diggers."

The combining of manganese and the impure sand must be conducted under oxidizing conditions (in this case, exposure to ultraviolet light). As early as 1948, Angus-Butterworth (1948:58) noted, "reducing agents destroy the purple tint." Reducing may be accomplished by heating the glass to a temperature between 450° and 500° F. This reverses the chemical change created by the exposure to solar radiation, and sun-colored amethyst glass becomes colorless once more. It should be noted that these temperatures are perilously close to the point where glass becomes plastic and the sample can become damaged (Weyl 1959:508–509; Paul 1982:261).

Early Investigations, Gaffield's Observations, and Gortner's Experiment

Chemists have been interested in color changes in glass caused by solar irradiation since the early-19th century. Scientists began discussing the phenomenon at least as early as 1823, although the controversy at that time centered around window glass rather than containers. The change of color in British windows was already becoming obvious early in the century (Gaffield 1867:244–252, 1881:4; Weyl 1959:498–500).

Thomas Gaffield (1867) conducted what may be the first actual testing of the effects of solarization on window and plate glass. He first placed what he called "really *colored* glasses, red, green, yellow, blue, and purple [emphasis in original]," in the sun but noticed little change except for the purple glass which "became slightly darker" (Gaffield 1867:245). He then exposed "white" (colorless) glass and lightly tinted glasses to sunlight and was rewarded by an increase in tint, mostly to a light-bluish or yellowish color with some pinks. He did not test any container glass.

Gaffield began his second set of experiments in 1870 and presented his findings in 1880 to the American Association for the Advancement of Science meeting in Boston (Gaffield 1881:7). He exposed "rough and polished plate; crown and sheet window glass; flint and crown optical

glass; glass ware and glass in the rough metal" to sunlight over a 10-year period. Gaffield "witnessed a perceptible change in a single hour of sunlight exposure upon the top of a post in a country garden, at noontime, on a clear and hot day of August." Other changes took place much more slowly. He observed changes in most types of glass except some "fine glassware and optical glass" (Gaffield 1881:4–5). Again, he did not test any container glass.

Gaffield (1881:5) observed a variety of color changes, including "from white [colorless] to yellow," colorless to purple, and several changes in lightly tinted glass of various shades. It is important to note that even prior to 1880, other decolorants (besides manganese) were in use. Gaffield (1881:7) indicated the presence of other decolorants (even prior to 1880) when he stated, "a yellowish or purple color was produced" when colorless glass was "painted by the magic pencil of the sun." Manganese does not create a yellowish color. Gaffield (1881:9) correctly attributed the cause of the aqua coloration in most glass to "the presence of oxide of iron" and "oxide of magnesium" as "the great colorist in all of these changes [solarization to a purple color]."

Gaffield (1881:6) also noted that sun-colored fragments of glass could be "restored to their original color by being placed in the kiln during a single fire." In other words, heating the glass would reverse the sun's action and alter the specimens back to a colorless form (see the chemical discussion of this phenomenon above). He noted that this phenomenon had been reported as early as 1867.

The discussions on solarization virtually ceased after 1881 only to be rekindled in the early-20th century in debates over the color change in container glass. Avery (1905:909–910) and Charles Rueger (1905:1206) each published brief notes that suggested the likelihood that color change was caused by irradiation from the sun among other possible explanations.

Such discussions spurred Ross Gortner (1908) to seriously study the phenomenon. On 9 July 1906, he attached 22 colorless glass containers and other colorless glass objects (including a glass funnel, a laboratory flask, and pieces of glass tubing) to a board atop his roof to assess their susceptibility to sunlight. Some of the containers were filled with various ingredients including manganese dioxide, lampblack, potassium permanganate, and other substances. After one month, five items had begun to turn purple. He did not check the experiment again for almost a year, at which time he discovered 17 items had turned purple, 4 remained unchanged, and 1 had been "blown away by the wind" (Gortner 1908:159).

Gortner's results showed that some contents retarded the solarization on the backs of the bottles (but not the fronts) and some (notably lampblack) eliminated the coloration from the backs entirely. Gortner ground up the samples of glass he had placed on the roof and tested them to obtain the chemical composition of each container. All but one of the test items that remained colorless contained no manganese, but the unaltered Jena glass (laboratory glass) flask had a manganese component (Gortner 1908:159–161).

In conclusion, Gortner (1908:1962) demonstrated that when glass is "colored violet by the action of sunlight, proof is furnished that the glass contains manganese." He further confirmed that even glass containing small amounts of manganese will turn violet or purple after prolonged exposure and that length of exposure will deepen the color intensity. Finally, he established that some glass (notably Jena glass) contains a chemical combination that inhibits color change during solarization despite the inclusion of manganese dioxide in its composition (although it is likely that only a very tiny percentage of glass fits into this category).

Dating Solarized Amethyst Glass

Background Literature

Until recently, bottle-collector literature has been the major source for information and dating of glass containers by historians, archaeologists, and collectors alike. Although some collectors' literature is well written and well researched, much of it is compiled without scientific methodology or accuracy. While some collector dating and wisdom have been disproved (for example, the idea that the proximity of mold marks to the lip of a bottle is relevant to its relative age), the dating and history of solarized, manganese-bearing glass has not been seriously researched by archaeologists.

The first collector to attempt dating purple glass was Grace Kendrick (1963:54–56). Kendrick dated the phenomenon of "sun-colored glass" as lasting from 1880 to 1914. Although she provided no justification for her beginning date, she stated, "[w]ith the advent of World War I, our main source of manganese (German suppliers) was cut off" (Kendrick 1963:56), thereby providing an end date that has been more or less accepted (along with her beginning date) ever since. Zimmerman followed Kendrick a year later, referencing solarized purple, flat (window) glass and tableware along with bottles as being used between 1850 and 1910 (Zimmerman 1964:7,19). She noted that many innovations in the glass industry began about 1890 (Zimmerman 1964:20–21), and the changeover to selenium was a process that continued from about 1910 until about 1930. Although Cecil Munsey (1970:55) cited Zimmerman as one of his sources, he accepted Kendrick's basic dating scheme and added, "around 1880, . . . the demand for clear glass forced the manufacturers to perfect the technique of decolorizing with manganese." Rick Baldwin (1985:23) combined the Kendrick and Zimmerman dating schemes to suggest a beginning date of 1880 and an end date between 1915 and 1930. T. Stell Newman (1970:74) modified that range by adding 10 years to all dates to allow for industry transition; Olive Jones and Catherine Sullivan (1989:13) and Miller and Pacey (1985:44) generalized it; and Richard Fike (1987:13) ignored it completely.

Kendrick was only partially correct in her reasoning for the industry's cessation of the use of manganese. In 1910, the United States imported 4,928 long tons of manganese from Germany, 2.03% of our total import for the year. By 1915 that was reduced to 258 long tons (0.08% of total import), followed by a reduction to zero in 1916. It was not until 1920 that the U.S. returned to German suppliers, and then the total import was only 11 long tons. In other words, Germany was never an important supplier of manganese during the period in question. Prior to World War I, British India supplied the most manganese to the U.S.: 58.2% of the total import in 1910, decreasing to only 11.4% by 1915. Brazil had contributed 22.2% of U.S. manganese imports in 1910, increasing to 85.9% in 1915.

The United States itself became an important manganese supplier by the end of the war, generating 31.4% of its supply (an increase from less than 1% in 1910) (U.S. Geological Survey 1913:207–208, 1919:734–736, 1922: 274–276). The United States Tariff Commission (1918a:13) stated that clay, not manganese was a major import from Germany.

Import records failed to tell the complete story. The U.S. Tariff Commission conducted two hearings concerning the effects of the war on the glass industry in 1917. In the second meeting, representatives from "65 flint-glass manufacturing firms" (not all bottle manufacturers) met with government officials in December 1917 to discuss the state of U.S. glass production. Despite the evidence produced above, glass manufacturers imported most of their manganese from Russia, although some was imported from Germany along with a small amount from France. It is clear that war disruption played a significant role in the importation of manganese (U.S. Tariff Commission 1918b:32).

It is instructive to note that the disruption produced a very complex reaction from the glass industry, rather than the simplistic response posited by Kendrick. Not counting plate glass manufacturers, 43 representatives discussed imports. Of those, 25 discussed manganese. Nine discussants continued to use manganese derived from other sources. Most of these used domestic manganese, although a few were dissatisfied with its quality. Two imported manganese from countries (like Canada) where shipping was unaffected by the war. Three discussants discontinued the use of manganese with no replacement; three others substituted selenium. A single glassmaker continued to pay higher prices and was still using imported manganese. The final nine were using other decolorants in place of manganese (Table 1). Five of them substituted a decolorizer manufactured by the Frink Laboratories, Lancaster, Ohio (U.S. Tariff Commission 1918b:32–37). The U.S. Tariff Commission hearing makes two points clear: (1) a significant number of manufacturers (36% of those who discussed manganese use) continued to use manganese as a decolorant in 1917; and (2) by that point, selenium was only one of a number of substitutes for manganese.

Beginning Dates

Manganese was used as a coloring agent at least as early as 660 B.C. in Egypt (Angus-Butterworth 1948:49) and in Roman glass from the 4th century B.C. to the 9th century A.D. (Werner 1968:34A). Helen McKearin and Kenneth Wilson (1978:10) note that the decoloring properties of manganese were demonstrated prior to 1662. Scholes (1935:207) even claims that "it was used for hundreds of years as the only satisfactory decolorizer." Manganese appears in tableware at least as early as the 18th century (Jones and Sullivan 1989:13). Window glass that had solarized to a purple color was investigated in England as early as 1823 (Gaffield 1881:4) and 1825 (Weyl

TABLE 1

EFFECTS OF IMPORT DISRUPTION ON MANGANESE-USING GLASS MANUFACTURERS IN 1917*

Reaction to Import Disruption	N	%
Substituted other manganese sources (mostly domestic)	9	36.0
Discontinued use of decolorant	3	12.0
Substituted selenium	3	12.0
Continued to use existing imported supplies	1	4.0
Substituted various other decolorants**	9	36.0
Totals	25	100.0

* Data derived from U.S. Tariff Commission (1918b:32–37).

** Five glass manufacturers (20.0% of the total number) used a decolorant developed by Frink Laboratories, Lancaster, Ohio.

1959:498–500). Gaffield (1881:3) observed, "changes of some light colored plate glass to a purple" had been noted "after the beginning of this century [19th]," placing manganese use in flat glass about 1800 or shortly thereafter. Manganese-decolored flat glass was also in use in the United States prior to 1880. In his report for the 1880 census, Joseph Weeks (1883: 1062–1063) claimed,

> manganese is used to correct this greenish color, and is often termed "glass-maker's soap," but glass so decolorized is liable under the action of sunlight to acquire a purplish tint of "high color." Window glass in which manganese has been used often assumes this tint to such an extent as to lead to the belief that it was originally colored.

It becomes clear that manganese-bearing glass was in use long before 1880 and was used in the United States prior to that date.

Prior to the use of manganese-decolored glass, most containers were manufactured as cheaply as possible, a technique that retained the green, blue-green, aqua, yellow, or light blue colors associated with the presence of iron oxides in the glass mix. Contemporary sources that deal with glass colors (Fike 1987:13; Jones and Sullivan 1989:13) are strangely silent on the subject of the light blue bottles that appear primarily in pre-1917 contexts. Bamford (1977:51–52), Walter Rosenhain (1908:190), and Donald Sharp (1933:762) identify blue as a color associated with iron impurities in glass. In a 1929 experiment, B. Bogitch "obtained colours [of glass] varying from brown to blue according to the condition of the iron" (Gooding and Murgatroyd 1935:45). Biser ([1899]:13) described this glass as "coarse and inferior in quality, used extensively for the commonest grades of bottles and hollow-ware, and is usually of a greenish, amber, or black color."

Because color was often unimportant (Rosenhain 1908:196), certain types of bottles continued to be made from "naturally colored" (iron bearing) glass, notably soda and beer bottles. Although occasional beer bottles appear in light blue or colorless forms, most were amber from the last quarter of the 19th century. Soda bottles generally retained the green, aqua, or light blue tints caused by the iron impurities. Biser ([1899]:86) suggested that soda and beer bottles remained colored because of the fear that

"the liquid contents of a flint glass [colorless] bottle were seriously impaired in strength and in color by the actions of light, which a green or amber bottle excluded, and thus protected its contents." The use of unaltered glass was so common in the manufacture of bottles that green glass was synonymous with "bottle glass" (*Harpers* 1889:257).

Two factors confound the selection of a single date as a beginning for the use of manganese as a decolorant in the United States: process and terminology. Process is a problem because manufacturers rarely (if ever) all switch to a new technology simultaneously or even in a relatively short time (Newman 1970:70). Weeks (1883:1062–1063) reported the use of manganese decolorization in 1880, but he was very unclear about the context.

When Gaffield (1881:5) examined the effects of sunlight on glass in 1867 and 1881, he reported that he used "rough and polished plate; crown and sheet window glass; flint and crown optical glass; glassware and glass in the rough metal" for his experiments. Like Weeks (above), the lack of reference to container glass is significant. Although not conclusive, these references create a lack of clear context for early manganese use in container glass.

The second problem is terminology. In their justification for the use of the term "colourless," Jones and Sullivan (1989:13) state that "terms like 'clear,' 'white,' 'flint,' or 'crystal' . . . have not been used consistently by contemporary authors or in historical documents." Originally, the term *flint* was used to mean lead glass (or potash-lead glass), highly prized for tableware because it was "colourless, heavy, and lustrous" (Jones and Sullivan 1989:11; also McKearin and McKearin 1941:8). Because the process was more expensive, its use in containers was limited, although *Harpers* magazine (1889:257) noted that it was used in the U.S. to manufacture "fine bottles." Later, the use of the terms grew more lax, and *flint* or *white* often meant glass made from pure sand, glass manufactured by techniques such as that developed by William Leighton in 1864 (Jones and Sullivan 1989:11) or glass made with a decolorant. Leighton, working for the glasshouse of Hobbs, Brockunier and Co., developed a soda-lime glass (often called "lime" or "lime flint" glass) that was colorless, of high quality, and much cheaper than lead-flint glass

(McKearin and McKearin 1941:8; Douglas and Frank 1972:40). Frank Gessner (1891:54–56) presented recipes for "flint hollow-ware" that all contained manganese as a decolorant.

George Griffenhagen and Mary Bogard (1999:20,35) note that imported "flint glass" medicine bottles were offered for sale in the U.S. as early as 1773 and American-made flint glass containers by the 1850s. Edward Perrish wrote in 1856, "flint vials are considerably more expensive than the green, though they are far more elegant for prescription purposes" (Griffenhagen and Bogard 1999:27). Although Perrish was most likely talking about lead flint glass, a more expensive process, his statement is important because it shows that people in the U.S. were showing a desire for colorless glass (at least in pharmaceutical containers) by the mid-19th century.

Although Leighton's "lime-flint" glass was well known for its use in pressed table glass (Jones and Sullivan 1989:11), no reference is found for its use in containers. Although Julian Toulouse (1971:369–370,387–388), mentions the company several times, it is always in connection with pressed tableware and never in a context connoting containers. It is obvious, that some form of colorless glass was used to produce medicinal containers in the U.S., possibly just glass made from essentially pure sand.

The combination of process and terminology creates a final hurdle that must be cleared before an understanding of when the use of manganese-decolored glass began among glassmakers can be achieved. The combined aspect centers around container type. Makers of different types of containers appear to have adopted glass decolorized by manganese at different times. Whitall Tatum & Co., for example, opened a "flint glasshouse" in 1864. Initially, the company used William Leighton's formula for colorless glass (without manganese), although it only met with limited success (Pepper 1971: 228–232). By 1870 the process had improved at Whitall Tatum through the use of manganese dioxide (Horner 1969:98). Personal communication with numerous collectors of drug store bottles indicates that, regardless of manufacture date, virtually all pre-1924 Whitall Tatum colorless drug store bottles (generally oval-shaped, pharmacy bottles with plate molds identifying local drug stores) will solarize to a light amethyst color. Attempting to quantify collector data is difficult. The author observed one collection of about 1,850 drugstore bottles, about half of which were marked with the Whitall Tatum logo. All were solarized to a light amethyst. Various collectors have reported looking at hundreds of drug store bottles from Whitall Tatum that showed similar characteristics.

By 1904, Whitall Tatum had developed a semiautomatic machine for wide-mouth containers and had one for narrow-mouth bottles operational by 1912 (Toulouse 1971:544–547); however, these were not used for drug store bottles. Because of the use of plate molds, these bottles were available to local storeowners at a slight additional charge and were popular during the late-19th and early-20th centuries. For drug store bottles (and, presumably other medicinals) the beginning date is about 1870.

An examination of soft drink bottles shows a different pattern completely. As stated above, most soda bottles were allowed to retain whatever colors the natural impurities in the glass mix created. The use of manganese-bearing, colorless glass in soft drink bottles seems to have begun sometime in the mid-1890s (William Lindsey and numerous bottle collectors 2004, pers. comm.). Less information is available for other bottle types, although beer bottles, even today, are generally not colorless.

Personal communication with collectors also indicates that many of the early milk bottles, most of which were made of colorless glass, will solarize to varying shades of amethyst or purple. Although the record of the earliest milk bottles is unclear, when the Thatcher milk bottles were first made in 1886, they were formed of colorless glass (Tutton [1996]:6). Colorless glass continued to be the industry standard until glass milk bottles were almost completely replaced by waxed paper and plastic containers.

Apparently, at least with Hemingray Glass Co., jar manufacturers did not begin using manganese to any strong degree until after 1893. Although Hemingray was best known for the making of insulators, the company, like its predecessors Hemingray Brothers & Co. and Gray & Hemingray, made such items as tableware, tumblers, chemical apparatus, perfume bottles, pickle bottles, fruit jars, and other bottle types (Toulouse 1971:224–225,246). Bob Genheimer (2004, pers. comm.) described his excavation of the Hemingray Glass Co. in 1986. In a large excavation unit (2.5 x 2.5 m), Genheimer found sizeable quantities of broken glass discarded by the factory. Although 52.7% of the broken glass was colorless, only 0.9% was a solarized amethyst. This may suggest the beginning of manganese use as a decolorant by the company by 1893 (the date the factory moved and ceased production on the site). Alternatively, the small amount of manganese glass could be from *cullet* (broken glass used to "prime" the furnace) collected from other factories.

Despite the unsupported references to 1880 found in the early collectors' literature, documentary sources discuss the appearance of manganese-decolored glass as a part of a general trend toward technological improvement beginning about 1890. Although specific inventions were unmentioned, *Harpers* magazine (1889) touted the innovations and modern techniques then taking place within the glass industry. Biser ([1899]:86) noted, the "so-called 'lime flint' bottle glass" was becoming more common and "the past decade [since ca. 1889] has wrought a revolution in so far as to give flint glass bottles much prestige." Scholes (1935:217) likewise stated: "From the first attempts to produce crystal glass in continuous tanks in the 1890's to the development of decolorizing by selenium twenty years later, glass makers struggled to maintain good color by manganese treatment." Zimmerman (1964:20–21) noticed the importance of the industrial development around 1890 but failed to link it to the early use of manganese in container glass. Although these sources are a bit unclear as to the date of entry of manganese-bearing glass, Gessner established the certainty that it was in use by 1891. In his *Glassmakers' Hand-Book*, Gessner (1891:7) notes, "the use of manganese has, however, been largely abandoned in European factories during latter years, especially in the manufacture of window glass and fine flint ware" because it changed color. For bottle glass he included manganese in all of his "flint hollow-ware" recipes. Gessner (1891:54) also states:

> flint hollow-ware has grown to immense proportions during recent years, and in many cases has largely displaced green glass. Fruit jars, the use of which is growing more extensive each year, especially those of large size to displace the shape and color of the contents, are now, to a large extent, made of flint [manganese-decolored glass], which is preferred on account of its greater clearness and transparency.

This suggests that, by 1891, manganese-bearing glass had been in use for at least a few years and was growing in popularity.

Biser ([1899]:86) also noted another interesting development near the end of the 1880s, "For a long time flint glass bottles were regarded with disfavor, inasmuch as their cost alone excluded them from beer and soda trade, to say nothing of the current belief rife among the bottling fraternity that flint glass lacked the strength and resistance of green glass." The sentence implies that the resistance was by then no longer prevalent. Although this may suggest other new techniques as well, it seems to describe the process of conversion to manganese decolorization. The use of manganese as a decolorant would have left the glass as strong and resilient as its predecessor, green (or aqua) bottle glass.

Although developed by manufacturers of drug store bottles more than a decade earlier, use of the technique for manganese decolorization was therefore probably widely in use by the late 1880s. The actual dates of inception for the technique seem tied to container type. Three different methods, then, may be used for determining a beginning date for the use of manganese-decolored glass. First, the earliest known date for use in the United States is 1870 (at Whitall Tatum & Co.). Second, the most practical "general use" date is the late 1880s. Finally, more specific dates need to be researched for specific types of glass containers. Currently, that includes 1870 for drug store bottles (and probably other pharmaceuticals), the mid-1880s for milk bottles, and the mid-1890s for soft drink bottles.

A slight postscript about beginning dates must be added. In his excavation of the Johnson's Island Civil War Prison, David R. Bush (2004, pers. comm.) discovered "numerous examples of solarized glass from contexts that date from the Civil War." While this questions the veracity of the dates discussed above, there are two mitigating circumstances. First, manganese was used in tableware throughout much of the 19th century; second, manganese has also been used as a colorant. McKearin and Wilson (1978:591) describe a style of flask that is found in both amethyst and deep amethyst (black) colors as well as various shades of green, blue, and yellow. A second style (McKearin and Wilson (1978:597) was colorless and "colorless, lavender tint." Although solarization is a possibility, the first bottle described was almost certainly made from amethyst glass intentionally, and the second probably obtained its tint accidentally through cullet or impurities. McKearin and Wilson (1978:592) also note a flask that is "amethyst and clear in striations, the overall effect being of brilliant amethyst." Other flasks are described as colorless, clear, or colorless with light shading of various colors ("clear light green" or "clear yellow green"). All of these are obviously not solarized. Future research should stress close observation of glass from the Civil War period for indications that might address solarization.

End Dates

As with a beginning date, the end date expresses a process. As noted above, the change from manganese dioxide to selenium and other decoloring agents was not caused by a shortage of manganese from Germany (although World War I did create a shortage of manganese, along with most other resources). The change was actually a result of technological improvements in the glass industry and is closely connected to the conversion to automatic bottle machines. McSwiney (1925b:53–57) and Miller and Pacey (1985:44–45) provide a concise summary of technological events that resulted in the transition to selenium usage, although they are vague as to the actual dating. Manganese dioxide performs best in crucibles, such as those used in the production of hand-blown glass, because of its need for an oxidizing environment. It is much less effective in open tanks, such as those required for the Owen Automatic Bottling Machine and others of its type. Even though manganese was more difficult to obtain during World War I, and selenium was cheaper to use, the improvement in technology (the popularity of semi-automatic and automatic bottle blowing machines) was the major reason for the change in decoloring agents. Because of the problem with manganese, many of the early machine-made bottles were aqua in color, a convenient way of avoiding the problem, as no decolorant was needed.

Scholes (1935:217) places the initial use of selenium about 1910. McSwiney (1925b:53,55) suggests the earliest use of selenium at "a few years before the war" but adds, "up to ten years ago [1915] the only decolorizer used to any considerable extent for the production of colorless soda lime glass was manganese." Weyl (1959:283) contends that the use of selenium began in the early 1890s. Sources more contemporary with the change declared, "in 1917, selenium, a domestic by-product of copper, was substituted for manganese" (U.S. Tariff Commission 1918a:32) and "manganese is one of the important decolorizers employed by the glass manufacturer" (Fettke 1918:82). These sources indicate that selenium was in use by at least 1910 (possibly earlier) but did not become popular until about 1917.

The term *popular* needs to be clarified. Since the popularity of selenium use (and, therefore, the end of prominence for manganese) closely follows the development of the automatic bottle machine, the significance of the term concerning automation of the glass industry must be examined. The use of automatic bottle machines had increased in popularity to the point that, in 1917, approximately half of all bottles in the United States were made by the Owens Automatic Bottle Machine. Additional containers were made on a variety of semi-automatic machines. Although machine production increased in popularity, hand-blown bottles continued to be manufactured until the early 1930s (Miller and Sullivan 1984:86–89). Machines were more efficient for producing bottles in quantity, so the more popular container styles (beer, soda, and food bottles) were the earliest made by the new process. By approximately 1920, most of the popular types of bottles were machine made.

Also following the machine production trend, manganese use as a decolorant continued in the smaller, hand-production glasshouses and for specialty bottles in the larger plants. These small-run, specialty bottle producers still used crucibles and had no reason to make the transition to selenium. In 1926, Alexander Silverman (1926:897) commented, "selenium has also largely displaced manganese dioxide as a decolorizer." By 1933, Sharp (1933:763) noted, "selenium is almost invariably used as the decolorizer in bottle glass because of the relatively constant results to be obtained. Manganese is still employed for high-grade pot glass." Although manganese use continued past 1920, its widespread use had clearly come to an end.

End dating specific container types provides a postscript to the dating discussion. As with beginning dates, not all bottle types or glass houses adopted selenium or other decolorants at the same time. Drug store bottles (pharmaceutical bottles, usually oval in shape and containing embossed plate molds with the names of local druggists), probably the earliest to show the adoption of manganese as a decolorant, were also some of the last to abandon the technique. Whitall Tatum continued to make drug store bottles by hand blowing until about 1924 (beginning about 1924, all pharmaceutical bottles at Whitall Tatum were machine-made and embossed with a different logo) and therefore continued to use manganese as a decoloring agent until that time. Cost may have been a deciding factor for druggists. Machine manufacture required a minimum order. Often, that minimal requirement resulted in an order too large to fit the needs of most druggists (Miller and Pacey 1985:42). As a result, the machine manufacture of bottles created a cost beyond the practical reach of many businesses. The day of the individually marked drug store bottle was at an end.

Soft drink bottles rarely showed the presence of manganese after the advent of machine usage in that field, between about 1912 and 1915. Some of the pint- and fifth-size preprohibition liquor bottles with no manufacturer's mark and those with the *B* (with serifs) mark made by the Charles Boldt Glass Co. from 1910 to 1919 solarize to light amethyst color, indicating the use of manganese. Yet these same bottles have the distinctive Owens scars that indicate the use of the Owens Automatic Bottle Machine. According to Miller and McNichol (2002:3,6–7), only Boldt and the Illinois Glass Co. were issued licenses to make whiskey bottles prior to the cessation of the Owens patents in the mid-1920s. Because Boldt did not include date codes on his bottles, the date range when he discontinued the use of manganese is unknown. Many early milk bottles (ca. 1900–ca. 1912), including some made with Owens machines by the Thatcher Glass Manufacturing Co. as late as 1914 (by date code on the base), have solarized to varying shades up to a rich, dark purple.

Conclusion

Both historical and empirical evidence indicate that the previously accepted earlier date (1880) for the beginning of popularity of colorless glass container use in the United States as suggested by bottle collectors may be slightly incorrect. Popular use seems to have begun by at least the mid-1870s and was solidly in place by 1890. This dating cannot be generalized to all glass artifacts. Manganese was used in tableware by 1865 and in flat (window) glass in the U.S. long before 1880. A practical end date for manganese use in all but specialty bottles is about 1920, although some use continued until the early 1930s. The end of manganese use is generally concurrent with the end of mouth-blown bottle production.

Acknowledgments

I would like to particularly thank George Miller for his many suggestions and for recommending sources. An important group consists of archaeologists (especially Bob Genheimer) who shared their findings with me through the HISTARCH listserv and numerous bottle collectors who inspected their collections for solarized bottles and gave me their candid views. A bouquet of gratitude also to my wife, Wanda Wakkinen, for listening to my endless hours of speculation.

References

ANGUS-BUTTERWORTH, L. M.
  1948 *The Manufacture of Glass.* Putnam, New York, NY.

AVERY, S.
  1905 Changes of Color Caused by the Action of Certain Rays on Glass. *Journal of the American Chemical Society* 27(7):909–910.

BALDWIN, RICK
  1985 Decolorizing Glass with Manganese. *Crown Jewels of the Wire* 17(7):23–25.

BAMFORD, C. R.
  1977 *Colour Generation and Control in Glass.* Elsevice Scientific, New York, NY.

BISER, BENJAMIN F.
[1899] *Elements of Glass and Glassmaking: A Treatise Designed for the Practical Glassmaker, Comprising Facts, Figures, Recipes, and Formulas for the Manufacture of Glass, Plain and Colored.* Glass and Pottery, Pittsburgh, PA.

DOUGLAS, R. W., AND SUSAN FRANK
1972 *A History of Glassmaking.* G. T. Foulis & Co., Henley-on-Thames, Oxfordshire, England.

FETTKE, CHARLES REINHARD
1918 *Glass Manufacture and the Glass Sand Industry of Pennsylvania.* Report no. 12, Topographic and Geologic Survey of Pennsylvania, Harrisburg.

FIKE, RICHARD E.
1987 *The Bottle Book: A Comprehensive Guide to Historic, Embossed Medicine Bottles.* Peregrine Smith, Salt Lake City, UT.

FOWLER, RON
1986 *Washington Sodas: The Illustrated History of Washington's Soft Drink Industry.* Dolphin Point Writing Works, Seattle, WA.

GAFFIELD, THOMAS
1867 The Action of Sunlight on Glass. *American Journal of Science and Arts* 94:244–252.
1881 *The Action of Sunlight on Glass.* Salem Press, Salem, MA. [From a paper presented to the American Association for the Advancement of Science, Boston, 27 August 1880.]

GESSNER, FRANK M.
1891 *Glassmakers' Hand-Book: Containing Recipes for Making Flint, Bottle, Window, and Architectural Glass. Plain and in Colors: Plate Glass–American, French, Belgian, German, and Bohemian Formulas: Also Recipes for Strass and Artificial Gems.* George E. Williams, Pittsburgh, PA.

GOODING, E. J., AND J. B. MURGATROYD
1935 An Investigation of Selenium Decolorising. *Journal of the Society of Glass Technology* 19:43–103.

GORTNER, ROSS AIKEN
1908 Some Effects of Sunlight upon Colorless Glass. *American Chemical Journal* 34(2):158–162.

GRIFFENHAGEN, GEORGE, AND MARY BOGARD
1999 *History of Drug Containers and Their Labels.* American Institute of the History of Pharmacy, Madison, WI.

HARPERS
1889 Great American Industries, VIII, A Piece of Glass. *Harpers* 79:245–264.

HARRINGTON, J. C.
1952 *Glassmaking at Jamestown: America's First Industry.* Dietz Press, Richmond, VA.

HODKIN, F. W., AND COUSEN, A.
1925 *A Textbook of Glass Technology.* Constable & Company, London, England.

HORNER, ROY
1969 *Tempo, the Glass Folks of South Jersey.* Reprinted in 1985 by Gloucester County Historical Society, Woodbury, NJ.

HUNT, CHARLES B.
1959 Dating of Mining Camps with Tin Cans and Bottles. *Geo Times* 3(8):8–10,34.

JONES, OLIVE, AND CATHERINE SULLIVAN
1989 *The Parks Canada Glass Glossary for the Description of Containers, Tableware, Flat Glass, and Closures.* Parks Canada, Ottawa, Canada.

KENDRICK, GRACE
1963 *The Antique Bottle Collector.* Reprinted in 1971 by Old Time Bottle, Salem, OR.

MCKEARIN, HELEN, AND GEORGE MCKEARIN
1941 *American Glass.* Crown Publishers, New York, NY.

MCKEARIN, HELEN, AND KENNETH M. WILSON
1978 *American Bottles & Flasks and Their Ancestry.* Crown Publishers, New York, NY.

MCSWINEY, D. J.
1925a The Decolorization of Glass. *The Glass Industry* 6(2):23–26.
1925b The Decolorization of Glass. *The Glass Industry* 6(3):53–57.

MILLER, GEORGE L., AND TONY MCNICHOL
2002 Dates for Suction Scarred Bottoms: Chronological Changes in Owens Machine-Made Bottles. Paper presented at the 2002 Annual Meeting of The Society for Historical Archaeology, Mobile, AL.

MILLER, GEORGE L., AND ANTONY PACEY
1985 Impact of Mechanization in the Glass Container Industry: The Dominion Glass Company of Montreal, a Case Study. *Historical Archaeology* 19(1):38–50.

MILLER, GEORGE L., AND CATHERINE SULLIVAN
1984 Machine-Made Glass Containers and the End of Production for Mouth-Blown Bottles. *Historical Archaeology* 18(2):83–96.

MUNSEY, CECIL
1970 *The Illustrated Guide to Collecting Bottles.* Hawthorn, New York, NY.
1972 *The Illustrated Guide to the Collectibles of Coca-Cola.* Hawthorn, New York, NY.

NEWMAN, T. STELL
1970 A Dating Key for Post-Eighteenth-Century Bottles. *Historical Archaeology* 4:70–75.

PAUL, A.
    1982   *Chemistry of Glass*. Chapman and Hall, New York,
           NY.

PEPPER, ADELINE
    1971   *Glass Gaffers of New Jersey*. Scribner's Sons, New
           York, NY.

ROSENHAIN, WALTER
    1908   *Glass Manufacture*. Archibald Constable & Co.,
           London, England.

RUEGER, CHARLES E.
    1905   Changes of Color Caused by the Action of Certain Rays
           on Glass. *Journal of the American Chemical Society*
           28(9):1206.

SCHOLES, SAMUEL R.
    1935   *Modern Glass Practice*. Reprinted in 1952 by Industrial
           Publications, Ind., Chicago, IL.

SCOVILLE, WARREN C.
    1948   *Revolution in Glassmaking: Entrpreneurship and
           Technological Change in the American Industry,
           1880–1920*. Harvard University Press, Cambridge,
           MA.

SHARP, DONALD E.
    1933   Chemical Composition of Commercial Glasses.
           Industrial and Engineering Chemistry 25(7):755–764.

SILVERMAN, ALEXANDER
    1926   Fifty Years of Glass-Making. *Journal of Industrial
           and Engineering Chemistry* 18(9):896–899.

TOULOUSE, JULIAN HARRISON
    1971   *Bottle Makers and Their Marks*. Thomas Nelson, New
           York, NY.

TUTTON, JOHN
    [1996] *Udderly Beautiful: A Pictorial Guide to the
           Pyroglazed or Painted Milkbottle*. Privately Printed,
           Front Royal, VA.

UNITED STATES GEOLOGICAL SURVEY
    1913   *Mineral Resources of the United States, Calendar
           Year 1912, Part 1—Metals*. U.S. Geological Survey,
           Washington, DC.
    1919   *Mineral Resources of the United States, Calendar
           Year 1916, Part 1—Metals*. U.S. Geological Survey,
           Washington, DC.

    1922   *Mineral Resources of the United States, Calendar
           Year 1920, Part 1—Metals*. U.S. Geological Survey,
           Washington, DC.

UNITED STATES TARIFF COMMISSION
    1918a *The Glass Industry as Affected by the War*. Tariff
           Information Series, No. 4. U.S. Tariff Commission,
           Washington, DC.
    1918b *The Glass Industry as Affected by the War*. Tariff
           Information Series, No. 5. U.S. Tariff Commission,
           Washington, DC.

WEEKS, JOSEPH D.
    1883   Report on the Manufacture of Glass. *Report
           on the Manufactures of the United States at the
           Tenth Census (June 1, 1880), Embracing General
           Statistics and Monographs on Power used in
           Manufactures, the Factory System, Interchangeable
           Mechanism, Hardware, Cutlery, etc., Iron and Steel,
           Silk Manufacture, Cotton Manufacture, Woolen
           Manufacture, Chemical Products, Glass Manufacture*.
           Bureau of the Census, Washington, DC.

WERNER, A. E. A.
    1968   Analytical Methods in Archaeology. *Analytical
           Chemistry* 40(2):28A–42A.

WEYL, WOLDEMAR
    1959   *Coloured Glasses*. Dawson's of Pall Mall, London,
           England.

WHITE, J. F., AND W. B. SILVERMAN
    1950   Some Studies on the Solarization of Glass. *Journal of
           the American Ceramic Society* 33(8):252–257.

ZIMMERMAN, MARY J.
    1964   *Sun-Colored Glass: Its Lure and Lore*. "Ole" Empty
           Bottle House, Amadore City, CA.

ZUMWALT, BETTY
    1980   *Ketchup Pickles Sauces: Nineteenth-Century Food in
           Glass*. Mark West Publications, Fulton, CA.

BILL LOCKHART
DEPT. OF BUSINESS, HUMANITIES, AND
SOCIAL SCIENCES
NEW MEXICO STATE UNIVERSITY AT ALAMOGORDO
2400 SCENIC DR.
ALAMOGORDO, NM 88310

Manganese, Glass Technology, and the Giant Hand, 1914–1918

Peter D. Schulz

The supreme test of the nation has come. We must all speak, act and serve together.
~Woodrow Wilson, 15 April 1917 [taken from Wilson 1918]

The events of the war years were so convulsively abnormal that to narrate them in detail would be to overload and distort the story which this book aims to tell (Allen 1935:193).

Archaeologists and collectors have long had considerable interest in the transition from manganese to selenium as the dominant agent in decolorizing glass, in large part because of its implications for chronology and interpretation. Upon exposure to sunlight, bottles decolorized with manganese dioxide will turn a light pink or lavender to moderately dark amethyst (purple), depending on the amount of manganese and amount of ultraviolet (UV) light. Archaeological literature often notes "sun-purpled" or "sun colored amethyst" glass, with

the assumption that most of these bottles (with some exceptions) date to ca. 1890–1919.

Bill Lockhart (2006; reprinted this volume) provides an excellent overview of the use of manganese as a decolorizer in American container glass factories in the 19th and early-20th centuries. In regard to the general abandonment of manganese in the second decade of the latter century, Lockhart adopts the interpretation of George Miller and Anthony Pacey (1985:44–45) that it was technological evolution, rather than material supply problems that led to the change:

> [T]he change from manganese dioxide to selenium and other decoloring agents was not caused by a shortage of manganese from Germany (although World War I did create a shortage of manganese, along with most other resources). The change was actually a result of technological improvements in the glass industry and is closely connected to the conversion to

automatic bottle machines... Manganese dioxide performs best in crucibles, such as those used in the production of hand-blown glass, because of its need for an oxidizing environment. It is much less effective in open tanks, such as those required for the [Owens] Machine and others of its type. Even though manganese was more difficult to obtain during World War I, and selenium was cheaper to use, the improvement in technology (the popularity of semi-automatic and automatic bottle blowing machines) was the major reason for the change in decoloring agents (Lockhart 2006:45).

This interpretation is based on a sound understanding of industrial evolution. It is especially attractive since it relates a shift in materials use to concurrent changes in technology and identifies the functional relationships that link the two; however, this interpretation is incomplete as an understanding of historical developments. The principal caveat that inspires this suggestion derives from a simple fact: the technological-cause interpretation was not held by glass manufacturers of the time.

An introduction to this issue can be found in a small article published in a glass trade journal in 1929. A purpled-glass hand-blown food bottle had been picked up in Death Valley and sent to the Owens-Illinois Glass Company as a curiosity. The response of company vice-president James Morrison, as relayed in the journal, is interesting. Morrison notes the former use of manganese as a decolorizer, and the effects of solar radiation in producing the purple color. He then turns to the shift in decoloring agents:

> [A]fter the war cut off the supply of Russian manganese, American glass makers turned to selenium combined with arsenic and cobalt for a decolorizer as a substitute. Experimentation and development improved the selenium combination to a point where it was far more stable and certain in action than the Russian manganese. For that reason, Russian manganese has since lost most of its market in the glass industry (*Glass Container* 1929)

A similar assessment was made several years earlier by F. C. Flint (1922:9), chief chemist for the Hazel-Atlas Glass Company:

> Manganese of sufficient purity for glassmakers' use came chiefly from the Caucasus mountain district, so that during the war the United States

glassmakers were hard put for decolorizer, for our own source of manganese, though very good for steel and iron use, contained too much iron in itself to be valuable for glassmaking. It was at this time that selenium came into active use as a decolorizing ingredient for glass. Selenium was first developed in Germany... in 1892. A number of patents were brought out at this time. However, these were practically forgotten because of the prohibitive price of these materials then, but during the war, in the United States, price was no object as it was a case of anything or nothing, so selenium was developed to its present state as a decolorizer. Since then efficient use of the material and development of new sources have made it the standard decolorizer used in glass.

Similar, if briefer, comments are available from others familiar with the industry in the U.S. and Great Britain (Williams 1918:460; Lehner 1920:597; Shively 1924a:371). Given these recollections from men who were intimately involved in the change, it is worth reviewing the state of the industry at the time, the role of the principal chemical agents involved, and the cultural and economic context provided by the war.

This article suggests that the manganese-selenium shift was a symptom of larger industrial changes brought about by the war. The elements of this argument are that (1) before the war the glass industry at large, for all its technological advances, was pre-scientific; (2) the problem with manganese was not merely shortages, but that the glass industry was a minor consumer having special requirements but lacking priority access; (3) the decolorizer problem co-occurred with other shortages that could be overcome only by a new and explicit focus on chemical research; and (4) all this occurred in a political climate in which national governments were, for the first time in some cases, directly involved in all aspects of the economy, encouraging research to develop domestic substitutes for foreign industrial materials.

GLASS IN THE PALEOTECHNIC ERA

The opening years of the 20th century witnessed a revolution in glass container technology—particularly the development of the Owens machine—similar in impact to the transformative breakthroughs in window glass technology (Anderson and Tushman 1990). Because of the importance of this transformation, which ultimately led to the science-based industry with which many of its historians were intimately familiar, researchers are tempted to view this as a "scientific" revolution. It would be more realistic to view it as a mechanical one, occurring in an industry that valued innovations with obvious economic rewards but had little tolerance for theory. Michael Owens and his coworkers and competitors, for all their brilliance, were practical mechanics, not trained engineers. Their understanding of glass was based on years of observation, not on a thorough understanding of its chemistry or physics. The automatic bottle machine, although it took several years to perfect, offered labor-saving (that is, labor-*cost*-saving) advantages readily apparent to those who funded its development.

For a perspective on the industrial context of the day, it is useful to begin with Lewis Mumford (1934:194), an early historian of technology:

> Within the industrial plant scientific knowledge was at a discount. The practical man, contemptuous of theory, scornful of exact training, ignorant of science, was uppermost. Trade secrets, sometimes important, sometimes merely childish empiricism, retarded the cooperative extension of knowledge which has been the basis of all our major technical advances...Right down to the World War an unwillingness to avail itself of scientific knowledge or to promote scientific research characterized paleotechnic industry throughout the world.

This acerbic view will doubtless strike many modern readers as unfairly negative, even though it can be matched by the comments of contemporary chemists (e.g., Hesse 1915:295–296; Bacon 1916:232). Its kindest expression is probably that on the part of manufacturers there was "a perfectly reasonable feeling of fear that academically trained chemists constituted a pure speculation" (Whitney 1916).

The question here, of course, is whether this criticism fairly applies to the American glass industry. References are few, but according to one technically trained observer:

> I found that glass-making today is carried on with no regard to definite proportions or consistent methods of operation; that it is void of any true knowledge, and is essentially an industry based and operated upon and subservient to personal opinions and prejudice, poisoned by legendary ideas and jealousies, and made generally unwholesome by lack of progressiveness or any initiative on the part of those who might, if they would, arise from this quagmire and put themselves on a basis of scientific fact...One frequently hears the remark that a chemist or scientist is of no use in a glass factory. This, no doubt, in a measure is true, for it is seldom, if ever, that a chemist or scientist will be able to find a manufacturer or owner, who would for a moment think of wasting time or money in the consideration or adoption of the suggestions of such individuals, at least not until they are confronted with a situation that legend, sorcery, prejudice, and guesswork can not account for or overcome (Frink 1909:304, 308; cf. Frink 1907).

A second chemist, citing several examples from his personal experience, rated glass manufacture as characterized by "singular and childish incompetence," constituting "a story of confusion and waste." One large manufacturer, for example, used "in accordance with a recipe that he had inherited from prehistoric days, seventy-five dollars' worth of nitre per day in the manufacture of a glass where it had no imaginable function whatever." He concludes, "the ignorance of the scientific conditions governing glass-making is found from top to bottom in the manufacture" (Duncan 1907:111–119). A third chemist, though more restrained, makes the same point:

> Of the many manufacturing industries in which secret processes are developed, there is perhaps hardly another which equals that of glass manufacture, and there is little doubt in the minds of those familiar with its methods that the formulas in actual use may be counted by thousands or even tens of thousands. Each manufacturer has made some change in a formula, either to follow the dictates of his fancy, or on the basis of sound scientific principles. Most of these changes belong to the former class, hence the thousands of recipes (Silverman 1912:818; cf. Silverman 1910).

When the Department of Commerce surveyed the nation's glassworks in 1916, it found manufacturers focused on "perfecting the mechanical end of the business and developing improved machinery." As for the composition of the metal itself, the manufacturer "made glass as his father made it before him (empirically) or as his competitor made it." Only about 5% of American glass factories employed a chemist of any kind, and only one plant in the country had a chemical physicist (Palmer 1917:23, 316). Similarly, at the outset of the war, the number of chemists and engineers employed in all the glassworks of the United Kingdom was estimated at 20 (Turner 1922:145).

References to a secretive prewar industry "run on rule of thumb methods" are available from those with first-hand understanding of both U.S. and British practice (Colne 1912; Washburn 1919; Hess 1922; Hostetter and Marshall 1933), including Owens himself (in Scoville 1948:197).

Given the anthropological interest in risk and innovation in technological evolution, researchers should be leery of the dysphemistic tenor of these contemporary assessments. An antipathy toward investing in chemical or physical research may indeed have reflected a realistic assessment of cost and return at the time. Such a perspective would have been especially relevant for small manufacturers, and it is not surprising that it was primarily the largest concerns that employed the industry's few chemists (Palmer 1917:316). The point here is that the industry at large, until the disruptions brought on by the war, viewed a scientific understanding of glass as unnecessary and investment in obtaining it as being of unlikely benefit.

THE GIANT HAND

The outbreak of the Great War in summer 1914 found Western nations involved in a world economy that favored international trade in basic commodities. This resulted from several factors. Large capital dominated all the major economies, and many large manufacturers looked to exports for a significant portion of their product. The development of steam power had led to increasing efficiency of national and international transportation systems, making the export of raw materials and mass-produced goods competitive with home products. The European powers had not been involved in a general war for a century, and most citizens of the industrialized world had come to believe such conflagrations were all but unthinkable.

The war was initially incomprehensible to most Americans. Although the U.S., as a neutral, was not initially drawn into the conflict, its economy—heavily dependent on imported materials for its basic industries—was almost immediately affected. By the

end of the year, Turkey had entered the war and closed the Dardanelles to shipping from Russian Black Sea ports, while the British navy was blockading the North Sea, cutting off most imports from Germany. Germany responded with submarine warfare, including the sinking of merchant vessels, which, in turn, reduced imports from Britain and the continent and inflated prices on those materials that were transported.

Well before entering the war, it was apparent to the American government that it would be necessary to substantially reorganize much of the economy in order to divert large numbers of men into the military and to ensure that industries crucial to the war effort had priority access to supplies, transportation, energy, and labor. By the time war was declared in April 1917, much of the theoretical groundwork had been laid. In July, the War Industries Board was created, subsuming or replacing a variety of previous boards and committees. Its nominal charge was to act as a clearinghouse for war industry needs. In fact the board—and the myriad of other boards and commissions that it oversaw or coordinated—adopted a wider mandate, setting prices, allocating resources, coordinating transportation, and establishing labor standards.

One aspect of this effort was the attempt to distinguish important war materials and manufactures from "nonessentials." This classification brought to a point the ultimate effects of war prioritization in the economy: was the government willing to eliminate industries that contributed obliquely at best to the war effort? The government ultimately identified 25 nonessential industries. Although the container glass industry escaped stigmatization, the glass tableware and window glass industries did not. This classification, even though never openly and officially sanctioned, was important since it meant that those industries were considered reservoirs of labor that could better be diverted elsewhere—industries whose supply needs were of minimal account, whose processes competed for energy with more valuable needs, and whose products took up space in a railroad system already overburdened with movement of more crucial products. By the end of the year, the government was considering cutting off coal and electricity to such operations (*New York Times* 1917a; 1917b), and by the next spring bankers were being urged to deny capital to the stigmatized industries (Stewart 1918).

For the glass trade, the nonessentials issue was of grave concern. Clearly, much of their output could fall under this category. The news from abroad was not encouraging: all the European belligerents placed controls of various kinds on their glass manufactures, and in fall 1917, word was received that the Netherlands was considering total shutdown of its glass industry to conserve coal (Mahin 1917). In November, the industry learned that the Fuel Administration and the Priority Board were considering an official list of eleven nonessential commodities, among which glass tableware and window glass were included (*New York Times* 1917a)—a classification that would clearly have popular support (Browne 1918).

This classification led to a 5 December 1917 meeting among 65 glass manufacturers to discuss the threat. (Interestingly, officials of the Flint Glass Workers Union were invited as well.) The meeting inspired a written brief sent to the Fuel Administrator, presenting the industry's case against nonessential classification. The brief noted the crucial importance of glassworks to many communities and the impracticality of temporary shutdowns in an industry in which pots had to be gradually heated for two weeks before they could be put to use. It then argued for the necessity in the war effort of illuminating, chemical, and optical glassware and of food and medicinal containers (Clarke 1918).

In spring 1918 automatic-machine bottle manufacturers agreed with the Fuel Administration to curtail production, "both in the interest of fuel conservation and to give the utmost possible opportunity for the manufacture of glass jars and other food containers." All factories not entirely devoted to food containers were to cut back total production by 15%, the reduction to effect the less essential portion of their output (American Flint 1918). During the war, the government would have primary control of mobilization and industry. Glass manufacturers were by no means the only industry affected. In December 1917, the President nationalized the railroads (Wilson 1918; Baruch 1941), the backbone of the transportation industry.

THE MANGANESE SHORTAGE

By all accounts, manganese was the most common decolorizer used prior to the war. The *National Glass Budget* (1903a) noted its use as "formerly universal," but that it had in recent years been largely eliminated

from the production of plate and window glass. It was still "extensively used" in hollowware of all kinds and, as late as 1917, was the principal decoloring agent (*National Glass Budget* 1912; Palmer 1917:41; McSwiney 1925). Use in the container industry was undoubtedly growing due to the increased demand for colorless ("white") glass, especially for food containers.

Notwithstanding later claims of its unsuitability for use in tank furnaces, it was used in tank as well as pot production. In 1903, for example, the H. L. Dixon Co. of Pittsburgh was offering manganese "granulated for tank furnaces, or powdered for pot furnaces," and this differentiation became standard in the industry (*National Glass Budget* 1903b; Phalen 1920:21). Although it was eventually realized that the operation of manganese—regardless of form—was more difficult to control in continuous tanks, this was met with practical response: "To guard against fluctuations of purity of the raw materials, we use a little more manganese than necessary, and add a small amount of powder blue [cobalt] to mask pink color" (Takahashi 1911:254). The difficulties did not trigger an active search for alternative decolorizers.

The outbreak of war in summer 1914 led almost immediately to a crisis of supply. In the face of shortages, prices dramatically rose. Manganese not only was more expensive, but glass factories had to compete for good quality manganese with other industries that had war priority. By the end of August, the glass trade was reported as "hysterical," and most reports indicate manufacturers and chemical suppliers with only about a four-months' supply on hand (*National Glass Budget* 1914). Scarcity for the glass industry only worsened over the next several years. In the manganese market, the glass industry was a minor consumer with especially rigid quality requirements, and other industrial consumers were wealthier, had greater volume demands, and had strategic priority recognized by the government— especially once the U.S. entered the war, and manganese became a "war mineral."

By far the majority of manganese (at least 90%; by some accounts 96%) used in the U.S. was consumed in the steel industry, where it used in part to deoxidize iron. For this use, manganese was employed in the form of one of two alloys: spiegeleisen (about 20% manganese, 5% carbon, 75% iron), used in the Bessemer process and ferromanganese (80%

manganese, 6% carbon, 14% iron), used in the open-hearth process. Total consumption of both alloys varied with steel production, which fluctuated with the market, but ferromanganese increased steadily from about 20% of consumption at the beginning of the century to more than 60% after 1912. The alloys were either imported from England and Germany or prepared in the U.S. from imported manganese. Regardless, the bulk of the manganese came originally from Georgia in the Russian Caucasus and from India or Brazil. Importantly, supplies from the latter two countries were too high in iron to be useful to the glass trade (Johnson 1917; Ghambashidze 1919).

Scarcity led to efforts by the U.S. government and private interests to identify domestic supplies of manganese ore. The majority of the new sources provided low-grade material that could be used for spiegeleisen but not for ferromanganese. Government standards for ferromanganese were consequently lowered to 70% manganese to allow use of more domestic ores for steel production.

Of the manganese not consumed by the steel industry, the bulk was evidently used by the glass industry and in the production of dry cell batteries. By 1917, demand for manganese in production of batteries and glass was about 25,000 tons per year, reaching 35,000 tons in 1918 and 1919 (Hewett 1917:32; 1921a:677–678; 1921b:632; 1922:107–108). Other users included manufacturers of chlorine and bromine as a drier for varnishes, a coloring material in pottery and brick manufacture, and a colorant in the production of paint (U.S. Tariff Commission 1918:126).

Most U.S. domestic sources were too high in iron. To be useful as a glass decolorizer, the mineral, generally as manganese dioxide (MnO_2), had to be nearly free (preferably less than 1%) of iron. Restrictions in the dry battery industry were even more stringent. Few sources could supply material of this quality. The most prolific source of material that met these standards was from Georgia, then part of the Russian Empire and the source of "Russian manganese" touted by the glass trade. The only serious competitor before the war was "Saxony manganese." Since Germany produced little domestic manganese, the source of Saxony manganese may have also been Georgia.

SELENIUM

Use of selenium, primarily to produce red glass but also as a decolorizer was developed in Germany in the late-19th century, and a German patent for this was awarded in 1891. It is unclear how extensively selenium was used as a decolorant in the next two decades, even in Germany. Its primary use—both in Europe and North America—seems to have been in the production of red glass. Nicholas Kopp is reported to have made the first selenium ruby glass in the U.S. in 1894 (Shively 1924b). The *National Glass Budget* (1903a) lists it as a potential decolorizer but does not say that it was actually being employed for that purpose in American factories. Walter Rosenhain (1908:190) reported that selenium was "finding some use" as a decoloring agent, although whether British or continental industry is meant is not stated.

Difficulties in practical use led to experiments by Fritz Kraze (1912), who was the first to identify arsenic as an agent to reduce the red tint when selenium was employed as a decolorant. An American abstract of this article noted that "selenium-manganese" was then being manufactured in the U.S. as a decolorizer (*Journal of Industrial and Engineering Chemistry* 1912), but it seems to have found little employment.

As late as spring 1916, S. R. Scholes, a prominent American glass chemist, concluded that selenium offered great difficulties, and it was unlikely to ever find much use as a decolorizer (*Metallurgical and Chemical Engineering* 1916). In July of that year, however, advertisements in the *National Glass Budget* announced that the Frink Laboratories of Lancaster, Ohio, were producing a new decolorizer offering "stable and constant results in tank furnaces without using Manganese, Arsenic, Antimony, Blue or other chemicals" at costs 50% to 75% less than manganese. Later reports indicate that the Frink decolorizer was a selenium product (U.S. Tariff Commission 1918:32).

Use of selenium as a decolorizer seems to have been modest until mid-1917. With the difficulties of obtaining manganese that accompanied outbreak of the war, chemists on both sides of the Atlantic began active experimentation on the use of this and other alternatives. There was a greatly increased demand in the glass trade in the latter part of the year (amounting to 50,000–60,000 lbs.) and the price doubled during that period (*Engineering and Mining Journal* 1918; Williams 1918:460; Umpleby 1921).

DISCUSSION

In his study of the economic forces in American political life between the 1890s and the Great

Depression, Frederick Allen (1935:195) noted that "the war dwarfed every other enterprise, submerged every other issue, distorted the organization of American life, colored every emotion." For the glass industry, the forces unleashed by the war in many respects exacerbated trends already evident and resulting from the operations of the market. The industry underwent a quantum change.

Simply, the war created shortages of crucial materials—not only manganese but potash and pot clay as well— that had been the basis of an industry "run on rule-of-thumb methods" (William Turner, in Douglas 1964:327). The shortages corresponded with governmental imperatives regarding the development of chemical and optical glass, increased efficiency in production for industry in general, and improved scientific understanding of industrial materials. For the glass industry, chemical knowledge became crucial. Furthermore, these changes occurred at a time when prices of fuel, chemicals, sand, and labor were all precipitously increasing (Mitchell 1919), and the federal government was directly inserting itself into the operations of the market. Although prices of glass products were also increasing rapidly, some segments of the glass industry were threatened by the fact that they were not essential to the war.

The advent of WWI and its effect on the global economy witnessed a period of exponential growth in the research of glass chemistry in the U.S. and (especially) Britain. This research perfected the use of selenium as a decoloring agent. It is noteworthy that demonstration of the relative advantages of selenium and manganese in tank and pot furnaces, respectively, *followed* the war. Thus the bulk of the shift to selenium occurred *before* its advantages in automatic bottle manufacture were known.

Would the shift have happened anyway? While the adoption of automatic bottle manufacture resulted in immediate and substantial savings in labor cost, changes in decolorizing agents never offered comparable benefits. Disruption in manganese supply directly caused the search for alternative agents. Simultaneous disruption in potash supply reinforced the imperative need to focus on glass chemistry.

CONCLUSION

During WWI, manganese lost its position as the preeminent decolorizer in container glass production and was largely replaced by selenium. This shift seems to have been rapid and to have begun in late 1917. While selenium was better suited than manganese to the continuous tank furnace, which by that time produced the bulk of the nation's container glass, this advantage was unknown prior to the war and even several years thereafter. Effective and widespread use of selenium was made possible by research into the chemistry of glass production that was in fact inspired by wartime shortages. Prior to the war, the American and British glass industries were focused on innovation in mechanical—not chemical—processes.

The broadening of industrial focus to include chemistry and related physical sciences was not brought about primarily by shortages in the supply of useable manganese. Rather, those shortages co-occurred with shortages in other essential materials (such as pot clay and potash) and with national needs to establish domestic production of chemical and optical glassware industries to serve the war effort. Although little studied, the scientific research carried out during the war effectively reoriented the industry, converting it into an enterprise based on the scientific understanding of physical processes.

REFERENCES

Allen, Frederick Lewis
1935   *The Lords of Creation*. Harper and Brothers, New York, NY.

American Flint
1918   Bottle Makers Agree to Curtail. *American Flint* 9(7):4–5.

Anderson, Philip, and M. L. Tushman
1990   Technological Discontinuities and Dominant Designs: A Cyclical Model of Technological Change. *Administrative Science Quarterly* 35(4):604–633.

Bacon, Raymond F.
1916   Industrial Research in America. *Scientific Monthly* 2(3):226–233.

Baruch, Bernard
1941   *American Industry in the War*. Prentice-Hall, New York, NY.

Browne, Lewis Allen
1918   Is Your Business Essential? *Forum* 2:165–180.

Clarke, William P.
1918   The Glass Industry Is Peculiar to Itself. *American Flint* 9(4):1–5.

Colne, Charles

1912   Wherein We Are Deficit. *National Glass Budget* 28(21):1.

Douglas, R. W.

1964   William Ernest Stephen Turner, 1881-1963. *Biographical Memoirs of Fellows of the Royal Society* 10:325-355.

Duncan, Robert Kennedy

1907   *The Chemistry of Commerce.* Harper & Brothers, New York, NY.

Engineering and Mining Journal

1918   Unusual Ores and Metals in 1917. *Engineering and Mining Journal* 105(2):134-135.

Flint, F. C.

1922   The Color of Glass for Packers' Ware. *Glass Container* 1(7):9,24.

Frink, R. L.

1907   The Scientific Side. *Commoner and Glass-worker* 26(2):6.

1909   Some Fallacies and Facts Pertaining to Glass Making. *American Ceramic Society, Transactions* 11:296-319.

Ghambashidze, D.

1919   *Mineral Resources of Georgia and Caucasia, Manganese Industry of Georgia.* George Allen & Unwin, London, England, UK.

Glass Container

1929   Humble Container Acquires Brilliant Color. *Glass Container* 8(11):37-38.

Hess, Henry W.

1922   How Evolution Has Affected Glass Industry "Secrets." *Glass Worker* 42(12):13.

Hesse, Bernhard C.

1915   Contributions of the Chemist to the Industrial Development of the United States—A Record of Achievement. *Journal of Industrial and Engineering Chemistry* 7(4):293-302.

Hewett, D. F.

1917   *Manganese and Manganiferous Ores in 1915.* U.S. Geological Survey, Mineral Resources of the U.S., 1915:29-43.

1921a   *Manganese and Manganiferous Ores in 1917.* U.S. Geological Survey, Mineral Resources of the U.S., 1917:665-696.

1921b   *Manganese and Manganiferous Ores in 1918.* U.S. Geological Survey, Mineral Resources of the U.S., 1918:607-656.

1922   *Manganese and Manganiferous Ores in 1919.* U.S. Geological Survey, Mineral Resources of the U.S., 1919:93-148.

Hostetter, J. C., and A. E. Marshall

1933   Glass Manufacture Changes from an Art to a Science. In *Twenty-five Years of Chemical Engineering Progress*, S. D. Kirkpatrick, editor, pp. 248-261. Van Nostrand, New York, NY.

Johnson, J. E.

1917   The Situation in Regard to Manganese, Sulpher, Pyrite, and Some Other War Minerals. *Proceedings of the Engineers' Society of Western Pennsylvania* 33:643-652.

Journal of Industrial and Engineering Chemistry

1912   Selenium Glass. *Journal of Industrial and Engineering Chemistry* 47(7):539-540.

Kraze, Fritz

1912   Selenglas (Selenium Glass). *Sprechsaal* 45:214-216, 227-228.

Lehner, Victor

1920   Selenium and Tellurium. *Journal of Industrial and Engineering Chemistry* 12(6):597-598.

Lockhart, Bill

2006   The Color Purple: Dating Solarized Amethyst Container Glass. *Historical Archaeology* 40(2):37-48.

Mahin, Frank W.

1917   Threatened Suspension of the Dutch Glass Industry. *American Flint* 9(2):6.

McSwiney, D. J.

1925   The Decolorization of Glass. *Glass Industry* 6(2):23-26; and 6(3):53-57.

Metallurgical and Chemical Engineering

1916   The Glass Industry. *Metallurgical and Chemical Engineering* 14(7):357-358.

Miller, George L., and Anthony Pacey

1985   Impact of Mechanization in the Glass Container Industry: The Dominion Glass Company of Montreal, a Case Study. *Historical Archaeology* 19(1):38-50.

Mitchell, Wesley C.

1919   History of Prices during the War: Summary. *War Industries Board Price Bulletin* 1:1-96.

Mumford, Lewis
1934 *Technics and Civilization.* Harcourt, Brace and World, New York, NY.

National Glass Budget
1903a The Decoloration of Glass. *National Glass Budget* 19(20):2–3.

1903b Flattening Stones and Manganese. *National Glass Budget* 19(7):6.

1912 Principles of Glass Making. *National Glass Budget* 28(1):11.

1914 Oxide of Manganese Supply. *National Glass Budget* 30(22):6.

New York Times
1917a Consider Embargo on Non-Essentials: Fuel for the Manufacture of Eleven Commodities Likely to be Curtailed. *New York Times,* 24 Nov. 1917:1.

1917b Factories to Be Closed: Pittsburgh Makers of Nonessentials Will Get No Current. *New York Times,* 16 Dec. 1917:4.

Palmer, Walter B.
1917 *The Glass Industry: Report on the Cost of Production of Glass in the United States.* U.S. Department of Commerce, Bureau of Foreign and Domestic Commerce, Miscellaneous Series 60:1–430.

Phalen, W. C.
1920 Uses of Manganese Other Than in Steel Making. *United States Bureau of Mines Bulletin* 173:15–26.

Rosenhain, Walter
1908 *Glass Manufacture.* Van Nostrand, New York, NY.

Scoville, Warren C.
1948 *Revolution in Glassmaking.* Harvard University Press, Cambridge, MA.

Shively, R. R.
1924a Principles of Glass Making: Use of Selenium in Glass. *Ceramist* 4:371–374.

1924b The Use of Selenium as a Decolorizer. *Glass Industry* 5(2):26–27.

Silverman, Alexander
1910 The Chemist and the Glass Manufacturer. *Transactions of the American Ceramic Society* 12:186–195.

1912 Glass Formulas: A Criticism. *Journal of Industrial and Engineering Chemistry* 4(11):818–820.

Stewart, John R.
1918 Why Bankers Should Withdraw Capital from the Field of Non-Essentials. *American Bankers Association Journal* 10(7):516–517.

Takahashi, K.
1911 Some Experiments on the Color of Soda-Lime Glass. *Transactions of the American Ceramic Society* 13:251–258.

Turner, W. E. S.
1922 The British Glass Industry: Its Development and Outlook. *Journal of the Society of Glass Technology* 6:108–147.

Umpleby, Joseph B.
1921 *Selenium in 1917.* United States Geological Survey, Mineral Resources of the United States, 1917:33.

U.S. Tariff Commission
1918 *The Glass Industry As Affected by the War.* United States Tariff Commission, Tariff Information Series 5:1–147.

Washburn, Edward W.
1919 Some Aspects of Scientific Research in Relation to the Glass Industry. *Journal of the American Ceramic Society* 2(11):855–864.

Whitney, Willis R.
1916 Research as a National Duty. *Journal of Industrial and Engineering Chemistry* 8:533–537.

Williams, F. E.
1918 Minerals and Power. *Scientific Monthly* 7(5):457–464.

Wilson, Woodrow
1918 *In Our First Year of War.* Harper & Brothers, New York, NY.

4
FINISHES AND CLOSURES

THE ANNUAL SUMMER SHUT-DOWN

Is of the greatest interest to users of private mould bottles. All such should *always* have their orders placed before May 1st for enough ware to carry on their business from July to October. Nearly all glass factories close from July 1st to about Sept. 1st, on account of the summer heat and for needed repairs of furnaces. Thousands of dollars are lost every summer by those who have failed to properly anticipate their needs for special ware.

FINISH.

The ordinary varieties of finish for bottles are given below, which, with slight modifications or combinations of two or more styles, will meet almost every requirement.

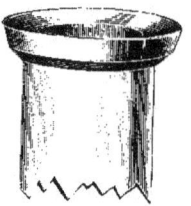
Prescription Lip.

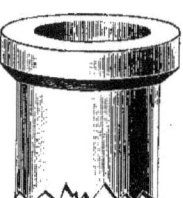
Extract Lip.

Packer Lip.

Flare Mouth

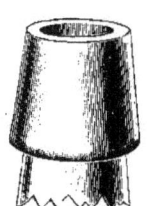
Oil Fniish.

Double Ring.

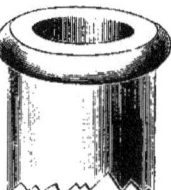
Bead Finish.

Brandy Finish.

Bottles of Every Description. (Illinois Glass Company, 1903–04 Catalog.)

Articles

"The Finishing Touch": A Primer on Mouth-Blown Bottle Finishing Methods
with an Emphasis on "Applied" vs. "Tooled" Finish Manufacturing
[**Reprint** from 2010, *Society for Historical Archaeology, Historic Bottle Website*
<http://www.sha.org/bottle/pdffiles/finishingtoucharticle.pdf>.]
Bill Lindsey

Catalog Reproductions: Finishes
[**Reprints** are selections from Kearns-Gorsuch and Illinois Bottle Company catalogs from the years 1916–1917,
1919–1920, and 1926. Entire volumes available at <http://www.sha.org/bottle/pdffiles/finishingtoucharticle.pdf>.]

The Parks Canada Glass Glossary: Part IV. Closures
[**Reprint** from 1989, *The Parks Canada Glass Glossary*, revised edition, pp. 147–167, Studies in Archaeology,
Architecture, and History, Canadian Parks Service, Ottawa, ONT, Canada.]
Olive Jones and Catherine Sullivan

Bottle Stoppers
[**Reprint** from 1900, *National Glass Budget* 16(13):4.]
National Glass Budget

Modern Closures a Significant Feature of Sanitary and Convenient Packing
[**Reprint** from 1923, *Glass Container* 2(11):5–9, 34, 40, 42.]
Glass Container

A Study of Glass Finishes for Metal Closures
[**Reprint** from 1930, *Glass Packer* 3(7):329–331.]
Glass Packer

Selecting a Wide Mouth Closure to Meet Exact Packing Conditions
[**Reprint** from 1930, *Glass Packer* 3(8):379–394.]
Glass Packer

Narrow Mouth Closures, An Analysis of Representative Types
[**Reprint** from 1930, *Glass Packer* 3(9):431–434.]
Glass Packer

The How and Why of Liners as the Most Important Factor in Securing a Perfect Seal
[**Reprint** from 1930, *Glass Packer* 3(10):475–478.]
Glass Packer

All Caps Have Changed Since 1928, and Some Are Entirely New
[**Reprint** from 1938, *Glass Packer* 17(11):685–694, 734, 736.]
Glass Packer

The Manufacture, Function, and Handling of Bottle Crowns
[**Reprint** from 1950, *Brewers Digest* 25(9):73–75.]
Clyde O. Hess

"The Finishing Touch": A Primer on Mouth-Blown Bottle Finishing Methods with an Emphasis on "Applied" vs. "Tooled" Finish Manufacturing

Bill Lindsey

"THE FINISHING TOUCH"
A Primer on Mouth-Blown Bottle Finishing Methods with an Emphasis on "Applied" vs. "Tooled" Finish Manufacturing

Bill Lindsey
Author of the *Historic Glass Bottle Identification & Information Website*
Copyright © 2010

ABSTRACT

The final step in forming a mouth-blown bottle was to finish it by forming a lip (the "finish" in glassmaker terminology) which would properly accept some type of sealing closure. Many different processes were utilized to accomplish this task, from the simple to the complex. This paper looks at the major finishing techniques used for American made mouth-blown bottles produced during the late 18th, 19th, and early 20th centuries. Emphasis is given to the Applied and Tooled finishing methods which are defined and described in detail. Knowing how to identify the specific finishing methods of a mouth-blown bottle is a significant step towards the dating of these bottles based on observable, manufacturing related, diagnostic features.

(Author's Note: This paper is a condensation of the bottle finishing methods information contained within the **Historic Glass Bottle Identification & Information Website** (or *Historic Bottle Website* for short) which is a part of the *Society for Historical Archaeology* web presence. The *Historic Bottle Website's* primary goals are to guide users towards determining the approximate age of manufacture ("dating") and typical use ("typing" or "typology") of American-made bottles produced from about 1800 to the 1950s [Lindsey 2009]. Please consult that website for more information on the fascinating world of historic bottles at: **www.sha.org/bottle/index.htm**. The glass making terminology used in this paper is defined on the *Historic Bottle Website's* "Glossary" page at: **www.sha.org/bottle/glossary.htm**)

Introduction

Simply put, the "finish" is the glassmaker's term for the "top part of the neck of a bottle or jar made to suit the cap, cork, or other closure" (Jones and Sullivan 1989:78). This term originated with the mouth-blown bottle production process where the last step in physically completing a bottle was to "finish the lip." Other alternative names for the finish besides "lip" were "top," "mouth," or "corkage" (Howard 1950; White 1978). Conversely, with semi-automatic and fully automatic bottle machines, the finish was (and still is) the first step in the bottle making process. The finish is fully formed in the "ring mold" as the remainder of the bottle is only pre-formed in the "blank" mold. Completion of the body shape occurs subsequently in the "blow" mold (Pearson 1929; Miller and Sullivan 1984; Miller and Moran 2004; Schulz and Miller, this volume).

Some authors, unfortunately, have included the entire neck above the shoulder as part of their definition of a finish (Ketchum 1975; White 1978:62). In hand production, however, the neck has already been completed before finish forming begins, and typically only its uppermost portion is affected. Consequently, it is not included as part of the finish (Toulouse 1969b; Deiss

1981; Creswick 1987; Jones and Sullivan 1989; Fike 1998; Lindsey 2009; many others). The use of the word "finish" has carried on to this day and is the preferred term for describing the entire lip and collar, indeed everything clearly above the upper terminus of the neck, for all bottles, both mouth-blown and machine-made (Holscher 1953:304, 311-312; Owens-Illinois Glass Co. 2009). The components of the finish are illustrated in **Figure 1**.

(Figure 1 [to right]. The general morphological features—or anatomy—of a stylized mid-19th century mineral water bottle including the primary finish components. If a two-part finish, the lip is also frequently referred to simply as the "upper part" and the collar as the "lower part." If the finish has three distinct parts, the middle part is referred to as such - the "middle part" [Jones and Sullivan 1989; Lindsey 2009].)

Determining the method employed in finishing a mouth-blown bottle can be one of the more useful diagnostic tools in determining its approximate manufacturing date range. Of particular interest – and an emphasis in this paper – are the

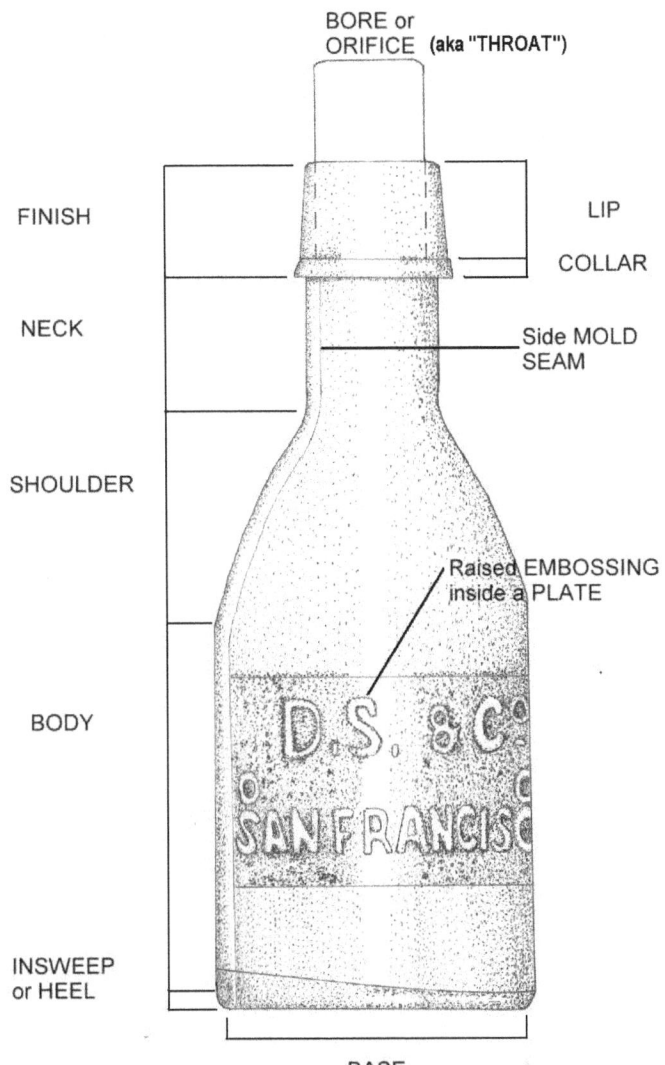

Applied and Tooled Finishing methods and the time periods that these two distinctive mouth-blown finishing techniques were used. Before delving into those subjects it is useful to first briefly describe some glass making processes and early finishing methods.

Blowpipe Removal Methods

Prior to finishing a mouth-blown bottle, the fully expanded bottle had to be removed from the blowpipe. This was done by one of three primary methods: the "cracking-off" process, the "bursting-off" method, or by "shearing" (cutting) the neck off the blowpipe. These methods of blowpipe detachment are usually indistinguishable from each other on the finished item since the vast majority of bottles received post-blowpipe manipulation at the removal point, i.e., "finishing" (Munsey 1970). However, all three of these methods resulted in a cursory "finish" that was sometimes left as is with little or no further manipulation.

With the exception of the "bursting-off" method, in order for the blowpipe to be detached a bottle first had to be held securely by the base, typically with the use of some type of pontil rod (earlier) or snap or snap case tool (later). (These subjects are covered by Toulouse 1968 and Lindsey 2009) The following briefly discusses these three blowpipe removal methods.

Cracking-off

Cracking-off (or "wetting off") was the process of applying a small amount of water—usually via a wet wooden paddle or a cold or wet piece of iron—to the point on the hot, just blown, bottle neck where the glassmaker wished to remove it from the blowpipe. This weakened the glass at the point of application, and a sharp tap on the pipe with one of the glassmaker's tools severed the bottle from the blowpipe

(Modes 1887; Kendrick 1968; Innes 1976). The result was a variably rough and sharp tubular end to the neck (**Fig. 2**) that could be fire polished or otherwise finished as discussed in this paper.

*(**Figure 2 [above right]**. A non-fire-polished, cracked-off finish on a 1850s era "scroll" flask [McKearin and Wilson 1978:422-423, 518-519].)*

For some early American bottles this was the rough, but complete, finish. Based on empirical observations, American-made bottles with this most cursory of finishes rarely date after the 1850s.

Bursting-off

The bursting-off (or "blow-over") blowpipe removal method resulted in a similar, roughly broken off, unfinished appearance to the bore. This process entailed the blowing of a relatively large bubble in the glass just above the mold top, i.e., above the upper end of the bottle neck beyond the mold edge. This thinned the glass sufficiently to allow the bubble to "burst"—with either a subtle twist of the blowpipe or a larger puff of air from the blower—detaching the blowpipe (Howard 1950). The bottle would then be removed from the mold using tongs, a metal rod, or wooden stick stuck in the bore. If further finishing was to be done (typically the case) then the bottle base would have to be held by either a pontil rod or a snap-case tool of some type while it was reheated and finished.

Sometimes, however, the burst-off necks were left unmodified (**Fig. 3**). While perhaps never common, the latter approach was used occasionally through the Civil War period (Russell 1998) and more rarely beyond (empirical observations). For example, three cases of such bottles were recovered from the Steamboat *Bertrand* which sank in the Missouri River in 1865 (Switzer 1974:61, 64). The author has also observed small schoolhouse shaped ink bottles with Burst-Off finishes which were produced by a Western American glass works in the 1870s.

(Figure 3 [to right]. A raw, non-manipulated, burst-off finish on an early 20th century English ink bottle. This looks very similar to the raw, cracked-off finish (Fig. 2) but does have some subtly differing characteristics. These are described in Lindsey [2009]. The same source includes a period film clip [very early 1900s] of a mouth-blown "shop" blowing bottles using the burst-off method to detach the blowpipe.)

Shearing

As with the previous two methods, shearing was both a blowpipe removal method and a type of simple finish. It entailed detaching the blowpipe from the bottle with some type of shears—similar to tin snips or sheep shears—that cut the hot glass analogous to cutting thick plastic with scissors (Barber 1900:21). The resulting finish – which usually received some simple tool work to smooth out the edge - is called a Sheared Lip or Sheared Finish (**Fig. 4**).

(Figure 4 [to left]. An early American pattern molded flask [ca. 1790-1830] with what is often referred to as a sheared finish, although that cannot be positively ascertained since it also received post-blowpipe fire-polishing and possible simple tooling.)

The term sheared lip is commonly used by collectors and archaeologists to refer indiscriminately to Cracked-Off, Burst-Off, and true Sheared Finishes which were subsequently fire polished—a process that typically makes the blowpipe removal method indeterminate (Munsey 1970; McKearin and Wilson 1978; Fike 1987). Sheared Finish bottles date similarly to the cracked-off finishes, usually prior to 1870 (empirical observations).

Once removed from the blowpipe, a vast majority of mouth-blown bottles received additional manipulation devoted to forming a finish that made the bottle opening (bore) more uniform and suitable for some closure method. The earliest of these methods are briefly described in the section which follows.

Early Simple Finishing Methods

Fire Polished Finish

Once the bottle was removed from the blowpipe, one additional finishing step was often taken, even if no specific finish type was to be formed. The upper neck of the bottle was reheated to smooth out the crude or sharp edges where the blowpipe was detached. The result of fire polishing (**Fig. 5**) is a finish or lip edge that is smooth and glossy with the rim being rounded and slightly thickened (Jones and Sullivan 1989:40). This method of completed finish--cracking-off, bursting-off, or shearing, followed by fire polishing—was commonly used on figured flasks dating from the first half of the 19th century and is rarely found on bottles produced after the early to mid-1860s (Deiss 1981:20-21; empirical observations).

*(**Figure 5 [above]**. A fire polished finish on an early American [1820s] "sunburst" flask produced by a New England glasshouse [McKearin and Wilson 1978:420-421].)*

For clarity, fire polishing (or fire finishing) should probably be distinguished from reheating. In the forming of mold blown bottles, these processes were operationally identical (taking the bottle to the furnace or glory hole to soften the glass of the finish area), but differed in purpose and in the stage at which they occurred. *Reheating* was a necessary step carried out to prepare the glass for further tool manipulation to create a finish, including most of those discussed in the following sections. *Fire polishing* was a final treatment sometimes used to smooth out any irregularities in a finish that had already been formed, particularly in its sealing surface, and to achieve a polished appearance. It could be used on finishes as simple as the type just described, or on more complex finishes, and was probably an option as long as hand production continued. Even after the introduction of machines, fire polishing was used for some types of finishes (Lockhart et al. 2009:51).

Ground Rim Finish

Along with fire polishing, the grinding down of the burst-off (occasionally cracked-off; rarely sheared) top surface of the lip or rim was one of the simplest methods for finishing a bottle since the functional structure of these finishes were fully mold-formed and not tooled to shape. Once removed from the blowpipe and annealed, the rough rim was ground down flat and even to finish the bottle or jar (**Fig. 6**).

(Figure 6 [to right]. A ground finish rim on a Lightning canning jar dating from between 1882 and the early 1900s.)

Ground rims were very common on a wide array of mouth-blown canning jars—and occasionally other bottle types—produced from the late 1850s until the 1910s (Toulouse 1969a; Creswick 1987). The sealing surface for such jars was not the ground rim surface itself. Instead, a thin rubber gasket was placed on a lower horizontal ledge. This was a typical—although not universal—configuration for ground rim canning jars including the famous Mason 1858 Patent jar which sealed on the shoulder ledge below the external screw threads and likely where this type finish originated (Deiss 1981).

This finishing process produces the following diagnostic characteristics: the extreme upper horizontal surface of the lip (rim) is flat (not rounded at all) and slightly rough to the touch, like fine grit sandpaper; there are usually tiny chips or roughness along the inside and outside edges resulting from the grinding process; the ground surface has a slightly opaque appearance; and the vertical side mold seams end right at the top outside edge of the ground rim and do not curl over the top of the rim.

Laid-On Ring Finish

Once the blowpipe was removed, a string or band of glass could be laid around the outside of the extreme upper neck forming the Laid-on Ring or String Rim finish **(Figure 7)**.

(Figure 7 [to right]. Laid-on finish on a mid-19th century French "Muscat" wine bottle showing the crudeness typical of this type finish where no post-application tooling was performed. This bottle was free-blown (not molded) and almost certainly cracked-off from the blowpipe leaving a rough, sharp rim that was not fire polished. There are many variations on the theme of the laid-on ring finish, and examples are illustrated in Jones [1986: 49-71] and Jones and Sullivan [1989: 95-96].)

Once applied, this string of glass received little if any tool manipulation though was often fire polished (Jones 1986; empirical observations). The entire finish is comprised of the applied glass and cracked-off, burst-off, or sheared bore. This ring of glass performed at least two functions: to give strength reinforcement to the bore of the bottle and to provide an anchor for wiring down a cork, if necessary (Jones and Sullivan 1989). This method of finishing produced primitive applied finishes which are the precursors to the true Applied Finishes covered later.

Laid-on Ring Finishes are particularly common on bottles made prior to 1850 and were first used at least as early as the mid-1600s (Deiss 1981; Jones 1986; Van den Bossche 2001). Be aware that there are many finishes that initially appear to be Laid-on Rings, but that actually were Applied or Tooled Finishes as defined later in this paper. The subtle variations differentiating these can be difficult to even the trained eye, although the true laid-on ring is usually crudely asymmetrical (**Figure 7**), has no horizontally concentric tooling marks in evidence, and simply looks as though a strip of glass was wrapped around the upper neck just below the bore with little other handwork done, which is just what was done.

Rolled or Folded Finish

This method of producing a finish entailed the use of some type of simple tool to turn the hot plastic glass at the neck terminus back onto itself. As with the other early finishing methods, the Rolled Finish did not involve the specialized lipping or finishing tools required for the Applied and Tooled Finishes discussed later. Once the blowpipe was removed from the bottle, the hot glass at the removal point was reheated as necessary, then either rolled/folded into the bore of the bottle or folded out onto the extreme upper neck, probably using a tool like a "jack," to smooth out and form this simple finish (Jones and Sullivan 1989). This folding certainly provided extra strength to the rim and upper bore of the bottle by "doubling" over the glass.

This type of finish (**Fig. 8**) is most common on early figured flasks, and especially medicine and food bottles dating from the first decade of the 19th century to the 1870s (Deiss 1981; Jones and Sullivan 1989; empirical observations). When rolled to the inside, this finish is also called an "infolded" lip or finish (White 1978).

(Figure 8 [above]. A crudely rolled or folded-in finish on a 1850s era [the base is pontil scarred] hair tonic bottle. The finish on the pictured bottle is crude enough so that parts of it appear to be rolled outwards, although when in hand it is obviously rolled into the bore.)

Flared Finish

The Flared or Flanged Finishing method also entailed the use of some type of simple tool to manipulate the hot glass at the end of the neck, creating a relatively thin finish which projects away from the top of the bore at a more or less 90° angle (**Fig. 9**). According to Kendrick (1968:139, 142-143), the mouth of a bottle "...could be expanded to form the flared lip, either by the use of a jack, or by inserting a cone-shaped plug into the mouth of the bottle as the pliable mass [of glass] rotated." A "jack" was a simple tongs-like tool that appears to be the precursor to the later, more specialized, finishing tools discussed later (Lindsey 2009).

(Figure 9 [above right]. A flared finish on an ink or utility bottle produced by an eastern American glasshouse ca. 1840-1860.)

Based primarily on empirical observations, but also corroborated in Deiss (1981), this method of finishing was most commonly used in the United States between the 1820s and about 1870, though it can date back much further in Europe (Toulouse 1969b; Van den Bossche 2001). These early Flared Finishes can be difficult to discriminate from similar-appearing finishes produced by the methods covered later. To the experienced eye it can be distinguished from applied or tooled flaring finishes by the thinness of the glass that forms the flared portion - much thinner glass than produced by these other later finishing tool methods.

Although this type of finish was "tooled" in the sense that it was manipulated with a simple tool and formed from the reheated glass at the blowpipe removal point, the process and the results were quite different from the later Tooled Finishing method employing a specialized "finishing tool." Both the Rolled and Flared Finishes were formed by working the reheated glass at the blowpipe detachment area but did not involve the application of additional, glass (Toulouse 1969b). This, in part, differentiates these simple tooling methods from the process covered next – the Applied Glass Finishing method.

Applied Glass Finishing Method

Manufacturing Processes

Between the early 1800s and the late 1880s - particularly between about 1830 and 1885 - the most common way of finishing an American-made bottle entailed an application of additional

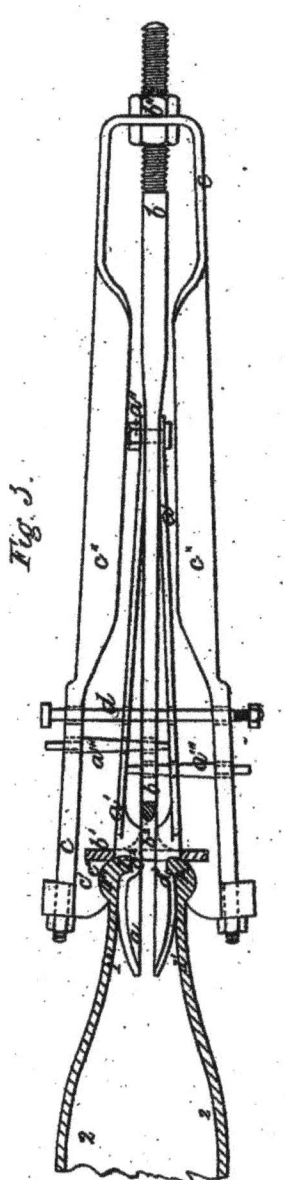

glass which was then shaped with a specialized tool (Hemingray 1860; Howard 1950; Jones 1986). Specifically, a variably thick (depending on the finish type and size desired) strip of hot glass was added at the blowpipe removal point using a pontil rod or other tool ("ring iron"). This was done as the bottle was rotated by another glassworker holding it by the base using either a pontil rod or a snap ("snap-case") tool (McKearin and Wilson 1978:13-14; Jones and Sullivan 1989:21).

This applied hot glass was then manipulated with a specialized "finishing tool" ("rounding tool" or "lipping tool") to form a wide variety of different finish types that could be more complex and variable than the earlier finishes noted above which were formed with very simple but versatile tools (Stone 1855, 1856; Sheldon and Lynn 1893; Munsey 1970:32). The finishing tool (**Figure 10**) was clearly more specialized: not only was its use restricted to creating finishes, but the jaws of every such tool had to be specifically designed for a particular size and profile of finish.

*(**Figure 10 [to left].** Illustration from an 1876 patent showing a fairly typical, calipers-type finishing tool used to create a type of applied, one-part "blob" finish used for carbonated beverages, the purpose of this design being to create a throat wider than the aperture [Lamont 1876].)*

This finishing method produced what is referred to as an Applied Finish, an example of which is illustrated by **Figure 11**. This image also shows the significant "slop-over" of the applied glass onto the upper neck beyond the reach of the finishing tool - a very common attribute and diagnostic feature of Applied Finishes (discussed later).

*(**Figure 11 [to right].** A two-part applied finish showing two characteristic features: slop-over of excess glass, and the vertical mold seam continuing to the bottom of the finish.)*

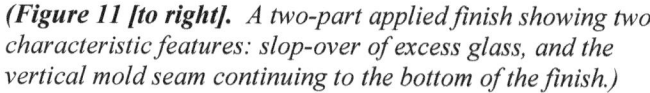

The earliest finishing tools—that is, those for Applied Finishes—only formed the dimensions of the finish itself and generally did not affect the upper neck. This is an important distinction when comparing the Applied Finishes to the Tooled Finishes discussed later.

What is probably the earliest form of specialized finishing tool (**Fig. 12**) is described in an 1842 explanation of the process of applying and forming a finish, beginning from the point where the bottle is detached from the blowpipe:

> The finisher then warms the bottle at the furnace, and taking out a small quantity of metal [i.e., glass] on what is termed a ring iron, he turns it once round the mouth forming the ring seen at the mouth of bottles. He then employs the shears [finishing tool] to give shape to the neck. One of the blades of the shears has a piece of brass in the center, tapered like a common cork, which forms the mouth [bore or inside of the finish], to the other blade is attached a piece of brass, used to form the ring [outside of the finish]. (quoted in McKearin and Wilson 1978:217)

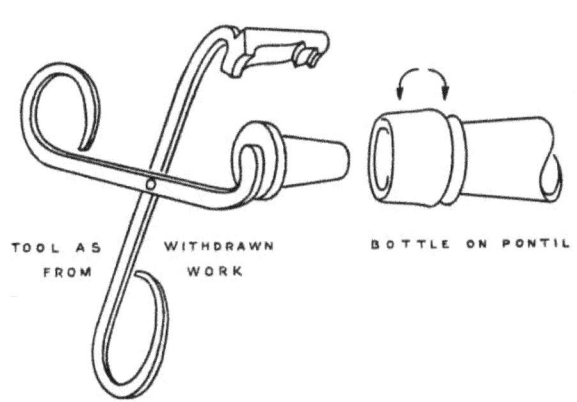

TOOL AS FROM   *WITHDRAWN WORK*   *BOTTLE ON PONTIL*

(Figure 12 [to left]. Artist's rendition of the lipping shears, probably the first form of specialized finishing tool [McKearin and Wilson 1978:Fig. 53a].)

These early finishing shears quickly evolved into the calipers-type finishing tools (**Fig. 10**) that dominated the industry by the 1850s. The *"piece of brass in the center"*—analogous to the plug shown on the illustrated caliper-type finishing tools— fit into the bore of the bottle. The *"piece of brass used to form the ring"* is analogous to the pair of jaws, one at the end of each caliper arm. The various finishing tool illustrations in this paper help to visualize these parts.

The following excerpt from an 1860 patent describes the mouth-blown production of jars with Applied Finishes. At that time the most common finish type on jars was the groove ring wax seal finish (**Figs. 13, 14**) although the process for forming and finishing most bottle types at the time was identical to that described:

> ...it has been customary to mold the body and neck of the jar in molds of two parts... After the jar has been thus formed and removed from the mold a portion of melted glass is taken and united to the top of the jar and the...[finish]...is

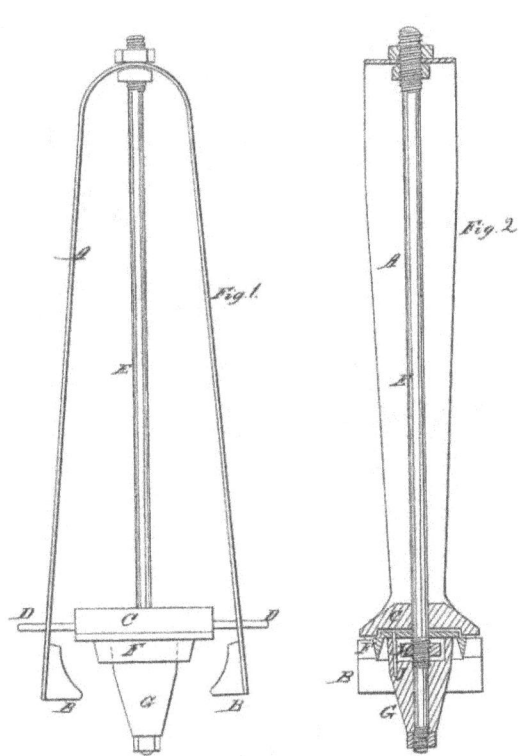

then...[formed with]...the plastic glass by a tool adapted to the purpose. This process is necessarily slow and laborious and the work when completed is not so uniform and complete as when the jar is finished in the mold and at one operation...[the latter of which was the purpose of the specific patent] (Hemingray 1860).

(Figure 13 [previous page to right]. Illustration of a finishing tool for making grooved ring fruit jars [Stone 1856], one of the first two American finishing tool patents. B indicates the jaws of the tool, which form the outside of the finish; F is a wedge-shaped blade to form the groove in the upper rim [Fig. 13].)

This clearly describes the application of glass and subsequent tooling for an Applied Finish and even notes the crudity ("*...not so uniform...*") that is often a result of such an operation. The more advanced tools used for finish glass manipulation and generally more complex design of most Applied Finishes is what differentiates this method of finishing from the simple, one-part "laid-on ring" finish described earlier.

The first patents for finishing tools in the United States were issued in the mid-1850s, although similar domestic and imported finishing tools were already long in use (Stone 1855, 1856; Toulouse 1969b:533; empirical observations). The patents were not for the concept itself, since such tools were no longer patentable by that time. Rather the patents were for new ways of constructing

them, or for designs that were particularly useful for distinctive forms of finish. The 1856 patent (**Fig. 13**), for example, was for forming an applied, groove-ring finish on wax seal canning jars (**Fig. 14**). The patented tool was for producing the "groove" in the groove-finish (**Fig. 13: part "F"**). The "jaws" (**Fig. 13: part "B"**) of these tools formed the outside of the finish when rotated and just barely, if at all, touched the upper neck of the bottle.

(Figure 14 [above right]. A groove-ring finish on a fruit jar, the product of a finishing tool like that shown in the previous figure. The vertical lip of the cap fit into the grooves, which were filled with wax to affect the seal.)

Regardless of the particular design of these early finishing tools, their use after the application of added glass constitutes a distinctive category of finish. The diagnostic characteristics of Applied Finishes will be discussed after a brief note on the terminology.

History of Terminology

The term Applied Finishes has its basis as a collector term. These could also be termed Applied & Tooled Finishes since special tooling of the added glass was necessary to create the desired finish shape and size (Deiss 1981:51; Roller 1983:463). This type of finish additionally goes by an array of collector-originated terms including "crudely applied lip," "glob top," "globby top," "drippy top," etc. It should be noted that applied finishes - especially earlier (1830s to 1860s) examples - tend to be more substantial, bulky and/or crude compared to later applied finishes, though there are many exceptions. This is likely because of the quickly improving techniques and tools during the last half of the 19th century, a period of explosive innovation in the American glass industry (Scoville 1948; Deiss pers. comm. 2003).

Some authors have criticized the use of the term Applied Lip as telling *"nothing of the method"* used to produce the finish (Toulouse 1969b:533) or that "...the term is so broadly interpreted as to render it meaningless" (Jones and Sullivan 1989:75). This certainly has been true. Many people - collectors and archaeologists alike—have too broadly used the term Applied Lip or Applied Finish in referring to any finish on a mouth-blown bottle where the side mold seam does not terminate at the very top of the finish. The origin of this broad interpretation appears to have come from Tibbitts (1964:3) who described an Applied Lip

> ...to include any lip or mouth that was hand worked after the bottle was broken off from the blowpipe. Among others, it includes sheared lip, rolled lip, applied collar on sheared lip, applied collar below sheared lip, applied blob, etc.

Tibbitts so broadly defined an Applied Lip as to include virtually any finish on a mouth-blown bottle including what is more properly referred to as a Tooled Finish. The production of a Tooled Finish entailed a different manufacturing process than an Applied Finish.

It is, however, important and useful to clearly differentiate Applied and Tooled Finishes from each other, and from other finishes, for dating utility. Simply expressed, and as described here, both of these finishes—and only these finishes—employed a finishing tool; an Applied Finish entailed the application of additional glass; a Tooled Finish did not.

Diagnostic Characteristics of Applied Finishes

The observable diagnostic characteristics of an Applied Finish include several or all of the following attributes:

1. The side mold seams end abruptly on the neck at the lower edge of the finish (Figs. 11, 15, 16). This feature is

True Applied Finish - The side mold seam ends abruptly (i.e. disappears) right at the lower edge of the finish.

Mold seam ends here

Often there is glass "slop-over" or "drip" just below the finish.

Side Mold Seam

usually quite reliable, though there are exceptions. For instance, the mold seams in the upper neck portions of an Applied Finish bottle can be hard to detect due to neck reheating prior to the finish application process. In addition, sometimes—especially with bottles from the first half of the 19th century—all or a portion of the neck had been formed by the skill of the glassblower since only the base, body, and shoulder were formed in the mold. No neck side mold seam would be possible on these bottles. Conversely, if the side mold seams extend perceptibly into the structure of the finish itself—and the bottle does not have a ground rim or a sheared/cracked-off finish—it is always a Tooled Finish (next section).

(Figure 15 [on previous page]. Applied finish on a proprietary medicine bottle, showing excess glass below the finish and relation to side seams, which end at the bottom of the finish.)

2. There is usually a small quantity of excess glass slopping over onto the upper neck of the bottle just below the finish (Figs. 11, 15, 16). Sometimes the excess slop-over is not evident or the applied glass was inadequate in quantity resulting in a finish that is missing some portions. This is evidenced by unfilled spots on the finish rim and/or a ragged unevenness or waviness at the base of the finish. In general, the appearance of an Applied Finish is less vertically (and sometimes horizontally) symmetrical than a Tooled Finish.

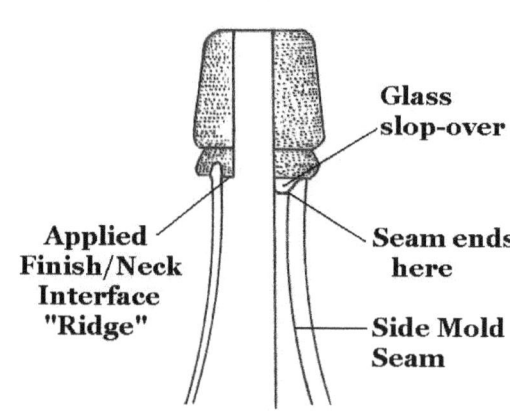

Glass slop-over

Seam ends here

Side Mold Seam

Applied Finish/Neck Interface "Ridge"

(Figure 16 [to right]. Partial section of an applied finish showing the relationship of original and added glass [after Deiss 1981:Fig. 17].)

3. The presence of a horizontal line or ridge within the throat of the bottle that can often be felt by inserting the little finger into the bore, if it will fit. (Fig. 16) This line or ridge marks the interface between the blowpipe severing point and the separately applied finish glass; it can vary from obvious to non-existent (Boow 1991:64).

4. Concentric horizontal tooling marks from the finishing tool *may* be present on the finish itself but *not* on the upper neck just below the finish (Fig. 22). The rotation of the finishing tool often left its mark on the outside surface of Applied Finishes very similar to those on Tooled Finishes. These tooling rings are rarely ever visible on the extreme upper neck of Applied Finishes – an extremely common attribute of Tooled Finishes - since the jaws did not extend beyond the base of the finish. Finishing tools for other Applied Finish types or styles (e.g., mineral finish, blob finish, etc.) had differently shaped "jaws" than that shown in this illustration.

5. Some applied finishes will exhibit a few to a grouping of small, short fissures or cracks ("crazing lines") in the area where the glass was applied to the raw neck end. This feature is very unusual, though not unknown, on Tooled Finishes and can be quite indicative of the presence of an applied finish. This feature is the result of the difference in temperature between the applied finishing glass (hot from the glass pot) and the glass of the upper neck which, though reheated, would have been cooler than the new viscous glass being added.

Few Applied Finishes will have all five of the features above in evidence. A combination of features **1** and **2** is the most commonly observed, with feature **3** being felt frequently if a finger will fit into the bottle bore, and feature **4** frequently observed upon close inspection. Sometimes a very well executed Applied Finish ("neatly applied" in collector jargon) will only show the side mold seam disappearing at the base of the finish (feature **1**) with maybe some faint tooling marks on the finish itself (feature **4**).

The specific dating guidelines for bottles with Applied Finishes are covered after the next section on the Tooled Finishing method. The dating of the transition from Applied to Tooled Finishes is somewhat bottle-type specific and the subject of Tooled Finishes needs to be covered first.

Tooled Finishing Method

Manufacturing Processes

This finish manufacturing method is the result of the glass for the finish-to-be being blown with the rest of the bottle, not added in a separate hand application as with the Applied Finishing method described previously. Specifically, once the blowpipe was removed from the bottle neck, the finish was formed and made smooth and precise by the reheating of the end of the neck—*with no additional glass added*—and tooled to the desired shape with a finishing tool (Deiss 1981; Roller 1983; Ring and Ham 1998). Tooled Finishes are also called Wiped Finishes by some - a fairly descriptive term, for the process sometimes "wipes" out a portion of the upper mold seams; a subject discussed later in this paper (Preble 1987; Fike 1998).

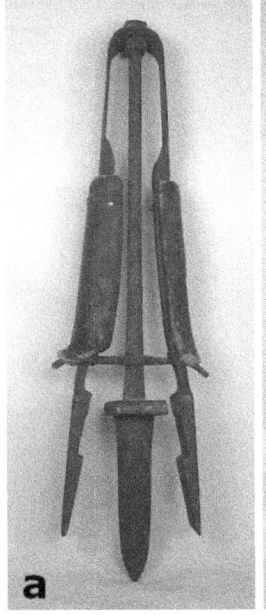

It is important to note that the term Tooled Finish is not used here to describe the primitive tooling of the simple finishes noted earlier in this paper, i.e., the Flared Finish, Rolled Finish, and often the sheared/cracked-off and Fire Polished Finish. Indeed, these earlier finishes were typically at least partially formed with the use of simple tools so are in a sense a type of Tooled Finish. Instead, the term Tooled Finish here refers to the more distinctive finishes fully formed without adding new glass, by the use of compression finishing tools like those in **Figures 17** and **19**. This distinction has important ramifications for the proper dating of bottles.

(Figure 17 (three images on previous page). A typical finishing tool used for tooled finish forming: (a): Complete tool; (b): Detail of jaws in open position allowing tool to be slipped over the unmodified bottle, and to be removed after forming the finish; (c): Detail of jaws in working position. The conformation of this tool indicates that it was used for the forming of a tooled finish as the jaws extend well beyond the base of the finish. This would have resulted in faint horizontal, concentric rings on the finish and upper neck.)

This process entailed an important change in the finishing tools themselves that permitted the forming of Tooled Finishes. In the forming of Applied Finishes the goal had been to align the base of the finish with the already existing neck, so the jaws were limited to the area of the finish itself. With the development of the tooled finish, this goal changed. Now the reheated glass of the upper neck itself had to be modified, in order to assure a proper transition to the new finish. Consequently, the jaws were lengthened to extend beyond the finish to the upper neck, and the central plug was extended with them to maintain alignment.

The result can be seen in a typical finishing tool for the new process, a tool for finishing demijohns from the *Illinois Glass Company* probably dating between 1890 and 1910 (**Fig. 17**). As with earlier tools, its central plug or spindle was inserted into the neck of the bottle and the bottle rotated with the finishing tool held steady while squeezing the jaws tightly against the plastic upper neck glass to compress and form the desired finish (Kendrick 1968:144). The conformation of this tool indicates that it was used for the forming of a Tooled Finish as the jaws extend well beyond the base of the finish. This would have resulted in faint horizontal, concentric rings on the finish and upper neck. The finish would have resembled **Figure 18**.

(Figure 18 [to right above]. A tooled single-part finish, such as would be produced by the tool in Fig. 17. Note the horizontal striations on the finish and upper neck.)

Another illustration of a tool of this type (**Fig. 19**) can be seen in an 1893 patent for a "Finishing-tool for Glass Bottles" (Sheldon and Lynn 1893). This tool was clearly designed to form Tooled Finishes with no application of additional glass. The patent narrative states the following about the tool's use, which includes an excellent description of the Tooled Finishing process:

The manner of operating our device is as follows: The bottles, which have been completed, and whose necks, mouths and extensions it is desired to finish, *are heated to such an extent that the necks become soft and plastic to a degree as to be readily formed or molded in any desired shape.* The spindle of the finishing tool is then inserted in the mouth of the bottle, and the spring jaws gradually closed until the finishing dies [i.e., the "jaws."] come in contact with the glass. At the same time the bottle is turned, the dies operating on the outside of the bottle neck, and gradually bringing it in the shape of the dies... After the end of the bottle has been finished off as mentioned, by releasing the pressure of the spring jaws [the tool] may be drawn out of the bottle, which is done and cold enough to retain its shape and may then be removed, and another bottle operated on (Sheldon and Lynn 1893; emphasis added)

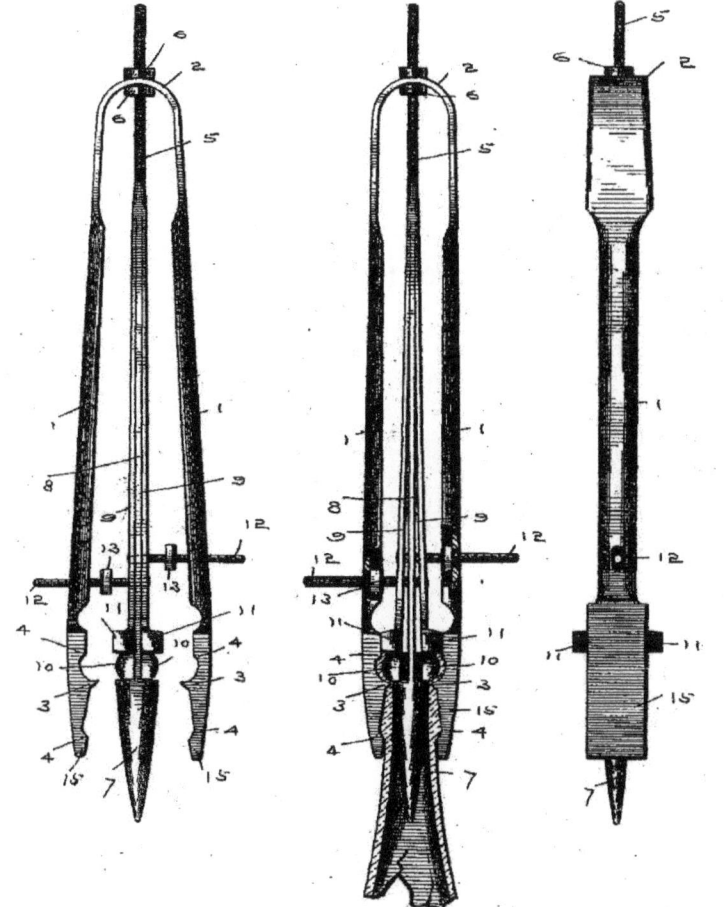

(Figure 19 [to right]. Illustration from an 1893 patent for a finishing tool for tooled finishes [Sheldon and Lynn 1893]. The patent application notes that the tool was used without added glass, and the jaws extend onto the upper neck.)

Categories of Tooled Finishes

Empirical observations by the author indicate that there were two distinct manufacturing methods for Tooled Finish formation based on mold conformation and finishing activity. These were the "Standard" and the "Improved" Tooled Finishes—both of which can be accurately referred to as Tooled Finishes. By distinguishing between the two variations, further bottle dating refinements are possible. The two methods are described as follows:

"Standard" Tooled Finish: This tooled finishing method is typically just called a Tooled Finish." The older of the two varieties, this method involved a mold in which the finish conformation was <u>not</u> significantly pre-formed in the mold. The shape of the base, body, and neck of the bottle were formed by the mold but not the precise shape of the finish. To put it differently, there was limited (or no) pre-forming of the finish by the mold itself as the finishing tool was utilized to completely form the finish conformation. Although the earlier of the two tooling methods, it also continued in use until hand production was replaced by machines, overlapping the "improved" tooling method described next. The Standard Tooled Finish was first used as early as the 1860s with some smaller bottles, although it became the dominant finishing method on just about all bottles by the 1890s. (More on dating later in this paper.)

The Standard Tooled Finish is identified by a side mold seam that ends or fades out on the neck distinctly below the bottom edge of the finish (**Figs. 20, 22a**). Bottles with such finishes are formed in two-piece "open molds" (**Fig. 21**) where the upper portion of the mold only forms the neck, not the finish (Kendrick 1963). This type of mold could have produced a bottle finished with either an Applied Finish (using glass applied to the neck end which was tooled to shape) or a Tooled Finish (by re-heating and compression tooling the end of the straight neck without additional glass added). With the latter process, the glassblower would have removed the blowpipe in a way which left enough "extra" glass to work with in creating the finish by reheating and compression tooling.

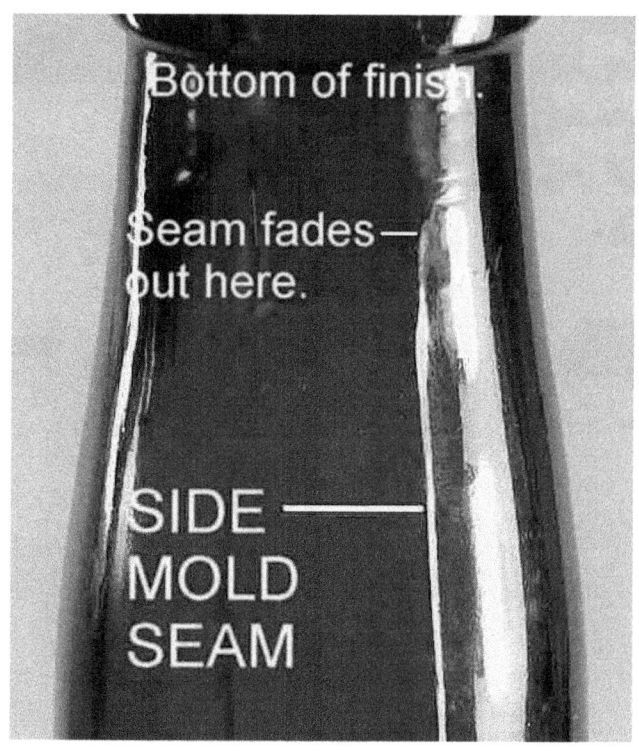

(Figure 20 [to right]. Neck of a bottle, showing horizontal striations eliminating the upper end of the vertical side seam below the finish, a characteristic indication of a tooled finish.)

(Figure 21 [below]. Drawing of a two-piece "open" mold, in which the entire neck, but not the finish, is formed in the mold.)

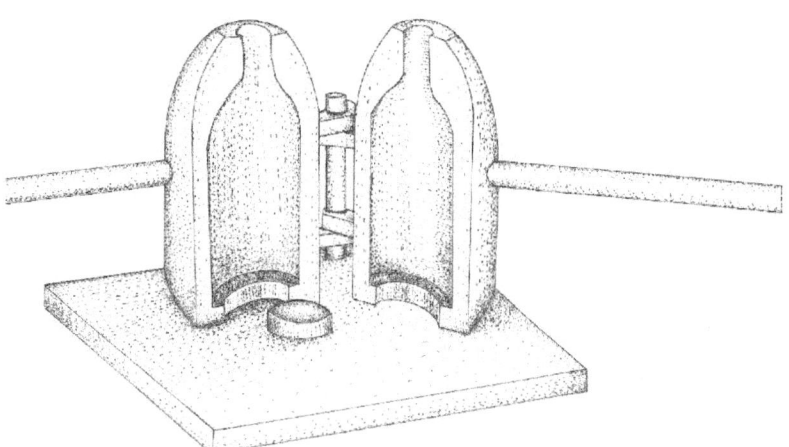

Two-piece "post bottom" mold with separate base plate.

The Standard Tooled Finish could be considered a transition type of Tooled Finish that was easily adapted to bottles produced in molds that were previously finished with an Applied Finish. **Figure 22** shows the finishes of two mid-1880 *Peruvian Bitters* bottles (San Francisco, CA.) which were blown in the same exact mold but one has an Applied Finish (right) and the other (left) a Standard Tooled Finish (Wilson and Wilson 1969; Wichmann 1999; empirical observations). Bottle molds produced with the intention of using the Tooled Finishing method were almost certainly made with a slightly longer neck in order to provide adequate glass for the process. The following quote is from a 1904 publication (*National*

Glass Budget) indicating such along with a reference to the former method of producing Applied Finishes:

> Formerly the bottle lip was finished by laying on a thread of hot glass, and each blower finished his own bottle. This method of finishing was slow, and required skill and strength of arm, ***so that when the neck was lengthened*** *and the bottle finished at the glory hole by stoving back the reheated neck so as to form the ring,* it increased the output, and made the work lighter (Anonymous 1904; emphasis added).

(Figure 22 [to right]. Two 19th century bottles [Peruvian Bitters] showing the different effects of tooled and applied finishes.)

"Improved" Tooled Finish: Towards the end of the mouth-blown era (late 1890s through the 1910s) many bottle molds did form most or all of the finish, because the upper portion of the mold cavity had the finish shape included. Kendrick (1963) called this type mold a "closed mold" as versus an "open mold"

Peruvian Bitters (San Francisco, CA.)

Tooled Finish

Applied Finish

Seam Ends

Seam Ends

2 cm

(**Fig. 21**) which did not form any of the actual finish. After the bottle was removed from the mold, the finish shape and bore conformation was made more precise—to ensure proper closure fit—with minor re-firing and/or tooling of the extreme upper portion of the finish (Deiss 1981).

(Figure 23 [to left]. An improved tooled finish on an early 20th century liquor bottle. The lower part of the finish is formed in the mold, and only the upper portion is tooled.)

The Improved Tooled Finish is identified by a side mold seam that ends or fades out well into the conformation of the finish itself, often just short of the finish rim. **Figure 23** shows the Improved Tooled Finish characteristics close-up. The location of the seam on this bottle makes it readily apparent that the basic finish form, including the lower ring, was formed by the mold without the addition of added glass. Horizontal tooling marks are evident only in the upper portion of the finish where the finish received

Concentric Tooling Marks on the upper finish portion.

Seam Ends Here

Side Mold Seam

cursory tooling to standardize the conformation and, in particular, the bore size in order to facilitate efficient corking with one size of cork. The pictured finish is on an *Oregon Importing Company* (Portland, OR.) cylinder liquor bottle that dates from between 1904 and 1915 (Thomas 1998a). The Improved Tooled Finish almost always identifies a bottle as having been produced *after* about 1895, with most dating after 1900 (empirical observations).

(Figure 24 [below]. Drawing of a two-piece "closed" mold in which the details of the finish (in this case external screw threads) are formed in the mold.)

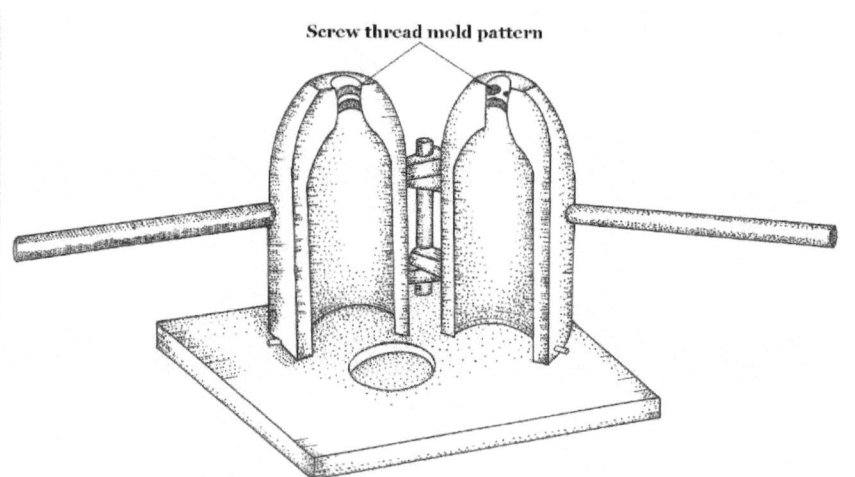

Closed mold where the conformation of the finish (in this case external screw threads) are formed by the mold itself.

An example of this type of production can be seen in an illustration of a "closed mold" which has the conformation of an external screw thread finish incorporated into the mold itself (**Fig. 24**)—a type of Improved Tooled Finish. A bottle produced in this type of mold would have required either some post-blowpipe reheating and/or tooling to the extreme upper portion above the screw threads, or the lip surface (i.e., rim) would have been ground flat to remove the rough edges created when the blowpipe was removed. One of these processes would have been necessary to make the upper finish suitably smooth and consistent enough to reliably seal with a screw cap (**Fig. 25**).

(Figure 25. Improved tooled finish on a 1905-1915 liquor flask with screw threads formed in the mold [Wilson and Wilson 1968:46, 49]. Tooling affects only the area above the threads.)

Side mold seam ends here

Additional Tooled Finish Information

As already noted, Tooled Finishes usually show some concentric tooling marks, with the Standard Tooled Finish having these marks extending onto the neck below the finish. Due to the amount of tooling on most bottles produced with this finishing method, the upper side mold seam is often substantially "wiped out" making it difficult to determine how much shape forming the finish received in the mold versus how much was purely from the tooling actions. Empirical evidence indicates that many bottles with Tooled Finishes had at least the basic finish conformation pre-formed in the mold. However, the subsequent re-firing and finishing tool action to complete the finish eradicated most or all of the signs of the side mold seam for as far as the tool reached on the outside of the neck. The absence of the mold seam in the finish itself likely makes many Improved Tooled Finishes actually appear to be Standard Tooled Finishes. In other words, if the mold seam <u>is evident</u> within the finish, one knows that it is an Improved Tooled Finish; if the side mold seam <u>is not evident</u> in the finish then one can not say for sure that the finish was not partially molded; only that physically it is a Tooled Finish. This is belaboring a fine point, but it does have dating implications which will be summarized later.

In any event, the actual finish glass for Tooled Finishes was not added to the neck terminus as with an Applied Finish. To picture the difference in these finish classes another way, the blowpipe detachment point on an Applied Finish was at or just above the point where the finish and neck meet in the finished bottle. The blowpipe detachment point on Tooled Finishes was (or became) the top surface of the finish. The Tooled Finish was a major innovation in that the bore and upper neck of bottle could be made smoother, more properly tapered, and of more uniform dimensions as compared to the Applied Finish. This allowed for more reliable sealing of the bottle with a cork in particular since more of the inside surface of the finish was in contact with the closure (Deiss pers. comm. 2003).

*(**Figure 26 [below right]**. Ground lip on a Mason jar.)*

Almost certainly the first important, fully molded finish was in 1858 with the invention and production of the Mason canning jar (Deiss 1981). (**Fig. 26**) These revolutionary jars were produced in a blow-over mold where the outside screw thread finish was molded along with the body and base. This was a mold conformation very similar to **Figure 24** except for a

differently shaped bottle with a wider mouth or bore. The rough cracked-off top surface of this finish was subsequently ground off to make it uniform and flat, i.e., a ground rim. In general, with the exception of simple straight finishes (simply sheared or cracked-off upper neck ends which were mold-formed) and canning jars, bottle molds with incorporated finishes (in whole or in part) were little used until the late 1870s, receiving only limited use until the 1890s when they became fairly common with some bottle styles until machine manufacture dominated the bottle making world by the mid to late 1910s (Deiss 1981; empirical observations).

Diagnostic Characteristics of Tooled Finishes

The observable diagnostic characteristics of a Tooled Finish include several or all of the following:

1. The side mold seam distinctly fades out on the neck of the bottle, usually below the bottom of the finish (Standard Tooled Finish; **Figs. 20, 27**). Frequently, with later mouth-blown bottles (early 20th century), the side seam will disappear *within* the confines of the finish itself (Improved Tooled Finish; see **Figs. 23, 25**), though it will not touch the outside edge finish rim unless the rim is ground down. (Note: There are some later, press-and-blown machine-made milk bottles that have fading upper side mold seams, and that, upon first appearance, appear to have Tooled Finishes.)

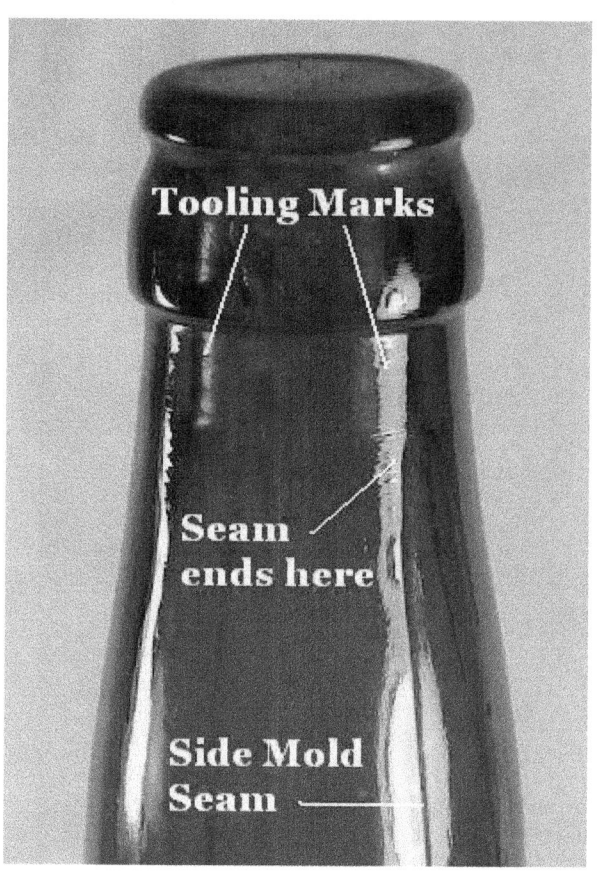

*(**Figure 27 [to right]**. A crown finish illustrating the characteristics of the tooled finish.)*

2. Concentric horizontal tooling marks are usually present on both the finish and the upper portion of the neck above where the side mold seam fades or disappears (Fig. 27).

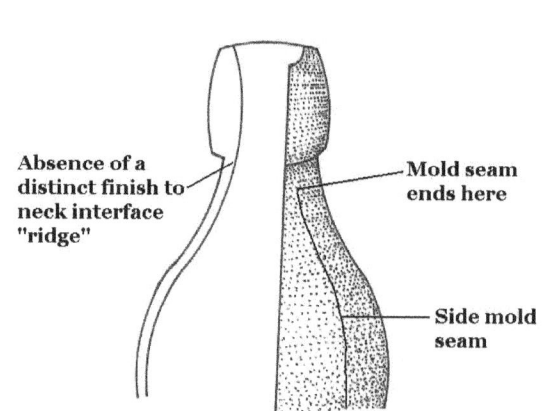

Absence of a distinct finish to neck interface "ridge"

Mold seam ends here

Side mold seam

Sometimes the side mold seams can be observed faintly "underneath" or within the tooling marks or rings. The side mold seam can also occasionally proceed faintly almost all the way to the top of the finish. This residual side mold seam is likely a result of the glass beginning to cool and solidify while being hand tooled, allowing mold seam traces to remain in the finish. The presence of the side mold seam in the finish itself on a mouth-blown bottle positively identifies the finish glass as having been mold blown and not applied.

*(**Figure 28 [to left]**. Illustration of the characteristics of tooled finishes.)*

3. The absence of a distinct line or ridge inside the finish - as would be found on an Applied Finish - since there was no separate application of finishing glass. (Fig. 28) The glass inside the neck at the finish/neck interface feels smooth to the touch with no distinct ridge or groove evident. Do not mistake the hump discussed next for the applied finish/neck interface ridge (#3 in the Applied Finish diagnostic characteristics noted earlier).

4. When viewing the upper neck and finish from the side, there is often a visible change in the thickness of the glass on each side of the bottle neck in the vicinity of where the side mold seam disappears and the tooling marks begin. (Fig. 29) Often this is just a subtle smooth "hump" on the inside surface of the glass within the throat or bore where the central plug or spindle of the finishing tool stopped.

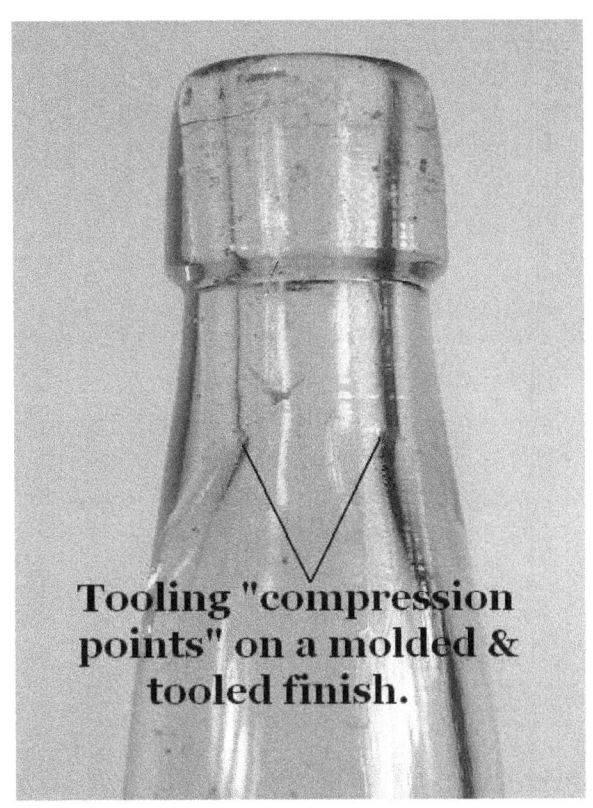

Tooling "compression points" on a molded & tooled finish.

(Figure 29 [to right]. Tooled finish of a Hawaiian export style beer bottle dating between 1908 and 1911 [Elliot and Gould 1988]. The compression points in the throat left by the spindle of the finishing tool, shown clearly here, are usually difficult to photograph.)

5. The absence of any glass drip or slop-over immediately below the base of the finish - as is commonly observed on Applied Finishes - since there was no separate application of finishing glass.

Bottle Type Specific Dating Guidelines

The changeover from Applied to Tooled Finishes was a relatively significant technological shift in bottle manufacturing. This changeover can often provide a useful dating break for bottles made during the last quarter of the 19th century. However, there was considerable time variation in making this transition depending on the specific type or class of bottles. There were also variations among the different glass makers, although these are usually impossible to ascertain as most bottles can not be firmly attributed to a particular glass factory during this era. Empirical observations indicate that the mid 1870s was when the transition from Applied Finishes to the more technologically advanced and efficient Tooled Finishes significantly commenced. Few bottles known to pre-date the mid-1870s have the Tooled Finish as defined here. Those that are known are primarily smaller bottles – a subject discussed below. Likewise, by the mid-1890s the changeover from Applied Finishes was largely complete, and a very large majority of American-made bottles dating after that time have Tooled Finishes. (Foreign bottles followed a different timeline; this is briefly covered later.)

The following information provides general dating guidelines for the transition from Applied to Tooled Finishes categorized by types or classes of bottles. It is based on the author's extensive empirical observations in conjunction with a wide array of published references which provide relatively precise company dating for various types and styles of historic bottles. (Major sources are noted in the "References" section of this paper.) As there are many exceptions to these general trends, dating accuracy can only be achieved by using these date ranges in conjunction with other diagnostic features (Lindsey 2009). However, the following information is considered accurate for a majority of bottles within the classes listed. Readers interested in this complex subject are encouraged to visit the various *Bottle Typing (Typology) & Diagnostic Shapes* pages on the *Historic Bottle Website* (Lindsey 2009) for much more in-depth finish manufacturing related dating information pertinent to specific bottle types.

Dating notes on the transition from Applied to Tooled Finishes

1. In general, it is clear that the smaller the bottle, the earlier that Tooled Finishes were first used. The total transition time from Applied to Tooled Finishes is from the mid-1870s to the mid-1890s in the United States. This is discussed in the points that follow. Why smaller bottles were tooled sooner than larger ones is not known, though the trend is very evident in the observation of many thousands of bottles by the author. It is, however, certainly related to some type of manufacturing efficiencies inherent in the production methods of different bottle sizes.

2. Smaller drug store bottles appear to have almost completely made the changeover to Tooled Finishes by the late 1870s. The author has studied hundreds of examples of Oregon druggist bottles in conjunction with business directory listings and has found that tooled "prescription" style finishes dominate such bottles by the late 1870s (Whitall Tatum & Co. 1879, 1880:7). Prior to the mid-1870s druggist bottles tended to have either a distinct Applied Finish or the older thin Flared Finish described earlier. These latter bottles are also often pontil scarred (Davis 1949; Deiss pers. comm. 2003; empirical observations). A typical late 19th century "Philadelphia Oval" style druggist bottle (embossed *BLUMAUER & HEUBNER / PHARMACISTS / PORTLAND, OREGON*) is illustrated as **Figure 30**. This example has a tooled finish, no evidence of mold air venting, and is known to date from 1878-1879 based on the short partnership period of the proprietors noted in period business directories.

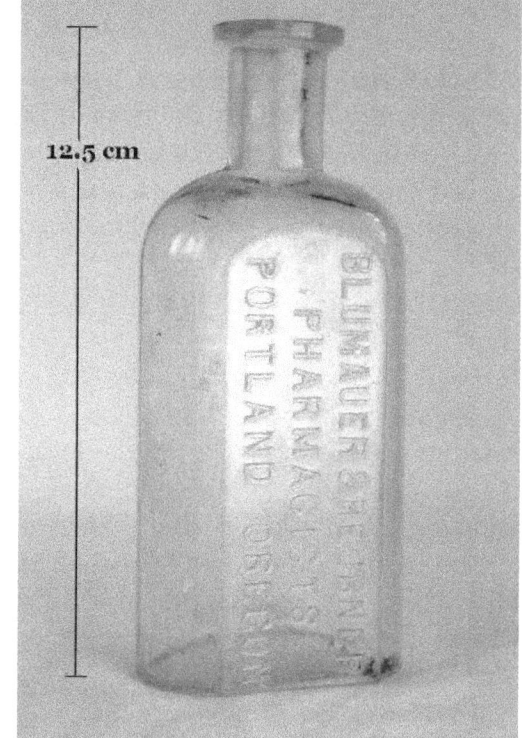

12.5 cm

(Figure 30 [to right]. Pharmacy bottle (1878-1879) with a tooled finish.)

3. Ink bottles and small (<7 inches tall) patent medicines appear to have followed a transition timeline similar to druggist bottles. Tooled Finishes dominate these classes of bottles by the late 1870s.

4. Larger, narrow bore medicinals (>7-8 inches tall) and soda and mineral water bottles appear to fall in the change to Tooled Finishes in the mid-1880s. Very few Applied Finishes were being produced on these types after about 1890.

5. The majority of medium sized (8-10 inches tall) oval, rectangular, cylindrical, "flask" shaped, and square medicinals, bitters, liquor, and other relatively narrow bore bottles appear to have changed to Tooled Finishes by the mid to late 1880s. For example, it appears that all of the liquor bottles from the South Carolina State Dispensary-- made from 1893 to 1907 and largely in this size and shape range—have exclusively Tooled Finishes (Huggins 1997; Teal and Wallace 2005).

6. Larger (>10 inches tall or with wide or large capacity bodies) liquor, beer, mineral water, and most sizes of wide-mouth food bottles—including wax sealed canning jars—seem to have begun the change to Tooled Finishes in the mid-1880s, with the majority tooled by the early to mid-1890s. Large capacity beer bottles (22-26 oz.) in particular were almost certainly still being produced by some factories with Applied Finishes as late as 1895 (Lockhart 2007). These are some of the latest American-made bottles to commonly incorporate Applied Finishes. Bottles within these types that are known to date after 1900 and have Applied Finishes are most likely imported bottles, as discussed below.

7. Any bottles exhibiting the features of the Improved Tooled Finish—and which do not have molded external screw threads with a ground rim—will virtually always post-date 1895 and most likely date from between 1900 and the end of the mouth-blown era in the early 1920s. Not all mouth-blown bottles from this era have the Improved Tooled Finish, but virtually all bottles with this finish are from the early 20th century.

Note on European-made mouth-blown bottles

(Figure 31 [to right]. Early 20th century [1914 or later] Dutch gin bottle with an applied finish.)

European-made mouth-blown bottles tend to have Applied Finishes much later than American-made bottles, lasting into at least the second decade of the 20th century. For example, the crudely applied one-part finish in **Figure 31** is on a Dutch gin bottle that bears a label identifying it as

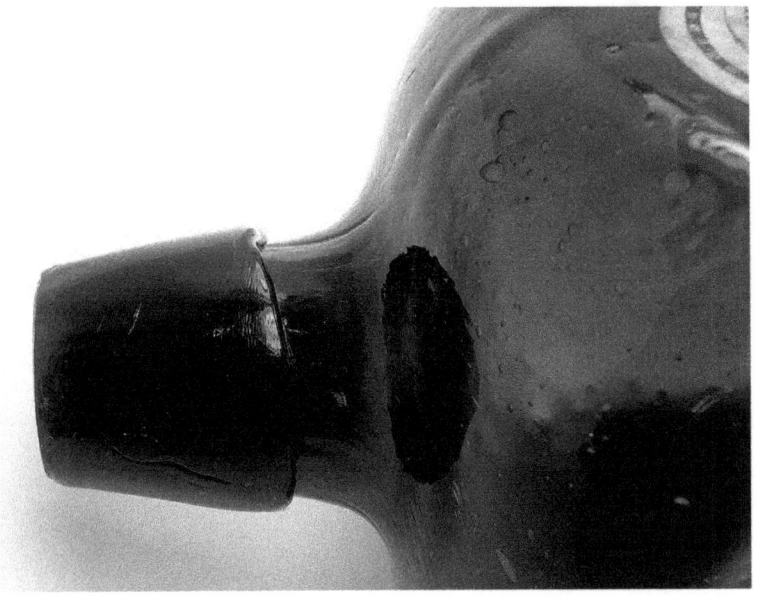

having been bottled no earlier than 1914 when an elephant became the trademark for *H. H. Melchers* - the Schiedam producer that utilized this bottle (Vermeulen 2000; Vermeulen pers. comm. 2008). This bottle also has additional body crudity to it (wavy bubble laden glass), a lack of mold air venting along with an absence of a pontil scar that would diagnostically date it from the 1860s to 1880s if produced in the U. S.

One of the many dating exceptions is the occasionally encountered bottles with obviously American company and/or product embossing and/or labeling that were actually manufactured in and imported from Europe. Of particular note are some soda, beer, and liquor bottles. For example, some cylinder bottles made for California liquor companies display diagnostic characteristics of American-made bottles from the 1870s or early 1880s—even though they were actually made in Germany as late as the early 1900s (Thomas 2002).

Summary

As previously noted, the dating of historic bottles is a complex subject that emphasizes the need to consider as many physical manufacturing-related diagnostic characteristics as possible—as well as product or company research where possible—in arriving at a reliable likely manufacturing date range. Being able to identify the finishing methods for mouth-blown bottles is but one of an assortment of attributes that can be used to help date bottles with a relatively high degree of reliability.

As with most of the discussions in this paper, the *Historic Bottle Website* (Lindsey 2009) may be consulted for an in-depth discussion of finish shapes or styles (not the subject of this paper). That website also has a full overview of other manufacturing related diagnostic features that can be quite useful in arriving at an approximate manufacturing date for just about any American-made bottle. For those interested in more information on finishing methods, please visit the following *Historic Bottle Website* pages: the "Bottle Finishes & Closures" main page at **www.sha.org/bottle/finishes.htm** and the "Glassmaking & Glassmakers" page at **www.sha.org/bottle/glassmaking.htm**.

Acknowledgments

I would like to thank Peggy Corson for the excellent illustrations prepared for the *Historic Bottle Website* – only a few of which were used in this paper. Also thanks must go to Dr. Pete Schulz who provided much warranted (and appreciated) critiques, suggestions and feedback on this paper.

References

Anonymous
1904   *Finishing a Bottle.* National Glass Budget 19(40):1

Barber, Edwin A.
1900   *American Glassware Old and New.* David McKay & Co., Philadelphia, PA.

Boow, James
1991   *Early Australian Commercial Glass: Manufacturing Processes.* The Heritage Council of New South Wales.

Borton, Warren
1988   *Historical Bottles of Wyoming 1868-1915.* Privately published, Midvale, UT.

Burggraaf, Mike & Tom Southard
1998   *The Antique Bottles of Iowa 1846-1915.* Privately published, Ohio Wholesale Copy Service, Northfield, OH.

Chapman, Tom L.
2003   *Bottles of Eastern California.* Hungry Coyote Publishing Company, Bishop, CA.

Clint, David K.
1976   *Colorado Historical Bottles & Etc. 1859-1915.* Antique Bottle Collectors of Colorado, Johnson Printing Co., Boulder, CO.

Creswick, Alice M.
1987   *The Fruit Jar Works Vol. 1 & 2.* Privately published, Grand Rapids, MI.

Davis, Pearce
1949   *The Development of the American Glass Industry.* Harvard University Press, Cambridge, MA.

Deiss, Ronald W.
1981   The Development and Application of a Chronology for American Glass. Master's thesis, Illinois State University, Normal, IL.

Elliott, Rex R. and Stephen C. Gould
1988   *Hawaiian Bottles of Long Ago.* Hawaiian Service Inc., Honolulu, HI.

Feldhaus, Ron
1986   *The Bottles, Breweriana and Advertising Jugs of Minnesota 1850-1920, Volume 1: Beer, Soda, Household.* Privately published, Edina, MN.

1987   *The Bottles, Breweriana and Advertising Jugs of Minnesota 1850-1920, Volume 2: Whiskey, Druggist, Medicine.* Privately published, Edina, MN.

Fike, Richard E.
1987   *The Bottle Book: A Comprehensive Guide to Historic Embossed Medicine Bottles.* Gibbs M. Smith, Inc., Peregrine Smith Press, Salt Lake City, UT.

1998   *A Guide to the Identification and Dating of Historic Glass Bottles.* Bureau of Land Management, Montrose, CO.

Fletcher, Johnnie W.
1994   *Kansas Bottles - 1854 to 1915*. Privately published, Mustang, OK.

2006   *Oklahoma Bottles – 1889 to 1920*. Privately published, Mustang, OK.

Fowler, Ronald R.
1981   *Ice-Cold Soda Pop 5¢ - An Illustrated History of Oregon Soda Pop Bottling*. Seattle History Company, Seattle, WA.

1986   *Washington Sodas – The Illustrated History of Washington's Soft Drink Industry*. Seattle History Company, Seattle, WA.

Frank, Himan
1872   Tool for Forming Mouths of Bottles, &c. Patent 130,207, patented Aug. 6, 1872. United States Patent Office, Washington. [Patent available at Lindsey 2009]

Hemingray, R.
1860   Mold for Glass Jars. Patent 30,063, patented Sept. 18, 1860. United States Patent Office, Washington. [Patent available at Lindsey 2009]

Holabird, Fred and Jack Haddock
1979   *The Nevada Bottle Book*. Privately published, Reno, NV.

Holscher, Harry H.
1953   Feeding and Forming. In *Handbook of Glass Manufacture*, edited by Fay V. Tooley, pp. 299-387. Ogden Publishing, New York.

Howard, George E.
1950   Glass Containers. *Glass Industry* 31(4):183-190, 214, 216, 218.

Huggins, Phillip K.
1997   *The South Carolina Dispensary: A Bottle Collector's Atlas and History of the System*. Sandlapper Press Co., Inc., Columbia, SC.

Illinois Glass Company
1906   *Illustrated Catalogue and Price List, Illinois Glass Company - Manufacturers of Bottles and Glass Containers of Every Kind*. Illinois Glass Co., Alton, IL. (Scans of this entire 1906 catalog are available on the *Historic Bottle Website* at the following URL: http://www.sha.org/bottle/igco_1906.htm)

Innes, Lowell
1976   *Pittsburgh Glass 1797-1891: A History and Guide for Collectors*. Houghton Mifflin, Boston, MA.

Jones, Olive R.

1986   *Cylindrical English Wine and Beer Bottles, 1735-1850.* National Historic Parks and Sites Branch, Parks Canada, Ottawa, Ontario.

Jones, Olive and Catherine Sullivan
1989   *The Parks Canada Glass Glossary for the Description of Containers, Tableware, Flat Glass, and Closures.* Studies in Archaeology, Architecture, and History. National Historic Parks and Sites Branch, Parks Canada, Ottawa, Ontario.

Kendrick, Grace
1963   *The Antique Bottle Collector.* Western Printing & Publishing Co., Sparks, NV.

1968   *The Mouth-Blown Bottle.* Edwards Brothers, Ann Arbor, MI.

Ketchum, William C. Jr.
1975   *A Treasury of American Bottles.* Bobbs-Merrill, New York.

Kyte, David L.
2005   *Early Utah Soda Bottles: 1870-1915 – A Bottling History & Guide.* Privately published, Midvale, UT.

Lamont, John
1876   Improvement in Glass-Tools. Patent 183,267, patented Oct. 17, 1876. United States Patent Office, Washington. [Patent available at Lindsey 2009]

Lindsey, Bill
2009   *Historic Glass Bottle Identification & Information Website.* Contained within the Society for Historical Archaeology Website, University of Montana, Missoula, MT. **http://www.sha.org/bottle/index.htm**

Lockhart, Bill
2007   The Origins and Life of the Export Beer Bottle. *Bottles and Extras* 18(3):49-57, 59.

Lockhart, Bill, Bill Lindsey, David Whitten, and Carol Serr
2005   The Dating Game: The Illinois Glass Company. *Bottles and Extras* 16(1):54-60.

Lockhart, Bill, et al.
2009   The Dating Game—Southern Glass Co. *Bottles and Extras* 20(6):50-61.

Markota, Peck and Audie Markota
1994   *Western Blob Top Soda and Mineral Water Bottles – Second Edition.* Privately published, Sacramento, CA.

1999   *A Look at California Hutchinson Type Soda Bottles.* Privately Published, Sacramento, CA.

McKearin, Helen and Kenneth M. Wilson

1978   *American Bottles & Flasks and Their Ancestry.* Crown Publishers, Inc., New York, NY.

Miller, George L. and Catherine Sullivan
1984   Machine-made Glass Containers and the End of Production for Mouth-Blown Bottles. *Historical Archaeology* 18(2):83-96.

Miller, George L. and Ed Moran
2004   A Household Cleanup Assemblage from Ca. 1938-1941, Raritan Landing, New Jersey, site 28Mil78: Feature 8, the well. Unpublished notes from Miller & Moran dated June 14, 2004.

Miller, Michael R.
1999   *A Collector's Guide to Arizona Bottles & Stoneware – A History of Merchant Containers in Arizona.* Privately published, Peoria, AZ.

2008   *A Collector's Guide to Arizona Bottles & Stoneware – A History of Merchant Containers in Arizona.* Privately published, Peoria, AZ. (Expanded 2nd edition.)

Modes, William F.
1887   Mold for Blowing Turned Bottles. Patent 364,840, patented June 14, 1887. United States Patent Office, Washington. [Patent available at Lindsey 2009]

Munsey, Cecil
1970   *The Illustrated Guide to Collecting Bottles.* Hawthorne Books, Inc. New York.

Odell, John
1997   *Indian Bottles & Brands.* Privately published.

2000   *Digger Odell's Pontil Medicine Encyclopedia: A Look at America's Pre-Civil War Medicine Bottles.* Privately published.

Oppelt, Norman T.
2005   *Soda and Mineral Water Bottles and Bottlers of Colorado, 1860 to 1915.* Oppelt Publications, Greeley, CO.

Owens-Illinois Glass Company
2009   *O-I Company North American website.* O-I (Owens-Illinois) Glass Co., U. S. A.

Pearson, B. M.
1928   Aspects of Bottle Machine Operations. *Glass Industry* 9(7):145-148.

Peters, Roger M.
1996   *Wisconsin Soda Water Bottles 1845-1910.* Wild Goose Press, Madison, WI.

Pollard, Gordon
1993   *Bottles and Business in Plattsburgh, New York: 100 Years of Embossed Bottles as Historical Artifacts.* Clinton County Historical Association, NY.

Preble, Glen R.
1987   *Impressed in Time – Colorado Beverage Bottles, Jugs, etc. 1859-1915.* Antique Bottle Collectors of Colorado, Johnson Printing Co., Boulder, CO.

2002   *The Rise & Demise of Colorado Drugstores 1859-1915.* Antique Bottle Collectors of Colorado, Englewood, CO.

Ring, Carlyn and Bill Ham
1998   *Bitters Bottles.* Boyertown Publishing Co., Boyertown, PA.

Roller, Dick
1983   *The Standard Fruit Jar Reference.* Acorn Press, Paris, IL.

Russell, Mike.
1998   *The Collector's Guide to Civil War Era Bottles and Jars.* Privately published, Herndon, VA.

Sheldon, Thomas K. and M. N. Lynn
1893   Finishing Tool for Glass Bottles. Patent 500,960, patented July 4, 1893. United States Patent Office, Washington. [Patent available at Lindsey 2009]

Shimko, Phyllis
1969   *Sarsaparilla Bottle Encyclopedia.* Privately published, Aurora, OR.

Stone, Amasa
1855   Forming Screw Threads, &c., in the Necks of Glass Bottles and Similar Articles. Patent 13,402, patented Aug. 7, 1855. United States Patent Office, Washington. [Patent available at Lindsey 2009]

1856   Tool for Making Glass Bottles. Patent 15,788, patented Sept. 23, 1856. United States Patent Office, Washington. [Patent available at Lindsey 2009]

Switzer, Ronald R.
1974   *The Bertrand Bottles – A Study of 19th Century Glass and Ceramic Containers.* National Park Service, Washington, D.C.

Synnott, Thomas W.
1875   Improvement in Bottles. Patent 162,117, patented April 13, 1875. United States Patent Office, Washington. [Patent available at Lindsey 2009]

Teal, Harvey S. and Rita Foster Walker
2005   *The South Carolina Dispensary & Embossed S. C. Whiskey Bottles & Jugs 1865-1915.* Privately published, Columbia, S.C.

Thomas, John

1974   *Picnics, Coffins, Shoo-Flies.* Preuss Press, San Luis Obispo, CA.

1977   *Whiskey Bottles of the Old West.* Maverick Publications, Bend Oregon.

1998a *Whiskey Bottles and Liquor Containers from the State of Oregon.* Privately published, Capitola, CA.

1998b *Whiskey Bottles and Liquor Containers from the State of Washington.* Ananta Printing & Publishing, Soquel, CA.

2002   *Whiskey Bottles of the Old West.* Boyertown Publishing Company, Boyertown, PA.

Tibbitts, John C.
1964   *1200 Bottles Priced: A Bottle Price Guide, Catalogue, and Classification System.* The Little Glass Shack, Sacramento, CA.

Toulouse, Julian H.
1967   When Did Hand Bottle Blowing Stop? *Western Collector* 5(8):41-45. San Francisco.

1968   Empontilling: a History. *Glass Industry* 49(3):137-142, (4):204-205.

1969a *Fruit Jars.* Thomas Nelson & Sons, New York.

1969b A Primer on Mold Seams. *Western Collector* 7(11):526-535, (12):578-587. San Francisco.

Van den Bossche, Willy
2001   *Antique Glass Bottles: Their History and Evolution (1500-1850).* Antique Collectors Club, Suffolk, England.

Vermeulen, Peter
2000   Melchers. *Antique Bottle & Glass Collector* 16(10):34-37

Whitall, Tatum & Co.
1879   *Whitall, Tatum & Co. Glass Ware 1879.* Whitall, Tatum & Co., Philadelphia.

1880   *Whitall, Tatum & Co. 1880.* Whitall, Tatum & Co., Philadelphia. Reprinted 1971 by Pyne Press, Princeton.

White, John R.
1978   Bottle Nomenclature: A Glossary of Landmark Terminology for the Archaeologist. *Historical Archaeology* 12:58-67.

Wichmann, Jeff
1999   *The Best of the West: Antique Western Bitters Bottles.* Pacific Glass Books, Sacramento, CA.

Willis, Keith
1972   *Antique Bottles Book 1: Washington-Oregon Whiskies*. Privately published. Duvall, WA.

Wilson, Bill and Betty Wilson
1968   *Spirits Bottles of the Old West*. Henington Publishing Co, Wolfe City, TX.

1969   *Western Bitters*. Northwestern Printing Co., Santa Rosa, CA.

1971   *19th Century Medicine in Glass*. 19th Century Hobby & Publishing Co., Amador City, CA.

Wilson, Joseph B.
1884   Tool for Forming Bottle Lips and Necks. Patent 295,848, patented March 25, 1884. United States Patent Office, Washington.

Wilson, Rex L.
1981   *Bottles on the Western Frontier*. University of Arizona Press, Tucson, AZ.

Zumwalt, Betty
1980   *Ketchup, Pickles, Sauces - 19th Century Food in Glass*. Mark West Publishers, Fulton, CA.

Bill Lindsey
Bureau of Land Management (BLM - retired) &
Author of the SHA/BLM *Historic Glass Bottle Identification & Information Website* – **www.sha.org/bottle/index.htm**
Klamath Falls, OR.

Catalog Reproductions: Finishes

Trade journals and catalogs are an excellent source for researching the evolution of manufacturing techniques as well as style changes over time. Both of these considerations make for useful dating tools. The pages that follow highlight finishes and closures; they are reproduced from the following catalogs, which are available in their entirety on the *SHA/BLM Historic Glass Bottle Identification and Information Website* <http://www.sha.org/bottle/index.htm>:

The Packers' Handy Reference Book, Issue of 1916–1917. Kearns-Gorsuch Bottle Company, Zanesville, OH <http://www.sha.org/bottle/kgbco1916.htm>.

"Finishes Produced by the Automatic Machine." *Bottle Catalog, 1919–1920, General Catalog A.* Illinois Glass Company, Alton, IL <http://www.sha.org/bottle/igco1920.htm>.

10   THE KEARNS-GORSUCH BOTTLE COMPANY

VARIOUS STYLES OF FINISH

Prescription Lip

Panel Lip

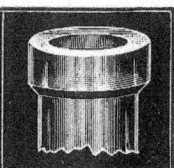
Packer Lip

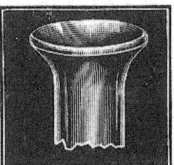
Flare Mouth

Oil Finish

Double Ring Finish

Bead Finish

Saucer Shape Prescription Lip

Brandy Finish

The above finishes are those ordinarily used.
Any special finish we will make to your liking.

NOTE

Finishes—Under this heading the abbreviation S. T. denotes Spring Top; A. denotes American Cap; P. denotes Phoenix Cap or Perfection Cap.

Example:—On page 18 we can make No. 31 8-oz. Olympia for No. 53 Spring Top, No. 53 Phoenix or Perfection Cap or No. 48 American Cap finishes.

Citrate of Magnesia
(PRIOF FINISH)

CITRATE of Magnesia Bottles on this page and the next are shown with three different finishes.

The Priof Finish, shown at the left, utilizes that positive and economical closure — the ordinary crown cap. A knife, coin, key or any flat piece of metal can be inserted between the skirt of the cap and the hump on the Priof Ledge, and used as a lever to pry the cap off.

When the crown is pried off in this way it isn't mutilated and sprung as by the ordinary crown opener, and hence, can be snapped back on again as an effective, although not a permanent reseal.

This is a simple yet superior finish for Citrate of Magnesia and is rapidly growing in popularity.

CITRATE OF MAGNESIA

Mould No.	Size	Quant. per Corr. Box	Weight per Gross
72	12 oz.	1 doz.	150 lbs.
		4 doz.	140 lbs.
		Quantity per Crate	
T-300	7 oz.	1½ gro.	90 lbs.

We are always glad to supply samples for your inspection.

Illustrating our one dozen Corrugated Reshipping Box for Citrates.

Citrate of Magnesia

(BLUE METAL CAP AND OTHER FINISHES)

THE Blue Metal Screw Cap is another practical, good looking closure for Citrate. It holds well under pressure and caps can be applied and removed by hand.

Glass or Porcelain Stoppers, Plain Crown Finish or Kork-N-Seal are other finishes with which these bottles can be supplied, if desired.

The split size, 7 oz., single dose bottle is a package individual with us.

Citrates are generally sold in quantities to Jobbers and included in their regular cars of Prescription Ware.

A four-dozen Corrugated Box for Citrates.

Illinois Glass Company

The All Glass Sprinkler Top Finish

THE All Glass Sprinkler Top Finish is a clean, sanitary, practical, good looking finish that has gained great favor among the manufacturers of hair tonics and toilet waters during the few years since its introduction.

Its one-piece all-glass construction makes it practically non-refillable.

As only a small one-piece metal screw cap is required for sealing this package, a substantial saving is accomplished through its use.

If machinery for filling bottles equipped with this style of finish is desired, we can furnish it through our Machinery Division.

Many other styles of bottles, in addition to those illustrated, are manufactured with this finish.

Page 111

The Variable Ledge Priof Finish

This finish may be applied to any of the jars in the ensuing section.

A New Finish for Wide-Mouth Jars

THIS new and better finish for glass jars extends to the wide mouth Food Products line the many advantages of that economical and positive closure — the crown cap.

The sloping, variable Priof ledge permits any flat metal instrument to be used as a lever in prying off the cap. With this finish the crown opener, while still effective, is no longer essential.

Not only that, but the cap may be removed without bending or mutilating — thus permitting the crown to be used as a reseal during the life of the package.

Special composition liners have been developed for the 37, 45, 54 and 70 millimeter crowns, which now make them suitable for sealing, either with or without vacuum.

Permit us to submit samples and discuss in detail what this finish means applied to your particular package.

Illinois Glass Company

The Priof Finish

*A New Finish That Will
Save You Money By
Saving Your Bottles*

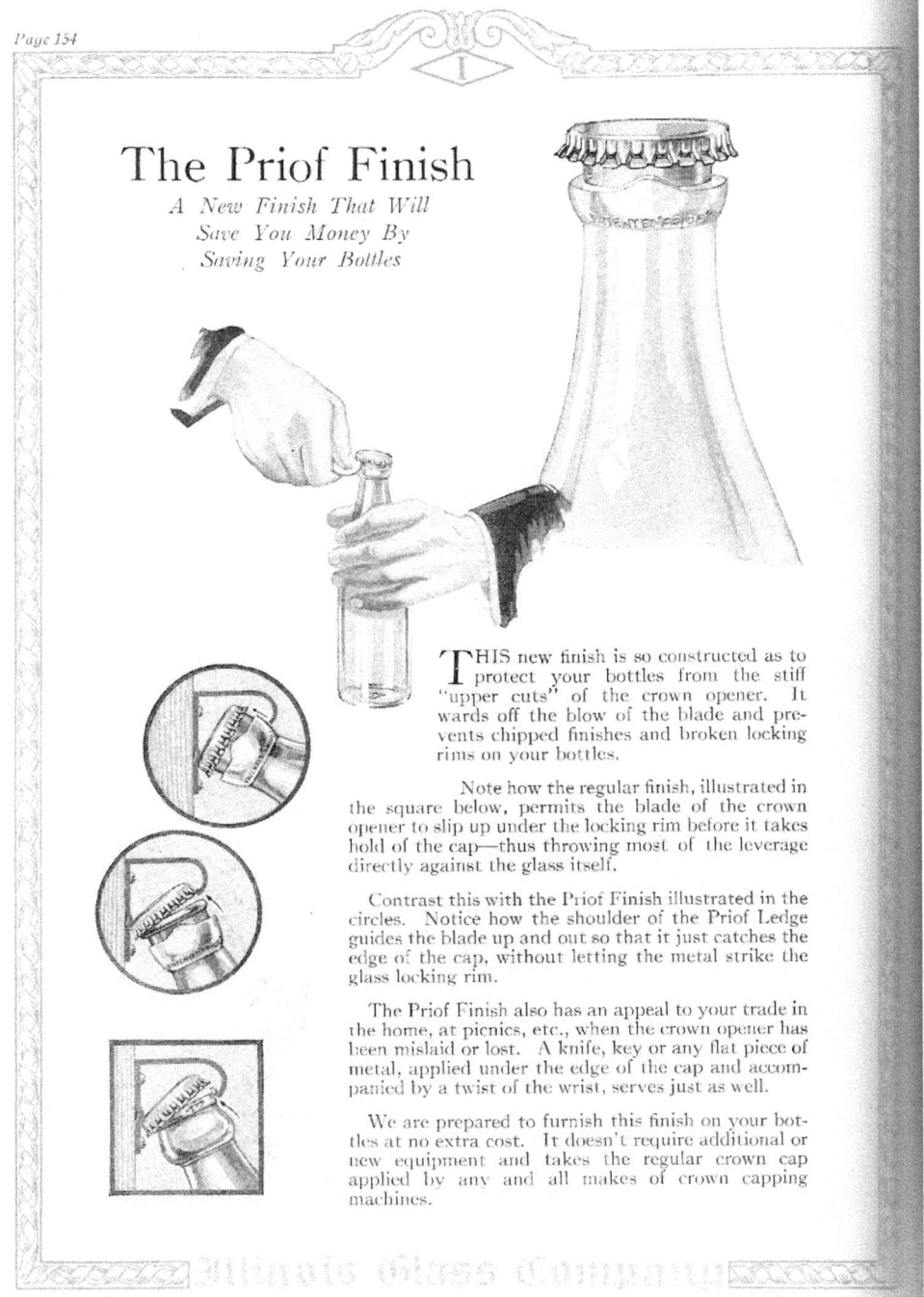

THIS new finish is so constructed as to protect your bottles from the stiff "upper cuts" of the crown opener. It wards off the blow of the blade and prevents chipped finishes and broken locking rims on your bottles.

Note how the regular finish, illustrated in the square below, permits the blade of the crown opener to slip up under the locking rim before it takes hold of the cap—thus throwing most of the leverage directly against the glass itself.

Contrast this with the Priof Finish illustrated in the circles. Notice how the shoulder of the Priof Ledge guides the blade up and out so that it just catches the edge of the cap, without letting the metal strike the glass locking rim.

The Priof Finish also has an appeal to your trade in the home, at picnics, etc., when the crown opener has been mislaid or lost. A knife, key or any flat piece of metal, applied under the edge of the cap and accompanied by a twist of the wrist, serves just as well.

We are prepared to furnish this finish on your bottles at no extra cost. It doesn't require additional or new equipment and takes the regular crown cap applied by any and all makes of crown capping machines.

Illinois Glass Company

5 Gallon Semi-Wide Mouth

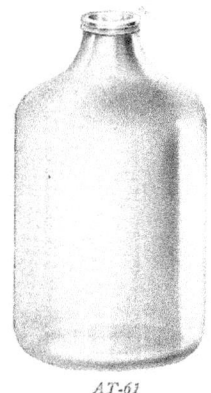

AT-61
5-Gallon

THIS package is much used for the storage of pulps, fruits, vegetables, and pickles, and as a container for powders, tablets, heavy liquids and compounds. Laboratories find it valuable for a number of purposes.

A Wide Mouth, Cork Finish Line

THE Wide Mouth Cork Finish Line is our Big Bottle addition to the "Diamond I" line of Round Wide Mouth Prescription Bottles.

Manufacturing Chemists and Jobbing Druggists find these bottles excellent for the storage of crystals and other soluble materials.

In addition to the protection afforded, these bottles enable stocks on hand to be determined at a glance.

AT-60   *AT-3*   *AT-32*
5-Gallon   *3-Gallon*   *2-Gallon*

The Parks Canada Glass Glossary: Part IV. Closures
Olive Jones and Catherine Sullivan

The Parks Canada

GLASS GLOSSARY

for the description of containers, tableware, flat glass, and closures

Olive Jones and Catherine Sullivan,
with contributions by
George L. Miller
E. Ann Smith
Jane E. Harris
Kevin Lunn

Revised Edition

Studies in Archaeology
Architecture and History

National Historic Parks and Sites
Canadian Parks Service
Environment Canada

CATEGORY

Closures — Closures are separate items used to cover the mouth of a vessel to protect the contents from dust, spilling, evaporation, and, sometimes, to exclude the air completely. Closures can be strictly functional, e.g. a wad of paper stuffed into the mouth of a bottle, or they can combine beauty with utility. Closures for glass tableware items tend to be limited to stoppers for decanters and cruets, fitments such as sprinklers and spouts for castors, and covers for tumblers, bowls, and stemmed drinking glasses. Closures for containers are much more varied and include stoppers, lids, caps, fitments such as sprinklers, sifters, sprayers, spouts, droppers, and pour-outs, as well as some complex patented closures.

SUBCATEGORY

Stoppers

A stopper is a plug which is inserted into the neck of a vessel to effect a seal from within the vessel. The stopper types discussed below are those that occur most regularly on our sites. Some specialized or unusual stoppers, e.g. glass balls, which are found less frequently will be discussed in Patented Closures.

CORK

Cork is the bark of the cork oak tree. Cork's ability to resume its original size and shape after compression makes closures of this material effective seals. Closures of cork can take three distinct forms: cork can be used as a stopper on its own; shell cork as a disk or in a sheet can be added to another type of closure; a cork stopper can be hollowed out and used as the medium by which a fitment is inserted into the mouth of an object, e.g. sprinklers.

Cork as a stopper seems to have become a standard closure for small-mouthed containers beginning in the 16th and 17th centuries, supplanting other sealing substances and maintaining its supremacy almost to the present day. The demand for good quality cork stoppers encouraged a large-scale industry in Spain and Portugal to produce these items. However large pieces were too expensive and difficult to obtain for cork to be used commonly as a stopper for large-mouthed jars.

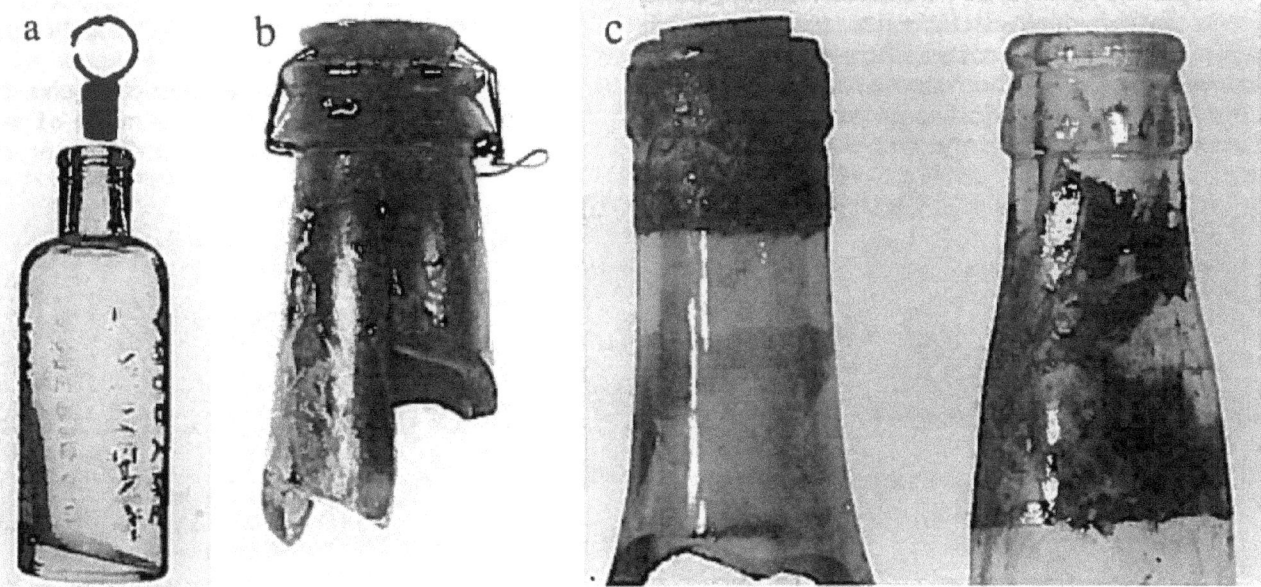

Figure 123. Cork closure. (a) Medicine bottle with cork closure and cork ring for removing the stopper. (b) "Wine" bottle neck with cork wired in position. (c) Two bottle necks, both of which were originally stoppered with cork and encased in a capsule.

149

Cork stoppers can be cut from a single block of cork, several strips of cork can be glued together to form the stopper, or, after the beginning of the 20th century, the stopper can be made of composition cork (see Nurnberg 1967: 13-14). Its shape can be cylindrical or tapered; some authorities feel that the tapered shape is earlier, the cylindrical requiring a special tool for its removal and thus dating after the invention of the corkscrew sometime in the 17th century (Gilbey Ltd. 1957: item 316).

Sealing practices involving cork stoppers can include a proprietor's brand stamped on the cork, wire or packthread to secure the cork, a grey metal or foil capsule, or wax, or composition with or without an impressed seal, to cover the cork. In addition, in the late-19th and early 20th centuries druggists' bottles stoppered with cork were often sold with a single-use cork ring, which, once inserted into the cork, acted as a handle for the stopper. Cork stoppers with composition heads were also available during the 19th century and are still used, plastic having replaced the composition.

Cork is not usually used as a stopper for tableware items.

The term "cork" has come to be used generically but should not be employed without qualifiers to describe something that is not true cork.

Interesting aspects of a cork stopper found in a bottle neck include its length, which determines to some extent how full the bottle could have been, whether the cork is a single chunk or a series of strips, whether the cork was driven flush or only part way, whether or not the top of the cork was cut off after insertion, the shape of the cork (tapered or cylindrical), and the diameter, as it will be impossible to measure the bore of the bottle without removing the cork. Also interesting is any additional treatment like wiring or enclosing the cork in a capsule or wax. The presence of a composition head or a cork ring can also be noted.

SPRINKLERS, POWDER TUBES, AND SQUIRT TOPS

These are closure/dispensers that fit into a bottle neck to regulate and direct the flow of liquid or powdered contents out of the bottle. They consist of a hollow shank which is inserted into the bottle neck, a horizontal projection which acts as a ledge or stop to sit on the bottle lip, and a hollow tube which may or may not have a cap or plug. Illustrations of squirt tops and powder tubes in 19th century catalogues show them on table glass and commercial containers: cruets, sauce bottles, colognes, tooth powders, barbers' bottles, and essence and bitters bottles. The design of all types of squirt tops is very similar, although they can be composed of different materials and those used on bottles with rapidly evaporating contents often have a cap or plug for the tube (Whitall, Tatum & Co. 1971: 62; Antiques Research Publications 1968: 5; Pyne Press 1972: 28, 123; Maw 1913: 67, 485; Budde & Westermann 1913: 38, 84).

Some 18th century examples of squirt tops in Parks Canada's collection are made of wood and have shanks large enough in diameter that

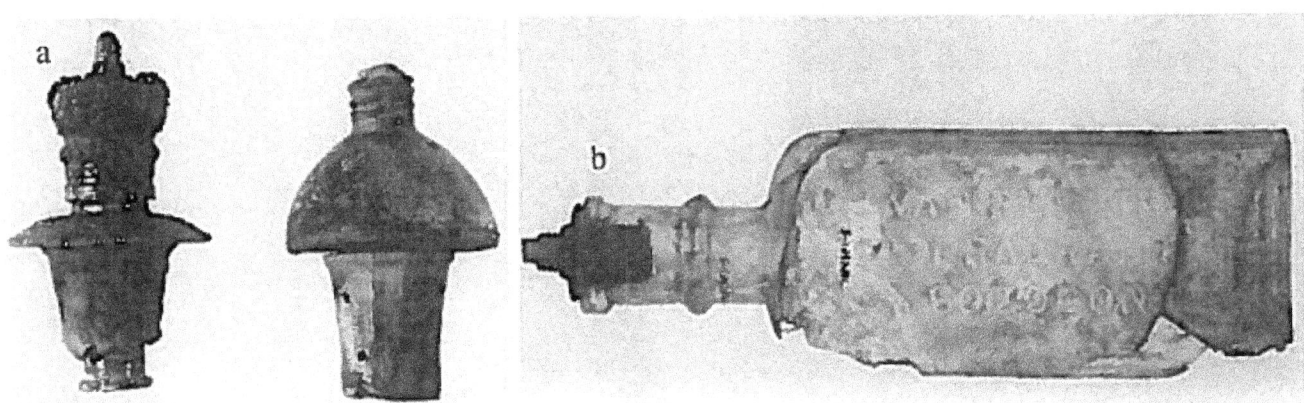

Figure 124. (a) Two metal sprinklers with shell cork on their shanks. (b) A bottle with its sprinkler in position.

150

Figure 125. Three stoppered glass bottles.

they may have been forced into a bottle with the intention that they not be removed; metal examples in Figure 124 have cork around a narrow shank and were probably transferable from one bottle to another.

GLASS STOPPERS

Glass stoppers consist of a shank, which is the plug, and a finial, the portion by which the stopper is grasped for removal. These two parts may be joined by a neck.

To prevent the stopper from slipping into the vessel, the shank may have screw threads to twist into place inside the neck or the finial portion of the stopper may rest on the lip of the container. If airtightness is desired in the closure, to prohibit evaporation for example, the shank may be ground to fit the bore or a strip of shell cork may be wrapped around the shank. An early reference to grinding glass stoppers is quoted by Helen McKearin (1971: 123) and dates from 1665. Loose or unground glass stoppers have been dated as early as 1500 B.C. (Holscher 1965: 467).

The finial portion of the stopper, if it is intended for an item of tableware or decorative glassware, may be decorated in a style complementary to the item; if for a commercial container the finial may have commercial markings, usually on its top.

Stopper shanks are usually tapered; their bottoms may be squared or rounded. This shape may be obscured by jagged glass or by a pontil mark.

Glass stoppers for tableware and decorative glassware items are not uncommon in the 18th and 19th centuries. Until 1841 they were individually manufactured; in that year an American mould was patented that allowed 10 stoppers to be press moulded at one time (Watkins 1942: 370). However, moulding the stopper was a minor part of the expense of production. Because each ground glass stopper is a unique fit to the bottle with which it is ground, manufacturing cost is rather high compared with other available types of stoppers; this restricted the use of glass stoppers for commercial containers. For example, in the 1880 Whitall, Tatum & Company catalogue prescription ware in the 1/2-ounce to 8-ounce

151

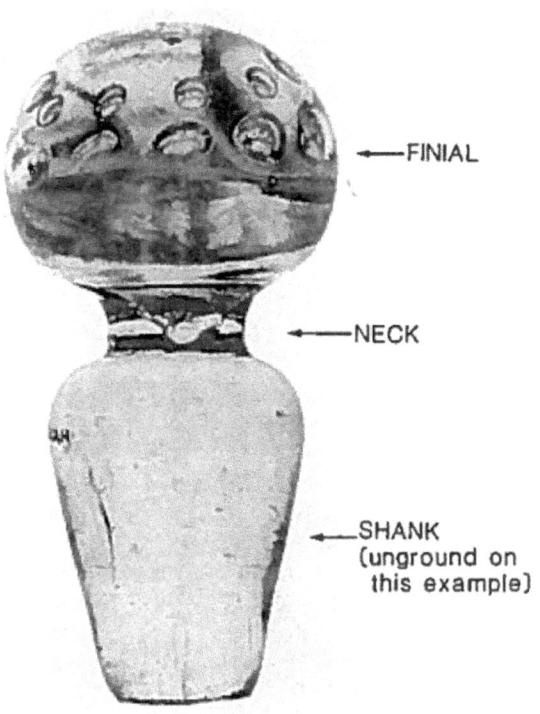

FINIAL

NECK

SHANK
(unground on
this example)

Figure 126. Glass stopper nomenclature.

sizes with ground stoppers were double or triple the cost of the bottles without stoppers (Whitall, Tatum & Co. 1971: 13). Glass stoppers found with commercial containers are usually not ground but fitted into a cork with a hole through its centre.

A glass stopper for a commercial container would be more useful than one of cork in a bottle of a product which was not to be used all at once, or in a bottle which could be or was intended to be reused, like a flask. A cork stopper removed many times would be inclined to break and require replacing. Glass stoppers are not likely to be associated with bottles whose contents were used all at once, e.g. small, single-dose medicines, beer and soft drink bottles (due also to the carbonation), and the majority of liquor bottles.

Glass stoppers should be described by the shape of the finial (using one of the standard shape names found on the following pages or a name from a catalogue or pattern book plus reference), the finial decoration, and any shank treatment, such as grinding, hollow blow, etc. As well, an indication should be given of the stopper's overall height and a

shank diameter, a clue to the size of vessel mouth for which the stopper was intended.

Glass Stopper Shapes

"Club sauce," club sauce type — Although glass catalogues of the late-19th and early-20th centuries advertise for sale a variety of glass stopper shapes, by far the most commonly occurring on our sites is the club sauce type. This stopper is for small-mouthed commercial bottles. It has a circular top, horizontally oriented; there may be a depression in the centre of the top, sometimes with lettering (e.g. Lea & Perrins) around the depression, or the top can be flat without a depression or dome-shaped; the edge of the top is bevelled or rounded; the sides are flat; the underside of the top is flat. The shank is cylindrical for a distance, indicating the area which could be wrapped in shell cork, and the lower portion of the shank is tapered. There is no neck between the shank and the finial. Although this stopper shape is often found with associated sauce bottles or with embossing that identifies it as a sauce bottle stopper, it is suggested that the name be used with qualification, i.e. club sauce type. The same kind of stopper has been seen on bottles intended for toilet vinegar (Maw Son & Sons 1903: 169) and under a grey metal capsule marked "Scotch Whiskey." As well, Whitall, Tatum & Co. (1896: 8-9) advertise their "club sauce" stopper to fit bottles of 1/2 pint, pint, and quart capacity only (compared with stoppers which come in "all sizes" or those that fit bottles of capacities from 1/2 pint to 1/2 gallon), suggesting that true "club sauce" stoppers may be limited in size. Club sauce type stoppers have no such restrictions; those in our collections range in height from 24 to 37 mm. This stopper shape was one commonly used in commercial packaging, if the incidence of its occurrence on our sites is any indication. The flat top fits under a capsule almost as conveniently as a cork stopper and could probably have been wired or tied in position. As well, the top of the stopper has a large exposed area on which to emboss commercial marks. The shape has no inherent weak spots such as can be found on stoppers with necks, and club sauce type stoppers are often excavated intact.

152

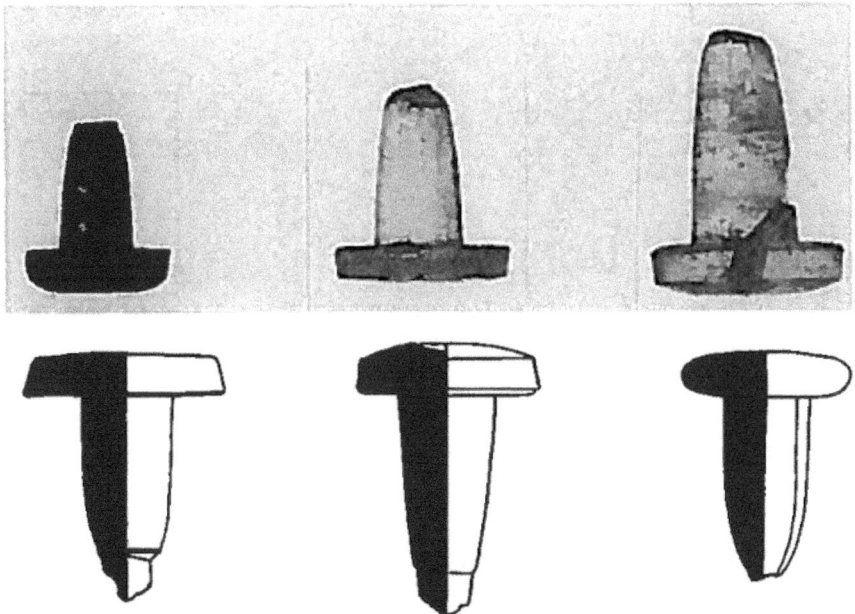

Figure 127. Six examples of club sauce type stoppers, with variations in size and shape. None of the specimens is embossed.

Eno's-type — This stopper is commonly found with Eno's fruit salt bottles, which have mouths that are larger than normal small-mouthed containers but smaller than jars. The stopper could be considered an enlarged version of the club sauce type in that it has a circular top, horizontally oriented, a tapered shank, and no neck. The Eno examples in the Parks Canada collection have a large flat circular depression in the centre of the top, embossed lettering on a raised band around this depression, and the sides of the top are flat. The shank is short and tapered. This stopper shape is sometimes called "mushroom" in druggists' catalogues, but that term is used in modern collecting literature to describe a fancy tableware stopper (Fig. 132) and should not be used to indicate a stopper for a commercial package.

Jar stoppers — This could be considered another, larger version of the club sauce type stopper. The wide raised band around the circular depression in the centre of the top often has embossed markings.

Flat oblong head stoppers — The finial is flat and rectangular and is vertically oriented; it may broaden slightly towards the shank or narrow to form a neck. The edges of

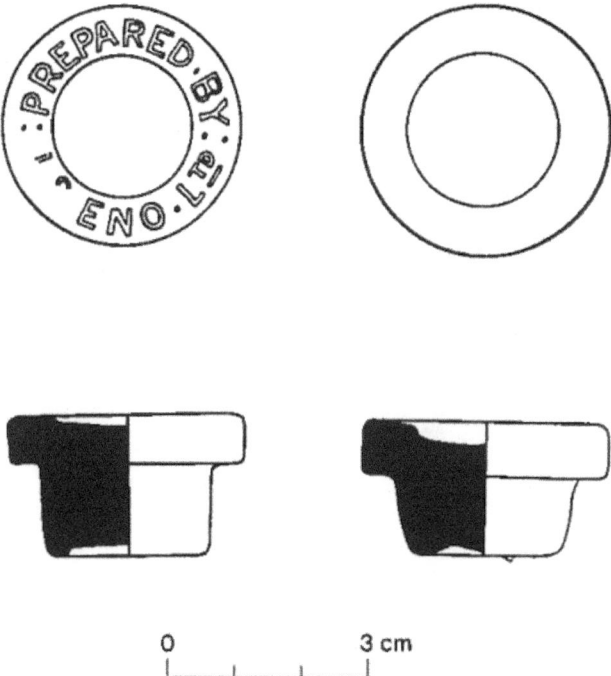

Figure 128. Eno's-type stopper.

the shank may be bevelled. If the top of the shank is wider than the finial, it forms a shoulder on which the finial sits. The five examples illustrated in Figure 130

153

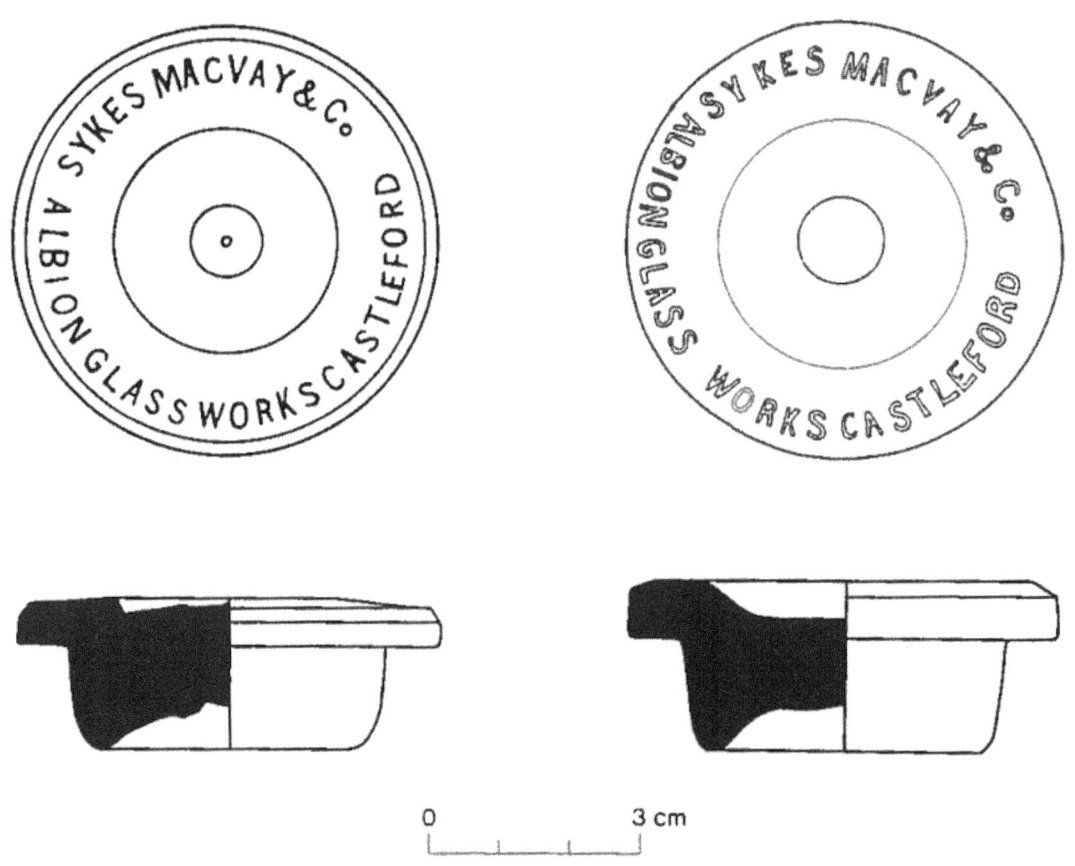

Figure 129. Jar stoppers.

Figure 130. Flat oblong head stoppers. The largest of these stoppers has a hollow shank; all five have ground shanks.

indicate a variety of bottle types for which this shape was made. Although it is not expected that this stopper style was used for tableware items, it figures prominently in the S. Maw 1913 catalogue of druggists' glassware for dispensaries, medicine chest bottles, and druggists' bottles (Maw 1913: 636-37, 61-65).

154

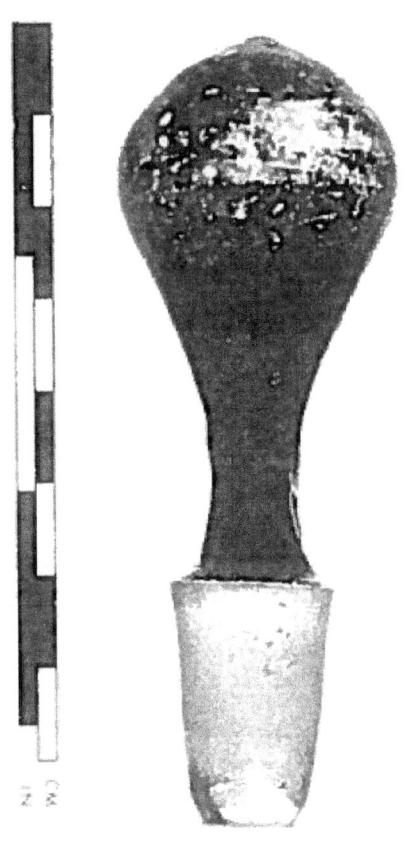

Figure 131. Ball stopper.

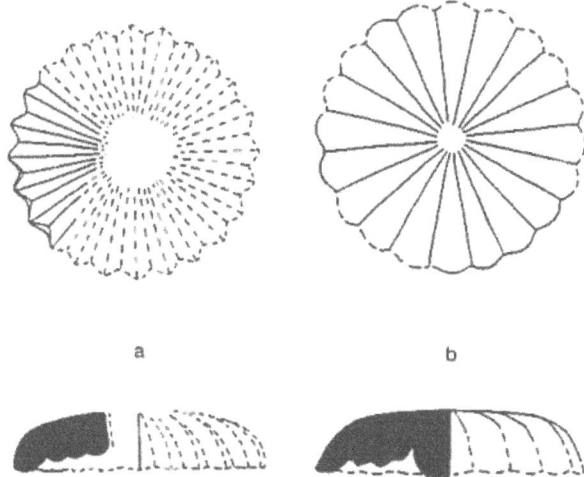

Figure 132. Mushroom stoppers.

Ball stopper — The finial is round or roundish on all sides. The example in Figure 131 has been decorated by staining, has an unusually long neck, and a small mamelon on its top. Although this specimen was a decanter stopper, the shape was also used on commercial containers and display bottles, and is also called "globe" shaped.

Mushroom stopper — The flat or dome-topped finial sits horizontally on the shank or on a globular knop or on a neck. The name mushroom is also occasionally applied to stoppers for commercial containers which we prefer to call "Eno's-type" and "club sauce type." It is suggested that "mushroom stopper" is more commonly understood to describe the fancy tableware closure illustrated in Figure 132 than the commercial container variety. A very common decoration for mushroom stoppers in our collection is moulded ribs radiating from the centre of the top to the edge of the finial, forming a sunburst motif (see also McKearin and McKearin 1948: Pl. 114, No. 19).

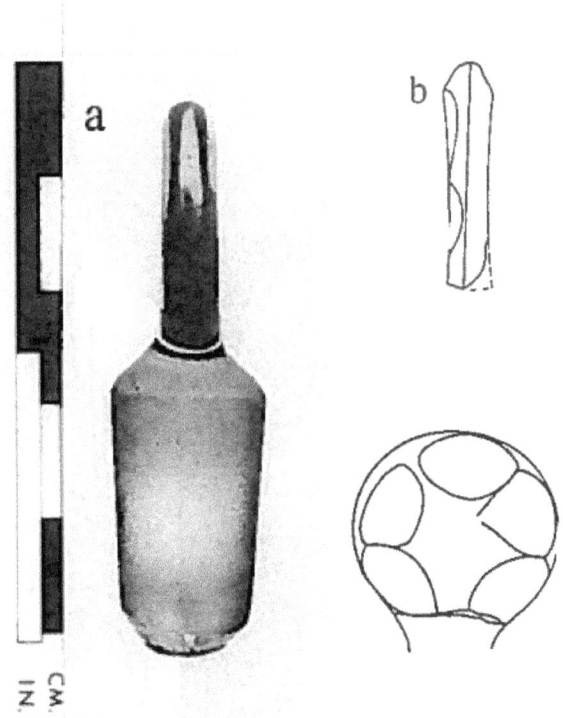

Figure 133. Disc stoppers. (a) A plain disc stopper with a ground shank. (b) A disc stopper decorated with cut facets.

Disc stopper — The finial is a vertical flat circle and the shape is also called "wheel."

155

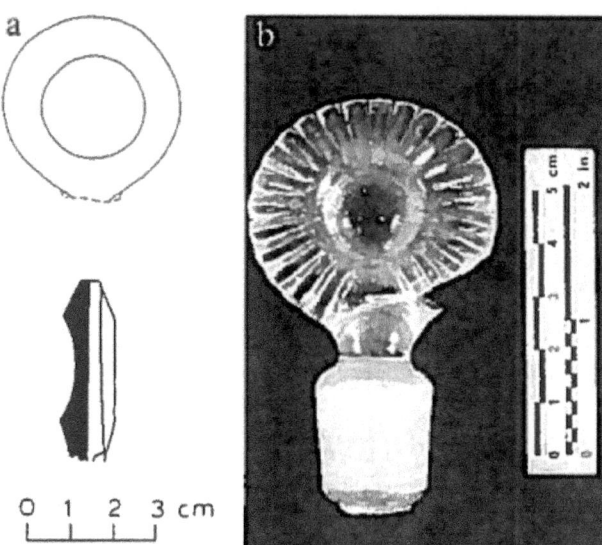

Figure 134. Target stoppers. (a) A plain style. (b) Has been pinched or pinch moulded to decorate the basic shape.

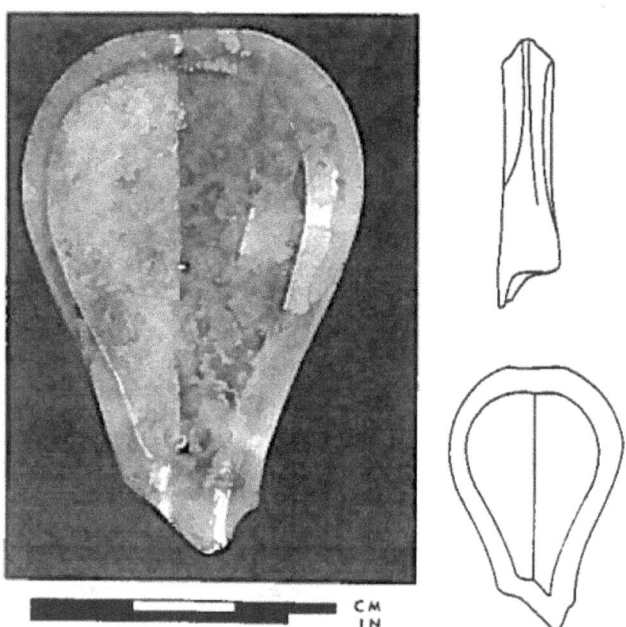

Figure 135. A lozenge stopper which has been decorated to form bevelled edges and to emphasize the lozenge shape. The lower portion of the neck and shank are missing.

Target stopper — This stopper is a variation on the disc stopper, but inherent in the name "target," or "bull's eye," as it is also called, is a depression in the centre of the disc, a feature that in this case is not viewed as decoration.

Lozenge stopper — The finial is a vertical flat baluster shape.

Miscellaneous Glass Stopper Features

Ground shanks — Grinding the shank of a stopper is done to achieve a close fit between it and the inside of the neck of a container. Grinding of glass stoppers has been noted as early as 1665 (McKearin 1971: 123) but apparently it became common practice in England in ca. 1745 (Hughes 1958: 254). Because each stopper is ground to fit the neck of the container with which it will be sold, each stopper is a unique fit.

Hollow, hollow shank — The whole stopper may be hollow with or without an opening at the bottom. Stoppers intended for large-mouthed vessels may have hollow shanks as a result of manufacturing or cost considerations; chemical jars were sometimes advertised with hollow shanks and finials to comfortably fit over a measuring spoon which remained inside the jar, or open hollow stoppers may have been used as a drinking vessel (Newman 1977: 300). In addition the finial can have been blown hollow as decoration, while the shank is solid; this would be referred to as a hollow ball stopper.

Screw-thread stoppers — The stopper shank is threaded; in the example in Figure 138 the threads twist into a hollowed cork. The collar at the base of the neck acts as a stop and sits on top of the cork. These items are called "peg stoppers" in an Illinois Glass Co. catalogue from 1911 and could be covered with corks to fit particular sizes of bottle mouths (Putnam 1965: 81-82). The cork, once jammed into the mouth of the bottle, is expected to be permanently fixed while the glass stopper can be removed and replaced to pour out the contents. The closure is intended to be airtight (see also "Sprinklers, Powder Tubes, and Squirt Tops). Although none are illustrated in this glossary, screw-threaded

156

Figure 136. Miscellaneous stopper features. Ground shank. The shank of (b) has not been ground.

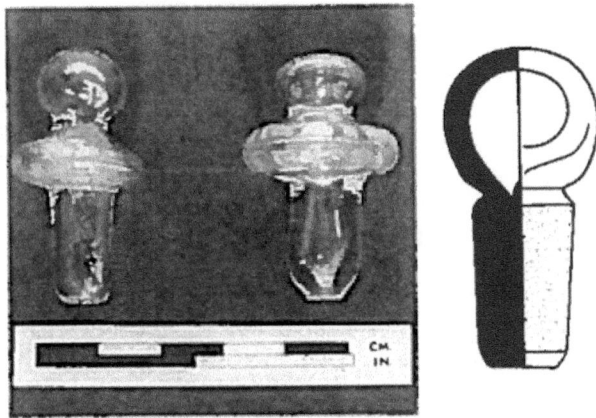

Figure 137. Miscellaneous stopper features: hollow finial.

Figure 138. Miscellaneous stopper features. Screw threads. In this example the threads twist into a hollowed cork.

glass stoppers intended to fit a correspondingly threaded bottle bore are advertised in glass catalogues of the late-19th century. Occasionally screw-threaded bottle bores do appear in assemblages from our sites.

Covers

Although the terms "cover" and "lid" are often used interchangeably in glass literature, we prefer to describe as a "cover" the glass item that sits over the mouth or top of an item of glassware that we categorize as tableware. A "lid" in our terminology performs this function for a bottle or jar. In addition to protecting the contents of a dish, bowl, tumbler, stemmed drinking glass, etc., a glass cover is also an ornamental piece and has been

157

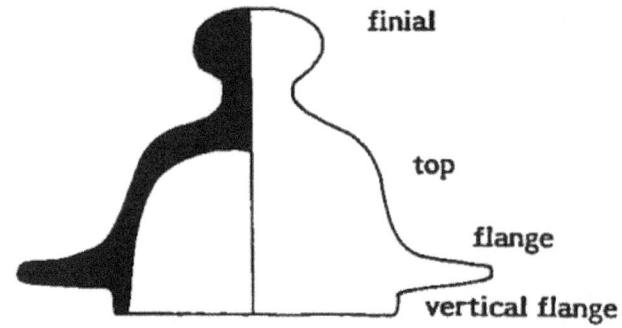

Figure 139. Cover nomenclature.

finial

top

flange

vertical flange

designed to complement the object it covers in shape and decoration. The tableware object may have a ledge into which or onto which the glass cover was intended to fit.

In describing glass covers one may want to consider the following features: the shape of the top (e.g. dome, flat dome, conical, etc.) and its decoration, interior and/or exterior; the finial or knob shape, for which stopper finial shapes may be applicable, and its decoration; the shape of the rim (e.g. plain, scalloped, etc.); and the length of the vertical flange, whether it is ground, and on which

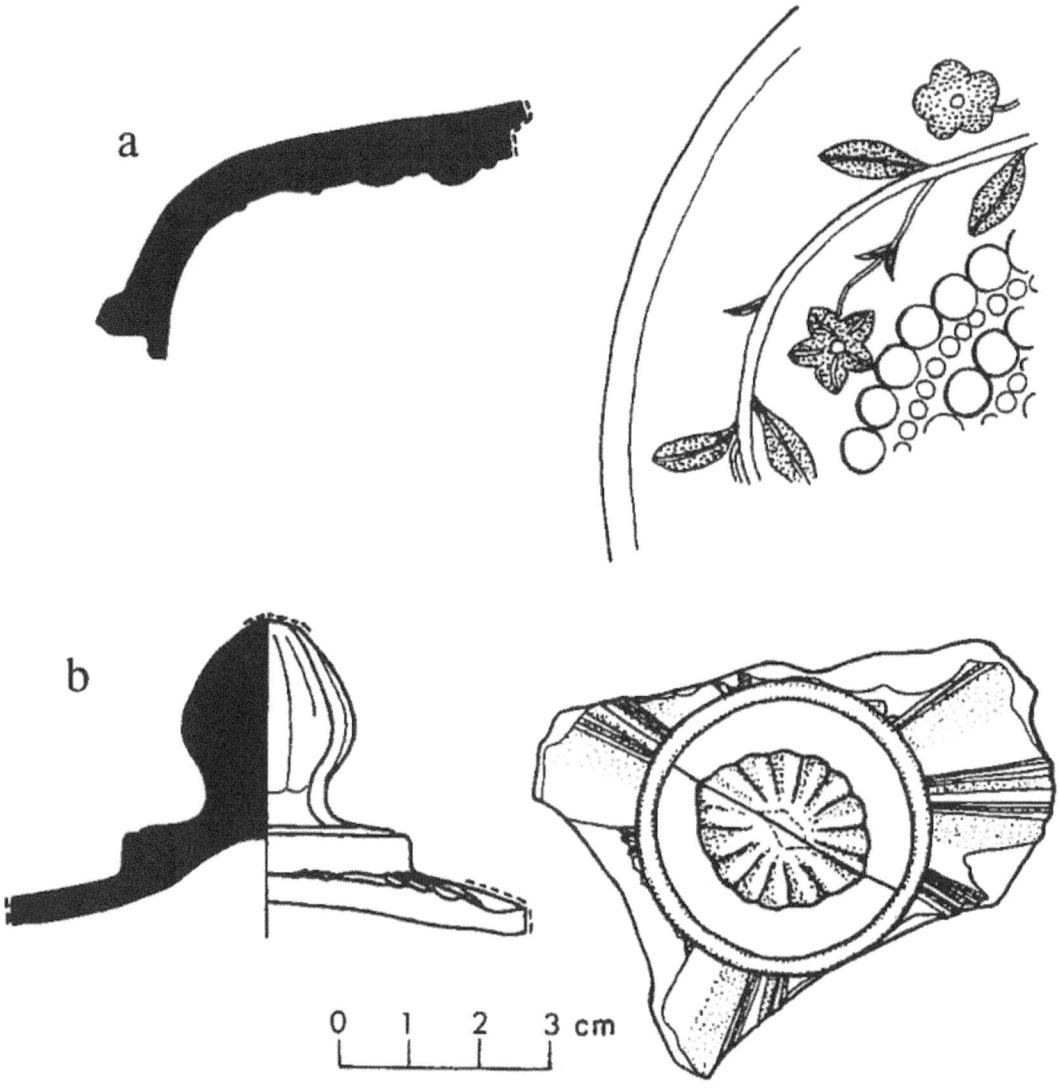

a

b

0   1   2   3 cm

Figure 140. Glass cover fragments. (a) Has a rim, vertical flange, and decoration on the interior surface. (b) The finial on this cover is spire-shaped and decorated and sits on a raised platform or step.

158

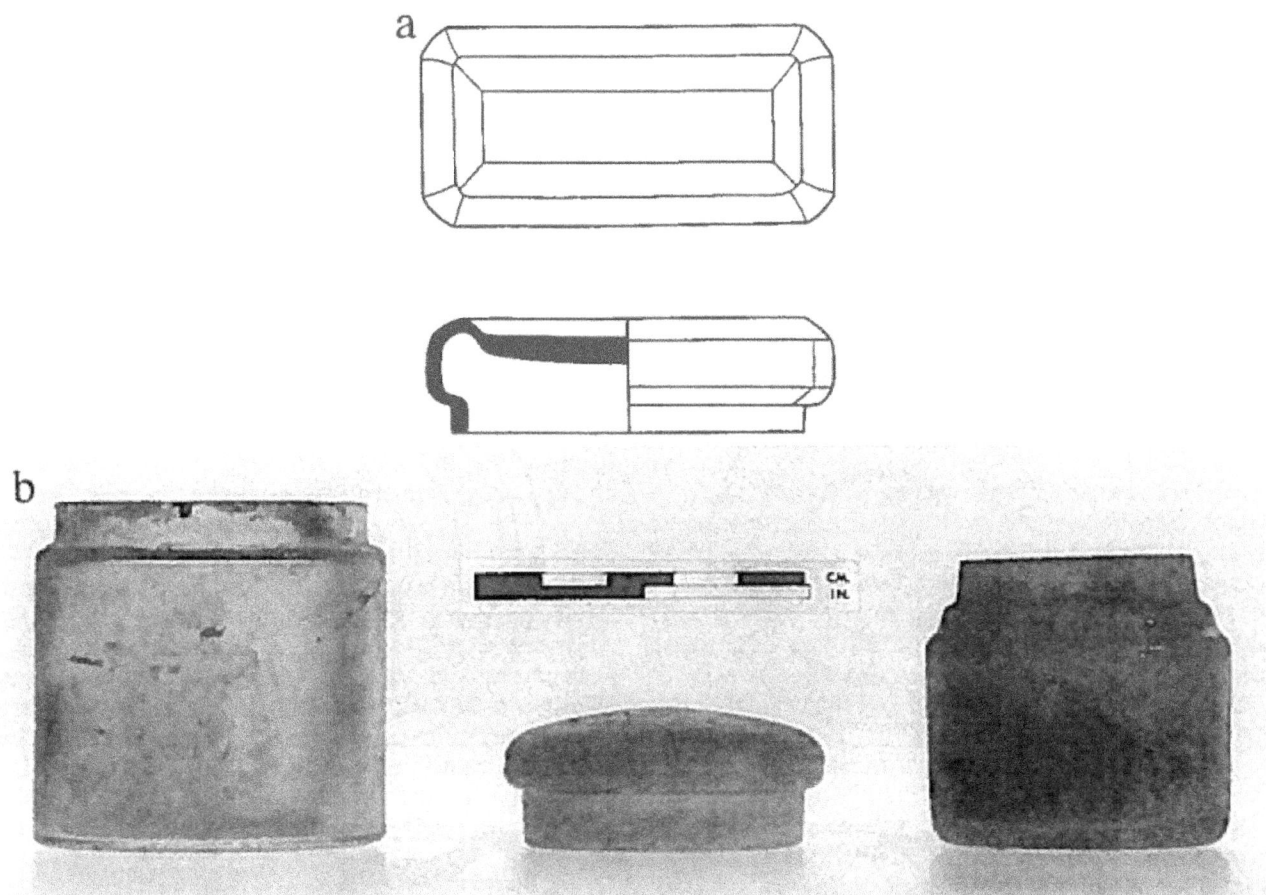

Figure 141. (a) Rectangular-shaped lid with a moulded panel on top and bevelled at the edge of the top and at the rim. (b) Two colourless glass jars and a glass lid which could belong to either jar.

surface. This latter feature would indicate whether the cover was intended to sit on or fit into an object.

Glass covers are not a common find on Parks Canada sites and the fragments from these objects could easily be misidentified, e.g. cover fragments from Grassy Island (12B) resemble pieces of a stemware foot fragment with a folded edge. Generally the presence of a vertical flange and oddly directed glass at the base of the finial are the most telling indications of a glass cover.

Lids

To reduce the confusion caused by the indiscriminate labelling of the glass items which fit over the top of glass vessels as "liner," "lid," or "cover," we suggest that a "liner" is part of a complex closure, a "cover" is the top of a tableware item, and a "lid" is the cover for a container, usually a jar, pot, or box. As a closure the lid stands alone.

The vertical flange of the lid may rest on a ledge part way down the outside of the neck of the container, or the flange may fit inside the lip of the vessel. This flange may have special features such as screw threads or ground surfaces, either internally or externally, to fit the bore of the container.

Descriptions of glass lids should include the horizontal shape (a round lid and a rectangular one are illustrated in Figure 141), the vertical shape (domed, panelled, etc.), decoration, treatment of the vertical flange (e.g. ground on internal surface and bottom), and finial shape, if there is a finial. As well an indication of the lid's dimensions should be noted in an attempt to establish the size of the pot for which the lid was intended.

Glass lids are not common in our collection, probably because other more durable types of closures were preferred.

159

Liners

A liner is part of a more complex closure and is therefore not a closure on its own. The glass liner was developed in the United States before 1869 (Toulouse 1969a: 350). Its purpose was to shield the food in fruit jars from the metallic taste imparted by direct contact with a metal cap. The glass liner, sandwiched between a metal cap and a rubber ring, was held in place by a screw band or solid cap made of metal. The entire unit supposedly made an airtight seal.

The glass liner in various forms was a part of several patented closures. Liners were made with different types of moulded configurations, depending on the device used to hold them in position on the jar. These configura-

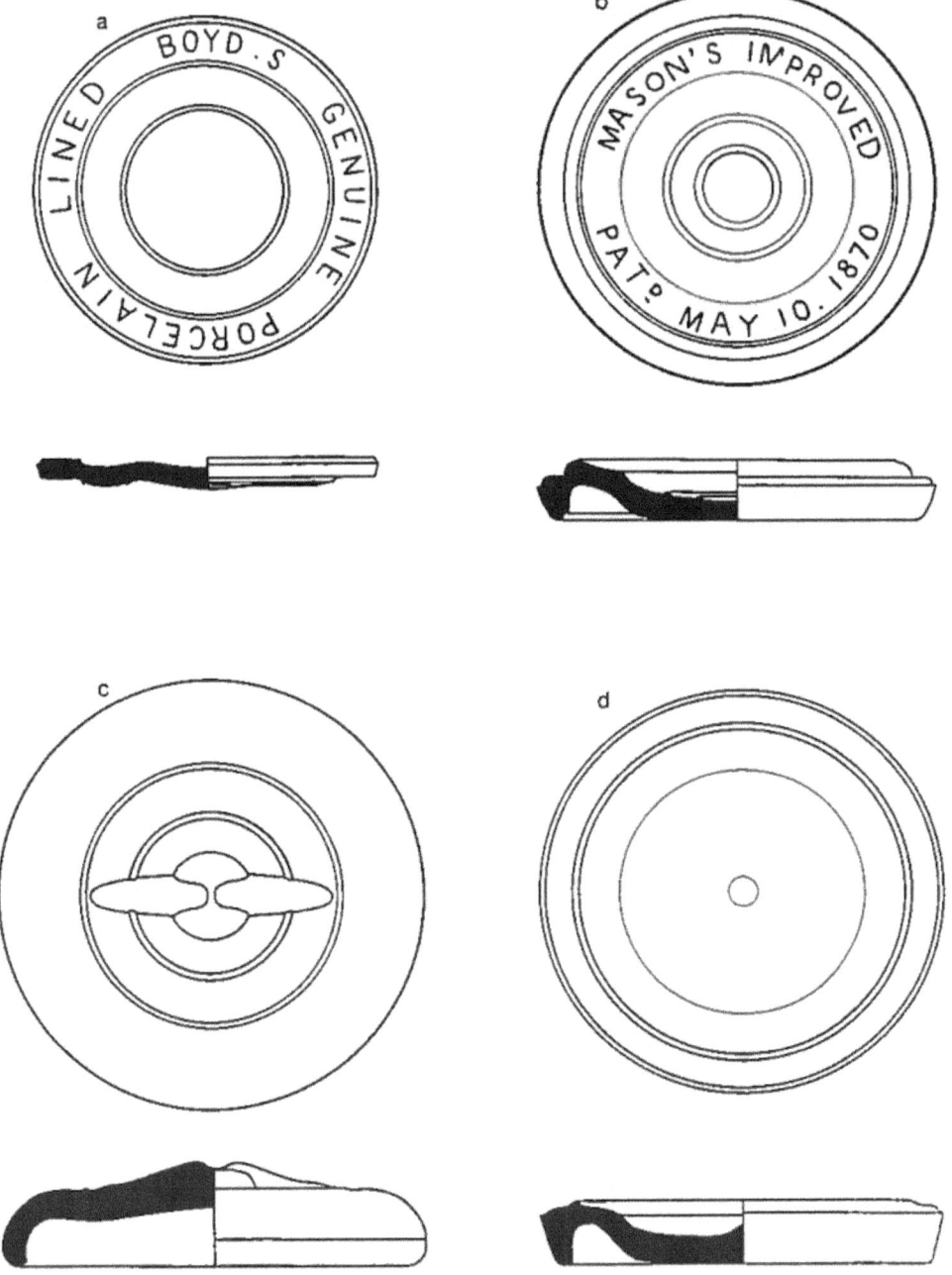

Figure 142. Glass liners. (a) Boyd's Genuine Porcelain Liner in opaque white glass. (b) Mason's improved liner. (c) Liner from a lightning closure showing the moulded centring configuration. (d) Plain glass liner with mamelon.

160

tions include a central upward projection called a "boss," threaded externally to be covered by a cap (the boss could be perforated to vent air during the food processing), moulded arrangements for centring various wire bails or yokes, and a moulded hole in a raised bump into which a metal thumbscrew on a metal yoke could be fitted. Liners intended to be held in place by a screw band or metal cap can be plain, with or without a vertical flange. The top of the liner may be flat or bevelled towards the centre for snap clips to attach to. Liners can have commercial markings; the glass liner may have been purchased separately from the glass or ceramic jar and the commercial markings may not match.

The individual design on each liner may be of interest in a concentrated study of these items, but for normal cataloguing these details are not usually dealt with. For the present, important features seem to be the commercial marks and their location (e.g. marks on the Boyd's porcelain liner are on the underside of the liner), whether or not the liner has a vertical flange, configurations for a specialized clamp, and the diameter of the liner.

Patented Closures

During the 19th century interest was shown in the improvement of containers and closures, particularly in those intended as packages for foods and beverages. The intent of the various inventors was to produce an airtight package that would not affect the taste and appearance of the contents, to make the package cheaply, and to ensure reliable sizes. The problems encountered with hand-made glass bottles and jars, including variations in the sizes of containers of the same capacity and inconsistent finishes which would not fit standard-size closures, were eventually minimized and eliminated by bottlemaking machines. Until that time invention flourished in Europe and North America, and many and varied were the results.

The patentees' approach to the problem varied. Some, like Mason, developed a bottle-making mould to produce a finish that would fit the closure; others invented a stoppering device to fit existing finish configurations. Thus it is not always possible to determine the sort of closure that a container was intended to take.

Patented closures can be fitted into a typology, as has been done by Toulouse (1969a); some of these have been selected for inclusion in this glossary. As well, the Dominion Glass Co. Ltd. (post-1913), in a catalogue dating from after 1913, advertises its packers' ware with a limited selection of finish styles to accommodate various closures, and some of these are included here. However, although this group was made by Dominion Glass at this period, it must be remembered that not every foreign patent was licensed to be made in Canada and Canadian glass factories alone did not supply the Canadian market.

Also detailed below are closures that became famous, those that are recovered from Parks Canada's sites with some frequency, and those that required specially adapted finishes. The concentration is on closures that were developed and patented in the late-19th century, although many of these were in use into the 20th century. Some, like the crown closure, are still in use today, either in the original form or in a modified version.

Discs — One of the simplest sorts of closure available is the unparaffined cardboard disc or plug cap used for milk bottles. These require a ledge inside the mouth of the bottle on which to rest (Fig. 56) and are not intended for long distance travelling or long storage. The first American patent for this closure is probably ca. 1901 (Toulouse 1969a: 426). A second type of disc was the Bernardin Metal Cap (the disc) and Neckband, intended to be used over a cork stopper instead of wire. The tin cap portion was round and flat with a central hole; it covered the cork and held it in place without digging into the cork as does taut wire. The neck band was a wide strip of metal attached to the cap, which wrapped around the bottle neck under the string rim. Discs were widely used on beer and ginger ale bottles. Bernardin's closure was patented sometime in the 1880s (Lief 1965: 15).

Codd's ball stopper — The Codd closure required a bottle neck with a complicated internal shape, a glass marble, and a ring of cork or rubber. When the bottle was filled, the ring or washer and the marble were pushed against the groove on the inside of the neck. The contents of the bottle had to be a carbonated beverage to

161

Figure 143. Codd's ball stopper.

Figure 144. Hutchinson spring stopper.

hold the marble stopper in place. The invention was an English one, patented in 1870, and was not popular in the United States although it was much used in England and her colonies (Lief 1965: 14).

Hutchinson spring stopper — The Hutchinson's Patent Spring Soda Bottle Stopper, patented in 1879 in the United States, consists of a loop of heavy wire attached to a rubber gasket. The device sits inside the bottle neck with the tip of the wire loop protruding from the mouth. Once the bottle has been filled the closure is pulled into place, a seal effected internally at the neck-shoulder junction, and the carbonation in the contents keeps the stopper in place. Bottles designed to take this stopper must have shortish necks. The bottle is opened by delivering a sharp blow to the top of the loop. The Hutchinson stopper was adaptable to available bottles with three wire lengths and five washer or gasket sizes and could be re-used until the rubber seal wore out. It was a very successful closure but eventually gave way to the crown, although the two competed into

the 20th century. Although the original invention was Hutchinson's, an Illinois Glass Co. catalogue of 1911 advertises it as a "Spring Stopper" (Putnam 1965: 195).

Lightning-type closure — An enormously successful bottle closure of the late-19th and early-20th centuries was the Lightning stopper and its variations. The basic invention was originally patented in the United States in 1875 (Toulouse 1969a: 465). A stopper of rubber or porcelain is attached to a wire bail which pivots on either side of the neck under the finish. The lever wire, which hooks into loops in a neck tie-wire used to keep the closure on the bottle, moves up and down to loosen or

162

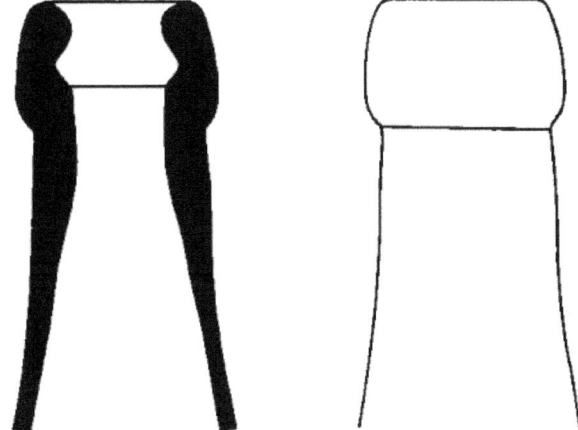

Figure 146. A bottle with a finish for an internal gasket, possibly the Baltimore Loop Seal, patented in the late-19th century by William Painter (Lief 1965: 16-17).

vertised in catalogues in 1911 for beer (Illinois) and after 1913 for ale (Dominion). Lightning-type closures are still used on a limited scale for effervescent beverages in modern times.

Internal gasket — See example in Figure 146.

Crown finish and cap — Patented in 1892 in the United States by William Painter (Lief 1965: 17), the crown cap proved to be the ideal single-use closure for carbonated beverages. The original crowns were plain, unmarked metal, one or both sides lacquered, with approximately 20 corrugations and an internal disc of natural cork. Later crowns had proprietors' marks on them and discs of composition cork, or, in the cap of one of Painter's competitors, linoleum discs. Modern ones may have plastic liners. The crown finish was part of the original patent and is distinctive in appearance. It is a two-part finish with a lip that has a flat top and rounded sides over which the skirt or flange of the crown will hook. Originally crown finishes were hand-made with a finishing tool, and foot-operated crowning machines could reconcile slight variations in lip shapes and sizes to standard crowns. Crown closures appear to have been made in only one size to fit small-mouthed bottles such as sodas and beers. Note: there should not be

Figure 145. Lightning-type closure. The example illustrated is on a beer bottle (Smithsonian Institute Negative No. 72-7155, Collection No. 65.510).

tighten the pivoting wire bail. This closure was apparently too expensive to be used for soft drink bottles but was popular for beer and ale bottles (Lief 1965: 16; Nurnberg 1967: 3). The necessary finish configurations are not complicated, and the Lightning was made in more than one size and in porcelain to fit different sized bottle mouths. There were other Lightning-type closures for small-mouthed bottles patented in the late-19th century, including the Triumph, the Magic, and the Electric, but all worked on the same principle. Lightning-type closures appear ad-

163

Figure 147. Crown finish and cap.

any confusion between the closure used on crown fruit jars and the crown finish and cap.

Kork-n-seal — The kork-n-seal requires a finish with a narrow, protruding lip over which to hook the skirt of the cap. The finish usually has a second part which varies in shape and seems to be largely decorative; there may be other features in addition to these two. The kork-n-seal closure first appears in glassmakers' catalogues of the early-20th century, advertised in sizes to fit bottle openings of 5/8, 1, and 1 1/4 inches. The kork-n-seal was still being supplied and called by that name in recent times (Moody 1963: 185, 190). Its selling point is to the consumer, who can re-use the closure indefinitely on bottles with still or effervescent contents.

Wax sealer — This type was one of the earliest glass jars for home canning, used to preserve foods that were processed after being put in the jar. The grooved lip received hot wax, and a stopper or liner of glass, cork, or metal would be pushed into the wax. Glass liners used for this purpose may show signs of use, e.g. nicks or gouges from being pried off congealed wax. This sort of jar was being produced in glass before 1854 (Toulouse 1969a: 415).

Liner with cap or screw band — Mason's patent of 1858 is generally regarded as the first workable seal of its type (Lief 1965: 9-13). His finish-forming bottle mould produced a jar with embossed threads which began below the top of the bottle and ended above the shoulder. The lip was then ground, without interfering with the

164

Figure 148. Kork-n-seal finish. The bottle illustrated has a finish designed to take a kork-n-seal lever-type cap.

Figure 149. Wax sealer.

threads, and the jar seal was effected externally, at the shoulder. Originally Mason's jar was intended to take a zinc metal cap, a closure that completely covered and sealed the mouth. However the metallic taste was imparted to the food and was unacceptable, so in 1869 Boyd patented a glass liner for the cap, first in colourless glass, later in opaque white glass called "porcelain" (Toulouse 1969a: 350). There were several fruit jar makers who used Mason's jar patent and his closure or a variation, the most popular of which was a glass liner sitting on a rubber ring and held in place with a screw band, a metal cap without a centre, patented in 1865. The name "Mason" became a generic term for fruit jars with a screw thread finish. Several glassmakers produced their own Mason jars, as Ball Mason's Patent, Ball Perfect Mason, Drey Perfect Mason, Samco Genuine Mason, Anchor Hocking Mason, and so on. Replacement zinc closures were readily available, manufactured as a line of production by a company that did not make the jars; therefore the jar and glass or metal liner may have different commercial marks. The Dominion Glass Company in an early-20th century catalogue offers the following varieties of jar that require such a closure: Improved Gem jars, jars for honey and marmalade, Diamond jars, crown fruit jars (not to be confused with crown finishes and closures), Mason fruit jars, Best jars, and some jelly

165

Figure 150. Two Mason jars. The earlier version on the left took a zinc metal cap; after 1869 this jar could be had with a glass liner. The jar on the right is a later variation and can still be found in use today.

Figure 151. Liner and metal yoke. The illustrated jar has four mould-blown lugs on the neck, sloping and thicker at an end, and might have been intended for a liner and yoke closure.

jars. As well, their pickle and olive jars could be ordered to take any style of closure, including, presumably, this one.

Liner and metal yoke — The elements of this closure type are a glass or metal liner held tightly in place by a wire yoke that lays across the top of the liner. This yoke hooks under helical (i.e. continuous or interrupted spiralling) or flat lugs, on the neck of the jar. Sometimes the lugs have stops to hold the yoke in place; some have serrated bottoms to keep the yoke from slipping. To tighten the closure the yoke is twisted in a motion like a screw cap or band.

Liner and spring clip — This closure type seems to be a variation on the liner and

metal yoke type in that the spring clip slides into place, whereas the yoke type twists. This difference will probably be most obvious on the neck of the jar. A jar intended to take a spring clip should have a well-defined bead or ledge encircling the exterior surface of the neck, over which to hook the clip.

Liner and metal yoke with thumbscrew or lever — There are several closure types grouped in this category together; Toulouse (1969a) defines each type and may be consulted if this information is required. Generally these closures consist of a liner of glass or metal and a flat metal or wire yoke that sits over the liner, hooking under two beaded lugs on the neck of the jar or wrapping around two moulded buttons on the jar neck. The yoke is tightened in position either by a thumbscrew in the centre of the yoke, which presses down the

Figure 152. Lightning-type closure. Illustrated is a Perfect Seal jar with Lightning-type closure and glass liner.

liner in its centre, or by a lever or two on the top or side of the jar, which, by lowering, takes up the slack in the yoke (see Toulouse 1969a: 48–96).

Liner and spring bail — The spring bail is a wire member fastened to the jar in such a way that it can be moved back and forth. The wire may be attached to buttons on the neck, it may hook into dimples in the jar, or the bail may be anchored to the jar by passing through a groove in the base of the jar. The bail is tightened on the jar by being forced over a projection on the liner and held in place by a groove in the projection. These projections can take some rather odd forms and are very distinctive in appearance (see Toulouse 1969a: 471–73).

Lightning-type closure — Working on concepts originally incorporated in a patented closure for bottles, the Lightning closure appeared on fruit jars of the same name by 1877 (Toulouse 1969a: 466). To be used on jars, the closure requires an independent glass liner with a moulded central ridge to hold the wire bail in position. The bail and lever wire work in the same way as on bottles. The closure was very successful for fruit jars and for bottles, and its imitators replaced the neck tie-wires with moulded dimples or moulded buttons on the neck of the jar. Lightning clamps were also adapted to hold down other glass liners (see Toulouse 1969a: 184).

167

Bottle Stoppers
National Glass Budget

National Glass Budget 16(13):4. August 18, 1900

BOTTLE STOPPERS

Many attempts have been made to displace cork for bottle closures, owing both to the cost of cork, and the variation in the finish or aperture of the bottle neck.

For wine bottles, the use of cork of superior quality and density has been found to be indispensible, owing to its cleanliness, tastelessness, and imperviousness to the action of acids. For export beer bottles and the finer brands of beer, which are Pasteurized in the bottle, cork stoppers are still adhered to, since rubber inclosures impart an objectionable flavor to beer which has been bottled more than a few weeks. The levered lightning stopper for beer bottles for home consumption was in great favor 10 and 15 years ago, but owing to its cost was displaced largely by the introduction of the Baltimore seal, which was a rubber closure easily inserted and withdrawn, and was used fresh for each filling. During late years the cheaper Crown seal, consisting of a tin cap with an interior lining of shaved cork, fastened to the bottle by bending over the ring the saw tooth edge of the tin cap, has grown greatly in favor, not only in the United States, but in England and Germany. Like the Baltimore seal the Crown seal is used but once, being cheap enough to throw away after being removed. The Crown seal possesses the cleanliness and tastelessness of a cork stopper, and is much less expensive.

The bottles for both the Baltimore seal and Crown seal have a peculiar finish, the former being a mitred inside finish with an irregular aperture, and the latter having a clearly defined lower edged ring, over which the tin cap is bent. Both bottles are made in a manner unfitting them for other than their special closures, which must be applied by machinery. For this reason the bottles thus made are as a rule useless to the consumer, and are in the main returned.

The wire stopper is, however, again coming into general use, since the introduction of the porcelain stopper, with a thin lining of rubber, which is only partially exposed to the bottle contents. The wired stopper is clean, easily opened and closed, and readily thrown aside on its hinges to enable the bottle to be interiorly washed by machinery, and as a result, it is being more extensively used for spring and mineral water bottles, club soda and beers, and in pop and soda bottles is largely displacing all other stoppers.

Modern Closures a Significant Feature of Sanitary and Convenient Packing

Glass Container

 **The Glass Container**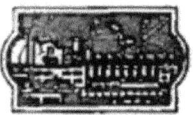

Vol. 2   Contents Copyrighted, 1923   **SEPTEMBER, 1923**   By The Glass Container Association   No. 11

The monthly magazine of The Glass Container Association of America, 70 Fifth Avenue, New York, N. Y., published in the interests of all makers and users of glass containers, and of the contributing industries.

Modern Closures a Significant Feature of Sanitary and Convenient Packing

*A description of the many different types
of effective closures used on today's package*

EDITOR'S NOTE: *This is the second of a series of articles devoted to showing how the equipment manufacturers, through research and invention, have been able to serve more adequately the user of glass containers. The third article will appear in the October issue and will deal with labeling and shipping.*

A FEW decades ago, there was no such thing obtainable as a perfect and convenient closure. When the food preserving industry began back in the time of Nicholas Appert, a great deal of difficulty was experienced by all those who desired to preserve foods and beverages from the action of the air. It is almost impossible, in this day when vacuum closures and perfect seals are in so wide a use, to think that there ever was a time when these were unknown and unavailable. It has become classic to quote the experiences of Nicholas Appert in all the experiences with details in early food preserving, and perhaps in no way did he encounter more difficulty than in adapting the closures of his day to the wide mouth jar that he may be said to have invented.

"Therefore, I have had bottles made expressly, having large openings and with contractions, that is to say, with a ridge extending into the interior of the opening below the cord-line (or ring). My object was that the cork introduced with force upon the bottle holder, of which I have spoken, with the assistance of the pallet, up to three-quarters of its length, was constricted through the middle. . . .

"The objects arranged, I draw the bottle holder between my legs, and introduce into the bottle a suitable stopper after having wet half of it in the vessel of water, so that it may enter more easily, and after having wiped the end, I press it in this position with my left hand which I hold steady so that the bottle may be perpendicular. I take the pallet with my right hand so as to push the cork in with force. When I feel after the first or second blow that the cork has entered a little, I stop so as to take the neck of the bottle in that hand, which I hold firm and perpendicular upon the bottle holder, and with repeated blows of the pallet, I continue forcing the stopper into three-fourths of its length.

"The quarter of the stopper which should always extend beyond the bottle after having resisted the repeated blows of the pallet assures me on the one hand that the bottle is closed perfectly, and on the other hand, this excess is necessary for the cork to support the two crossed wires or two strings so as to hold it. . . . One cannot be too careful in attaining a good closure; no small details should be neglected in order that the substance which is to be preserved should be rigorously excluded from contact with the air, since it is the destructive agent most to be feared."

This explains fully the laborious and slow method necessary for successful preserving a hundred years ago—for ordinary bottle. Appert had greater difficulties with his wide mouth jars, for which he had to make stoppers of three, four, and five layers of cork, which he "glued with good sense, that is to say, the pores of the cork placed horizontally, with fish glue." He prepared his own glue from a formula which he discovered to be the most efficient. In many cases, after all his painstaking details, he found it advisable to apply a coat of tar over the cork after its insertion, and the bottle neck as well, in order to insure an hermetic seal.

As far as one can trace, American glass manufacturers were the first to experiment with metal closures. Baron Steigel, who was one of the more important early American glass manufacturers, did a great deal of experimenting with problems pertaining to glass and to glass containers, and was probably the first manufacturer in America, and perhaps in the world, to produce a bottle with a metallic closure.

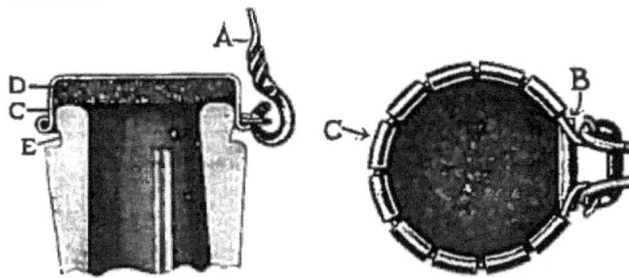

Williams Kork-N-Seal—in relation to bottle before closure. A, lever; B, contracting ring; C, metal skirt expanding; D, cork liner; E, bottle top

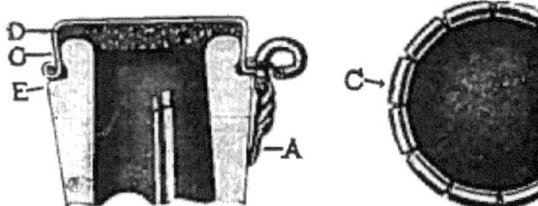

Williams Kork-N-Seal contracted, making seal, when lever is down

The Bernardin Bottle Cap Company's one-piece long skirt cap

The American Dan bottle seal machine

The Dan seal   The Armstrong embossed corks

The Closure Service Corporation's bottle seal

The Phoenix cap manufactured by the Phoenix Hermetic Company. It is but one of their extensive line

Type R A sealing machine manufactured by the Aluminum Company of America

The Adriance power crowning machine manufactured by the Adriance Machine Works, Inc.

 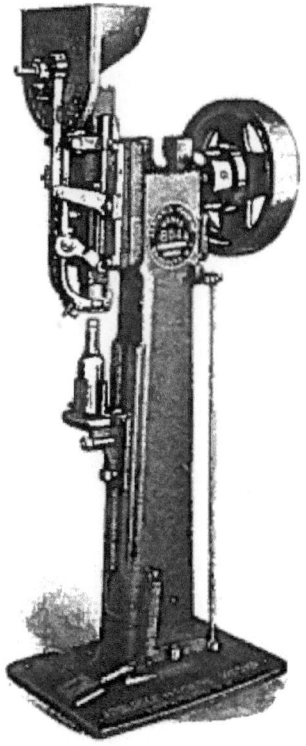

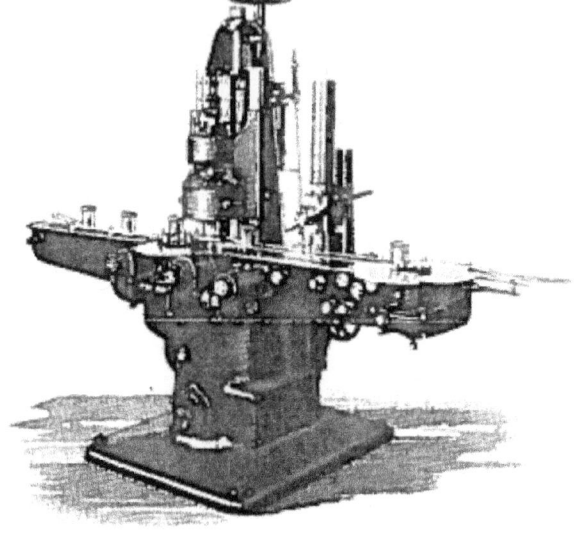

Anchor single head sealing machine

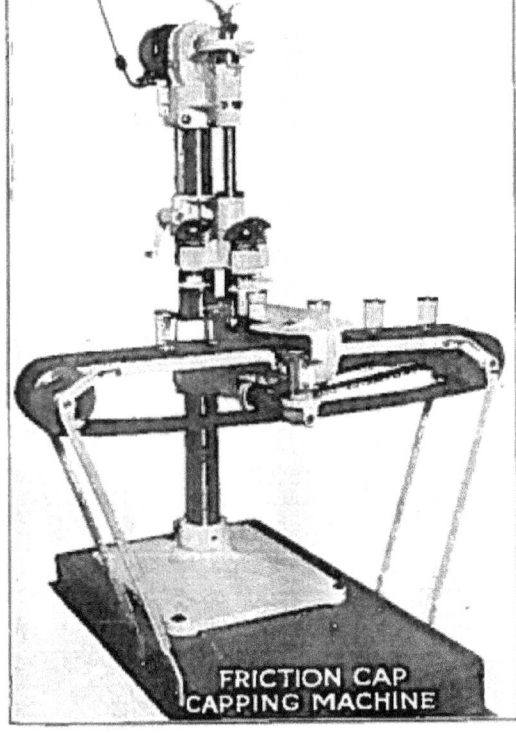

American Metal Cap Co.'s friction cap machine—Dexeal cap and Wire-Edge cap

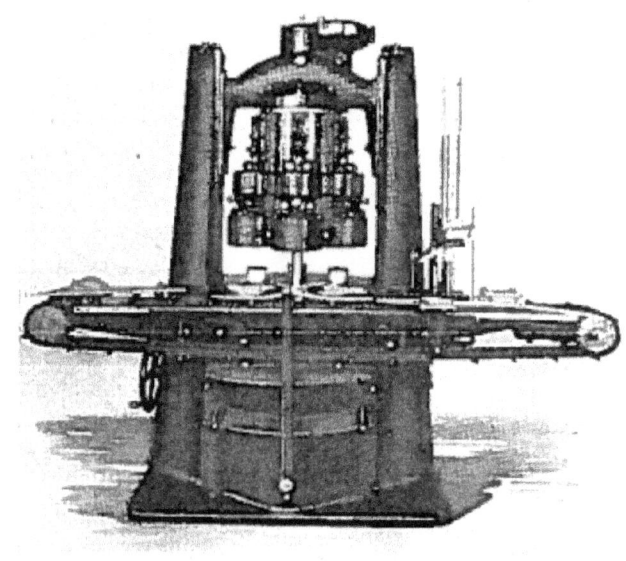

Anchor multiple head sealing machine of the Anchor Cap & Closure Corporation, manufacturers of the Anchor caps

The Upressit cap made by the Upressit Products Corporation

The glass bottle-stopper manufactured by the Whitall-Tatum Co.

The machines of the National Seal Co., manufacturers of the Duplex Seal, shown below

To trace the history of the evolution of the vacuum cap or hermetic seal of our day from these early beginnings would be a very interesting thing to do, but it can scarcely come within the compass of this article.

The food packer, the bottler, and all who are engaged in preserving foods, enjoying the convenience and the security of the modern container with its modern closure, owe a tremendous debt of gratitude to the inventive geniuses all along the line who have made the modern jar and seal possible.

There are various types of closures, developed to fill a particular need, and meeting these requirements as perhaps no other type could.

For sealing beverage bottles, the crown seal has long been in popular use. It is affixed to the bottle by a pressure capping machine, which operates in connection with the filling machine, making filling and capping practically one operation. This closure is manufactured by a large number of companies and is produced by millions every year. In fact, this closure is in such wide use that the crowns, after they are used, become the coin of the realm of childhood, and are one of the great mediums of exchange in small boys' bartering.

Another type of closure in use for many years is the bottle stopper, made either of glass, porcelain, or hard rubber, and secured to the bottle neck by wires. This is an effective seal, and is opened and closed by an ingenious lever device. This is at present widely used by bottlers of mineral waters and pharmaceuticals, particularly in bottles of a fairly large capacity. It is manufactured by several companies of which perhaps the best known are the Whitall-Tatum Co. and Karl Hutter, Inc.

There are many important modern seals or closures, invented to answer a particular need, and they are all remarkably ingenious, simply effective, and in very wide practical use. A study of each individually will perhaps be the clearest means of description, and will obviate the confusion that might arise by comparisons.

For the small mouthed bottles, such as those used for ketchup, beverages, syrups, vinegar, and the like, the Goldy Seals, made by the Aluminum Company of America, the American Dan Bottle Seal, the Closure Service Corporation's bottle closure, the Handycap, made by the Handycap Manufacturing Corporation, and the Kork-N-Seal, made by the Williams Sealing Corporation, are undoubtedly the best known and the most popular in use.

The Goldy Seals of the Aluminum Company of America are made of pure aluminum, and are affixed to the bottle completely by automatic sealing machines, ranging in output from twenty-five to over a hundred bottles per minute. The Goldy Seal is opened by lifting a flat aluminum tab, which tears easily, making it very convenient.

The Aluminum Company of America have produced a new type of automatic sealing machine, Type SA. It is designed for the packer who requires a completely automatic machine, that can handle various sizes of bottles and caps with but little time needed for adjustment. In Type SA, speed in sealing has been obtained in a simple and rugged machine construction. With only one sealing head, this machine can be changed from one size of cap or bottle to another size quickly and easily. Type SA will handle bottles from 4 to 12 in. in height, caps from 26½ mm to 92 mm in diameter and will seal 24,000 bottles per day of 10 hours. This machine automatically takes bottles from the filler, delivers them to the capping head, and passes them on to the conveyor or labeling machine.

The Dan seal, manufactured by the American Dan Bottle Seal Corporation, is a malleable metal cap made of one piece of thin aluminum, formed to provide one or more lobes, or ears. The metal being thin, the tearing of the cap from the mouth of the bottle dispenses with the necessity of a tool. The malleable cap may be provided with a cork, paper or other gasket.

The Dan system of sealing includes a machine which makes the seal from a ribbon of aluminum and applies it to the bottle at a rate up to ninety per minute. The machine is fully automatic; the seals are made, the corks or liners are introduced, and the capping effected in one operation, at a cost comparatively small. The machine is so designed that the trade-mark, or legend, is embossed upon the aluminum cap at the time the cap is made by means of embossing dies, which may be changed in less than five minutes.

The Closure Service Corporation manufacture a very effective seal, used extensively on ketchup bottles and those of similar types. It is made of thin metal, and opens easily by tearing a strip around the base of the cap by means of the provided tab. It has an oil paper lining, and has been claimed for very wide use by packers.

The Handycap, made by the Handycap Manufacturing Corporation, is made of thin metal, and is opened by lifting a center tab and tearing down over the edge. It is very simple and effective, and enjoys a merited popularity.

The Williams Kork-N-Seal features its convenience in resealing, and so is a popular cap for products that are consumed gradually. They are manufactured in five sizes, covering bottle opening diameters from 7/16 in. to 1¼ in. It can be easily removed, and reseals perfectly, by means of the little lever at one side. The Williams capping machines that apply the caps to the bottle range from the bench machines for plants having a comparatively small output to the Rotary machines with a capacity up to seventy bottles per minute.

The manufacture of bottle caps has more than kept pace with the improvement of containers for bottle packs. It has only been a few years that packers have desired a cap to cover the inner seal, yet food bottles are usually seen on the shelves of the retailer with a decorated cap.

The Bernardin Bottle Cap Co., Evansville, Ind., experimented many years before a machine was finally perfected that would draw a cap with a long skirt—the entire cap being made from one piece of tin.

To further perfect machines which would deep draw sheet tin that had been laquered or lithographed in colors without breaking or otherwise damaging the colors was still a greater problem.

Deep drawn bottle caps may be had in as many colors as necessary to reproduce a trade-mark or other design, and at popular prices.

There are many packers who believe the most attractive cap is that which always has a bright appearance. Plate tin as it comes from the rolling mills is subject to corrosion and does not have a finish that retains its bright appearance; therefore, to complete a cap to retain its brightness and be perfectly sanitary, the cap is first drawn with the same machinery as the lithographed cap and then dipped by hand and retinned. This retinning process makes a cap with all the appearance of nickel plating. Trade-marks may be embossed on such caps, which preserves the identity of the packer indefinitely.

A great change has taken place within the last twenty years in the manufacture of wide mouth food containers, and in the making of caps and closures to fit them. Before the days of automatic machinery, it was practically impossible for the glass manufacturer to furnish perfectly finished containers, but now this is completely changed. Specifications can be followed minutely, and a standard product results, which makes possible a co-operation between the glass manufacturer and the cap and seal manufacturer. There has also been a great progress in cap manufacturing. Remarkable development has taken place in the making of capping machinery. In the old days, the machines were crude and worked imperfectly. But within a period of fifteen years, the "vacuum closure has come from practically nothing to a point where it is considered almost indispensable on the majority of food packs."

The American Metal Cap Co., the Anchor Cap and Closure Corporation, the Hazel-Atlas Glass Co., the National Seal Co., Inc., the Phoenix-Hermetic Co., and the Upressit Products Corporation are the best known makers of caps for wide mouth food containers, jars for such products as fruits and vegetables, fish, meat products, condiments, peanut butter, and table specialties.

The American Metal Cap Co. manufactures an extensive line of metal closures for both narrow and wide mouth jars and for tumblers, but they feature the American Wire Edge Cap and the Dexeal closures, the Wire Edge Cap being used largely for sealing jams, jellies, mustard, pickles, and other products, while the Dexeal closures are adapted to toilet creams, cosmetics, writing inks, and other products where a reseal is desired.

The American Wire Edge Cap is a four notched cap and the Dexeal closure is of the two-notch type. In both closures the notches are equally distanced which enables the notches of the closures to take hold simultaneously on the threads of the bottle or jar and to exert an equalized downward pressure under all threads until the seal or closure is effected. In both closures the four or two points of sealing efficiency deliver a tightly sealed package and in consequence their positive points of sealing contact on the threads of the finish obviate all danger of binding action of the threads.

The Friction Cap made by this company, as illustrated, is a type of closure that is applied to both bottles and tumblers. The caps are supplied with all combinations of liners and are applied to the jars and tumblers by an automatic machine, as illustrated.

The Anchor Cap and Closure Corporation is one of the largest and best-known manufacturers in the closure industry, and their products are varied to meet the demands of different types of containers. The tin plate used in the Anchor Cap is given a coating of sanitary vegetable gold lacquer which is baked into the pores of the tin at great heat. A tight hermetic seal is made upon affixing the cap to the container by means of the side seal and the heavy gasket sealing ring.

This company manufactures a popular type of clipper cap, used for sealing jams, jellies, peanut butter, and like products, a four-thread screw cap, and a continuous thread cap, used quite extensively by packers of various food products. Their sealing machines are of the completely automatic type, and have a speed of sealing 100 jars per minute.

Lithographing trade-marks upon the caps, in various color combinations, is done by practically all the cap manufacturers, some of the details differing perhaps in the various plants, but practically the same in result to all intents and purposes. This lithographing is usually done while the metal is still in the sheet form before being stamped into caps. This adds greatly to the appearance of the cap, and individualizes it with the packer's trade-mark, name or emblem. It is another advertising feature, and has come into very wide use.

The Hazel-Atlas Glass Co. manufactures the Hazel Vacuum Cap which is very popular among the food packers.

The Hazel Vacuum Cap is applied to the container in series of from sixteen to twenty-four jars or tumblers at 15 to 20 seconds for each complete operation—in this way, enabling the packer to close from 7000 to 10,000 jars or tumblers per eight-hour day with one machine operator, in this way reducing the labor expense to the minimum. When the container is taken out of the closet, the cap, which is held on the jar or tumbler by vacuum or atmospheric pressure, gives absolute evidence whether the seal is defective, thus guaranteeing to the packer the perfect condition of the contents when it reaches the consumer.

The Hazel Vacuum Cap is removed very easily by the housewife. The metal from which it is made is pliable and can be readily torn with the fingers. Two ears or tabs are provided on the sides of the cap to insure convenience and ease in opening. It is a convenient and simple seal, economical, and widely known in the food packing trades. (*Continued on page* 34)

Modern Closures a Significant Feature of Sanitary Packing

(Continued from page 9)

The National Seal Co., Inc., are the manufacturers of the Duplex Seal, and have in the market two types of closing machines designed for affixing Duplex Seals.

The larger of these is a Multiple Power Closing Machine, strongly built, and of the Rotary type. It has interchangeable closing heads, all of which can be raised or lowered to accommodate bottles of different heights. This machine operates at a speed of from sixty to ninety sealings per minute, according to the size and shape of the bottles or jars that are being filled.

This Rotary Capper is so designed that where needed, it can be used in conjunction with an automatic feeder whereby all of the seals are placed on the bottles automatically prior to being fed into the machine for closing operation. There has been little demand for these automatic hoppers and feeders, however, as manufacturers find that as the bottles travel along the conveyor belt on their way to the machine, Duplex Seals can be dropped in place by hand so rapidly that they are at all times ahead of the closing operation.

For the smaller manufacturer of medium production, a single power closing machine is manufactured. Its operations and effects are all the same as those of the large Rotary type referred to above with the exception that it is a single head power driven machine, controlled by tripping a foot treadle while the large Rotary is a six-head machine, the operation of which is continuous. This machine has a speed of from twenty-five to thirty sealings per minute, according to the shapes and sizes of bottles. Both of these machines are operated by belt driven pulleys or by self-contained electric motors.

This seal company also has a hand closing device for users who do not fill more than fifteen bottles or jars per minute. It is made of aluminum and shaped to fit the operator's hand. It seems to be proving satisfactory wherever used by small manufacturers.

The Phoenix-Hermetic Co. manufactures a wide variety of caps, used chiefly in sealing food products, fruits and vegetables, jams, jellies, peanut butter, meat products, and other well known commodities. The Phoenix Cap, used in illustration, is the widely known band type, an hermetic closure, which is opened easily by removing the band. It is very simply constructed in three parts, the top, and a composition ring which is vulcanized to the top, and the outside band which seals it and fastens it to the container. Other caps manufactured by the Phoenix-Hermetic Co. are the Two-Piece Compo Screw Cap, the Vacuum Jar Cap, the Snap Cap, Presto, and Tip Top Caps. They are all adapted to certain types of containers and products and are applied by automatic closing machinery.

The Upressit Cap, made by the Upressit Products Corporation, operates on an entirely different principle. By squeezing the edge of the cap, it closes and forms an hermetic seal. It is released by depressing the center of the cap, which, due to the special hardened metal used, forces the side outward. It is therefore a very simple seal and reseal device, and is used in various sizes varying from the smaller ones up to those 4½ in. in diameter. For assembling Upressit Caps, large bottlers use standard capping machines with specially built hoppers, feeds, and heads.

The Security Metal Products Co. are owners of a process which they term the "Porcenam Process," by which a porcelain-like finish is applied to bottle and jar caps after they are formed. Through this method it is possible to produce a beautiful lustrous finish on the sides as well as the top of the cap.

Corks have been used for ages as a closure for bottles with small openings, and the modern cork closure adds a decorative value to the container it seals. The Armstrong Cork Co. manufactures Embossed Top Corks with tops of tough hardwood, colored to harmonize with the package and with a plain or glossy finish. They can be embossed with the bottler's name, trade-mark or design, and have proved very satisfactory in their great field.

For milk bottles, the most popular cap is the paper-board cap, which is inexpensive and convenient for the milk bottler's purpose. The paper-board is made from spruce logs, and are thoroughly sanitary in every way. They are used in quantities of many millions yearly, being used practically universally. The Sealright Co. manufactures a special milk bottle cap which they call the Pouring-Pull Cap. It has the added features of a pull handle or tab, and at the same time, an opening through the cap. The cap can thus be removed by pulling the tab; the tab can be lifted without removing the cap, and the milk poured without spilling or exposure .

There are, as it may be readily seen, many closures for many products, all of them excellent, all of them serving a necessary and important purpose, and all helping the packer in his great mission of preserving foods, drugs, or beverages to further the health and pleasurable living for humankind.

———————

A Study of Glass Finishes for Metal Closures

Glass Packer

A Study of Glass Finishes

For Metal Closures

A Wide Variety of Caps Necessitates a Wide Variety of Finishes
The First of a Series of Articles Devoted to a Discussion of Closures

DEVELOPMENTS within this century in the manufacturing of glass containers and the fabrication of closures have made possible the tremendous advance of glass as a container for various products of commerce. Many articles already appearing in journals have recorded the progress in the field of glass technology. Even the radio has carried the story of glass as a modern material proving suitable for numerous applications of exacting requirements. Closures, however, have received far less attention although the advances in the manufacturing of metal closures have been no less noteworthy. In fact, the position now attained by the glass container is due very largely to the ability of the modern closure to meet all the requirements placed upon it.

One can not deny that for attractive appearance, simplicity of operation both in application and removal, and serviceability, the present day closure matches the glass jar in every respect. Together they afford the user a thoroughly modern, reliable container. The purpose of these articles therefore is primarily to present the results of the cap manufacturer's efforts in developing his closure. There will be no attempt to give a history, but rather to offer a complete discussion of those closures now available for the packer.

In presenting this material the authors realize that they are venturing into a highly competitive field with the risk of appearing partisan. On the contrary, it is their earnest desire to be absolutely impartial and to deal justly with every closure. Naturally, in an exposition of this sort certain adjectives and superlatives must be deleted regardless of any convictions. No doubt our efforts will be a failure as far as those loyal salesmen or packers whose experience apparently justifies their beliefs are concerned. Still with due apologies and for the express purpose of presenting the modern closure as the partner of the modern glass jar, the attempt is made.

In this series of articles on caps and closures, THE GLASS PACKER believes it has collected information that has never before been available to those interested in the processing and packing of food products. While the subject has often been treated in manufacturers' catalogues, and now and then trade journals have touched upon phases of it, with this series it appears in its entirety for the first time. The series will include four articles beginning with the subject of "Finishes". Following on successive months will come articles on "Closures for Wide Mouth Containers", "Closures for Narrow Mouth Containers" and "Liners", each equally important in its bearing upon the food packing trade. In preparing these articles every effort has been made to cover the ground thoroughly. Cap and glass and liner manufacturers from coast to coast have given their hearty cooperation, which added to the splendid advice and aid received from research laboratories, and individual food packers, has furnished a source of valuable information that will make this series an asset to the library of every food manufacturer.

A glass container considered as a package consists of three equally important units—the metal closure, the liner, and the glass. While the closure and liner seem comparatively simple things there are numerous problems incident to their production which demand the utmost diligence and technical study. In the earlier days the cap manufacturer was compelled to employ whatever material appeared best suited to his need, but now the metal, lacquers, liner materials, are prepared exclusively for his use and to his specifications.

When the requirements set before the cap manufacturer are considered, his task does not appear simple. The first consideration is, of course, a hermetic closure. There are some applications where a strictly hermetic closure is not required but they represent exceptions. A hermetic seal is far from the whole story, as those familiar with this field realize. Appearance, is a major consideration. The user demands a pleasing contour and a lustrous finish and frequently brilliant colors of extreme durability. Strength sufficient to resist the numerous operations of sealing and processing is an important feature. To assure proper fit they must be uniform and built to exact dimensions. The packer imposes certain demands as to method of application and the consumer expects to readily and easily accomplish its removal. One can hardly comprehend the diversity of demands which

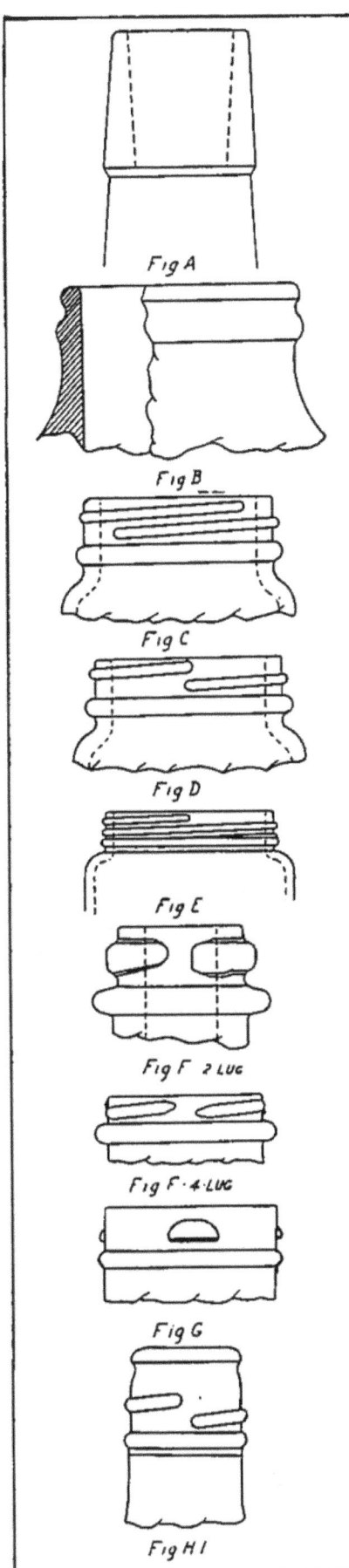

Fig A

Fig B

Fig C

Fig D

Fig E

Fig F 2 LUG

Fig F · 4 · LUG

Fig G

Fig H I

confront the closure manufacturer.

In the manufacturing operations many problems have been encountered. Not the least of these was in connection with the raw metals from which the closures are formed. From experience in the working properties of tin plate, rigid specifications have been formulated to assure proper metal. Automatic machines have been designed to perform the various drawing and stamping operations without seriously weakening the metal even though sharp bending of the metal is necessary.

Several metals are employed. Tin plate which is a steel rolled very thin and given a coating of tin is the most common. Tin serves as a protective coating for the steel against corrosion and rust. A bright metallic appearance also results from the tin coating. Because of its ductility, strength and relatively low cost it is admirably suited for cap construction.

Aluminum is another metal which because of the ease of tearing finds rather extensive application in the closure field. Other properties which make it suitable for closures are: greater resistance to corrosion, ductility, lightness, and resistance to food products.

A third metal employed for closures is zinc. This also is a softer metal than tin plate with the same non-rusting property as aluminum. This particular metal is familiar to many in the form of the Mason cap.

Other metals such as brass, monel metal, and various alloys find a limited application. Nickel plated caps are examples of another metal finish available for the user.

While there may be closures constructed of the raw material without additional finish, generally some added protective coating is applied upon which the resistance of the completed closure depends. Usually some form of lacquer is applied to the raw metal after cleaning and is baked on at high temperature. These lacquers not only afford additional protection against moisture and the contents of the container, but also give the metal an attractive appearance. The compounding of these lacquers and their application is another accomplishment of the closure manufacturers and those concerns who supply them with raw materials. Not the least important item is the improvement in the ovens which bake the lacquered sheets producing an even finish.

As previously pointed out the glass package consists of three elements and probably the most important element is the liner. It would be a difficult task indeed to secure a tight seal between glass and metal without the liner. In fact, remove the liner from the modern closure and a hermetic seal is impossible. In effect, the closure only serves to maintain the liner in contact with the glass finish and as a covering for the container. Because of the importance of the liners a special section of this article will be devoted exclusively to their consideration.

While it may seem an odd concept for many, in our discussion of closures we will assume their function to be principally a means of securing the liner. This will permit consideration of the mechanical features, method of application and removal; holding in abeyance the question of liners until all the various types of closures have received attention.

In order to secure the closures to the glass jar some form of thread, ring, lobe, or surface is required. This is known as the finish. Since the finish on the container is an important part of the complete seal, an examination of the various finishes will assist in the general appreciation of the subject of closures.

The finish is formed independent of the size or shape of the container. Theoretically, it would be possible to obtain any finish on any glass container. Practically, however, this is not true as certain combinations would hardly be suitable for commercial use. In some cases the mechanical features of the closure or the lack of suitability of the closure for the product ordinarily packed in a particular container have limited the combinations manufactured.

In presenting the various finishes the purpose is to acquaint the reader with the general appearance without discussing the operation of the closure employed with the finish. While the stopper as a closure is familiar to everyone, it is included and naturally heads the list as the oldest form of seal. In fact, when Nicholas Appert reported in 1810 on his inventions of preserving foods in glass containers by heat, he employed the cork stopper which he constructed of laminated cork. Figure A shows a bottle with a stopper finish. The sealing surface is naturally the inner surface of the neck opening.

Perhaps the second type of closure familiar to most everyone is the crown. Here in figure B is a simple finish with a top sealing surface against which the liner is secured.

Another type of closure of extensive application and one which has witnessed several modifications from the original design is that employing the principle of the screw thread. Several closures may be included under this heading, but the finish for each is quite different in appearance. The sealing surface is indicated in the various sketches.

Two common finishes are the deep and shallow (C T) continuous thread. These are illustrated in Figures C and D. A continuous thread just below the top engages the closure.

Figure E represents the R O (roll on) finish—a slight modification of the continuous thread necessitated by the unique method of securing the R O seal.

A variation of this closure is the divided thread designed to reduce the amount of turning action required to bring the cap against the seat. In Figure F is shown the 4-lug reseal finish; and a 2-lug Amerseal also made in two and six lug depending upon the size of the container.

A different finish scarcely resembling the others but for a closure operating on the divided screw thread principle is the Duplex seal finish. A four lobe finish is illustrated in sketch G.

For those containers on which a combination of hermetic seal and loose fitting overall cap is employed

finishes such as shown in Figure H are available. Here is a special screw or friction finish on the top with a crown finish below. This finish is employed on condiment bottles.

Another class of closure employs what is termed an anchor or friction finish. The form illustrated in Figures I, 1 and 2, has a smooth surface with no projections. The sealing surface of this finish is on the side. Two illustrations show the manner in which the finish is applied to a jar and tumbler.

A special provision for removal of the seal illustrated in Figures J, 1 and 2, is a pry-off finish which consists of a ledge or shoulder formed on the container below the regular closure finish. The illustration shows two applications of the pry-off arrangement, one on a friction finish and the other a variable ledge "priof" finish combined with a crown finish.

The band cap utilizes a heavy ring around the top of the container with the sealing surface on the top of the jar. Figure K is a drawing of the band finish and it can be observed that there is a slight inward slope toward the top to the outer surface which affords a means of identification.

The Atlas closure, an all aluminum cap, employs the finish shown in Figure L. This consists of two rings, the upper one of which serves as the sealing surface.

A special finish suitable for the Goldy seal, sketch M, represents a variation in the crown finish designed especially for this seal. A top sealing surface is employed with this closure.

Another special adaptation of the crown is the supercrown. The finish used represents a distinct variation from the usual crown finish as Figure N shows. Instead of a top sealing surface a double surface is utilized.

Save-A-Seal—a special type of closure utilizes still another variation in glass finish as may be observed in sketch O 1. A modification of this finish is illustrated in sketch. The purpose of this variation which is designed for the Super Seal will be discussed under closure operation.

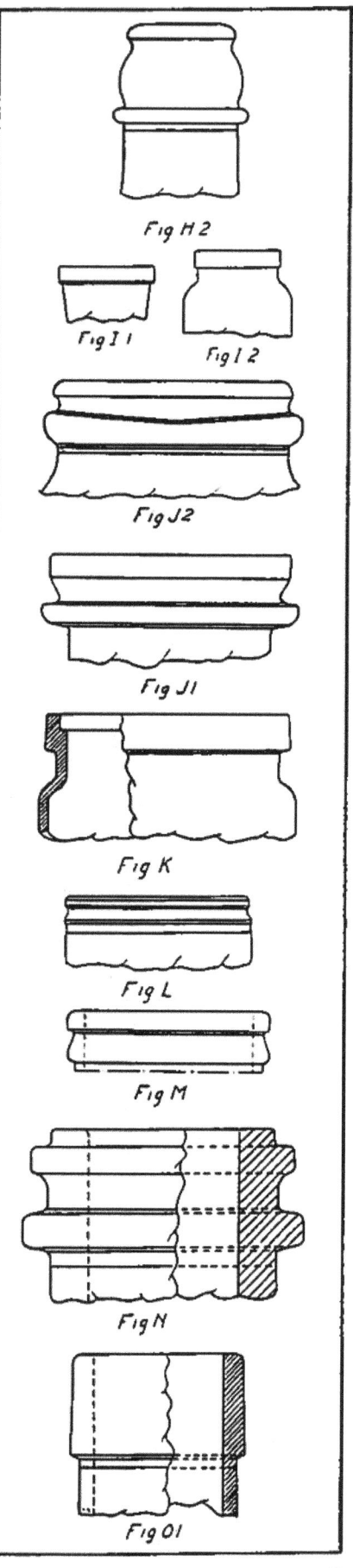

Fig H 2

Fig I 1

Fig I 2

Fig J2

Fig J1

Fig K

Fig L

Fig M

Fig N

Fig O1

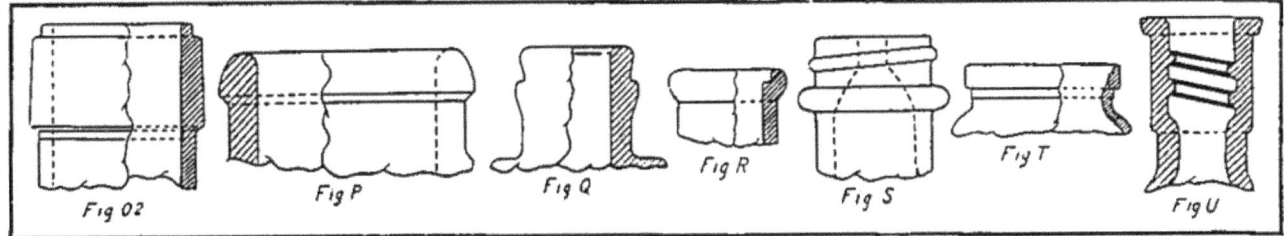

Fig O2   Fig P   Fig Q   Fig R   Fig S   Fig T   Fig U

Upressit, another closure with a name suggestive of the method of application, employs the finish pictured in sketch P.

One closure which possesses a characteristic feature is the Kork-N-Seal employing the finish given in Figure Q.

A finish, Figure R, with which everyone is familiar is that used on the milk bottle. An inside sealing surface is employed with the ordinary paper milk bottle seal. The outside finish sometimes holds a cover cap used to protect the pouring lip.

The all glass sprinkler top which replaces the stopper sprinkler represents a finish which can be employed with various caps embodying the screw principle. This is clearly illustrated in Figure S with a CT thread.

Figure T shows the finish used for the Vacuum Seal, all-glass cap, employing an inside sealing surface, and U illustrates the principle involved in finishing a bottle for a Spring Stopper closure. This, incidently, is the only closure for which threads are placed on the inside of the mouth.

While some closures have doubtless been omitted, and new ones are almost constantly making their appearance, practically every principle of wide and narrow mouth finish is here represented, and with the next article of this series which will appear in the August issue of THE GLASS PACKER the classification of caps and their various applications will be considered.

Selecting a Wide Mouth Closure to Meet Exact Packing Conditions

Glass Packer

Selecting a Wide Mouth Closure

To Meet Exact Packing Conditions

The Second Article of a Series Designed to Acquaint the Reader With the Various Types of Closures for Glass Containers

THE fundamental purpose of a closure is to confine the product within the container. To accomplish this requires more than physically retaining it within the jar. There must be no influx of air or liquid with the likelihood of re-infection of the product. When the container is sealed under a vacuum, this vacuum must be retained indefinitely. Furthermore, no reaction should occur between the product and the metal, liner, lacquer, or protective coating.

A closure is assumed to consist of three separate elements — the metal cap, the liner, and the finish of the glass. The purpose of the metal cap is to hold the liner in place, and no seal would be effective without a liner. In discussing the cap, we are interested chiefly in the manner in which it secures the liner in place, and also the manner in which the metal cap is removed; for it is in these features that metal caps differ.

Possibly before discussing the construction of metal caps, it may be advisable to briefly outline the various operations to which a closure may be subjected in the food packing field. Since we are concerned chiefly in this installment with the mechanical and physical features of the cap, no attention will be given to the liner or gasket.

There may be specific reasons in the mind of the packer on which he bases his selection of closure. Such are likely to be appearance, method of removal, or some other particular feature which in itself is logical, but does not take into account the manner in which the closure functions in every step of his packing operation. The packer should base his selection on an analytical study of his requirements and not on one particular feature of the closure in question.

Many failures in cap operation can be accredited directly to the use of a closure not suited to the type of processing employed. Failure may have been due to the inability of the liner to retain its shape at high temperature, or for instance in using a two-piece-screw cap in a water bath to have water retained in between the shell and the disc, causing rusting or discoloration. In effect, the two-piece screw cap gives an adequate seal, but the water retained above the disc ruins its appearance.

As a guide for the packer who wishes to make his selection on an analysis of his exact needs, an outline of the various conditions of sealing, processing, storage, and removal, which effect cap operation, is presented. The purpose of this outline is to illustrate the method of selection.

The outline gives the various conditions in four operations which might effect the behavior of a closure. If a closure under consideration is examined as to its behavior under each of these conditions, proper selection is assured.

Assume for instance, the selection of closures for products such as hard candy, coffee; mayonnaise, salad dressings; peanut butter; pickles, green olives, frankfurters and sauerkraut, vegetables, chicken and catsup; cider vinegar, fruit juices carbonated beverages. Each of these is packed processed, stored and opened under different conditions which determines the type of closure. They also have different chemical properties which require that the liner, gasket, or lacquer have the necessary resistance.

To make the outline more comprehensive a number of products have been selected which are packed under different methods and which differ in their action on the liner or lacquer. The various conditions effecting closure operation are given across the top of the table and the conditions applying to each product in the left-hand column indicated by check marks or notations. If a packer adds his product to this outline and indicates the conditions in a similar manner, he will be in a position to examine the closures considered in every detail of the required performance.

Under sealing, there is the nature of the product—

OUTLINE OF CONDITIONS EFFECTING CLOSURE OPERATIONS

Before selecting the closure for one's product, the conditions affecting closure operations should be analyzed. Using this chart as a guide such conditions may be readily outlined

Fig. 1.   One piece C. T. cap

Fig. 2.   Two piece cap and disc

Fig. 3.   Two piece ring and disc

whether it is an acidified brine, an oil, or a neutral liquid, a dry product, the temperature of the product and jar at time of sealing, whether packed under vacuum or atmospheric pressure. Each one of these will have some bearing on the selection. The temperature of processing and the internal pressure developed are also important factors to which due consideration must be given. It may be advantageous to employ a closure which will vent during process and thus relieve excessive internal pressure, but the cap must reseal after release of pressure to give a tight seal. No doubt there will be considerable variation in the diligence with which individual packers analyze the closure requirements. However, if such are reduced to an outline, it will not only afford an aggressive cap salesman increased opportunities to present the features of his closure, but it will assist the packer in understanding the closure operations, a lack of which has resulted in losses.

The mechanical features of the various closures have been the subject of but few articles, and so far no author has attempted to classify them. Since it is impossible to adequately consider all closures in one article, a division based on their use for wide or narrow mouth containers is made. In this case, narrow mouth is assumed to include up to 40 mm. sizes. This grouping is purely arbitrary, as certain closures are employed on both wide and narrow mouth containers.

SCREW CAPS

The cap employing the screw principle is perhaps the best known closure, and may properly head the list.

Fig. 4

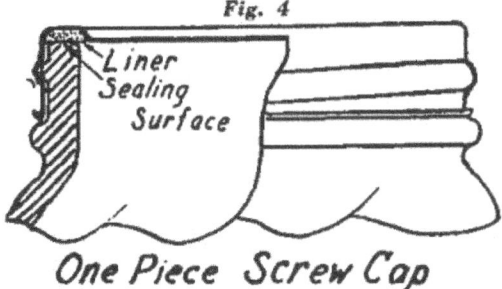

Liner
Sealing
Surface

One Piece Screw Cap

There are several variations grouped under this heading and collectively they represent a large portion of the closures used.

The screw cap, secured or removed by turning, is

the zenith of simplicity. No one can deny that the method of removal is obvious, which factor in a measure may account for its popularity. It also affords an excellent reseal or even reuse, both of which may have considerable merit, especially for certain products. As the closure for the Mason jar, it probably became familiar to many of us long before we gave any serious thought to closures. Its application is simple, and both manual or machine sealing operation may be employed.

Any one who remembers the early screw caps with their raw edges and uneven finishes will appreciate the advances in closures as exemplified by the modern C. T. (continuous thread) caps. By rolling the lower edge to give a wire finish, the sharpness has been eliminated. Knurled edges and pleasing designs contribute to the attractiveness of the complete package.

Three forms of the C. T. cap are available. First, the one piece cap which consists of a single metal shell with the thread turned on the metal skirt. The liner is generally a single disc covering the entire inner surface of the cap, although a ring or gasket of sufficient width to cover the upper surface of the jar may be employed. These are illustrated in Fig. 1.

The second form consists of a shell like the first, but there is an inner metal disc to which the gasket is secured. By using a separate disc the shell serves only to secure the disc and liner against the glass, and consequently, there is no hindrance to its removal due to any tendency of the liner to adhere to the glass. In Fig. 2 a complete cap and the separated disc and shell are shown.

A third form, Fig. 3, similar to the second, uses a ring instead of the whole cap to secure the disc. This form is generally employed as a vacuum seal and is so designated by some manufacturers.

In the C. T. caps, the sealing surface is on the top of the glass as illustrated in the sketch, Fig. 4. This also holds true for the modification of the screw cap with but one exception which will be mentioned later.

Several modifications of the C. T. cap intended to facilitate the removal of the cap are illustrated in Fig. 5.

On the extreme right is the Sur-Off cap. An embossed wavy bead which is directly over the contact of the liner and glass, when it is crushed, spreads the cap, loosening the pressure on the surface as well as

Fig. 5. Designed for easy removal   *Fig. 6. Divided thread caps*   *Fig. 7. Vacuum Amerseal cap*

the contact of the threads on the glass. This is claimed to positively break the seal.

In the center, is the Adams cap which has four humps or projections also intended for easy removal.

Still another modification is the Swan cap, illustrated on the left. In this cap, vertical ribs standing out from the thread give an additional grip for turning the cap. For those instances where this does not suffice, a light metal wrench which fits over the ribs gives still more leverage which can hardly fail to loosen the cap.

A modification is the manner of applying the screw principle. Illustrating the ingenuity of the cap manufacturers, is the divided thread. The purpose of this is to reduce the amount of twisting necessary to secure the cap. Actually, only a quarter turn is required to apply or remove a divided thread cap.

The Amerseal cap, formerly manufactured by the American Metal Cap Company, is a divided thread cap which made its bid for fame on the proposition that because of the quarter turn the product within the jar is easily accessible, and also that speed of cap application is increased. In form this closure resembles the C. T. cap except for the fact that instead of a thread on the skirt, there are two or three indentations or lugs which engage gradually pitched projections or sections of thread on the glass. Three forms—one-piece, two-piece, disc and ring are available. Several of these caps are illustrated in Fig. 6. One special form of the

Amerseal is known as the Vacuum Amerseal, illustrated in Fig. 7.

The Duplex cap, Fig. 8, utilizes the quarter turn. A pitch is given the three or four lugs on the cap, while the lobes on the glass finish are straight. By bending in sections of the skirt, the lugs are formed in such a manner that the skirt is absolutely smooth and devoid of indentations, although a knurled edge is employed on some caps. Several forms of this cap may be obtained to serve special purposes and may be employed for vacuum sealing. This closure is made both in one and two piece caps.

R. O. seals are, in the final analysis, screw caps, but caps which utilize a unique method applying to a screw finish. The cap as received by the packer, resembles a screw cap with the thread omitted. They are placed on the container, and in the sealing machine, the threads are rolled on the cap in conjunction with the thread on the bottle. It is in effect a "tailored" cap, not "ready cut." It is claimed that this method of securing the cap takes care of imperfections in the finish. Fig. 9 shows the cap as received, and after the thread has been rolled on the cap. These caps consist of an inner disc of tin plate, and an outer ring or capsule of light aluminum which can be readily shaped in the sealing machine. The disc carries the gasket or liner which makes the seal, as in other screw caps.

Another modification which concerns solely the seal-

Fig. 8. The Duplex cap

Fig. 9. R. O. seals

Fig. 10. Everseal caps

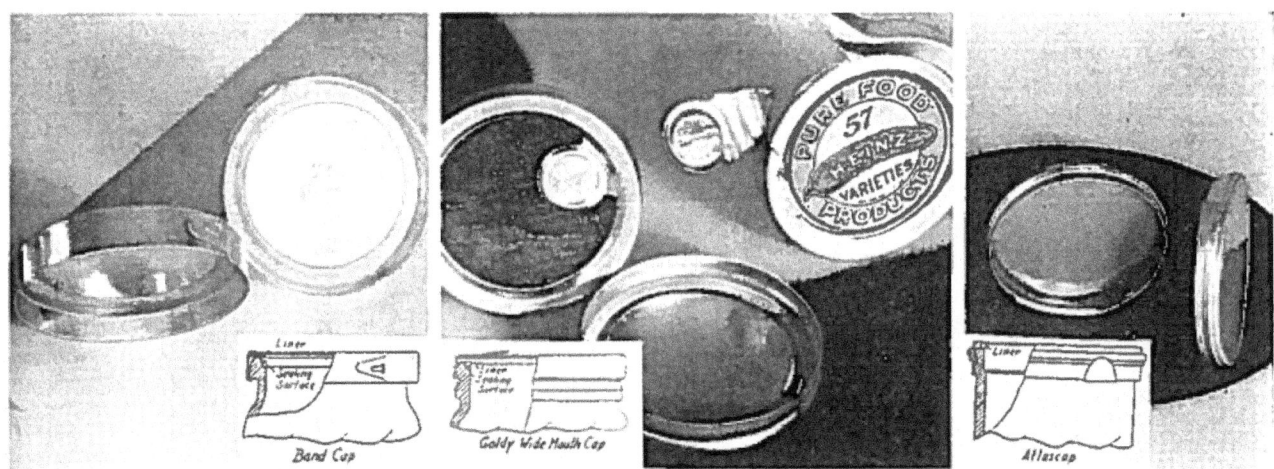

Fig. 11. The band cap   Fig. 12. The Goldy cap   Fig. 13. Atlas cap

ing surface is observed in the Everseal cap. A "double seal" feature is claimed by using the forms of glass finish shown in Fig. 10. The sealing surfaces are claimed to be the bottom and side of the ledge, instead of the single sealing surface on the top as with the ordinary screw cap. In all other respects, this closure corresponds to the ordinary C. T. cap.

The tremendous advance in the application of glass to food products requiring processing in the container is due in no small part to the development of special closures. Both the tightness of the seal and ease of removal are common characteristics which are, however, obtained by different methods. A tight seal is a comparatively simple proposition, but the removal is quite another matter. It is in this phase of closure operation, that the ingenuity and progressiveness of the cap manufacturer is evident. An excellent idea is worthless unless it can be built into a simple piece of metal, and it is particularly in the fabrication of metal caps, that the developments in technique have occurred. The proper shape, thickness of metal, correct dimensions, working of the metal without introducing weakness, and introduction of automatic machinery are accomplishments in this field.

These caps when equipped with the proper liner or gasket may be used in process either for pasteurization or sterilization. When employed on containers processed above 212° F. under pressure additional air pressure is generally employed to offset the internal pressure. None of these closures are limited to the process field. They can also be applied under vacuum for either hot or cold vacuumization. Generally, when employed as process caps they are vacuum sealed or applied to the product packed hot or given an exhaust. This is to reduce the internal pressure produced during processing.

BAND CAP

The band cap, a familiar closure, is a two-piece cap consisting of a metal disc and a band made with a clasp, both of tin plate. The disc carries the liner or gasket and is held in place by the ring the lower edge of which is rolled under the finish as illustrated in the sketch Fig. 11. To remove the cap, the clasp is opened freeing the ring and the disc pried off. The sealing surface is on the upper surface of the jar. Various types of liners can be employed and for processing, a composition rubber ring gasket is supplied as illustrated in the photograph.

GOLDY CAP

The Goldy cap is very similar in general construction to the band cap but utilizes a tearing action to remove the ring. This cap consists of a tin plate disc with a light aluminum ring with a tab. To apply the cap, a slight head pressure forces the liner against the finish and while in this position, the aluminum ring is rolled against the finish on the container thus securing the cap in place. As shown in the illustration, Figure 12,

Fig. 14. Upressit cap

Fig. 15. Anchor cap and opener

Fig. 16. Friction caps

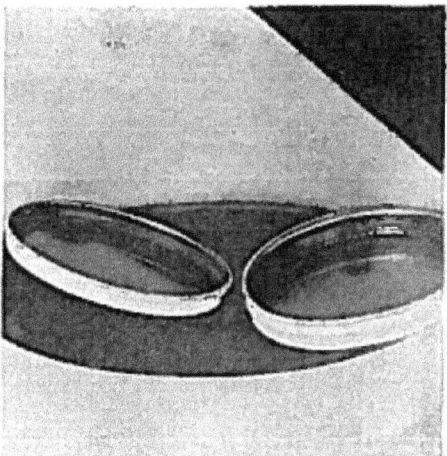

Fig. 17. Hazel cap   Fig. 18. The White cap   Fig. 19. The Swan cap

the tab tears down separating the ring, and the disc is pried off. Here also either liner or gasket may be used as desired depending upon whether the cap is employed for cold, hot, or processed products.

ATLAS CAP

The Atlas is a cap offered as a solution of the removal problem. A light aluminum one-piece cap with a rubber ring inserted in the side is applied under vacuum solely by top pressure. As the cap is forced in place, this rubber slips down over the finish, Figure 13, and when the vacuum in the chamber is released, the excess atmospheric pushes against the cap slightly flexing it inward. This action aids in tightening the seal. The removal of the cap is accomplished by pulling out one of the tabs and tearing off a strip near the edge until the cap is free. Since it is made of light aluminum and might be deformed by excessive pressure differences during processing, a special pressure control for controlling the balance pressure has been devised. The unit keeps a balanced pressure throughout the process.

UPRESSIT CAP

The Upressit cap is removed and applied exactly as its name suggests, Figure 14. It is constructed of fairly heavy tin plate with a fluted skirt turned under at the bottom. By pressing in the center, the skirt is forced away from the finish removing the cap. Pressing against the skirt snaps the center up, bringing the skirt against the glass. The sealing surface is against the top of the finish and a disc liner is employed. As a means of securing the seal, a ring with a tab for removal is employed.

FRICTION CAP

The Anchor or friction finish serves as the anchorage for a variety of metal caps differing in appearance, method of application and method of removal. As the name of the finish implies these closures are secured primarily by the friction grip against the side wall of the container. In most cases, a vacuum seal is used and the air pressure against the cap furnishes additional holding power. All the closures discussed in this group may be applied with or without vacuum.

Since the finish is named for the Anchor, this closure naturally heads the list. This is a one piece cap with the gasket inserted in a groove formed in the skirt. Before sealing, the cap fits loosely over the container

finish and its seal is effected by means of sealing chucks, dies, or rollers which vertically compress the skirt of the cap, thus forcing the sealing gasket in against the side surface of the container as illustrated in Figure 15. When employed on a process container, counterbalanced air pressure is employed to prevent failure of the closure. A special opener shown with the caps is widely distributed.

In addition to the above caps, there are the Anchor Clipper Caps—A, P, and R and the P. H. Snap Cap illustrated in Fig. 16. These caps are made with either a disc liner or a composition gasket for vacuum sealing. Head pressure applied to the caps forces it down over the glass where it is held in place by friction or vacuum. When a liner is used, the sealing surface is on the top and with a gasket on the side or outer edge. To remove the cap, it is pried off or if vacuum sealed, punctured and pried off.

Another closure employing the same finish but made of light aluminum is the Hazel Cap. This cap of one piece is forced in place by head pressure and the gasket which is located in the skirt as shown in Figure 17, is compressed as the cap slips over the container finish. No mechanical action other than head pressure is required to seat the cap. It is removed by tearing away a strip from the lower section of the skirt relieving pressure against the liner.

The White cap is one of the newer closures in this group. Here is a one-piece tin plate cap of unusual shape which is also solely applied by head pressure. Figure 18 gives an illustration of the closure applied to a container with the pry off finish. The gasket, a composition rubber ring, is in the skirt where it presses against the side of the container. It is claimed that this closure has unusual merit as a reseal friction cap.

The Swan Cap, Figure 19, is a recent addition to the list. The unique feature of this cap is the annular bead which when compressed reduces the diameter of the cap at this section bringing the metal in contact with the glass. The gasket is so located that the seal is made against the top and side. No mechanical action other than the compressing of the annular bead is required to effect the seal. There is no packing between the glass and metal where the grip is made.

A development in the Anchor cap to increase the holding power as a means of overcoming loss of clos-

(Continued on page 394)

Selecting a Closure

(Continued from page 383)

ures due to internal pressure is illustrated in Figure 15. A bead forming a ring around the glass is located so that the gasket is forced against it. The skirt of the cap is increased and turned under the gasket to prevent it from being blown out. This closure known as the Anchor D has increased resistance to internal pressure because of the positive grip secured by the bead.

No doubt much more could be written concerning every cap listed and the advantages or disadvantages of each might be thoroughly discussed, but much more space would be required. An attempt has been made to show by illustration the features of nearly every cap mentioned in this section of the article. It has been, however, impossible to bring out details, leaving this to the salesman who will, no doubt, zealously follow up any inquiries which may arise. In justice to all it might be stated that any closure of correct dimensions, provided liner and lacquer are right, and glass finish to G. C. A. specification should afford a satisfactory seal. The main differences lie in method and speed of application and means of removal.

The September issue of THE GLASS PACKER will bring the third article of this closure series, the subject to be, "Narrow Mouth Closures".

THE GLASS PACKER

Narrow Mouth Closures,
An Analysis of Representative Types

Glass Packer

Narrow Mouth Closures

An Analysis of Representative Types

Sealing Principles and the Relation Between Cap and Product
Are Studied in This Article—The Third of a Series on Caps and Closures

"WHAT closures are best suited for my product?" Some packers ask themselves this question and are stumped from the start; others ignor it entirely and blunder upon the first stopper that comes to their mind; still others make it a serious study and are rewarded by a better preserved product, less leakage and a more attractive and serviceable package. In this discussion of closures for narrow mouth containers, we shall take the packer's angle, and clear for him, as best we may, this perplexing closure problem.

In most cases more than one type of closure will serve a particular purpose, and therefore individual characteristics of all closures will be outlined. Originally any product placed in a narrow mouth container was retained by means of the stopper. This developed from a tapered section of natural cork into an extremely ornamental and useful closure. There is shown in figure 1 a series of cork stoppers. The tappered stopper (1) is the most common form, and its action is familiar to every one. Products which are constantly being used and which are more or less impervious to atmospheric conditions are best sealed with this type closure because of the ease of reseal. In cases where a hermetic seal is required the quality of the cork must be good. If it contains many connecting air spaces, "breathing" may occur. To offset this a special type of protective coating, made from cellulose products, is applied to the cork. This material comes in the shape of a cap which is dropped over the cork in a moist condition, and as it dries out, it shrinks tightly over the neck and stopper.

When a product is packed in an exceptionally large container, a larger size stopper (2) may be employed. It is simply a tapered stopper made of high quality

Which closure? For the sealing of one's product there are many from which to choose

cork. In the case of beverages or other products which are to be stoppered under pressure, the straight stopper (3) is serviceable. This will fit well down into the neck of the container and withstand high internal pressure.

For bottling a commodity that must have more than the ordinary care due to perhaps rough handling or the likelihood of staining, special stoppers (4, 5, 6) are commonly used. The wood, cork or composition top is added to make a closer fitting seal which is not easily dislodged. An appeal to the artistic is made through cork stoppers fashioned in out of the ordinary shapes (7, 8). Some decorative coating is often applied which adds to the appearance.

Every one who is interested in packing meat sauces or vinegar will recognize the cork shell (9) used in conjunction with a glass top in sprinkler top bottles. Ammonia and strong chemical solutions are usually stoppered with a rubber seal (10). When a bottle contains substances such as shoe polish or a solution which is used carefully and sparingly, a stopper of cork or rubber (11, 12) allows for application with the minimum possibility of undesired contact and waste.

Such commodities as iodine, manicure preparations, mercurochrome, etc., which are likely to evaporate or stain, can be effectively sealed with stoppers such as are included in figure 2. Their important feature is the employment of an inside thread instead of depending upon friction between the stopper and the glass. In the case of such products as mentioned there is added an applicator rod which is moulded in one piece with the seal and stopper. The illustration shows the clear glass stopper with an outside thread which is brought in contact with the top surface of the container by the action of the screw thread. Mineral oils, liquid shampoos. etc.. are examples of products using this latter type of stopper. Other types are made of

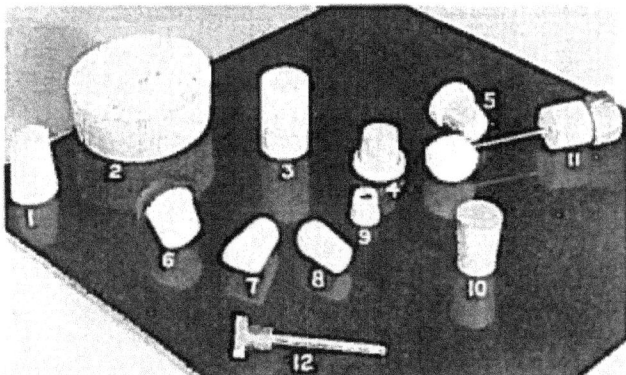

Fig. 1. *Various cork stoppers*

porcelain and composition materials such as Durez and Bakelite.

The bottler of carbonated beverages, pasteurized milk, chocolate milk drinks, distilled water, etc., needs no introduction to the crown type of cap. It hardly seems necessary to say anything about its application or removal. It consists of a single piece of metal with a turned over, fluted skirt which is forced down around the finish of the bottle by the action of a metal throat through which the cap is forced. The seal is

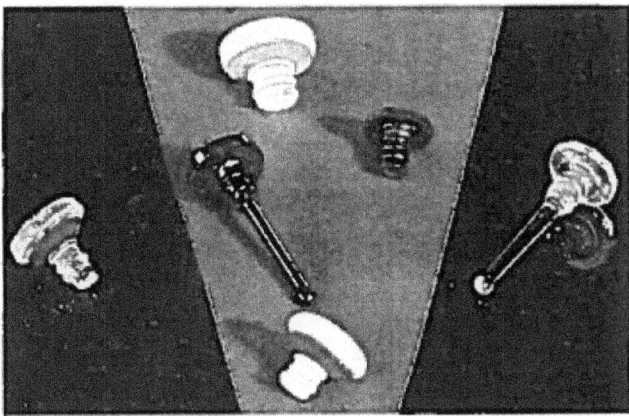

Fig. 2. *Stoppers employing an inside thread*

made against the top surface. The cap is applied with high head pressure, thereby compressing the gasket or liner which in the ordinary crown is a compo cork or natural cork disk. This particular closure, because of the crimping action under the ring forming the finish. will withstand very high internal pressure. and therefore is used almost universally as a closure for carbonated beverages.

Several varieties of crown caps are illustrated in figure 3. The one shown at the extreme right is a modification of the ordinary crown. known as the supper crown. This particular closure has a long skirt and the gasket is a rubber ring which seats against the ledge on the outside of the top, giving a double seal. This particular closure because of the long skirt can also withstand considerable internal pressure. It is

made in sizes from 44 mm. to 80 mm. which really puts it in the wide mouth class, but as it was developed from the ordinary crown closure, it is included in this article. Figure 3 also pictures a small size anchor cap which will fit the crown finish. This style of cap has been discussed in a preceding article.

Another cap. designed for use on milk bottles, and known as the Saniseal, shown in figure 3. is essentially a crown, though somewhat altered to suit the milk bottle finish, and serve as a protection for the lip. This

Fig. 3. *Crowns*

is easily removed and can be used as a cover cap in place of the paper.

A packer usually has two or three factors to take into consideration when selecting his closure. If he depends chiefly upon the appearance of his product, as a sales factor, he must have a closure that is especially harmonious to the container and product insofar as size, shape and finish are concerned. If. on the other hand, service and easy access to the commodity are prime considerations, he must pick a closure that is of sturdy construction and able to withstand much usage

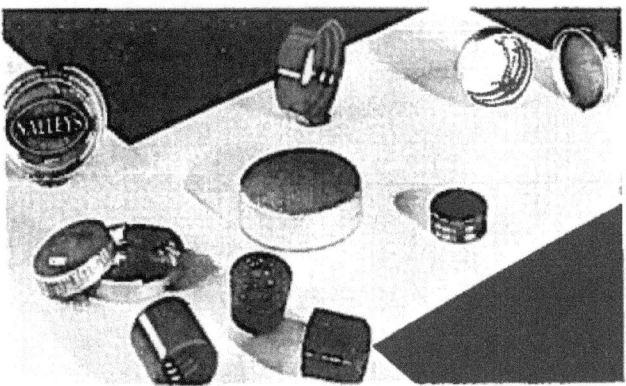

Fig. 4. *Many types are available*

without sacrificing an attractive appearance. Perhaps for competitive reasons, it is necessary for him to keep down the price of his product, in which case he will want an inexpensive yet reliable closure. Whatever the requirement may be, the packer can secure among others a variety of closures of the screw cap type. This form of closure has long been a popular one. Products ranging from beauty preparations and medicinal oils to sauces and dressings besides countless other articles are sealed under various screw caps. Such caps are made from tin plate, aluminum, brass, nickel plate, bakelite, durez or composition materials utilizing several kinds of liners. They range in size from 14 mm. up to 38 mm. Both the C T cap and the divided thread cap are available in sizes for narrow mouth containers (figure 4). Three other types of caps, the R O which is applied to the screw finish, the Goldy seal and the Upressit cap, are also made in small sizes for narrow mouth containers.

While the screw caps are used for a great diversity of products, there are, however, some unique caps which have special features making them exceptionally efficient in satisfying exacting requirements and personal tastes. One example is the Williams Kork-N-Seal (figure 5). Containers for oil, French Dressings, beverages, cider, vinegar, etc., use this rather unusual type of closure. The Williams cap has a perforated metal skirt with the ends of the flaps rolled over to secure a metal wire run through the skirt and hooked at each end. A heavier wire, so made that by turning it down the wire in the cap is drawn together, firmly clamps the skirt of the cap in against the finish. When this cap is applied, head pressure forces the glass up tightly against the gasket or liner and a device pushing down the metal, clamps the cap on securely. To remove the cap it is only necessary to pry up this lever which loosens the wire and the cap is free to be removed.

The new Goldy lug seal has the advantages of the Goldy seal plus the reseal feature. The tin disc used in the closure is equipped with metal lubs which hold the disk down against the top surface of the jar and allow for replacement after the capsule has been torn off.

To seal bottles containing powders and similar dry products, there has been evolved a heavy paper seal. This has a cork shape center which fits into the neck of the bottle and continues up and over the edge of the mouth. The paper has tiny corrugations which give it elasticity and hold in against the top ring of the bottle. To remove this the edge of the cap is gently forced up (see figure 5).

A cap known as the Sterling Closure employs 3 or more lugs to effect engagement with the bottle. A downward pressure is applied at the time the cap is rotated ¼ turn to a stop. While the cap is still under pressure the annular ring is compressed slightly, after which the pressure is removed and a seal results. The cap can be removed by hand and provides a reseal (see figure 5).

The Save-a-seal and Super seal caps are special types of narrow mouth closures designed so that they can be removed without destroying the reseal possibilities of the closure. The Save-a-seal utilizes the top sealing surface, and the Superseal is essentially the same cap but with a modification of the closure so that a ledge below the top seal is employed rather than the top sealing surface. This closure is secured to the container by rolling under the lower edge of the skirt. A metal tab permits the lower edge of the skirt which is scored to be drawn off, thus freeing the seal. This cap may be slipped over the top of the container as a reseal.

To catsup and condiment packers the closure illustrated in figure 6 will be familiar. It consists of a cover cap which is intended to fit as a reseal after the original seal has been removed. There are two types, a friction or snap cap, and a screw cap. They are planned for use over a crown, goldy or handycap. This type of closure furnishes an excellent seal for any product which if allowed to run over on the threads, might harden and cause difficulty in removing. A combination Goldy seal and loose fitting screw cover cap illustrates the possibilities of this arrangement. The Goldy cap gives the original seal, and when opened by removing the ring, the screw cover cap can be used to force the disc in place for reseal purposes.

On products where it is desired to show that the contents have not been tampered with, a seal used in connection with the R O closure is employed such as is illustrated in figure 7. This consists of an ordinary R O seal, which has already been discussed, but attached to it is a metal skirt with two flaps which can be covered by the label or any other means to prevent interference with the seal without visible evidence.

There are one or two specially constructed caps which are good examples of how caps can be adapted to meet various needs. A familiar one is that used for

Fig. 5. Special feature caps   *Fig. 6. Cover caps*   *Fig. 7. Tamper-proof*

paste bottles. It is the usual screw cap with a raised hood in the center which permits the brush to remain in the jar after sealing. Another is the one which includes a rubber bulb and medicine dropper as part of the closure. Cork stoppers and bakelite caps sometimes have brushes inserted at the base thereby using the

Fig. 8. Special closures

closure as a handle. Examples of special closures are shown in figure 8.

Two types of all glass containers which are used extensively for home canning but are sometimes employed commercially are the Mason and Lightning. The seal in the Mason jar is usually made on a sealing shoulder about ¾ in. below the top of the jar. The tops are made of either glass or porcelain with a screw cap to hold the cover in position. This screw cap sometimes fits just around the neck of the bottle and over the edge of the glass top or else comes further

up to cover most of the glass top. Two types of this jar are shown in figure 9.

The Lightning jar effects a seal by means of a rubber ring fitted on the sealing shoulder and a glass cover placed over it. A heavy wire passes over the top fitting into a notch in the center of the cover and is held down to the top by a wire clamp at the side of the jar.

A container similar to the Lightning is the Vacuum Seal jar which utilizes the unique feature of a valve action top. This is obtained by having a sloping inside wall at the neck of the jar and using this side wall as the sealing surface, with a light spring clamp over the top holding the gasket against the sealing surface. The seal is produced solely by the vacuum created by exhausting with the cover in place relying upon the valve action of the top to permit the escape of vapor, but preventing the entrance of vapor or liquid. It is opened by prying out the rubber gasket to break the vacuum (figure 9).

The Presto jar is similar to the Mason, using a light aluminum ring to secure the glass top in place. A rubber ring, forced against the sealing surface by screwing down on the metal ring accomplishes the seal.

Another type of all-glass containers is the bottle used for salts, chemicals, etc., which has a glass stopper the base of which is ground to the inside surface of the neck of the bottle. With a slight pressure this stopper becomes firmly fixed. A knob at the top of the stopper facilitates removal.

The October issue of THE GLASS PACKER will bring the fourth article of this closure series, the subject to be, "Lacquers and Liners"

Fig. 9. Mason, Presto, Lightning and Vacuum Seal jars

The How and Why of Liners as the Most Important Factor in Securing a Perfect Seal

Glass Packer

The How and Why of Liners

As the Most Important Factor in Securing a Perfect Seal

The Fourth Article of a Series Dealing With Closures
Which Will Help the Packer Select Them More Intelligently

OF the three elements of a closure, the glass finish, the metal cap, and the liner, the last is decidedly first in importance to a perfect seal. The liner unites the glass finish and the metal cap and determines the tightness of the seal. There is no doubt that the major portion of closure failures can be attributed to the improper liner, and therefore a closure selection made with due regard to the suitability of the liner should reduce the probability of closure failures.

However, in order to prevent any rash conclusions regarding closure failures, it is stated that insufficient headspace, poor filling machine operation, and various other causes may be solely responsible. With the ever increasing complexity of products sealed in glass, the cap manufacturer is called upon to meet very unusual conditions. He certainly cannot be expected to produce a closure capable of withstanding some of the abuse a packer may thoughtlessly give it.

In this series of articles the one predominant thought has been to assist the packer in selecting his closure. Obviously he alone must make the final decision, as personal tastes and price carry considerable weight. In some instances probably too much weight. Therefore, in presenting this material the authors who know by experience the attitude of both packer and cap salesman, have stressed suitability of the closure for the particular job from start to finish—from sealing to opening—considering the various factors in sealing operation, sales appeal, method of opening, and reseal.

Everything that has been said on the subject of selection of caps holds true for liners. Since this element actually accomplishes the seal, determines the tightness, protects the products and in fact stands guard against internal or external contamination, it is obvious

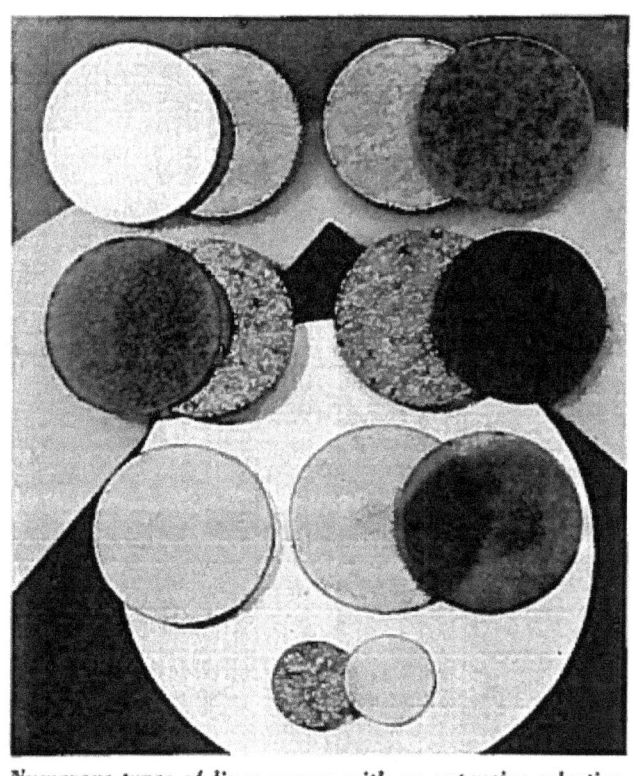

Numerous types of liner papers with an extensive selection of backings meet every packing requirement

that much depends upon the proper selection. There is, of course, the suitability of the liner for the particular closure in question; but that is distinctly the cap manufacturer's problem and should not concern the packer. There have been instances, however, where cap manufacturers have been at fault due primarily to the meager information given them by the packer, and in some cases their limited knowledge of the processes employed.

One entirely erroneous conclusion on the part of the packer is that just because a certain particular liner is being used for a specified product, that is proof of its suitability. On the contrary, price, appearance, or lack of knowledge may have determined the selection, and therefore the only safe procedure is to obtain definite assurance based on extensive experience or laboratory tests. Many of the cap companies, as well as the Glass Container Association, have laboratories which are available to the packer for conducting suitable liner tests. There should be no legitimate excuse.

Whatever the material employed to complete the closure, the first requisite is naturally proper functioning to produce a tight seal. Considering the variety of metal caps with different means of securing them to the container, different sealing surfaces, different head pressures, there can be no wonder that there is no universal medium, but rather a similar variety of material. Considering also the multitude of products, all varying in chemical and physical characteristics, and subjected to processing temperatures ranging from 150° F. to 250° F., it is apparent that such a multiplicity of conditions can only be met by a wide range of materials. Even to enumerate these would require considerable space. It will be necessary to confine the article to representative types.

By way of introduction it may be advisable to differentiate between liner and gasket, as there is apparently some confusion regarding the difference. A liner is a disc which covers the entire inside surface of the metal cap, protecting the cap surface, and extending over the sealing surface. A gasket is a ring only of sufficient size to cover the sealing surface. The inner surface of the cap is unprotected except by the lacquer.

Since liners, more than gaskets, are the immediate concern of the packer, they will be considered first. It appears that many packers think of the liner solely as the means of giving an air tight seal. Primarily this is one object to be accomplished; but actually it is only a small part of the whole story. The liner must protect the product against contamination; it must in no way affect the product or be effected by it; and the appearance must be satisfactory after long storage periods. When the multiplicity of products is considered this is no small task for the liner manufacturer. One other important item is the storage life of unused closures. The liner must retain its usable properties under what are sometimes extremely unfavorable conditions. All these requirements demand a fairly sizeable list of material stock in the cap manufacturer's plant and therefore represents an expense. No doubt, a universal liner would be welcomed by the entire industry.

Assume, for instance, the ordinary screw cap. The liner, a disc, is inserted in the cap. The center section is in contact with the product. The outer section is pressed against the glass. In order to give a satisfactory seal the liner itself or the backing must have sufficient resiliency to take up slight variations in the glass finish and also to retain the original tightness of the seal against lessening of the cap pressure due to temperature changes.

When the screw cap is twisted into position the liner must slide easily over the glass. Likewise, after storage and when opened there should be no sticking of the liner to the glass hindering the removal of the cap. With two piece caps or the R. O. seal there is no sliding action and this does not have to be considered.

What has been said regarding the requirements of liner materials is necessarily sketchy, but it is ample to enable the packer to appreciate the closure problem as it concerns the liner. The next logical step is to discuss the liner materials available.

In order to produce a disc to cover the entire jar opening of the wide mouth type, practically the only material of reasonable cost available is paper or a paper pulp product. Untreated paper would not be practical for many applications, and therefore various treatments and coatings have been developed to give the necessary physical and chemical characteristics. While there are a large number of such papers of different types, it will only be necessary to discuss a relatively small number to illustrate them.

The simplest type of paper liner is a wax treated paper. Such a coating tends to eliminate any minor defects in the neck of the jar. It does, of course, have definite limitations as to temperature since the melting point of wax is much below some packing processes. Such a coating tends to prevent excessive moisture evaporation. Wax treated liners are produced as a thin paper backed by some resilient material, or a heavy pulp board, wax coated on one side only. Wax or parafine imparts no odor or flavor and the clean appearance of white wax is a distinct advantage.

Other types of paper finding extensive application in the food and drug industry are varnished paper. To a very large degree these appear to be the universal liner material, subject, however to definite limitations based on processes. Such paper must meet the following general requirements. It must not be affected by or affect the product. It must be non-porous and prohibit the passage of air or gases. Moisture effects should be as low as possible. In order to produce a satisfactory seal it must be flexible and should have considerable resistance to abrasion. These papers, generally termed oiled papers, are extensively employed for jams, jellies, pickles, mayonnaise and similar products. By careful selection of the base papers successive varnish film can be baked on without producing a brittle product. In general some form of vegetable drying oil with possibly the addition of some gum constitute the varnish. They do, however, show a somewhat high evaporation loss, and in some instances are wax coated as a means of further increasing their resistance to moisture.

A third type is the black varnished paper having an asphaltic base, or like products compounded with certain types of oils baked on. This liner has certain advantages such as a lower moisture absorption, resistance to practically everything that any other liner is resistant to, and a deal more. Its greater expense and color are handicaps, although its superior resistance is an advantage for products containing alkalies and alcohols.

One of these has a white coating made from a special oil, possesses a high degree of chemical inertness and toughness. This is claimed to be due to the fact that the oil sets by condensation rather than exidation producing a film of different nature.

Where papers fail, metal foils enter. Liners of tin foil, combinations of tin and lead, and aluminum foil, are used with a backing for products which affect papers. Pure tin foil must be employed when the chemical reaction of the product is such that it corrodes lead and not tin, or where the use of lead would be objectionable. In fact there would be a saving in employing a composition foil. Such composition foils range from low percentages of lead up to 97 per cent lead and 3 per cent tin.

Pure tin foil is employed on beverages, especially with waters, where it is believed by some that varnished papers have a tendency to taint the water. It finds application on a few food products and those pharmaceuticals of such chemical composition that tin-lead alloys would be impractical.

There is one serious drawback to a metal foil liner and that is that any roughness on the glass finish cuts holes in it, and corrosion may take place. The same objection holds true for varnished papers when the caps are applied under heavy head pressure. This is sometimes overcome by the use of a spot, or smaller disc covering only the center portion of the cap back-

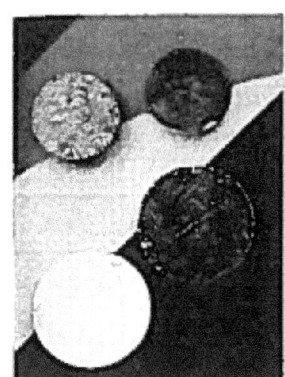   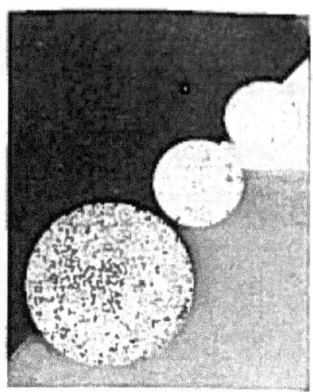

Liners and backings for both wide and narrow mouth closures. Note the extensive use of cork and varnished paper "spot" liners for certain products sealed with crowns

ing, and not extending over the sealing surface. One special example of this is the paper or metal spot employed on carbonated beverage caps.

The use of a wax coating on paper or heavy pulp liners has already been mentioned. In some instances this wax coating is applied to the surface of the backing to prevent that moisture which penetrates the paper liner from affecting the backing. In the sealing of oils which show a tendency to creep, special coatings, one of which is casein, are applied to the metal liner.

Since paper or foil is very thin, it is necessary to employ some sort of backing to give resiliency. These backing or padding materials consist of heavy pulp, composition cork, or felt. What type is employed depends upon the type of cap, and size, since larger cap size means relatively higher cap cost, and consequently increased cost of his product. Here the packer must cooperate with the cap manufacturer to obtain the proper combination.

One of the most common materials which serves both as a liner and padding is cork. Here is a product with a long record of use as a sealing material. It served as the earliest seal, and even today ranks as an important member of the list of sealing materials.

The cork oak bark as removed from the tree contains both good and poor materials. As the new product contains the pores of the bark, careful selection and cleaning is necessary to produce natural cork liners of perfect qualities. The difficulties in accomplishing this at a reasonable cost resulted in the foundation of the composition cork type of liner.

There has not as yet appeared any substitute for cork, and improvements in methods of manufacturing composition cork have strengthened its position. In place of the original process of grinding the cork to pass through a definite size screen, the present highly developed method produces particles of special shape which laboratory studies have shown to be best adapted for composition cork uses. A close-up structure is obtained by mixing definite proportions of varying sized particles. Repeated treatments rid the cork of all hard particles.

Binders consist of some albuminous product such as glue, albumen or casein, mixed with water and glycerine. A small amount of some formaldehyde producing chemical may be added to the mix. Recently a new binder, a synthetic resin material, has been introduced.

It is obvious that any binder consisting of albuminous materials is liable to mold. Also, if the binder itself has a relatively low softening point sterilization of the sealed container may give trouble. Special binders of synthetic resins eliminate the possibility of mold growth and show greater resistance in processing.

As a backing, composition cork furnishes a resilient material especially suitable for many closures. As a liner, depending upon the binder and whether it is wax coated or not, it fulfills the requirement of many products.

For backing material besides pulp and composition cork, there is felt which can be obtained in several forms to meet special requirements.

One rather interesting and unique development in liners is Filmaseal. By employing a transparent cellulose product fixed to the sealing surface of the glass container with an adhesive, the product is retained behind a hermetic seal which becomes a part of the con-

Where a protective lacquer shields the metal surface of the cap a rubber ring or gasket over the glass finish usually makes an efficient seal. Types of rings, rubber and cork gaskets and flow-in rubber gaskets are illustrated

tainer independent of the closure. This material in the form of a disc fits inside the metal cap over the conventional liner. By applying the adhesive to the glass the Filmaseal disc is secured to the glass when the cap is applied. As illustrated, removing the cap leaves the film seal as a transparent cover easily cut or torn out with the original liner intact for reseal purposes.

Many cap manufacturers who make a sincere effort to supply their customers with the best results obtainable carry an extensive stock of liner materials. Other manufacturers believe that relatively few materials are sufficient to meet the needs of the users of glass containers. Most cap manufacturers, where liners are concerned, have lists of products giving the first and second choice. When such lists are based on laboratory tests or successful operations their reliability cannot be questioned and the packer will be wise in listening to the advice of the cap manufacturer. When it comes to new products a laboratory test is the only reliable procedure.

There are other liners or combinations available such as composition rubber for small size caps, heavy paper liners for crowns, and oil paper pulp backed liners with a rubber gasket. These few illustrations will convey the possibilities of special combination.

GASKETS

Many caps are used without liners, depending upon the protective coating on the metal. Such coatings or

A new type of seal—the mouth of the container is sealed with cellophane

lacquers are generally vegetable products applied to the whole sheet metal before the cap is formed. These sheets are run through ovens and baked. To give special resistance, several coats of lacquer may be employed. Many manufacturers have compounded special lacquers and they employ whichever one is best suited for the product to be sealed. In general the base of these lacquers is some vegetable gum although other materials, sometimes synthetic, may be added to toughen or increase the chemical resistance.

When greater resistance is required the inner surface of the cap may be coated with an enamel. For special acid food products such enamels afford excellent protection.

In one of the earlier articles on metal caps the use of a gasket fitted into the cap and pressed against the sealing surface was discussed. Such gaskets may be made of composition cork, rubber, or compo or special sealing compounds.

As composition cork has already been discussed it is only necessary to say that such a gasket consists of a ring covering the sealing surface and fixed to the cap by some adhesive.

Rubber gaskets are known to everyone since many of the present day closures employ them. As sealing rings for the home canning jar they are widely known. Since rubber is exceptionally resilient, it takes up irregularities, and being inert toward many products, it contributes to the operation of many closures.

Composition rubber rings or gaskets are made in special shapes and of definite composition to meet the specific requirements of the closure with which they are employed. This composition rubber is essentially a mixture of rubber with special filler softened by solvents such as gasoline or benzol. Much work has been done on these materials to give them the proper physical charactertistics and increase their life. This material is generally produced in the form of a ring which is inserted in the cap and held in place by the shape of the cap or an adhesive.

Still another form of gasket of which there are two general types, is the flowed-in rubber compounds. These materials are applied as a heavy liquid and the solvent dried out in an oven. The major differences of these two materials has been established by advertising and the sales effort of the interested concerns. Much development work has been done with these materials to meet the various requirements of the packing industry. In the developing of these compounds special attention has been given to the requirements of various types of closures. With the screw cap there is a sliding action to eliminate the tendency to adhere to the closure, and therefore make easier the removal of the seal; for those caps where there is an exceptionally high head pressure, it is possible to so adjust the compound that there will not be excessive flowing of the material and thus a loosening of the seal.

In presenting this article we have covered the various types of material employed for liners and gaskets. No attempt has been made to lay down any exact statements for their particular use, since there apparently is no real agreement between cap manufacturers, and no hard and fast rules available. The differences in closures, in the metals of which they are constructed, the method in which they are sealed, and other factors so complicate the whole question that it would be practically impossible to set up any definite rules. To the packer we might make the following suggestion: that if he has confidence in the reliability of the cap manufacturer, he give attention to his recommendations, not permitting the question of price to be the sole deciding factor, since loss of the product might more than offset the additional gain in production cost.

All Caps Have Changed Since 1928, and Some Are Entirely New

Glass Packer

All Caps Have Changed Since 1928

and Some are Entirely New

FIGURE 1.

No matter what you work at—purchasing, production, or sales—you need all the information you can get about the materials you work with.

This thought certainly should apply to packages, and especially to closures, which are available in such a variety as to be rather confusing, when viewed *en masse*. Besides, the closure user has another problem—to keep up with the changes and improvements which are constantly being made. There is not one seal on the market today which has not been changed in some important way during the past ten years, and during the same length of time a number of new caps have come on the market which were entirely unknown before 1928.

A closure, of any kind, looks like a simple invention, but like a lot of other simple things which are taken for granted, it is a complex development—the product of many minds—and usually has reached its present form by a process of evolution. There is no better way to learn what is new and significant in closures than to study this evolutionary process and see what American inventive and technical ability have been doing to one of the "important little things of life," the bottle cap.

It would, of course, be possible to begin at the beginning, and a very fascinating "history of the art of sealing" could be written, covering the subject from ancient times down to the present day. But this would hardly be as useful to the reader as a discussion of what has happened during recent years. For it is a fact that the last ten years have marked a new era in closure methods. Some very far-reaching changes and innovations have come to pass in that period. Most of these, resulting from continued research by the closure manufacturer, have been gradual improvements, so that their advent has been less spectacular than practical and the total effect of all these changes is apt to be lost sight of in the general picture as it exists today.

Coming of the molded closure

Ten years ago the molded closure was unknown. In a surprisingly short time it became widely used[1] and was a factor stimulating improvements in other types of closures. At first the relatively high cost of the resinoid molding compounds and the lack of high-speed molding equipment limited the use of molded caps to high priced drugs and toilet articles. Many of the early molded caps were made to fit special mold bottles and it was some time before threads were standardized to GCA specifications.[2] Thus, history of the molded cap paralleled that

---

[1] Production by 1933 had risen to 439,092,000 caps for that year. Four years later, in 1937, molders turned out 704,803,000 closures.

of early metal screw caps, which did not become widely used until threads had been standardized. And like the metal screw cap, the molded closure was helped along the road to success by its adoption for prescription ware, which not only provided a large market but made the public familiar with its advantages. Molded caps are now made in a great variety of styles suitable for a very long list of products. (Fig. 1)

Molded caps have been improved in a great many ways since their first appearance. Probably in no other branch of the cap industry have such rapid strides been made. Better molding compounds have been developed, and certain molders now produce these caps by means of completely automatic machines which permit an accurately regulated time cycle for the molding and curing process,

as well as uniform wall thickness resulting in stronger and better appearing closures. Construction for holding liners in place has been improved. The range of colors has been tremendously broadened. The first caps were made of phenol formaldehyde materials, which limited the colors. Urea formaldehyde materials are used today to provide white, ivory and pastel shades. Both transparent and opaque molded caps can now be made in every color of the spectrum. Design is possible in almost any kind of surface molding to harmonize with the form of the completed package, thus advancing the trend to "streamlining" of packages. The fact that molded caps are inert to the chemical action of many products, has also contributed in no small measure to their rapidly increased usage. Still another advantage, perhaps not so important as it was in the beginning, is that molded plastic threads "slip" easily on glass threads, making a closure that is very easy to remove.

That the molded cap was a competitive force in the improvement of metal caps would be readily admitted by any cap man. Its cost alone kept it from becoming a serious threat to one of the oldest, and the most widely used of all commercial closures, the metal screw cap.

[2] First known user of a molded closure was The Mennen Co., on collapsible tubes, in 1920. The method of manufacture then used was too costly to permit more than a trial of this cap. Several years later, E. R. Squibb & Sons, Colt's Patent Fire Arms Mfg. Co. and General Plastics, Inc., joined in successful development of closures for tubes, and later, for bottles. It is believed that McIlhenny's Tabasco Sauce was the first glass packed product to carry a molded cap, which was supplied by Colt's. A line of stock molded closures with GCA standard thread was first advertised by Anchor Cap & Closure Corporation in 1931. One of the first very large users of molded caps on bottles was the Pepsodent Co., whose antiseptic, advertised by Amos 'n' Andy, was placed on the market in 1931.

Improvements in Metal Screw Caps

Great improvements have been made in metal screw closures, and an analysis of these provides an insight into cap lore which is illuminating, to say the least.

Perhaps the most noteworthy innovation in these closures in the past ten years, were the caps with concealed threads or lugs (Fig. 2), in which group the double shell is particularly prominent. The first general announcements of this cap came in 1931.[3] Molded closures had helped to make manufacturers in certain fields "style conscious," and the makers of metal caps responded with the double shell cap, an efficient and substantial closure, possessing an attractive appearance not possible in a cap with visible threads. The double shell prospered because it has much of the beauty of the molded closure, with certain advantages of its own, particularly strength, which was not always adequate in early molded caps, especially in the larger sizes. It also had a distinct advantage in adaptability for decoration by coatings and lithography.

One-piece shell

The one-piece or single shell closures[4] with concealed lugs or threads deserve special mention, particularly as they represent a high degree of mechanical ingenuity on the part of the closure manufacturer and make available, at less cost to the user, a cap in which the sealing mecha-

nism is not visible, and which can therefore assume its share in "smoothing out" the package design. In construction of these caps, deserved attention is given to the matter of sealing efficiency, since a closure that fails even in part to perform this function, is a liability, regardless of its external appearance. Single shell closures with concealed lugs are truly effective in this respect, a fact sometimes doubted by prospective users unfamiliar with the attention given to this feature by the manufacturer, who goes to considerable lengths to insure the rugged lug construction embodied in this type of cap. (*Continued on page 691*)

FIG. 2. *Concealed thread and concealed lug caps, both single and double shell, are today available in any color, plain or decorated, with various types of dome aand skirt design.*

[3] THE GLASS PACKER, Oct., 1931, p. 544, carried announcements of this type of closure by Phoenix-Hermetic Co. (now Phoenix Metal Cap Co.) and by National Seal Co. It was also stated that the new type of cap would also be supplied by Closure Service Corporation (now a division of Owens-Illinois Glass Co.) A patent was granted to Phoenix on March 15, 1932. Various patents have since been granted on different methods of assembling the two cap shells.

[4] The first one-piece metal cap with concealed lugs was the Duplex, of National Seal Co., which has been on the market considerably more than the ten years covered by this survey. In Jan., 1935, the Unishell was advertised in THE GLASS PACKER, being the first one-piece metal cap with concealed screw threads.
New types of concealed lug caps were subsequently introduced by other manufacturers.

FIG. 3. *These visible thread caps are types which were unknown ten years ago. Illustrated are new forms of dome construction, thread design and such features as the turned in edge and elimination of knurling to improve appearance.*

Very important changes have been made in thread construction of metal screw cap (Fig. 3), which can readily be seen by comparing a standard visible thread cap of today with a similar closure of 1928. Changes in shape and contour, making a more sharply indented thread, have made screw closures more efficient—by which is meant that more of the force of application is utilized in making a seal and less of it wasted in friction. This means, from a practical standpoint, that closures with the more highly developed thread, while making a better seal, are in addition considerably easier to remove. In this connection, attention should be directed to the "lubricated" gasket materials which have helped to make certain screw closures easy to remove.

A further development in thread design was the more *abrupt*, as contrasted with the older tapered, or gradual,

CO-AUTHORS OF THIS SYMPOSIUM

This group of articles on ten years' progress in glass container closures is probably the most comprehensive treatment of the general subject of closures ever published. It would not have been possible without the cooperation of a group of men who gave unsparingly the benefits of their long experience in the industry.

THE GLASS PACKER wishes to acknowledge particularly the help of the following individuals and companies:

D. M. Gray, Closure Division, Hazel-Atlas Glass Co; H. J. Higdon and Lindsay Crabbe, Phoenix Metal Cap Co; R. F. Delaplane, Closure Sales Division, Owens-Illinois Glass Co; George P. White and C. M. Roberts, White Cap Co; L. C. McAuliffe, Mundet Cork Corporation; P. C. Doyle, Ferdinand Gutmann & Co; J. H. Gilliley, Anchor-Hocking Glass Corporation; George P. Edmonds, Bond Manufacturing Corporation; J. E. Sharp. Norman Olsen and G. H. Fitch, Aluminum Seal Co; H. S. Spencer, General Plastics, Inc; M. Stewart Ireys and Clark Samuel, Armstrong Cork Products Co; L. L. Lauve and John Kastendyke, Crown Cork & Seal Co; P. S. O'Reilly, National Seal Co, Don Masson, The Bakelite Corporation.

start of the thread. This is said to have much to do with positive engagement of the cap thread and the glass finish. A tapered thread might "ride up" on the glass thread, but the abrupt thread must engage under the finish thread or it is not engaged at all.[5]

To maintain standards of thread contour and also to study actual cap and glass thread contact and engagement, use is made of contour projection apparatus which provides a greatly magnified outline of the conditions inside the closure. Optically enlarging comparators are therefore utilized not only for research but also for production control and inspection.[6] (Fig. 4)

The shape or form of the top of a closure is also a factor of some importance and one to which considerable study has been given. The top, whether flat or domed, indented or raised, or of the numerous other forms or combinations available, determines in many instances the degree of sealing effectiveness and removability of the entire closure. Many new ideas on top construction of metal screw caps have been tried out in the past ten years, and a number have been highly successful.

From the appearance standpoint, screw caps have benefited in many instances by elimination of the knurling which formerly was found on virtually all closures of this type. Still another improvement was the turned-in edge,[7] replacing the "wire rolled edge" of older types of screw caps. The turned under edge makes it possible to bring the cap decoration clear down and under the skirt of the cap, whereas the wire edge forms a bright metal border around the bottom of the cap.

In the metallurgical field, the development of ductile tin plate within recent years is a contribution of vast

[5]The question of thread construction is subject to some variation of opinion, with competing closure manufacturers supporting several different theories as to the exact type of thread deemed most desirable.
[6]Introduced by Poenix Metal Cap Co., in 1928
[7]The first patent on a completely curled-in edge was granted to American Metal Cap Co. (now Anchor Cap & Closure Corporation) in 1926.

REPRINT—ALL CAPS HAVE CHANGED SINCE 1928, AND SOME ARE ENTIRELY NEW

THE GLASS PACKER : NOVEMBER, 1938 : **691**

398

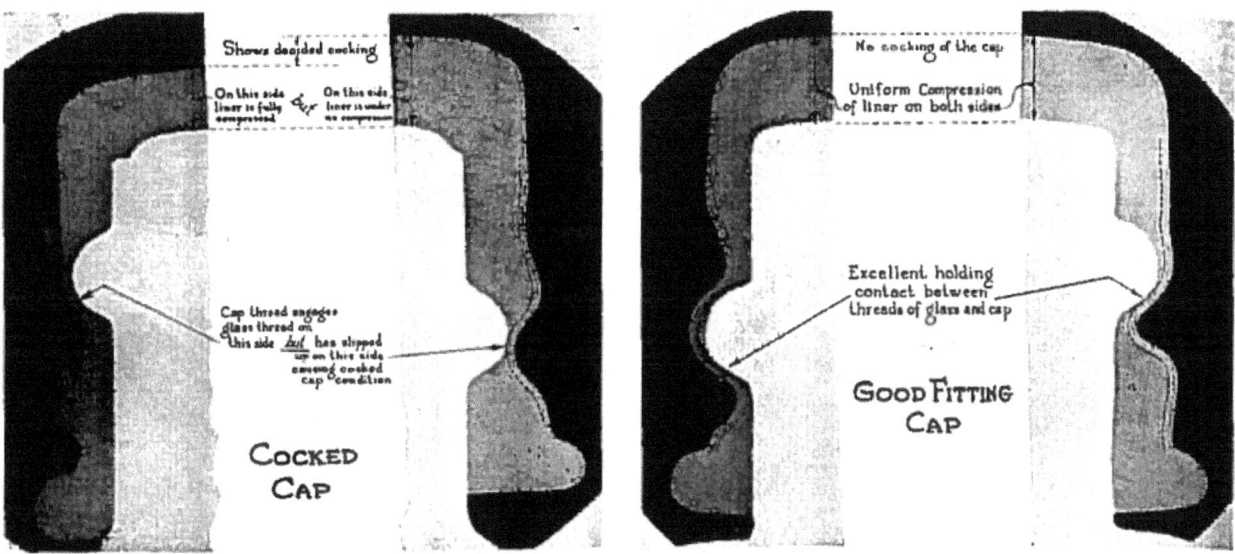

FIG. 4. *Illustrating how the optically enlarging comparator can be used to study sealing efficiency. More complicated conditions than this can be disclosed with these instruments and corrected by the closure manufacturer.*

importance to the closure industry. Since practically all metal closures are fabricated by forming a flat sheet into a cylindrical shape, the drawing properties of the metal are of the utmost importance. Improvements in the manufacture of steel by the cold roll process have given the cap manufacturer a much more ductile material to work with. Prior to the availability of ductile metal the drawing operation frequently produced a shell with a corner instead of the desired round flange. When curled, this uneven flange sometimes produced a ragged edge on the bottom of the closure. Today, deeper draws, in fewer drawing steps, are possible, which in turn makes it possible to supply caps at lower cost to the user. Of equal importance is the fact that many styles of closures now on the market would not be in existence if they had to be made of the old type of tin plate. In addition, better corrosion resistance is shown by some of the types of ductile tin plate.

New Packages, New Problems, New Closures

A man who wants to "keep track" of all the new ideas in glass packaging may find his Waterloo in the field of closure specialties—the many types of seals which have been developed and are constantly being added to, for capping particular types of containers and products. Some of these closures have limited, though very important use, like the new "Bulk Bacterin Safety Seal" used by Abbott Laboratories, for vaccine. Others, like the tamper-proof closures for liquor, have such extensive use that they can hardly be called specialties. At present we can only go down the line, pointing out some of the more outstanding successes of the past 10 years.

Capping the thin re-usable tumbler

In 1928, use of thin tumblers, either blown or pressed, for commercial packages, was still unknown. Since this type of container had decided advantages from a re-use standpoint, it was not surprising that glass and closure manufacturers soon realized its possibilities, and that packers were quick to adopt it as a merchandising device. The first use was for the packing of cottage cheese, which was made practical by the invention of a light weight aluminum foil cap and a suitable machine for crimping the foil under the bead of the tumbler.[8] Soon other tumbler caps were developed, suitable for sealing products requiring a more substantial closure than the foil

used on cottage cheese. One of the first to use an hermetic seal on a light weight tumbler was the Red Wing Co., of Fredonia, N. Y., packer of jams and jellies. These products in the new package[9] were exhibited for the first time at the 1933 Canners' Convention.

Development of suitable sealing compounds and gaskets for the light metal caps used on thin tumblers was an important factor in the success of this type of package. Vacuum caps were devised for both mechanical (crimped on) application, and for top sealing with the closure held on by atmospheric pressure.

Related to the first use of foil caps on tumblers, was the invention of the aluminum foil hood and suitable bottle finish for milk.[10]

Repeal brings new closures

One of the most significant influences on all types of closures in the United States was the repeal of Prohibition in 1933. Previously, rampant bootlegging had led Canadian distillers to look for means of tamper-proofing their containers and thereby putting a stop to the havoc raised by illegal practices. During the 1929-32 period

[8]Introduced by Aluminum Seal Co., in 1934.
[9]Joint development, Sterling Aluminum Co. (cap), Libby Glass Co. (tumbler), and Dewey and Almy Chemical Co. (sealing compound).
[10]By J. E. Sharp, Aluminum Seal Co. (1929). Mr. Sharp was also the inventor of the "roll-on" method widely used in applying various types of aluminum closures (1923).

several types of tamper-proof seals were invented, all employing the roll-on type of aluminum cap, with protecting band which had to be broken before the seal could be removed. Other styles of tamper-proof closures have since been developed, the metal varieties being made almost entirely of aluminum on account of the adaptability of this metal for such closures.

At least one molded tamper-proof cap has been successfully marketed,[11] and the use of tamper-proof cellulose sealing bands to be slipped over various types of closures has been an outstanding feature of wine and liquor packaging. Bands with transparent side panels have been developed,[12] and these are almost universally used by rectifiers and distillers to protect government tax stamps. The range of colors has been recently broadened (five colors) and improvements in printing now permit the reproduction of almost any trade-mark.

Another development, new to this country, has been the perfection of aluminum foil capsules and the machinery for their application.[12] These capsules compete successfully with imported foil capsules.

Before leaving the subject of tamper-proof closures, it should be of interest to comment on a Repeal development which was not without its humorous side. This was the revival of nationwide effort by inventors in all strata of society to produce the "non-refillable bottle." Like perpetual motion, this long-lived goal of the gadgeteer has sent hundreds of drawings and models around the country and into the Patent Office in Washington. About 1934-35 some very convincing demonstrations were put on by the promoters of certain "non-refillables" which employed rather complicated closure devices to accomplish their purpose. Like many another bright packaging idea, there seems to have been too much "Rube Goldberg" in these *apparatii* to permit practical use.

Almost the opposite of the complicated non-refillable closure, was the improvement which Repeal brought to the oldest of all commercial closures, and one of the best for many purposes—the cork. Long years before Prohibition, all-cork flange corks were used, especially on

bar packages. Their simplicity and convenience for high speed serving kept these closures very much in the running, and when the molded top flange cork was developed[14] the bartender was quick to agree with the closure man, that "he had something, there." In effect, the molded top put "a handle on the cork," made it unbreakable, and a decorative addition to the package. A problem with this closure was to secure a satisfactory bond between the adhesive and the molded part. This was overcome by changing the method of applying the cork to the molded piece by inserting a peg into the cork and the cork into the flange.

Metal top flange corks were also introduced during the past 10 years, with the metal spun over a wood base in which the cork is inserted with an adhesive. Embossed wood top corks, once found almost entirely on ink bottles, also enjoyed a new popularity as a result of Repeal, and were improved by new methods of embossing, new alcohol resistant coatings, and two color decoration. The latest development in corks is the straight cork with chamfered edge, especially suitable for the new choke-neck liquor bottles.

Numerous styles of applicator caps have appeared on the market since 1928, the most widely used being the dropper cap which combines a glass medicine dropper with a molded or metal screw cap. Applicator caps have made a long list of bottled medicinal and toilet preparations vastly more convenient to use. It is safe to say that consumers would revolt, perhaps violently, should there be any attempt to return to the closures formerly used for these products. Applicator tops are made with glass rods, brushes and various types of fabric, sponge and rubber daubers and dispensers.

The applicator idea has in some cases been carried to a high degree of specialization. Examples might be the caps used on certain brands of nail polish, which provide the user with more than one applicator in a single closure; or the seals used on hospital packages of intravenous solutions, which are devised to permit sterile transfer of the solution from the bottle to the surgeon's needle.[15]

Intimately related to the development and use of several highly successful closures for food products was the building, in 1929, of the first Vapor-vacuum Sealing machine.[16] Taking advantage of the principle of air

---

[11]By Anchor Cap & Closure Corporation.
[12]By E. I. du Pont de Nemours, Inc., Cellophane Division.
[13]By Aluminum Seal Co., 1934.
[14]By Mundet Cork Corporation, in 1934
[15]Developed by Aluminum Seal Co and Baxter Laboratories, Inc.
[16]By the White Cap Co First announcement and public exhibition at the Canning Machinery & Supplies Exposition, Chicago, Jan., 1931.

FIG. 5. *Used for food products, most of these closures are types which did not exist before 1928, and the others include important features which have been developed during the past ten years. Seven pry-off types are represented, with three side seals and four top seals. A lug cap and a C.T. are lined with "lubricated" rubber gaskets vulcanized in place. All but one of these caps were designed for vacuum packing.*

displacement by steam, a new and revolutionary method of vacuum capping was made possible, using a press-on type of side seal closure. In this machine, steam is injected into the headspace of the package, forcing out the air and sterilizing the top surface of the product and the inner surface of the container finish. The cap is then pressed on, and the condensation of the water vapor on cooling, produces a high vacuum.

A number of press-on and top seal closures were developed for bottles and jars of all sizes, and these are all being applied by the vapor-vacuum machine at speeds up to 300 per minute. A large volume of glass packed food products are now sealed by this method. The principle of vacuum creation by steam condensation has also been utilized in automatic application of a lug type closure[17] which was placed on the market in January, 1936. A number of new caps suitable for vacuum capping are shown in Fig. 5.

[17]The V.P.O. Cap of Crown Cork & Seal Co., first shown at the Canning Machinery & Supplies Exposition, Chicago, Jan., 1936.

Lacquers and Coatings

The most evident feature of any closure is its decoration, and yet developments in the field of finishes, decorative and protective, are not at once evident to those unfamiliar with the manufacturing end of the closure industry. Very notable advances have been made in recent years in the synthetic resin industry, which have made available lacquers and varnishes unthought of ten years ago. Closure manufacturers were quick to avail themselves of these new raw materials for cap coatings.

Naturally, a tremendous amount of research was involved to formulate and adapt these new materials to the specific requirements of closure finishes. Since the majority of closures are decorated while the metal is in flat sheet form, the coating must pass successfully through the various drawing, threading and forming operations necessary to fabricate the metal into finished cap. The requirements of a closure coating do not, however, end at this point, for it must meet a multitude of further requirements, even more difficult than fabrication ability. The coating must naturally possess a high degree of adhesion to the metal base, but it must also have a quality, which for want of a better term, may be called "abrasion resistance." The increased use of automatic capping machinery, even with the present day refinements in this equipment, make the matter of abrasion resistance of the closure finish of utmost importance. The finishes of ten years ago would fare sadly indeed in a modern automatic capping line. Likewise, since the closure has assumed its added role of styling the package, less damage or marring of the finish can be tolerated. In this important matter of abrasion resistance, synthetic[18] resins have come to play a most vital part.

In line with its present position in decorating the package, the closure has rapidly developed in the matter of color. Since this color (in metal closures) is provided by the coating or lacquer, color possibilities, both as to design and solid colors, have come to be a major

interest of the closure manufacturer. Close control of color is becoming increasingly necessary and variations in color, taken as a matter of course several years ago, are now no longer tolerable. In color control and standardization, new color analyzing and recording instruments, such as the General Electric Recording Spectrophotometer,* have been found very helpful, since they remove the human element in color matching and also provide permanent and unchanging standards and records. The trend toward color in closures during the past ten years has been quite pronounced. One leading manufacturer reports that decorated production rose from about 25 per cent in 1928 to approximately 70 per cent in 1938, of the total closures manufactured.

Alcohol and acid resistant coatings

The repeal of Prohibition and the subsequent wide use of metal closures on alcoholic beverages, brought a host of problems in providing alcohol resistant finishes. These finishes—both protective (on the inside of the closure) and decorative (on the outside)—had to be formulated to withstand the softening action of alcohol, a material notorious for its disturbing effect on lacquers and varnishes. In this connection, synthetic resins again made possible, in many instances, finishes with a truly remarkable degree of alcohol resistance. In addition, these finishes had also to meet requirements of a decorative nature. Unquestionably, the development of alcohol resistant finishes, made possible by the resin developments of the past seven years, is largely responsible for the use of metal closures on alcoholic beverages.

Concurrently with the development of alcohol resistant coating materials, came the special finishes designed to protect the inside of the closure from attack, and consequently to improve the ease of removal and general appearance of the closure. One division of this particular class of finishes is known as the "Acid Resisting." Frequently this appears as a white enamel, having special acid resistant features. The white appearance is of very definite sales value, as it testifies to the general cleanly and sanitary merits of the seal, and hence, of the entire package and its contents.

The rapid growth of the cosmetic industry and the consequent widespread use of metal closures, of both the double and single shell varieties, in this field, gave rise logically to special problems in protective and decorative coatings and lacquers. Protective coatings were formulated with the special feature of "cosmetic resistance,"—that is, the ability to withstand the action of the many and varied materials which may quite properly be included in a cosmetic product formula. Some creams and lotions are mildly alkaline, others slightly acid, still others oily or containing fats; some cosmetic products
(Continued on page 734)

[18]The term "synthetic," as applied to these resins is really a misnomer, since most of them have no natural counterpart possessing the same unique properties. In nature, for example, there is no material remotely resembling the widely used vinyl resins or the phenolaldehyde resins, of which latter group Bakelite is a familiar example. Both of these materials, either alone or modified with oils or other resins, are of extreme value to the closure manufacturer in the formulation of his finishes and enable him to provide the cap user with a product of corresponding advantages. It should not be inferred that no further fields for improvement exist in this direction, as continued research will undoubtedly bring advances comparable with those attained in the ten years just past.
*Introduced in the closure industry this year by Metal Closure Division, Hazel-Atlas Glass Co.

All caps have changed since 1928

(Continued from page 694)

contain detergents to assist their cleansing action, and special other agents along these lines to provide a specific function. The user of closures, examining the finished article, does not always realize the very considerable amount of thought and research which has gone into the development of a coating or enamel, to have it perform its functions perfectly, without succumbing to the effect of single or combined ingredients in the product, which may have a special "appetite" for ordinary coating materials.

Lithograph design and photocomposing

The use of individualized lithographed designs on closures has shown a marked increase during the past ten years, and as a consequence, developments in this particular branch of closure manufacture have not lagged behind. The use of photocomposed press plates is perhaps the most notable trend in improvement, of a mechanical nature, in the lithographing part of closure manufacture. Photocomposing—a high degree of mechanical precision combined with a photographic process —enables lithograph designs to be reproduced in detail and with fidelity on closures.

A recent advance of note is the development of the so-called "quick-drying" lithograph inks, by the use of which baking or drying of the lithograph design, formerly comparatively slower in tin printing than paper printing, has been speeded. Of more significance to the closure user is the clearer, denser, and harder image obtainable with these new inks. Here again, synthetic resins have provided a vehicle for the coloring material of the ink, which opens up new possibilities which as yet have not been entirely explored.

Closures on their packages are frequently subjected to the sterilizing action of heat, usually in the form of hot water or steam, and the use of synthetic resin vehicles in the lithograph ink used for the design opens possibilities for decoration in a field which up to now has been limited, because of the severe action of steam and hot water on the older types of ink.

Improvements in Liners

A totally different branch of closure manufacture is represented by that of the liner—the unseen part of the closure vitally responsible for the seal. It is the liner of the cap which actually is the sealing mechanism, the closure itself being really the mechanical contrivance for holding the liner securely to the opening of the glass container.

The available liner materials of some 10 years back were comparatively few in number. That most commonly used was oiled or varnished paper—a material originally made as an insulating material for electrical equipment and borrowed for use in closures[19] because of its waterproof qualities. The oiled paper of 10 years ago was a very different product than that in use today. Closure and liner manufacturers had at that time begun

to appreciate keenly that a material suitable for electrical purposes had quite a few shortcomings for closure purposes. Research and development over the years have continuously improved this product, so that today the oiled or varnished paper, supplied in closures, represents about the zenith of development of which the basic materials are capable. But newer products and more stringent requirements in existing ones still find present-day varnished paper lacking in many respects. Particularly is this true of chemical resistance and resistance to transmission of moisture.

In over 90 per cent of the total packages of glass packed products, prevention of excessive moisture loss is a matter for consideration. Due to developments in the past ten years in the liner field, this no longer presents the problem it did some years ago, thanks to liner materials of comparatively recent origin. There is as yet no so-called "universal" liner material, and probably never will be, but both Vinylite[20] and Pliofilm come closer to meeting the theoretical requirements of such a material than was thought possible only a few years ago. Both of these materials have low moisture transmission characteristics, which make them outstanding materials for liner usage. It stands as a matter of course that these materials must also have the other necessary requisites of a satisfactory liner material—such as, permanent flexibility, light or white color, freedom from taste or odor, chemical resistance, commercial availability, and reasonable cost.

The advent of these materials in the liner field was not accidental, but was the result of many years of research. Comparative studies of various liner materials, in which the actual amount of moisture evaporation from capped containers was determined by weighing periodically on delicate balances, show the superiority of Vinylite liner material over various "papers" commonly in use. The table of actual evaporation losses taken from test data is typical of this material.

Evaporation Losses
in 8 oz. Jars Sealed with 58 MM. C.T. Caps
After 4 Weeks at 98°F.
(Pulpboard Backing for All Liners)

Facing Material	Evap. loss on water	Evap. loss on 50% grain alcohol
Vinylite (E)	0.32 grams*	0.30 grams*
Vinylite Plain	1.40 "	1.28 "
Pale Yellow Oil Paper	2.66 "	7.60 "
White Enameled Oil Paper	2.68 "	4.17 "
Light Brown Oil Paper	2.59 "	3.77 "
Black Alkali Resisting Paper	1.98 "	2.09 "
Pliofilm	0.58 "	0.48 "

*1.0 gram = 1/28 ounce

There are, of course, products where evaporation loss is not a problem, but where a consideration of cost is the governing factor; and in such instances, the use of Vinylite and similar newly available materials is not mandatory. However, for the majority of products packed in glass containers, which majority also contain more or less moisture, these newer materials afford advantages that make their use well worth while in spite of their slightly higher cost.

Under the heading of "liners" it is appropriate to men-

[19] The term "insulated," from this source, is still found in liner specifications today.
[20] Offered under several trade names.

tion what might properly be called a new method of liner application. Introduced in 1929,[20] this was a method of cementing a thin film of liner material to the top of the bottle finish, using a suitable adhesive. The result was an air-tight and liquid-tight seal which functions satisfactorily on such products as mineral oil and others which are difficult to "hold." This closure has also been adapted to use for tamper-proof sealing of such products as wines and certain pharmaceuticals where it is important to assure customers that the package has not been opened since it left the packer's plant. Many different liners and cements have been developed.

A good example of the development of liners as applied to a single type of closure, can be found in the well-known beverage crown. For many years prior to 1928, the closures generally used on carbonated beverages were the natural cork crown or the composition cork crown. Since that time the spot crown has become very widely used. This was made possible by the invention of automatic machinery which punches the spot out of a roll of liner material and cements it to the face of the cork disc inside assembled closure. Also important was the formulation of suitable water resistant cements.

The spot eliminated the trouble which the beverage industry had with acid drinks, such as gingerale. Even with the finest grades of natural cork, used on gingerale of the better qualities, there was a tendency of the tinplate to pinhole. The spot prevented this.

With the return of beer, the aluminum foil spot was introduced. Its function was to keep the beer from coming in contact with the cork which may contain enough tannic acid to affect the flavor of the beer.

The synthetic resins, such as Vinylite, also find an important use in spot crowns, and synthetic resin binders have made composition cork a much improved material for crowns used on such products as catsup, which is highly acid and is pasteurized during the packing operation. At the same time, cheaper compositions have been perfected using a protein type binder, to be used for spotted cork liners. Such combination liners, due to the unsurpassed resiliency of cork, make a tight and extremely satisfactory seal.

Liner standardization

Developments during the 10 years past have not been confined by any means to Vinylite and Pliofilm, though these two are most widely used in closures today. Various liner materials of all types and descriptions have appeared on the market, practically all of them developed for some special purpose or product or to meet some rather limited set of special requirements. Frequently these special materials were sponsored by the closure manufacturer who introduced them, and while many of them had merit, the result was a rather confusing and bewildering array of materials, particularly evident after the comparative dearth existing some 10 or 12 years before. Quite recently, a concerted effort has been made to standardize liner materials and to eliminate unnecessary variations in a single group of materials. This move, when carried to its logical conclusion, will effect substantial savings to the closure user and manufacturer alike, and in addition, will remove much of the unnecessary confusion and misunderstanding in regard to liner materials employed today. The users of closures will find it very much to their own benefit to cooperate to the fullest in this simplificaton and standardization effort.

---

[20] The Filma-Seal of Ferdinand Gutmann Co.

The Manufacture, Function, and Handling of Bottle Crowns

Clyde O. Hess

ALTHOUGH a bottle crown may be small, it is the big difference between bottled beer that is refreshing and delectable and bottled beer that is flat, without flavor, and distasteful.

Brewers know that it's the small things that count, for the tiny crown that's not much bigger than a 25-cent piece holds the key to a million dollars worth of flavor. With such a responsibility, crown manufacturers demand that their crowns meet rigid specifications. Each crown must be "as perfect as a watch." One imperfect crown in a bottler's capping machine may cause a clogged chute and halt production or it may mean a "leaker" and the loss of flavor in the beer or ale.

The Manufacture, Function and Handling of
Bottle Crowns

By Clyde O. Hess
Armstrong Cork Company

*This is one in a series of articles devoted to the general subject of beer packaging.

The Making of Crowns

The making of crowns, or bottle caps as they are more familiarly known, is a far more complicated task than one would imagine from a casual examination of the finished product. To produce a new crown design, a skilled designer, with a knowledge of lithography as well as merchandising, prepares a hand-drawn color sketch in which eye appeal and product or brand identity are first considerations.

When the color sketch is approved, production artists prepare accurate, (two or three times the actual crown size) black and white master drawings for each color to be printed. The enlarged drawings are photographically reduced to positives of actual size and a photo composing machine makes 288 uniform prints on a sensitized zinc printing plate which is then chemically etched to produce the multiple design images. Next, the zinc plates are mounted on a cylinder of the lithographing press.

Meanwhile, a color specialist mixes printing inks. There are certain combinations anyone can follow, but perfection calls for long experience and highly specialized knowledge because mixing printing inks is much like blending flavors.

The application of each printing color normally requires a separate run through the printing process. Perfect register of multi-color designs is a must and that means that each color has to be in its proper place with no perceptible overlap.

The shell of the crown begins with a steel sheet that is closely controlled in gauge, temper, and ductility. The sheet is coated with a layer of metallic tin to prevent rust and to provide a base for exterior lithography and interior sanitary coatings.

After each run through the lithographing press, the tin sheets are sent through a 96-foot oven with a temperature ranging from 200 to 450 degrees Fahrenheit. The sheets are on an endless chain which is synchronized with the speed of the press. An evaporative water cooling system is used to reduce the temperature of the metal sheets to room temperature after they are discharged from the oven.

After decorating the tin sheets has been completed according to the de-

(All photographs by the makers of Armstrong's Crowns)
Before the actual manufacturing of crowns begins, a skilled designer blends his ingenuity and talent to design a crown that has eye-appeal and originality.

The crown design is reproduced 288 times on one lithograph plate by a photographic process. Rigid standards are demanded so that each crown will be a perfect reproduction of the original design.

Printing the crowns on the metal requires a separate run through the presses for each color. Perfect register must be obtained so that each color will be in its proper place with no perceptible overlap.

Giant presses punch out sixteen individual crown shells with each stroke. The huge press, which weighs approximately eight tons, must be accurate to 5 thousandths of an inch. The metal sheets are fed automatically into the press from the left.

sired trademark or design, they are transferred to the "punching" operation. Here a press weighing approximately eight tons punches out sixteen individual shells with each stroke. Here, too, accuracy is demanded and, despite the natural vibration, the formation must be accurate to 5 thousandths of an inch so that the decoration will not "hang over the side" of the crown.

Following the punching operation, the metal shells are individually inspected and transferred to assembly machines for installation of the cork disc inside the shell. The cork disc is highly important. It's the seal of protection that sets up a secure lock on the lip of the bottle.

The Cork Liner

The first cork disc or liner used for beer packages was composed of natural cork. The crown industry, however, grew so fast that the cork-growing countries, centered around the Mediterranean Sea, could not produce enough high quality cork discs to supply the demand. Natural cork was expensive, too.

Composition cork liners for crowns were developed making it possible to use by-product cork from manufacture of various natural cork products such as wine and pharmaceutical closures. To make these, the cork is put through a grinding and classification operation and then mixed with suitable binders.

The mixed material is extruded through tubes and baked to form a rod of composition cork about one inch in diameter. After an aging period, the rods are sliced into discs for assembly in the decorated metal crown shells.

A tasteless and odorless adhesive is applied to the inside of the metal shell in which the cork disc is inserted. A combination of pressure and heat assures positive adhesion of the cork to the metal shell.

The first binders used to make cork composition set up a new problem in beer and malted beverage crowns. A haze was found to develop in beer, sometimes just a few weeks after it was bottled. This trouble was traced back to the binders.

The Aluminum Spot

Chemists attacked the problem, and it was partially solved with the use of a special, chemically inert binder. However, the development of the aluminum foil spot really solved the problem. Aluminum was found to be free from reaction with beer, and placing the spot over the composition cork liner prevented contact between the liner and the beer.

The aluminum spot does not cover the entire area of the cork disc for a good reason. When a liner covering the entire disc area is used to seal beer, loss of gas pressure is apt to result. It is essential that the top of the glass bottle be sealed by the surface of the compressed cellular cork body. When the crown is crimped down on the bottle, the uncovered cork around the edge of the liner disc is highly compressed and forms a gas-tight sealing

Constant inspection and tests are made to control to close tolerances the over-all height, inside diameter, and outside diameter of the crowns. Every crown is inspected on the assembly line and, in addition, spot checks like the one shown above are frequently made to insure top quality.

These sausage-like objects are rods of cork that eventually become discs to fit inside the metal shell of a bottle crown. After running through a shaving machine which shapes them to the exact size, the rods will be sliced into discs of the desired thickness.

rim, while the aluminum spot is interposed at the bottle mouth between the cork liner and the beer.

Aluminum foil was chosen as a spotting material because it is both tasteless and odorless and does not alter brew flavor after the beer leaves the pasteurizer. The adhesive used is generally a thermoplastic adhesive that is tasteless, odorless, and non-oxidizing.

Some unspotted crowns are still used in the beer industry, but they are usually found only on beer that is locally distributed and quickly sold. For this service the plain cork composition liners with special binders produce satisfactory results.

Each crown is inspected after the punching operation, after the cork discs are inserted, and again after the aluminum spots are placed. In addition, periodical random inspections are made during the entire manufacturing process. The over-all height, inside diameter, and outside diameter must be controlled to close tolerances. The crowns are then counted automatically and placed into shipping cartons.

Although the manufacturing process has been completed and the crowns are in perfect condition, there's still plenty of possibilities for them to be damaged before they are capped on a bottle. Careless handling or storage of the crowns may cause costly production line interruptions and "leakers."

Storage of Crowns

The crowns should be stored in a clean, dry place where the temperature remains reasonably constant. Prolonged exposure to heat will dry out the cork liners, make them lose their resiliency, and possibly cause poor sealing.

It also is urged that all precautions be made to keep the crowns clean and sanitary. Before opening a carton, any dust and dirt that may have accumulated during storage should be wiped off the carton. To prevent damage to the crowns, the cartons should be handled with a minimum of abuse. They should never be thrown or dropped from a truck or the top of a storage pile.

Careful Handling Essential

Furthermore, the rough handling of scoops may bend some of the shells, causing interrupted feeding and line shutdowns. It is best to pour them into the hopper or the container that feeds the hopper right from the carton. As a final precaution, the crowns should not be left in the hopper when washing up the equipment at the end of the day's run. Sprayed water or cleaning solutions may discolor the discs and may transfer foreign matter into the beer.

To assure maximum efficiency in operation it is recommended that the hopper be emptied and the crowns returned to their original box at the end of each day's operation. The hopper, sorter, and crown track should then be brushed thoroughly to remove any foreign particles that might have accumulated during the day's production.

By following these precautions, the crown will best be able to perform its service of protecting the flavor and appearance of bottled beer and ale.

5
GLASS CONTAINER DESIGN

Advertisement for the Goldy seal. (Western Canner and Packer, 1934.)

Articles

Standardization in the Glass Container Industry
[**Reprint** from 1922, *Glass Container* 2(2):5–7, 16, 18, 20.]
Irwin G. Jennings

The Factor of Breakage in Odd Shaped Glass Containers
[**Reprint** from 1927, *Canning Age* 8:431–433.]
J. S. Algeo

Making the Most of Glass
[**Reprint** from 1935, *Glass Packer* 14(5):285–288, 321.]
John T. Ogden

Improving the Strength of Glass Containers through Design
[**Reprint** from 1939, *Glass Industry* 20(12):443–448.]
Leonard G. Ghering

Modern Styling in Bottles for Beer
[**Reprint** from 1937, *Brewers Technical Review* 12(9):344–345.]
J. H. Toulouse

The Standardization of Bottles for Beer and Ale
[**Reprint** from 1941, *Brewers Digest* 16(10):173–177, 181.]
J. H. Toulouse

The Development of the One-Way Bottle for Beer
[**Reprint** from 1945, *Brewers Digest* 20(9):45–47.]
Julian Harrison Toulouse

Principles of Glass Container Design
[**Reprint** from 1949, *Modern Packaging Encyclopedia*, pp. 443–445.
Packaging Catalog Corporation, New York, NY.]
J. S. Algeo

Standardization in the Glass Container Industry
Irwin G. Jennings

The Glass Container

Vol. 2   Contents Copyrighted, 1922   DECEMBER, 1922   By The Glass Container Association   No. 2

The monthly magazine of The Glass Container Association of America, 70 Fifth Avenue, New York, N. Y., published in the interests of all makers and users of glass containers, and of the contributing industries.

Standardization in the Glass Container Industry

Analyzed Conditions Show How Users Are Accountable for the Evolution of Standardization in the Glass Container Industry

An address by
IRWIN G. JENNINGS
at the National Exposition of Chemical Industries

IT is fair to assume that there are at least the average number of practical and progressive men in the glass container industry, and among them there is scarcely a man who does not see many advantages to the public and industry in the adoption in general of standardization or simplification methods and processes, and specifically, in their application to the glass container industry itself.

But there are certain things involved in the standardization of glass containers which must be well understood and dealt with before beginning upon any active program for this purpose. Either this, or great injustice may be done to the manufacturers of containers, their customers and the public.

The glass-container industry is one of the oldest in the world's history. The manufacture of glass has always been considered one of the highest of industrial arts. The glass manufacturers and blowers of past centuries were held in great esteem. Their returns and wages were large; a certain air of mystery surrounded the trade, and everything possible was done to protect trade

ARTICLES on Standardization of glass containers are by no means a novelty. The subject is so pertinent to every maker and user of glass containers that all wide-awake men in the several allied industries are closely following everything written on it.

There are many angles to the standardization problem. We feel that this article treats of the matter in an entirely new way and is therefore at least supplemental toward placing all the facts of standardization before the many who are interested.—THE EDITOR.

secrets, and to maintain the rather unique position of the glass workers.

Real Advancement Shown

However, the early part of the present century saw the development and utilization in the industry of several practical automatic devices and machines. Since that time, during the past fifteen years, there has been more real advancement in the application of economical and uniform methods to glass manufacture than in all the ages before. I think it would be safe to say that the manufacture of glass containers has developed more rapidly and surely, relatively speaking, than that of almost any other well-established human necessity.

Along with the progress that has been made in the manufacture of glass containers, a progress just as great has been going on in the attitude of the various manufacturers toward their industry, their customers, the users of glass containers and the public. Neither the money nor the time of these manufacturers has been spared in organizing their industry along such lines as will extend to the twenty or more great national groups

of these users, the greatest possible public service.

Among other things, this has been done by studying how they might make progressively better containers in harmony with the users' demands, by maintaining research laboratories and placing them at the service of the users to help them in obtaining better products, by creating agencies for developing safer packing methods for shipping their glass containers, by standardizing bottle finishes and thus guaranteeing for their products better-fitting caps, by organizing a traffic department to encourage the united effort of the users of containers to obtain better traffic conditions and more favorable railroad rates for their shipments, by inaugurating a publication department to acquaint all interested users of glass containers with the progress being made in the industry, by stimulating educational and publicity measures throughout the industries of both the manufacturers and users to cause a better appreciation by the public of the glass container and products contained therein, and by maintaining a business and publicity department to bring about co-ordination of effort throughout the whole movement.. In the development of their associated activities, the greatest consideration has been given always to both the users of containers and the public.

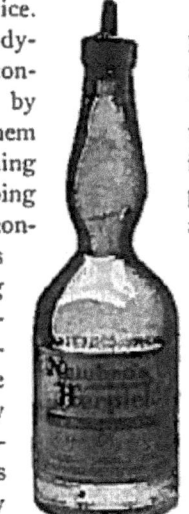

Good-Will the Keynote

This organizing has been carried on not only by the glass men, and the makers of caps and closures, but also in conjunction with the manufacturers of raw material and equipment for glass factories. Its primary object has been to create good-will with the various groups of users of containers, and thus to win their confidence, to consult their interests, to study and fill their needs, and to co-operate with them to the end that they, too, shall progress. Of course, the ultimate object of it all has been that more glass containers shall be sold and with them more glass-contained products, to the mutual benefit of both the manufacturers and users.

Must Consider Intelligent Program

The best assurance of standardization of glass containers is their large and increasing use; the greatest obstacle is their limited use, thus causing a possibility that certain manufacturers, in spite of desirable standards which may ultimately be agreed upon, in order to run their factories, will make any kind of containers ordered, though they do not conform to the agreed standards. It is obvious, also, that in addition to the development of markets, the mere fact that there is an organized glass-container industry is reassuring to advocates of standardization, for without organization to encourage it, practical standardization would be impossible. The pressure of the above associated activities, together with the individual initiative in the industry itself, is bound to make itself felt.

Therefore, it would seem that an intelligently planned and controlled program of standardization should be considered by our industry after a careful analysis of the above conditions and forces, together with the uses to which the glass container is put, the extent of their use and the nature of the product contained therein, and thus expedite standardization where it is desirable, and fix certain limits where it would result destructively in impairing some of those well-known virtues of glass containers, which, in many cases of their use, are invaluable to those industries which commit their product to them.

But first as to the meaning and application of the term standardization itself as related to the glass container industry. A mere name should not be allowed to cloud the minds of those who are seeking progress. Call it simplification if necessary to banish a prejudice, for standardization is almost synonymous with the simplification of methods and processes made necessary by constructive progress and increased demand. When the demand for glass-contained products becomes so large that packers and bottlers begin to study costs and efficient production, a demand for standardization will arise. That this demand is now present is one of the propitious signs in our industry.

Three Factors to Consider

In the standardization of glass containers, three factors must be taken into consideration, and are here named in the order of their importance: The manufacturers of glass containers, the users of glass containers and the public. The glass-container manufacturers must consider the needs and desires of the users of containers, and the users must study very carefully the wants and demands of the consumer. There is thus a double check on the glass manufacturers in any program of standardization, developed by themselves or suggested to them without the sanction of the users or a reasonable assurance that the public will acquiesce. Obviously, the users themselves are checked by public approval.

Standardization of the glass container may be applied to the inside dimensions, the outside measurements, the shape, the design, the weight of glass, the top finish, the length of the neck, the width of the cap seat, the filling height, the markings, the color, etc. Our research laboratories have already given considerable attention to the standardization of finishes. They have also done work in filling heights, leaky caps and other related subjects.

Characteristics of Glass Container

And now, perhaps, a discussion of the characteristics of the glass container and its uses will aid in appraising the value of and setting the limits to standardization in other respects.

The glass container is practically unique in at

least four respects. First, it is transparent. While studying the public welfare as to standardization, it may be well to call attention to the value to the public of being able to see what it buys, the exact nature and character of the contents of the package as revealed by the glass container, the guarantee to the public of honesty and goodness of product through this transparency. Second, for all practical purposes it is impervious to acids and alkalis. This characteristic, together with its transparency, has made the glass container not only a most valued aid in the development of science, but the ideal, sanitary container for foods and drinks. Third, in its plastic state it can be molded readily into various shapes and designs, at times producing most beautiful effects. Herein seems to be the rub with most of those who think that standardization is backward in our industry, largely because they do not understand and appreciate how far it has gone already. Fourth, it is capable of complete inside and outside sterilization, with consequent adaptability to re-use.

An Important Consideration

Of these four characteristics of the glass container, the first two are not affected by standardization, but the last two require further consideration.

Were these containers empty and unlabeled any child would recognize the use for which they were intended

Now, a most important consideration, which, on the one hand urges the necessity for standardization of the glass container, and, on the other hand, limits its utility and desirability, is the use that is made of it. Roughly, glass containers are used for preserving and containing foods, drugs, drinks and miscellaneous products, such as chemicals, perfumes, flavoring extracts, pastes, inks, etc. The first two characteristics noted above make glass containers peculiarly valuable for foods and drinks, and it is here that the subject of standardization can be approached with greatest assurance of success. In such products as drugs, perfumes and flavoring extracts, quantity is far less a consideration than strength and efficiency, and specially designed bottles for these products are not only desirable but expected by the public. Much of the pleasure in using perfumes lies in our admiration of the beautiful designs of perfume bottles, and the housewife would be lost in her kitchen without the familiar panel bottles containing flavoring extracts.

But there is one thing that is rarely taken into consideration in discussing standardization of glass containers. It would seem to be truly futile and illogical to insist upon the standardization of containers when there is no standardized conception in the minds of the users of what the container should be or an organized and active sentiment among them to support the glass-container manufacturers in developing and maintaining standardization by their ordering only standardized designs. The

There are still other valuable characteristics, more or less unique, to the glass container, such as its adaptability to hand-cutting and other individual treatment, but among these its capability of being capped, filled and otherwise handled by automatic machinery is the most pertinent, so far as the matter of standardization is concerned.

(Continued on page 16)

Standardization in the Glass Industry

(Continued from page 7)

maintenance of organizations among the users of containers who will co-operate with the glass manufacturers in the inauguration and development of standardization is thus very necessary to its success. It is rarely considered good business to resist the demands of the trade, and only the active co-operation of the users in supporting agreed-upon standardization would keep the glass-container manufacturers from filling their customers' orders for unstandardized bottles, especially if such orders became an appreciable part of their business.

Much Work Still To Be Done

Among the users, then, of glass containers there is much work, organization and education to be done before standardization of the containers can be assured. The glass-container manufacturers will be glad to join with the users in working out proper standards. By the same token they feel that there are so many outstanding advantages of the glass container over other containers which standardization would not adversely affect, that they can afford to go the limit in standardization, providing the users in dominating groups agree on what they want. Where the use of containers is very large, the manufacturers of containers themselves might bring some pressure by refusing to make other than standardized types, but such tactics would not be entirely satisfactory and, in general, glass-container manufacturers will be disposed to fill their customers' orders.

And now, in discussing standardization specifically, let us confine ourselves to food and drink containers, and even though, as we have seen before, glass containers may be standardized in several different particulars, let us further limit our discussion to the standardization of sizes and shapes, for this method will probably be most indicative of the whole problem.

By size herein we mean the inside capacity. There is positively no justification for any shape, size or design of glass container, if it were possible, which will deceive the public. But a very sharp distinction must be made between what in reality deceives the public and what might possibly be decided by inspectors of the government as tending to deceive under such regulatory legislation as, for instance, the proposed Haugen Bill.

Opposition to Haugen Bill

The glass-container industry is bitterly opposed to the Haugen Bill and other bills of its class, not only because of their unwarranted interference with business and the losses they may cause if they should become laws, but because of the fact that in the Haugen Bill particularly the possible lack of experience and judgment of inspectors, the changing personnel of public officials charged with the enforcement of such a law and their self-interest

to make a good showing in their work, might tend to bar out many excellent glass containers, hold up the sale of preserved products, and thus cause irreparable mischief to the glass men and the packers.

The best way, however, to avert all trouble is for the manufacturers and users to take steps co-operatively, and in advance, to provide for intelligent, if at first moderate, standardization. Let the users of the glass container, through committees of their various associations, meet the Standardization Committee of the Glass Container Association, already appointed and functioning, and provide for a reasonable number of popular and useful standardized sizes of containers. It is obvious, however, that such standardization of sizes must be consented to and adopted as a business practice by the very great majority of the individual firms in each group of users in order to be practical, or to impose any binding obligation on the makers of glass containers. This co-operation on the part of the manufacturers and users should always have the aid and support of those departments of the government who are interested, and perhaps better yet, the movement might be inaugurated in conjunction with these departments. Certainly standardization should never be made the subject of legal regulation. The only power the government rightly possesses in business practices of this kind is that of co-operating with an industry or suggesting the advantages of eliminating abuses of this nature where they exist.

Standardization of Shapes

And now as to the standardization of the shapes of glass containers. As has been said before, the very nature of glass invites an effort to utilize its beauty and the capabilities of its being molded into various shapes, as a sales advantage. The subject of this address was supposed to have been "The Reasons for the Varieties of Shapes and Sizes of Glass Container." There is only one real reason, so far as the glass-container manufacturers are concerned, why there are various shapes and sizes, and that is because the packers and bottlers have given orders for that kind of bottles. This of itself would have been a perfect answer to the question.

Many packers and bottlers have found that in those fields in which the sale of their products is somewhat limited and where there are opportunities to build up a special demand for them based on quality and appearance, specially shaped glass containers have appreciable sales value. They have, therefore, built their own individual ideas into their designs which, after a period of years, have acquired very large trade-mark value. So, there is the sales reason, the trade-mark reason, reasons of beauty, strength and adaptability to product. But

(Continued on page 18)

Standardization in the Glass Industry

(Continued from page 16)

these are reasons operating in the minds of the user. And who can say they are not good ones?

It would be rather difficult to convince the Heinz Company that the care and study they have made to produce bottles of distinctive and attractive design have been thrown away and useless. The business men in the Coca-Cola Company are progressive enough to know something about the value of standardization, and yet they order, and we make for them a distinctive Coca-Cola bottle. There is something, too, that must be remembered, and that is this: That once having devised and produced the necessary molds, it is possible to make the distinctive bottle in our factories about as rapidly and economically as the plainer containers. This is especially so if the orders are very large, thus permitting the factories which make the distinctive containers to be run at something like capacity. On the other hand, this very fact might cause some disappointment among the advocates of standardization as to the economies realized by its application to bottle making.

Again, if large use and the acquiescence of the users and the public in sizes and shapes is any criterion of standardization, the glass-container industry has already made tremendous strides in this direction. Every child can identify a soda bottle, a milk bottle, a catsup bottle, by the style, and the difference in design between bottles used by various packers and bottlers is a privilege that cannot be rightfully denied without their approval.

Trade-Mark Value of Bottles

It must be considered that certain bottles and containers have been used for so long a time that they really have large trade-mark values, and it is not possible nor proper to throw this value into the junk heap. The panel bottle has long been used for flavoring extracts. There is no justification for the panel bottle that has practically no inside capacity, *i.e.*, where the sides almost adhere because they are so close together. But there should be no objection to a reasonable panel bottle. It permits more attractive labeling and is the type of bottle in which most people expect to find certain kinds of products. There was a time when bottles were manufactured for champagne that had a large amount of glass in the bottom. It has been supposed by some critics that this extra glass was put in the bottle for the purpose of deceiving the public, but certainly this was not the case. The primary reasons for making this type of bottle were: First, to produce greater stability; second, to make it better withstand the pressure of the gas within; and, third, to facilitate the settling of grounds from the wines contained, if any, to the bottom. There is no excuse, however, for using these bottles for such things as cider or vinegar and other like products. The fact of the matter is that

a canvass of the glass manufacturers shows that this type of bottle has not been manufactured in this country for years. The glass-container industry is solidly opposed to any practice that will deceive the public.

So, there is a very grave question whether or not this sales initiative on the part of the users of glass containers, unquestionably taken after their study of the public demand, should be discouraged, by relegating them to a standardized shape of container.

There is something very attractive, after all, about the olive bottle, the pickle bottle, the mustard jar and the jam and honey jar, even though some of them may be tall and others squatty. What pleasing, appetizing appeals are made by jelly glasses, jars of marmalade, of bacon, of peas, of salad dressing!

For a few cents one may go into a lunch stand and purchase a luncheon that will contain as many calories as a meal costing five times as much in a first-class restaurant. Cleanliness and appearance count with food, and people pay added prices for the satisfaction they bring. The same thing applies to individuality in glass containers. Meat packers invariably select containers to fit their product as in the case of tongue, or to display them temptingly as in the case of sliced bacon. Tongue or bacon can be cut up into uninviting bits and placed in any kind of a container, but carefully chosen glass jars may be designed to show these products to their best advantage.

All these distinctive containers have come into being as the result of that same type of pride which causes a man to select a well-fitting suit or a lady to dress her hair attractively. There is reason, pride, satisfaction, joy, behind this individuality in glass containers.

Makers and Users in Unison

May we not, therefore, reach this most reasonable conclusion? That at least no arbitrary stand on the part of the glass manufacturers in refusing to make these very popular styles of glass containers could be justified or expected unless there was a clear acquiescence in the matter by the various users of containers after the most careful consideration of the subject by the several interests involved, including the attitude of the public. Then if a decision should be made which provides, at its beginnings, for moderate standardization, both makers and users should pledge themselves to strictly adhere for the good of the public as well as themselves to the standards adapted.

I am perfectly aware that I have not touched upon the standardization of chemists' ware, but the glass-container industry is here this evening with an open mind. We have thought it better to show you that even in those

(Concluded on page 20)

Standardization in the Glass Industry

(Concluded from page 18)

fields in which standardization would seem to be most valuable and appropriate, there are still problems to be solved. The suggestions of the chemical industry will be heard with the greatest interest and respect by our industry. At first blush it would appear that here, more than in most other fields, the chemists themselves must take the initiative and decide what they want. Beakers and flasks are in the nature of tools for the laboratory, and individual preferences, it would seem to us, are bound to occur. It is in conferences like these, where men of intelligence and understanding meet together with open minds to give something and perhaps to receive something that not only industry but the great American people can hope to have its problems settled sanely and successfully.

Let us, therefore, hope that some suggestions of real value for the public good and for us all may be the result of this evening's meeting.

The Factor of Breakage in Odd Shaped Glass Containers

J. S. Algeo

The Glass-Pack Age

A Section of Canning Age Devoted to Food Packers Using Glass Containers

The Factor of Breakage in Odd Shaped Glass Containers

How the Craving for Individuality Can Be Satisfied Without Recourse to the Fantastic

By J. S. ALGEO
Hazel Atlas Glass Company

THE making of glass is almost as old as civilization itself. There has been more progress made in glass manufacturing in the past twenty-five years than in all the preceding centuries. In these past twenty-five years the making of glass bottles and jars has been revolutionized—but still a lot has to be done. Glass is brittle; it will break; and we will have problems to solve as long as we have to work with glass. Every once in a while you read something about unbreakable glass. I am sure everyone will be glad when that time comes; but it is not here yet.

I have not much to say about the composition of glass containers; that is the formulae of glass. Glass today is the same as it was centuries ago; that is, it is made of the same constituents; sand, soda ash and lime. Up until a few years ago glass was made by the rule of thumb method; today our chemists have developed it into a really fine art. Much has been done in a scientific manner in refining the formulae; in selecting the grades of material best suited for the purpose; in melting; annealing etc.; all of which make a more uniform and stronger glass. I do want to say something about the styles of glass containers and to try to show why certain styles are more apt to break than others. The glass manufacturer handles glass at a temperature of about 2400 degrees. It is melted in a liquid form and in that form we have to handle it. In other words, glass is not stamped out the same as steel or tin plate. Therefore, the glass manufacturer has a different sort of problem to solve than the man

who makes something out of metal and yet the glass manufacturer has to take that glass at a temperature of 2400 degrees which is almost of a watery consistency and work it into bottles and jars which vary from one another by only a very few thousandths of an inch in dimensions and by only small fractions of ounces in capacity. On a pound jam jar, we work within a quarter of an ounce variation in capacity.

The principle by which all bottles and jars are made is exactly the same, no matter by whom made nor by what process. There are two main operations: (1) Making the blank, represented by Fig. 2 (2) Blowing the completed article, represented by Fig. 3.

In Fig. 2, the cross-hatched portion represents the glass. The area partially surrounding it represents the mold—this mold is usually called the "blank mold." This mold is filled with glass and a plunger is inserted into the glass. The unshaded area represents the plunger or rather where the plunger was before it was withdrawn. After this first operation is completed the blank mold is taken away and the finishing mold (see Fig. 3) closes around the glass. After the finishing mold closes around the glass, compressed air is blown down through the opening made by the plunger. The glass of course has cooled down considerably but is still semi-liquid and something like thick molasses. When the compressed air is forced into the glass the glass spreads out until it comes into contact with the inside of the finishing mold.

Now this glass expands evenly. By virtue of that fact, the glass in the sides and bottoms will be thick or thin, even or uneven,

Fig. 1

Cross section of a round jar, the "perfect" package from the manufacturer's standpoint. When this container was blown, the glass had to travel the same distance in all directions to reach the side of the mold. As a result of this uniform distribution, there are no thin spots in the glass to break in the handling.

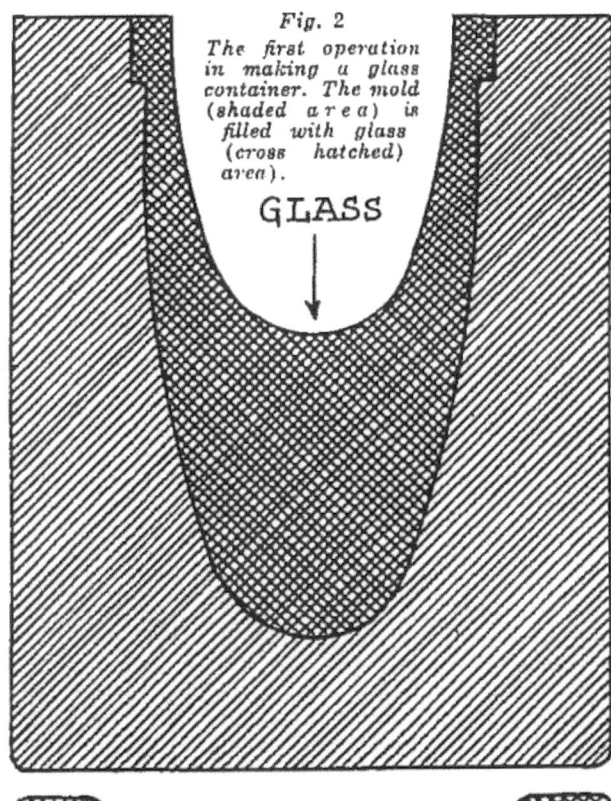

Fig. 2
The first operation in making a glass container. The mold (shaded area) is filled with glass (cross hatched) area).

GLASS

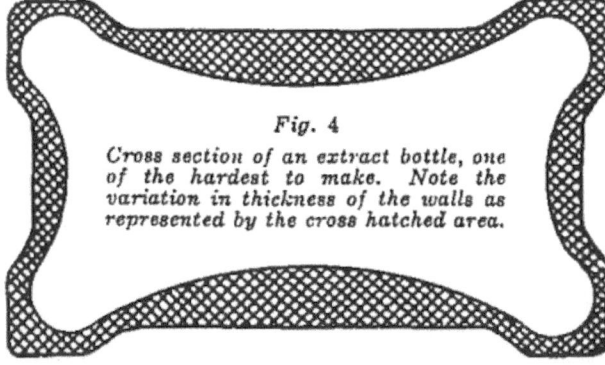

Fig. 4
Cross section of an extract bottle, one of the hardest to make. Note the variation in thickness of the walls as represented by the cross hatched area.

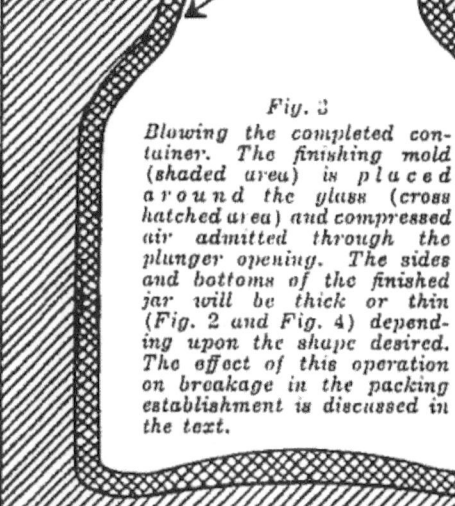

GLASS

Fig. 3
Blowing the completed container. The finishing mold (shaded area) is placed around the glass (cross hatched area) and compressed air admitted through the plunger opening. The sides and bottoms of the finished jar will be thick or thin (Fig. 2 and Fig. 4) depending upon the shape desired. The effect of this operation on breakage in the packing establishment is discussed in the text.

depending upon the shape of the bottle or jar. If the bottle or jar is round, the glass in the sides and bottoms will be fairly uniform in thickness. Fig. 1 shows a cross section through the sides of a round jar. To see the extreme in the other direction, see Fig. 4, which represents a cross section of an extract bottle—a difficult shape to make. In Fig. 1, the sides are equidistant from the center, consequently the glass has to travel the same distance in all directions to reach the sides of the mold and as a result the distribution of the glass is uniform. In Fig. 4 the glass has to travel much farther to reach the corners than to reach the sides and as a result the glass in the sides is very thick and in the corners very thin.

From the glass manufactures' point of view the thing to make is a plain round bottle or jar. The farther you get away from the plain round the more difficulty the glass manufacturer is going to have and the more difficulty the packer is going to have. It is all relative. If you have a square jar, you will have more uneven distribution than if you have a round jar. If you have an octagon jar you will have more even distribution than if you have a square jar. And if you have a twelve sided jar you will have more even distribution than if you have an octagon.

Now these different shapes of jars and bottles cause the manufacturer trouble and they cause you trouble. If we have to work with sharp cornered jars we will have trouble, because a great deal of the glass will blow so thin that we cannot pack it. Consequently our loss in packing is great. Moreover this glass is handled many times in a glass plant. It is carried from the machine to the lehrs or annealing ovens. It is taken from the lehrs, selected, and then packed. It is then carried to the warehouse and from there to the cars. Then the railroads get a chance at it. After you get it you handle it several times. The point I want to bring out is that these jars and bottles are handled many times and that there is breakage every time they are handled and that the more nearly they approximate a round shape the less breakage there will be. I wouldn't attempt to say what the loss is in handling glass in a glass plant but I venture to say that it is a great deal more than you have any idea it is. Our Company does not pack 99½ per cent of the glass it makes nor does any other manufacturer. The loss runs into very large figures.

From the glass manufacturers' point of view, therefore, the nearer you approximate a round article the better we are going to like it: the less loss we will have and the greater production we will have. This saving will be passed along to you and you can pass it along to your customers. And the cheaper you can sell your product the more you are going to sell.

Another thing that causes or prevents breakage is the annealing or tempering of ware. Poorly annealed glass will break easily when subjected to a shock such as a sudden change in temperature; as, for example, pouring hot jam or jelly into it. Annealing is simply the process of slowly and gradually cooling the glass from a temperature of about 1400 or 1500 degrees, at which temperature it comes from the mold, to the room temperature. Prior to a few years ago the degree of heat was regulated by the eye. Great advance has been made in that art and now almost every factory is equipped with instruments which automatically register and record the degree of heat. There is much less chance of poorly annealed ware getting out to the user than formerly, although it still does happen occasionally. Poorly annealed glass is a source of exasperation and loss both to the user and to the glass manufacturer but the latter is constantly improving his methods.

I would like to say a few words about how the preserver can help the glass manufacturer. Part of this will have no direct bearing on the subject of breakage. He can help in a great many ways. One thing he can do is to give up the idea of using fantastic shapes and getting as near to the round article as possible. It helps us in a hundred different ways and helps the packer likewise. Another way you can help us is in standardizing to a certain extent. There has been a great deal of talk in the National Preservers' Association about adopting one standard jam jar. I do not believe your industry is ready for anything of that kind; I do not believe it could be put across. But one thing the preserver could do is to standardize on sizes. Our Company for example, has dozens of sizes of preserve jars that run within three-quarters of an ounce in capacity. We have a jar that holds eleven ounces, another 11⅛, another 11¼, another 11½, another 11¾ etc., all of the same style but a little different in size. These molds cost a lot of money and some one has to pay for them. It would be a wonderful thing if the preservers could standardize on sizes and it would help the Glass Industry enormously, not only because it would save many thousands of dollars which are now spent for molds but more important because it would enable us to get greater production from the standard molds due to the less frequent changing and to the longer periods of operation. If you fellows could standardize on sizes you would confer a benefit on the glass manufacturer, on yourselves and on your trade.

I have been asked how much would be saved by adopting one standard jam jar. It would be impossible for me or anyone else to tell exactly how much less the cost would be for larger quantities. This question of cost is all relative. It is perfectly obvious, of course, that the more articles you make of the same kind the lower the cost will be; but there is a limit to that cheapness. No matter how many articles of one kind you make the material cost is no less. The material cost is not effected by quantity but remains exactly the same. The fuel cost is not effected by quantity and the cost of fuel and material constitute a very large part of the total cost. When you get down to packages, of course, economies would be effected by virtue of the fact that packages would be purchased in larger quantities.

The point I want to make is that there is a limit. A thousand gross of jars of different type will cost so much money. Ten thousand gross of the same jars will cost a little bit less; how much, I do not know. It depends altogether on conditions at that time. If we have enough of one article to keep one machine busy all the time making that article, we get a further reduction; because if we have one machine operating continuously on one article we can equip ourselves for handling that article automatically. If the production is increased still further and we are able to run a whole furnace on one article then the cost would be still further reduced because we could then equip a whole furnace for automatically handling the same article, and you gentlemen all know the relative cost in handling goods when labor saving devices can be used. Going still further, if two or three furnaces—that is to say a whole factory—could be devoted to making one article there would be still further reduction.

Making the Most of Glass

John T. Ogden

Making the Most of Glass

By JOHN T. OGDEN
Publisher of GLASS INDUSTRY, and of THE GLASS PACKER

BECAUSE of its versatility, glass is one of the most interesting materials to work with in planning a package. Colorless itself, it lends itself ideally to any conceivable color scheme; either through its transparency, which permits the natural color of the product to be utilized; through the treatment of the labels and closures; through the use of colored glass; or by applying color to the glass surface. In its natural state, glass is plastic, making it possible to mold the container into an inconceivable number of shapes and forms, both decorative and utilitarian. And it is a material entirely acceptable to consumer psychology, since the man or woman buyer is well accustomed to drinking his beverages, eating his food, or taking his medicaments from glass because it is the most cleanly and agreeable material which he knows of for these purposes.

In the hands of a skillful package designer, these many properties of glass may be utilized with telling effect. In some instances—notably the Hoffman Club Soda bottle which this year won the Wolf award—designers are alert to these opportunities. All too often, however, the designer muffs the ball. And the reason, as it seems to me, is because he does not understand sufficiently the material with which he is working. Glass container design requires more than a pencil or draughting board. I hope that all my readers will take note of this statement; too many people are of the opinion that glass container design—any container design—is simply a matter of draughtsmanship; of line and proportion, which any clever student in a high school art class is capable of accomplishing successfully. I mean this literally, for I know of companies employing artists to design their packages who have never even been in a glass factory. Although this comment is pertinent to many container materials it is particularly true of glass. Why this is so I shall try to explain very briefly by a series of simple illustrations. The first step in the making of a glass container is to put the hot glass in a blank, or parison mold. Fig. 1 represents the parison mold with the hot glass in the middle of it. One of the most important functions of the blank is to get the hot glass in such a shape that when it is transferred to the blow mold, the glass will be evenly distributed and its temperature will be evenly distributed. A mold maker recently remarked that he did not think a person is competent to design a good glass container until he can design a good blank. Perhaps it is requiring too much of a package designer to ask him to design a good blank; but I quote this remark simply to indicate how important it is to start right.

The glass next goes into the blow mold (Figure 2), and here it is formed into the particular shape you wish it to assume when it appears finally as a finished container. If the blank has been properly made and if your design is practical, the compressed air admitted into the blow mold will cause the glass to distribute itself evenly to all parts of the mold in the period of time allotted to this operation, and that, of course, means the distribution of glass will be even in the finished container. If the design of your container is such that it will not permit even distribution, there will be trouble. A few examples will make this clear.

Square shoulders make trouble. Please understand that when I say they "make trouble" I do not mean this cannot be overcome, but that it presents difficulty. It slows down production. It makes the container more expensive. When you blow air into a mass of hot glass, its natural tendency is to assume the form of a sphere just as when you blow up a balloon it becomes round. When the mold is square the glass reaches the bottom of the mold before it gets to the corners. (Fig. 3.) Look at a cross section of a mold (Fig. 4), with the glass in it. If a glass maker does not exercise care it is difficult to keep the glass from being thin at A and thick at B. Generally it is good to avoid square corners. To make a good container it is necessary to keep

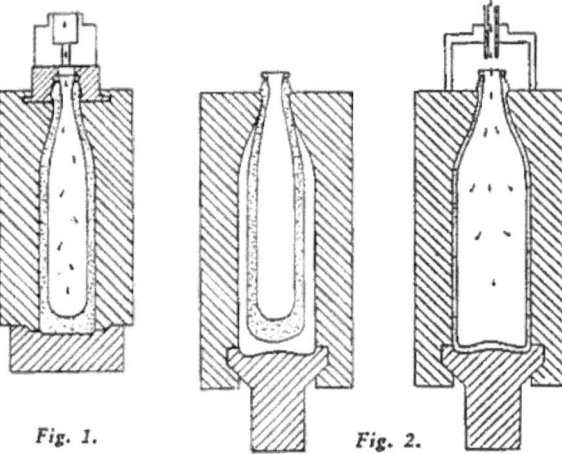

Fig. 1.

Fig. 2.

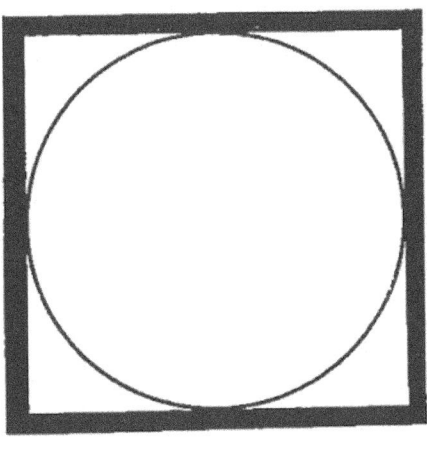

Fig. 3.

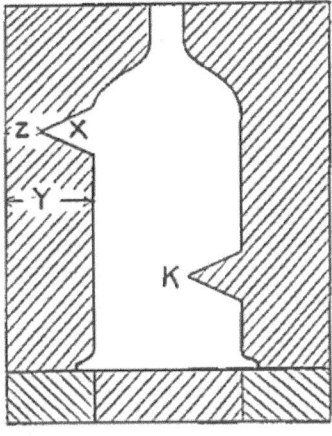

Fig. 5.

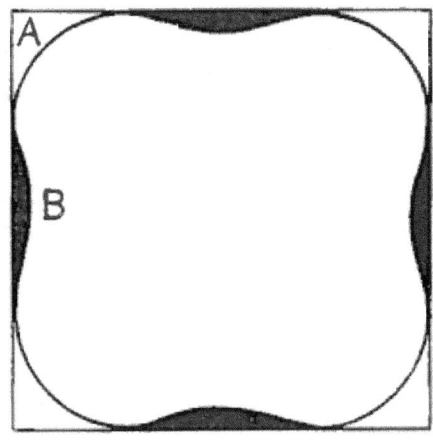

Fig. 4.

the hot glass at an even temperature throughout its entire mass. I remember the case of a manufacturer who made a shampoo for dogs and conceived the bright idea of shaping his container like a poodle dog. Now dogs have noses. In this drawing (Fig. 5), let us assume that X represents the dog's snout. The thickness of the mold wall at X is greater than at Z; consequently the mold is apt to cool off more quickly at Z. Rapid cooling retards the flow of the glass; the glass does not flow into the snout (X) easily and consequently the glass is apt to be thin at this point. Suppose you had a design just reversing this illustration, and in place of a projection, there was an indentation at the point K. Because the mold is thicker at K it keeps its heat longer; consequently the glass, being more "liquid," flows away from K and the glass is apt to be thin here.

If you are designing a container for a crown closure, remember it will have to be sealed under a crowning head, and if you have ever seen a crowning machine in operation you know that the pressure exerted on a container is considerable. So if you were to design a container for a crown closure, and give the bottle a square shoulder, you would have real difficulties, because when the force of the crowning machine is applied to the cap there would be nothing to support the neck. To provide the necessary support the manufacturer would have to build up the wall of the glass at the point M—not an entirely satisfactory solution, and one that would add needless weight to the container. Fig. 5.

This leads to another problem of container design. How much glass are you going to use in your container? If your design is ably done, with due consideration to all the factors involved in glass making, the mold will take the required amount of glass and no more. But if you have to build up thick spots in your glass you are going to add to the weight of the container and, naturally, to its cost. The bottle manufacturer must also have a reasonable tolerance in dimensions in order that the volume of glass and the capacity of the bottle may not conflict with the dimensions in his specifications. He should be allowed a slight leeway in the weight of the bottle in order that the weight of glass which will form most effectively for that particular shape of bottle may be chosen.

Consider the container finish. By "finish," I am not referring to the surface of the glass, but to the closure finish. A crown finish must have a long neck. A crown closure has to be applied by putting the neck of the bottle into a chuck, and the bottle neck cannot get into that chuck unless you provide enough room.

Containers must come out of the mold easily. Some of the causes of trouble in this respect are sharp reverse curves and sharp corners. Fig. 6 shows a cross-section, looking down, of a bottle which you may recognize. The sharp reverse curves at X make it quite difficult to get the container out of the mold. A good rule is to avoid sharp angles on any part of a bottle. (Sharp angles are also a frequent cause of "checks" or cracks in forming.) Furthermore, designs or decorations blown in the glass should not be heavy on the shoulder or upper areas of a bottle, and when a decorative effect of any kind is present it must be very faint at the seams of the mold in order that the bottle may be discharged from the mold freely and without injury to it.

The bottle in Fig. 6, incidentally, illustrates other difficulties arising from design. Fig. 4 showed how the flow of glass would be retarded by a sharp projection in the container. The same is true in Fig. 5. Here the glass is apt to flow into the projection more slowly, and a thin spot may result at X. When the design is such as to require the walls of the container to be of uneven thickness, as at X, Y and Z, the glass will cool more slowly where the glass is thicker and the result may easily be a poorly annealed container.

When designing a glass container, the designer must also take the product into consideration. He must know how it is manufactured. A few years ago, before prohibition was repealed, there was quite a vogue for flasks. Packers would buy the flasks, pack them with their products, and sell them to the consumer, because the consumer could re-use the containers for liquor. Some of the flasks were curved to fit the hip, and some were straight sided. A packer of tomato juice cocktail conceived the idea that he would pack his product in a flask, and without consulting the glass container manufacturer, he loaded up and processed an entire retort. Every bottle broke; I think there were 1,200 bottles in the lot. A second lot, also of 1,200 bottles, all broke.

What had happened? During the process, which involved the application of heat, the product naturally expanded. There being only a short neck on the flask, with no room for expansion, something had to give way; i. e. the container. If the packer had wanted to use that flask for tomato juice he would have had to fill far below the shoulder, which would make the package unmerchandisable. The package was not suitable for tomato juice cocktail.

While the case just cited is somewhat extreme it is important that any bottle to be filled with liquid have a proper expansion space above the correct filling point in order to allow for the expansion of the liquid without giving rise to excessive pressures. There are oils which at increased temperatures have an expansion coefficient three times as great as that of water, and when these oils are filled into bottles the pressure is excessive at only 80-90°F.

Remember that a bottle should preferably have a reasonable ratio of width to thickness. Thin, flat bottles are not conducive to ease of manufacture nor do they have as great strength as bottles with a smaller ratio of width to thickness. Remember also that if you pack under pressure, a curved container is ideal. The C & C Club Soda bottle is a good type of bottle to withstand high internal pressure.

Free-pouring liquids pour best from long-necked bottles. Whenever water goes over the lip of a container it tends to spread sidewise over quite a wide area. So if you want to pour water in small quantities, give the water enough room or time to "chase itself" down the bottle neck. By contrast, a viscous product, such as catsup, or some hand lotions, tends to pile up on itself, and does not require such a long neck for pouring.

Incidentally, in connection with catsup, there has always been quite a controversy as to its pourability—in what kind of bottle will it pour best? The Glass Container Association made a study of that problem a few years ago and found that two factors are responsible: the catsup and the container. Both factors are important, and you must consider them together. As far as the catsup is concerned, the finish is what counts. A well-finished, smooth catsup will pour out of almost any kind of bottle. If it is poorly finished, it will clog the neck no matter what you do about it. Considering the other factor, the bottle—the real secret is the slope of the shoulder. If the slope is abrupt, the catsup will not pour as freely as if the shoulder slopes gradually.

You may pack your product by weight. Suppose you want to sell a package containing six ounces of a product, for which you order a six-ounce bottle. Bottle capacities are all figured in terms of water, hence it is important to know the relation of your product to water, its specific gravity, so as to obtain a container that will hold just the required amount.

Tall Jars. A tall jar may have excellent display value, but I often think that manufacturers lay too much stress on the height of bottles in their effort to secure good shelf value; often a squatty container will give just as good results, and will save endless trouble, not only in the glass plant but especially in your own factory and when placed on display.

Two more points are well worth remembering: One, proper consideration should be given to the size and spacing of areas on which labels are to be placed and labels should always be provided with a smooth space. Secondly, the type and size of closure should be properly selected to conform to the character of product with which the bottle is to be filled.

I have given you these illustrations to indicate just a few of the problems involved in the design of a glass container. May I say once more that I do not mean to infer, for example, that all square bottles and all tall bottles have weak spots. These points that I have covered are points which should be considered in designing glass containers. Otherwise production may be slow, difficulties may arise, and needless expense be incurred.

I have used just a few illustrations showing that to design a glass container one must know something about glass. Something about the product, too. And, I believe, you will agree that very few designers outside of the glass companies themselves, and the mold makers, are familiar with such details.

No matter how good looking a package may be to the eye, if it is not designed correctly from a production standpoint, it will prove in the long run a costly package. Costly—not because the glass container manufacturer cannot overcome such problems; he does this every day. But costly because production may be slowed down; because shipping weight may be increased; because the packages may not handle well on

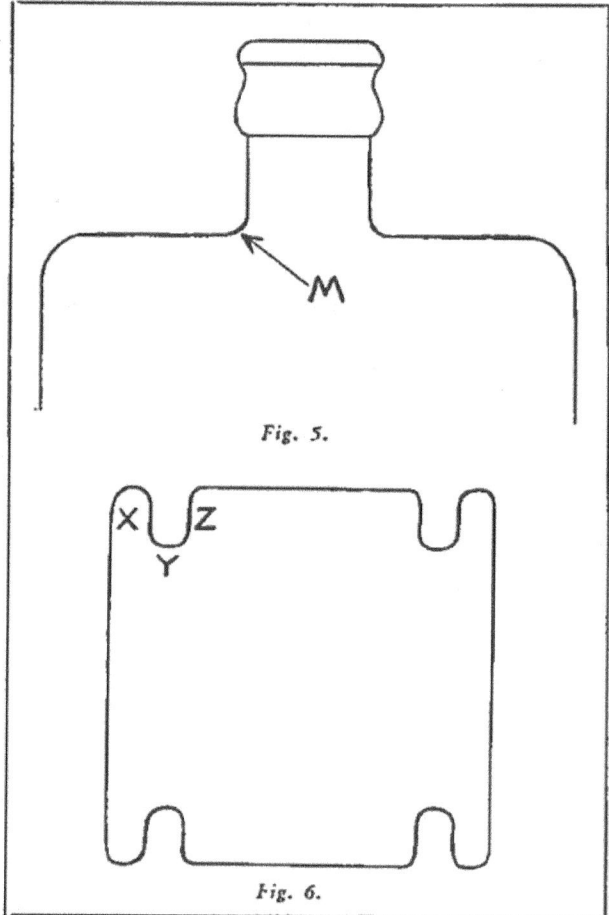

Fig. 5.

Fig. 6.

your production lines, or for innumerable reasons that add directly or indirectly to packaging costs. If you are designing a container why not design a good one while you are about it?

So if you have a particular design which you wish to see translated into glass, take it to a practical glass man and permit him to check it. His experience will tell him how to avoid these difficulties. And very often, by a few minor changes that do not destroy the spirit of your design, he will give you a good production package.

My opening statements alluded to the versatility of glass. One of its most interesting properties, is the number of finishes with which glass containers may be manufactured. By finish, I am referring now not to the closure finish but to treatment of the glass surface.

Stippled Finishes.—These are particularly desirable when a partial masking of the contents is desired as in the case of clam juice, which deposits a sediment; tomato juice, particularly when not manufactured by a process that prevents separation of the solids. Effects suggestive of coolness may be obtained, of which we have such a splendid example in the Hoffman Club Soda bottle. Stippled finishes are inexpensive, inasmuch as they are produced in the blowing operation and require no extra labor. The surface of the mold is roughened to conform with the design required on the finished bottle.

Frosted Glass.—This finish is sometimes referred to as matted, etched, or satin finish. It is produced by allowing hydrofluoric acid to dissolve the glass surface. Because it involves an extra operation frosted glass is naturally more expensive.

Sand Blasted Ware.—This closely resembles frosted ware. It is made by blowing sand against the glass surface, the impact of the sand causing minute particles of the glass to break away from the surface.

Iridescent Ware.—This finish is not difficult to make, and beautiful effects can be secured. Certain metallic salts are sprayed against the red hot bottles as they leave the forming machine. The cost of iridescent glass depends largely on the cost of the salts themselves. Iridescent ware has not proved popular. Its use is limited and demand has dwindled almost to the vanishing point.

I have mentioned these different types of glass finishes in order to make the record complete. In the great majority of cases, the manufacturer is well advised to stick to clear flint glass.

Container Colors.—Closely allied with finishes are the colored glasses. These may be either transpa nt, as when the glass itself is colored, or opaque, wher the color is applied. The standard colors are green, an'er, blue and opal (white). Normally two types of gieen are available, light and dark, though during the past year or so some manufacturers have developed other green colors.

The wisdom of sticking to the machine production colors is self evident. Within certain limits, however, almost any color can be secured by resorting to applied colors. These are opaque and will not permit the contents to be seen. This type of finish is made by apply-

ing lacquers to the glass and baking the color on.

In connection with applied colors I should call attention to a new development which has taken place within the past year or so that can be utilized in many ways and for excellent purposes. I refer to application in color of designs, names, and trademarks. These designs will not come off—and if any of you know the severe treatments to which some bottles are subjected in washing, the "fastness" of the color under such conditions is impressive.

Color and the Effect of Light.—The subject of colored glasses brings up a matter in which many readers are interested; namely, spoilage. Some two years ago, a chemist of the Bureau of Chemistry announced that his experiments had proved that light rays were an important factor in the deterioration of many products, and that a certain "grass green" or "chlorophyl" green glass would prevent that deterioration. The result was that literally dozens of manufacturers began writing THE GLASS PACKER to ask where they could buy "grass green glass." Everybody became upset over an announcement that was truly misinformation. I would like here to set the matter straight.

It is true that light rays of themselves do cause many products—if not most products—to spoil. But let me state with the utmost emphasis that the fact can still be true and still be a matter almost of indifference to the manufacturer whose products are protected by glass containers. The truth is that products of commerce are never exposed to high powered lamps and almost never to direct sunlight when they are so exposed, the flint glass of which the container is made will filter out the ultra-violet rays, which cause most of the harm. Moreover, it is a well established fact that both *heat* and *oxygen* play a part in decomposition. These experiments lost sight of the fact entirely that products packed in glass containers are not exposed to air.

I have tried to deal with a very intricate subject in very simple words. One cannot deal with so technical a subject in so few words and still maintain strict scientific accuracy. So for all practical purposes, the packer should just remember this one thing: the number of products which will deteriorate when packed in glass and exposed to light is so few that they can almost be numbered on the fingers of your hands. The vast majority who pack in glass are well advised if they forget the matter entirely.

In conclusion, let me go back to the point at which I began—the mold. To anyone at all interested in package design or package merchandising, it is obvious that so far as glass containers are concerned, the past four years have been four years of rugged individualism. By that I mean, manufacturers have gone to great length to secure private molds. I wonder if in all instances this has been necessary?

A mold costs several hundred dollars. A set of molds, several thousand dollars. Believe it or not, the purchaser of the container pays for these molds. Perhaps the expense is concealed, like the suit of clothes in the expense account. On a long run, say of many carloads, the container manufacturer may "absorb the

(*Continued on page 321*)

MAKING THE MOST OF GLASS

(Continued from page 288)

cost." But if he does absorb the cost, what does he really do? It goes into his overhead, and with glass, as with other merchandise, overhead figures in the sales price. One of the larger glass companies told me a few years ago that his investment in molds alone was some $750,000, if I remember the figures rightly. Could he, or could anyone, afford to forget that sum of money, and really absorb it?

My reason for mentioning this is that many of the containers we see today, instead of being designed with a real merchandising idea behind them, are selected simply because they are "different." I know of cases where simply gorgeous packages were thrown into the discard in order to have something new. This theory of packing finds perhaps its widest expression in the vinegar industry, where some vinegar manufacturers have an established policy of "bringing out a new piece" every Fall.

Novelty is a good thing. There is also a good merchandising reason for developing re-use containers; such as lamps, vases, refrigerator bottles, etc; since, as between two competitive items, the consumer often would choose the lamp base. But there are definite limitations to this plan of selling. Eventually, the consumer gets her home filled up with gadgets, and is out of that market. Moreover, constant change absolutely precludes establishing package identity.

My thought is not to decry the private mold. It is frequently advisable if not a downright necessity. But it exacts a price. There are some lovely stock containers available, and the smart designer—or so it seems to me—is the man who can take the package which others are using, and by giving real thought to the label and cap treatment, evolve something that is distinctive as well as beautiful. That is real package design!

Improving the Strength of
Glass Containers through Design

Leonard G. Ghering

IMPROVING THE STRENGTH OF GLASS CONTAINERS THROUGH DESIGN

By LEONARD G. GHERING

PRESTON LABORATORIES, Butler, Pa.

CYLINDER	SPHERE	PRISM	CUBE
⅛″ wall	⅛″ wall	³⁄₁₆″ wall	³⁄₁₆″ wall
95 sq. in. surface	82 sq. in. surface	131 sq. in. surface	112 sq. in. surface
11.3 cu. in. glass	9.8 cu. in. glass	22.5 cu. in. glass	19.2 cu. in glass
16 oz. glass	14 oz. glass	32 oz. glass	27 oz. glass

Photograph 1: All models are based on a capacity, inside walls, of 60 cu. in. The dimensions of the Prism are arbitrary. Wall thicknesses are comparative to give approximately the same strength. The photograph illustrates the fact that redesign of the container to give lower ratios of surface-to-volume allows lighter weight without sacrificing strength.

It is hardly an exaggeration to say that the variety of modern designs, sizes and shapes of glass bottles and jars is exceeded only by the variety of the fragments in a pile of cullet. And, although the artistic designer and the adaptation of glass to private molds, "distinctive packages," and "attractive packages," account for much of the variety and most of the frills and decoration in modern design, many other factors are very important. Some customers ask for all sorts of emblems and complicated lettering molded into their bottles, and usually insist on their own ideas as to where these adornments should be located, and specify certain types of labels.

Bottle design must be adapted to a great variety of mechanical handling devices—washing machines, washing machine pockets, brush spindles. inside brushes. fillers, filling tubes, cappers, pasteurizers, labelers, conveyors and cartoners, most of these units existing in many makes and models often differing widely.

A variety of types of closures is in existence. Head space and filling point have to be considered. Sometimes compact shapes are necessary for efficiency of packing or storage space.

Another factor of great importance recently has been that the weight of the containers must be a minimum in order to reduce their initial cost as well as freight and handling charges.

Although modern forming machines are sufficiently flexible to meet most of these demands, there are numerous angular shapes, sharp edges, and cut glass design imitations that are impractical or impossible to fabricate; the attainment of uniform distributions of the glass is sometimes a very critical matter. Consequently, in order to obtain high quality and efficient machine production, the packing department, the mold shop, and the fabrication foreman necessarily impose many more restrictions on design. Compromises have to be effected between what is wanted and what can be made.

Because of these demands, difficulties. and restrictions with respect to design, it is small wonder that the designing of bottles for maximum mechanical strength is as yet

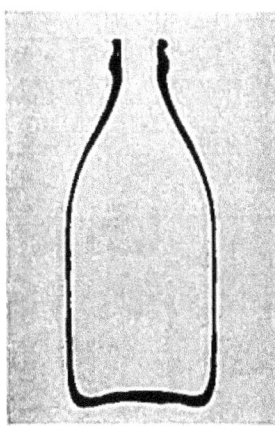

Fig. 1. No Deposit Beer showing bulged shoulder and rounded sidewall base junction. This design, even on light weights, tends to give good internal pressure, thermal shock, and impact strength.

Fig. 2. This design on a pint juice bottle gives good strength with a minimum of glass.

an undeveloped technique in the industry. Day by day, however, this situation is rapidly changing, mainly for two reasons:

1. Several laboratories and engineering departments connected with the industry are making careful comparative strength tests and accumulating data on all types of bottles. In some instances systematic programs have been instituted. The recent development of more accurate testing equipment has been helpful in this respect. Also the application of the comparatively new technique of locating the origins of fractures has enabled testing departments to identify the weak spots in a container.

2. The demands for lighter weight containers in the industry has focussed everyone's attention on the possibility of getting equivalent or even greater mechanical strength with less glass through improvement in the design and in the distribution of the glass in the container.

The purpose of this article is to discuss some of the definitely established general principles with respect to design and its relation to strength from the theoretical as well as from the practical point of view.

Theoretical Aspects of Design for Economy of Material

Any carpenter ought to be familiar with the fact that it takes more lumber to build a long rectangular box than to build a cubical box to hold a given volume. The same idea applies to glass containers; the surface area and the weight of glass required to enclose a given volume with, say, $\frac{3}{16}$" wall thickness depends on the form or shape of the container. The exact relationship between form and weight is given by the surface-to-volume ratios of the various simple geometric shapes. In a recent article Dr. J. H. Toulouse* illustrated the relation between form and design with photographs of four wooden models. These are reproduced in Photograph 1.

*"The Glass Industry Charts a New Course in Design," The Glass Packer, April, 1939.

The legend with the photograph gives the surface area required for a sphere, cylinder, prism and cube respectively, to enclose a volume of 60 cu. in. (about 1 quart). Also the weight of glass required for these various shapes is given.

From the data with the photograph it is seen that the container form most economical of container material is a perfect sphere, the surface required to enclose a given volume being a minimum. Of the four illustrated forms the next most economical of material is the short cylinder. In practice this is approximated in a round half-pint mason jar. The cube and prism are still less economical in the order named.

Economy of Glass in Practice

In practice the ideal spherical shape cannot be used for a container. Although it is approached in many designs, in general it is not well adapted to machine handling and other practical requirements.

On the other hand, short cylinders, fortunately, are well adapted to most practical requirements for containers. Theoretically, the cylinder most economical of material is one whose weight approximately equals its diameter. However, since a bottle has a shoulder, finish, and relatively thick base, its height should be somewhat greater than its diameter. Also, in practice the height and shape of the shoulder and neck are an important consideration. Although the amount of glass required for the finish is usually constant, this is not true for the neck and shoulder. The amount required for the latter depends on the shape and contour. By way of illustration, the amount of glass in the shoulder, neck and finish of a 10-oz. weight, 12-oz. capacity beer steinie is ½ oz. greater than that in the 12-oz. stubbie. Along the same lines of reasoning, it is obvious that the 12-oz. capacity ginger ale type bottle has too long a neck and is otherwise too tall to take full advantage of the theoretical possibilities of economy of glass in the neck and shoulder.

Also, by modifying the lower part of cylindrical bottles economies of material can be gained in practice. If the lower sidewall and base sidewall junction is rounded off, the ideal spherical curvature is being approached for at least that part of the container. Fig. 1 is an example of economical curvatures both in the shoulder and near the base. Fig. 2 and 3 show greater modifications in the lower part.

Likewise glass can be saved in the rectangular shapes if the factory designer is permitted to round off the edges of the sidewall. Even greater savings can be made in the shoulder and basal regions. The great difference between the glass required for an unmodified rectangle as compared with a sphere is illustrated by Toulouse's calculations (legend, Photograph 1). Although the savings accomplished by rounding off the edges are rather meagre compared with those occurring from the use of a different shape, they are none the less worthwhile.

The Theoretical Effect of Shape on Strength

The container shapes which are the most economical of material are the strongest containers in one sense: they give the maximum wall thickness for a given weight of glass. Theoretically, however, the stress developed in a container by an imposed force depends not only on the wall thickness but also on the dimensions and form of the container.

The amount of stress developed by a given internal pressure in containers of equal wall thickness and contents, but of different forms and shapes, is of particular interest. This stress will be a minimum in the sphere. It will be somewhat higher in an ellipsoid or other curved surface characterized by "double curvature"; the less the radii of curvature, the greater the strength (for equal wall thicknesses and volumes). In a short cylinder the stresses will be still higher, partly because of lower strength of the "single curvature" in the sidewall and partly because of the flat "drum-skins" at the ends. The latter cause particularly high localized bending stresses at the junction of the end and sidewall. It is because of the inherent weakness of flat ends, and the localized stress at the right-angle edge, that cylindrical metal high pressure containers such as steam boilers normally have dome-shaped ends (double curvature). However, we cannot put a dome end (base) in a bottle because the flat surface is necessary to allow the bottle to stand upright.

Because of all these stress relationships, the best choice of height-diameter ratio for maximum strength of a cylinder is not the same as that for minimum surface-to-volume ratio, but requires a somewhat taller bottle.

The stress developed in cubes and prisms is still higher than that for cylindrically shaped bottles (assuming equal internal pressures, wall thicknesses, and volumes). The cube is better than the rectangle since the area of its longest and widest panel is a minimum. Bottles having wide, flat panels are hopeless for pressure containers.

The mechanical stresses produced by thermal shock are different from those just described for internal pressure. For a given wall thickness, the thermal shock stresses in a sphere are a minimum because of the absence of corners and edges.

In cylindrical bottles, the greatest stresses develop at the junction of the base and sidewall due to the fact that the peripheral stresses in the lower part of the sidewall combine with the radial stress of the base at this junction. In rectangular shapes the thermal shock stresses are greater than for the other shapes; the stresses reach their maximum at the end-sidewall junctions because of the combined effects at the corners and edges.

With respect to the stresses produced by mechanical impact, thick-walled convex low-radius "double curvature" surfaces would be ideal. This is illustrated by the young lad who is unable to break an eggshell when squeezing it hard between his knees and distributing the force uniformly on the two ends by the use of the palms of his hands.

Practical Aspects of Strength and Design

The rudiments of the above theoretical principles have been recognized by the industry. This is shown by the predominance of cylindrical bottles over square and rectangular ones for pressure containers. Also the industry has shown a preference for broad and rounded shoulders, edges and corners.

Practically speaking, there is a lot more involved in the designing of containers for strength than the mere theoretical considerations and principles. Glass as a material conforms with the strength of materials' principles, as outlined in textbooks, up to its elastic limit.

If this limit is not exceeded, glass is a very strong structural material. However, when the elastic limit is reached, glass differs from most other materials in that there is no plastic flow; glass is brittle rather than plastic, and fractures once started are readily propagated.

Glass in the form of a container has further unique properties: it is fabricated in a mold by a specialized process; the surfaces are as unique as they are important in the strength of the article; there are several types of fabrication defects which have practical importance; and even in the best present practice the distribution of the glass, i. e., uniformity of wall thickness, is seldom ideal. Further, the container itself is unique in its details of shape and form; it must have a finish, a neck, a base, a shoulder, molded adornments, etc.

Internal Pressure Strength in Practice

For pressure containers, in practice, we are most interested in cylindrical shapes, and modifications thereof. In order to attain the strongest possible container, we are interested in the effect of height to diameter ratio on strength and the effect of length of neck and shoulder contour on strength. We are particularly interested in the effect of various curvatures in the junction of the base and sidewall and other basal modifications on strength. Theory does not give the complete answer to these questions. Rather, it is necessary to fall back on experimental bottles and empirical testing for several reasons:

1. The finish, neck and shoulder curvatures are too complicated to lend themselves to theoretical stress calculations.

2. The curvatures, both inside and outside, of the base and lower part of the sidewall of the cylindrical bottles are also complex, and theoretical calculations are further complicated by the rather large variations

Fig. 3. The well rounded lower sidewall on this quart milk bottle tends to give good thermal shock and impact strength.

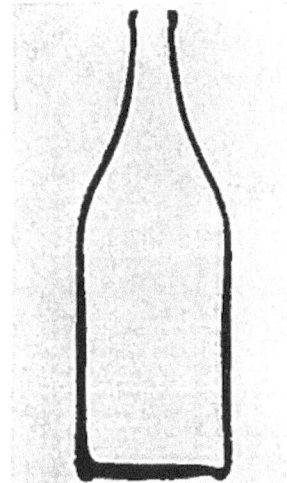

Fig. 4. In this quart beverage bottle the rings and lettering in the Murgatroyd Belt region are particularly bad. A bump check can easily be driven through the thin spot in the lower sidewall on the thin side.

in thickness of the glass usually produced by most fabricating machines in this region (heel taps, etc.).

3. The same variations in thickness and inside curvature in the base and lower part of the bottle make it virtually impossible to calculate accurately the ideal height to diameter ratio for a given volume.

Furthermore, fabrication irregularities and defects and the condition of the surface of the glass make a two or three-fold difference in the strength of the container. One type of defect is an "invisible check" in the glass at the contact point in the base (portion of the base which touches any flat surface upon which the bottle is sitting). Such an invisible check may cut the pressure strength by half or more, and is capable of detection only by an internal pressure test on the bottle or by etching with hydrofluoric acid, or other specialized laboratory techniques. Whether or not such a defect is formed may depend on the design or thickness of the basal portion of the bottle, and seems to be unpredictable in the present stage of the strength designer's experience. The remedy for such checks lies essentially in proper temperature control of the glass and the conveyor belt and is more of a practical problem than a theoretical one of design. However, design may enter into the final solution.

Another type of defect is a "cold fillet" of glass along the blank mold seam which does not flow freely or "blow out" in the finish mold, and therefore produces a "baffle mark." These baffle marks may or may not affect the strength, and the exact effect can be determined only by testing the bottle. Also the position of this baffle mark in the base may be a determining factor in the strength of the bottle. The correction of baffle marks is essentially the job of the mold shop and the machine operator rather than the designer.

The effect of slight "heel taps" and other variations in the basal thickness on the pressure strength depends to a great extent on all the details of the finish mold design and the thickness. In one design a heel tap may be particularly serious, whereas in another it may not. The strength of the base is most critical when the base is large or the height-to-diameter ratio small. In determining the maximum width of a bottle to hold a given volume, it is therefore again necessary to supplement

all theoretical considerations of surface to volume economy with empirical data on the pressure strength.

The condition of the surface of the glass may double or halve the pressure strength of a container. Plant inspectors usually roll two or more together in their inspection. Both the position and seriousness of the damage, as well as the resulting loss of strength, depends on the weight, size and design of the bottle. Increasing strength thus becomes a matter of preventing damage. Sometimes changing the design will help to prevent the damage (Figs. 4 and 6).

Also of great importance on the pressure strength of bottles is the uniformity of thickness or the excellence of the distribution of the glass attainable in the fabrication of a particular design. Obviously, unless the particular design of bottle can be made well, it is worthless in spite of any theoretical good points.

For maximum pressure strength in practice the ideal distribution seems to be a slightly greater thickness of sidewall in the lower part (Fig. 1). The No-Deposit Beer design shown in this figure is excellent in economy of glass, distribution of glass, and strength. Also, this bottle has good stress distribution and illustrates the "double curvature" bulging shoulder, short neck, and rounded sidewall base junction. Fig. 2 shows a similar design on a non-pressure container.

Fig. 6. This is an improved design of a carbonated beverage Steinie. Note that the lower sidewall is rounded off and the rings are moved up to the top of the Murgatroyd Belt where they do considerably less damage than lower down as in Figure 4. This design has good thermal shock strength.

In order to attain better stress distribution on prism-shaped and panelled bottles the same ideas may be applied. Although drastic changes from panels to single curvature or double curvature may not be possible, it may still be possible to salvage a few modest improvements by rounding off edges and corners and shortening straight panels.

Practical Design for High Thermal Shock Strength

To a great extent practical experience in thermal shock strength follows theory. Thick walls and junctions break more easily than thin ones; large diameter bases weaken the container; and acute angles and small radii curvatures at junctions give higher localized stresses than well-rounded edges.

Figs. 1, 2, 3 and 6 illustrate designs having good thermal shock strength.

Just as was the case in internal pressure strength, commercial bottles often develop unexpected weaknesses in thermal shock, and for much the same reasons. Bad

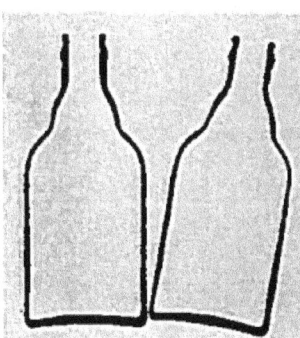

Fig. 5. (a) Two square base Steinies showing how the base of one can easily drive a bump check through the vulnerable Murgatroyd Belt region of the other.

Fig. 5 (b) Similar Steinies with rounded bases showing how the convex surfaces in this region cannot inflict localized blows and therefore do not produce bump checks or other damage.

baffle marks have long been recognized as a source of difficulty, but the machine operators' problem may sometimes be simplified by modifications in design.

Checks will also ruin the thermal shock strength, a check orientated peripherally in the base-sidewall junction being the most serious. This differs from pressure strength checks in that the latter are most serious if they have a radial direction.

Of perhaps even greater practical importance in the thermal shock strength is the condition of the surface. Damage in the lowest ½ in. to 1 in. of the sidewall was found by Murgatroyd to be particularly serious. Scratches and bruises on the outside in this region do more damage than in any other part of the bottle. The region is sometimes referred to as the "Murgatroyd Belt." For a bottle having a square sidewall-base junction, deep bruises, and even "bump checks" can be easily driven into the glass by the inspector, especially if he inspects the bottle while still hot. Further damage

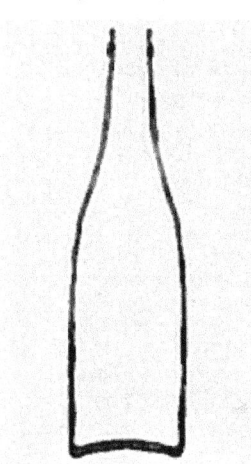

Fig. 7. A square base beverage bottle with a slight heel tap in the lower sidewall adjacent to the rigidly supporting base. An impact at this thin spot in the lower sidewall easily produces breakage.

is caused in bulk pack shipping cartons and in all subsequent handling in service. Rings and lettering or other adornments in the Murgatroyd Belt region are particularly bad (Fig. 4).

Much of the damage in the Murgatroyd Belt can be avoided by changing the design of the bottle. Undercut the lower part of the sidewall (or round off the base-sidewall junction) so that when two bottles are bumped side by side they do not inflict damage in this important region (Fig. 5). The prevention of the damage increases both the pressure and thermal shock strength, the thermal shock strength being particularly sensitive to the presence or absence of damage in this region.

Furthermore, rounding off the base usually gives a thinner sidewall-base junction, which increases the thermal shock strength. Also, the smaller diameter of the flat portion of the base is favorable (Fig. 6).

Effect of Design on Impact Strength

Theoretically it is difficult to predict just how or where or what shape container will break most easily when subjected to mechanical impact. In general one would expect that low radius double curvature and thick walls would be favorable for great strength. However, our greatest practical interest lies in the essentially cylindrical (single curvature) bottles with or without rounded bases. The strength at the various points along the straight part of the sidewall is therefore important.

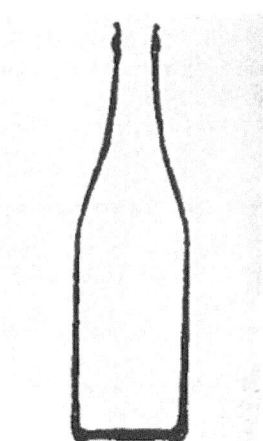

Fig. 8. A square base beverage bottle with relatively thick lower sidewalls which tend to increase the bottle's resistance to external impact.

Various types of impact testing equipment have been used from time to time. In the Butler Laboratory we have been using a newly designed semi automatic ball dropper. In this test, for example, on 12-oz. steinies, 16 steel balls ¾ in. diameter are dropped successively by an automatic magnetic release. The bottle (lying on its side) is rotated by the machine so that the 16 impacts are in the form of a spiral around the barrel of the bottle, starting at the shoulder and extending to the edge of the base. The impact can be varied by changing the height from which the balls are dropped.

In a bottle with a straight rather than an undercut lower sidewall, and with even distribution up and down and round the sidewall, breakage in a typical case will not occur with the first 14 balls; but it will very likely be broken by one of the last two which strike the lower part of the sidewall. This is the part which is rigidly supported by the base. The explanation probably is that in the center of the barrel of the bottle the glass can give when it is impacted, much as a window-pane will give if one pushes it with their finger in the center of the panel. If one strikes either the window or a bottle at a point adjacent to its rigid support, in the lower sidewall next to the base in the case of the bottle, and near the edge in the case of the window pane, it will break easily.

A bottle which has a thin spot in the sidewall adjacent to the base is very weak; the thin spot is more serious there than at any other part of the barrel (Fig. 7).

On the other hand, the barrel of a bottle may be surprisingly thin, providing it is uniform, and still not break in the center of the barrel. Breakage near the rigidly supported base may be decreased if the glass is a bit thicker in the lower sidewall (Fig. 8).

Let us now consider the effect of a rounded base design. It is harder to strike the bottle, either in the test or in service, at this point with other than a glancing blow. Furthermore, the stress distribution on the rounded surface is more favorable. Also the Murgatroyd Belt is not as easily damaged by the inspector. Many types of light weight bottles having this undercut design have shown excellent impact strength in the above test.

The Relation of Distribution and Design to Lighter Weight

Having chosen the proper design and determined the ideal distribution of glass, high strength is assured if

(Continued on page 472)

IMPROVING THE STRENGTH OF GLASS
CONTAINERS (Continued from page 447)

this ideal distribution can be obtained by the machine operator in practice (and other fabrication irregularities eliminated). That is not as big an "if" as it might seem. Fabrication machines, blank mold design, and operating technique, are constantly being improved.

Weight may be reduced and the strength may be increased by eliminating dead weight in the form of thick bases and corners, by employment of lower surface to volume ratio shapes, and by generous use of double curvatures, without decreasing the wall thickness. Weight may also be reduced by decreasing the wall thickness. Sometimes both are done. If the wall thickness is radically decreased, then there is grave danger that the strength will be impaired (radical shape changes excepted) unless compensating improvements in the quality of the distribution are made simultaneously. It is in such instances that lighter weight is vitally dependent upon the attainment of ideal distribution. Fortunately, it is just those rounded shapes and bulging double curvatures that increase strength and decrease weight that are also the joy of the mold shop and the machine operator. These are the shapes that are naturally adapted to the attainment of ideal distribution in practice.

Modern Styling in Bottles for Beer

J. H. Toulouse

Modern Styling in Bottles for Beer

J. H. Toulouse, Ph. D., Ch. E.

Packaging Research Division, Owens-Illinois Glass Company

MODERN streamlining includes the modern bottles. It has lighter weight but with rugged strength, shorter height for less space in storage, increased girth which means greater speed possibilities in handling, and larger sizes—which mean —PROFITABLE VOLUME.

Never before has a bottle of beer been given a name which the consumer so immediately accepted and used. Never before have beers been named *after* the bottle which contained them. Yet these things are being done today and accepted as a matter of course.

Thirty months ago a new thought in packaging of beer was inaugurated. A bottle was made with the shortest possible height and lowest weight to which modern beer filling lines could be adapted. This was the "Stubby" bottle for beer. Soon after appeared the "Steinie" which combined tradition with modern styling.

Bottle Types and Standardization

"Steinie" was not the product of an overnight effort. Over six months were required to assemble machine parts of all kinds which might influence the shape—soaker pockets, rinsing devices, filling tubes, crowning throats, pasteurizer pockets and labeler parts. Then the bottle was painstakingly tailored to fit with each one of over one hundred different pieces of equipment which would handle it. "Steinie" could step into any filling line almost overnight so few were the changes and adjustments needed.

The net result of the "Steinie" and "Stubby" development was lighter weight, less bulk and lower operating costs. A typical case of bottles, filled, weighs only 36½ lbs., as compared with 51½ lbs. for the older style bottle and wood case—a savings of 30%. Five hundred cases of "Steinies" occupy the same space as three hundred cases of the old bottle, a further savings of 40%.

The lighter weight encouraged sales "by the case." More bottles in the refrigerator meant more sales. More cases in the truck, or in the carload, meant lower shipping costs and greater shipping volume.

That "Steinie" was accepted is a matter of history —history that recorded itself with breath-taking speed. In less than sixteen months' time, *half* of all beer bottle production swung to the "Steinie" and "Stubby" bottle. Some brewers are bottling in these new bottles who never before packed beer in any bottle.

The style of bottle is by no means the only change. Prior to repeal, a great deal of confusion existed. Bottle sizes were by no means standard. Twelve, twelve and one-half, thirteen and fifteen ounce sizes were in competition with each other. After much effort these have become standardized as the twelve

ounce size, except on the Pacific Coast. New York State has standardized in steps of four ounces for the smaller sizes—as eight, twelve, and sixteen ounces.

The twelve ounce size is by no means the only size. Quarts and half-gallons had been used, the former pasteurized, the latter, not. Newer developments have changed the aspects of both.

There have been two developments in the quart size. The first has been the adoption of the "Steinie" shape — both for reduction in weight, and for the compactness that it offered. At the present time a considerable portion of the quart volume is going into this style of container. The second development was purely technical and will be discussed later in this article.

It is in the half-gallon size that the greatest changes have taken place—both in style, handling and merchandising.

Shortly after repeal, a few breweries started placing beer in tall half-gallon bottles, keeping it cold and selling it without pasteurizing for immediate consumption. In some cases this was done by filling the bottles from keg beer—even as a sideline at the bar. In time it had grown to a sizable volume, centered in the Chicago-Milwaukee, Northwest and the New York areas.

Soon the state of Washington demanded that all bottled beer be pasteurized. Efforts to pasteurize in the tall shape showed that more weight and more headspace were required. About this time the "Steinie" shape was being introduced so that efforts were made to try the new design in the half-gallon size. By the use of the proper amount of headspace, and the proper weight, it was possible to produce a bottle to hold a full half-gallon of beer, pasteurized to keep indefinitely before sale.

This package was so popular that soon an identical shape was produced for beer that was not pasteurized. Still another development, just completed, is a "Steinie" shape for *full automatic pasteurizing operation*, handled exactly like the smaller sizes. With these advances, the volume of beer going into the half-gallon size has approached five percent of the total of all beer produced. In the city of Chicago it represents 25% of all packaged beer.

Another inovation in the packaging of beer is applied color lettering, the permanent, fused-on colored glass design that is part of the bottle, itself. This eliminates labels and insures the return of the bottle to the brewery. It would probably be difficult for a shipping brewer to use bottles with these fused-in labels, but where the business is sectional or local, it undoubtedly offers a most interesting merchandising prospect for the future.

Pressure in Pasteurization

Pasteurization of beer has called for a study of that operation. Theoretically, pasteurization could produce a pressure of over one hundred pounds per square inch—practically only about eighty pounds is reached where the bottle is not agitated during pasteurization and ninety pounds per square inch in automatic types which turn the bottles over when the chain reverses direction. Pasteurization of half-gallon bottles resulted in the finding that these bottles could not be laid on their sides because the slight swinging action of the basket gave a "sloshing" agitation that increased the pressure to unsafe limits.

Expansion Factor

Another pasteurization discovery was the effect of high alcoholic content on the expansion of the beer during heating. High alcoholic beers have about thirty percent greater expansion when heated than low alcoholic beers. The older beers expanded about two percent during pasteurization; the newer "high-power" beers expand from 2.75% to 3%. Because overfilling reduces the headspace safety, we have adopted four percent as the minimum allowable, with 6¼% as the average, depending on the size of the container.

The old style quart bottle had too little headspace for pasteurized beers. It has been difficult at times to have the breweries realize the necessity of a safety factor for expansion of liquids particularly under conditions of pasteurization.

The bottle manufacturer must produce bottle styled to be used under the worst conditions rather than the average for which reason the new quart had to be made to take high-power beers even though often used for beers of lesser alcoholic strength or for unpasteurized beers.

AN EVOLUTION IN BOTTLES

THE "STUBBY"

POPULAR HALF-GALLON "STEINIES"

The Standardization of Bottles for Beer and Ale

J. H. Toulouse

The new standard bottle (in center) compared with previous designs. Note differences in height and thickness and variable styles of bulb design.

The Standardization of Bottles For Beer and Ale

By

J. H. Toulouse, Ph. D.

Owens-Illinois Glass Company, Toledo, Ohio

THE outstanding event for the bottling of beer in 1941 was the promulgation, during May of this year, of the standards for beer bottle design developed by the joint committees of the United States Brewers Association, and of the Glass Container Association. These committees began their work in April of 1940, and considered the matter for a full year in developing the final standards adopted. The work has the support of the United States Bureau of Standards in carrying out the program of standardization.

The writer does not represent the committee, nor was he a party to any of its deliberations. Any material given herein, except by the way of direct quotation, is used as a matter of his own opinion, and as his interpretation, only, of the good to come from the program.

Several years ago we were asked to design a bottle shape that could be recommended as a weight saving, space saving, and cost saving bottle for beer. The result was the Steinie shape, now in current use. The shape of the bulb was determined by securing drawings of those machine parts that made contact with the bottle. These drawings were superimposed, with the finish (or crown holding part) of the bottle sketched in its limiting position. The bulb was then drawn in as a graceful curve, carrying out the tradition of this neck shape

used so long in the industry. The point to emphasize here is that machinery for handling bottles was closely considered.

Better adaptation to the machinery that must handle the bottle seems to be the prime motivation of the present standardization committee's work. Increased speed of handling means that bottles must be more closely alike in height and diameter. The shape of the bulb influences the apparent filling height, and the appearance of foils on the neck. The changing of filling tubes between beer and ale runs, or between 11 fluid ounce capacity and 12 fluid ounce capacity and the like, is a time consuming, and therefore, costly matter if done during the day's run.

We can take up the issues of standardization, as they appear to us, under these several headings:

Height and Diameter

The specifications for height and diameter are not necessarily new. For long years the height of the 12 fluid ounce beer has been 9½ inches. Diameters varied somewhat with differing heights of shoulder, shape of neck, and weight of glass. With the adoption of a *standard shape, or contour*, not just height and diameter, the diameters are now fixed within the usual tolerances for variations necessary

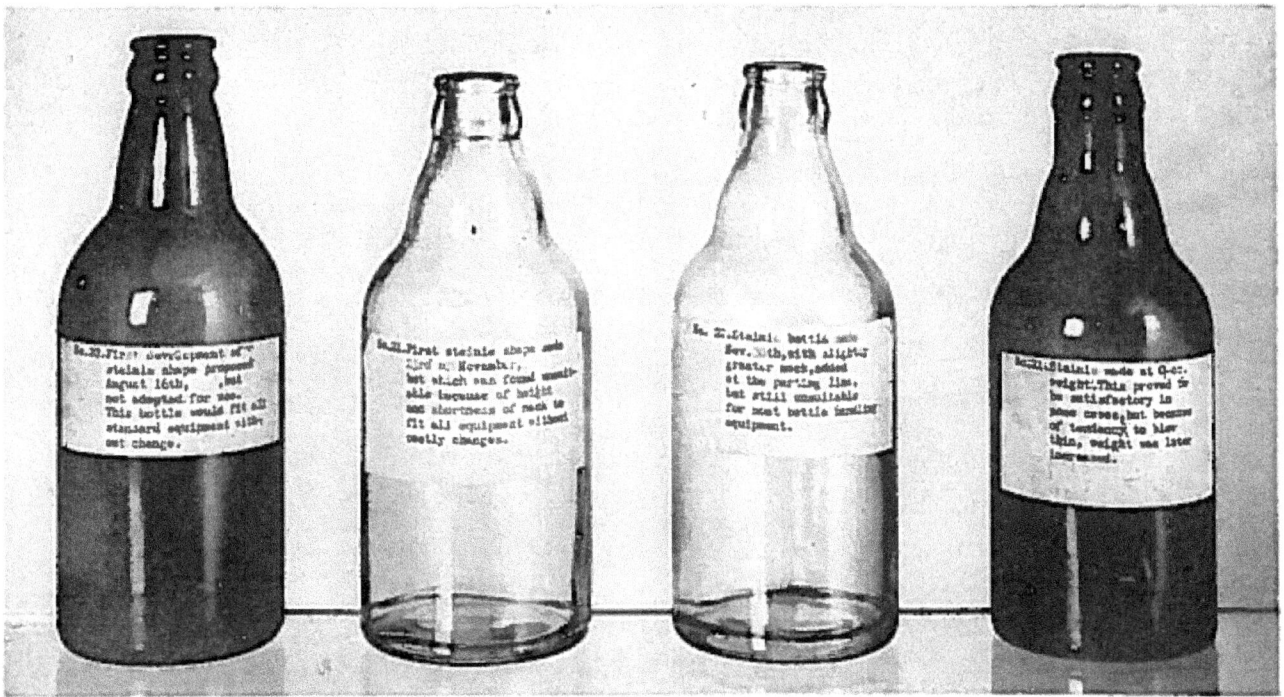

Evolution of the Steinie design (from left to right): the first development of the steinie shape which would fit almost all brewery equipment without change. Next is an attempt to make a shorter and fatter neck. The third bottle repre- sents a change by one-eighth of an inch but the bottle still would not fit standard brewery filling equipment. At right is a standard bottle, one-eighth of an inch taller than the bottle to its left.

with the glass container. These tolerances are standard in the industry and represent the unavoid- able difference due to the high temperature of the bottle at the time of forming, and the reasonable wear of a set of molds during its normal and useful life.

Thus, for example, the diameters of the "Ex- port," "Select," and "Ale" shapes in the 12 fluid ounce series are 2-15/32″, 2-17/32″ and 2-27/64″ re- spectively. There is no reason why bottles with this overall spread of 9/64″ from widest to narrowest cannot go down the same filling line without chang- ing guide rails, starwheels, and filling tubes, if a brewer wants to fill these three shapes with cor- responding differing products alternately during the day. And since the 11 fluid ounce capacity bot- tles have the same respective widths in the Export shape and in the Select shape as the 12 fluid ounce series, they also can be handled at differing periods of a day's run, without loss of time other than changing labels and crowns.

The importance of widths is apparent in some breweries. A thoroughly modern high speed filling line in a Toledo brewery has had difficulty because of some of the "fat" heavy weight bottles of twenty-five to thirty years ago that still come back to them, still sound and strong, and ready for an- other trip. (I wonder how many trips a bottle makes in thirty years!)

Height of the 11 Fluid Ounce Bottle

A factor of importance is the specified difference in heights of the 12 fluid ounce, and the 11 fluid ounce container. Untold hardship has been brought about by those who insisted on the same height for both bottles. When the bottles were mixed in the trade, no power on earth could separate these bot- tles as they passed down the filling line at 100 to 160 bottles per minute. Even the use of a bead was not too effective, as the time allotted for examina- tion could never be sufficient. As a result, bottles made for, and filled with eleven fluid ounces were labeled 12 fluid ounces, and 12 fluid ounce bottles were so filled but labeled 11 fluid ounces. The dan- gers in this are real, and costly, as the brewery could be subject to stiff penalties for such mislabel- ing. To name a case in point, one brewery had a shipment of second hand bottles come over a thou- sand miles, only to find they were an ounce too small. For this reason the writer hails the fore- sight of the committee in fixing the standard dif- ference of ¼ inch between the heights of the 11 and 12 fluid ounce bottles, the more so that it enables diameters to remain equal.

Bulb Dimensions Specified

Of equal importance is the fact that the specifica- tion of critical dimensions also extends to the bulb diameter. The point specified is the diameter at the approximate filling point. This is of major impor- tance in securing a uniform filling level under the present provisions of specifying overflow capacity.

The need for a standard bulb shape is very press- ing. Only recently we were confronted with the fact that one type of bottle washing machine, whose pocket fitted the contour of the bulb very closely, would not handle one of the standard bottles. Quite possibly the manufacturer of the machine used a random bottle for fixing the dimensions of the pocket. Quite possibly, also, the bottle chosen was one with a narrow bulb. A redesign on our part made a bottle that failed to fit the pocket by what amounted to about 1/32" or less in height. Since a number of the machines were in use, we had to alter our bottle design. Had there been at that time a limiting *contour for the bulb* which we would not exceed in one direction, and which the machinery manufacturers would not exceed in the other direction, such troubles would not have been encountered.

Bulb dimension specification has other benefits. By the gradual elimination of the larger diameters previously made by various bottle makers, foil sizes can become more uniform and saving of material. The headspace, or volume above the filling point, is more uniform, and the result is more uniform filling quantities as well as heights. There will always be assured an adequate expansion space for pasteurization without this old-time possibility of questionable overflow capacity; brewers need no longer tolerate overfilling and its loss in value of filled goods.

Head Space and Overflow Capacity

A new provision of these standards is the abandonment of "filling height" for "overflow capacity" as a basis of measurement. A very real engineering need brought this about.

Hitherto Ale, Select and Export shapes had the same filling points, about 2¼ inches down from the top of the bottle. But the Export shape had a large bulb, the Ale shape a straight taper neck, and the Select shape a long narrow neck. The resulting headspace was longer in the export bottle, smaller in the Ale shape, and still smaller in the Select shape. *These bottles could not previously be filled correctly using the same filling tubes of the "displacement" type, but could be filled with tubes filling to a height.*

The differing headspace remaining gave a real problem. Beer expands greatly in volume during pasteurization. The more alcohol present, and the less dissolved solids, the greater will be the expansion. The result is that Ale, with generally a higher alcohol content than most beers, and therefore with the greater expansion, had the least space in which to expand within the sealed bottle.

By adopting a uniform *overflow* capacity for *each* size bottle, the committee made an outstanding step forward. They made it possible to so regulate filling that the same filling tubes can be used for several products and bottles, filling each with the same number of fluid ounces, and having identical headspaces for expansion during pasteurization. This safety factor is important in reducing bottle breakage and product losses during the operation of pasteurization.

(The writer does not share the view that the standardization program will allow the same tubes in every instance to be used with the Steinie shapes, as with the corresponding taller shapes. The Steinie

Maintaining tradition in the brewery bottle family. At left is a 50 year old, hand-made Anheuser-Busch bottle. Next is a Schlitz bottle 35 years old made with automatic equipment. The next three are developments in the steinie design.

bottle cannot take the same long tubes as used in certain types of filling. Neither can it be filled to the same filling level by the fillers that "fill to a level." For this reason he feels that the 7 bottle sizes stated in the G.C.A. report of the beer bottle standardization to be filled by 1 set of tubes should be decreased to 5, and that a new tube designation be set up to handle Steinie bottles. With all respect to the committee's work, the writer feels that this particular problem cannot be solved because of physical reasons.)

To analyze this matter further, we must consider that there are in general two methods of filling:

1. Those filling machines that fill to the top of the bottle, then remove a tube whose volume equals the desired headspace.

2. Those filling machines that fill to a given level, regardless of headspace.

Throughout many years there has been every incentive to develop machines that filled to a line. Bottle capacities have been designated by the volume at given heights. The uniformity of the filled heights of a group of bottles has been greatly stressed.

Of the filler types that filled the bottle to the top with a long filling tube, and then "pulled out the hole," the syphon filler is the earliest type. The bottle would fill to the top, and could remain on the filling rack almost indefinitely, until the operator got around to taking it off. When the long tube was pulled out, the liquid level dropped down to the approximate level desired.

Gravity fillers of the diaphragm compensator type also filled bottles to the top, and then withdrew the tube. The water check type of filler also filled to the top of the bottle as usually employed, but it should be recognized that these fillers fundamentally *fill to a level*, with the level chosen as the top of the bottle only for convenience, and for the purpose of air elimination. If necessary to secure greater headspace, a simple adjustment of the water check was all that was needed.

Changing design in brewery bottles. At left is a cork finish pint, hand-made about 50 years ago—at right, a cork finish bottle of the same age. Note striking resemblance to present stainie.

Bottles of 80 years ago (left—1858, right—1866) made for Thomson's Aerated Water, Dunedin, Scotland. Even as long ago the bulb shaped neck was an element of design.

The important thing about the above is that all three types depend upon the volume displaced by the filling tube as a means of securing the proper headspace. For filling the newly standardized 12 fluid ounce bottles all that is needed is to see that the tubes displace 23/32 of a fluid ounce. With this properly done, all 9½″ tall bottles, and all 9¼″ tall bottles will be properly filled, since all are arranged to have 12-23/32 or 11-23/32 fluid ounces overflow capacity respectively.

The other type of filler, filling to a level and without using a long filling tube presents another problem. It cannot work on the overflow principal. Hitherto its chief requisite has been that bottles have the same filling height. Because of this, it is necessary to further specify that the diameter at the *approximate* filling height for 12 fluid ounces for example be maintained in all makes of bottles within the ordinary dimensional tolerances for glass.

The writer is not sure how the differing shapes of bottles as Export, Select, and Ale, can be handled interchangeably on this type without change or adjustment of tube's length down to the air inlet valve, unless something can be done by means of adjustable pressure or jetting. Since the heights of fill, in distances down from the top, vary from 2-15/32″ in the Export shape, to 2⅝″ in the Ale shape, and to 2-23/32″ in the Select shape, there is a change in filling height of ¼″ necessarily due to bottle shape.

The fact that problems still exist does not detract from the outstanding work of the committee. The

outstanding total of almost one hundred different *stock* molds has been reduced to twenty-two. Eighteen existing designs for the 12 fluid ounce capacity, the weights, heights, and other dimensions differing, have been reduced to four, of two heights and of two weights only (for Steinie and tall bottles respectively).

The goal of the joint committee was stated as follows in its report of May 1, 1941:

"The advantages to the Industry in complying with this standard list are many: Briefly the following are manifest:

1. It should eliminate nearly 80% of the present large variety of bottles manufactured for the sale of beer (it being estimated that 85% of the bottled beer is sold in about five glass containers);
2. The reduction of the weight of the containers should effect savings in freight charges;
3. The cost of bottles should react favorably;
4. It will tend to eliminate the costly adventures in new style bottles that very frequently prove unprofitable.
5. It will avoid the costly obsolescence heretofore experienced due to lack of standards;
6. It will provide the brewers with advance, expert advice on the advisability of initiating a new container, and will not interfere with progress and technical advancement in this field;
7. It may assist in simplification of the laws and regulations affecting containers."

In further statement regarding its list of standards, the committee states:

"(a) This list of standards adopted, together with approved blue prints applying thereto, set forth weights, dimensions and fill points for bottles of the type and capacities listed;
(b) This list shall not be interpreted as an indication that all bottles of the capacities designated are recommended for general use nor interpreted as an interference with the right of brewers to order bottles not listed but now in use by such brewers;

REPRINT—THE STANDARDIZATION OF BOTTLES FOR BEER AND ALE

Capacity in Ounces	Overflow in Ounces	Weight in Ounces	Height in Inches	Diameter in Inches
EXPORT SHAPES—(Drawing No. C-146)				
7	7$\frac{19}{32}$	8	7$\frac{1}{8}$	2$\frac{9}{64}$
8	8$\frac{31}{64}$	9	8$\frac{1}{4}$	2$\frac{3}{16}$
11	11$\frac{23}{32}$	12	9$\frac{1}{4}$	2$\frac{15}{32}$
12	12$\frac{23}{32}$	12	9$\frac{1}{2}$	2$\frac{15}{32}$
24	25$\frac{15}{64}$	22	11$\frac{1}{2}$	3$\frac{9}{32}$
32	33$\frac{3}{4}$	28	12	3$\frac{9}{16}$
STEINIE SHAPES—(Drawing C-128)				
7	7$\frac{19}{32}$	10	7	2$\frac{9}{32}$
11	11$\frac{23}{32}$	9$\frac{1}{2}$	6$\frac{3}{4}$	2$\frac{49}{64}$
12	12$\frac{23}{32}$	9$\frac{3}{4}$	7	2$\frac{13}{16}$
32	33$\frac{3}{4}$	20	9$\frac{7}{8}$	3$\frac{11}{16}$
64 Unpast.	66$\frac{1}{2}$	34	11$\frac{3}{32}$	4$\frac{13}{16}$
64 Past.	68	39	11$\frac{3}{32}$	4$\frac{15}{16}$
SELECT SHAPES—(Drawing C-150)				
8	8$\frac{31}{64}$	9	8$\frac{1}{4}$	2$\frac{17}{64}$
11	11$\frac{23}{32}$	12	9$\frac{1}{4}$	2$\frac{17}{32}$
12	12$\frac{23}{32}$	12	9$\frac{1}{2}$	2$\frac{17}{32}$
CHAMPAGNE SHAPES—(Drawing No. C-190)				
64 Unpast.	66$\frac{1}{2}$	36	13$\frac{3}{4}$	4$\frac{33}{64}$
64 Past.	68	39	13$\frac{3}{4}$	4$\frac{31}{64}$

(Author's Note: The difference in the 64 fluid ounce capacities is due to the necessity of having ample headspace for the expansion of beer during pasteurization.)

ALE SHAPES—(Drawing No. C-130)				
6	6$\frac{1}{4}$	8	7$\frac{1}{4}$	2$\frac{1}{16}$
7	7$\frac{19}{32}$	8	7$\frac{1}{8}$	2$\frac{7}{64}$
8	8$\frac{31}{64}$	9	8$\frac{1}{4}$	2$\frac{11}{64}$
12	12$\frac{23}{64}$	12	9$\frac{1}{4}$	2$\frac{27}{64}$
32	33$\frac{3}{4}$	28	12	3$\frac{9}{16}$

(c) It is intended to be a guide to brewers in the elimination of all bottles for which standards are not given;

(d) This standard list must be kept distinct and not in conflict with any Governmental regulation or control now existing or hereafter promulgated;

(e) That the weights which appear on the standard list are in the interest of economic uniformity and are commercially adequate for the purposes intended;

(f) That all single trip bottles shall be of such shape and design that they will be readily distinguishable from standard deposit bottles or multi-trip bottles. Single trip bottles must be lettered on shoulder, 'NOT TO BE REFILLED—NO DEPOSIT —NO RETURN'."

The designation of standard sizes is tabulated in the above table.

The Brewers' Containers Committee and the Glass Containers Committee are standing committees and any brewer or glass manufacturer who feels he would benefit through the use of a container which differs from those on the adopted list and not now in use should submit his design to the joint Committee for its approval or disapproval before making any attempt to have the same manufactured. By this cooperation, efficient business harmony and economy will be maintained in this highly important field.

In their communication to the Glass Industry, the Glass Container Association further states:

"In addition to establishing uniformity of bottle designs, the new specifications are set up to simplify filling operations and reduce the number of filling tubes and the labor required to change them. The new specifications, while they indicate approximate filling points, are made to give correct headspace by displacement of the tube after overflow filling. Reducing the number of standard designs eliminates much of the filling spout complication, and care in setting up the specifications has simplified it still further. All 12 oz. capacity bottles, for instance, are designed with the same overflow capacity and can be filled with the same tube."

(Authors Note: The last statement cannot apply to Steinie and tall bottles of the same size interchangeably.)

All 22 standardized bottles can be filled with eight filling spouts, as follows:

Displacement of Spout in Fluid Ounces		No. of Standard Bottles Filled
$\frac{1}{2}$	....	1
3$\frac{1}{64}$	....	3
1$\frac{9}{32}$	....	3
2$\frac{3}{32}$	....	7
1$\frac{43}{64}$	....	1
1$\frac{3}{4}$	....	3
2$\frac{1}{2}$	....	2
4	....	2

The U. S. Bureau of Standards, which has assisted in the simplification and standardization of articles of many industries in the United States, has pledged its support to the present program of beer bottle standardization. The glass companies, having contributed to erecting the standards are also pledged to carrying the program into effect. The brewers of the country will cooperate by adhering to the standards which have been established by their Committee.

What the Standardization Means to Brewers

1. The standardized bottles recommended by the Brewers' Containers Committee and the Glass

(Please turn to page 41)

The Standardization of Bottles for Beer and Ale

(Continued from page 37)

Container Committee reduce the present variety of glass beer containers, numbering approximately a hundred, to 22.

2. Elimination of little-used variants will lead to longer runs and better manufacturing of beer bottles, with a favorable reaction in costs.

3. Adherence to standards will tend to discourage expensive adventures into new styles of bottles which often prove unprofitable.

4. The Standardization Program provides the industry with a committee of expert consultants who can pass on the advisability of initiating a new container from the standpoint of the brewing industry as a whole.

5. Establishment of standard bottles and the cooperation of the brewing industry in maintaining the standard will prevent costly obsolescence of container stocks.

6. The Standardization Program may assist in simplifying the laws and regulations affecting containers.

7. Specifically, adherence to the standard glass containers recommended will lead to substantial economies in the sorting and storing operations of breweries.

8. Further, and most important in its immediate effects, the Standardization Program will lead to important economies in the filling operation, assuring a supply of bottles of uniform height requiring a uniform headspace, and avoiding time and labor wasted in changing filling tubes for non-uniform bottles.

9. The Standardization Program is tangible evidence of cooperation with the Administration's policy of simplifying shapes and styles. The adoption of these standards should reduce the need for machine changes and thereby make these machine facilities available for important Defense work, a trend speeded by recent action of the OPM. The Beer Bottle Standardization Program is therefore a contribution to the Defense Program.

‹ ›

The Development of the One-Way Bottle for Beer

Julian Harrison Toulouse

WHILE the chief interest of this discussion is the glass container for beer, including the one-way bottle for the armed forces, it is difficult to discuss the development of the newer beer bottle without showing how it fits into the general picture of glass in the war effort.

Glass is serving an important part, not only in the many forms in which it is used, but also in the distinct field of glass containers. Many materials, such as acids, corrosive fluids heavy chemicals, and the like, can use only glass. When the ultimate in purity is needed, as in blood plasma, intravenous solutions, drugs and hospital supplies, glass was the essential package. The front line soldier carried his personal kit of insect repellent and water purification tablets in glass. When he turned to relaxation, bottled beer was one of the things waiting for him.

Record of Glass Containers

The record of shipments of beer has been astounding. The fact has been that the glass bottle, so frequently labeled as "fragile," can take it as ruggedly as any other container when used for its own purpose and in the proper way. We were told of shipments of sixty thousand cases arriving with only a case of bottles broken. We were told how glass was the one container to withstand the high temperature (including higher pressures) of the tropics. We were told that glass, in direct contact with the beer it contained, was the answer to the problem of the necessarily long storage of beer in the container during shipment in the freighter's hot holds over long distances.

But space in any freighter was at a premium, and we were asked to develop an even more compact container over the space-saving Packie to save space, weight and paper. This discussion centers about the changes that make the several one-trip beer containers practically synonomous in size. The story is one of engineering, planning and production.

When the Quartermaster Corps first presented the problem, we surveyed the limits of the present Packie bottle. Certain design features are fundamental in smooth filling line operations, such as rounded containers, absence of beads, rolls, or pronounced decorations, and low centers of gravity. One essential for smooth transfer of a container from machine to machine is that the diameter at top and bottom never be greater than the diameter of the principal portion.

The Development of

The One-Way Bottle for Beer

By Julian Harrison Toulouse

Chief Specifications & Service Engineer
Owens-Illinois Glass Company, Toledo, Ohio

Modifications in Design

On these principles, the height of the bottle could be reduced through the use of smaller radii at heel and shoulder. Diameter was practically unchanged. The result gave much of the reduction needed.

The next design feature was in the finish and the crowning ring. In the early days of bottle making, a rugged reinforcing ring became standard because of the use of this portion of the bottle as a centering tool for filling and crowning operations. Improvements in bottle handling machinery make such design unnecessary for light weight, one-way bottles. As a result a new design of finish has been developed, shorter, lighter, and completely satisfactory. It appears in accompanying photographs, and

Fig. 1. One-way beer bottle in Preston hydrostatic pressure testing machine, approved by A.S.T.M. Bottle is placed under hydrostatic pressure by rotation of the machine.

completes the effort toward shorter height and space savings.

The question of color also came up, but the answer was the present well known amber, giving needed protection to beer from action of light. The reason is shown in the light transmission data.

The question of light and its effect on beer and other products has been the subject of much speculation, vague generalizations, and some nonsense. The general public thinks of light in terms of that visible in daylight, but visible light is made up of many rays of various color. The harmful rays are in the invisible ultra-violet and, to some extent in the violet, blue violet, and blue green, none of which passes through an amber bottle. It is not what we see outside the bottle, but what gets through, that counts, and the light that get through amber is less than 5% of the total light, and at that, only a portion of the red and orange. Red is the color largely used as a photographic "safe light" for the very same reason. It is a "heat ray" with little or no photo-chemical effect. Gray Stone, and Rothchild reported in April 1941 (Wallerstein Lab. Vol. IV, No. 2) that hardly any effect was produced on beer by orange and red light, and this scientific report should settle the question on the basis of fact.

With the design and color crystallized, the next step was elaborate sampling and testing. Long sampling runs were made to determine the suitability of the bottle and its forming characteristics. From these studies the ideal weight was determined to be six and one-half ounces.

Tests show that the bottle has all the strength characteristics demanded by beer. The ability of glass con-

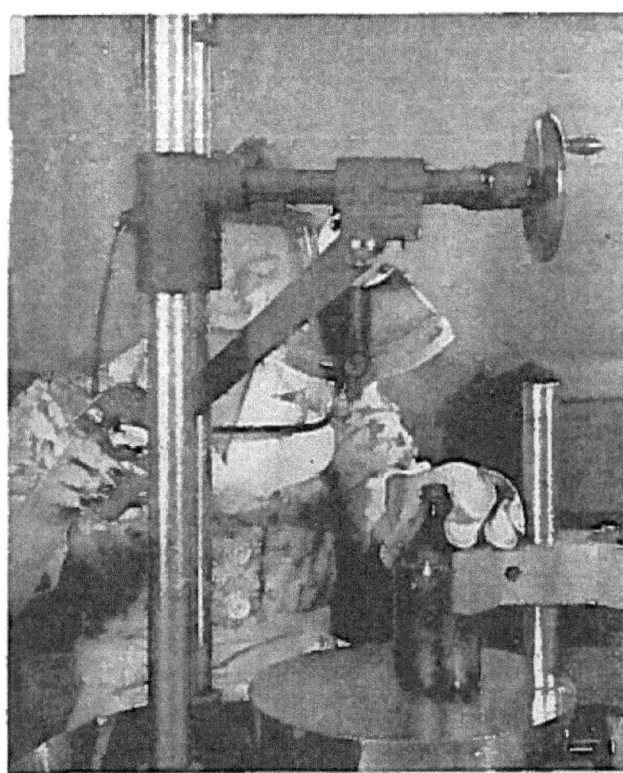

Fig. 2. One-way beer bottle in impact machine. Impacted with steel hammer used to improve bottle strength.

Fig. 3. Standard Export beer bottle in vertical pressure test. This bottle is shown undergoing 6000 lbs. load. Shield around bottle for protection during test.

tainers to hold the pressure of pasteurization is unsurpassed. Figure I shows the new bottle in the Preston standard hydrostatic pressure testing apparatus approved by the American Society for testing Materials, one of the fundamental tests used. Impact tests were made on the apparatus shown in Figure II. Resistance to vertical pressure was made as shown in Figure III, where a regular export beer is shown supporting a load of three tons. (Individual export beers have held as high as five and one-half tons.) The average crowning device imposes a load of only 200 to 750 pounds! The strength of the bottle is shown by its ability to carry the weight of a Jeep, using a single bottle on each corner.

Other tests were of the bottle, filled with beer, and enclosed in the W-5-C carton, packed in accordance with Army specifications for over-seas shipment. The photo in Figure IV shows five of these cases which averaged 510 falls in the drum test, before any bottle broke. The carton shows the extreme punishment they have taken especially when the average of 510 falls is compared with the 25 to 40 that would be adequate for normal commercial use.

Following this, a number of brewery trials were made, first on a short run basis, and later on larger runs. Without exception, these have been good. Permission was given for semi-production runs, and these were made in four of our factories, including the West Coast, as well as by other glass companies. The glass industry has approved the bottle from a manufacturing standpoint and the brewing industry is ready to use it for domestic trade.

Fig. 4. W-5-C cartons containing one-way beer bottles, after test. Cases of bottle filled with beer averaged 510 falls in drum test. (25 to 40 falls considered adequate normal resistance.)

Advantages of One-Way Bottle

On completion of these tests, recommendations were made to the

SEPTEMBER, 1945

Quartermaster Corps for use of the new one-way bottle. We now find the following advantages:

1. Overall package weight reduced 17.2%.
2. Space reduction 11.4%.
3. Considerable reduction in paper.

We hope that, following the trial runs and shipments already made, the bottle will be generally adopted for overseas armed forces. It is now being used by the armed forces in this country. In the meantime, as soon as war front demands are modified, the bottle is ready for civilian use, and will be available from all the usual beer bottle manufacturers.

Principles of Glass Container Design
J. S. Algeo

Modern packaging

ENCYCLOPEDIA

1949

Edited and published by the Staff of Modern Packaging Magazine

Published by the Packaging Catalog Corporation, 122 East 42nd
Street, New York 17, N. Y.; 221 N. La Salle Street, Chicago 1,
Ill.; 815 Superior Ave., Cleveland 14, Ohio; 2412 West 7th Street,
Los Angeles 5, Calif.; 1085 Monadnoc Bldg., San Francisco, Calif.

Principles of glass container design

by J. S. ALGEO

A properly designed glass container must necessarily represent a compromise in the views of the three principal parties concerned: the glass manufacturer, the packer and the consumer. The transportation company might be considered as a fourth party, but if the container is designed to meet the needs of the other three, then it automatically will be proper from the standpoint of the carrier.

In the past it was too often true that a container was designed purely from a supposed merchandising angle and little or no attention was paid to the other problems involved. The resulting package, in too many cases, was impractical to manufacture and to handle through packing lines and, in addition, too often ugly.

Glass is a beautiful and versatile substance. Among others, it has three outstanding qualities: visibility, rigidity and the ability to be molded into an infinite variety of shapes. Because of these qualities, it can be formed into containers having utilitarian as well as artistic features. It was only during the past ten years that an effort was made to reconcile the conflicting viewpoints of the principal parties involved in the development of containers in order to take full advantage

of the inherent qualities of glass. Great progress has been made, but much remains to be done. The expert designer has become a full-fledged member of the staff of glass manufacturing companies. The designer has reconciled differences between the various parties. He has utilized the qualities of glass as well as the improvement in glass-making techniques.

Today, we have containers which are much lighter, much stronger and much more beautiful than their counterparts of two decades ago. Lighter weights have come about for two reasons. First, the manufacturer has learned that the elimination of sharp corners and depressed panels will permit a weight reduction with added strength. Second, improved processes have enabled the manufacturer to blow glass with more even distribution, so that but little compensation need be made for thin and thick spots.

Improvement in design has come about because skilled designers have applied their artistry. The designer has gained a knowledge of the needs and limitations of the glass manufacturer, the packer and the consumer. He has succeeded in creating packages which the manufacturer can make in lighter weights and at

1—Designs for jars: (A) Ideal relation of height to thickness is shown by round plan with tapered shoulders and pulled-in foot; (B) Oval plan increases heaviness; (C) Addition of paneling lessens desirability; (D) Reduced manufacturing speed and added weight result from increased height, taper to wide bottom and sharp corners at base; (E) Bad example is rectangular plan with sharp corners and foot resulting in a poor distribution of glass, or an excessive amount of glass may be used with the resultant loss of manufacturing speed; (F) Disproportionately tall cylinder causes unsatisfactory weight, from which (G) also suffers; (H) Sharp corners and foot handicap manufacture—plain shape with well-rounded shoulder and minus foot, in this proportion, is considered far preferable

DRAWING, COURTESY HAZEL-ATLAS GLASS CO.

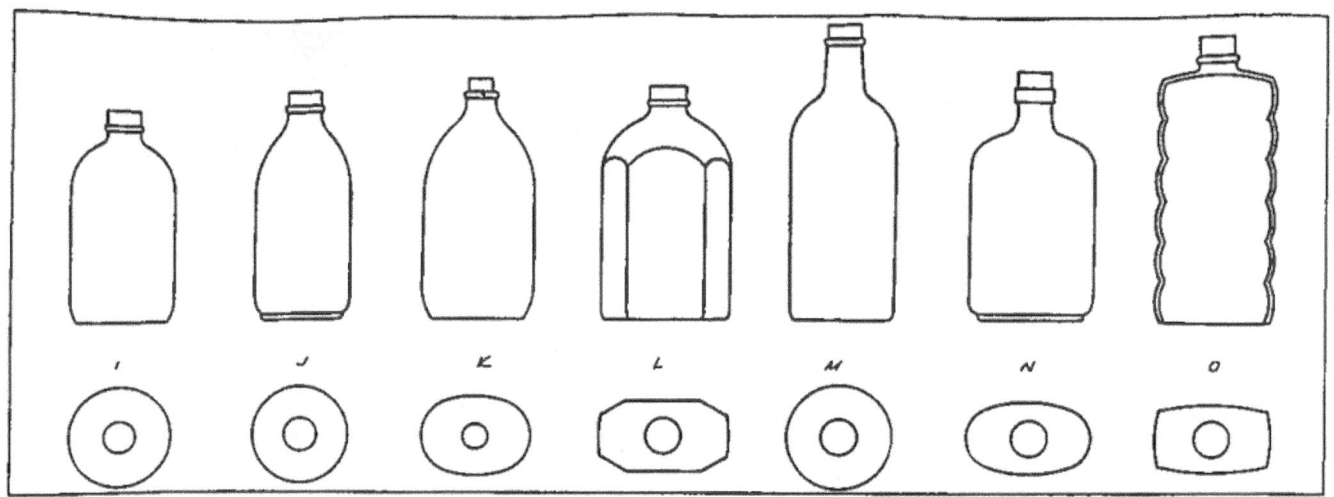

DRAWINGS 1 AND 3, COURTESY HAZEL-ATLAS GLASS CO.

2—Bottle designs: (I) Ideal shape is illustrated by round plan with well-rounded foot and shoulder; (J) Slightly increased height makes this bottle less acceptable; (K) Greater height and oval plan decrease desirability but not efficiency; (L) Manufacturing speed is retarded and weight is added by greater width, less thickness, use of panels and square corners at base; (M) Despite round plan, greater height and long neck reduce efficiency; (N) Comparatively thin oval plan, plus the neck, require a fairly high weight for this bottle; (O) Extreme height in addition to relative thinness and decorated ends which restrict pouring, make high-speed production of this type fairly difficult

higher speeds; which the packer can put through his lines at high speeds, at minimum costs, with little breakage; which the consumer finds more useful and more beautiful.

Glass containers are made by two processes—the simple "pressing" method and another method which is a combination of pressing and blowing and which is usually spoken of as the "press and blow" method. Since by far the greater volume is made by the "press and blow" method, this article will deal with such containers, although many of the remarks will apply as well to those made by pressing.

Without going into a technical explanation, it will be sufficient to say that a glass container is made by pouring molten glass at a temperature of 2400 to 2600 deg. F. into a mold and then blowing it out by means of compressed air. The glass flows evenly from the center line. The farther it is blown, the thinner the wall becomes. If it is blown farther in one direction than in another, as in the case of a rectangular shape, it is thinner on one side than on the other. If it is blown into a sharp corner, it blows thinner to a greater degree.

It follows that the most practical and economical design is a plain round with well-rounded shoulders and heels (the curve between the side and bottom), without depressed panels, with perpendicular sides and with the proper relationship between height and width. In the case of jars, the neck should be enough smaller in diameter than the body to produce a pronounced shoulder. In order to achieve the lightest, strongest and therefore the most economical container, the proportions of height to width must be properly related. Roughly, the most economical jar is one whose height is $1\frac{1}{2}$ to 2 times the diameter. In the most economical bottle, the height should be 2 to $2\frac{1}{2}$ times the diameter. As the height increases beyond these ratios, the weight likewise

increases and machine speeds decrease. As the ratios decrease, other complications arise. For instance, if the neck opening is narrow in relationship to the body diameter, the glass will blow too thin in the shoulders, thus requiring extra weight to compensate. It is not to be construed that a container is impractical to make if these ratios are not observed. Generally speaking, the farther away from this happy medium a container is, the more it will cost to produce.

When a departure is made from a plain round container, sharp corners, depressed panels and excessive decoration should be avoided whenever possible. In oval and rectangular shapes, there should be a low ratio between the two diameters; the relationship between height and diameter should be as near to the stated proportions as the particular circumstances will permit; and the sides as nearly perpendicular as possible.

In considering a glass container, the packer naturally has two objectives. The first is to use a container which will go through his factory operations at the lowest cost, which means at the highest speed, with the fewest operations, and with the least breakage. The second is to use a package pleasing to the consumer.

Fortunately, the packer's interests coincide with the glass manufacturer's so far as the first objective is concerned. The manager of the packer's factory wants exactly the container which the glass manufacturer prefers. He wants a container with perpendicular sides and a low center of gravity so that it will ride on his conveyors without tipping over and go through his filling, capping and labeling machines at high speeds without jamming or breaking. He wants containers with sufficiently wide openings so that the maximum filling speeds can be attained, and he wants plenty of labeling area so that, if necessary, labels of different sizes may be used. The needs of the packer, from his factory standpoint, are nearly identical with those of the glass manufacturer.

However, the packer cannot use exactly the containers that his plant manager prefers, because the consumer, usually a woman, comes into the picture.

In the final analysis the fate of the container is held in the hands of the consumer. If she has a choice, she often buys or fails to buy because of the appearance of the container. She looks for various features, depending upon the product. A great number of products are packed in glass, and these products or classes of products necessitate differing features in the container. When staple products, such as foods, household chemicals or polishes are packed, the utilitarian feature outweighs the artistic feature. For these products, she wants a container from which the contents can easily be removed either by pouring or by the use of such handy kitchen utensils as spoons or knives. She wants a container which will fit on refrigerator or pantry shelves without tipping over. She wants a container with a large label area so that a conspicuous label can be applied. Above all, she wants a container which will not break.

At the other end of the line are high priced cosmetics, such as perfumes. For this class of product, the artistic appearance is primary and the utilitarian feature is secondary. The cost of the glass and the cost of filling it constitute but a small portion of the price which the consumer pays, therefore less attention need be paid to the problems of the other two parties. Nevertheless, even in designing containers for the most expensive cosmetics, account must be taken of the packer and the glass manufacturer, although to a lesser degree than in the case of low cost staples.

Medicinal, liquor, wine and other products occupy a position between staples and cosmetics, and for that reason the utilitarian feature is of somewhat less importance than for staples, but more important than for cosmetics. The reverse is true for the artistic feature.

As to re-use containers, the trend in milk bottles is toward designs which can be made in lighter weights and which will take up the least room on refrigerator shelves, but which will still be sufficiently strong to withstand many trips. The trend toward space saving is especially pronounced and should be kept in mind in designing such containers.

There seems to be no change in the trend of design for re-use beverage (soft drink) bottles. Such bottles are made of individualistic shapes, and designs are usually patented. They are made in heavy weights and of sturdy construction to withstand many returns, together with extremely rough handling. There is little likelihood of any degree of standardization of this class of bottle in the near future because the bottle cost per drink is exceedingly small and because of the enormous expense that would be involved in changing plant lines, cases, trucks, advertising copy, and so on, in order to use radically different bottles.

The trend in returnable beer bottles is toward complete standardization so that bottles made by numerous manufacturers may be run through packing lines without adjustments being required. The standard shapes are plain rounds, well designed from the glass manufacturer's point of view, and comparatively heavy in order to withstand many return trips.

The glass container industry has not yet developed to a mass production level. Until the past few years it conducted its business pretty much on a "job" basis although its plants and equipment were more suitable for mass production. Ten years ago it started to redesign its containers in order to get stronger containers at lower costs and to simplify and standardize them.

A great impetus was given to standardization and simplification by the necessities of war, and the movement will continue to have its effect upon design. However, it must not be thought that all glass containers will be standardized. The cost of containers for certain products which are widely used, such as staple foods, household chemicals and some beverages, constitutes a considerable portion of the total cost. Of necessity, these products will be packed in the most economical containers, and the containers will be produced by mass production methods.

In those cases where the merchandising of a product depends greatly upon its style or artistic effect, there will be little or no effort toward standardization. In designing such containers, it will be desirable to keep in mind the limitations of the glass man and packer to the greatest degree possible without minimizing the sales appeal for the consumer.

Although this article pertains to the glass container only, it must be remembered that the label and closure are parts of the package. Because of the use of containers of generalized shape for staple or low-cost products, it seems reasonable to assume that more effort than ever will be made in the future to gain distinctiveness and individuality by means of greater emphasis on design of closures and labels.

3—Machine speed must be sacrificed to produce the variety of bottle shapes shown here which depart from the ideal and present manufacturing problems

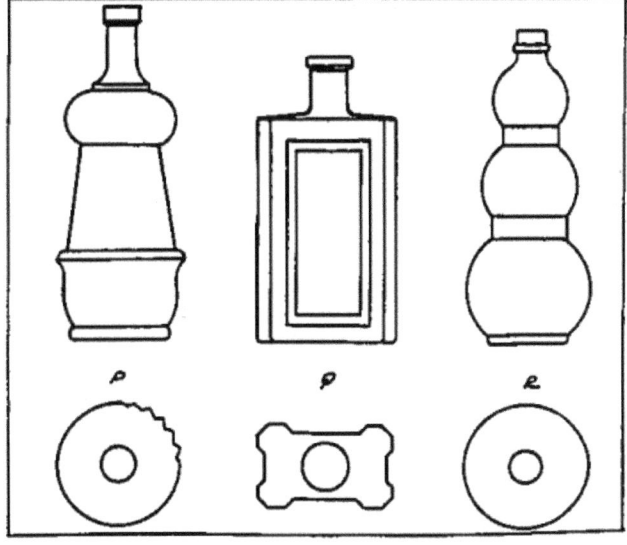

6
LABELS AND MARKS

The Berkshire Bitters bottle is one of the most unusual containers in the collection recovered in Old Sacramen-to SHP in 1978, manufactured by Amann & Co—a firm started by Anthony and Edmund Amann in Cincinnati, 1869. This dark amber glass in the form of a pig is embossed on the side with the words "BERKSHIRE BITTERS// AMANN & CO/CINCINNATI O. ("Bottle Type Collection Photo Gallery," California Department of Parks and Recreation, Sacramento, CA <http://www.parks.ca.gov/?page_id=22425>.)

Articles

Liquor Bottle Regulations, Summarized for *Glass Packer* Readers
[**Reprint** from 1934, *Glass Packer* 13(8):502–503.]
Glass Packer

OnIzed Applied Color Milk Bottles
 [**Reprint** from ca. 1935, brochure, Owens-Illinois Glass Co., Toledo, OH.]
Owens-Illinois Glass Company

Spotting Labels on Round Bottles
[**Reprint** from 1940, *Glass Packer* 19(3):182–183.]
Glass Packer

The Bewildering Array of Owens-Illinois Glass Co. Logos and Codes
[**Reprint** from 2015, *SHA/BLM Historic Glass Bottle Identification & Information Website*,
< http://www.sha.org/bottle/index.htm>.]
Bill Lockhart and Russ Hoenig

Rim Codes: A Pacific Coast Dating System for Milk Bottles
[**Reprint** from 2009, *Historical Archaeology* 43(2):30–39.]
Peter D. Schulz, Bill Lockhart, Carol Serr, and Bill Lindsey

Liquor Bottle Regulations, Summarized for *Glass Packer* Readers

Glass Packer

Liquor Bottle Regulations summarized for GLASS PACKER readers

STRIKING at the traffic in used and counterfeit liquor containers, the Treasury Department has now formally issued regulations licensing all manufacturers and users of liquor bottles. Starting Aug. 1, any person intending to engage in the manufacture of liquor bottles must apply to the Supervisor of the district in which his principal place of business is situated for an appropriate permit, and no person thereafter may manufacture, ship, or consign liquor bottles unless in accordance with the terms of such a permit. Furthermore, all buyers of liquor ware must be certified or shipments to them cannot be made.

Regarding the bottle itself, either in the body or on the bottom of it, there must be blown the permit number of the manufacturer, the year of manufacture, and a symbol assigned by the Supervisor to represent the name of the buyer. Blown into the shoulder of the bottle must be the words, "Federal Law Forbids Sale or Re-Use of This Bottle." Bottles for liqueurs, cordials, bitters and other specialties as may be specified from time to time do not fall under the ruling. Nips, or containers of less than one-half pint capacity, are also exempt.

On the part of the liquor manufacturer, after Nov. 1 it will be illegal for him to use bottles except those as defined and conforming to the regulations. He cannot accept shipment or delivery of liquor bottles except from persons holding permits under the regulations, nor can he use his bottles for any purpose other than as containers for liquor after they are delivered.

The new regulations call for detailed reports from both the bottle manufacturer and the distiller. A certified copy of each order must give the name of the manufacturer-consignor, date of the order, shipping or delivery destination, name and address of the consignee, the method of forwarding, and the shipment date requested by the consignee. This information the distiller must forward to the Supervisor of the district in which the consignee's place of business is situated at the time the order is placed. A similar report that must check in detail with the distiller's order, must also be forwarded to the Supervisor by the bottle manufacturer. Also a certified copy of the report must accompany the shipment or delivery.

Upon receiving a shipment of bottles, the distiller must make another report to the Supervisor in his own district, again listing the name of the bottle manufacturer, date of the order, date of delivery, date of receipt, method of forwarding, the destination, the number of packages and the size, quantity and description of the bottles received. Distillers were also required to furnish the Supervisor with an inventory of all bottles designed for the packaging of distilled spirits on hand July 31, at their respective plants, and must supply such subsequent inventories and records as the Supervisor may from time to time require. Records shall at all times be available for inspection.

After Nov. 1, the importation of empty bottles will be prohibited except by special permit, and bottles thus imported must have blown into the bottom of each bottle the name, and the name of the city and address of the importer, and also the same wording as is required on the shoulder of domestic bottles.

After Jan. 1, 1935, there must be blown, either in the bottom or in the body of all filled liquor bottles imported from foreign countries the name and the name of the city or country of the manufacturer of the spirits, or of the exporter abroad; or the name, and the name of the city or address, of the importer in the United States. The same shoulder legend is also required. Containers of distilled spirits exported in bond will not be subject to these regulations, provided application is first made to the Supervisor and a permit is issued.

In the securing of all permits application must first be filed with the Supervisor. The Supervisor then investigates and either issues or refuses a permit according to his findings. In case a permit is refused, the applicant may file a request for a hearing. Failure to file such a request within 15 days renders the refusal final. If a hearing is requested, the Supervisor designates the date and place of the hearing, and notifies the applicant at least 15 days in advance. If from the findings of the hearing the original decision against the applicant is reversed, a permit is promptly granted. If the original disapproval is affirmed, the applicant may still request a review of the record by the Commissioner. The Commissioner may either review the case himself, or request the Supervisor to grant the applicant a third hearing.

In case of violation of any of the provisions of the Resolution (enabling act under which the regulations are drawn) the permittee will be ordered to appear and show cause why his permit shall not be suspended. The Supervisor passes on the hearing, and if violation is found, re-hearings are granted, if desired. When a permit is suspended, stocks of liquor bottles on hand must be disposed of as directed by the Commissioner.

Under the regulations, trade in used bottles, or the possession of large quantities of used bottles, is prohibited. The Deputy Commissioners in Charge of the Alcohol Tax Unit are, under the direction of the Commissioner, charged with the administration and enforcement of the Resolution.

How Liquor Bottles Must Be Marked

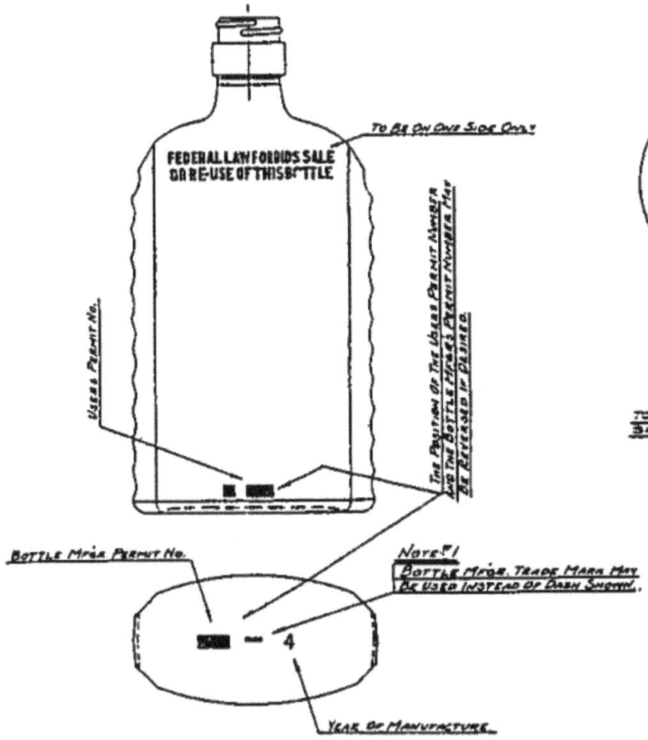

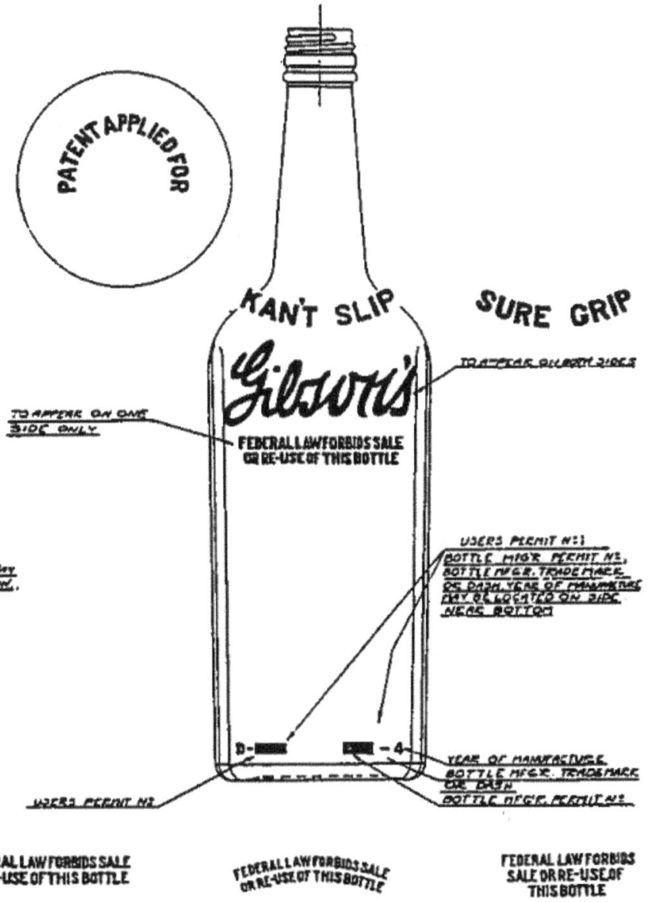

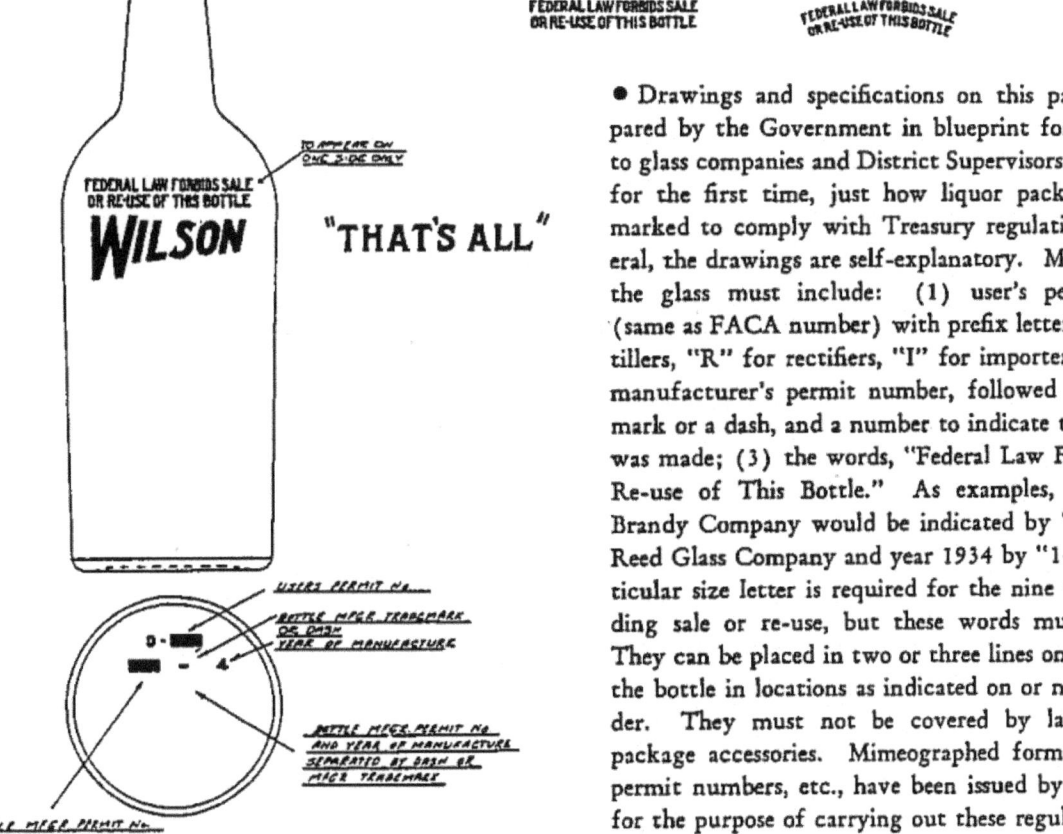

PATENT APPLIED FOR

KAN'T SLIP — SURE GRIP

Gibson's

FEDERAL LAW FORBIDS SALE OR RE-USE OF THIS BOTTLE

WILSON

"THAT'S ALL"

FEDERAL LAW FORBIDS SALE OR RE-USE OF THIS BOTTLE

FEDERAL LAW FORBIDS SALE OR RE-USE OF THIS BOTTLE

FEDERAL LAW FORBIDS SALE OR RE-USE OF THIS BOTTLE

● Drawings and specifications on this page were prepared by the Government in blueprint form and issued to glass companies and District Supervisors. They show, for the first time, just how liquor packages must be marked to comply with Treasury regulations. In general, the drawings are self-explanatory. Marks blown in the glass must include: (1) user's permit number (same as FACA number) with prefix letter "D" for distillers, "R" for rectifiers, "I" for importers; (2) bottle manufacturer's permit number, followed by his trademark or a dash, and a number to indicate the year bottle was made; (3) the words, "Federal Law Forbids Sale or Re-use of This Bottle." As examples, the Abbott's Brandy Company would be indicated by "D-435," and Reed Glass Company and year 1934 by "1-4." No particular size letter is required for the nine words forbidding sale or re-use, but these words must be legible. They can be placed in two or three lines on either side of the bottle in locations as indicated on or near the shoulder. They must not be covered by labels or other package accessories. Mimeographed forms and lists of permit numbers, etc., have been issued by the Treasury for the purpose of carrying out these regulations.

Onlzed Applied Color Milk Bottles
Owens-Illinois Glass Company

The Juliette K. and Leonard S.
Rakow Research Library

CM
OG Corning Museum of Glass

* A. C. L.

A typical group of milk, cream and cottage cheese containers with *OnIzed* Applied Color Lettering and Merchandising appeals. A different slogan or sales appeal on each container. A distinct family resemblance for the entire group.

*Applied Color Lettering.

Applied Color Lettering on Milk Bottles

Introduced by

Owens-Illinois Glass Company

Designs on On1zed Applied Color containers for dairies are executed by our own designers who have had years of experience in developing designs that do a merchandising job. Designs or trademarks may be adapted from your present advertising or our designers will create other suitable copy for reproduction on the bottles.

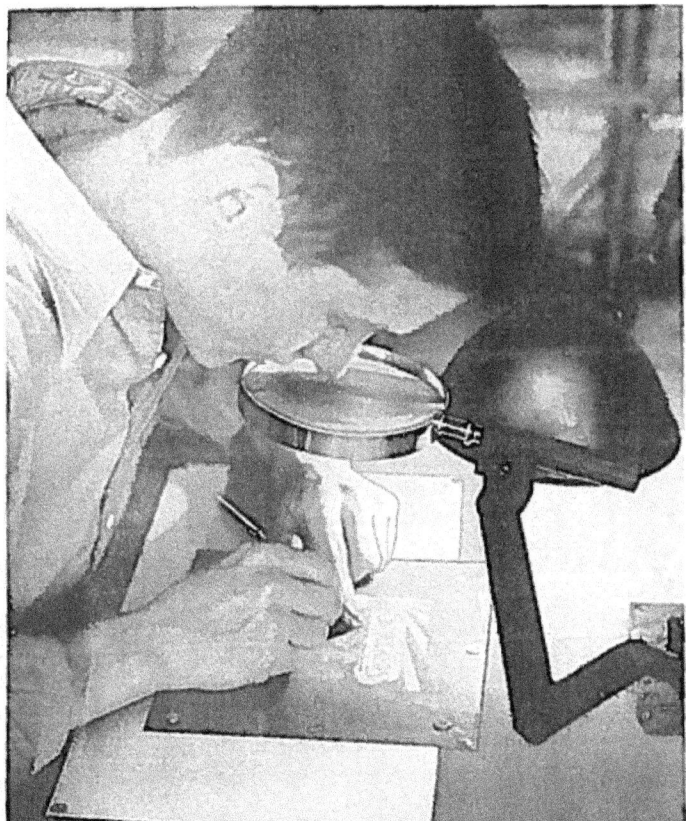

Cutting A.C.L. Screens

After the creation of the design on paper it must be transferred to the silk screen. This is accomplished by covering the silk with "profilm" (a thin paint resistant paper of special texture) into which the design is cut by a small sharp knife so that the silk is exposed in the design form, thus the paint later applied reaches the bottle only through the exposed portions of the silk surface.

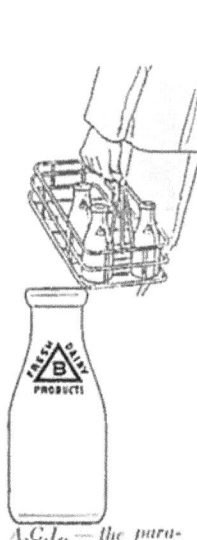

A.C.L. — the para-mount achievement in milk packaging.

Applying Profilm to A.C.L. Screens

Ironing-in the profilm after the design has been cut out. Profilm is of such a composition that when heat is applied it becomes a part of the silk screen and permits the special paint to pass only through the silk surfaces where the design has been cut out of the profilm.

Completed A.C.L. Screens

Typical screens as used on bottles for some of the large dairies. The two lower ones are for applying color designs on bottle shoulders and the other three for applying color designs on the body. This illustration shows the wooden frames with design-cut profilm applied to the silk and ready for use on the machines illustrated on pages 8 and 9.

Your advertisement on A.C.L. bottles is read by housewives right at meal time.

A.C.L. bottles attract attention to your milk and display your name or advertise your other products.

Grinding A.C.L. Colors

Two of the large battery of these machines in one of our factories. All paint used in the Onized A.C.L. process is composed of glass making material and specially ground in our own plants. Color experts check each grinding to assure a uniform color on every job.

A.C.L. bottles are impervious to ordinary caustic solution—the color is permanent.

Close Up of A.C.L. Body Decorating Machine

Applying the design to the body of the bottle. This machine is one of a large battery in one plant. Here the bottle is placed under the silk screen and the paint is forced through the open design onto the body of the bottle. Both sides of bottle may be decorated in one operation with the same or different designs.

Do dairies and customers like A.C.L. bottles? — Ask any user or his customer.

Decorating the Shoulder

Machines of a special type are required to decorate the shoulders of bottles. The above illustrates one of our machines making an A.C.L. application onto the shoulder of a bottle.

Group of A.C.L. Machines

Four of the battery of machines in one of our plants applying color designs to our milk bottles. After the bottles are decorated on these machines they are placed on the conveyor at left which carries them to the lehr in the extreme background of the illustration.

The best advertising space is on your bottle and it is FREE —use it for slogans or to advertise other products.

A.C.L. bottles are an attractive advertisement wherever they are seen.

A.C.L. Bottles Entering Lehr

Entering the lehr. After the bottles have been decorated they are carried to the lehr on the conveyor. Here they are again inspected and placed in this lehr and move slowly through this long, tunnel-like, heat chamber, during which travel they are heated to a high temperature so that the applied color actually becomes a part of the glass.

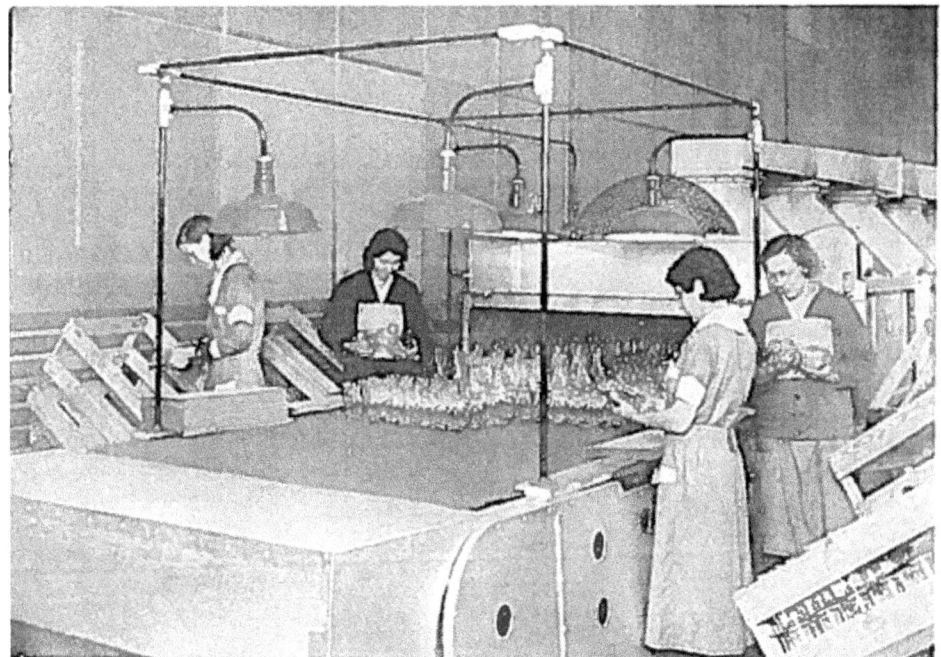

Inspection and Packing of A.C.L. Bottles

Onized Applied Color Milk Bottles emerging from the annealing lehr. These bottles have been heated to a high temperature to fuse the color into the glass which makes Onized A.C.L. bottles impervious to scratching and caustic resistant.

Sloganize with A.C.L., use the reverse side for a slogan that sells milk.

A Section of One of Our A.C.L. Departments

Note the decorating machines and conveyor in the foreground. The annealing lehr is in the background. Straight line production permits us to sell Onized A.C.L. bottles at but a slight increase in price over plain or blown lettered ware.

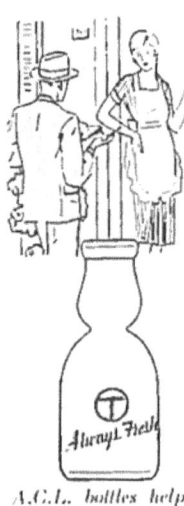

A.C.L. bottles help salesmen get new accounts and sell more to old ones.

Onized APPLIED COLOR MILK BOTTLES

ACL Milk Bottles—the paramount achievement in milk packaging—were developed by Owens-Illinois Glass Company and introduced to the dairy industry as the greatest improvement in the packaging of milk since the advent of the first glass milk container.

In the relatively short time since these bottles have been on the market, dairies, both large and small, in all sections of the country have proved by experience that Onized ACL Milk Bottles are truly what we claim for them—the paramount achievement in milk packaging.

The use of applied color lettering (ACL) on milk bottles is especially timely in this age of color when the entire nation is color conscious. Second only to a better product is a better or more attractive package. Onized ACL Milk Bottles afford the dairy business many advantages.

INCREASED TRIPPAGE

Due to conspicuous and easy identification with name in color Onized ACL Milk Bottles are handled with more care and returned to the original dairy without delay. Other dairies hesitate to use competitors' bottles with the dairy name so conspicuously displayed in color.

ADVERTISE OTHER DAIRY PRODUCTS

The space on a milk bottle is the most valuable advertising medium a dairy can use and it is FREE. When using Onized ACL Milk Bottles for the purpose of displaying the name in color, the reverse side may be devoted to advertising other dairy products such as cottage cheese, butter, chocolate milk, buttermilk, ice cream and coffee cream. This advertising is read by customers at meal-time when they are in the most receptive mood to menu suggestions.

SLOGANIZE WITH ACL

If preferred, slogans may be used on the reverse side of ACL Milk Bottles to advertise the health-giving qualities of milk such as: "Milk Is Nature's Most Perfect Food," "Milk Promotes Restful Sleep," "Milk Promotes Sound Teeth and Bone Growth in Children," etc.

The small additional cost of *OnIzed* ACL Milk Bottles is offset in several different ways.

1. They make more trips than plain or blown lettered bottles.

2. They advertise other dairy products.

3. They are ideal for trade-marking special brands of milk.

4. Because of being especially attractive, retailers display milk in prominent positions in their stores.

5. They assist the driver-salesman when soliciting new business because they convey the impression that the dairy using them is aggressive and up to the minute.

Each of our milk bottle plants is strategically located for your convenience and quick service—each is completely equipped to apply colored lettering and designs to milk bottles. *OnIzed* Glass Milk Bottles—the ideal containers for milk—with *OnIzed* ACL offer the perfect package for milk and dairy products. Send us a sample of your present bottle and copies of your letterhead or advertising material and we will, without obligation to you, submit suggestions as to how the *OnIzed* ACL Milk Bottle can be adapted to your own individual needs.

OWENS-ILLINOIS GLASS COMPANY

TOLEDO · · · · · OHIO

Spotting Labels on Round Bottles
Glass Packer

Spotting labels on round bottles

Five ways to secure close registry of labels on round containers or others whose shape is such that bottle supports or conveyors will not present them in the best position for label placement.

At one time spot labeling on bottles or jars with a label panel was a job for hand work if neatness was desired. Close registry of the label in the label space was accomplished by careful placement, followed by wiping. In recent years the versatility of labeling machinery has been extended so that a great deal of close register work is done on semi-automatic and automatic labeling machines. Lately some new tricks have been tried, with the result that labels are spotted mechanically on round bottles or jars, and on oval shaped containers whose shape is such that bottle supports cannot be made to hold the containers in the exact position for precise register of the labels. The purpose of this article is to detail some of the methods that have come to the notice of THE GLASS PACKER. There may be others, of which we have not heard, and these will be given suitable publicity if called to our attention.

(1) BOTTOM SLOT, CENTERED

This is a very simple but effective method for use with semi-automatic (hand fed) labeling machines. A lug or projection is cut on the bottom plate of the bottle mold, forming a slot in the thicker central portion of the bottom of the bottle. A suitable projection is mounted on the bottle rest of the labeling machine (Fig. 1), and the operator, when placing the container in the bottle rest, merely turns it enough to engage the peg with the slot. As a matter of fact, it is hardly necessary to turn the bottle, for the slot and peg are so shaped that forward pressure on the bottle causes it to turn on its axis until the label space is centered correctly. Movable mounting of the bottle rest makes it possible to adjust quickly for correct height and to straighten labels vertically. If a back label is also used, it can be perfectly centered 180° from the front label.

It has been suggested that this method of label spotting might be used to make labels "face front" on round containers with large size lithographed caps, particularly screw caps or lug caps. This is impractical, due to the fact that cap lugs or threads are not formed in register with lithographed decorations. Furthermore, the amount of turn to effect seal will vary. Careful work on the part of operators seems to be the only way to secure alignment of cap and label designs.

(2) SLOT OR GROOVE ACROSS BOTTOM

This would serve in the same way as the slot described in No. 1 (above) except that it applies the idea to automatically labeled containers. A slot or groove at one side of the base of the bottle engages a guide rail at the side of the conveyor chain. This device stops rota-

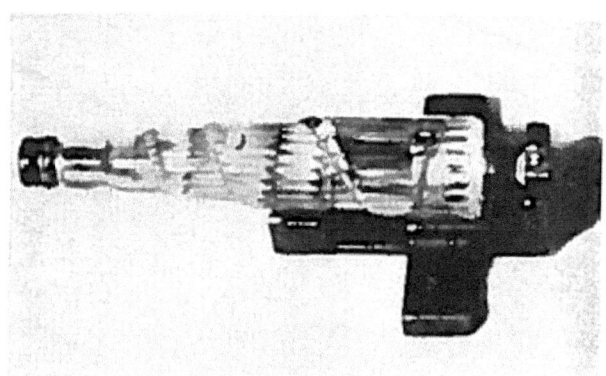

FIG. 1. *Private mold bottle of Ayash Refining Co. in position to engage peg on bottle rest. This bottle labeled on Pony Labelrite of New Jersey Machine Corporation. Below: Location and approximate dimensions of slot.*

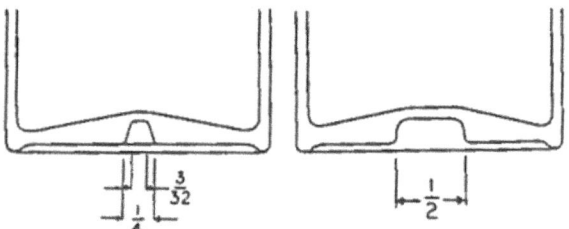

tion and keeps each bottle lined up and facing in the right direction as it is moved into the labeling machine. One manufacturer is reported to use this method to insure placement of labels on round bottles at the side opposite the pouring lip which is incorporated in his particular containers. Thus there is little chance that the label will ever be marked by drops running down what would otherwise be the front of the package.

Location of the slot or groove has not been limited to the extreme sides of the base. Instances are reported of use of grooves across the center from one side to the other. This would seriously weaken bottles in most instances, and require excessive glass.

(3) SLOTS AT BOTH SIDES OF BASE

Here is a method used by a face cream manufacturer to insure proper placement of labels on private mold jars, using an automatic front and back labeling machine. The label space is not closely outlined on these containers but nevertheless is sharply limited by the rather formal decorations on either side. Off center and crooked labels look particularly bad on packages of this type. The registry problem was solved by putting slots on the jars to fit a track just above the conveyor chain leading

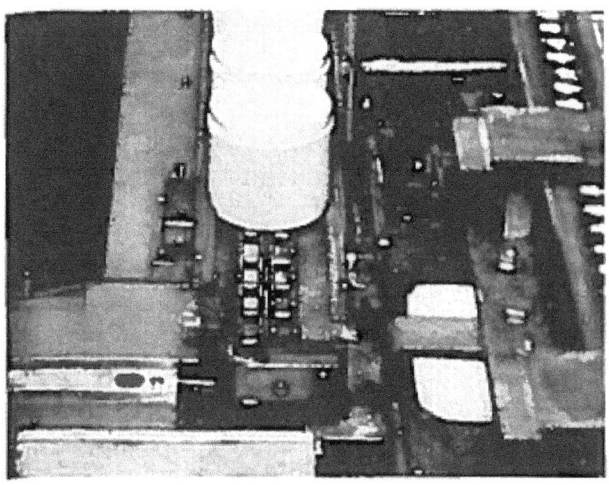

FIG. 2. *Face cream jars riding track into McDonald labeling machine. Note slots at each side of jars engaging track which keeps them from turning while on conveyor. The pusher mechanism which transfers jars to labeling machine conveyor contacts flat surface of slot on the left side of the jar (see photo) thereby preventing any rotation of jar during this movement. Daggett & Ramsdell, New York.*

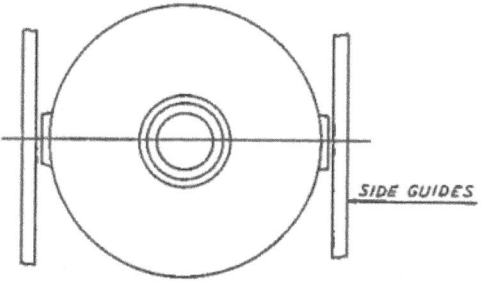

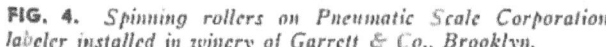

SIDE GUIDES

FIG. 3. *Cross-section near base of round bottle with parallel lugs designed to prevent rotation of container while on conveyor leading to labeling machine.*

FIG. 4. *Spinning rollers on Pneumatic Scale Corporation labeler installed in winery of Garrett & Co., Brooklyn.*

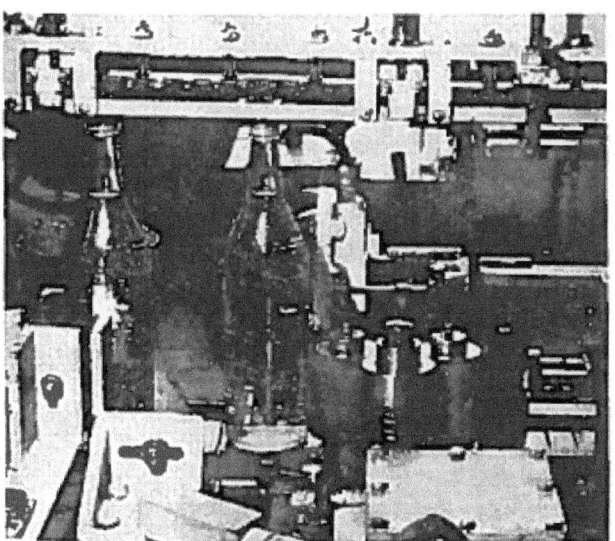

to the labeling machine. The jars rest on the conveyor, and are kept in line by means of the track which engages the slots on both sides of the jars. An operator turns the jars to put them on the track, after which they cannot turn on their axes until the labels have been affixed and pressed down securely. (Fig. 2)

(4) PARALLEL LUGS, AT BASE OF BOTTLE

Another version of the method just described calls for the use of parallel lugs blown in on both sides, near the base. (See Fig. 3). A round bottle would be kept from turning by the contact between the lugs and guide rails of the conveyor. A possible objection to this method is the amount of glass required to blow a bottle with perfectly formed lugs. A better method might be to flatten the sides of the bottle enough to prevent turning while on the conveyor. Care might have to be taken to design a shape that will not wedge in conveyors or star wheels. Parallel flat sides can be used to prevent rotation either by contact with guide rails or by contact with other bottles on the conveyor. This is perhaps the most commonly used method of all.

(5) SPINNING ROLLERS TO FACE BOTTLES "FRONT"

An entirely different method from those above has been found practical for round bottles that bear blown-in decoration or lettering and therefore require accurate placement of labels. All that is asked of the container is that it have a small knob or bar in the proper location on the back. This bar need not be more than .050" high and ⅜" in length. When the bottle enters the labeling machine a pair of cork-covered rollers spin it around on its axis until the little projection strikes a small roller on the end of a contact finger. This electrically or mechanically disengages the clutch which controls the movement of the spinning rollers, and the bottle stops turning at the correct position for placement of the label. (Fig. 4)

The Bewildering Array of Owens-Illinois Glass Co. Logos and Codes

Bill Lockhart and Russ Hoenig

The Bewildering Array of Owens-Illinois Glass Co. Logos and Codes

Bill Lockhart and Russ Hoenig

[In 2004, Lockhart wrote similar articles about maker's marks and codes used by the Owens-Illinois Glass Co. for the Society for Historical Archaeology Newsletter and a collectors' magazine. While these articles contained more detailed information than earlier works (e.g., Toulouse 1971), there were still problems with some of the identifications. The current study corrects the issues and explains past discrepancies. Parts of this study were taken from Lockhart 2007 (online version of 2004 article).]

From its beginning in 1929, the Owens-Illinois Glass Co. has been a giant in the bottle and jar industry. Its history (see below) is filled with growth and innovation. As a result, there is probably no way to even estimate the billions of bottles that Owens-Illinois has produced during the more than 80 years of its tenure. That means, of course, that the Owens-Illinois manufacturer's mark and codes are the most common of all logos found by historical archaeologists in excavations and surveys of post 1930 sites.

The study of these marks and codes are therefore of great interest to archaeologists studying material culture. Bottle collectors were the first group outside of the bottle industry to be introduced to the Owens-Illinois codes via a letter from Julian Harrison Toulouse to May Jones, published in Volume 5 of *The Bottle Trail* (1965). Toulouse served his entire career as an employee of Owens-Illinois, and, as his retirement neared, he wrote numerous articles and two books aimed at bottle collectors. He joined a large group of collectors under the umbrella of May Jones to simultaneously disseminate and collect bottle information.

Although Jones was the first to publish the relationships between the Owen-Illinois mark and the numbers surrounding it, her newsletters reached a very limited audience. Toulouse (1971:406) wrote his now famous *Bottle Makers and Their Marks* and explained in more detail the relationship between the company, date, and mold codes and the Owens-Illinois logos. The Bottle Research Group (BRG) began following up the study of manufacturer's marks in the mid-1990s with a goal of updating the Toulouse research.

1

As part of the BRG studies, I wrote an article about the Owens-Illinois history and marks for a collectors' magazine in 1994. Later that year, I published a similar article in the Society for Historical Archaeology Newsletter, currently (i.e., in 2015) available online (Lockhart 2007). Unfortunately, my understanding of the marks – although correct as far as it went at that time – was quite incomplete. As it turns out, the codes are much more complex than I had any way to know at that time, as attested by hundreds of e-mails I have received during the last decade. The following study will address the variations and errors commonly found in these marks and codes.

Owens-Illinois Glass Co. History

The Owens-Illinois Glass Co. began with the merger of two of the industry giants: the Illinois Glass Co. and the Owens Glass Co. The Illinois Glass Co. was incorporated in March 1873 and began business in August. The company was successful and made virtually every type of bottle. By 1911, Illinois Glass had obtained the first of three Owens Automatic Bottle Machine licenses and made many other containers from semiautomatic machines. The firm expanded until the merger with Owens (see Lockhart et al. 2005a for a discussion of the company and its marks).

The Owens Bottle Co. (1911-1929) grew from a series of companies that began with the Toledo Glass Co. (1896-1903). The Toledo company was succeeded by both the Owens Bottle Machine Co. (1903-1911) that made and sold the Owens Automatic Bottle Machine and the Northwestern Ohio Bottle Co. (1904-1908), a company to make bottles. The firm dropped the "Machine" designation in 1919, heralding a shift in emphasis from the sale of machines to the manufacture of bottles. In 1929, the firm merged with one of its major competitors, the Illinois Glass Co. to form the largest glass company in the industry.

The merger between the Owens Glass Co. and the Illinois Glass Co. brought under the Owens umbrella the "largest individual bottle plant in the world" (Paquett 1994:71). The merger was formally approved on April 17, 1929 (Paquette 1994:70). On March 25, 1931, the firm was incorporated in California as the Owens-Illinois Glass Co., Ltd. The newly-renamed organization purchased the Illinois-Pacific Coast Co., the largest glass manufacturer on the West Coast on November 30 of the same year. The name of the West Coast operation was changed to the Owens-Illinois Pacific Coast Co. on April 23, 1932 (Lockhart et al. 2005b; Paquette 1994:81-

2

82). According to Paquette (1994:81), Owens-Illinois introduced Applied Color Lettering (ACL) in 1931, although other sources place the date of the practical application at 1934. The firm absorbed numerous smaller glass houses and pioneered considerable change in the industry. Owens-Illinois purchased Brockway, Inc. in 1988, renaming the glass container operation as Owens-Brockway, a subsidiary of Owens-Illinois (O-I 2005). The firm remains a major glass production center in 2015.[1]

The Basic Logo and Code Formats

Toulouse established the basic code/logo sequence in 1965 (Jones 1965) as well as in his book (Toulouse 1971:406) in 1971 (Figure 1). The original manufacturer's mark used by Owens-Illinois was a merger of logos, similar to the merger of the firms. The Illinois Glass Co. had used the Diamond-I logo ("I" enclosed by a horizontally elongated diamond) since 1915, although the

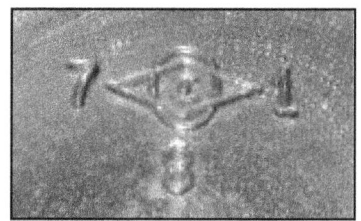

Figure 1 – Owens-Illinois codes (eBay)

business had used a diamond

Figure 2 – Second logo

surrounding catalog numbers as early as 1897. The Owens Bottle Co. had used the Box-O (O in a square) logo since 1919. The new firm selected the entire Illinois Glass mark and superimposed an "O" – that extended beyond the top and bottom of the diamond – around the "I." Generally, the "O" was shaped as an upright oval, although the configuration could vary. Although Owens-Illinois continued to use the old molds from both former companies until they wore out – probably no longer than ca. 1931 – the new firm began using its recently adopted mark almost immediately. Because the merger occurred late in the year – in a transition lasting most of the month of September – very few bottles had the new logo in 1929.

In 1954, Owens-Illinois adopted a new logo that eliminated the diamond (Figure 2). Some plants adopted this I-in-an-Oval mark almost immediately, and some delayed. We have

---

[1] When the *Encyclopedia of Manufacturer's Marks on Glass Containers* reaches the "O" Volume, we will present a *much* more complex and complete history of Owens-Illinois.

3

recorded the old logo on bottles made at least into 1966. Russ Hoenig remembered a time in the late 1960s or early 1970s, when the main office told him to use baseplates with the older logo. Thus, there was more than a decade overlap from 1954 to at least 1966, when each logo could have been used. The second mark was used into the 21st century when it began transformation into an OI joined together by a short line (Figure 3).

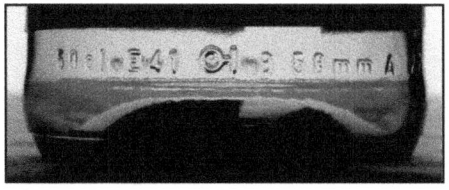

Figure 3 – Recent logo

The code positions shown by Toulouse in his original postings (Jones 1965; Toulouse 1971:406) are correct with some advisement. The code to the left of the logo generally represents the factory of manufacture with a one- or two-digit number. However, codes on liquor bottles made between 1934 and 1964 follow the federal requirements rather than the Owens sequence (see the section on liquor codes below). Left codes on packer and medicinal bottles also do not follow the same rule for the left code.

The code to the right of the logo was a date code, and this pattern was generally followed by almost all glass manufacturers from the 1930s (often earlier) to the present – although some firms failed to include date codes until sometime during the 1970s, and a few used their own positioning or even letter codes. With a very few exceptions (discussed in the liquor section), Owens-Illinois date codes were always positioned to the right of the logo. When I wrote the 2004 article, however, I was unduly influenced by soda bottles, so I addressed the date codes on those containers as if they applied to all Owens-Illinois bottles. Reality is much more complex. On some bottle types, the single-digit date code was used into the 1960s, likely into the 1970s, and possibly even into the 1980s. See the individual bottle sections below for date code variations on each type.

Below the logo was a one- or two-digit mold cavity code. These were of interest to quality control people in the factories but have little relevance to archaeologists. A final code on later bottles was a catalog or model code. These identified each bottle according to a model number in the catalog, or, with private molds, an identifying number for an individual bottler. These can be useful where the number is known, although a study of relevant codes is beyond the scope of this work. To make these identifications even more challenging, the West Coast plans used different codes than factories in the rest of the country – for the same bottle styles.

4

In addition, the following Mold Prefixes were used in most of the U.S.:

Liquors – L, LP, W, WP

Food – C, D, E, F, T, AT

Beverage – G, GB

Packers & Preservers – A, B, P, R, CH, FB

Milk – M, ML, CL

The same codes appeared as suffixes on glassware made in the Owens-Illinois West Coast plants (Owens-Illinois 1941). The firm adopted additional model codes over time.

The Trademark that Never Was

The decade after World War II was rife with change. The non-returnable bottle had been developed in 1935 and was extensively used during the war – and this led to a renewed interest in lighter, stronger bottles. The federal government sued Owens-Illinois for price gouging and unfair profit from war work. The use of waxed-paper milk cartons was cutting into the profits at Owens-Illinois, and the management began to move toward single-trip containers for every use. With this change in marketing strategy, the firm began looking at ways to alter its image.

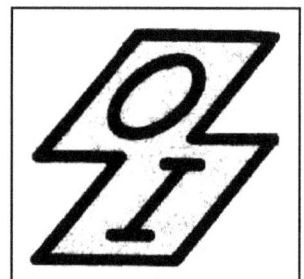

E. L. Randle proposed or presented a new trade mark on July 22, 1952 (Figure 4). After investigating the increased area needed and the costs involved in changing the logo, Owens-Illinois determined that it would cost between $225,000 and $750,000 to make the conversion (Owens-Illinois 1952). Probably because of the expense, the mark was never adopted, although there is a small chance that it was embossed on a few trial bottles that may someday be found. The simpler "I" in an "O" – already part of the older logo – was a much easier to change.

Figure 4 – The never-used logo

Owens-Illinois Factories

When Toulouse (1971:395) published his Owens-Illinois factory number list, he opened up an area of vast confusion. Even though he was an "insider," many of his dates were

5

incorrect, and he missed quite a few plants – some of which opened after his book was published. One of the problems that Toulouse faced was the availability of information. Much of the data on individual plants was scattered around, rather than being in a central repository, making collection of the needed dates very difficult. In addition, the entire 1971 book is riddled with typographic errors in dates. Since Toulouse was receiving much of his data in handwritten format, much of this can be forgiven, but much also just appears to be error.[2] One final issue makes correct dating difficult. Often, the erection of factories continued for as long as three years, and, often, sources cited the date when construction began. The important date is when production commenced. We have used the production date whenever it was available, although sometimes our only source failed to specify which date it used.

Table 1 was compiled by the BRG in conjunction with two former Owens-Illinois employees, Russ Hoenig and Phil Perry. We began with the Toulouse table and traced every date through internet searches, while Russ and Phil searched Owens-Illinois documents. We spent hours discussing the often conflicting results and sorting production dates from inception dates. While a few entries remain somewhat speculative, the vast majority are solidly backed by Owens-Illinois records. Kudos for this research go to Russ and Phil.

Table 1 – Plant Numbers – Owens-Illinois Glass Co.

No.	Location 1	Dates	Location 2	Dates
1	Toledo, OH	1930-1950		
2	Huntington, WV	1930-1990		
3	Fairmont, WV	1930-1980	Muskogee, OK	1988-present
4	Clarksburg, WV	1930-1944 (idle)	Brockport, NY	1961-1984
5	Cincinnati, OH	1930-1933 (idle)	Charlotte, MI	1963-2010
6	Charleston, WV	1930-1962	Winston-Salem, NC	1980-present
7	Alton, IL	1930-1983		

---

[2] In one case, I wrote that Toulouse dates were often incorrect by a year, frequently off by a decade, and even inaccurate by a century in two places. A friend e-mailed me that I had written 1988 instead of 1888 in the very next line!

6

No.	Location 1	Dates	Location 2	Dates
8	Glassboro, NJ	1930-1940 [1]	New Orleans Lapel, IN	1961-1984 1988-present
9	Streator, IL	1930-present		
10	Newark, OH	1930-1938 [2]	Atlanta, GA	1957-present [3]
11	Evansville, IN	1930-1939 (idle)	North Bergen, NJ Freehold, NJ	1963-1982 1988-1991
12	Gas City, IN	1930-1982	Zanesville, OH	1988-present
13	Chicago Heights, IL	1930-1939 [4]	Montgomery, AL	1988-1991
14	Bridgeton, NJ	1930-1984		
15	Okmulgee, OK	1930-1939 [5]	Waco, TX	1944-present
16	Minotola, NJ	1930-1933	Lakeland, FL	1965-2001
17	Clarion, PA	1930-2010		
18	Columbus, OH	1930-1948 [6]	Brockway, PA	1988-present
19	Hazelhurst, PA	1930-1931 (idle)	Crenshaw, PA	1988-present
20	Brackinridge, PA	1930-1940 (idle) [7]	Oakland, CA	1936-present
21	San Francisco, CA	1932-1937	Portland, OR	1956-present
22	San Francisco, CA	1932-1937	Tracy CA	1962-present
23	Los Angeles, CA	1932-present		
24	Los Angeles, CA	1932-1937	Mansfield, MA Ada, OK	1975-1981 1988-1991
25	Terre Haute, IN	1934-1950 [8]	Volney, NY	1985-2001
26	Muncie, IN	1933-1943 [9]	Toano, VA	1990-present
27	Toledo [10]	1960-1970s	Oakland South, CA	1988-1989
28	Pomona, CA	1988-1994	Windsor, CO	2005-present
29	Danville, VA	1988-present		

No.	Location 1	Dates	Location 2	Dates
30	Toronto, Ont. [11]	1997-2009		
31	Brampton [11]	1997-present		
32	unknown			
33	Chicago Heights, IL [12]	1949-1997	Milton	1997-2003
34	Montreal [11]	1997-present		
35	Auburn, NY	1994-present		
36	Scoudouc [11]	1997-2009		
37	Lavington [11]	1997-2009		
51	Antiock, CA	1997-1997		
52	San Jose de Las Tajas, Cuba	1953-ca. 1960	Hayward, CA	1997-2001
55	R.M.B.C. CO [13]	1988-present		
65	Vega Alta, Puerto Rico	1975-2008		

[1] Glassboro plant was altered to make closures in 1936 so it could not produce glass containers after that.

[2] Newark closed July 1, 1930; idle until 1934; then produced fiberglass

[3] Plans were made for the Atlanta plant on May 13, 1944.

[4] The Kimble Glass Co. purchased the Chicago Heights plant in 1939. When Owens-Illinois acquired the Kimble factories in 1949, Chicago Heights returned as Plant No. 33.

[5] Idle after 1932

[6] Converted to TV tubes in 1949

[7] The plant was idled 8-31 and never restarted until WWII when it made land mine top covers.

[8] Idle after 1936; rebuilt in 1941; restarted in 1942; 3rd furnace added in 1944

[9] Muncie was idle in 1940; converted to glass block in 1943; still open in 1950+.

[10] A Libby Glass Co. plant temporarily made liquor containers (possibly only a few) at Toledo in the 1960 and possibly 1970s. It was assigned Plant #27.

[11] These Canadian plants (formerly Consumer's Glass Co.) were not given Owens-Illinois numbers until 2001.

[12] Phil Perry made the following comments about the Chicago Heights plant but noted that much

of it was speculation: The factory was sold to Gerrsheimer as they were the only distributor for the plant's total output (i.e., Borosilicate glass). It was originally plant No. 13 until it was sold to Kimble. When it was later repurchased, it had to be given a different number (No. 33) as the old No. 13 had been reassigned to another factory.

[13] Joint venture – was Coors Beer and Anchor Glass; now Coors Beer and Owens-Illinois

Soda and Beer Bottles

The original article centered around soda and beer bottles, and most of the details were accurate. At least one Hutchinson soda bottle – one of the few of that type made by an automatic bottle machine, and one of the last ones produced – was made in 1929 and marked with the new Owens-Illinois logo. There is thus no question that the mark was in use from the beginning. As noted in the original article, two major changes in basemarks on beer and soda bottles occurred in 1940.

The term "Duraglas" was first embossed in cursive on bottle bases at some point during the year – so expect bottles with "0" date codes both with and without the word. Duraglas was a glass formula that was stronger than most previous glass mixtures. The story of this development is worth presenting. In the 1930s, accountants studied the cost of manufacturing a ton of glass in each factory and suggested that profits could be maximized by using less glass. Prior to that time, the only consideration was each plant's perception of what amount of glass was needed to produce a quality container. Since management now had data on which to base profitability, it required the engineering departments to create a new formula, glass design, and a new image (presented by the public relations departments) that would use less glass in container production. The result was Duraglas.

The formula and the embossed cursive "Duraglas" continued in use until 1964, although engravers occasionally included the mark as late as 1970 or later. The base in Figure 5 had both digits of the date code altered, so this may have been an old mold that was reused. At that point, Owens-Illinois developed a new coating for the bottles called DURAGLAS – in block capital letters. The name was never embossed on bottles.

Figure 5 – Duraglas (eBay)

9

The second 1940 innovation was basal stippling. This consisted of tiny dots poked into the baseplate of the mold. The dots became embossed stippling on the bottles. As with Duraglas, Owens-Illinois developed stippling at some point during 1940, so the plants made bottles during the year both with and without this feature. The process aided in preventing "checks" or shallow cracks in the base due to rapid cooling. The glass industry called this process "bottom plate knurling." It actually included stippling, chain stippling, BPMR (bottom plate metal removal, a series of concentric circles of dots) and others that were in use in the early days.

Other glass houses rapidly adopted the idea, and virtually all beer and soda bottles eventually appeared with stippled bases. For the discerning archaeologist, the stippling – originally applied by hand – shifted to machine application in the early to mid-1940s. This can be recognized by its evenly spaced appearance, although various shops adopted the process at different times. Figure 6 shows hand stippling on the left and machine stippling on the right.

Figure 6 – Basal stippling (Patricia McFarland)

At some point during the 1970s (currently unresearched), the industry began experimenting with other forms of stippling. The most common alternative was tiny crescents that looked like a single parenthesis ["("] in a line encircling the resting point of the base (Figure 7). It is important to know, however, that some bottles made after 1940 lacked stippling and the Duraglas logo. Some bottles were not made with the Duraglas process. The presence of either feature is datable; the absence is not.

Figure 7 – Alternative stippling (eBay)

The three codes on soda and beer bottles followed the typical Owens-Illinois format, with factory code to the left, date to the right, and mold cavity code below the logo. By the late 1930s, many bottles also showed catalog codes. The major issue, of course, was the date code.

10

As discussed in the earlier study, the initial date codes were single-digit numbers. While "9" could indicate either 1929 or 1939, *very* few bottles were made by the Owens-Illinois plants with 1929 date codes (Figure 8).

The problem was at the other end. These were returnable bottles, with a typical life of about five years – with some bottles still in use more than a decade after manufacture.

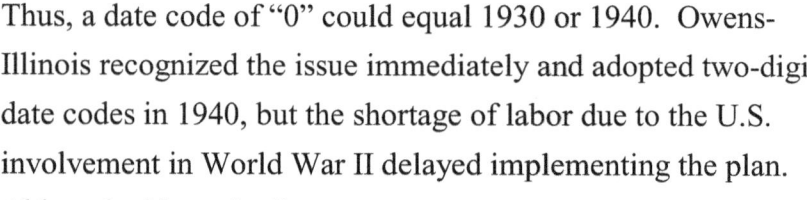

Figure 8 – 1939 date code

Figure 9 – Stippling and dot

Thus, date codes on returnable bottles could easily overlap. Thus, a date code of "0" could equal 1930 or 1940. Owens-Illinois recognized the issue immediately and adopted two-digit date codes in 1940, but the shortage of labor due to the U.S. involvement in World War II delayed implementing the plan. Although either stippling or "Duraglas" would set the code as 1940, the lack of those features would not necessarily indicate 1930. By 1941, the Owens-Illinois engravers came up with an easy fix; they added a dot at the end of the single-digit date code to indicate the 1940s.

Thus, a code of "1." indicates 1941. In some cases, however, the mold maker ignored (or forgot) the dot. In addition, the dot can get lost in the stippling (Figure 9).

Figure 10 – Inserted "4" (eBay)

The dot system began to be phased out almost immediately. By 1943, the engravers began using the two-digit date system, occasionally inserting a "4" in front of and slightly above the single-digit code (Figure 10). Between 1943 and 1946, a given bottle may have a dot code or a double-digit number. Thus, a bottle made in 1944 may be coded "44" or "4." It is important to remember that the dot system *only* applies to soda and beer bottles. We have not discovered the dot dating system on other bottle types. To add to the confusion, some Owens-Illinois plants used a system of dots on some other bottle types, notably prescriptions bottles. In some cases, these *may* have indicated the month or quarter of manufacture, but we received no consensus of

11

opinion from Owens-Illinois sources. Therefore, a dot following a date code on a prescription bottle is *not* indicative of a 1940s manufacture.

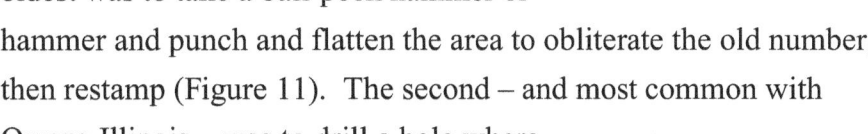

Figure 11 – Peened date code (eBay)

Often, when the same mold was used for more than one year, the engravers changed the date codes. This was done in one of three ways. The oldest was to take a ball-peen hammer or hammer and punch and flatten the area to obliterate the old number, then restamp (Figure 11). The second – and most common with Owens-Illinois – was to drill a hole where the number was stamped, insert a cast iron rod, saw the rod off flush with the

Figure 12 – Drilled date

mold surface, grind it to fit, then stamp the new number (Figure 12). The final option was to just stamp the new number atop the old one. Figure 13 shows a real mess. The mold was moved from Plant No. 7 to Plant No. 3 (with a "7" engraved over the "3") and a "1" stamped over a "7" that was stamped over a "6."

Figure 13 – Stamped date code (eBay)

Figure 14 – O.I.G. logo (Andy Higgs)

An odd early mark only appeared on a few soda bottles: O.I.G. We have only found a single bottle with a base embossed "O.I.G. / X / 31F" (Figure 14). The "X" may have been a designation for an experimental bottle, "31" was a date code for 1931, and "F" indicated the Fairmont, West Virginia, plant. The date and plant codes in this position appeared frequently on bottles of this type that were made between 1925 and 1931 by the American Bottle Co., a subsidiary of the Owens Bottle Co. The American Bottle Co. plants at Streator, Illinois, and Newark, Ohio, became Owens-Illinois factories in 1929, but the date/plant code configuration was used by at least two other plants (including Fairmont) in 1930 and 1931. It therefore, becomes clear that "O.I.G." equals Owens-Illinois Glass." While these are unusual, we have had this same bottle reported to us twice in different venues.

12

Coka-Cola Bottles

The Coca-Cola Bottling Co., based at Atlanta, Georgia, required all glass houses making Coke bottles to follow its pattern for manufacturer and date codes. Early in the century – possibly as early as 1900 – Coca-Cola apparently asked or demanded that the manufacturer's of the bottles emboss their logos on the heel or bases. For more information on early Coke bottles, see Porter

Figure 15 – Heel code

(2012). By the time the firm adopted the hobble-skirt bottles, that requirement seems to have been forgotten. Coca-Cola reinstated the demand and revised the original configuration twice, each necessitating immediate compliance. The four periods are summarized in Table 2.

Figure 16 – First skirt code

A July 23, 1919, letter from the Coca-Cola home office required a manufacturer's mark and the year of production to be embossed on the heels of the bottles. The date code was always two digits. Owens-Illinois used the Diamond-OI logo, and both the mark and date code were usually in fine-line embossing and are often difficult to see on a worn bottle (Figure 15). This practice continued until 1930 (Lockhart & Porter 2010).

Figure 17 – Second skirt code

In 1930, the code system migrated to the "skirt" of the hobble-skirt bottle, although a few bottles escaped notice and retained the old system mark during 1931. The mark now had a two-digit date code to the left of the logo and the two-digit mold code to the right (Figure 16). A code of 42 <0> 16 would mean the bottle was produced in 1942 in mold #16. The next shift placed the logo back on the base and transferred the date code to the left position – still on the skirt – with a hyphen between the two codes (Figure 17). A code of 52-16 now indicated a manufacture in 1952 with mold #16 (Lockhart 2010:340-343).

13

Table 2 – Coca-Cola Glass Manufacturer Logo and Code Requirements

Dates	Requirement	Bottle Type
ca. 1900-ca. 1917	Logo*	Straight-Sided
1919-1930	Logo and date code on heel	Hobble-Skirt
1930-1952	Mold code, logo, & date code on skirt	Hobble-Skirt
1952-at least 1990s	Mold code & date code on skirt; logo on base	Hobble-Skirt

* This is extrapolated from empirical evidence; we have no documentary confirmation.

Pepsi-Cola Bottles

Until the firm adopted Applied Color Label (ACL) bottles in 1943, Pepsi-Cola had no logo or code requirements for its bottle manufacturers. During that year, however, Pepsi instituted a complex code. An example (Figure 18) will help to explain. The base of this bottle was embossed "DES. PAT. 120,277 (arch) / 14 B 48 / 9 {Diamond-OI logo} / Duraglas (cursive) / G1170 / 8." From the top, the design patent number identified the patent used for the bottle. The left number on the next line may be a manufacturer's

Figure 18 – First Pepsi code

code. On our sample, 14 seems to indicate Owens-Illinois; 15 for Laurens Glass Works, and 16 for Brockway Glass Co. The capital letter in the center (almost always A or B) *may* indicate the factory within the glass company (e.g., 14 B *might* mean the Streator plant of Owens-Illinois), but the final two digits are the date code – 1948 in this case.

The one- or two-digit number to the left of the logo on the second horizontal line *is* the plant code (Plant No. 9 at Streator, Illinois, in the example), and Duraglas (next line) was discussed above. G1170 was the code for the bottle style, and "8." was a mold cavity code. This same configuration (including the patent number) was used until Owens-Illinois adopted the new logo in 1954.

Figure 19 – Second Pepsi code

The next format was similar but a bit simpler as shown in Figure 19. The patent number was now so out of date as to be

14

meaningless, so it had been removed. The example base was embossed "14 B 56 / 15 {OI logo} 6 / Duraglas (cursive) / G1170." Again, we cannot explain the "14" or "B," but "56" was the date code for 1956, and "15" was the plant code for the Waco, Texas, factory; "6" was a mold number. The Duraglas mark and style code remained the same. This format continued into the 1960s, probably later.

Liquor Bottles and Flasks

In early 1934, the *Glass Packer* (1934:502-503) reported that the Treasury Dept. had passed a law requiring several changes in the embossing on the bases or heels and the shoulders of liquor bottles and flasks. Glass manufacturers wishing to produce liquor containers had to obtain a federal licence and number and to conform to these regulations on all items made after August 1, 1934. Distilleries, rectifiers, or importers had to also procure federal numbers and permits, and they were required to use the newly marked bottles by November 1.

The requirements called for a specific code sequence on bases, with the distiller number (beginning with D), rectifier number (beginning with R), or import number (beginning with I) on top, followed by a second line with the glass house (federal) number to the left, followed by either a dash or the manufacturer's logo (Figure 20). If a dash were used, the logo had to appear elsewhere on the base. The number to the left was a date

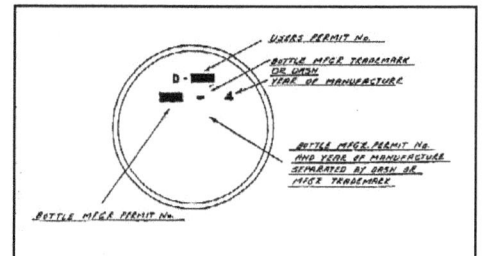

Figure 20 – Liquor Codes (*Glass Packer* 1934:503)

code, and two-digit numbers were required during 1940 (in a different ordinance). The configuration for flask bases or bottle heels were very similar. In addition, the shoulder of the bottles had to be embossed "FEDERAL LAW FORBIDS SALE OR RE-USE OF THIS BOTTLE." The requirements were not rescinded until 1964.

Typically, each glass manufacturer was assigned a single number, although a few amassed extra numbers as they purchased or absorbed smaller factories. Because of its vast size and numerous plants Owens-Illinois received a large quantity of numbers. According to an Owens-Illinois 1969 internal list of liquor permit numbers, the firm received numbers 54-55, 57-

15

58, 60, 64-65, 88, 100, 111, 159, 171, 175, 177, 179, 180, 182, 202, 221, and 222 (see Lindsey 2015 to view the 1969 document). In addition, we have recorded 56 and 62 associated with

Figure 21 – OI liquor codes (Tucson Urban Renewal and Paul Demers)

Diamond-OI logos. These probably represent plants that had been closed by 1969. Figure 21 compares a typical flask base from 1942 with one made prior to Prohibition. The codes speak for themselves.

Figure 22 – OI heelcode (Tom Alex)

Although much less common, Owens-Illinois occasionally used heelcodes (Figure 22). Another fairly common variation was the "factory code - date code" format with the Diamond-OI mark to the side and rotated 90 degrees (Figure 23). A final unusual but fairly common configuration was to stack

Figure 24 – Variation code

Figure 23 – Variation code (eBay)

the codes. In the example in Figure 24, the top code (64) is the plant number, the center (D-1) is the distiller's code, and the bottom number (45) is the date code for 1945. These and other variations are relatively common, so the government must not have been too concerned with order.

Milk Bottles

Owens-Illinois made milk bottles in two basic cross-sectional shapes: round and square. Round milk bottles were used long before the 1929 merger and were still made at least into the 1980s, possibly later. The earliest of these had the typical Owens-Illinois codes, with plant codes to the left of the Diamond-OI logo and single-digit date codes to the right. However,

16

especially with West Coast factories (Plants 21-24), the single-digit codes extended to ca. 1946 with no dot delimiter (Figure 25). These plants did not fall under the Owens-Illinois envelope until 1932. Frequently, these had no stippling or Duraglas mark, so date codes of 2, 3, 4, 5, and 6 should be approached with caution.

Figure 25 – Round milk bottle base

The large letter in Figure 25 was a sorter's code or sorter's letter. Each of these was typically the first letter in the name of the dairy (P = Price's Dairy in the example). When milk bottles were returned to the dairy, they were first sorted to remove bottles that belonged to other dairies. The sorter's letter made that task much easier.

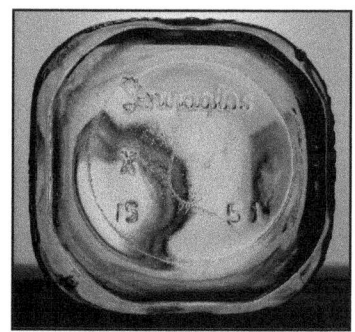

Figure 26 – Square milk bottle base

Although two other inventors had earlier patented milk bottles that were square in cross-section, they were ahead of their time. Roy Blunt of the Buck Glass Co. invented the first truly successful square milk bottle in 1942, although Owens-Illinois designed its own brand – called the Handi-Square – the following year. Although some of the early square milk bottles followed the same pattern as the round ones, the logo soon migrated to the heel of the bottle, along with terms like "REGISTERED," "SEALED," or other words. The base was generally embossed "Duraglas" (cursive) until after 1964, a capital letter, and two numbers. The left number was a one- or two-digit plant code, while the right one was the date code (Figure 26). See Lockhart (2014) for a discussion of the inventions, patents, finishes, and other attributes of milk bottles over time.

Another set of codes, found on milk bottle heels, began with the letter "M":

"M"=Gallon milks
"MH"=light weight milk
"ML"=standard weight milks
"MX" or "MLX"= standard weight milks with headspace ¼" below cap seat
"MY" or "MHX"= light weight milks with headspace ¼" below cap seat
"MZ"= non-returnable milk

17

Prescription Bottles

Owens-Illinois rapidly became one of the most prolific producers of prescription bottles in the United States. Both ancestral firms had carried their own brands of prescription bottles, and the new company adopted the flagship brand from each of them.

Owens Ovals

A full study of the Owens Ovals would fill a chapter by itself and is thus beyond the scope of this work. Although we have no early catalogs, date codes show that the Owens Bottle Co. offered the model by at least 1918. When Owens Bottle adopted the Box-O logo in 1919, it used that mark until the late 1920s (Figure 27), then added "WENS" to the right side of the box to make "OWENS" with the "O" in the box (Figure 28).

Figure 27 – Box-O logo (eBay)

Figure 28 – Box-O + WENS

With the merger, the base was embossed "OWENS / {number} {Diamond-OI logo} {number}. The number to the left of the logo in this case is a mold number, *not* a plant code – although the number to the right *is* a date code. An example from 1939 (Figure 29) was embossed "OWENS / 12. Diamond-OI 9 (followed by 3 dots in an "L" shape)." One or more dots follows either of the numbers, sometimes both – as in Figure 29.

The dot system was developed because of the sensitive nature of prescriptions bottles. Once manufactured, they cannot be stored for too long a time because of the risk of contamination. As a result, several runs of each type of prescription bottle were made each year. The dots indicate the number of the runs, with a single dot indicating the first run, two dots for the second, etc.

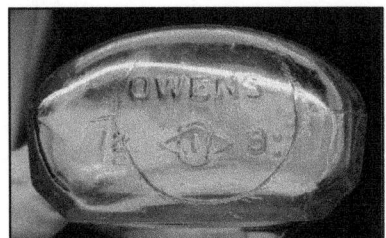

Figure 29 – Owens Oval base

18

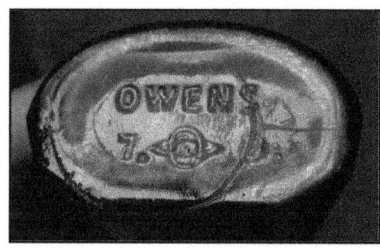

Figure 30 – Dot codes

When dots followed the mold codes, they would designate the machine position on multi-cavity molds. If the mold number was "7," for example, the front cavity would have no dot. The back cavity on a dual cavity

Figure 31 – Unexplained dots

mold, however, would be "7•"; or in the case of a triple cavity mold, the code would be "7••" for the center cavity. In Figure 30, "7•" indicates mold the back cavity of mold number 7. The right code shows that the bottle was made in the third run in 1939. Although the dots should follow the number and be centered, on small bottles, they were often placed wherever the engraver could fit them. We have no explanation for some extraneous dots (Figure 31).

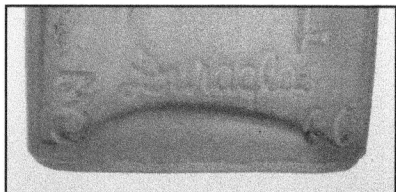

Figure 32 – Duraglas (Fort Bliss)

Figure 34 – Owens Oval – plastic

From 1940s, most bottles also had "Duraglas" (cursive) embossed on the front heel, back heel, or both (Figure 32). From the inception of Owens-Illinois, the firm offered the bottles in both prescription and continuous-thread finishes (Figure 33), and with or without graduations. The plants also made other slight variations. By the end of 1949, the plants removed the word "OWENS" from the base, although it was clearly the same bottle.

Figure 33 – Finishes (Owens-Illinois 1930 catalog)

By the 1950s or 1960s, Owens-Illinois added a code to these bottles that indicated the capacity in ounces (10, 20, 30, 40, etc.). Sometimes, the engravers would get confused and change the "0" to a "1" – thinking these were date codes. The error could be repeated. Russ Hoenig discovered one example that was embossed "94" – but was not made in 1994. This could easily create confusion for archaeologists

19

finding later bottles.   In 2015, the same Owens Oval bottle style – long out of patent protection – is still used in plastic format (Figure 34).

Illinois Ovals

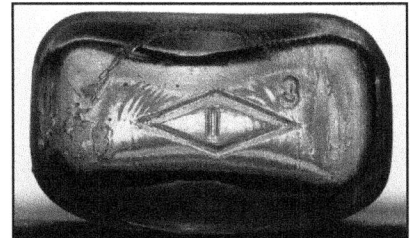

Figure 36 – Diamond-I logo

Figure 37 – Lyric Oval (Illinois Glass Co., 1906 catalog)

C.M. Schofield invented the Lyric Oval in 1912 and assigned the patent to the Sheldon-Foster Glass Co. the following year (Figure 35). Sheldon-Foster sold the Chicago Heights plant to the Chicago Heights Glass Co. later in 1913, and the new firm made the first Lyric Oval bottles. By the end of the year, the Illinois Glass Co. had acquired the factory and patent rights.

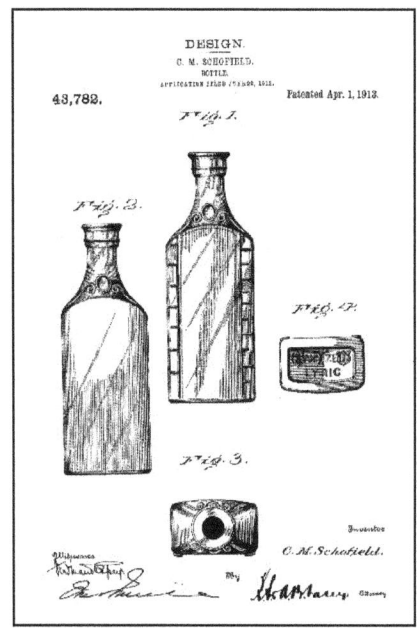

Figure 35 – Lyric Oval (Schoefield 1913 patent)

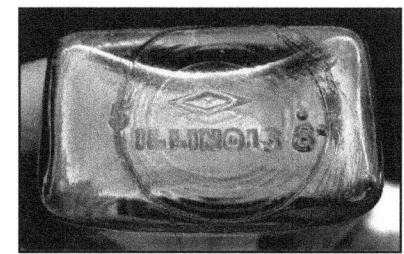

Figure 38 – ILLINOIS base

Illinois Glass made the bottles, still using the Lyric trademark along with the Diamond-I logo, until the 1929 merger (Figures 36 & 37). Toward the end of the 1920s, the firm added the word "ILLINOIS" (Figure 38). Owens-Illinois called the same bottle the Illinois Oval and added the typical Owens-Illinois codes (although the left code *still* was not a factory number). The company continued to produce the Illinois Ovals until 1949 (Figure 39).

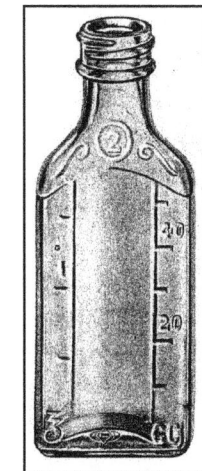

Figure 39 – Illinois Oval bottle (O-I 1930 catalog)

20

Packers, Product Bottles and Jars

Typically called packers in the industry, these were bottles and jars used to hold food, medicines, household items, and a variety of other things. Until the 1970s, these were only lightly regulated. This lack of regulation means that the typical code and logo arrangement was generally followed, although one of the codes might by missing on any given jar or product bottle. Smaller bottles often only had a single-digit date code until at least the mid-1970s, and the lone digit may have extended into the 1980s (Figure 40). Many of the odder logo variations (see below) occurred on this type of container.

Figure 40 – Packer base

The Final Codes

Figure 41 – AGR Peanut Code

The American Glass Research (AGR) created the Cavity Identification Detection code system in the 1970s. Commonly called the peanut code, these consisted of a series of squares made of dots that were embossed in a circular format on the bases of bottles and jars.

Figure 42 – OI ring codes

Each square could have between one and four dots representing a numerical combination that could only be read by machines leased by AGR. Eventually, the "peanuts" evolved into two dots (Figure 41).

In 1978, Owens-Illinois adopted a system of concentric circles – since AGR had patented the dot codes. Originally the Owens-Illinois system used eight rings but that was reduced to seven rings later (Figure 42). Using a combination of missing rings and the distance between rings, Owens-Illinois was able to develop its own machines to read the code as a number. Like

21

other "mold" codes, these were used for quality control. Owens-Illinois adopted its own dot code – located on the heels of the containers – in the early 1990s (Figure 43).

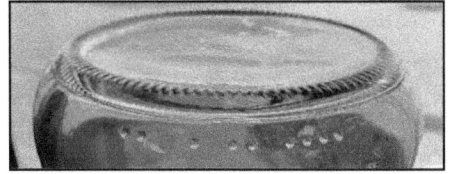

Figure 43 – Dot heelcodes

Oddities

Engravers sometimes had bad days or were under other pressure. A mold shop foreman disclosed me that he was occasionally told to forget the date change (or other last-minute finishing touches because they needed the molds on the floor – NOW. The older types of errors – like letters missing, letters or numbers backward, or a complete misspelling – were mostly eliminated by the time that Owens-Illinois was formed. What remained were odd variations in the logos. These included a dot in center of the diamond instead of an "I"; an empty diamond; a large "O" and small diamond; tilted or offset "I"; unusual shapes, and variations in the "I." Figure 43 shows some examples.

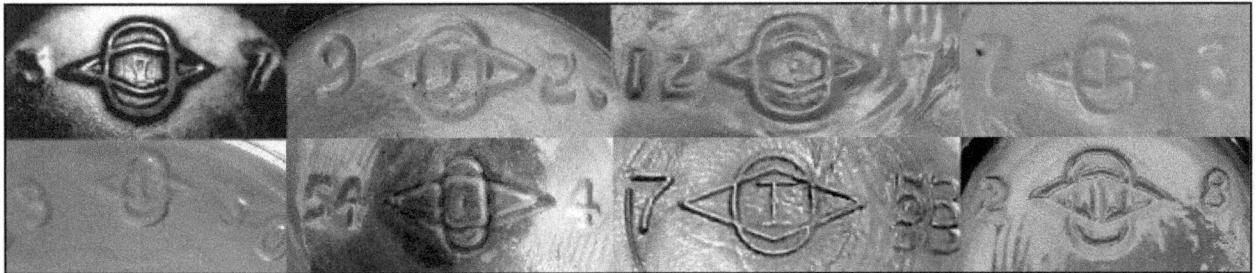

Figure 44 – Oddities

Conclusion

This study takes us as far beyond my 2004 article as that one did from Toulouse (1971). But, this will not be the end. There are already tantalizing hints that we are only beginning to observe. For example, it may be possible to tie certain design and/or technique changes to specific plants. We now have the big picture; it is time to fill in the nuances.

Acknowledgments

Our gratitude to Phil Perry. Like Russ Hoenig, Phil was a former employee of the Owens-Illinois Glass Co. Phil contacted Bill Lindsey with a question *he* had for Bill. Bill, of

22

course, had questions to ask Phil, and soon brought in the rest of the Bottle Rearch Group. Phil suggested Russ, who was conducting his own research into the Pennsylvania Owens-Illinois plants. Phil and Russ provided a huge volume of non-proprietary information on Owens-Illinois and its ancestral factories. Our relationship has been a good match.

Sources

Glass Packer
> 1934 "Liquor Bottle Regulations Summarized for Glass Packer Readers." 13(8):502-503.

Hoenig, Russ, Bill Lockhart, Pete Schulz, Carol Serr, Les Jordan, Bill Lindsey, and Phil Perry
> 2008 "The Dating Game: Berney-Bond Glass Company." *Bottles and Extras* 19(3):33-42. [This issue is misnumbered; the cover states that it is No. 3; inside, however, it is listed as No (no period) 4. The actual issue is No. 5.]

Jones, May
> 1965 *The Bottle Trail, Volume 5*. Nara Vista, New Mexico.

Lindsey, Bill
> 2015 "Historic Glass Bottle Identification & Information Website." http://www.sha.org/bottle/index.htm

Lockhart, Bill
> 2004 "The Dating Game: Owens-Illinois Glass Co." *Bottles and Extras* 15(3):24-27.

> 2007 "Owens-Illinois Glass Company." Society for Historical Archaeology http://www.sha.org/index.php/view/page/owens-Illinois_article

> 2010 *Bottles on the Border: The History and Bottles of the Soft Drink Industry in El Paso, Texas, 1881-2000*. Historic Glass Bottle Identification & Information Website: Reference Sources/Bibliography. http://www.sha.org/bottle/References.htm

> 2014 *Milk Bottles and the El Paso Dairy Industry*. Privately published.

Lockhart, Bill, Bill Lindsey, David Whitten, and Carol Serr

 2005a "The Dating Game: The Illinois Glass Company." *Bottles and Extras* 16(1):54-60.

Lockhart, Bill, Michael R. Miller, Bill Lindsey, Carol Serr, and David Whitten

 2005b "The Dating Game: Illinois Pacific – A Division of the Illinois Glass Co." *Bottles and Extras* 16(4):73-80.

Lockhart, Bill and Bill Porter

 2010 "The Dating Game: Tracking the Hobble-Skirt Coca-Cola Bottle." *Bottles and Extras* 21(5):46-61.

 1952 "Owens-Illinois Trademark." Internal document.

Owens-Illinois Glass Co.

 1941 "Mold Schedule Desk, Routines & Practices." General Service Dept.

Paquette, Jack K.

 1994 *The Glassmakers: A History of Owens-Illinois, Incorporated*. Trumpeting Angel Press, Toledo, Ohio.

Porter, Bill

 2012 "Dating and Identifying Early Coca-Cola Bottles: Focusing (Mainly) of Florida and Georgia Bottles." *Bottles and Extras* 23(4):14-15, 54-63.

Toulouse, Julian Harrison

 1971 *Bottle Makers and Their Marks*. Thomas Nelson, New York.

Rim Codes: A Pacific Coast Dating System for Milk Bottles

Peter D. Schulz, Bill Lockhart, Carol Serr, and Bill Lindsey

Peter D. Schulz
Bill Lockhart
Carol Serr
Bill Lindsey

Rim Codes: A Pacific Coast Dating System for Milk Bottles

ABSTRACT

Milk bottles from the western United States sometimes exhibit embossed numbers on the upper surface of the finish. Physical and historical evidence indicate that these numbers constitute a unique date code, indicating the month and year of production. Examination of more than 1,200 milk bottles from this region (227 with the code) demonstrates that the code was used by five California glass factories between 1924 and 1933. It appears that in a region with intense competition among glass factories, this dating system was developed to help dairies track bottle loss—a significant problem at that time. The code was discontinued after most of the region's milk bottle production was concentrated in a single company.

Introduction

Historic archaeologists have long been interested in the use of makers' marks and associated codes for dating bottles and contexts in which they occur. Known date codes share several characteristics: they are usually found on the heel or base of the bottle, indicate the year of production, and specify individual glass manufacturers (Toulouse 1971; Lockhart 2004; Lockhart et al. 2007). An ongoing study of bottle manufacturers' marks, however, encountered a previously unreported date code system that exhibits none of these characteristics: a code indicating both the month and year of manufacture, placed on the bottle finish, and shared by several Pacific Coast glassworks.

The code was first encountered on a California milk bottle embossed on the rim (lip) of the cap-seat finish with two numbers: "2" on the left and "5" directly opposite on the right. Research led to no previous reports of such marks in the archaeological or collectors' literature. Examination of additional collections indi-

cates that such rim codes were commonly used by Pacific Coast glass factories in the 1920s and early 1930s but were evidently unknown elsewhere. Historical research confirms that the codes were intended to address an important problem in the dairy industry by indicating the production date of each bottle.

Materials and Methods

To determine the geographical and temporal distribution of rim codes, the authors examined milk bottles in numerous archaeological, museum, and private collections, the largest single collection being the 1,200+ bottles in the State Dairy Collection maintained by the California Department of Parks and Recreation. Contact with other archaeologists and collectors throughout the country found no one who had noticed the codes or anyone with a clear understanding of what they represented.

During examination of rim-coded bottles, other features were noted as well. These features included the nature of the finish, the bottle capacity, the dairy label and whether it was embossed or applied color, the maker's mark, any other codes present, and the manufacturing technique. Simultaneously, one of the authors reviewed the literature on milk-bottle production and use, focusing on national and regional dairy trade journals produced throughout the first half of the 20th century.

Results

Rim codes were found on 227 bottles with capacities ranging from one-quarter pint to a quart. The codes were embossed only on cap-seat finishes, the upper face of the lip sometimes being flattened slightly to accommodate them. The numbers are well formed and usually quite distinct but are only about 1/8-inch (3 mm) tall. As in the initial example, they always occur in pairs: one number on the left side of the rim, the other directly opposite it on the right (Figure 1). Left-side numbers range from 1 to 12. Those on the right occur in both single-

Historical Archaeology, 2009, 43(2):30–39.
Accepted for publication 2 June 2008.
Permission to reprint required.

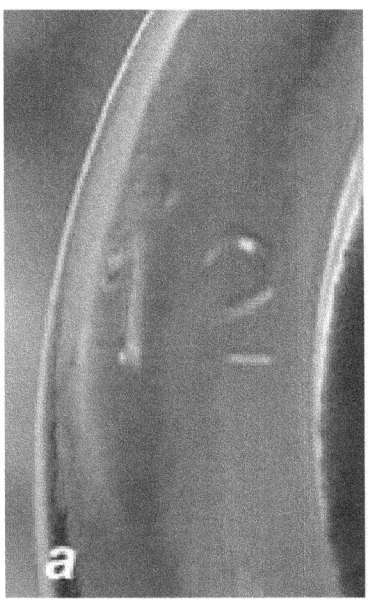 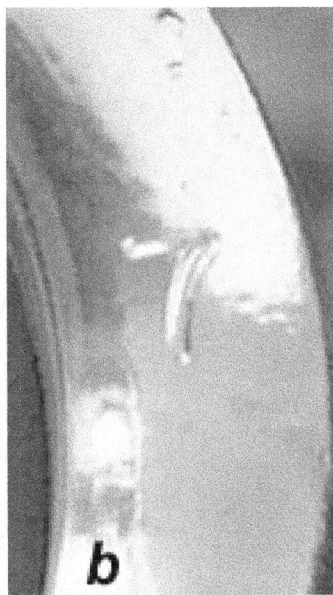 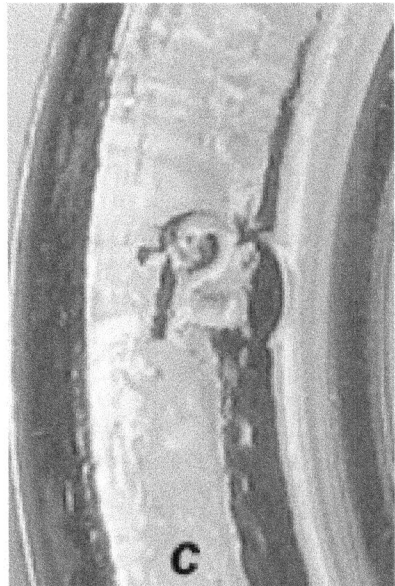

FIGURE 1. Rim codes on milk bottle finishes: (*a–b*) left and right side numbers from the same bottle; (*c*) result of peening out and replacing a number ("10" replaced by "2"). (Photos by B. Lindsey.)

digit (0–9) as well as double-digit (25–26) form. This observation strongly implies that the left/right combination represents a month/year code, and that single- and double-digit codes were used variably to indicate the year.

All bottles with rim codes were machine made. This conclusion was expected since hand production of cap-seat finishes required use of a lipping tool, which would preclude any embossing on the finish. Bottles from both blow-and-blow and press-and-blow machines were represented (see Miller and Sullivan [1984] for distinguishing features), although the latter were far more common. Additionally, all dairy labels on rim-code bottles were embossed with only one bottle having an additional applied color label (discussed below). This suggests that rim codes were popular prior to the widespread introduction of applied color labels in the mid-9   .

Rim codes were observed on bottles made by at least five glass companies (Table 1). Although all the code-using glass factories were in California, dairies employing the codes were located in California, Hawaii, Nevada, Oregon, and Utah. Factory operation dates indicate the codes must have been in use before 1930 and must have continued until at least 1932. Bottles made for West Coast dairies by eastern factories, in the same era, exhibited no rim codes.

Assuming a month/year designation for the codes, it was initially unclear whether they indicated the date the mold was made or the time of the bottle manufacture—that is, whether the intended user was the glass factory or the dairy. Physical evidence, however, demonstrates that the codes were sometimes peened out, and newer ones were applied to the molds (Figure 1*c*). This would have made no sense if the code were intended to track the mold.

The codes in fact indicate the date of manufacture and were intended to help track the bottles. This purpose is intimated by an advertisement from one of the California glass manufacturers (Illinois-Pacific Glass Company), noting that their bottles were "stronger and give longer service," which was "why each one bears its own date" (*Pacific Dairy Review* 1925). An advertisement a few months later is definitive:

> Keeping Books on Milk Bottles. How do you know a bottle has earned its cost unless it is dated? Look at the top of the finish for date of manufacture. If it is there the maker believes in his own bottle (*Pacific Dairy Review* 1926).

A similar message from the same company touted the durability of its bottles and alleged that they "live practically twice as long [as] ordinary milk bottles." Milk distributors were

TABLE 1
DISTRIBUTION OF RIM CODES BY MANUFACTURER AND DATE

Glass Company	Location	Operation	No.	Code Range
Blake-Hart (only)[a]	Sacramento		15	Dec. 1925–Dec. 1929
Illinois-Pacific Glass Co.	S.F. and L.A.	1926–1930	126	Jan. 1925–Jul. 1933
Latchford Glass Co.	Los Angeles	1925–1938	5	Sep. 1932–Oct. 1932
Owens-Illinois Glass Co.[b]	San Francisco	1932–1937	1	Jul. 1932
Pacific Coast Glass Co.	S.F. and L.A.	1919–1930	46	Jun. 1926–Nov. 1932
Southern Glass Co.	Los Angeles	1917–1931	15	Oct. 1924–Sep. 1930
None or unknown			19	Dec. 1925–Sep. 1930
Total			227	

[a]Blake-Hart bottles were made by Illinois-Pacific Glass and Pacific Coast Glass. Only those lacking a separate glass company mark are listed under Blake-Hart.
[b]Owens-Illinois Factory 21.

advised that the bottles "are dated on the top of the finish so you can figure for yourself" (*Western Milk Dealer* 1926).

Rim codes thus indicate the month and year of manufacture, likely practical because the limited number of bottle sizes and styles allowed ring (finish) molds to be manufactured or retooled each month and then used with a variety of previously made blow molds.

Manufacturers and Dating Problems

Of the 227 code-marked bottles, 85% can be assigned to five manufacturers, based on makers' marks (Table 1). The remaining code-marked bottles have no perceptible makers' marks but probably derive from the Illinois-Pacific Glass Company and the Pacific Coast Glass Company. The heel marks of both these companies are often quite faint. It is likely that in some cases the molds were not sufficiently well cut to provide a clear impression or that the heel marks lost their clarity faster than the body labels.

About half of the bottles with no perceptible maker's mark do, however, exhibit the mark of the Blake-Hart Company (Giarde 1980:16–17). This Sacramento partnership patented a design for a square milk bottle (Blake and Hart 1927), which was actually manufactured by both Illinois-Pacific Glass and Pacific Coast Glass during the 1920s. (Two Blake-Hart bottles that exhibit an Illinois-Pacific factory mark are included with that

company's bottles in Table 1. It may be noted that 7 of the remaining 15 Blake-Hart bottles have year codes of "25" or "26" on the rim—a double-digit year code otherwise used only by Pacific Coast Glass and only in those two years.)

The remaining bottles have makers' marks. All are identified by Julian Harrison Toulouse (1971), although in some cases more recent investigations modify chronologies proposed by him. All date codes from bottles made by Latchford Glass Company, Southern Glass Company, and Owens-Illinois (Plant 21) fall within the temporal range of those companies (Table 1), but the same is not true of the other two manufacturers.

Pacific Coast Glass Works was incorporated as the Pacific Coast Glass Company in 1924, but it used the same marks before and after the reorganization. The rim codes provide no information on these changes. Two of the rim codes, however, date after the company's merger with Illinois-Pacific in September 1930, to form the Illinois Pacific Coast Company. A third code (November 1932) even postdates the latter firm's acquisition by Owens-Illinois in July 1932 (*Western Milk Dealer* 1930; Porter 1933:294–296). These seeming discrepancies are almost certainly due to retention and continued use of old private blow molds by the new firms operating the old factories. Only the ring (finish) molds were being updated.

Obvious discrepancies also occur with the Illinois-Pacific Glass Company marks. All bottles with rim codes exhibit the company's initials in a triangle. This Triangle-IPG mark dates to the later years of the company's operation and suggests that it was introduced when the company incorporated in 1926 (Lockhart et al. 2005:76–78). The association of this mark with rim codes dating as early January 1925 indicates that the mark was in use at least a year before incorporation. As with the Pacific Coast Glass Company bottles, the Illinois-Pacific rim codes continue past the 1930 merger and even the 1932 acquisition by Owens-Illinois. Eight bottles have rim codes dating to the Illinois Pacific Coast period, and an additional three postdate the 1932 acquisition. These changes again can be attributed to reuse of old private blow molds with new ring molds.

One of the Illinois-Pacific bottles is particularly interesting. It has a rim code of "2 // 1" and a circular plate-mold label for Brant Rancho, Owensmouth, California. The opposite face has an applied color label—the only example of such a label found on a rim-code bottle—with similar information, but this label locates the dairy in Canoga Park. The change in location reflects the fact that Owensmouth changed its name to Canoga Park on 1 March 1931 (*Van Nuys News* 1931). Thus both the rim code and the embossing should predate the applied color label. Presence of a color label is initially confusing since the technology was not introduced until the mid-1930s.

Owens-Illinois introduced applied color labels on milk bottles beginning in mid-1933, offering them only from its Huntington, West Virginia, factory. The process was expanded to the Columbus, Ohio, factory in 1934 and then to other plants (*Milk Dealer* 1933; *Modern Packaging* 1948:122). Color-labeled bottles were available from Owens-Illinois California plants (including the former Illinois-Pacific plants) beginning in fall 1934 and were heavily advertised by 1935 (*California Milk News* 1934; *Los Angeles Times* 1935; *Milk Dealer* 1935; Owens-Illinois Glass Company 1935).

The important point here is that color labels could be applied to old bottles. In fact, the Owens-Illinois San Francisco factories did this experimentally in 1936, inviting local dairies to send in embossed bottles to have color labels applied to the opposite side (*Milk Dealer* 1936). It is quite possible that the Los Angeles plants did the same. Such a practice would result in

bottles with dual-embossed and color labels, and the present specimen seems to be an obvious example of this process.

A final limiting factor in interpreting the codes is that some pairs of numbers can be read upside down (for example, "6 // 8"), leaving a question as to which is the month and which is the year code. Sixteen specimens in the sample reflect this difficulty. While it might be argued that the earlier possible date is the one intended, it is also possible that the glass factories simply overlooked this problem. In only three cases was possible confusion eliminated by the addition of an underline.

Subtracting specimens with only partial codes or where uncertainty exists regarding the month-year interpretations leaves 207 bottles where the year is known and 209 with a known month. The annual and monthly distributions are shown in Figures 2 and 3.

"No Experience but Grief": Rim Codes and the Dairy Industry

The 1920s witnessed an increasing interest in bottle date codes among businesses relying on returnable bottles, that is, among dairy companies and beverage bottlers. Such companies had considerable capital tied up in containers that were prone to breakage, theft, or loss. Glass companies appealed for patronage through claims for the durability of their products, sometimes using date codes:

> The old saying of "The pitcher that goes to the well too often gets broken" can now be applied to your beverage bottles, but the Pacific Coast Glass Company has made it possible to keep track of the trips. It is now possible to get your bottles with the date of manufacture blown in them.
>
> This feature has many advantages. It gives the bottler an opportunity of keeping track of the life of a purchase of bottles and to determine just how long it takes to use up so many gross. He can always make up his orders ready so that he need not run short of bottles at the height of the season.
>
> Another advantage of this dating is to help keep accurate figures on costs. By knowing the life of a bottle it is possible to determine the average number of trips a bottle will make, and to determine an average cost of packing beverages. This is an advantage that should encourage every bottler to buy his bottles dated (*Pacific Bottler* 1928).

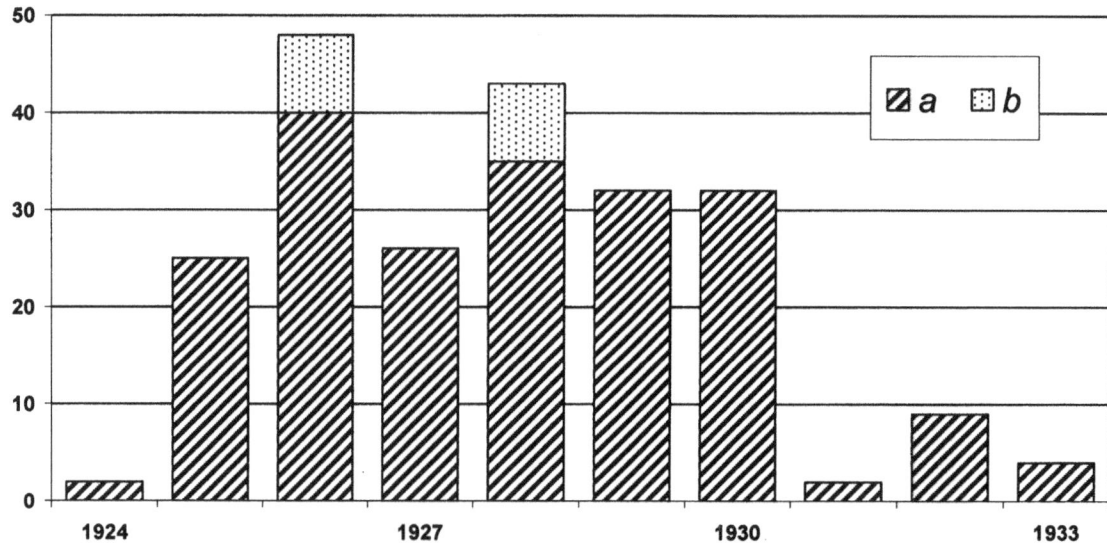

FIGURE 2. Annual distribution of codes in the present study: (*a*) distribution of 207 specimens for which the year is unequivocal; (*b*) distribution of 16 specimens for which alternative readings are possible, assuming the earlier year is intended. (Graph by authors.)

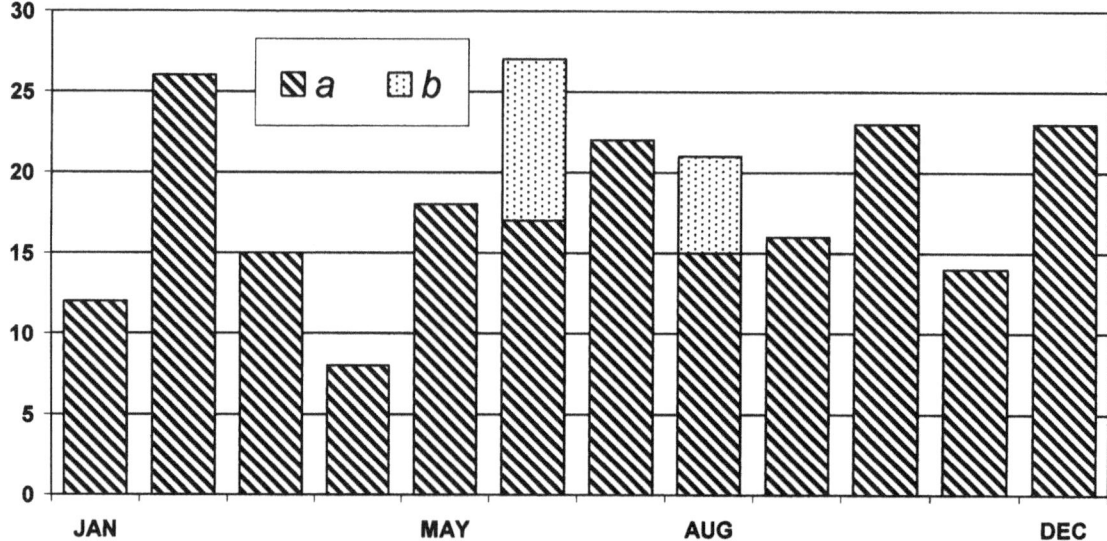

FIGURE 3. Monthly distribution of codes in the present study: (*a*) distribution of 209 specimens for which the month is unequivocal; (*b*) distribution of 16 specimens for which alternative readings are possible, assuming that the earlier month is intended. (Graph by authors.)

Intended for soda bottlers, this advice was old news to the fluid milk industry, which had been complaining about the functional lifespan of bottles for more than two decades while trying to devise practical solutions.

Creation of the modern dairy industry was based on an expanding market for its products, and this market depended on two crucial factors: an increasing perception of the nutritional values of milk and the increasing demand for sanitary rigor in its handling (DuPuis 2002). The "milk for health" campaigns of the 1920s depended on widespread insistence on inspection of dairy herds and milk plants by local health authorities. The perception of milk as valuable for the public health—especially the health of children—led to legal mandates for sanitary plants, pasteurization, and eventually to vitamin-augmentation of the milk supply. Importantly, these developments relied on the elimination of what was the nearly universal method of delivery in the 19th century: "loose milk," dipped from a communal milk pail to fill the customer's own receptacle. Sanitary processing of fluid milk—in the dairy—resulted in a product that was safe to consume. To ensure delivery of uncontaminated milk to consumers, local and state governments required that milk be sealed at the dairy in sanitary containers. Although there was some early interest in disposable paper containers (Winslow 1909:140–141), the overwhelming choice of distributors throughout the nation was to use returnable glass bottles.

Investment in milk bottles, however, was expensive, and the problem of bottle loss—and a corresponding interest in "trippage" (the number of round trips a bottle made from dairy to customer and back)—quickly became a focus of concern throughout the industry. In the early decades of the 20th century, loss of bottles through breakage, theft, or simply the failure of customers to return them was universally considered one of the most important problems that milk dealers had to face. Simultaneously, it was one of the few expenses potentially within their power to reduce (Spear 1907; Hagemann 1913; Lane 1913; Hood 1914; *Milk Dealer* 1915b; Parker 1917:326–327; Walker 1917, 1923; Traveler 1918; Kullman 1921; Smith 1921; Cochran 1923a, 1923b, 1923c; Clement 1924; Gardiner 1925). A national survey of distributors in the early 1920s reported an average daily loss of 4% of all bottles delivered, with an estimate of 13–21 trips per bottle (Kelly and Clement 1923:339–340).

An important element of the problem was breakage, either in the plant or upon delivery. For very small dairies, this was the most important source of loss. Concern focused on the contributing factors in handling by workers as well as breakage by poorly designed washing and bottling machines (Moon 1917; Clement 1923; Ford 1924a, 1924b, 1924c; *Certified Milk* 1927; *Milk Dealer* 1929, 1932; Clement et al. 1932). This concern also resulted in investigations of bottles themselves (Williams 1922; Gardiner

1925; Kouwenhoven 1926). It should come as no surprise that the durability of their products was the most commonly stressed feature of major milk bottle manufacturers in this era.

For larger distributors, the most important factor in bottle loss lay with retrieving empties. Customers discarded the bottles or diverted them to other uses; junkmen scavenged them for resale; or competing dairies pirated them for their own use. Surveys of how dairies met these problems typically found a limited number of solutions: charging deposits, forming bottle exchanges, legal action against junkmen, public information campaigns, creating local organizations to use "universal bottles," and either rewarding or penalizing the delivery drivers. A 1921 survey inspired comments from 50 dealers throughout the U.S. and Canada. All of these possible solutions and combinations of them found adherents or experimenters, and a few were satisfied with the results. Most dealers, however, were dissatisfied and frustrated, echoing at greater length the terse response from a California distributor: "No experience but grief. Do the best we can and buy more bottles" (Smith 1921:14).

Regardless of the nature of the loss, distributors could understand its source and extent only by maintaining appropriate records. The trade literature specifically encouraged such tracking (*Milk Dealer* 1913, 1915a; Whitcomb 1922) and prominently featured discussions of the bottle loss problem from dairymen who clearly were employing such methods and knew exactly the extent and nature of their losses (Hagemann 1913; Clement 1923, 1924; Cochran 1923a, 1923b, 1923c; Ewing 1923; Kelly and Clement 1923; Lindsey 1923; Walker 1923; Ford 1924a, 1924b, 1924c).

This was the nature of the trade into which rim codes were introduced in the early 1920s. It is interesting that the codes nearly escaped mention in the milk trade literature, but they were certainly popular enough that five California glass companies offered them. The situation in California appears to have been unusual in only two ways. First, the great majority of milk bottles were manufactured within the state, local production accounting for 82% of bottles purchased by California milk distributors (Hayden 1924:218). Second, the state government recognized the problem of bottle loss and actively supported attempts to reduce it, especially the formation of bottle exchanges (Frey 1925:241–242; Wademan 1930). It is clear that the glass companies (while obviously using the codes as an advertising technique to stress the quality of their products) recognized the great interest among distributors in reducing bottle loss.

The reasons for abandonment of the code system, on the other hand, are not so clear. It is true that after 1930 economic depression brought significant changes to the liquid milk industry: fluctuating demand, foreclosures of large dairies and distributorships that had overextended during the 1920s, difficulties in collecting debts, and a seemingly endless and incurable series of price wars that racked the industry (Tinley 1938). Yet, it is unclear how these changes would affect use of the code system. In spite of these conditions, the industry in California was successful in establishing bottle exchanges in virtually all major milk markets. By 1930, 10 regional exchanges were retrieving and repatriating 12,000,000 bottles annually (Wademan 1930). It is possible that this success reduced the felt need among distributors for tracking individual bottle loss.

The glass industry, meanwhile, had experienced a series of acquisitions and consolidations that ultimately left the majority of the state's container-glass production in the hands of a single company. Acquisition of the Illinois Pacific Coast Company by Owens-Illinois in mid-1932 meant that almost all the code-using factories were now controlled by a single corporation. (The one exception, Latchford Glass, was at best a minor producer of milk bottles.) Examination of more than 150 milk bottles produced in the 1930s by Owens-Illinois' California factories (Schulz et al. n.d.), undertaken in the course of this study, encountered no evidence for use of rim codes after 1933.

It is thus possible that reduction in competition eliminated the value of rim codes as an advertising tool, and no advantage was seen by the glass industry in perpetuating the extra expense of the codes. By this time, most large glass companies were already employing year codes, including both Owens-Illinois and the Thatcher Manufacturing Company, then the two largest producers of milk bottles for the national market (Lockhart 2004; Lockhart, Schulz et al. 2007; Schulz et al. n.d.).

Additionally, it is worth considering how useful the codes really were. While they are placed where they can be readily accessed even on full and sealed milk bottles, it is doubtful that they were ever systematically used in this condition. The numbers are so small that they are very difficult to see in any but the best light. They would be impossible to record expeditiously during sorting or on the filling line. In contrast, those marks that needed to be observed on a routine basis—the distributor's initials on the bottle base—are quite large, typically much larger than any lettering on the body. Consequently, it seems likely that the codes were useful only for recording the age of chipped or broken bottles, prior to discard.

Conclusion

In the 1920s, several California glass factories adopted an unusual date code system that was widely accepted by milk distributors throughout the far west. Judging from this research sample, the system was pioneered by the Southern Glass Company in 1924. Although American glass factories had been increasingly adopting date code systems since the turn of the century, the rim code system was unique in two ways: it included a code for the month as well as the year, and it was embossed on the upper surface (lip) of the finish. It seems clear that this combination of traits was possible only on milk bottles for three reasons. First, it required month-specific embossing only on ring molds, which could be interchanged with private blow molds for any number of dairies. Second, unlike the great majority of finishes, cap seat finishes could be embossed on the lip without interfering with the seal of the closure. Third, milk bottle lips were large enough to accommodate a legible code.

It should be noted that month-specific embossing was impractical for either the body or base components of blow molds because those mold components were intended for prolonged periods of use. Most factories offered multiple styles of bodies, in several sizes, so that even plate molds—featuring interchangeable dairy labels—could not be used for even a majority of orders. Additionally, base components of the blow molds commonly featured the initials of the dairy placing the order. These mold components were consequently used on limited-production runs but had to be available for future orders. The milk bottle cap and, hence, the cap seat, however, was standardized by the glass and dairy industries in mid-**?** at a single size, regardless of the size or style of the bottle (Little 1924). This meant that ring molds could potentially be used interchangeably with all the blow molds used by a factory, regardless of their size or style or any needed dairy labels. The rim-code system was introduced within six months after this standardization was announced.

The rim-code system was introduced at a time when bottle loss was a serious problem in the liquid milk industry and when tracking that loss and identifying its causes were seen as important goals for virtually all milk distributors. The system was abandoned a decade later, perhaps due to reduced competition in the glass container industry or because that industry, now dominated by national corporations, saw little value in perpetuating a regional dating system in addition to the year codes they had already adopted.

Acknowledgments

We thank Bruce Stiny for access to the State Dairy Collection, and Jeanette Schulz and Wanda Wakkinen for recording assistance. We also thank the Bonita Historical Society Museum, the Save Our Heritage Organization (San Diego), Doug Gisi, Kirby Johnson, G. Nicewonger, Frank Pekarek, and Sally Starling for providing examples of bottles; Gail Bardhan (Corning Museum of Glass) and George Miller for research assistance; and John Finnegan for computer assistance.

References

BLAKE, IRA J., AND HARRY H. HART
1927 Bottle. U.S. Patent 1,635,811, filed 13 Jan. 1925, issued 12 July 1927. U.S. Patent Office, Washington, DC.

CALIFORNIA MILK NEWS
1934 O. J. Weber Co. Advertisement. *California Milk News* 3(22):6.

CERTIFIED MILK
1927 Breakage of Bottles in Milk Plants. *Certified Milk* 6(3):20.

CLEMENT, C. E.
1923 Milk-Plant Operation. *Creamery and Milk Plant Monthly* 12(9):43–48.
1924 Milk Plant Costs. *Milk Dealer* 13(6):62–63,70.

CLEMENT, C. E., J. B. BAIN, AND F. M. GRANT
1932 *Effect of Plant Arrangement, Equipment, and Methods of Operation in Relation to Breakage of Bottles in Milk Plants.* U.S. Department of Agriculture Technical Bulletin, No. 280. Washington, DC.

[COCHRAN, HAMILTON]
1923a A Study of the Return and Breakage Problem of Milk Bottles. *Glass Container* 2(7):5–7,46.
1923b A Study of the Return and Breakage Problem of Milk Bottles. *Glass Container* 2(8):9–10,45.
1923c A Study of the Return and Breakage Problem of Milk Bottles. *Glass Container* 2(9):9–10,28.

DUPUIS, E. MELANIE
2002 *Nature's Perfect Food: How Milk Became America's Drink.* New York University Press, New York, NY.

EWING, C. OSCAR
1923 The Bottle Question in Louisville and Minneapolis. *Creamery and Milk Plant Monthly* 12(1):53.

FORD, KARL L.
1924a Milk Bottle Handling in Dairies. *Glass Container* 3(10):10–11,18,32,34.
1924b Milk Bottle Handling in Dairies. *Glass Container* 3(11):12–13,32–33,46.
1924c Milk Bottle Handling in Dairies. *Glass Container* 3(12):14–15,18.

FREY, J. J.
1925 Bureau of Dairy Control. *California Department of Agriculture Monthly Bulletin* 14(7-12):235–252.

GARDINER, A. B.
1925 The Strength and Weakness of the Milk Bottle. *Creamery and Milk Plant Monthly* 14(2):41–42.

GIARDE, JEFFERY L.
1980 *Glass Milk Bottles: Their Makers and Marks.* Time Travelers Press, Bryn Mawr, CA.

HAGEMANN, E. F.
1913 The Milk Bottle Question. *Milk Dealer* 2(11):38–39.

HAYDEN, CHAS. F.
1924 Division of Weights and Measures. *California Department of Agriculture Monthly Bulletin* 13(7-12):216–227.

HOOD, C. H.
1914 The Distribution of Milk. *Milk Dealer* 3(9):16–18.

KELLY, ERNEST, AND C. E. CLEMENT
1923 *Market Milk.* John Wiley & Sons, New York, NY.

KOUWENHOVEN, F. W.
  1926   The Testing of Milk Bottles. *Glass Industry* 7(6):137–138.

KULLMAN, F. H.
  1921   Bottle Exchange Operated by Chicago Milk Dealers. *Creamery and Milk Plant Monthly* 10(12):23–26.

LANE, C. B.
  ?   The Milk Bottler's Problems. *Milk Dealer* 2(11):

LINDSEY, H. A.
  1923   The City Milk Plant. *Milk Dealer* 12(8):42,44,46.

LITTLE, R. E.
  1924   Simplification of the Milk Bottle. *Milk Magazine* 12(3):7. Also published in *Creamery and Milk Plant Monthly* 13(6):47.

LOCKHART, BILL
  2004   The Dating Game: Owens-Illinois Glass Co. *Bottles and Extras* 15(3):24–27.

LOCKHART, BILL, M. R. MILLER, B. LINDSEY, C. SERR, AND D. WHITTEN
  2005   The Dating Game: Illinois Pacific—A Division of the Illinois Glass Co. *Bottles and Extras* 16(4):73–80.

LOCKHART, BILL, P. SCHULZ, B. LINDSEY, AND C. SERR
  2007   The Dating Game: Thatcher Glass Mfg. Co. *Bottles and Extras* 18(4):53–65.

LOS ANGELES TIMES
  1935   Adohr Dairies. Advertisement. *Los Angeles Times*, 2 April 1935:4.

MILK DEALER
  1913   Methods of Checking In and Out of Retail Wagons. *Milk Dealer* 2(4):10–11.
  1915a The Colvin Dairy Co. of Jackson, Mich. *Milk Dealer* 4(10):24–26.
  1915b The Way of the Milk Bottles. *Milk Dealer* 4(5):26–29.
  1929   Breakage of Bottles in Milk Plants. *Milk Dealer* 19(2):144.
  1932   Geo. J. Meyer Manufacturing Company. Advertisement. *Milk Dealer* 21(9):4.
  1933   Owens-Illinois. Advertisement. *Milk Dealer* 22(10):51.
  1935   Colored Lettering on Milk Bottles. *Milk Dealer* 24(7):62–63.
  1936   Nine Bottles Required for Each Quart of Milk Sold, Frisco Check-Up Shows. *Milk Dealer* 26(2):40.

MILLER, GEORGE L., AND CATHERINE SULLIVAN
  1984   Machine-Made Glass Containers and the End of Production for Mouth-Blown Bottles. *Historical Archaeology* 18(2):83–96.

MODERN PACKAGING
  1948   Ceramic Color Labeling. *Modern Packaging* 21(9):120–126,210.

MOON, H. A.
  1917   One Way to Reduce Your Bottle Losses. *Milk Trade Journal* 5(9):7,30.

OWENS-ILLINOIS GLASS COMPANY
  1935   *Applied Color Lettering on Milk Bottles.* Owens-Illinois Glass Company, Toledo, OH.

PACIFIC BOTTLER
  1928   Keep Track of Your Bottle Trips. *Pacific Bottler* 45(2):26.

PACIFIC DAIRY REVIEW
  1925   Illinois-Pacific Glass Company. Advertisement. *Pacific Dairy Review* 29(42):13.
  1926   Illinois-Pacific Glass Company. Advertisement. *Pacific Dairy Review* 30(1):5.

PARKER, HORATIO N.
  1917   *City Milk Supply.* McGraw-Hill, New York, NY.

PORTER, JOHN S.
  1933   *Moody's Manual of Investments, American and Foreign: Industrial Securities.* Moody's Investors Service, New York, NY.

SCHULZ, PETER D., B. LOCKHART, C. SERR, AND B. LINDSEY
  n.d.   Owens-Illinois Date Codes: A Study of Milk Bottles. *Historical Archaeology.* Forthcoming.

SMITH, R. E.
  1921   Milk Bottle Losses. *Milk Dealer* 10(10):14,16, 79–86.

SPEAR, JAMES A.
  1907   The Retail Milk Business. *Hoard's Dairyman* 38(30):773.

TINLEY, J. M.
  1938   *Public Regulation of Milk Marketing in California.* University of California Press, Berkeley.

TOULOUSE, JULIAN HARRISON
  1971   *Bottle Makers and Their Marks.* Thomas Nelson, New York, NY.

TRAVELER, A.
  1918   Putting the Milk Business on the Carpet. *Milk Dealer* 8(1):20–21.

VAN NUYS NEWS
  1931   Just a Little of This & That. *Van Nuys News*, 12 March 1931:1.

WADEMAN, G. F.
  1930   The Milk Bottle's Chaperon. *California Department of Agriculture Monthly Bulletin* 19(9-10):671–672.

WALKER, BERT H.
  1917   Curtailing Losses of Milk Bottles. *Milk Dealer* 6(5):6–7.

1923 System of Handling Milk Bottles. *Milk Dealer* 12(7):10,12,14.

WESTERN MILK DEALER
1926 Illinois-Pacific Glass Company. Advertisement. *Western Milk Dealer* 9(1):5.
1930 Illinois Pacific and Pacific Coast Glass Form Merger. *Western Milk Dealer* 13(5):20.

WHITCOMB, W. D.
1922 Uniform Accounting. *Creamery and Milk Plant Monthly* 11(6):35–37.

WILLIAMS, ARTHUR E.
1922 Disintegration of Soda Lime Glasses in Water. *Journal of the American Ceramic Society* 5(8):504–517.

WINSLOW, KENELM
1909 *The Production and Handling of Clean Milk*. William R. Jenkins, New York, NY.

PETER D. SCHULZ
ARCHAEOLOGY, HISTORY AND MUSEUMS DIVISION
CALIFORNIA STATE PARKS
2505 PORT STREET
WEST SACRAMENTO, CA 95691

BILL LOCKHART
DEPARTMENT OF HISTORY, SOCIAL SCIENCES, AND ENGLISH
NEW MEXICO STATE UNIVERSITY
2400 SCENIC DRIVE
ALAMOGORDO, NM 88310

CAROL SERR
CULTURAL RESOURCE MANAGEMENT DIVISION
ICF JONES & STOKES
9775 BUSINESSPARK AVENUE, SUITE 200
SAN DIEGO, CA 92131-1642

BILL LINDSEY
KLAMATH FALLS RESOURCE AREA
BUREAU OF LAND MANAGEMENT
2795 ANDERSON AVE., BLDG. 25
KLAMATH FALLS, OR 97603

7
REFERENCES

Bottle of Evil. (1848, source unknown [illustration by T. Horton & Co.].)

Articles

Glass Bottle Glossary
Peter D. Schulz and Jeanette K. Schulz

Glass Bottle Bibliography
Peter D. Schulz

Julian Harrison Toulouse: Selected Bibliography
Peter D. Schulz

Glass Bottle Glossary

Peter D. Schulz and Jeanette K. Schulz

Whether a certain bottle is a two ounce morphine, or a one ounce wide mouth, is what is bothering two Eastern locals of the American Flints. President Smith [of the union] has gathered samples of each, and it would take a microscope to tell 'tother from which (*American Glass Worker* 1886).

The following glossary attempts to clarify at least the more common terms that are, or have been, used in regard to the production and description of glass containers. This is, no doubt, an unachievable goal. As indicated in the foregoing quote, the need for commonly agreed-upon definitions has plagued the industry for more than a century and probably much longer than that. In spite of the fact that workers were paid different rates for different kinds of bottles and different kinds of finishes—all carefully listed in wage agreements—little effort was made at systematic definitions. Distinctions were generally left to the common understanding of the industry (e.g., Glass Bottle Blowers' Association 1913).

While this laissez faire approach periodically fed disputes that had to be settled on an ad hoc basis, it was probably inevitable. A largely common vernacular did indeed exist, favored by the long apprenticeships required of glassblowers, the tendency of blowers to migrate widely to obtain work, and the eventual growth of national unions, national trade associations, and national markets. Countervailing forces were also at work. Secrecy prevailed regarding production processes and glass formulas, regional traditions of nomenclature had evolved, and new styles of containers and new production equipment were continually being developed and marketed.

Additionally, until the second decade of the 20th century, manufacturers were generally loathe to employ chemists or engineers who might be expected to promote a common vocabulary, at least as related to glass composition and production. In these circumstances, the only reasonable forum for the development of systematic definitions was the pattern of annual labor-management conferences, but these were necessarily focused on the sharper interests of wages and working conditions.

The result can be seen in a discussion of the nomenclature of different forms of glass in the early 20th century:

> Anyone entering upon the study of glass technology for the first time is at once struck and often confused by the loose terminology employed. When referring to his materials, the glass-maker speaks of "manganese" for manganese dioxide, "lead" for red lead oxide, "arsenic" for arsenious oxide, "alkali" for sodium carbonate, and so on. Glass which is colourless he calls "white" glass, whilst that which is actually white in colour he terms "opal." Many of these terms are well established in the industry, a precise "glass" meaning, so to speak, having been attributed to each, and they are soon assimilated by the student and become part and parcel of his "glass" vocabulary. When he comes to the actual designation of different glasses, however, the student is often in deep water, for in literature and in discussion he may have the same glass referred to under a variety of names, or, *vice versa*, different glasses may be known by the same name (Peddle 1921:3).

Although this observation is from Britain, the situation in America was by no means better. Even though the subject of that observation involved the chemistry of glass, similar comments could have been directed toward production methods and products.

While the admonitions of Cyril Peddle (1921) and others inspired efforts at uniform descriptions of glass composition, it was not until the 1940s that an attempt was made by the Glass Division of the American Ceramic Society to compile a set of industry-wide definitions focused on the technical aspects of production (Holscher et al. 1948).

For archaeologists and students of glass history, the problem is even greater than that confronted by Peddle, Harry Holscher, and their colleagues. Researchers are faced with terms not only drawn from the earlier industry but also from bottlers and packers; end customers and the public; and collectors, historians, and other archaeologists. Any reasonable glossary must deal in some detail with container styles and form details, finish styles and closure types, physical evidence of production processes, and techniques of labeling and marking.

As an example, many archaeologists have drawn on manufacturers' catalogs for terminology used for finishes. To be sure, these primary sources have tremendous value, but they can also become beautifully illustrated examples of the difficulties noted above. While in many cases catalogs illustrate the widespread use of particular terms, just as often they vary at whim, leaving the reader unsure if the words used illustrate the factory's own terminology or some bowdlerized substitution thought to be more readily grasped by the uninitiated customer. For example, the evolution of finish styles has been of great interest to researchers, and probably no term has acquired more universal and specific acceptance in the glass container industry. Yet 19th- and 20th-century industry catalogs are as likely to refer to "lip styles" or even "neck styles" when describing variations in finish styles.

The present glossary was compiled to some extent by consulting previous glossaries and glass dictionaries, both published and web-based. It also draws heavily on the literature produced by the glass industry as well as the food and beverage industries, including trade journals and product catalogs. Archaeological and historical studies and the collectors' literature have been widely examined, in most cases fruitfully, although no attempt has made to repeat definitions that appear questionable or unfounded. Citations are necessarily sparse, since the goal has been to obtain multiple sources for the terms and definitions included here. While citations would surely be of benefit to those interested in particular terms, their systematic inclusion would quickly defeat the objective of ready consultation.

It is important, however, to highlight one source for definitions of bottle and finish forms and construction details related to forming—the *SHA/ BLM Historic Glass Bottle Identification & Information Website* <http://www.sha.org/bottle/>, maintained by the Society for Historical Archaeology. Far more comprehensive in those areas than is possible here, the website also has the ability to illustrate virtually all the terms included, describing them at length when necessary. The glossary in this volume strives, instead, toward briefer definitions and a broader inclusion of production processes, closures, and finishes.

Note: ALL WORDS IN SMALL CAPS INDICATE DEFINED ENTRIES IN THE DICTIONARY; words in parentheses are near grammatical matches.

ABM *See* AUTOMATIC BOTTLE MACHINE.

ACL *See* APPLIED COLOR LABEL.

annealing—controlled heating and cooling of newly manufactured glass objects in a special oven (LEHR), necessary to relieve internal stresses induced during and immediately after forming; without annealing, the glass may shatter upon the slightest impact or temperature change.

aperture—the opening in the top of the FINISH that allows a container to be filled or contents to be removed.

applied ceramic label *See* APPLIED COLOR LABEL.

applied color label (applied ceramic label, applied color lettering, PYROGLAZING)—a decorative and labeling technique, developed in the 1930s, that applies ceramic color decoration, originally via a silk-screen process, to a bottle after ANNEALING; this is followed by reheating to bake the decoration into the glass surface. Most commonly used on milk and soda bottles, it has also been used on other types of bottles and on inexpensive tablewares.

applied color lettering *See* APPLIED COLOR LABEL.

applied finish—in hand production, broadly, any FINISH that involves adding glass to the otherwise completed bottle. More strictly, it is a finish made by a LIPPING TOOL that includes added glass. Also see LAID-ON FINISH, TOOLED FINISH.

Arbogast patent—an 1882 U.S. patent by Philip Arbogast for forming containers using three molds and two sequential steps: a BLANK MOLD and RING MOLD combination were used to simultaneously form the PARISON and FINISH, followed by inflation of the body to final size and shape in a BLOW MOLD. This process was the basis for all successful bottle-forming machines.

Ashley machine *See* JOHNNY BULL MACHINE.

automatic bottle machine—a machine producing fully formed bottles without the help of human BLOWERS or GATHERERS. The first successful fully automatic machine was invented by Michael Owens at the beginning of the 20th century. Semiautomatic machines began to be converted to fully automatic status after the invention of compatible feeders. See also BLOW-AND-BLOW MACHINE, IS MACHINE, NARROW NECK PRESS-AND-BLOW MACHINE, OWENS BOTTLE MACHINE, PRESS-AND-BLOW MACHINE; compare to SEMIAUTOMATIC BOTTLE MACHINE.

baffle (BAFFLE PLATE)—modern industry vernacular for the bottom part of a TWO-PIECE MOLD.

baffle mark (parison mark)—the SEAM left on the PARISON that marks the junction of the BAFFLE PLATE and the BLANK MOLD. This line is found on the completed bottle in the form of a (usually off-center) circle occupying most of the base and may extend onto the heel. Like CUT-OFF SCARS (but unlike VALVE MARKS) it is joined by GHOST SEAMS on two opposite sides.

baffle plate (BAFFLE, BOTTOM PLATE)—the base plate or bottom part of a TWO-PIECE MOLD, forming the base of the bottle. Specifically in modern industry terminology, it refers to the base of the BLANK MOLD, while "BOTTOM PLATE" or "PLATE" is used for the corresponding portion of the BLOW MOLD.

ball neck—a neck featuring one or more broad rounded rings blown in the glass; most common on food and pharmacy bottles with rectangular bodies.

Baltimore loop seal (Baltimore seal)—a CLOSURE for carbonated beverages, consisting of a rubber gasket that fits into a tapered groove formed just within the APERTURE of the bottle. A metal stud extends through the gasket, becoming a loop that simplified opening the closure. This device was patented by William Painter in 1885 (no. 327,099, 29 September 1885).

Baltimore oval—a straight-sided ovoid pharmacy bottle in which the two broad faces and two narrow sides are relatively flat but are connected by broadly curving surfaces.

Baltimore seal *See* BALTIMORE LOOP SEAL.

band cap—a two-piece metal CLOSURE featuring a metal disk that covers the opening and forms the seal and a separate band that holds the disk in place. The disk is either lined on the underside or covers a further disk or gasket of compressible material to allow a perfect seal. Although the most familiar band caps today are those for home canning jars with a threaded band, far more common earlier in the 20th century were commercial closures, featuring a locking band or a tear band. The most common locking band was the PHOENIX CAP, while the GOLDY SEAL was the most popular tear band.

bare iron pontil (improved pontil, iron pontil)—a PONTIL with an expanded head that is heated and attached to the bottle base without attached glass to hold the vessel to the rod. The iron oxide from the tool leaves a flat dull-gray or rust-colored circle on the base of the bottle.

barrel mustard (French mustard)—bottle in the shape of a barrel and circled by raised beads blown in the glass in imitation of barrel hoops; usually used for French mustard.

batch—the properly apportioned mixture of materials used to compose the glass prior to melting. More broadly, it can refer to the METAL or molten glass but with the implied reference to the specific ingredients.

battledore—in hand production, a wooden paddle sometimes used to flatten parts of the vessel.

bead—a raised line (usually horizontal) on the bottle surface, either laid-on or embossed.

bead finish (button finish)—a short, single-part FINISH with rounded sides in the form of a BEAD or RING.

bearing surface—the perimeter of the base upon which the bottle actually rests.

BIM—collectors' abbreviation for "blown in a mold."

BIMAL—collectors' abbreviation for "blown in a mold with applied lip."

black glass—glass that appears black in reflected light; in transmitted light, it is usually dark olive, sometimes dark green or reddish brown; very common in the 19th century (and earlier), especially for bottles of liquor, ale, and bitters.

Blake—a rectangular pharmacy bottle lacking inset panels.

blank—the PARISON; in modern industry vernacular, the BLANK MOLD that forms the parison.

blank mold (BLANK, measuring mold, parison mold)—in machine production, it is the initial MOLD, made of cast iron, in which the PARISON is formed prior to being transferred to the BLOW MOLD, where the container assumes its final shape.

blast (fire)—in hand production, the portion of the of the glass industry year when work ceased for a summer break; a blast typically ran from mid-August to mid-June, but timing and duration was greatly dependant on local traditions, union agreements, demand for product, and need for repairs at individual factories.

blob top—a thick and broad, single-part rounded FINISH commonly used on 19th-century American soda water and ale bottles; sometimes used by collectors to mean any single-part finish on mold-blown bottles.

block mold—a one-piece MOLD, open at the top. See DIP MOLD.

blow-and-blow machine—a forming machine that relies on compressed air rather than the pressing action of a plunger to form the PARISON in the BLANK MOLD. A GOB is dropped into the blank mold, and a puff of compressed air forms the neck. A second blast forms the parison that is then inverted (flipped over) into the BLOW MOLD, and compressed air or a vacuum completes the bottle-forming process. As in most all bottle-forming machines, compressed air is the most common method used to inflate the vessel to full size in the blow mold. See also NARROW NECK PRESS-AND-BLOW MACHINE.

blow back See BLOW OVER.

blower—in hand production, a worker who forms a PARISON from the GATHER on the end of a BLOWPIPE (or receives the parison from the GATHERER), then blows the container, either offhand or in a MOLD; the parison is typically reheated before passing to the FINISHER.

blowing iron See BLOWPIPE.

blow mold (FINISHING MOLD, form mold, forming mold)—in machine production, the final mold, made of cast iron, bronze, or occasionally stainless steel, in which the body of a bottle is blown. In modern industry vernacular, it is simply the MOLD.

blow over (blow back, bust and grind)—in hand production, the blowing of jars in a MOLD that included the entire FINISH plus additional glass above it, which was typically bulbous with a thin lower portion where the glass could be separated without cracking the retained glass below; the extra glass was ground down to the intended level of the LIP or rim. This technique was used in the latter half of the 19th and early-20th centuries for complex finishes (e.g., CONTINUOUS THREAD FINISH or LUG FINISH), especially on fruit jars, to ensure that the glass threads accurately met those of the mass-produced metal lids (see Toulouse, "Primer on Mold Seams," this volume). While originally carried out by hand, machines were being developed by the late 1860s to complete the grinding more accurately. Also see GROUND LIP and MINARD MACHINE.

blowpipe (blowing iron, pipe)—in hand production, use of an iron tube 4 to 6 feet long with a knob at each end to form hollow glass vessels.

blowpipe pontil mark (OPEN PONTIL MARK)—in hand production, use of a BLOWPIPE as a PONTIL leaves a characteristic scar on the bottle base that consists of a hollow ring of glass with a broken face.

Blue machine—a PRESS-AND-BLOW MACHINE for manufacture of wide-mouth bottles and jars, patented by Charles E. Blue in 1896. This first really successful SEMIAUTOMATIC BOTTLE MACHINE on the North American market was placed in operation by the Atlas Glass Works the same year and was subsequently used by other factories in North America, Europe, Australia, and New Zealand.

bocksbeutel—the traditional bottle for *Steinwein* from the Franconian wine region of Germany, in use from the 18th century until the present; a type of bottle with a flattened bulbous body (oval in horizontal section), a long tapering neck, and a modest PUSH UP.

Boker bitters bottle (LADY'S LEG BOTTLE)—cylindrical BLACK GLASS bottle with a distinctive neck that constricts at the shoulder, expands, and then constricts again at the FINISH; named after a well-known mid-19th century bitters brand that popularized this bottle style.

boot—a rounded hood of fire clay that surrounds a gathering hole on the inside of the GATHERING CHAMBER and extends down to the bottom of the glass bath as an oval cylinder. An opening near the bottom of the hood admits fluid glass into this reservoir for the continual use of the GATHERER, avoiding excessive heat or contaminating the main source and also avoiding contamination of the fluid glass from the surface scum of the glass bath itself.

bore (corkway, throat)—the opening in the top of a bottle, from the APERTURE to the interior of the FINISH, including the SEALING SURFACE of cork or stopper finishes and any interior configurations that may be intended to seat or seal the CLOSURE.

borosilicate glass—a high silicate glass with at least 5% boron oxide, used especially for heat resistant glassware. Also see PYREX.

bottle factory—the larger bottle works are generally several melting furnaces, but each is complete in itself, a unit from which a larger or smaller plant may be constructed according to need. Each is housed in its own building with a tall chimney rising from the center of the roof. In the interiors, bottle making progresses in an orderly fashion, starting with the mixing room, on to the melting FURNACE, and then to the GATHERING CHAMBER where BLOWERS draw their supply of molten glass. The glass is quickly blown into shape in a MOLD, and carried off by dexterous boys to be given a FINISH, and finally placed in the ANNEALING LEHR to be cooled into the finished bottle.

bottle maker—in America, either a worker involved in bottle making or a manufacturer who operated a bottle factory; in Britain, a FINISHER

bottom plate—the separate lower portion of a part MOLD, which forms the base of a vessel and sometimes the heel. Specifically in modern industry, refers to the lower component of a BLOW MOLD; the corresponding part of the BLANK MOLD being called a "BAFFLE." Also see CUP MOLD, POST MOLD.

brandy finish—a two-part FINISH featuring a relatively tall COLLAR above a RING or BEAD.

burst off *See* BURST OVER.

burst over (burst off, STEM METHOD)—in hand production, a form of mold blowing that (unlike CRACKING OFF or whetting off) automatically separates the BLOWPIPE from the neck of the formed bottle. The bottle is blown in the MOLD but when complete, the pipe is raised or pulled aside slightly to form a bubble that bursts between mold and pipe, separating the two. The bottle is then removed for tooling or grinding the FINISH.

bust-and-grind *See* BLOW OVER.

bust-and-grind finish *See* GROUND LIP.

button finish *See* BEAD FINISH.

cap—a term now usually used for metal or molded CLOSURES that cover the top and at least the upper sides of the FINISH. This definition is not exclusive, since the term was universally used for the LIGNEOUS DISKS used to seal milk bottles. Also see BAND CAP, CAP SEAT, CROWN CAP, FLIP-TOP CAP, FRICTION CAP, KORK-AND-SEAL CAP, LUG CAP, PHOENIX CAP, RIP CAP, ROLL ON SEAL, VACUUM CAP.

capacity—the volume of contents that a container will hold in commercial filling. Since most contents require HEADSPACE and because inserted CLOSURES also occupy space, "capacity" in practice is less than the total volume or "overflow" capacity of an uncapped container.

cap seat—a once highly popular FINISH for milk bottles, consisting of an internal ledge below the LIP. On this ledge (seat) rests the CLOSURE, a flat disc made of paraffin-impregnated, pressed wood pulp. Also see COMMON-SENSE MILK BOTTLE.

carbonic oxide—created by burning coal in gas generators on heated inclined grates where it unites with oxygen to form carbonic-acid gas, which is reduced by heat to a condition of carbonic oxide; it is highly combustible, producing a blue flame. The oxide mixes with volatile hydrocarbons (fresh coal gas), and this mixture passes at once to three chambers above the MELTING TANK. Heated air is introduced just before the gas reaches the fire bridge to the melting tank, producing an intense and continuous heat.

carry-in boy (carrying in boy; carrying out boy)—a helper (usually a boy) in 19th- and early-20th-century hand production factories who carried finished bottles to the LEHR.

carrying-out boy See CARRY-IN BOY.

case bottle (case gin)—a square bottle that is broadest at the shoulders and tapers perceptibly toward the base, usually made in BLACK GLASS. The edges are usually somewhat rounded, unlike SCHNAPPS BOTTLES. Most often used for gin, the name evidently comes from the ability of these bottles to fit easily into an internally divided box or case.

case gin See CASE BOTTLE

cathedral pickle—a square bottle with a relatively large aperture, usually in aqua glass and of a quart size or larger, with inset panels on its faces resembling gothic church windows. These bottles were used for pickles, preserved fruit, and other condiments. Also see GOTHIC PEPPERSAUCE.

cave—in traditional hand factories, a subterranean passage extending beneath a glass furnace, providing a draft and allowing the clearing of cinders and other refuse from the fire above. A cave usually had four passages that met at right angles directly under the middle of the furnace.

cavity—in machine production, industry term for the NECK RING, BLANK MOLD, and BLOW MOLD combination used to create one bottle.

cavity codes—any embossed codes used by inspection machines to identify the CAVITY that produced a bottle. Also see CAVITY DOTS, CONCENTRIC RING CODES, PEANUT CODES.

cavity dots—in modern machine production, a line of small raised bumps on the heel of a bottle, spaced to provide a code that identifies the CAVITY (mold combination) in which a bottle was made. It is used for quality control in the factory, allowing identification of the MOLD in which defective bottles were made. Cavity dots were introduced in the late 1970s or early 1980s and have been systematically used since.

cavity rate—a measurement for machine production (particularly on IS MACHINES) that takes into consideration the fact that machines vary in the number of MOLDS operated. Cavity rate = bottles produced per minute/the number of cavities.

chair—in American hand production, a special chair in which the GAFFER sits while creating the FINISH of a bottle or adding additional glass to tableware vessels. The chair has two flat arms across which the PONTIL or SNAP is laid while the gaffer is working on the vessel; in Britain, used to mean SHOP.

champagne beer—a style of beer bottle somewhat popular in the late-19th and early-20th centuries that has a general similarity to a CHAMPAGNE BOTTLE, except for the FINISH and the absence of a high PUSH UP.

champagne bottle—a traditional style of bottle used for champagne with a relatively broad cylindrical body that features straight sides narrowing gradually to form a long neck, while the base features a pronounced PUSH-UP. Because of the need to resist internal pressure, the glass is thicker than in bottles for still wines. The FINISH consists of a neatly formed prominent band located somewhat below the LIP. See CHAMPAGNE FINISH.

champagne finish—originally a FINISH featuring a neatly squared band below the LIP, made by a LIPPING TOOL; the lip itself may be flattened or chamfered at the edge. Identically shaped finishes are made by machine. Developed in the 19th century for CHAMPAGNE BOTTLES because the internal pressure required the wiring for the cork to have an especially secure attachment.

cleaning-off boy See CRACKER-OFF BOY.

clean iron method—in hand production, a blowing

process, typically used for small bottles of 6 oz. CAPACITY or less, in which each BLOWER has several BLOWPIPES available so that a clean pipe is ready while the excess glass is knocked off the one just used. Also see STEM METHOD.

clear glass (COLORLESS GLASS)—a less accurate term for transparent glass.

closure—any CAP, lid, cork, stopper, or other means used to seal a bottle. The term is sometimes broadly used to include also the FINISH if it is designed to incorporate a special type of closure.

cobalt—a dark blue color sometimes used for containers, especially for medicinal bottles. This use perhaps got its impetus from the blue glass craze of the 1870s when it was widely used for skylights and windowpanes for the alleged health benefits of sunlight passing through the glass.

cobalt oxide—used as a colorant, or for DECOLORIZING with SELENIUM to mask the yellowish or straw tint sometimes produced by the latter. Also known as "smalt" when cobalt oxide colorant is mixed with silica and potash and used as a colorizer in ceramics and European oil painting pigments, especially in the 16th and 17th centuries.

coffin flask—a style of FLASK, especially popular in the late-19th and early-20th centuries, similar to the SHOO-FLY FLASK, except that the narrow sides are beveled, making the vessel hexagonal in horizontal section.

cold end treatment—any process for treating glass vessels after ANNEALING.

collar—FINISH or finish part with straight sides that may narrow toward the LIP.

colorless glass (CLEAR GLASS, FLINT GLASS)—transparent glass lacking visible color. Since the components of the BATCH generally contain elements (especially iron) that impart some color to glass, production of colorless glass traditionally requires addition of a DECOLORIZING element to the batch. For many centuries, MANGANESE served this function, but during the second decade of the 20th century other elements, particularly SELENIUM, rapidly displaced manganese in commercial production.

common sense milk bottle—a milk bottle with a CAP SEAT FINISH, that is, a finish featuring an internal ledge intended to be sealed by a paraffin-impregnated disk. Although often described as the first modern milk bottle and attributed to Dr. Hervey D. Thatcher, it was actually patented by two of his associates, Harvey and Samuel Barnhart, in 1889. The original bottle design featured high shoulders and a short neck, but more sloping shoulders and a longer neck were soon developed for ease of carrying and washing. This form was the most common milk container on the American market for the first four or five decades of the 20th century.

concentric ring code—a CAVITY CODE system introduced in 1977 consisting of variably spaced concentric rings on the bottle base. Subsequently, this code was replaced by CAVITY DOTS and PEANUT CODES.

cone—in traditional hand production, the conical chimney of a coal-fed furnace, usually made of brick.

continuous tank—a glass furnace in which the level of molten glass remains constant because BATCH is fed continuously to replace the glass that is withdrawn.

continuous thread finish (CT)—a FINISH featuring a continuous spiral ridge of glass on its exterior intended to mesh with the thread of a screw-type CLOSURE. Also see INTERRUPTED THREAD FINISH, LUG FINISH.

corker—a bottle designed to be sealed by insertion of a cork.

corkway *See* BORE.

counter blow—the charge of compressed air that inflates the PARISON in BLOW-AND-BLOW MACHINE forming; in many machines it follows the SETTLE BLOW, hence the term.

cracker-off boy (cleaning-off boy)—in 19th- and early-20th-century hand factories, a helper (often a boy) who cleaned the MOIL from BLOWPIPES.

cracking off (whetted, whetted off, water shrending)—in hand production, removing the bottle neck from the BLOWPIPE by touching the hot glass at the end of the pipe with a tool dipped in cold water. The bottle is placed into a "cradle" (dirt trough) or onto sand. Then the blowpipe is repositioned onto the bottom as a PONTIL, leaving a rough ring of glass when finally removed after the LIP is finished.

crown cap (crown cork)—a CLOSURE consisting of a metal CAP with crenulated edges and a cork or plastic lining, used with a CROWN FINISH. William Painter patented the device in 1892. Within a couple of decades it had become the dominant form of closure used on beer and soda bottles. The closure forms the seal by compressing the lining against the top of the LIP (locking ring) of the bottle while edges of the metal shell are clamped over the LOCKING RING to secure it.

crown cork *See* CROWN CAP.

crown finish—a beverage bottle FINISH patented by William Painter in 1892, consisting of two parts: a rounded lower portion (the REINFORCING RING) for strength, and a smaller upper part (the LOCKING RING) precisely tooled to accept a special metal CLOSURE (crown cap) that is crimped over it. It may be noted that although this finish was developed for the CROWN CAP, and this has been its primary use ever since, it was sometimes used with other closures. In the late-19th and early-20th centuries, some brewing companies used corks to seal crown finishes, and in the early-20th century other kinds of closures were developed for the finish as well. Subsequent developments in the design of nonreturnable beer bottles, driven by the demand for lighter and shorter containers, led to modification of the crown finish itself. In 1944, the GB-6 beer bottle was introduced, featuring a REINFORCING RING barely larger than the LOCKING RING, and this modified form was subsequently used on other styles of no-return bottles. Introduced in 1958, the HANDY BOTTLE disposed of the reinforcing ring altogether. Still the original form of the crown finish continues in general use, except where it has been superseded by threaded finishes. Also see DACRO FINISH, PRIOF FINISH.

crown pulcap *See* FLIP-TOP CROWN.

crucible *See* POT.

CT *See* CONTINUOUS THREAD.

cullet—broken or scrap glass mixed with the BATCH, which lowers the melting temperature and saves fuel energy in production; used to describe both waste glass (MOIL), recovered after completion of a vessel, as well as recycled bottles (FOREIGN CULLET) bought by glassworks to add to their METAL.

cup-bottom mold *See* CUP MOLD.

cup mold (cup-bottom mold)—a bottle MOLD in which the detachable base (BOTTOM PLATE) forms the bottom of the bottle, including the heel. Cup bases are used on both hand and machine molds. See POST MOLD.

cut-off scar (Owens scar)—a somewhat circular scar produced on the base of bottles made in suction machines such as those of Owens or Roirant. The scar is made by the "knife" that slides across the bottom of the BLANK MOLD, separating the molten glass that has been sucked into the MOLD from that remaining in the POT. This process leaves a circular scar on the bottom of the PARISON, which is retained on the completed bottle. Many cut-off scars feature "feathered" edges due to wear on the knife or the nose of the blank; marks left by well-aligned and unworn equipment are probably indistinguishable from the BAFFLE MARKS produced by other machines. Like baffle marks but unlike VALVE MARKS, these scars are always connected to the GHOST SEAMS from the side of the blank mold.

dacro finish—a CROWN FINISH for milk bottles introduced in 1912. Early dacro finishes are similar in appearance to those used for beverage bottles, except that the diameter was 43 mm rather than 12 mm. Beginning in the early 1930s, the REINFORCING RING became more projecting, providing for a more secure grip when carrying the bottle.

day tank—a glass MELTING TANK made of refractory blocks, designed to be emptied each day of GATHERING and refilled at night with new BATCH, which would be melted by the next morning. Day tanks can hold more glass than POT furnaces and have the advantage that the type of glass can be readily changed. Day tanks were used for hand and, perhaps, semiautomatic production, but they are not compatible with 24-hour production made possible by CONTINUOUS TANKS.

decoloring *See* DECOLORIZING.

decolorizing (decoloring)—the process of producing a colorless appearance in glass, typically by adding chemicals that mask the natural pale green color produced by iron. Until the early- 20th century, decolorizing was usually accomplished by adding MANGANESE to the BATCH. During WWI, shortages of supply led to substitution of SELENIUM and arsenic for this purpose.

deep lip finish—a single-piece FINISH featuring a broad flat band with vertical (plumb) sides and a flat upper surface.

demijohn—a large cylindrical or globular narrow-necked container with a CAPACITY of about 2 to 5 gallons. Olive Jones and Catherine Sullivan (1985:72) suggest that "as most recovered archaeological specimens cannot be measured for capacity, the term demijohn can be used for all containers larger than a gallon."

dip mold (block mold, open mold)—a one-piece MOLD, open at the top. The essential feature of such molds is that they be narrower at the bottom than at the top, so that the formed article can be lifted out without interference. In common use until the mid-19th century, such molds form only the base and body of bottles, the shoulders and neck being formed offhand.

dipped—when sticking a bottle from the BLOWPIPE to the PONTIL, the end of the pontil is touched to the top of the molten glass but never actually "dipped" into the glass. This hot tip is then pressed against the bottom of the piece, trued, and set before being separated from the blowpipe.

discontinuous thread finish *See* INTERRUPTED THREAD FINISH.

domestic cullet—CULLET from operations within the factory. Also see FOREIGN CULLET.

dope—a chemical component added to a BATCH in an attempt to correct the consistency or color of the glass; also used for various materials placed on MOLD surfaces to avoid friction, sticking of the glass to metal, checking, oxidation, or other defects.

double strike—a doubled and overlapping embossed impression sometimes found on the bases of mold-blown bottles, created when the BLOWER places the PARISON in the MOLD so that it touches the base, then withdraws the parison before blowing it to full size.

drop blank system—a system of MOLD transfer used in early PRESS-AND-BLOW MACHINES, in which the BLANK MOLD is nested inside the BLOW MOLD during charging and while the PARISON is being pressed. The blank mold then drops out the bottom of the blow mold, leaving the parison suspended from the RING MOLD while the base plate swings into place prior to blowing. This system was first patented by J. R. Windmill in Britain in 1886 (in the U.S. in 1889), and for a decade or two it was more popular than the SET-OVER TRANSFER system developed earlier by Philip Arbogast. Also see ARBOGAST PATENT.

dummy—in hand production, a mechanical device, operated by the blower's feet, for opening and closing the MOLD. In TURN-MOLD production, the dummy also wets the mold. Also see TREADLE MOLD.

Duraglas—a trade name adopted by the Owens-Illinois Glass Company in 1940 to indicate the quality of its glass containers.

embossing—raised lettering or figural designs on the surface of a bottle, produced by corresponding designs cut in the MOLD.

empontilling—in hand production, use of a PONTIL to hold the bottle during finishing.

export beer bottle—a type of bottle developed for exporting pasteurized lager beer to the Western territories or foreign countries. Originating in 1873, these bottles feature a slightly bulbous neck and are usually amber or aqua. Eventually, this form became the most common bottle style used by the American brewing industry and is commonly used today.

extract finish—a single-part FINISH consisting of a relatively narrow flat band with a flat upper surface.

eye—a grate-covered opening in the middle of a POT furnace through which the flame enters. The eye connects to the CAVE below, allowing cinders and ash to be cleaned out of the furnace.

Ferrari furnace—a continuous tank FURNACE, first used in the Glassboro, NJ, that has large fire clay tanks rather than separate crucible POTS for the molten glass and employs gaseous fuel rather than solid. Compact and easier to operate but more inexpensive compared to the old style, they require less repair and eliminate the need to frequently replace the old-style pots every few months.

fin—an exaggerated MOLD seam or parting line that forms a thin raised ridge. This is a defect that not only detracts from appearance but also, depending on its location, may interfere with the CLOSURE or weaken the container by concentrating thermal or impact forces.

finish—the uppermost part of a bottle from the LIP to the upper part of the neck, including any modifications to strengthen the opening or adapt it to a particular CLOSURE. In hand production, it means adding or tooling glass in this area to form a useable opening as the final modification before the bottle is completely formed, hence the name. In machine production, the finish is the first part of the bottle to be formed. Also see APPLIED FINISH, BEAD FINISH, BLOB TOP FINISH, BRAND FINISH, CHAMPAGNE FINISH, CONTINUOUS THREAD FINISH, CROWN FINISH, DACRO FINISH, DEEP FINISH, EXTRACT FINISH, FLAT LIP FINISH, GOLDY FINISH, GROUND LIP, KORK-AND-SEAL FINISH, INTERRUPTED LAID-ON FINISH, LUG FINISH, OIL FINISH, PACKER FINISH, PRESCRIPTION FINISH, PRIOF FINISH, STRING FINISH, THREAD FINISH, TOOLED FINISH.

finisher—in hand production, a worker who forms the FINISH of a bottle, often the senior member of a SHOP and sometimes referred to as a GAFFER in America or as a BOTTLE MAKER in Britain. In some factories, the role was simply rotated in turn among the three blowers in a shop.

finish forming tool *See* LIPPING TOOL.

finishing (MAKING)—in hand production, forming the FINISH on the otherwise completed bottle.

finishing mold—British term for BLOW MOLD, being the MOLD in which the bottle takes its final shape. Note, however, that this mold plays no role in forming the FINISH.

finishing tool *See* LIPPING TOOL.

fire *See* BLAST.

fire finishing *See* FIRE POLISHING.

fireman (teaser)—in hand production, a worker who tends the fire in a glass furnace.

fire polishing (fire finishing)—reheating a completed vessel or portion thereof (usually the FINISH), to remove marks left by molds or tools, or to obtain a smoother surface.

flaconage—British term for cosmetic and pharmaceutical containers.

flask—a container, usually for liquor, having a broad flattened body, designed to be carried in the pocket. Also see COFFIN FLASK, JO-JO FLASK, PICNIC FLASK, PUMPKINSEED FLASK, SHOO-FLY FLASK, UNION OVAL FLASK.

flat lip finish—a single-piece FINISH, consisting of a narrow flat band with vertical (plumb) sides and a flat upper surface.

flint—a skilled worker in the FLINT GLASS industry, often specifically a member of the Flint Glass Workers Union during the late-19th and early-20th centuries (Green Glass Blowers Association 1913).

flint glass—originally, glass made with silica of flints; subsequently, a synonym for LEAD GLASS; since the latter-19th century, for LIME GLASS or for any COLORLESS GLASS used for containers or tableware. Commonly known as crystal.

flip-top crown—a variety of CROWN CAP, introduced in 1963, featuring a perimeter tab which, when pulled up, tears the side of the crown, thus breaking the SEAL and allowing easy removal. The CROWN PULCAP, introduced about the same time, resembles the old GOLDY SEAL in that a circular tab is mounted atop the CROWN that can be pulled up and out to break the seal.

foot bench—in hand production, a raised platform surrounding or adjacent to the FURNACE, on which workmen stand to GATHER glass and blow bottles. Molds were set on the floor just outside the foot bench so that the BLOWPIPE could be held vertically as the PARISON is placed in the MOLD.

forebay *See* FOREHEARTH.

forehearth (forebay)—an extension or forebay of a tank FURNACE that continuously receives the molten glass from the main melting furnace and cools it to the proper and uniform temperature and viscosity while reducing impurities. GOBS are removed by various means (dipping, suction, etc.) and transferred to the forming machines. Depending on the type of furnace and machine forming apparatus, the forehearth can variously be a covered trough, channel, chamber, or refractory tank.

foreign cullet—CULLET from outside the factory. Also see DOMESTIC CULLET.

form mold, forming mold *See* BLOW MOLD.

flux—an oxide that interacts with other oxides in the BATCH to promote fusion and thus speeding melting.

free blowing *See* OFFHAND BLOWING.

French mustard *See* BARREL MUSTARD.

French square—a square prescription bottle lacking inset panels.

friction cap—a CLOSURE used in packaging dry, loose, or liquid products that require multiple openings and closings. Such caps must not fall off when a container is inverted but must be loose enough for easy removal, although some force is required for proper use. Most such containers are made of metal, given its malleable properties and ability to be maintained within narrow limits of size. Paint cans, spice tins, coffee tins, talcum powder containers, and similar items use friction cap CLOSURES. Glass jelly jars have metal lids that can be carefully prized off and then snapped back on to store the remaining contents.

frit—BATCH material that has been previously melted and then ground. Prior to the early-19th century, conversion of the batch to frit was a necessary initial process since the furnaces available could not attain the temperatures necessary for direct melting.

furnace—the center of a glass factory where the ground and mixed crude materials are heated in POTS or tanks to produce molten glass for the works.

gaffer—in hand production, the head workman in a SHOP or the superintendent of a small glass factory.

gaffer team *See* SHOP.

gather (GATHERING)—a portion of molten glass, sufficient for a single vessel, collected on the end of the BLOWPIPE or GATHERING IRON as the first step in hand or semiautomatic machine blowing; equivalent to the GOB of machine production.

gatherer—in hand or semiautomatic production, a worker who, using a BLOWPIPE or GATHERING IRON, collects the GATHER from a POT or tank and passes it to the blower or the machine.

gathering—British term for GATHER.

gathering chamber—the section, point, or area of a glass FURNACE where the molten glass has been conditioned in temperature and viscosity for consistency and from which GOBS or MOLD charges are gathered by various means and transferred for forming. In hand production, the gathering chamber can be the crucible that is also the melting POT. In machine production, it can be various extensions such as channels, chambers, refractory tanks, and FOREHEARTHS or forebays.

gathering iron (PUNTY)—a solid iron rod used to GATHER molten glass for SEMIAUTOMATIC BOTTLE MACHINES.

gathering ring *See* RING.

GB-6—a style of nonreturnable beer bottle introduced by Owens-Illinois in 1944 that is similar to the earlier PACKIE but is shorter and features a CROWN FINISH in which the REINFORCING RING was reduced almost to the size of the LOCKING RING.

ghosting—a collectors' term for EMBOSSING that has been peened out of a metal MOLD, often with new embossing nearby or covering the "ghosted" letters. These appear on bottles or jars as faint lettering, hence a "ghost" of the former label.

ghost seams—in machine production, vertical MOLD seams left on the bottle body that reflect the joins of a two-part BLANK MOLD.

glass can—beer brewing industry term for the nonreturnable HANDY BOTTLE.

glassmaker's soap—MANGANESE used for DECOLORIZING.

glory hole—in hand production, originally an opening to the hot interior of the FURNACE and, later, a separate small furnace used for reheating ware, especially prior to FINISHING. Skill is required to heat only the neck and not distort the shoulders of bottles being tooled.

gob—in machine production, a portion of hot glass, sufficient for a single vessel, delivered by a feeder. Equivalent to the GATHER of hand and semiautomatic production, the two terms are sometimes used interchangeably.

Goldy finish—resembles a CROWN FINISH with only a very subtle difference in the upper BEAD. Indeed, the industry produced several finishes, identified as "combination finishes," that were designed to accept multiple CLOSURES, including the CROWN, Goldy, and screw CAP.

Goldy seal—a CLOSURE popular for food containers in the 1920s and 1930s with a BAND CAP. A lacquered tinned steel disk that folds slightly over the LIP of the FINISH provides the seal, which is secured by an aluminum band whose edges snug under the BEAD of the finish and over the top of the disk. A rounded tab lays atop the disk that, when pulled, tears across the aluminum band, leaving the disk to be removed by hand. Beginning in 1934, some disks were made with four flat perimeter tabs that allowed more secure reclosing of the containers. Especially popular for catsup bottles, a special double CAP was developed to cover the bottle after initial unsealing.

gothic peppersauce—a square or hexagonal bottle (usually 6 or 8 oz CAPACITY) with ornate inset panels resembling gothic church windows. Panel designs resemble those on CATHEDRAL PICKLE BOTTLES, but these are much smaller bottles, relatively tall and slender with long necks and narrow APERTURES. Be aware that both "gothic" and "cathedral" are sometimes used interchangeably for either type of bottle.

graduated bottle—a bottle, usually for medicines, having a vertical graduated scale for volume embossed or otherwise marked on the side.

green—a skilled worker in the green-glass bottle industry, often specifically a member of the Glass Bottle Blowers Association. Also see FLINT.

green glass—traditionally, glass in its natural state, neither made colorless nor artificially colored. More broadly, any container glass other than COLORLESS GLASS (FLINT); generally made from coarser materials, usually with soda (or potash) plus lime as its alkaline bases. The green or aqua color results from iron in the sand employed. Used for common wares in the 19th and very early-20th centuries.

groove ring fruit jar *See* WAX SEALER.

ground lip (bust-and-grind finish)—in hand production, a form of FINISH blown in a MOLD that includes the finish and an area immediately above it; the LIP then is ground down to the correct height. This technique was most commonly used on fruit jars but was occasionally used on narrow-neck ware as well. It eliminates the need for tooling to complete the finish and allows the production of more exact heights for threaded finishes.

handy bottle (GLASS CAN)—a short, nearly neckless, nonreturnable beer-bottle design, featuring a single-ring CROWN FINISH, introduced in 1958. Originally entirely straight-sided and smooth-surfaced, the design was modified in 1962 to provide stippled shock bands at the heel and shoulder, separated by a slightly recessed label panel. Immensely popular for several years after its introduction, the style was reported in 1961 to be "the most frequently formed glass container in the world."

headspace—the unoccupied space within a bottle between the top of the contents and the bottom of the CLOSURE. Traditionally, this space is necessary to allow sufficient compressible air for the cork to be driven into the FINISH, but it is likewise essential for containers of products in which pressure can develop. Additionally, headspace allows predetermined volumes, even when there is variability in bottle CAPACITY. It is necessary when the bottle is to be capped before the contents have settled or cooled. In modern packing operations, the air from the headspace may be exhausted and replaced with steam.

hinge mold—a bottle MOLD formed with a hinge *across the bottom*. Molds hinged *at the side* are simply designated by the number of parts, not including the BOTTOM PLATE.

hoch bottle *See* HOCK BOTTLE.

hock bottle (hoch bottle, SCHLEGELFLASCHE)—a tall, narrow WINE BOTTLE having a gradually curved shoulder that is almost imperceptibly distinguished from the body and neck and traditionally used in the Rhine, Mosel, and Alsace regions of Germany. Rhine bottles are most often dark amber or reddish brown glass, while those from the Mosel and Alsace are traditionally olive green. The form became recognizable in the early-19th century, at which time the bottle is characterized by a high PUSH-UP. This feature became gradually less pronounced, so that by the 1860s push-ups are modest and usually MOLD formed (May 1991).

holding-mold boy *See* MOLD BOY.

hole—British term for SHOP.

hollow ware—a broad term that includes glass containers and tableware as well as illuminating ware in the broadest sense (glass lanterns, globes and chimneys, light bulbs, radio and television tubes, etc.).

hot end—the portion of a factory creating and processing molten or hot glass, including the FURNACE, forming processes, and ANNEALING.

hot end treatment—any process for treating glass vessels after forming and before ANNEALING.

Hutchinson stopper—a CLOSURE for carbonated beverage bottles patented by Charles Hutchinson in 1879. Hutchinson bottles are basically BLOB-TOP bottles having virtually no neck, the shoulder being immediately below the FINISH. The CLOSURE is a flat disk and rubber gasket surmounted by a metal loop. The gasket rests inside the bottle at the junction of the shoulders and finish and is designed to be held in place by carbonation pressure. Hutchinson stoppers were extremely popular for carbonated beverages in late-19th and early-20th centuries but were generally superseded by CROWN CAPS by about 1912.

improved pontil *See* BARE-IRON PONTIL.

individual section machine *See* IS MACHINE.

interrupted thread finish—a FINISH featuring a set of spiral ridges on the exterior, none of which extends entirely around it or are connected. The ridges are intended to mesh with the thread of a screw-type CLOSURE that generally has lugs. Also see CONTINUOUS THREAD FINISH and LUG FINISH.

iron pontil *See* BARE-IRON PONTIL.

IS machine—industry abbreviation for individual section machine, first introduced commercially by the Hartford-Empire Company in 1925. These machines now account for almost all commercial production of glass containers. Unlike most forming machines, which place the MOLDS on rotating tables or frames, IS machines set the molds in stationary banks or sections, allowing changes or repairs to an individual bank while the remaining banks continue to operate. For many years IS machines were BLOW-AND-BLOW, but PRESS-AND-BLOW models were developed between the late 1880s to 1905 for WIDE-MOUTH ware and from about the mid-1900s to 1910 for narrow-neck ware.

Johnny Bull machine (Ashley machine, United machine)—the first practical mechanical SEMIAUTOMATIC BOTTLE MACHINE was invented and placed in production by a Yorkshireman, H. M. Ashley, a manager of an iron foundry. Given an English patent in 1886, it is also called the "plank machine" because of being mounted on a wooden board. Between 1887 and 1889, Ashley filed patents in the U.S. Its unique method of bottle production results in no basal machine scars, and its short production span can be aids to dating bottles produced on these machines. "Johnny Bull" was a popular English figure, representing the English working man, hence the machine's nickname. The Ashley machine was popular in America for about a decade before being out-competed, starting around 1915, for production speed by the OWENS BOTTLE MACHINE.

jo jo flask—a liquor FLASK with flat panels front and back, distinctly rounded shoulders, and matching rounded base in a half-pint or pint size; the flat panels may be embossed. A famous jo jo flask was produced by the South Carolina Dispensary system, a state-run liquor monopoly operating from 1893 until 1907. It features an embossed Palmetto Tree or the S.C.D. monogram on the panel body and the word "Dispensary" curved across the bottom of the panel.

jug—a narrow-neck container with a relatively broad cylindrical body and a short neck, adjacent to which, on the upper shoulder, are one or two ring-shaped handles, also known as "ears."

junk bottle—a 19th-century vernacular term for a cylindrical BLACK GLASS bottle used primarily for malt beverages and other liquors. At the end of the century, in the midst of lobbying efforts by glassworkers to ban the refilling of bottles, the term came to mean used bottles, especially those supplied by junk dealers to brewers, distillers, and packers for refilling.

key mold—a HINGE MOLD in which the bottom portions of the two halves feature a semicircular projection and a corresponding CAVITY on the opposing face, thus promoting the alignment of the two halves when the MOLD is closed.

kick or **kick up** *See* PUSH-UP.

knife edge union oval *See* UNION OVAL FLASK.

knurling—short vertical ridges on the perimeter of metal or plastic CAPS to facilitate opening. Also see STIPPLING.

kork-n-seal cap—a reusable CROWN CAP, designed to easily reseal liquids in bottles by means of a wire loop around the cap skirt that is connected to a hinged-wire toggle on one side. The toggle is snapped down, which tightens the wire loop to hold the cap in place by compressing the skirt. Sometimes these CLOSURES were given out separately as promotional items.

kork-n-seal finish—this FINISH typically looks like the upper BEAD part of a CROWN FINISH, but the collar or lower part varies and is largely decorative and not related to sealing. It was used on narrow to moderately wide bottles.

lady's leg bottle—a collectors' term for the BOKER BITTERS BOTTLE.

laid-on finish—in hand production, a FINISH made by applying a BEAD, string, or band of glass at or below the LIP but without use of a LIPPING TOOL. Also see APPLIED FINISH, TOOLED FINISH.

lead glass (FLINT GLASS)—glass made with oxide of lead, which gives it a more crystalline appearance than SODA GLASS or GREEN GLASS; usually used for tableware rather than bottles.

lear *See* LEHR.

leer *See* LEHR.

lehr (leer, lear)—an ANNEALING oven that cools bottles slowly to relieve stresses, thereby strengthening them.

ligneous disk—the original term for the flat disk used to SEAL the COMMON SENSE MILK BOTTLES. Also see CAP SEAT.

lime glass—a variety of soda glass developed in the 1860s to imitate LEAD GLASS, using bicarbonate of soda and new proportions of lime. It is as clear as lead glass but not as heavy and is much cheaper to produce. Like lead glass, it is often called FLINT GLASS.

lip (rim)—a vernacular and industry term for that portion of the FINISH (the upper edge) that surrounds the APERTURE. The lip often, although by no means always, serves as the sealing surface for the CLOSURE. Among archaeologists and collectors, the term is sometimes used for the entire upper portion of a two-part finish, since this element evolved from the tooled-out or rolled over lip of 18th-century bottles (Jones and Sullivan 1985; Jones 1986). In the latter context, this usage has some historical justification. However on bottles with an APPLIED FINISH or TOOLED FINISH or on machine-made bottles, it would seem to court confusion. Note "lip" is sometimes used in bottle manufacturer's catalogs as a popular synonym for finish but so is "neck."

lip maker *See* LIPPING TOOL.

lipping tool (finishing tool, finish forming tool, rounding tool, lip maker)—a tool consisting of a central spindle and two adjustable arms. Once the bottle is removed from the BLOWPIPE, the upper end is reheated, the end of the spindle is inserted in the opening, and the tool is rotated so that the arms shape the FINISH. If glass is added at or around the opening before the operation, the product is called an APPLIED FINISH; if the tool is used with no additional glass, it is called a TOOLED FINISH.

locking ring—the upper part of a CROWN FINISH or the aluminum band of a GOLDY SEAL.

lug cap—a CLOSURE with evenly spaced protrusions on the interior of the CAP skirt that mesh with spaced threads on a container and require only a few degrees of rotation to close firmly.

lug finish—a glass container FINISH identified by discontinuous horizontal and tapering protruding ridges of glass that permit specially shaped compatible edges of a CLOSURE to slide between the protruding lugs and fasten securely with a partial turn.

maker's mark (punt mark)—a permanent label (words, abbreviation, or symbol) that indicates the manufacturer of a glass vessel. Such marks are typically embossed, although etching is common in some kinds of scientific and other glassware.

making—British term for FINISHING.

mallet bottle—a form of free-blown WINE BOTTLE of the early-18th century, featuring a broad body with relatively straight sides, a long tapering neck, and a pronounced PUSH-UP.

manganese—as manganese dioxide (MnO_2), used sometimes as a colorant but more often as a DECOLORIZER to mask the greenish tint produced by iron. When exposed to solar radiation for protracted periods, the manganese affects a purpling of the glass, sometimes called "SUN-COLORED AMETHYST."

marver—in hand production, a metal block or a table with a metal top used for rough-shaping a vessel during free hand blowing or for rolling, shaping, and cooling the PARISON before inserting it in a MOLD.

Matthews stopper—a CLOSURE for carbonated beverage bottles, patented by John Matthews in 1864. Matthews bottles are basically BLOB-TOP bottles having a very short necks. The closure is a glass rod incased in a rubber stopper that is inserted inside the bottle and held in place at the top of the shoulders by the pressure of the carbonation.

measuring mold *See* BLANK MOLD.

melting tank—a fire clay tank or POT that holds the BATCH and CULLET, which is then intensely heated until it liquefies into molten glass to be used to make bottles or other objects.

metal—refers to molten glass in the POT or tank, but its use is generally discouraged outside the trade because it can be misleading—glass is not a metallic substance.

Minard machine—a machine for grinding the LIPS of fruit jars, based on the Kelly and Samuel patent of 1869. The jars were positioned and removed by hand, each being ground as it turned on its own axis while all the jars revolved on two circular plates. Also see BLOW OVER, GROUND LIP.

moil (overblow)—any excess glass left over after vessel production; originally, extra glass left on the BLOWPIPE after the bottle was removed; the extra glass produced in BLOW OVER jar production or in the production of blown tableware. Some authors use "moil" specifically for unblown glass on the blowpipe, and "overblow" for glass that was part of the PARISON. Moil was saved for CULLET.

mold (MOULD)—any CAVITY into which molten glass is blown or pressed in order to create the shape of the vessel. Early bottle molds were made of wood or ceramic; metal molds (usually cast iron, sometimes bronze, now rarely stainless steel) were introduced in the late-18th century and became virtually universal by about the 1840s. In modern industry vernacular, this otherwise-generic term is used specifically for the BLOW MOLD that completes blowing the bottle after receiving the PARISON from the BLANK MOLD, which may be referred to simply as the BLANK. Also see DIP MOLD, THREE-PIECE MOLD, TWO-PIECE MOLD,

mold boy (holding-mold boy)—in 19th- and early-20th-century hand production, a helper, usually a boy, who opened and shut the MOLD for the BLOWER.

mold seam—used by the glass industry, for lines reflecting the adjoining surfaces marking where the halves of a TWO-PIECE MOLD join. Mold seams are usually vertical and occur in matching pairs on opposite sides of the vessel. Also see SEAM, PARTING LINE.

monkey pot—glass factory slang for a covered POT for melting glass.

mould—British term for MOLD.

multisided—a large and varied class of bottles characterized by having more than four flattened body sides or panels. Most common are the conical bodies of UMBRELLA INK bottles, so-called because their bases roughly resemble open umbrellas. Typically 8-sided, but they also can be found with 6, 12 and, rarely, 16 sides. Another major group features vertical panels such as short ink and glue bottles. Taller multi-sided vertical panel bottles that are "ribbed" or "fluted" held catsups, sauces, and other food condiments.

Murgatroyd belt—the area of a bottle's body immediately above the heel, designated by J. B. Murgatroyd (1933) as a "dangerous area" because surface flaws in this area make bottles especially susceptible to thermal or impact stress. On modern bottles the Murgatroyd belt is equivalent to the lower SHOCK BAND.

narrow mouth—the FINISH of a glass container in which the opening diameter is small compared to the diameter of the body—generally less than 1-1/2 inches.

narrow neck press-and-blow machine—in machine production, the second of two major automatic bottle machine processes used to form a PARISON in the BLANK MOLD. The GOB is dropped into a MOLD where a plunger is pneumatically driven up into the gob to form the parison. Then the parison is inverted (flipped-over) into the BLOW MOLD where it is reheated, stretched, and given the final blow of compressed air to complete the bottle. Compare with BLOW-AND-BLOW MACHINE.

neck—the portion of a container in which the shoulder narrows to join the FINISH.

neck mold *See* NECK RING MOLD.

neck ring *See* NECK RING MOLD.

neck ring mold (neck mold, neck ring, ring mold)—in machine production, a separate MOLD part above the BLANK MOLD that forms the FINISH as the blank mold forms the PARISON. In the vast majority of machines, the neck ring mold is comprised of two pieces that open to release the completed finish. In some PRESS-AND-BLOW MACHINES, however, the neck ring mold may be a single piece with the solid mold being lifted or screwed off rather than opened. In most machines the parison is suspended from the neck ring mold while being transferred to the BLOW MOLD.

NNPB—industry abbreviation for NARROW NECK PRESS-AND-BLOW MACHINE.

NR—industry abbreviation for no-return bottles.

offhand blowing (free blowing)—in hand production, blowing vessels without use of MOLDs.

offware—containers that fail to meet all manufacturing criteria.

oil can—a glass bottle, intended to hold motor oil, topped with a CLOSURE that tapered to form a long funnel.

oil finish—a single-part FINISH consisting of a tall COLLAR.

one-piece mold—*See* BLOCK MOLD, DIP MOLD.

onion bottle—a form of free-blown WINE BOTTLE of the late-17th and early 18th centuries in which the base is broader, the sides somewhat less rounded, and the neck somewhat shorter than in the earlier SHAFT AND GLOBE BOTTLE.

open mold *See* DIP MOLD.

open pontil mark—in collectors' and archaeological literature, a BLOWPIPE PONTIL mark. See Julian H. Toulouse (1973) for meaning in the glass industry.

overblow *See* MOIL.

overflow capacity *See* CAPACITY.

Owens bottle machine—the first fully automatic bottle machine, invented by Michael Owens in 1903. This BLOW-AND-BLOW MACHINE featured a number of mold-carrying arms that revolved around a central axis. Glass was obtained by suction through the open bottom of the BLANK MOLDS, which dipped into a special revolving POT connected to the tank. As each blank mold rose from the pot, a blade slid across the base of the MOLD, severing the glass in the mold from that in the pot. Compressed air was then used to inflate the PARISON. The blank mold then opened, and the parison with its completed finish was transferred to a BLOW MOLD, using the NECK RING for the transfer. Once the body was blown to full size and shape in the blow mold, the bottle was automatically released. Thus suction GATHERING, blowing of the parison, transfer to the blow mold, and final inflation and take out, all occurred automatically and simultaneously as the machine revolved. Commercial production began in late 1904 or early 1905 with six-arm machines, but a variety of additional larger models were developed in the ensuing years. Initially used for NARROW-NECK ware such as beer and catsup bottles, the machine was also used for WIDE-MOUTH ware, including milk bottles (beginning in 1905) and fruit jars (beginning in 1909). By 1917, half of the glass containers made in America were produced on Owens machines. They eventually lost market share to GOB-feeder machines, especially IS MACHINES. The last Owens machine was decommissioned in 1982.

Owens scar *See* CUT-OFF SCAR.

packer—an industry term used to indicate either wide-mouth or narrow-mouth containers, particularly those made for the pharmaceutical or food-packing industries. It was apparently meant to indicate stock containers lacking distinctive designs or EMBOSSING.

packer finish—a single-part FINISH consisting of a relatively broad band with a flat upper surface.

packie—an industry term (used primarily by the Owens-Illinois Glass Company) for a short-necked, nonreturnable beer bottle introduced in 1939. This is the first style of beer bottle to feature stippled body surfaces and the embossed legend "NO DEPOSIT – NO RETURN." Also see GB-6, STEINIE, STUBBY.

panel—a flat recessed area on the surface of a bottle. On modern bottles it also refers to the recessed body surface on cylindrical bottles where SHOCK BANDS are formed at the heel and shoulder, slightly broader than the rest of the body.

panel bottle—a rectangular bottle featuring an inset PANEL on one or more faces, commonly used for liquid medicines, flavoring extracts, and household products in the 19th and early 20th centuries. More broadly, any bottle featuring inset panels.

parison (BLANK)—a glass object in the process of manufacture at the stage when the GATHER or GOB has been slightly inflated into a tube-like form, but the object has not yet been blown into shape. In machine production, the parison is formed in a separate MOLD (BLANK MOLD), prior to transfer to the BLOW MOLD where forming is completed.

parison mark *See* BAFFLE MARK.

parison mold *See* BLANK MOLD.

parting line—term used by the glass industry for lines reflecting the adjoining surfaces of two separate molds (such as the RING MOLD and the BLANK MOLD, or the BLOW MOLD and the BOTTOM PLATE), while MOLD SEAM is used for such lines marking where the halves of a TWO-PIECE MOLD come together. Parting lines are typically horizontal and encircle the bottle. Also see SEAM, MOLD SEAM.

part-size mold (pattern mold)—a DIP MOLD intended to form the shape or decoration of the body of a vessel, which after removal was then blown larger than the MOLD CAVITY.

paste mold *See* TURN MOLD.

pattern mold *See* PART-SIZE MOLD.

peanut code—a CAVITY CODE consisting of a ring of double (figure-8) dots embossed on the bottle base to identify the source CAVITY during machine quality inspection. This system was introduced about 1981 and is still in use.

peanut ware—modern industry vernacular for very small bottles.

pearl ash *See* POTASH.

phial *See* VIAL.

Philadelphia oval—a straight-sided oval pharmacy bottle having one flat face.

Phoenix cap—a once-popular CLOSURE consisting of a BAND CAP in which the upper and lower edges of the band are crimped over the disk and under a BEAD or exterior ledge on the FINISH, while the ends form a clamp that holds the band in place until the clamp is released. The idea for this form of CAP was patented in France in 1889 by Achille Weissenthanner and was brought to the U.S. four years later and patented by his son Alfred who organized the Phoenix Cap

Company in 1896 to produce one of the most common commercial closures through the 1930s.

picnic flask—a narrow oval FLASK, especially popular in the late-19th and early 20th centuries, featuring two broad flat faces and two narrow rounded sides, the flat faces being nearly circular. Also see PUMPKINSEED FLASK.

pig—in hand production, an iron rest for BLOWPIPES or PONTILS when not in use.

pipe See BLOWPIPE.

plate—the bottom segment of a MOLD, especially the base plate of a BLOW MOLD. Also, a removable plate set in the side of a mold to allow for different embossed labels from the same mold. Also see PLATE MOLD, SLUG PLATE.

plated mold See PLATE MOLD.

plate mold (plated mold)—a MOLD with an opening in the side or base where metal plates (SLUG PLATES) could be inserted, thus allowing the same body mold to be used with the embossed labels of multiple customers. The earliest plate molds were probably those used on the bases of RICKETTS BOTTLES. Later, they were commonly used on soda water and pharmacy bottles in the 19th century and on milk bottles in the 20th century.

pontil (GATHERING IRON, pontil iron, ponty, punting iron, PUNTY)—in hand production, an iron rod with an expanded end used to hold the bottle while the BLOWPIPE was detached and the FINISH was formed. This term was also used for the GATHERING IRON that fed glass to semiautomatic machines.

pontil iron See PONTIL.

pontil mark See PONTIL SCAR.

pontil scar (pontil mark)—a residue of glass, sand, or iron oxide left on the base of a bottle by a PONTIL.

ponty See PONTIL.

pop top See RIP CAP.

post mold—a MOLD in which the separate bottom portion (BOTTOM PLATE) forms the base of the bottle but no portion of the heel, which is formed by the lowest portion of the body mold. Post bottoms are found on both hand and machine molds, although on the latter they are decidedly less common than CUP MOLDS.

pot (crucible)—in hand production, a large clay vessel used to hold molten glass (METAL). Often constructed on site at glass factories, they were of two types: open pots, used in GREEN GLASS production; and covered pots, used in FLINT GLASS production.

potash (pearl ash)—various potassium compounds used as a FLUX.

pot ring (RING)—a refractory RING floated on top of the molten glass to provide a clean surface, free from cord, stones, etc., from which the glass can be gathered. Usually made from fired fireclay, each ring is made in two interlocking halves to simplify insertion into the POT or tank.

prescription—any tall cylindrical, oval, rectangular, or square bottle intended for medicines compounded by a druggist.

prescription finish—a one-part FINISH, used primarily on pharmacy bottles, in which the side of the finish flares upward, while the upper surface tapers inward.

press-and-blow machine—a machine in which the molten glass is shaped in the BLANK MOLD by pressing the glass with a plunger, forming the FINISH and creating a CAVITY that is inflated to form the PARISON, which is then ejected with a valve from below. Press-and-blow machines were used originally only for WIDE-MOUTH WARE but are now used for NARROW-NECK WARE as well. Also see VALVE MARK.

press liner—a disk of milk glass made to be inserted within the metal lid of fruit jars to form a better seal.

press mold—ordinarily, a MOLD used for pressing tableware, lenses, insulators, etc.; occasionally used for the BLANK MOLD in press-and-blow operations.

priof finish—a CROWN FINISH variant that features a projecting ledge (instead of a REINFORCING RING) below the LOCKING RING. A short vertical wall connects the RING to the ledge, the top of which varies in height, providing a space that allows a coin or other tool to be inserted to pry off the CAP. The priof finish appears in advertising after 1920 and fades out in the 1930s.

pulcellas (steel jack)—in hand production, a tweezer-like hand tool with blade-like prongs.

pull—British term for the quantity of glass delivered by a FURNACE in a given time, usually 24 hours.

pull-off boy—in 19th- and early-20th-century hand production, a helper who cleaned the MOIL from BLOWPIPES, sometimes using a foot-operated stripping device, especially in factories making beer bottles.

pull-off cap *See* RIP CAP.

pumpkinseed flask—a popular style of FLASK with a squat (compressed) oval shape and flattened face and back, stem-like neck, and oval foot, most commonly a half-pint. It may feature EMBOSSING on the face. Rarely also called the PICNIC FLASK.

punting iron *See* PONTIL.

punt mark *See* MAKER'S MARK.

punty (PONTIL)—British term for the SABOT after traditional punties were no longer in use.

push-up—the central part of a bottle base that is concave, often deeply so, as in traditional WINE BOTTLES. The push-up may be formed in a MOLD but originally was formed by a special tool that pushed in the base, which often created a bulge at the heel.

Pyrex—trade name for the borosilicate low-expansion glass developed by Corning Glass Co. in 1915. Used primarily for chemical and oven glassware, it was also used for nursing bottles.

pyroglazing—a term used by the Thatcher Manufacturing Co. for ceramic color labels. Also see APPLIED COLOR LABEL.

radius—a vertical curve in the shape of a bottle, as at the shoulder.

registration dimple *See* SPOTTING SLOT.

reinforcing ring—the lower part of a CROWN FINISH.

revolving pot—a revolving circular POT from which the Owens Bottle Machine gathered molten glass by suction. Other types of automatic machines obtain GOBs from the FOREHEARTH.

Ricketts mold—a particular type of THREE-PIECE MOLD patented in 1821 by Henry Ricketts, an English glass manufacturer. It features a base plate that dropped down when the shoulder section of the MOLD was opened. The bases of bottles made in Ricketts molds often feature a flat band surrounding a rounded concavity. This band provided an ideal place for an embossed legend, which many glassworks used for that purpose.

rim *See* LIP.

rim code—a month and year code embossed on the upper surface of the FINISH for milk bottles made in California glass factories from the mid-1920s to the early 1930s.

ring (gathering ring)—used to describe the number of working ports in a glass furnace or factory, i.e., a factory with 10 rings had either 10 pots or a tank with 10 ports; also, a bottle FINISH part with short rounded sides. *See* POT RING.

ring mold *See* NECK RING MOLD.

rip cap (pop top, pull-off cap)—a variety of opener-unneeded bottle CAPS put on the market beginning about 1964. These CLOSURES are used with the CROWN FINISH. Unlike traditional CROWN CAPS (and unlike the later twist-off caps that have the external appearance of crown caps), the cap edge lacks the crenellated rims and is simply rolled over the LOCKING RING of the crown finish. Because the edge is smooth and snugged under the locking ring, it cannot be opened with a bottle opener. The aluminum caps feature a pull tab (in various shapes, sometimes a pull ring) projecting from one side, while the body is scored to create the lines along which the tear would occur. Pulling the tab upward tears a band of metal across the top of the cap, breaking the SEAL, and allowing the cap to come off easily. Because of the tear, the cap cannot be used to reseal the bottle. The immediate inspiration for these closures was probably the success of pull-tab openers on beer cans, but they mirror the much earlier pull-tab features of the GOLDY SEAL and the ALKA CAP. Also see FLIP-TOP CROWN.

roll on seal (RO seal)—an aluminum threaded CLOSURE in which the unthreaded CAP is applied to the filled container, the cap's threads being then formed by a machine that rolls them into place over the glass threads of the FINISH.

RO seal *See* ROLL ON SEAL.

rounding tool *See* LIPPING TOOL.

sabot—in hand production, a metal sleeve on the end of a rod, used to hold a bottle while the incomplete top is reheated at the GLORY HOLE, and while the FINISH is formed. Also see SNAP, PUNTY.

sand pontil—a PONTIL whose head is coated with sand (rather than glass) before being applied to the bottle base, leaving tiny bits of sand and glass adhering to the base after detachment.

Schlegelflasche—German term for a HOCK BOTTLE.

schnapps bottle—usually in BLACK GLASS or dark amber glass, a square bottle with flat (not paneled) sides, the shoulders not visibly broader than the base, commonly used for gin (schnapps), bitters, and sarsaparilla. The edges are generally quite distinct and narrowly chamfered but not rounded as in CASE BOTTLES.

sealing surface—that portion of the FINISH against which the CLOSURE forms a SEAL. Often this is the LIP, but with some threaded closures it may be the sides of the FINISH or even the shoulder. Cork closures form the seal against the inside walls of the opening (BORE).

seam (PARTING LINE, MOLD SEAM)—used generically by archaeologists and collectors for a narrow line or slight ridge of glass on the bottle surface indicating a location where the parts of a MOLD adjoin or where two different abutting molds came together. The glass industry commonly differentiates with the more specific terms "parting line" or "mold seam."

selenium—an oxide first used as a colorant in the 1890s to produce ruby glass, but material shortages during WWI led to experiments with use of selenium as a DECOLORIZER. Selenium was eventually found to be more reliable than MANGANESE in the reducing conditions of tank furnaces.

semiautomatic bottle machine—any of a variety of bottle-making machines in use from the 1890s into the early 20th century. In all of them, however, the glass for each bottle is gathered and fed to the machine by hand, hence the term "semiautomatic." Also see BLUE MACHINE, JOHNNY BULL MACHINE.

set over transfer—in machine operation, the system of transferring the PARISON out of the BLANK MOLD to a separately located BLOW MOLD. This is the process originally patented by Philip Arbogast in 1882 and later used in most machines, including virtually all BLOW-AND-BLOW MACHINES. Among early PRESS-AND-BLOW MACHINES, however, it was less common than the DROP BLANK SYSTEM.

settle blow—in some forms of machine production, an injection of compressed air into the inverted BLANK MOLD, forcing the GOB firmly into NECK RING to form the FINISH.

shaft and globe bottle—a free-blown 17th-century WINE BOTTLE form, featuring a somewhat globular body and a long tapering neck.

shock bands—raised areas, often stippled, just above the heel and just below the shoulder of cylindrical bottles, positioned to take impact stresses and limit breakage.

shoo-fly flask—a style of FLASK, especially popular in the late 19th and early 20th centuries, with its narrow sides rounded and its flat broad faces being markedly wider at the shoulders than at the heel. Also see COFFIN FLASK.

shop (CHAIR, HOLE)—in late-19th and early-20th-century hand production, a group of glassmakers organized so that each is responsible for a different stage of production. Composition the group varied through time and in different factories, but the essential members were a GATHERER, a BLOWER, and a FINISHER—all assisted by unskilled helpers (usually boys) to carry out ancillary tasks. In some cases, a pair of men did both GATHERING and blowing, providing bottles for a single finisher.

shoulder seal—a blob of glass applied to the shoulder or side of a bottle immediately after forming and then impressed with the seal of the intended user. Eighteenth-century seals typically indicate the individual customer for whom the bottle is intended. Nineteenth-century seals are most often of wineries, olive oil manufacturers, or distillers.

siege—in hand production, the bench or floor inside a FURNACE upon which the POTS are set.

skin—a dulled surface on a glass vessel caused by contact with the MOLD during forming.

slug plate (PLATE)—a removable metal PLATE made to be inserted into a bottle MOLD so that the same mold could be used for multiple clients. Also see PLATE MOLD.

small help—industry term (19th- and early 20th centuries) for child labor. Also see CARRY-IN BOY, CRACKER-OFF BOY, MOLD BOY, PULL-OFF BOY, SNAP-UP BOY, TAKE-OUT BOY, THROW-OUT BOY.

smooth lip jar—collectors' term for a fruit jar with a threaded FINISH on which the upper edge is formed without grinding. Although special finishing tools were available in the 19th century to form threaded finishes, these were most often used on NARROW-MOUTH WARE. Fruit jars were generally made at the time with the GROUND LIP FINISH ("bust-and-grind" technique). Consequently, the term usually refers to machine-made jars.

snap (SNAP-DRAGON, SNAP CASE)—in hand production, a rod with an adjustable sleeve for holding a bottle while it is carried to the GLORY HOLE for reheating and while the FINISH is applied.

snap case—collectors' term for SNAP.

snap-dragon—glassworkers' term for SNAP.

snapper-up—*See* SNAP-UP BOY.

snap-up boy (snapper-up, sticker-up, sticker-up boy, sticking-up boy, warming-in boy)—in 19th- and early-20th-century hand production, a helper (usually a boy) who carried the unfinished bottle to the GLORY HOLE for reheating prior to being finished.

soda glass, soda lime glass (LIME GLASS)—glass made with silica, soda, and carbonate of lime and decolorized with MANGANESE. Used for tableware and druggists' ware, it is inexpensive, chemically stable, reasonably hard, and can be re-softened multiple times to be shaped to complete an object in steps.

spotting lug *See* SPOTTING SLOT.

spotting slot (spotting lug, registration dimple)—a distinct raised or indented area, typically on the heel or base of a bottle, used by the labeling machine to align the vessel so that the label can be mechanically applied to a specific surface area.

spun bottle—Australian term for a TWISTER.

steinie—a step-necked beer bottle introduced in 1936. Originally intended to be a nonreturnable bottle, it soon became a returnable container. Also see PACKIE, STUBBY.

stem method (BURST OVER)—in hand production, a blowing process (used for bottles over 6 oz. CAPACITY) in which the BLOWER uses a single pipe and does the GATHERING as well as the blowing. See CLEAN IRON METHOD.

> You would blow the bottles, pull your pipe away from the top of the mold and blow a bubble thinner than a cigarette paper, that would break. A stem of glass about six inches long would form between the bubble and the end of the pipe. You would dip this hot glass stem in water up to the end of the pipe, and the stem would drop off. You would then gather another lump of glass… (W. McLaughlin, in Padgett 1996:24).

sticker-up, sticking-up boy *See* SNAP-UP BOY.

stippling (KNURLING)—a surface of small raised bumps on bottle bodies or bases that adds to the strength of the glass by localizing the force of an impact. Perhaps the first use of this technique was in the PACKIE beer bottle, introduced in 1939, where the body and base are entirely stippled. Subsequently, the technique was more commonly restricted to SHOCK BANDS and, especially, to the BEARING SURFACE of the base.

strap side union oval *See* UNION OVAL FLASK.

string finish (string rim finish)—a laid-on FINISH in which the added glass is in the form of a narrow string of varying size, sometimes applied at the LIP or rim but more often wrapped around the neck below it. This simple form is generally quite uncommon on American-produced bottles within typical 19th-century historic production timeframes. Olive Jones and Catherine Sullivan (1985) used the term to describe a "string rim" as the protruding ledge or BEAD below the lip or thread of a formed finish, but, to avoid confusion, this element can be included as an integral part of the overall finish type or style. An exception to the rarity of this finish occurs on the West Coast during the Gold Rush period. Peter Schulz and colleagues (1980) note that WINE BOTTLEs recovered in Old Sacramento variously have "string-like laid-on rings" and that for Bordeaux wine bottles "the finish is usually a laid-on ring, quite casually applied." The appearance of these rudimentary finishes may be ascribed to the European tendency to ship everything available in their warehouses to the lucrative Gold Rush market, most likely including older bottles and wine.

string rim finish *See* STRING FINISH.

stubby (HANDY BOTTLE, GLASS CAN)—a compact beer bottle originating in 1935 with a very short neck, introduced to compete with the newly developed beer can. Originally intended to be a nonreturnable bottle, it eventually became a returnable container. Also see EXPORT BEER BOTTLE, GB-6, PACKIE, STEINIE.

suction-blow machine (suction machine)—a bottle machine in which the glass for the PARISON is obtained by suction and is performed on directly by the BLANK MOLD, which moves over the surface of the molten glass, draws in a sufficient amount, and then rises—a knife or shear blade severing its contents from the glass remaining below. The most important example is the OWENS BOTTLE MACHINE.

suction machine *See* SUCTION-BLOW MACHINE.

sun-colored amethyst—a purplish color produced by solar radiation in glass that has been decolorized with MANGANESE.

take-out boy—in 19th- and early-20th-century hand production, a helper (usually a boy) who removed the unfinished bottle from foot-activated MOLDS operated by the BLOWER.

teaser *See* FIREMAN.

teasing—in hand production, the practice of tossing coal by hand into the fire, which is heating POTS. Also see TEAZE HOLE.

teaze hole—in hand production, an opening for a chute that leads under the SIEGE and opens above the firebox of the FURNACE. Fuel (typically coal) is pushed through the teaze hole to feed the fire, which is heating the POTS. Also see TEASING.

three-piece mold (TREADLE MOLD)—a MOLD in which the body is formed in a single lower block, while the shoulders are formed by two hinged segments that close during blowing and open afterwards to release the bottle. The base may be formed by the lower block or by a separate hinged element, as in the RICKETTS MOLD.

throat *See* BORE.

throw-out boy—in 19th- and early-20th-century hand production, a helper (usually a boy) who removed the finished bottle from the SNAP and placed it on a stand for the CARRY-IN BOY.

toe in—the lateral distance between the side of a bottle and the bearing surface of the base.

tool—both the implement used to create the FINISH and the act of forming the neck and the finish of a bottle. A tool consists of a central stopper kept damp with oil that is placed in the mouth of the bottle for gauge and of two outside arms of iron, which by rotation form the smooth RING commonly used to complete bottles. Different finishes may be obtained by contouring the ends of the arms into different patterns. In hand production, this work is done by a GAFFER sitting in a chair while glasswork is brought to him by a stream of little boys who carry it away again to the LEHR in quick order.

tooled finish—in hand production, broadly, any FINISH that involves use of a LIPPING TOOL. More specifically, a lipping-tool finish that does not include the addition of extra glass for the finishing process, merely the reheating and modification of the otherwise complete bottle after removal from the BLOWPIPE. Also see APPLIED FINISH, LAID-ON FINISH.

torpedo bottle—a 19th- and early-20th-century bottle style featuring straight sides and a rounded bottom, typically used for soda water. The purpose of the rounded bottom was to ensure that the bottles were stored on their sides in order to keep the cork moist.

tramp iron—iron that enters (contaminates) the BATCH or the METAL from tools and equipment used to handle the materials or from the clay of the POT or tank.

treadle mold—in hand production, a part MOLD opened and shut by a lever activated by the blower's foot. In Britain, a THREE-PIECE MOLD.

turn—a work shift in the glass factory. The number of hours per turn varied through time.

turn mold (paste mold)—in hand production, a TWO-PIECE MOLD for cylindrical bottles in which the bottle is rotated during the blowing process, erasing any SEAM lines derived from the MOLD. Turn molds are immersed in water before each blowing, and the interior surface is brushed with a paste of resins and linseed oil which, when the hot glass is blown against it, forms a cushion of steam that allows the bottle to be turned in the mold. Also see TWISTER, SPUN BOTTLE.

twister (SPUN BOTTLE)—industry slang (late-19th and early 20th centuries) for a bottle made in a TURN MOLD.

two-piece mold—a MOLD in which two hinged sections form the body and shoulders of the bottle. The base is formed by a third section, unless the body sections are hinged at the bottom to open vertically. Also see BAFFLE, BAFFLE PLATE, TURN MOLD.

umbrella ink—popular collector's name for small, multisided bottles, usually of eight panels, that vaguely resemble open umbrellas, often used for ink. Also called "pyramid," "fluted pyramid" or "fluted cones," they are abundant in 19th-century sites and were made for a very long time starting around 1840 until about 1909. None appear to be machine-made, and finishes varied widely, although all have round short necks. Bases varied between early PONTIL scars to "key base" and cup-base molds. Produced in a variety of glass colors they are quite distinctive.

union oval—a straight-sided pharmacy bottle with two convex faces and two narrow flat sides.

union oval flask (strap side union oval, knife edge union oval)—a glassmaker's term for both liquor flasks and druggist bottles that are more or less oval in cross-section with flattish faces and a raised strap or band down the sides that is a common post-Civil War FLASK type. Usually druggist bottles are straight sided to the base, while the sides of the liquor union ovals typically narrow slightly from shoulder to heel. Collectors further classify union oval flasks based on details of side configuration, mostly being those with the raised strap or band down the side ("strap side union oval") and those that do not have the strap and are more or less rounded on the narrow side, simply called a "union oval" or "knife edge union oval" if the side comes to a bit sharper edge.

United machine *See* JOHNNY BULL MACHINE.

vacuum cap—a bottle CAP that allows air to escape when closing so that the bottle may be more easily closed and contents remain sanitary; a cap for hot-filled products that forms a vacuum upon cooling, which helps hold the cap in place. A small ramp on the glass FINISH thread is needed to lift the cap and break the vacuum seal upon opening. In canning, the term refers to multiple CLOSURE styles that rely on the cooling effect of the hot-pack process to press a SEAL against the sealing surface, which is the LIP portion of the finish that makes direct contact with the inside of the closure, sealing gasket, or liner. Variously, steam can be injected into the HEADSPACE as the cap is applied. When the steam cools, a vacuum is formed. "Tamper-proof" vacuum caps are metal caps with a center button that depresses during hot sealing and which pops-up if the vacuum seal is disturbed or compromised.

valve mark, valve scar—an indented circular ring made in some PRESS-AND-BLOW MACHINES on the base of bottles. This scar is produced by the ejection rod or valve that pushes the PARISON up from a one-piece BLANK MOLD so that it can be transferred to the BLOW MOLD. Unlike BAFFLE MARKS and suction scars, valve marks are not connected to GHOST SEAMS since one-piece blank molds do not leave such seams.

vent marks—small embossed dots on the surface of a bottle body indicating the location of air vents in the MOLD. An attempt was often made to conceal these vents by positioning them in embossed labels or along mold joints, although they are not uncommonly found on the otherwise unmarked areas of the surface. The purpose of the vents is to facilitate the escape of air that might otherwise be trapped against the wall of the mold, thus impeding contact of the glass with the mold wall. The technique seems to have been common in hand production in the very late-19th and early 20th centuries and is still used on machine molds today.

vial (phial)—very small glass vessels often used to store medications such as liquids, powders, or capsules. Most often cylindrical or four-sided, vials have a narrow neck that can be capped or plugged and a flat base, but other styles of small bottles also may be called vials.

warming-in boy *See* SNAP-UP BOY.

water shrending *See* CRACKING OFF.

wax sealer (groove ring fruit jar)—a fruit jar style, popular from about 1855 to about 1912, in which the top of the FINISH featured a groove into which fit a flange of the CLOSURE (usually a tin lid), the seal being provided by hot wax.

whetted, whetted off *See* CRACKING OFF.

white glass—although truly white glass (milk glass) was produced in the 19th century and was occasionally used for bottles (especially for toiletries), the term is generally used in commerce to mean colorless glass.

whittling—an uneven ("corrugated") bottle body surface traditionally attributed by collectors to production in wooden MOLDS but which actually results from metal molds that are too cold.

wide-mouth ware—glass containers in which the diameter of the FINISH (and of the APERTURE) is large relative to the diameter of the body. Usually, apertures wider than about 1-1/2 inches in diameter are considered "wide mouth."

wine bottle—a generic term for any bottle that held wine. It is often used to indicate the variety of BLACK GLASS bottles of English origin that evolved into the JUNK BOTTLE of the 19th century, including that form itself (Jones 1986). In latter 19th- and 20th-century contexts, it is more commonly associated with styles that developed in France and Germany. See BOCKSBEUTEL, HOCK BOTTLE, MALLET BOTTLE, ONION BOTTLE, SHAFT AND GLOBE BOTTLE.

work hole—an opening in the wall of a FURNACE that allows the GATHER to be extracted from a POT or tank.

REFERENCES

American Glass Worker
1886   [Untitled note.] *American Glass Worker*
1(23):1.

Green Glass Blowers' Association
1913   *Wage Scale and Working Rules Adopted by the Glass Bottle Blowers Association of the United States and Canada and the National Glass Vial and Bottle Manufacturers' Association, 1913-1914.* Magrath Publishing, Camden, NJ.

Holscher, Harry H., and American Ceramic Society Committee on Classification, Nomenclature, and Glossary
1948   Glass Glossary. *American Ceramic Society Bulletin* 27(9):353-362.

Jones, Olive
1986   *Cylindrical English Wine and Beer Bottles: 1735-1850.* National Historic Parks and Site Branch, Environment Canada, Ottawa, ONT.

Jones, Olive, and Catherine Sullivan
1985   *The Parks Canada Glass Glossary.* National Historic Parks and Site Branch, Environment Canada, Ottawa, ONT.

May, Degenhard
1991   *Zur Entwicklung der Weinflasche im 19. Jh. am Beispiel des südwestdeutschen Raums* [Development of the wine bottle in the 19th century: an example from southwest Germany]. Association Internationale pour l' Histoire du Verre, Annales du Congrès 12:529-540.

Murgatroyd, J. B.
1933   The Strength of Glass. *Journal of the Society of Glass Technology* 17(67):260-272.

Padgett, Fred
1996   *Dreams of Glass: The Story of William McLaughlin and His Glass Company.* Private Printing, Livermore, CA.

Peddle, C. J.
1921   The Nomenclature of Glasses. *Journal of the Society of Glass Technology* 5:3-16.

Schulz, Peter D., Betty J. Rivers, Mark M. Hales, Charles A. Litzinger, and Elizabeth A. McKee
1980   *The Bottles of Old Sacramento: A Study of Nineteenth-Century Glass and Ceramic Retail Containers. Part 1.* California Archaeological Report, No. 20. California Department of Parks and Recreation, Sacramento.

Toulouse, Julian H.
1973   *Bottle Makers and Their Marks.* Thomas Nelson, Inc., New York, NY.

Glass Bottle Bibliography
Peter D. Schulz

This glass bottle bibliography notes some of the sources that the editor has found most useful in clarifying a variety of issues related to bottle production, function, and dating. It is not an extensive bibliography of sources on all the varied aspects of the bottle industry or its products. That goal is already pursued on the *BLM/SHA Historic Bottle Identification & Information Website*, created and maintained by Bill Lindsey—readily available and continually updated <http://www.sha.org/bottle/index.htm> source that also provides an excellent and well-illustrated introduction to an amazing range of topics related to bottle identification.

Articles listed here by Julian H. Toulouse and by Olive Jones on processes and evidence of hand production are extremely helpful. Perhaps the most useful explanation of the process is provided by Grace Kendrick (1968), who illustrates hand production of bottles and tableware based on her observations and photographs at several Mexican factories. George

Miller offers the most comprehensive discussions of machine production. Ronald Switzer's (1974) *The Bertrand Bottles* is an excellent overview on form and function.

For the identification and chronology of glass bottle makers' marks, Toulouse's (1971) classic work is still unrivalled as a comprehensive volume. For archaeologists and collectors alike, it is probably the most frequently consulted work of any kind dealing with glass.

This bibliography is divided into eight sections, entitled (1) Bottle Basics: Dating and Contents; (2) Glass Industry: Hand Production Technology; (3) Glass Industry: Machine Technology; (4) Finishes and Closures; (5) Bottle Form: Design, Function, and Standardization; (6) Labels and Marks; (7) Reprinted Glassworks Catalogs; and (8) Archaeological Context Studies.

Note: ** after entry = reference included in this volume

1. BOTTLE BASICS: DATING AND CONTENTS

Baldwin, Joseph K.

A Collector's Guide to Patent and Proprietary Medicine Bottles of the Nineteenth Century. Thomas Nelson & Sons, New York, NY.

Baxter, R. Scott

2013   Stoneware Ale Bottles. In *Ceramic Identification in Historical Archaeology: The View from California 1822–1940*, Rebecca Allen, Julia E. Huddleson, Kimberly J. Wooten, and Glenn J. Farris, editors, pp. 303–314. Society for Historical Archaeology, Special Publication Series No. 11, Germantown, MD.

Blasi, Betty

1974   *A Bit About Balsams: A Chapter in the History of Nineteenth Century Medicine.* Farley-Goepper, Louisville, KY.

Fike, Richard

1987   *The Bottle Book: A Comprehensive Guide to Historic Embossed Medicine Bottles.* Gibbs M. Smith, Salt Lake City, UT.

Jones, Olive

1971   Glass Bottle Push-ups and Pontil Marks. *Historical Archaeology* 5:62–73.**

1983   The Contribution of the Ricketts' Mold to the Manufacture of the English "Wine" Bottle, 1820–1850 *Journal of Glass Studies* 25:167–175.**

1984   London Mustard Bottles. *Historical Archaeology* 17(1):69–84.

1986   *Cylindrical English Wine & Beer Bottles, 1735–1850.* National Historic Parks and Sites Branch, Environment Canada, Ottawa.

Jones, Olive, and E. Ann Smith

1985   *Glass of the British Military: 1755–1820.* National Historic Parks and Sites Branch, Environment Canada, Ottawa, ONT.

Jones, Olive, and C. Sullivan, G. L. Miller, E. A. Smith, J. E. Harris, K. Lunn

1989   *The Parks Canada Glass Glossary for the Description of Containers, Tableware, Flat Glass, and Closures.* National Historic Parks and Sites, Canadian Parks Service, Environment, Canada.** [Selection on Closures included in this volume.]

Leavitt, Robert C.

2004   Taking the Waters: Stoneware Jugs and the Taste of Home They Contained. Master's thesis, Department of Anthropology, University of Nevada, Reno.

2013   The Westerwald Jugs. In *Ceramic Identification in Historical Archaeology: The View from California 1822–1940*, Rebecca Allen, Julia E. Huddleson, Kimberly J. Wooten, and Glenn J. Farris, editors, pp. 323–333. Society for Historical Archaeology, Special Publication Series No. 11, Germantown, MD.

Lockhart, Bill, Bill Lindsey, David Whitten, and Carol Serr

2005   Debunking the Myth of the Side Seam Thermometer. *Bottles and Extras* 16(4):14–15, 41.**

Markota, Peck, and Audie Markota

1972   *Western Blob Top Soda and Mineral Water Bottles,* revised edition. Peck and Audie Markota, Fair Oaks, CA. Reprinted 2005.

Miller, George L., and Tony McNichol

2002   Dates for Suction Scarred Bottoms: Chronological Changes in Owens Machine-Made Bottles. *Northeast Historical Archaeologist,* Vol. 41:18–38.**

Munsey, Cecil

1970   *The Illustrated Guide to Collecting Bottles.* Hawthorn Books, New York, NY.

Orser, Charles E., and David W. Babson

1990   Tabasco Brand Pepper Sauce Bottles from Avery Island, Louisiana. *Historical Archaeology* 24(3):107–114.

Paul, John R., and Paul W. Parmalee

1973   *Soft Drink Bottling: A History with Special Reference to Illinois.* Illinois State Museum Society, Springfield.

Putnam, H. E.

1965   *Bottle Identification.* H. E. Putnam, Duarte, CA.

Roller, Dick

1983   *The Standard Fruit Jar Reference.* Acorn Press, Paris, IL.

Schulz, Peter, Betty Rivers, Mark Hales, Charles Litzinger, and Elizabeth McKee

1980   *The Bottles of Old Sacramento: A Study of Nineteenth-Century Glass and Ceramic Retail*

Containers, Part 1. California Archaeological Reports, No. 20. Department of Parks and Recreation, Sacramento.** [Selection included in this volume.]

Shimko, Phyllis
1969   *Sarsaparilla Bottle Encyclopedia.* Andrew and Phyllis Shimko, Aurora, OR.

Sullivan, Catherine
1994   Searching for Nineteenth Century Florida Water Bottles. *Historical Archaeology* 28(1):78–98.

Switzer, Ronald R.
1974   *The Bertrand Bottles: A Study of Nineteenth-Century Glass and Ceramic Containers.* National Park Service, Washington, DC.

Thomas, John L.
1977a   *Picnics, Coffins, Shoo-flies.* Maverick Publications, Bend, OR.

1977b   *Whiskey Bottles of the Old West.* Maverick Publications, Bend, OR.

Toulouse, Julian Harrison
1966   Whittled Molds. *Western Collector* 4(10):27–28.**

1967   When did Hand Bottle Blowing Stop? *Pioneer for Today's Collector* 5(8):41–45.**

1968   Empontilling: A History. *Glass Industry* 49(3):137–142, (4):204–205.**

1969a   *Fruit Jars.* Thomas Nelson & Sons, New Jersey and Everybody's Press, Hanover.

1969b   A Primer on Mold Seams. *Western Collector* 7(11):526–535; and 7(12):578–587.**

1973   The Pontil as a Tool for Holding Glassware During Finishing. *Federation of Historical Bottle Clubs Journal* 1(2):8–10.**

2001   *Bottle Makers and Their Marks.* Blackburn Press, Caldwell, NJ. [2001 copyright of 1971 edition.]

Watson, Richard
1965   *Bitters Bottles.* Thomas Nelson & Sons, New York, NY.

Wilson, Bill, and Betty Wilson
1968   *Spirit Bottles of the Old West.* Antique Hobby and Publishing, Amador City, CA.

1969   *Western Bitters.* Northwestern Printing Company, Santa Rosa, CA.

1971   *Nineteenth Century Medicine in Glass.* Nineteenth Century Hobby & Publishing Company, Amador City, CA.

Wilson, Rex
1981   *Bottles on the Western Frontier.* University of Arizona Press, Tucson.

Zumwalt, Betty
1980   *Ketchup, Pickles, Sauces: Nineteenth Century Food in Glass.* Mark West Publishers, Fulton, CA.

2. GLASS INDUSTRY: HAND PRODUCTION TECHNOLOGY

Boow, James
1991   *Early Australian Commercial Glass: Manufacturing Processes.* Heritage Council of New South Wales, Australia.

Cable, Michael
1998   The Operation of Wood Fired Glass Melting Furnaces. In *The Prehistory & History of Glassmaking Technology,* Patrick McCray, editor, pp. 315–329. American Ceramic Society, Cincinnati, OH.

Dodsworth, Roger
1982   *Glass and Glassmaking.* (Shire Album 83). Shire Publications, Aylesbury, England, UK.

Dralle, Robert
1911   *Die Glasfabrikation* (Glassmaking), Volume 2. R. Oldenburg, Munich, Germany.

Kendrick, Grace
1968   *The Mouth-Blown Bottle.* Edwards Brothers, Ann Arbor, MI.

Knapp, F.
1849   *Chemical Technology.* Lea and Blanchard, Philadelphia, PA.

Lardner, Dionysius
1832   *The Cabinet of Useful Arts: A Treatise on the Progressive Improvement and Present State of the Manufacture of Porcelain and Glass.* Longman, Rees, Orme, Brown, and Green, London, UK.

1972   *The Manufacture of Porcelain and Glass.* Noyes Press, Park Ridge, NJ. [Reprint of 1832 edition.]

Lovejoy, Owen R.
        Child Labor in the Glass Industry. *Annals of the American Academy of Political and Social Science* 27(2):42–53.

Markham, Edwin

1906   The Hoe-Man in the Making: II. Child-Wrecking in the Glass-Factories. *Cosmopolitan Magazine* 41(6):567–574.

McKearin, George S., and Helen McKearin

1948   *American Glass.* Crown Publishers, New York, NY.

McKearin, Helen, and Kenneth M. Wilson

1978   *American Bottles and Flasks and Their Ancestry.* Crown Publishers, New York, NY.

Neil, Chas. P.

1911   *Report on Condition of Woman and Child Wage-Earners in the United States: III. Glass Industry.* Sixty-First Congress, Second Session, Senate Document 645. Bureau of Foreign and Domestic Commerce, U.S. Department of Commerce, Washington, DC.

Pepper, Adeline

1971   *The Glass Gaffers of New Jersey.* Charles Scribner's Sons, New York, NY.

Rocheleau, W. F.

1900   *Great American Industries, Third Book: Manufactures.* A. Flanagan, Chicago, IL.

Society for Promoting Christian Knowledge

1845   *The Useful Arts and Manufactures of Great Britain: The Manufacture of Glass.* R. Clay, London, England, UK.

Trowbridge, J. T.

1870   *Lawrence's Adventures among the Ice-Cutters, Glass-Makers, Coal-Miners, Iron-Men, and Ship-Builders.* Henry T. Coates, Philadelphia, PA.

3. GLASS INDUSTRY: MACHINE TECHNOLOGY

Busch, Jane Celia

1983   The Throwaway Ethic in America. Doctoral dissertation, Department of American Civilization, University of Pennsylvania, Philadelphia.

Douglas, R. W., and Susan Frank

1972   *A History of Glassmaking.* G. T. Foulis & Co., Oxfordshire, England, UK.

Dralle, Robert

1911   *Die Glasfabrikation* (The Glass Factory), Vol. 2. R. Oldenburg, Munich, Germany.

Fones-Wolf

2007   *Glass Towns: Industry, Labor, and Political Economy in Appalachia, 1890–1930s.* University of Illinois Press, Urbana.

Haas, Paul F.

1970   The Glass Container Industry: A Case Study of Oligopoly and Antitrust. Doctoral dissertation, Boston College, Boston, MA.

Holscher, Harry H.

1953   Feeding and Forming. In *Handbook of Glass Manufacture,* F. V. Tooley, editor, pp. 299–387. Ogden Publishing Co., New York, NY. [In subsequent editions, revised versions of this chapter are called "The Processing of Bottles and Other Hollow Ware Articles."]

1965   *Hollow and Specialty Glass: Background and Challenge.* Owens-Illinois, Toledo, OH.

1972   *The Glass Primer.* Magazines for Industry, New York, NY.

Marson, Percival

1918   *Glass and Glass Manufacture.* Isaac Pitman & Sons, London, England, UK.

Meigh, Edward

1960   The Development of the Automatic Glass Bottle Machine: A Story of Some Early Pioneers. *Glass Technology* 1(1):25–48.

Miller, George L., and Antony Pacy

1985   Impact of Mechanization in the Glass Container Industry: The Dominion Glass Company of Montreal, a Case Study. *Historical Archaeology* 19(1):38–50.

Miller, George L., and Catherine Sullivan

1984   Machine-Made Glass Containers and the End of Production for Mouth-Blown Bottles. *Historical Archaeology* 18(2):83–96.**

Minton, Lee W.

1961   *Flame and Heart: A History of the Glass Bottle Blowers Association of the United States and Canada.* Glass Bottle Blowers Association of the United States and Canada, Philadelphia, PA.

Moll, William A.

1982   Bottles—Manufacture & Standards. In *Beer Packaging: A Manual for the Brewing and Beverage Industries,* edited by H. M. Broderick, pp. 83–109. Master Brewers Association of the Americas, Madison, WI.

[Parker, Walter B. et al.]

1917   *The Glass Industry: Report on the Cost of Production of Glass in the United States*, Miscellaneous Series No. 60:1-430. Bureau of Foreign and Domestic Commerce, U.S. Department of Commerce, Washington, DC.

Scoville, Warren C.

1948   *Revolution in Glassmaking*. Harvard University Press, Cambridge, MA.

Skrabec, Quentin R., Jr.

2007   *Michael Owens and the Glass Industry*. Pelican Publishing Co., Gretna, LA.

Stern, Boris

1927   Productivity of Labor in the Glass Industry. *U.S. Bureau of Labor Statistics Bulletin* 441:1-204.

Zembala, Dennis M.

1984   Machines in the Glasshouse: Transformation of Work in the Glass Industry, 1820-1915. Doctoral dissertation, Department of American Studies, George Washington University,

4. FINISHES AND CLOSURES

Canning Age

1929   Aluminum Seals. *Canning Age* 10(11):795-798.

Everett, J. F.

1982   Bottle Closures. In *Beer Packaging*, H. M. Broderick, editor, pp. 167-191. Master Brewers Association of the Americas, Madison, WI.

Girling, P. J.

2003   Packaging of Food in Glass Containers. In *Food Packaging Technology*, Richard Coles, Derek McDowell, and Mark J. Kirwan, editors, pp. 152-173. Blackwell Publishing, London, England, UK.

Glass Packer

1930a   The How and Why of Liners As the Most Important Factor in Securing a Perfect Seal. *Glass Packer* 3(10):475-478.**

1930b   Narrow Mouth Closures: An Analysis of Representative Types. *Glass Packer* 3(9):431-434.**

1930c   Selecting a Wide Mouth Closure to Meet Exact Packing Conditions. *Glass Packer* 3(8):379-383, 394.**

1930d   A Study of Glass Finishes for Metal Closures. *Glass Packer* 3(7):329-332.**

Lief, Alfred

1965   *A Close-Up of Closures*. Glass Container Manufacturers Institute, Madison, WI.

Modern Packaging

1942   Closures and the Bottleneck. *Modern Packaging* 16(1):37-52.

1975   Using Glass Containers Effectively. *Modern Packaging* 48(12):86-94.

Morrison, James

1929   The Modern Glass Container. *Canning Age* 10(9):673-674, 681.

Nairn, J. F., and T. M. Norpell

1986   Closures, Bottle and Jar. In *The Wiley Encyclopedia of Packaging Technology*, M. Bakker and D. Eckroth, editors, pp. 172-185. John Wiley & Sons, New York, NY.

Pacrette, Jean

1904   *The Art of Canning and Preserving as an Industry*. Henry I. Cain & Son, New York, NY.

Pitman, K.

1999   Closures in Beverage Packaging. In *Handbook of Beverage Packaging*, Geoff A. Giles, editor, pp. 207-2245. Sheffield Academic Press, Sheffield, England, UK.

Sterling, A. J.

1933   Closures. *Packaging Catalog*, 1933 edition, pp. 72-74. Beskin & Charlton, New York, NY.

1935   Types and Applications of Closures. *Packaging Catalog*, 1935 edition, pp. 70-73. Beskin & Charlton, New York, NY.**

Theobald, Nigel

2006a   Closures for Glass Containers. In *Packaging Closures and Sealing Systems*, Nigel Theobald and Belinda Winder, editor, pp. 101-117. CRC Press, Boca Raton, FL.

2006b   Push-on Closures. In *Packaging Closures and Sealing Systems*, Nigel Theobald and Belinda Winder, editors, pp. 183-204. CRC Press, Boca Raton, FL.

Von Till, L. A.

1963   The ABC's of Closures. *Glass Packaging* 42(12):24-31.

Wheaton, J. M.

1948   Closure Liners. *Modern Packaging* 21(8):184-185.

White, T. A.
1949   What Are the Factors of a Good Glasspacking Closure? *Food Packer* 30(10):28, 66–67.

Wright, Frank H.
1956   Glass Containers: In Food Products Manufacture. *Western Canner and Packer* 48(13):20–30.

5. BOTTLE FORM: DESIGN, FUNCTION AND STANDARDIZATION

Algeo, J. S.
1927   The Factor of Breakage in Odd Shaped Glass Containers. *Canning Age*, pp. 431–433.**

Foster, T. V.
1979   Containers. In *Glass Making Today*, edited by P. J. Doyle, pp. 197–211. Portcullis Press, Redhill, Surrey, England, UK.

Ghering, Leonard
1939   Improving the Strength of Glass Containers through Design. *Glass Industry* 20(12):443–448.**

Girling, P. J.
1999   Packaging of Beverages in Glass Bottles. In *Handbook of Beverage Packaging*, edited by Geoff A. Giles, pp. 53–70. Sheffield Academic Press, Sheffield, England, UK.

Glass Packer
1940   Breakage Control. *Glass Packer* 19(4):229–230.

Modern Packaging
1949   Glass Containers. *Modern Packaging Encyclopedia*. Packaging Catalog Corporation, New York, NY.

Murgatroyd, J. B.
1933   The Strength of Glass. *Journal of the Society of Glass Technology* 17(67):260–272.

Ogden, John T.
1935   Making the Most of Glass. *Glass Packer* 14(5):285–321.**

Toulouse, Julian Harrison
1937   Modern Styling in Bottles for Beer. *Brewers Technical Review* 12(9):344–345.

1941   The Standardization of Bottles for Beer and Ale. *Brewers Digest* 16(10):173–177, 181.**

1945   The Development of the One-Way Bottle for Beer. *Brewers Digest* 20(9):45–47.**

6. LABELS AND MARKS

Glass Packer
1934   Liquor Bottle Regulations summarized for *Glass Packer* Readers. *Glass Packer* 13(8):502–503.**

1940   Spotting Labels on Round Bottles. *Glass Packer* 19(3):182–183.**

Internal Revenue Department
1969   Industry Liquor Bottle Permit Numbers: Glass Container Manufacturers Authorized to Manufacture Liquor Bottles. Ms., Internal Revenue Department, Washington, DC.

Owens-Illinois Glass Company
[1935]   *OnIzed Applied Color Milk Bottles*. Brochure, Owens-Illinois Glass Co., Toledo, OH.**

Lockhart, Bill
2004   The Dating Game: Owens-Illinois Glass Co. *Bottles and Extras*:2–5.

7. REPRINTED GLASSWORKS CATALOGS

Collector Books
n.d.   *Illinois Glass Co.: Bottles of Every Description, 1903-4*. Alton, Ill. [Collector Books, Paducah, KY.]

Pacific Grove Press
n.d.   *1909 Price List, Robert J. Althier, Manufacturer of Druggists, Chemists and Perfumers' Glassware*. San Francisco, CA.

Pyne Press
1972   *Pennsylvania Glassware, 1870-1904.* [Pyne Press, Princeton, NJ.]

Whitall, Tatum & Co.
1971   *Whitall, Tatum & Co. 1880.* [Pyne Press, Princeton, NJ.]

8. ARCHAEOLOGICAL CONTEXT STUDIES

Berge, Dale
1980   *Simpson Springs Station: Historical Archaeology in Western Utah.* Cultural Resource Series No. 6. U.S. Bureau of Land Management, Salt Lake City, UT.

Busch, Jane
1987   Second Time Around: A Look at Bottle Reuse. *Historical Archaeology* 21(1):67–80.

Herskovitz, Robert M.
1978   *Fort Bowie Material Culture.* University of Arizona Anthropological Papers No. 31. University of Arizona Press, Tucson.

Larsen, Eric L.

1994   A Boardinghouse Madonna—Beyond the
        Aesthetics of a Portrait Created through
        Medicine Bottles. *Historical Archaeology*
        28(4):68–79.

Miller, George L., with contributions by Patricia
Samford, Ellen Shlasko, and Andrew Madsen

2000   Telling Time for Archaeologists. *Northeast
        Historical Archaeology* 29:1–22.

McDougall, Dennis P.

1990   The Bottles of the Hoff Store. In *The Hoff
        Store Site and Gold Rush Merchandise from
        San Francisco, California,* Allen G. Pastron
        and Eugene M. Hattori, editors, pp. 58–74.
        Society for Historical Archaeology, Special
        Publication No. 7. Braun-Brumfield, Ann
        Arbor, MI.

Petchey, Peter

2000   A Quick Note on the Tops of Bottles, or Boys
        Will Be Boys. *Archaeology in New Zealand*
        43(3):201–205.

Spude, Catherine H., Douglas D. Scott, Frank Norris,
David R. Hulesbeck, Linda S. Cummings, and
Kathryn Puseman

1993   *Father Turnell's Trash Pit*. Archeological
        Investigations in Skagway, Alaska, Volume 4.
        U.S. Department of the Interior, National Park
        Service, Denver, CO.

Staski, Edward

1984   Just What Can a 19th Century Bottle Tell Us?
        Historical Archaeology 18(1):38–51.**

Van Wormer, Stephen

1983   Beer, Wine and Sardines with a Dash of
        Pepper Sauce: An Analysis of the Glass and
        Tin Cans of the Encino Roadhouse. *Pacific
        Coast Archaeological Society Quarterly*
        19(1):47–66.

Julian Harrison Toulouse: Selected Bibliography
Peter D. Schulz

[Buchanan, J. H., E. E. Peterson, J. H. Toulouse, and M. Levine]

1927   Grading of Bottled Carbonated Beverages. *Beverage News* 19(4):16–18. [Reprinted in *Glass Container* 6(10):13, 26,30,32,36; reprinted as Bottled Beverages Should Be Graded Periodically. *Pacific Bottler* 45(6):16, 40, 42.]

[Levine, M., J. H. Toulouse, and J. H. Buchanan]

1928   Effect of Addition of Salts on the Germicidal Efficiency of Sodium Hydroxide. *Industrial and Engineering Chemistry* 20(2):179–181.

[Levine, M., J. H. Toulouse, E. E. Peterson, and J. H. Buchanan]

1927   The Place of Chlorine Solutions in the Bottled Beverage Plant. *Beverage News Journal* 18(6):18–20 (February).

Toulouse, Julian Harrison

1931   Locating Spoilage by a Flow Sheet Analysis. *Glass Packer* 10(13):649–651, 684.

1931   More Valuable Tables to Aid Bottlers. *Pacific Bottler* 49(8):7.

1932   To Insure Uniform Beverages—A Standard Is Needed for Citric Acid Solution. *Glass Packer* 11(4):232–233,256. [Reprinted as A Standard for Citric Acid Solution Is Needed to Insure Uniform Beverages. *Pacific Bottler* 50(4):8–9, 30.]

1932   Control of "Summer-End" Spoilage. *Pacific Bottler* 50(9):8, 12, 26.

1933   The Sugar/Acid Ratio—All Important Factor in Ginger Ale. *Glass Packer* 12(10):639–642.

1934   Citrus Fruit Juices from the Bottler's Standpoint. *Industrial and Engineering Chemistry* 26(7):765–768.

1934   Oxygen-Consuming Phenomena in Beverages. *Industrial and Engineering Chemistry* 26(7):769–770.

1934   Problems in the Bottling of Carbonated Fruit-Juice Beverages. *Food Industries* 6(6):249–251.

1937   Modern Styling in Bottles for Beer. *Brewers Technical Review* 12(9):344–345.

1939   Bottle Washing. *First Annual Blue Book of the National Carbonator and Bottler*, Sec. 2:1–4 (February).

1939   Bottles: Applied Color Labels. *First Annual Blue Book of the National Carbonator and Bottler*, February. [Reprinted in *Soda Net*, Jan., 1994:9–12.]

1939   The Glass Industry Charts a New Course in Design. *Glass Packer* 18(4):211–214. [Reprinted as Newest Bottle Developments. *Bottler and Packer* 13(6):62, 64, 66, 68.]

1939   Increasing Bottle Trippage. *Brewers Digest* 14(10):44–47. [tech. pp. 182–185] [Reprinted as Increasing Beer Bottle Trippage. *Bottler and Packer* 13(11):34, 36, 38.]

1940   Further Studies on Bottle Handling. *Brewers Digest* 15(11):68–70.

1941   The Standardization of Bottles for Beer and Ale. *Brewers Digest* 16(10):33–37, 41. [tech. pp. 173–177,181]

1944   Demonstration of Sampling Fluctuations in Drawings from a Bowl. [Abstract] *Glass Industry* 25(10):449.

1944   A Discussion of the Applicability of Control Charts to Glass Container Production. [Abstract] *Glass Industry* 25(10):448–449.

1945   The Development of the One-Way Bottle for Beer. *Brewers Digest* 20(9):45–47.

1948   Statistical Control. *Glass Industry* 29(2):79–80, 100, 102.

1950   The Manufacture of Beer and Ale Bottles. *Brewers Digest* 25(1):43–46; 25(2):48–50, 55; and 25(3):42–44, 50. [Reprinted in *Bottler & Packer* 24(10):113–115; and 24(11):112–116.]

1953   Quality Control in the Manufacturing of Glass Containers. *Glass Industry* 34(2):70.

1955   A Study of Industrial Use of Probability Statistics in the Physical Sciences. *Journal of the American Statistical Association* 50(272):1014–1021.

1966   Mason and Other Fruit Jars. Ms. at Rakow Library, Corning Museum of Glass, Corning, NY.

1966   Whittled Molds. *Western Collector* 4(10):27–28.

1967   Johnson & Johnson and the Fruit Jar. *Spinning Wheel* 23(4):22–23.

1967   When Did Hand Bottle Blowing Stop? *Western Collector* 5(8):41–45. [Reprinted in *Applied Lip*, October 1993:3–7.]

1968   Empontilling: A History. *Glass Industry* 49(3):137–142; and 49(4):204–205.

1968   The Men Behind the Fruit Jar. *Spinning Wheel* 24(9):18–20.

1968   San Francisco Bottle Makers. *Western Collector* 6(10):35–41.

1969   *Fruit Jars*. Thomas Nelson & Sons, New York, NY.

1969   A Primer on Mold Seams. *Western Collector* 7(11):526–535; and 7(12):578–587.

1969   Those Royal Ruby Beer Bottles. *Spinning Wheel* 25(7):14–15, 66. [Reprinted 1994 in *Applied Seals* 23(10):6.]

1969   What Mold Seams May Teach Us. Speech draft, 21 March 1969, on file at Rakow Library, Corning Museum of Glass, Corning, NY.

1970   Bottle Makers of the Pacific Northwest. *Western Collector* 8(7+8):32–37.

1970   High on the Hawg, or How the Western Miner Lived. *Historical Archaeology* 4:59–69. [Reprinted 1996 in *Bottles and Extras* 75:3–7.]

1971   *Bottle Makers and Their Marks*. Thomas Nelson, New York, NY. [Reprinted by Blackburn Press, 2004.]

1972   Bottle Makers of Southern California. *National Bottle Gazette* 2(7):3.

1972   A Three Hundred Year Evolution of a Bottle Design. Ms. at the Rakow Library, Corning Museum of Glass, Corning, NY.

1973   Glass Jelly Molds. *Spinning Wheel* 29(8):12ff.

1973   The Pontil As a Tool for Holding Glassware during Finishing. *Federation of Historical Bottle Clubs Journal* 1(2):8–10. [Reprinted in *Somers Antique Bottle Club News Views*, Winter, 1997:6–7.]

1973   There's a Glassmaker's Word for It. *Federation of Historical Bottle Clubs Journal* 1(1):28.

1975   How America's Western Pioneers Lived. *Federation of Historical Bottle Clubs Journal* 3(1):14–19.

[Toulouse, J. H., J. H. Buchanan, and M. Levine]

1931   New A.B.C.B. Tables Simplify Syrup Making. *Pacific Bottler* 49(6):7–10, 27.